# Artificial Intelligence in Biomaterials Design and Development

Woodhead Publishing Series in Biomaterials

# Artificial Intelligence in Biomaterials Design and Development

*Edited by*


*Payam Zarrintaj*

*Mohsen Khodadadi Yazdi*

*Sidi A. Bencherif*

*Mohammad Reza Saeb*

*Masoud Mozafari*



ELSEVIER

WP
WOODHEAD PUBLISHING
An imprint of Elsevier

Woodhead Publishing is an imprint of Elsevier
50 Hampshire Street, 5th Floor, Cambridge, MA 02139, United States
125 London Wall, London EC2Y 5AS, United Kingdom



ISBN: 978-0-323-95464-8 (print)

ISBN: 978-0-323-95465-5 (online)

For information on all Woodhead Publishing publications
visit our website at https://www.elsevier.com/books-and-journals

*Publisher:* Matthew Deans
*Acquisitions Editor:* Sabrina Webber
*Editorial Project Manager:* Anand Siddharth
*Production Project Manager:* Anitha Sivaraj
*Cover Designer:* Gopalakrishnan Venkatraman

Typeset by MPS Limited, Chennai, India

# Contents

# List of contributors

**Maryam Sadat Adibhosseini** Faculty of Chemical Engineering, Biomedical Engineering Division, Tarbiat Modares University, Tehran, Iran

**Mahnaz Ahmadi** Department of Tissue Engineering and Applied Cell Sciences, School of Advanced Technologies in Medicine, Shahid Beheshti University of Medical Sciences, Tehran, Iran

**Bahareh Alizadeh** Protein Technology Research Center, Shahid Beheshti University of Medical Sciences, Tehran, Iran

**Trinh Hai Anh** Department of Implantology, Ha Noi National Hospital of Odonto-Stomatology, Hanoi, Vietnam; Faculty of Dentistry, University of Medicine and Pharmacy, Hanoi National University, Hanoi, Vietnam

**Mohammad Ashrafuzzaman** Department of Biochemistry, College of Science, Doping Research Chair, Deanship of Scientific Research, King Saud University, Riyadh, Saudi Arabia

**Seyed Mohammad Ayyoubzadeh** Department of Health Information Management and Medical Informatics, School of Allied Medical Sciences, Tehran University of Medical Sciences, Tehran, Iran; Health Information Management Research Center, Tehran University of Medical Sciences, Tehran, Iran

**Nelson Barrios** Department of Forest Biomaterials, North Carolina State University, Raleigh, NC, United States

**Sidi A. Bencherif** Chemical Engineering Department, Northeastern University, Boston, MA, United States; Harvard John A. Paulson School of Engineering and Applied Sciences, Harvard University, Cambridge, MA, United States; CNRS, PBS UMR 6270, University Rouen Normandie, Rouen, France

**Hrishikesh S Bhardhwaj** Department of Biotechnology, R V College of Engineering, Bengaluru, Karnataka, India

**Shubhabrata Datta** Centre for Composite and Advanced Materials, Department of Mechanical Engineering, Faculty of Engineering and Technology, SRM Institute of Science and Technology, Chengalpattu, Tamil Nadu, India

**Kamyar Davarikia** Department of Pharmaceutics and Pharmaceutical Nanotechnology, School of Pharmacy, Shahid Beheshti University of Medical Sciences, Tehran, Iran

**Sara Etminanrezaeieh** Chemical Engineering Group, Faculty of Chemical Engineering and Advanced Materials, Urmia University of Technology, Urmia, Iran

**Praveen Kumar Gupta** Department of Biotechnology, R V College of Engineering, Bengaluru, Karnataka, India

**Artak Heboyan** Department of Prosthodontics, Faculty of Stomatology, Yerevan State Medical University after Mkhitar Heratsi, Yerevan, Armenia

**Soroush Heydari** Department of Health Information Management and Medical Informatics, School of Allied Medical Sciences, Tehran University of Medical Sciences, Tehran, Iran

**Ahmad Al Jaghsi** Clinical Sciences Department, College of Dentistry, Ajman University, Ajman, United Arab Emirates; Center of Medical and Bio-Allied Health Sciences Research, Ajman University, Ajman, United Arab Emirates; Department of Prosthodontics, Gerodontology, and Dental Materials, Greifswald University Medicine, Greifswald, Germany

**Rohan D. Jagtap** Division of Oral and Maxillofacial Radiology, Department of Care Planning and Restorative Sciences, School of Dentistry, University of Mississippi Medical Center (UMMC), Jackson, MS, United States

**M. Kamaraj** Centre for Composite and Advanced Materials, Department of Mechanical Engineering, Faculty of Engineering and Technology, SRM Institute of Science and Technology, Chengalpattu, Tamil Nadu, India

**Zohaib Khurshid** Department of Prosthodontics and Implantology, College of Dentistry, King Faisal University, Al-Hofuf, Saudi Arabia; Center of Excellence for Regenerative Dentistry, Department of Anatomy, Faculty of Dentistry, Chulalongkorn University, Bangkok, Thailand

**Hossein Madineh** Faculty of Chemical Engineering, Department of Polymer Engineering, Tarbiat Modares University, Tehran, Iran

**Fateme Mansourinia** Faculty of Chemical Engineering, Department of Polymer Engineering, Tarbiat Modares University, Tehran, Iran

**Ronald Marquez** Department of Forest Biomaterials, North Carolina State University, Raleigh, NC, United States; LEPAMAP-PRODIS Research group, University of Girona, C/Maria Aurèlia Capmany, Girona, Spain

**Anand Marya** Department of Orthodontics, Faculty of Dentistry, University of Puthisastra, Phnom Penh, Cambodia

**Masoud Mozafari** Research Unit of Health Sciences and Technology, Faculty of Medicine, University of Oulu, Oulu, Finland

**M.Z. Naser** Artificial Intelligence Research Institute for Science and Engineering (AIRISE), Clemson University, Clemson, SC, United States

**Mojtaba Nasirinezhad** Chemical Engineering Group, Faculty of Chemical Engineering and Advanced Materials, Urmia University of Technology, Urmia, Iran

**Lokendra Pal** Department of Forest Biomaterials, North Carolina State University, Raleigh, NC, United States

**Dinesh Rokaya** Clinical Sciences Department, College of Dentistry, Ajman University, Ajman, United Arab Emirates; Center of Medical and Bio-Allied Health Sciences Research, Ajman University, Ajman, United Arab Emirates

**Mohammad Reza Saeb** Department of Pharmaceutical Chemistry, Medical University of Gdańsk, Gdańsk, Poland

**Mariangeles Salas** Department of Forest Biomaterials, North Carolina State University, Raleigh, NC, United States

**Ali Samadi** Faculty of Engineering, Department of Polymer Engineering, Urmia University, Urmia, Iran

**Saeid SamadiDana** Department of Computer Science & IT, Austin Peay State University, Clarksville, TN, United States

**Saba Abbasi Sedaghat** Chemical Engineering Group, Faculty of Chemical Engineering and Advanced Materials, Urmia University of Technology, Urmia, Iran

**Diane Isabel Selvido** Academy of Research and Clinical Dentistry, Metro Manila, Philippines

**Pravin Kumar Shah** Boston University Henry M Goldman School of Dental Medicine, Boston, MA, United States

**Siddharth Kaushik L.S.** Department of Biotechnology, R V College of Engineering, Bengaluru, Karnataka, India

**Viritpon Srimaneepong** Department of Prosthodontics, Faculty of Dentistry, Chulalongkorn University, Bangkok, Thailand

**Shreya Subedi** Department of Restorative Dentistry, College of Dentistry, University of Illinois Chicago, Chicago, IL, United States

**Mohsen Tabibian** Center of Sciences, Wilmington College, Wilmington, OH, United States

**Thippa Reddy K.S.** Department of Biotechnology, R V College of Engineering, Bengaluru, Karnataka, India

**Laura Tolosa** School of Chemical Engineering, University of Los Andes, Merida, Venezuela

**James Tsoi** Dental Materials Science, Faculty of Dentistry, Division of Applied Oral Sciences and Community Dental Care, The University of Hong Kong, Pok Fu Lam, Hong Kong

**Snigdha Tutika** Department of Biotechnology, R V College of Engineering, Bengaluru, Karnataka, India

**Raine Viitala** Department of Mechanical Engineering, School of Engineering, Aalto University, Aalto, Finland

**Mohsen Khodadadi Yazdi** Advanced Materials Center, Gdańsk University of Technology, Gdańsk, Poland; Division of Electrochemistry and Surface Physical Chemistry, Faculty of Applied Physics and Mathematics, Gdańsk University of Technology, Gdańsk, Poland

**Sina Yousefi** Department of Data Science and Analytics, Georgia Institute and technology, San Jose, CA, United States

**Muhammad Sohail Zafar** Clinical Sciences Department, College of Dentistry, Ajman University, Ajman, United Arab Emirates; Center of Medical and Bio-Allied Health Sciences Research, Ajman University, Ajman, United Arab Emirates

**Sara Zaky Mohammed** Prosthodontics Department College of Dentistry, Ras Al Khaimah Medical and Health Science University, Ras Al Khaimah, United Arab Emirates

**Payam Zarrintaj** Independent Researcher, E3 LLC, Louisville, KY, United States

**Raha Zarrintaj** Department of Computer Science, Tabriz University, Tabriz, Iran

# Editors' Note

Biomaterials science is a field born from the intersection of curiosity and compassion, our desire to understand nature at its most fundamental level, and to use that understanding to heal, restore, and improve human life. Each generation of researchers has expanded this vision, from early advances in chemistry and metallurgy to the rise of biotechnology, nanoscience, and regenerative medicine. Now, we are witnessing yet another transformative chapter with the integration of artificial intelligence (AI) into the design and development of biomaterials.

This transformation is not only a technological evolution but also a conceptual revolution. AI is changing how we think, not just how we compute. It enables us to move from observing biological systems to anticipating them, from fabricating materials to teaching how to respond to them, and from analyzing data to learning from them. AI-driven tools can predict molecular interactions, simulate biological responses, and propose entirely new material architectures, sometimes ones that even surprise their human creators.

In this sense, AI is more than a scientific instrument; it is an intellectual partner that augments our ability to imagine and innovate. Yet, its power also challenges us to reflect on the essence of discovery itself. What does it mean when machines can learn the patterns of life faster than we can observe them? How do we ensure that such intelligence serves human goals for the betterment of health and quality of life? These are questions that science cannot easily answer on its own but which every scientist must continue to ask.

As we move into a future where data and design converge, our progress will depend on our ability to build bridges across domains. The next breakthroughs in biomaterials will not emerge from algorithms alone but from the synergy between machine intelligence and human insight, between digital precision and biological complexity. In this partnership, AI provides us with the means to model the unpredictable, to design the adaptable, and perhaps one day, to engineer materials that learn and evolve alongside the human body.

Looking ahead, I believe the integration of AI into biomaterials science will redefine not only how we create but also how we think about creation — and, more importantly, how we understand biological interactions. The materials of the future will not be passive implants or inert scaffolds; they will be more dynamic, sensing, responsive systems that interact with tissues, decode biological cues, and guide healing processes in real time. In this future, the boundary between materials and intelligence will blur, giving rise to a new class of "living materials" designed with human-centered intelligence at their core.

**Masoud Mozafari**
2025

# Preface

The accelerating use of artificial intelligencc (AI) in medicine is reshaping how we conceptualize, design, and apply materials for human health. Traditionally, the development of biomaterials relied heavily on experimental work. While these efforts have produced remarkable advances, from biocompatible polymers to sophisticated tissue-engineered constructs, the process has often been time consuming, expensive, and limited by the complexity of biological systems.

Today, the rise of AI-driven methodologies, including machine learning, deep neural networks, data analytics, and computational modeling, is transforming this landscape. These tools enable the prediction of structure–property relationships, the optimization of synthesis and processing parameters, and the discovery of new materials with desired functionalities, all before a single experiment is performed. By integrating massive datasets from materials characterization, biological assays, and clinical outcomes, AI offers a pathway toward predictive, adaptive, and even autonomous biomaterials design.

This book, *Artificial Intelligence in Biomaterials Design and Development*, brings together an international network of scientists, engineers, and clinicians who collectively explore how AI is redefining the boundaries of biomaterials research. Across its chapters, readers will encounter the diverse and rapidly evolving ways in which intelligent algorithms are being used to accelerate materials discovery, optimize fabrication processes, refine characterization techniques, and guide the clinical translation of next-generation biomaterials. The contributions span from fundamental aspects, such as dataset curation, algorithmic modeling, and neural network training, to advanced applications in drug delivery, tissue engineering, prosthodontics, and biopolymer design.

Our vision in developing this book was to create not merely a reference text but a cross-disciplinary dialogue between computational intelligence and materials science. The authors present both the technical depth of AI methodologies and the human creativity that drives progress in biomaterials. This interplay between data and discovery lies at the heart of scientific innovation. AI can help us recognize patterns invisible to the human eye, but it is still the researcher's curiosity, ethics, and imagination that give these discoveries purpose.

From predictive modeling of polymers and proteins to AI-assisted synthesis, intelligent drug delivery platforms, hard tissue implants, and even education enabled by product-based learning, this volume showcases the transformative potential of intelligent systems when thoughtfully applied to the complexities of biological materials science. By bridging disciplines, it envisions a future where AI not only accelerates progress but also enriches our fundamental understanding of how materials interact with living systems.

We are deeply grateful to all contributors for their dedication, expertise, and insight, and to Elsevier's editorial team for their professionalism and continued support throughout the publication process. Above all, we recognize the collective effort of the scientific community whose pioneering research has made this integration of AI and biomaterials possible.

It is our sincere hope that this book will inspire a new generation of researchers to embrace AI as an integral tool in biomaterials research. By combining the analytical power of algorithms with the imagination and empathy that define us as scientists, we can move closer to designing smarter, safer, and more sustainable materials for the benefit of human health and the future of medicine.

**Payam Zarrintaj**
**Mohsen Khodadadi Yazdi**
**Sidi A. Bencherif**
**Mohammad Reza Saeb**
**Masoud Mozafari**
*Editors* (2025)

# Acknowledgment

I gratefully acknowledge the profound and formative influence of Prof. Hamid Modarress, emeritus professor of Chemical Engineering at Tehran Polytechnic or Amirkabir University of Technology (AUT), Iran. During my undergraduate studies in physical chemistry at AUT, Prof. Modarress did far more than teach—he illuminated a scientific path forward. His distinctive approach to problem-solving, clarity of thought, and unwavering intellectual integrity were exactly what I had been seeking throughout my early academic life. In his classroom, I did not merely learn science; I found my scientific self. That transformative experience—deepened by the privilege of serving as his teaching assistant for 5 years—laid the foundation of my scientific identity and has since inspired countless creative and innovative pursuits in my research. The vision underpinning this volume owes much to the intellectual foundation he so generously helped me build.

***Mohammad Reza Saeb***

# The critical role of artificial intelligence in biomaterials design and development

**1**

*Payam Zarrintaj*[1], *Mohsen Khodadadi Yazdi*[2,3], *Sidi A. Bencherif*[4,5,6], *Mohammad Reza Saeb*[7], *and Masoud Mozafari*[8]
[1]Independent Researcher, E3 LLC, Louisville, KY, United States, [2]Division of Electrochemistry and Surface Physical Chemistry, Faculty of Applied Physics and Mathematics, Gdańsk University of Technology, Gdańsk, Poland, [3]Advanced Materials Center, Gdańsk University of Technology, Gdańsk, Poland, [4]Chemical Engineering Department, Northeastern University, Boston, MA, United States, [5]Harvard John A. Paulson School of Engineering and Applied Sciences, Harvard University, Cambridge, MA, United States, [6]CNRS, PBS UMR 6270, University Rouen Normandie, Rouen, France, [7]Department of Pharmaceutical Chemistry, Medical University of Gdańsk, Gdańsk, Poland, [8]Research Unit of Health Sciences and Technology, Faculty of Medicine, University of Oulu, Oulu, Finland

## 1.1 Introduction

Biomaterials have emerged as a crucial component of modern medicine, characterized by their biocompatibility, bioactivity, and degradability, which enable seamless integration into biological systems without adverse reactions [1]. These biomaterials, classified into ceramics [2], metals [3], polymers [4], and composites [5], serve various medical applications, including implants [6], prosthetics [7], and drug delivery systems [8]. Recent advancements highlight the development of biobased materials, which are sustainable and eco-friendly, addressing the growing demand for environmentally responsible options in biomedical applications [9–11]. The field has evolved significantly, incorporating insights from tissue engineering and materials science, leading to innovative biomaterials such as microbubbles and nanoparticles [12,13]. However, challenges persist, including the need to improve mechanical properties and optimize degradation rates to enhance functionality and longevity in medical applications [14,15]. Overall, ongoing research holds great promise for revolutionizing healthcare through the creation of advanced biomaterials that improve patient outcomes [16–18]. As the field of biomaterials continues to progress, the integration of cutting-edge technologies like artificial intelligence (AI) is becoming increasingly crucial in driving innovation and overcoming existing challenges.

AI plays a transformative role across various scientific domains, enhancing capabilities and efficiency. In education, AI facilitates intelligent tutoring systems that promote self-reflection and critical thinking among students, thereby improving learning outcomes [19]. In the medical field, AI technologies, particularly deep learning (DL) algorithms, are revolutionizing patient care by enabling accurate diagnoses and personalized treatment plans, although their integration into clinical practice faces resistance from

**Artificial Intelligence in Biomaterials Design and Development. DOI:** https://doi.org/10.1016/B978-0-323-95464-8.00015-3

healthcare professionals [20,21]. Furthermore, AI's applications extend to social and human sciences, where it aids in understanding complex human behaviors and enhances research quality by bridging gaps between different disciplines. Despite these advancements, challenges such as data privacy, bias, and the need for explainable AI remain critical issues that must be addressed to fully realize AI's potential in modern science [22]. Overall, AI is not only reshaping existing practices but also expanding the horizons of knowledge across multiple fields.

The intersection of AI and biomaterials represents a transformative frontier in both material science and biomedicine. AI technologies are revolutionizing biomaterial design by enabling rapid prediction of material properties and facilitating the discovery of novel materials through advanced algorithms such as machine learning (ML) and generative AI [23]. These tools not only enhance the efficiency of material discovery but also allow for bio-inspired designs that mimic nature's multifunctional materials, promoting sustainability [24]. Furthermore, AI-driven design processes, including text-to-image generation, are reshaping how biomaterials are conceptualized and visualized, although they raise ethical concerns regarding authorship and copyright [25]. While the integration of AI in biomaterials research offers significant opportunities for innovation, challenges such as interdisciplinary collaboration and ethical considerations must be addressed to fully realize its potential [25]. Overall, this emerging synergy is poised to accelerate advancements in both fields, fostering a new era of biomaterials development. In summary, the convergence of AI and biomaterials is not just advancing material science but also paving the way for groundbreaking innovations in healthcare.

## 1.2 Foundations of artificial intelligence and machine learning in biomaterials research

This section presents an in-depth introduction to the basics of AI and important subfields associated with it; major attention is paid to their relation and potential toward developing the field of biomaterials research. AI is indicated as being a very broad and dynamic domain with many subdomains, including ML, DL, natural language processing, and robotics—where each of the subdomains tends to develop a form of human cognitive function in machines [26,27]. These technologies make it possible for machines to perform many activities that normally require human intelligence, such as recognizing patterns, making decisions, and understanding language. AI includes a wide array of technologies aimed at replicating human intelligence, such as ML, which uses algorithms to allow computers to learn from data and make predictions [28–30].

The section kicks off by discussing ML as a critical subset of AI, within which work is focused on developing algorithms, allowing computers to learn through data and make predictions. Supervised learning (SL) is one of the primary approaches within ML, pertaining to the training of models on labeled data that can be used to predict outcomes for new, unseen data [31,32]. This is applied to a very large number of tasks, such as classification, where inputs are assigned to predefined categories, and regression, which feeds into an output of continuous values. This section focuses on the fact that the SL models are developed through the minimization of the loss function that measures the difference between predicted and actual outcomes through optimization algorithms, among them provision for optimization using algorithms like the gradient descent for fine-tuning the models [33,34]. Unsupervised learning (UL) allows you to discover the unknown structure in the data by yourself, without knowing what the outcomes for each data item are. In other words, finding the relationships that may exist in the data without predetermined labels is known as UL. Two common UL techniques usually mentioned in this subclass include clustering, which groups similar data points, and component analysis, which reduces the number of variables [28] (Fig. 1.1).

Reinforcement learning (RL) is a paradigm in which agents learn to select a sequence of actions based on their environment by interacting with it. Through this process of trial and error, they maximize cumulative rewards over time. RL is typically applied in dynamic and complex settings, such as robotics or game playing. This section also addresses several important challenges in RL, including the exploration-exploitation tradeoff, managing delayed rewards, and considerations of safety and ethics for real-world applications [28,35,36].

This approach is elaborated on by the authors and explains the most important specialized area of ML—DL—using a very deep, artificial, neural network-based learning from large datasets. The DL model, based on hierarchical data representations, has been shown to perform tremendously in tasks such as visual object recognition, image/speech recognition, and natural language understanding. The section presents related discussions considering various issues that arise in DL, including the high number of labeled examples, model interpretability, and high computational costs for training such models [28,37,38]. Techniques under research toward this end include transfer learning and semisupervised

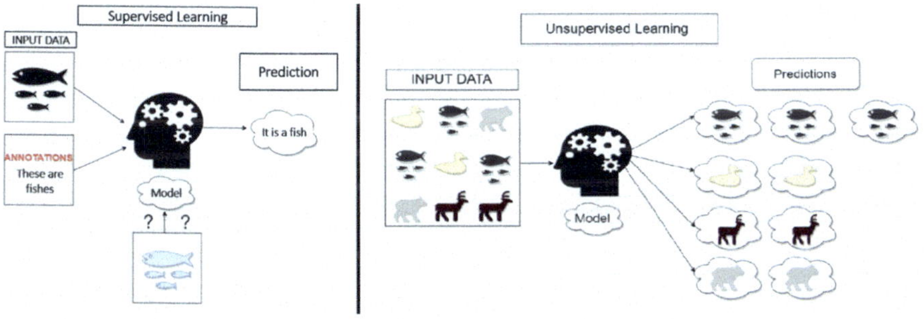


**Figure 1.1** Supervised learning (Left-hand image) versus unsupervised learning (Right-hand image). Comparison of supervised and unsupervised learning in machine learning. In supervised learning, the model is trained using labeled input data, where annotations guide the learning process to predict specific outcomes. In unsupervised learning, the model operates on unlabeled data, identifying hidden patterns or clusters without predefined labels and grouping similar items based on their inherent features (e.g., clustering different animals like fish, ducks, and goats). The figure illustrates the different learning approaches and their application in predictive modeling and pattern recognition.
Reprinted with permission from [28].

learning. Artificial neural networks (ANNs), including deep neural networks (DNNs), function by transforming data through interconnected nodes, much like the animal visual cortex. These networks learn by adjusting the weight of connections between nodes, a process known as backpropagation. This allows the network to improve its accuracy over time, similar to how brain plasticity strengthens neural connections. In DL, multiple hidden layers between the input and output enable the network to process data at increasingly abstract levels. With sufficient layers and computational power, DL models can autonomously learn complex patterns from data, making them highly effective for tasks like image recognition and object classification. Despite their sophistication, the underlying process of data transformation within these networks can be understood without requiring deep technical expertise (Fig. 1.2) [39–41] (Table 1.1).

It is evident that AI and its various subfields are crucial for the development of advanced intelligent systems. By enhancing capabilities in analyzing and interpreting complex data, these technologies drive innovation and push the boundaries of biomaterials research. This section sets the stage for applying AI methodologies to real-world problems, thereby significantly contributing to scientific discoveries and breakthroughs [43].

## 1.3 Current artificial intelligence integration

DL is rapidly advanced for healthcare, more particularly in big data areas that are less understood by human intuitions, such as genomics, gene expression analysis, and public health data. Such applications, such as clinical imaging, electronic health records, and wearable health-tracking devices, have made breakthroughs that would have been near impossible to reach without DL [44,45]. It enables extraction of features and patterns from data with very minimal previous knowledge in biology or medicine, for example, identifying medically relevant genetic variants, providing early detection of cancer, and relating cellular features to tumor pathology. For example, DL has already played a major role in medical imaging, a field with very complex and ambiguous data, for tasks such as tissue and organ segmentation. Presently, DL goes beyond this to abnormality detection, cell counting without invasion, and finally, predicting stem cell behavior [46].

In biomaterials science, ML, particularly DL, has significantly enhanced the design and optimization of three-dimensional scaffolds, which are crucial for controlling cell behavior in tissue engineering. By integrating DL, researchers can tailor biomaterials with patient-specific and trauma-specific parameters, optimizing topographical characteristics at both the microscale and nanoscale to influence cell migration, proliferation, and differentiation [42]. Recent advancements include using DL to accurately predict cell responses to various microtopographies, enabling more efficient and targeted biomaterial design. Notably, these advances were achieved with relatively small datasets, thanks to effective data augmentation techniques that expanded the dataset without compromising the model's generalization capability. This approach highlights the potential of DL in biomaterials research, particularly in reducing the time and resources needed for experimental validation while avoiding common pitfalls like overfitting. These findings suggest that DL can be successfully applied even in fields

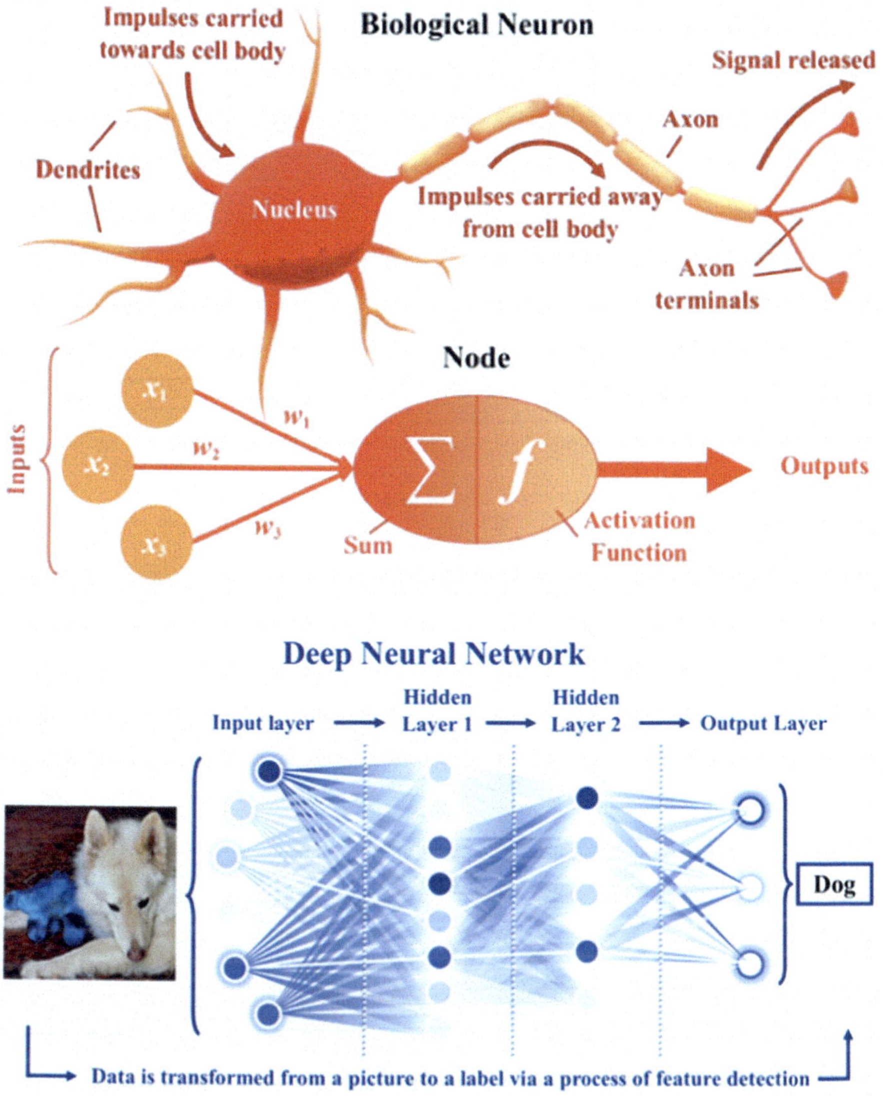


**Figure 1.2** Biological neurons versus artificial neural networks. (A) Biological neurons in the visual cortex and artificial nodes in neural networks function similarly. Both receive, process, and transmit information: neurons via dendrites, cell bodies, and axons, and artificial nodes through weighted inputs, activation functions, and outputs to subsequent layers. (B) In deep neural networks, input data is processed through multiple hidden layers, where it is weighted, summed, and transformed, enabling abstract feature extraction. The structure of the network, including the number of layers and nodes, is customizable.
Reprinted with permission from [39].

**Table 1.1** Examples of data mining and sampling, and algorithms commonly used for both supervised and unsupervised learnings [42].

| Category | Methods | Advantages | Weaknesses |
|---|---|---|---|
| Data mining, sampling, variable selection | – Random oversampling (RO) | – Simple to use, one of the most commonly used | – Ineffective against class imbalance |
| | – Synthetic Minority Oversampling Technique (SMOTE) | – Interpolation of data helps to reduce minority class imbalance | – Suffer in complex and hard-to-learn data |
| | – Adaptive synthetic (ADASYN) | – Effective to reduce class imbalance for hard-to-learn minority data | – Complex to use |
| | – Least absolute shrinkage and selection operator (LASSO) | – Simple and straightforward to use | – Limited number of variables, cannot do group selection |
| Supervised learning | – Random forest | – Robust to outliers, can handle large datasets, low risk of overfitting | – Can be slow with many trees |
| | – Gradient boosting | – Easy to read and interpretable, can handle overfitting | – Sensitive to outliers |
| | – Logistic regression | – Easy to use, simple, interpretable | – Overfitting |
| | – Support vector machine | – Effective in high-dimensional space | – Not effective to handle large datasets |
| | – Partial least squares (PLS) | – Lower sample size requirements | – Can be hard to interpret |

*(Continued)*

**Table 1.1** (Continued)

| Category | Methods | Advantages | Weaknesses |
|---|---|---|---|
| Unsupervised learning | – Artificial neural network (ANN) | – Robust against noisy data, fast | – Bad interpretability, nontractability |
| | – Convolutional neural network (CNN) | – Robust detection of feature importance | – Slow, computationally expensive |
| | – Principal component analysis (PCA) | – Remove correlated features, low risk of overfitting | – Need data standardization, information loss |

with limited data availability, offering promising avenues for future research and practical applications in tissue engineering [47].

The integration of machine intelligence with stem cell research extends beyond topographical response, aiding in understanding cell differentiation, reaction to micro-environmental cues, and quality control automation [48]. ML models have shown effectiveness in predicting outcomes in bioreactor-based experiments, such as the classification of cardiomyocyte content, and in quality control for stem cell cultures, although accuracy can vary based on data quality and complexity. Additionally, AI has improved the prediction and management of chronic graft-versus-host disease (GvHD) and stem cell mortality, enhancing clinical decision-making through predictive models [49]. The use of AI in animal-based research is also advancing the ethical principles of the 3Rs—replacement, refinement, and reduction of animal use—by improving the predictability of in vivo outcomes based on in vitro data, thereby reducing the reliance on extensive animal experimentation. This progress represents a significant step toward more efficient and ethical research practices in biomedical science [50] (Fig. 1.3).

## 1.4 How to integrate artificial intelligence?

Integrating DL into scientific research and practical application will have to be done with a structured and methodical approach. The first—and probably the most critical—step is the clear definition of the task that the network will carry out. The task must be well within the range of accomplishment with the available data and must have a payoff, like time or resource reduction, or an increase in the depth of scientific understanding. Selection of the data is a crucial part of this process. Apart from architecture choice, ensuring that the data is relevant and accessible is also very crucial for guaranteeing effective training of the network, such that it can finally

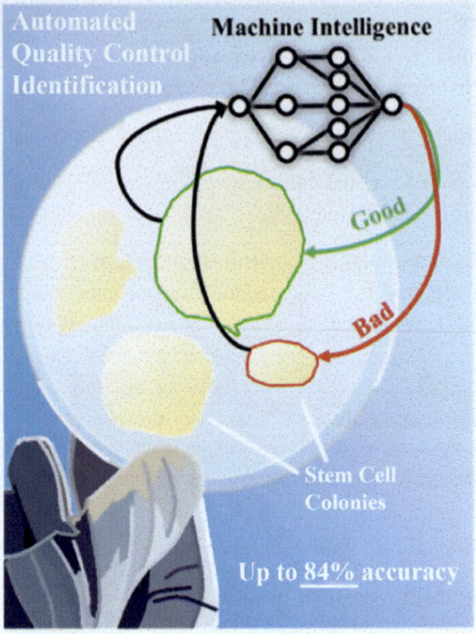


**Figure 1.3** AI-driven quality assessment. Machine intelligence can identify cell colony quality with up to 83.8% accuracy for "good" quality colonies. While accuracy for "semi-good" and "bad" requires further improvement before the system is capable of real-world application, there is a possibility for real-time noninvasive stem cell quality control through the use of AI. Reprinted with permission [39].

deploy in real-life scenarios. As an example, if DL network diagnosed COVID-19 from a selfie, it may not be up to the task, but with CT scans or X-rays of the chest, the relevant features are more evident, and the data can be accessed readily [51,52].

First, one defines the task and collects the suitable data and then comes the selection of a suitable network architecture. The choice of architecture is critical because it controls how the network processes the data to realize an end result. For example, the same architecture adopted for predicting stem cell responses with micro-patterned topographies is extendable to other jobs of biological imaging: 3D cell labeling or transforming optical microscope images into high resolution. This is because, in current DL practice, many architectures are often available, and all come with varying precisions and accuracies under different conditions. This would be very useful in cases of novel applications, where extensive experimentation with many architectures can be carried out. So, in general, a set of experiments with several architectures and data type experiments will have to be done before the optimal combination can be identified [53–55].

The selected network will have to be trained, and during the process, a procedure of meticulous fine-tuning for several hyperparameters is necessary to achieve an optimal performance. A few of these hyperparameters include the number of layers, the number of filters per layer, and the learning rate, which considerably alter the behavior of the network. Adding more layers with more filters in the model will be complex but, in turn, will increase the time needed for computations and require bigger computational power. The learning rate defines the step size of the network toward the minimization of errors and can be changed while training. In the case of a learning rate that is too high, the network may overshoot the optimal solution, and in the event of a rate that is too low, it may get stuck in a suboptimal state. Balancing these considerations is very important for the effective learning of the network and for yielding accurate results [56–58].

Arguably, the testing of this network forms the most critical step in the process because it validates not only the network's performance and accuracy while being trained but also the applicability of the network in real-life usage. High accuracy in training does not mean it will perform well in practice; hence, testing must be extensive. An ideal feature of testing data is that it should be very different from the features in the training data to avoid the overfitting of the features and that it should contain many features which are never going to be seen in the training data to evaluate the generalizability of the network. For example, if the network has been trained on X-rays from two hospitals, one might test it on data from a third hospital to see how it generalizes across different equipment, clinicians, and patient demographics. This helps check how well the network will adapt to new conditions and offload the expectation that it will be reliable even when deployed in considerably diverse real-world settings [59,60].

Incorporating DL research with everyday applications, therefore, balances task definition, data selection, architecture of the network, training, and rigorous testing at almost every step. Each step is interwoven with the others through the decisions made at each stage. This would mean that success will have to embody some meticulous planning and execution to assure that, more than an accurate network, the model developed will be applicable in the real world. But it is this above-mentioned fact that renders DL very relevant when looking for scientifically meaningful discoveries and practical applications; this process drives progress in many fields (Fig. 1.4).

## 1.5 Artificial intelligence application in biomaterial design

Abdallah et al. explored the integration of AI-generated images into the design process, specifically in the context of biomaterials research. The authors highlight the potential of AI text-to-image models, such as Midjourney and Stable Diffusion, to revolutionize design by rapidly generating high-fidelity and innovative visualizations of biomaterials. These models can create photorealistic renders that reflect the detailed physical characteristics of proposed biomaterials, from micro to macro scales, making them valuable tools for research-driven design. The article discusses the role of AI in augmenting the design process, particularly in form-finding, rendering, and visualization phases. It emphasizes the capacity of AI to synthesize complex data from various disciplines, contributing to innovative design solutions. However, the authors also address significant challenges, including the need for criteria to evaluate the efficiency of AI in design, issues of copyright and authorship, and the limitations of AI models in translating 2D images into 3D models for fabrication. Through the analysis of two case studies—one focused on bone tissue-inspired furniture and the other on pearl-inspired furniture—the article presents a SWOT analysis to evaluate

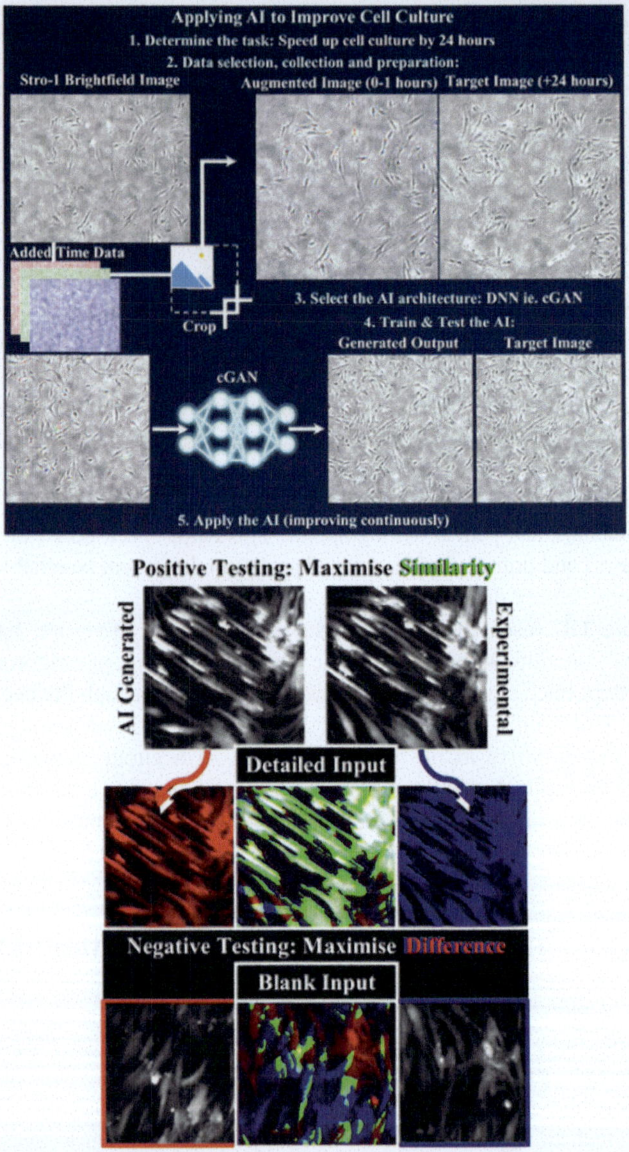


**Figure 1.4 AI-Enhanced Workflow for Optimizing Time-Consuming Tasks:** Top) Step-by-step example of applying AI to improve a time-consuming and resource-expensive task. Step 1 is determining a task that balances improvement with ease of data acquisition, such as reducing time needed for cell culture through AI-prediction of Stro-1 selected Human Bone Marrow Stromal Cells (HBMSCs) after an additional 24 h. Step 2 is selecting appropriate data (a brightfield image at time-points before and after 24 h), collecting the data (a continual time-lapse experiment at multiple positions with multiple cell cultures), and preparation (augmentation to provide maximum

(*Continued*)

the strengths, weaknesses, opportunities, and threats of AI integration in the design process. The findings suggest that while AI offers valuable tools for brainstorming and initial visualization, it still falls short in areas like technical drawings, simulation, and fabrication. The authors propose the development of auxiliary AI models for automatic referencing and protection of design copyrights, highlighting the need for further research to optimize the integration of AI in biomaterials-driven design [25,60].

ML can be used in nanomaterial synthesis, mostly within drug delivery systems and optoelectronics. The complexity of nanomaterials, which includes aspects such as composition, defects, shape, size, or surface characteristics, may be influenced by reaction conditions and experimental parameters [61]. This has been developed further through highly efficient flow chemistry coupled with ML to enable researchers to control the size and dispersity of quantum dots with perfection and adjust their composition and bandgap for optoelectronic applications. It can also be used to identify features that can be improved, such as performance-related features of nanoparticles. For instance, it has been used to predict the antibacterial properties of metal nanoparticles based on the size of their core and to track the in vivo fate of gold nanoparticles using mass spectroscopy coupled with supervised ML. In the field of drug delivery, ML has provided efficient screening of drug-excipient pairings for coaggregation into nanoparticles, bringing considerable improvements in the efficiency of drug loading [62,63]. Moreover, ML has been used to understand biological component-nanoparticle surface interactions. For example, it was applied in the study of the influence of surface chemistry on the adsorption of proteins onto PEGylated nanoparticles for the design of anti-fouling systems. This section highlighted that this work involves the predictive design of nanoparticle drug delivery systems by investigating changes in the nanoparticle, coating agent, and drug and by using large datasets along with ML models to optimize such components for better performance [64] (Fig. 1.5).

ML is enhancing and moving forward to design and develop polymer-based tissue engineering scaffolds. Polymers are materials used in making substitutes for tissues and organs [65]; however, it is essential to understand cell behaviors against

relevant data per input image and maximum images without overfitting). Images were processed here by combining 3 time-points and then performing randomized cropping. Step 3 is to decide on AI architecture(s), depending on both the task and the data acquired. For image data, a conditional Generative Adversarial Network (cGAN) is the starting-off architecture used here, as it has proven successful for similar tasks and code is readily available and open source. Step 4 is to train and then test the architecture, making multiple changes to both hyperparameters and the architecture until results can be trusted. The final step is to apply the AI, as the inclusion of new input and output data will reveal current limitations and provide improvement to the AI, while simultaneously saving 24 h of cell culture time. (Bottom) Comprehensive testing includes both positive and negative testing to determine both reliability and applicability. For cGANs, a successful positive test would include large areas of similarity (green) between the network-generated prediction (red) and experimentally obtained result (blue) to a detailed input. A negative test (blank input) should result in different results due to random network output, or the network has overfit to training data and is not applicable in real-world usage.
Reprinted with permission [39].

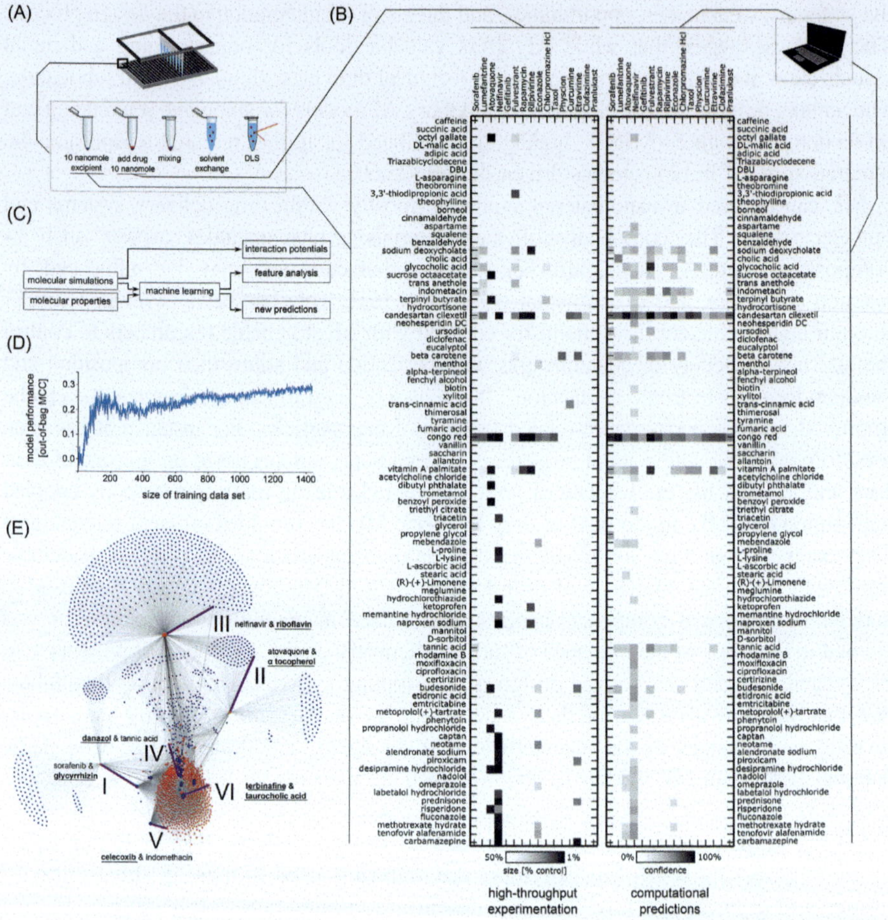


**Figure 1.5** High-throughput screening. (A) Schematic of high-throughput screening to create self-assembling drug nanoparticles. (B) High-throughput testing of all 1440 combinations of 16 drugs and 90 excipients (inactive ingredients, generally recognized-as-safe food and drug additives and other FDA-approved compounds). (C) Molecular properties of drug-excipient pairs are encoded, and molecular simulations (molecular dynamics) determine interaction potentials. These are fed into a random forest ML model to indicate important features and predict potential to coaggregate and form nanoparticles. (D) Out-of-bag performance analysis on different training dataset sizes with Matthews correlation coefficient showing convergence. (E) The ML model was used to model 2.1 million pairs of drugs and excipients for ability to coaggregate and form nanoparticles, and the six named pairs were validated experimentally. The novel component that was not part of the initial high-throughput screen in part A is underscored.

Reprinted with permission from [64].

these materials [66]. In developing scaffolds, some of the considerations that should be taken into consideration include wettability, chemistry, topography, and mechanical properties at the surface [67–69]. It demonstrated how surface topography can be utilized to direct cytokine secretion and support tendon cell phenotypes. Other work utilizing ML techniques, like partial least squares regression, remained focused on the interaction of human embryonic stem cells (hESC) adherence with polyacrylate polymers. A combinatorial approach delivered almost 500 polyacrylates, and ML models predicted primary fibroblast functions to a very high degree of accuracy from the surface properties alone, strongly correlated with the predicted values arising from the analysis of surface ions. The ability to predict biological interactions with polymer surfaces was further developed by nonlinear Bayesian regularized artificial neural network with a Laplacian prior (BRANNLP) and ANNs. ANN models then logically predicted very accurately protein adsorption on self-assembled monolayers and water contact angles. They also provided insight into the relevance of the chemical structure descriptors in guiding the material design through quantification of the contributions of specific molecular features [70] (Fig. 1.6).

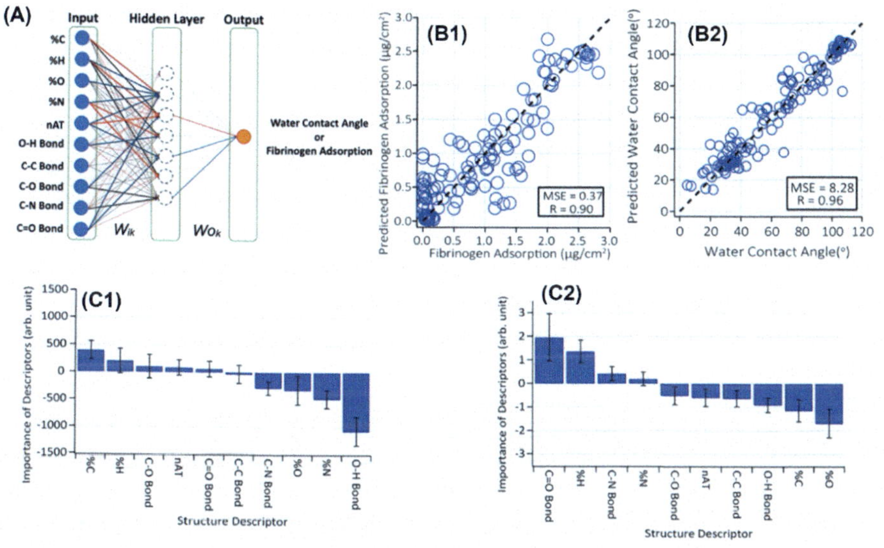


**Figure 1.6** ANN prediction model. (A) ANN model was used to evaluate and calculate the water contact angle and fibrinogen adsorption on the surfaces of self-assembled monolayers (SAM). The red and blue arrows illustrate positive and negative weights after the training, respectively. (B1–2) Amounts of adsorbed fibrinogen onto self- assembled monolayers (SAMs) predicted by the trained ANN plotted from multi- and single-lab data against corresponding experimental values, respectively. (C1–2) Results of analytical importance analysis of water contact angles and the one-laboratory data set training, respectively. Standard deviation (N=2000) is the standard error bar.
Reprinted with permission from [70].

## 1.6 Concluding remarks and future direction

The integration of AI into biomaterials research, combined with recent breakthroughs in the field, is now significantly enhancing the design and application of these materials. AI technologies, including ML and DL techniques, allow scientists to predict material properties, optimize designs, and improve the efficiency of development processes. These technologies facilitate the discovery of new materials, enable bio-inspired designs, and promote sustainability in biomaterials development. AI's potential impact is evident in the transformative synthesis of nanomaterials, drug delivery systems, and tissue engineering scaffolds. For instance, AI-powered models have shown significant improvements in predicting protein adsorption on SAMs, optimizing polymer scaffolds for tissue engineering, and designing nanoparticles with sophisticated nanofeatures.

In addition to AI, emerging technologies like blockchain are poised to make significant contributions to biomaterials research and healthcare. Blockchain technology, which underpins cryptocurrencies, is being explored in various sectors, including healthcare and biomaterials research. It has the potential to enhance transparency, traceability, and security in the supply chain for biomaterials, as well as to manage intellectual property and research data more efficiently. Decentralized platforms are being developed to explore applications in healthcare and biotechnology. For example, some blockchain projects focus on managing medical data, optimizing supply chains in the pharmaceutical industry, and incentivizing scientific research through tokenized rewards. While blockchain is not yet dedicated specifically to biomaterials, it could play a significant role in broader ecosystems that include biomaterials, contributing to innovations in transparency and data management.

However, despite the vast opportunities presented by AI and blockchain technologies, challenges remain—such as the need for interdisciplinary collaboration and addressing ethical considerations. While these obstacles are significant, the prospects for further integration of these technologies into biomaterials research, healthcare, and materials science are both promising and exciting. AI and blockchain's roles in revolutionizing future technologies offer the potential for improved patient outcomes and more efficient research methodologies.

Ultimately, the convergence of AI, blockchain, and biomaterials marks a new phase of scientific development and practical application. This integration holds the promise of overcoming current limitations and expanding the horizons for further advancements in the field. By embracing these emerging technologies and fostering collaborative efforts, the future of biomaterials research is poised for significant breakthroughs that will benefit both science and society.

## Acknowledgment

To the best of the Editors' knowledge and authors' claims, no generative AI tools were used for substantive writing of chapters. Any AI-assisted language editing, if applied, was limited to grammar or style suggestions and did not alter the scientific content.

## References


[1] Marin E, Boschetto F, Pezzotti G. Biomaterials and biocompatibility: An historical overview. *Journal of Biomedical Materials Research* 2020;108(8):1617–33.
[2] Zheng K, Boccaccini AR. Sol-gel processing of bioactive glass nanoparticles: A review. *Advances in Colloid and Interface Science* 2017;249:363–73.
[3] Chen Q, Thouas GA. Metallic implant biomaterials. *Materials Science and Engineering R: Reports* 2015;87(1):1–57.
[4] Banoriya D, Purohit R, Dwivedi RK. Advanced Application of Polymer based Biomaterials. *Materialstoday Proceedings* 2017;4(2):3534–41.
[5] Jagur-Grodzinski J. Polymers for tissue engineering, medical devices, and regenerative medicine. Concise general review of recent studies. *Polymers for advanced technologies* 2006;17(6):395–418.
[6] Teo AJT, Mishra F, Park I, Kim Y-J, Park W-T, Yoon Y-J. Polymeric materials for medical implants and devices. *ACS Biomaterials Science and Engineering* 2016;2(4):454–72.
[7] Heboyan A, Zafar MS, Rokaya D, Khurshid Z. Insights and advancements in biomaterials for prosthodontics and implant dentistry. *Molecules* 2022;27(16):5116.
[8] Ma W, Hua D, Xiong R, Huang C. Bio-based stimuli-responsive materials for biomedical applications. *Materials Advances* 2023;4(2):458–75.
[9] Birajdar MS, Joo H, Koh WG, Park H. Natural bio-based monomers for biomedical applications: a review. *Biomaterials Research* 2021;25(1):8.
[10] Wendels S, Avérous L. Biobased polyurethanes for biomedical applications. *Bioactive Materials* 2021;6(4):1083–106.
[11] Duceac IA, Balan V, Gheorghe D, Ailincai D, Nica V, Chibac A. Biobased materials for biomedical engineering. In: Thomas S, Durand JM, Chandra A, editors. Handbook of Biopolymer-Based Materials. Weinheim: Wiley-VCH; 2021.
[12] Esmaeili J, Rezaei FS, Mahmoudi Beram F, Barati A. Integration of microbubbles with biomaterials in tissue engineering for pharmaceutical purposes. *Heliyon* 2020;6(1):e04189.
[13] Bapat RA, Joshi CP, Bapat P, Chaubal TV, Pandurangappa R, Jnanendrappa N, et al. The use of nanoparticles as biomaterials in dentistry. *Drug Discovery Today* 2019;24(1):85–98.
[14] Wang L, Wang C, Wu S, Fan Y, Li X. Influence of the mechanical properties of biomaterials on degradability, cell behaviors and signaling pathways: current progress and challenges. *Biomaterials Science* 2020;8(10):2714–33.
[15] Nair LS, Laurencin CT. Biodegradable polymers as biomaterials. *Progress in Polymer Science* 2007;32(8-9):762–98.
[16] Facklam AL, Volpatti LR, Anderson DG. Biomaterials for personalized cell Therapy. Advanced Materials 2020;32(13):1902005.
[17] Viswanath DI, Liu H-C, Huston DP, Chua CYX, Grattoni A. Emerging biomaterial-based strategies for personalized therapeutic in situ cancer vaccines. *Biomaterials* 2022;280(1):121297.
[18] Mirkhalaf M, Men Y, Wang R, No Y, Zreiqat H. Personalized 3D printed bone scaffolds: A review. *Acta Biomaterialia* 2023;156(15):110–24.
[19] Sabirovna MK. The role of artificial intelligence in modern education. *International Journal of Pedagogics* 2024;4(06):86–9.
[20] Barua R, Datta S. Artificial intelligence in modern medical science: a promising practice. Recent developments in machine and human intelligence. IGI Global; 2023. p. 1–12.

[21] Balasubramaniam K, Anitha L, Anandavalli R, Kumar V. Role of artificial intelligence in the medical field. Journal of Artificial Intelligence and Capsule Networks 2023;5(4):346–461.
[22] Williamson SM, Prybutok V. Balancing privacy and progress: a review of privacy challenges, systemic oversight, and patient perceptions in AI-driven healthcare. *Applied Sciences* 2024;14(2):675.
[23] Han S, Wu J. Artificial intelligence (AI) meets biomaterials and biomedicine. *Smart Materials in Medicine* 2024;5(2):251–5.
[24] Luu RK, Arevalo S, Lu W, Ni B, Yang Z, Shen SC, Berkovich J, Hsu YC, Zan S, Buehler MJ. Learning from nature to achieve material sustainability: generative AI for rigorous bio-inspired materials design. MIT Generative AI Initiative. 2024.
[25] Abdallah YK, Estévez AT. Biomaterials research-driven design visualized by AI text-prompt-generated images. *Designs* 2023;7(2):48.
[26] Li J, Lim K, Yang H, Ren Z, Raghavan S, Chen PY, Buonassisi T, Wang X. AI applications through the whole life cycle of material discovery. *Matter* 2020;3(2):393–432.
[27] DeCost BL, Hattrick-Simpers JR, Trautt Z, Kusne AG, Campo E, Green ML. Scientific AI in materials science: a path to a sustainable and scalable paradigm. *Machine Learning Science and Technology* 2020;1(3):033001.
[28] Gokcekuyu Y, Ekinci F, Guzel MS, Acici K, Aydin S, Asuroglu T. Artificial intelligence in biomaterials: a comprehensive review. *Applied Sciences* 2024;14(15):6590.
[29] Rojek I, Mikołajewski D, Dostatni E, Macko M. AI-optimized technological aspects of the material used in 3D printing processes for selected medical applications. *Materials* 2020;13(23):5437.
[30] Sha W, Edwards KL. The use of artificial neural networks in materials science based research. *Materials and Design* 2007;28(6):1747–52.
[31] Kopper AE, Apelian D. Predicting quality of castings via supervised learning method. *International Journal of Metalcasting* 2022;16(1):93–105.
[32] Tepla TL, Izonin IV, Duriagina ZA, Tkachenko RO, Trostianchyn AM, Lemishka IA, Kulyk VV, Kovbasyuk TM. Alloys selection based on the supervised learning technique for design of biocompatible medical materials. *Archives of Materials Science and Engineering* 2018;93(1):32–40.
[33] Metzger A, Toscani M. Unsupervised learning of haptic material properties. *Elife* 2022;11:e64876.
[34] D'urso P, De D'ursoGiovanni L. Unsupervised learning. In: Webster JG, editor. editor. Wiley Encyclopedia of Electrical and Electronics Engineering. Wiley; 2018.
[35] Sui F, Guo R, Zhang Z, Gu GX, Lin L. Deep reinforcement learning for digital materials design. *ACS Materials Letters* 2021;3(10):1433–9.
[36] Shawky D, Badawi A. A reinforcement learning-based adaptive learning system. The international conference on advanced machine learning technologies and applications (AMLTA2018). Springer; 2018. p. 221–31.
[37] Bhuvaneswari V, Priyadharshini M, Deepa C, Balaji D, Rajeshkumar L, Ramesh M. Deep learning for material synthesis and manufacturing systems: a review. *Materials Today* 2021;46:3263–9.
[38] Nash W, Drummond T, Birbilis NJn MD. A review of deep learning in the study of materials degradation. NPJ Materials Degradation 2018;2(1):37.
[39] Mackay BS, Marshall K, Grant-Jacob JA, Kanczler J, Eason RW, Oreffo ROC, Mills B. The future of bone regeneration: integrating AI into tissue engineering. *Biomedical Physics and Engineering Express* 2021;7(5):052002.
[40] Feng S, Zhou H, Dong HJM. Using deep neural network with small dataset to predict material defects. *Materials and Design* 2019;162:300–10.

[41] Jiang J, Chen M, Fan JA. Deep neural networks for the evaluation and design of photonic devices. *Nature Reviews Materials* 2021;6(8):679–700.
[42] Suwardi A, Wang F, Xue K, Han MY, Teo P, Wang P, Wang S, Liu Y, Ye E, Li Z, Loh XJ. Machine learning-driven biomaterials evolution. *Advanced Materials* 2022;34(1):2102703.
[43] Basu B, Gowtham N, Xiao Y, Kalidindi SR, Leong KW. Biomaterialomics: data science-driven pathways to develop fourth-generation biomaterials. *Acta Biomaterialia* 2022;143:1–25.
[44] Ravì D, Wong C, Deligianni F, Berthelot M, Andreu-Perez J, Lo B, Yang GZ. Deep learning for health informatics. *IEEE Journal of Biomedical and Health Informatics* 2016;21(1):4–21.
[45] Norgeot B, Glicksberg BS, Butte AJJ. A call for deep-learning healthcare. *Nature Medicine* 2019;25(1):14–5.
[46] Yang S, Zhu F, Ling X, Liu Q, Zhao P. Intelligent health care: applications of deep learning in computational medicine. *Frontiers in Genetics* 2021;12:607471.
[47] Ahmed E, Mulay P, Ramirez C, Tirado-Mansilla G, Cheong E, Gormley AJ. Mapping biomaterial complexity by machine learning. Tissue Engineering Part A 2024;30:662–80.
[48] Kim M, Hong SJT. Integrating artificial intelligence to biomedical science: new applications for innovative stem cell research and drug development. Technologies 2024;12(7):95.
[49] Gandelman JS, Byrne MT, Mistry AM, Polikowsky HG, Diggins KE, Chen H, Lee SJ, Arora M, Cutler C, Flowers M, Pidala J, Irish JM, Jagasia MH. Machine learning reveals chronic graft-versus-host disease phenotypes and stratifies survival after stem cell transplant for hematologic malignancies. Haematologica 2019;104(1):189.
[50] Rudroff T. Artificial intelligence as a replacement for animal experiments in neurology: potential, progress, and challenges. Neurology International 2024;16(4):805–20.
[51] Panwar H, Gupta P, Siddiqui MK, Morales-Menendez R, Singh V. Application of deep learning for fast detection of COVID-19 in X-Rays using nCOVnet. Chaos, Solitons and Fractals 2020;138:109944.
[52] Bhimbhai PP, Jagannath PN. Review on deep learning techniques for the diagnosis of corona virus using CT & X-ray images. Proceedings of the Advancement in Electronics and Communication Engineering 2022;9:1–9.
[53] Moen E, Bannon D, Kudo T, Graf W, Covert M, Van Valen D. Deep learning for cellular image analysis. *Nature Methods* 2019;16(12):1233–46.
[54] Guay M, Emam Z, Leapman R. and Microanalysis. Two-stage neural architecture search for microscopy image segmentation. *Microscopy and Microanalysis* 2019;25(S2):188–9.
[55] Christiansen EM, Yang SJ, Ando DM, Javaherian A, Skibinski G, Lipnick S, et al. In silico labeling: predicting fluorescent labels in unlabeled images. *Cell* 2018;173(3):792–803.e19.
[56] Talashilkar R, Tewari K. Analyzing the effects of hyperparameters on convolutional neural network & finding the optimal solution with a limited dataset. 2021 International Conference on Advances in Computing, Communication, and Control (ICAC3). IEEE; 2021. p. 1–5.
[57] Radiuk P. An approach to accelerate the training of convolutional neural networks by tuning the hyperparameters of learning. *International Journal of Computer Applications in Technology* 2020;2:31–6.
[58] Smith LN. A disciplined approach to neural network hyper-parameters: part 1—learning rate, batch size, momentum, and weight decay. arXiv 2018.
[59] Eche T, Schwartz LH, Mokrane F-Z, Dercle LJRAI. Toward generalizability in the deployment of artificial intelligence in radiology: role of computation stress testing to overcome underspecification. Radiology Artificial Intelligence 2021;3(6):e210097.
[60] Zhang M, Leung KH, Ma Z, Wen J, Avinash G. A generalized approach to determine confident samples for deep neural networks on unseen data. In *Uncertainty for Safe*

*Utilization of Machine Learning in Medical Imaging and Clinical Image-Based Procedures: First International Workshop, UNSURE 2019, and 8th International Workshop, CLIP 2019, Held in Conjunction with MICCAI 2019, Shenzhen, China, October 17, 2019, Proceedings*. Springer; 2019. p. 65-74.

[61] Harrison PJ, Wieslander H, Sabirsh A, Karlsson J, Malmsjö V, Hellander A, Wählby C, Spjuth O. Deep-learning models for lipid nanoparticle-based drug delivery. *Nanomedicine* 2021;16(13):1097–110.

[62] Alshawwa SZ, Kassem AA, Farid RM, Mostafa SK, Labib GS. Nanocarrier drug delivery systems: characterization, limitations, future perspectives and implementation of artificial intelligence. *Pharmaceutics* 2022;14(4):883.

[63] Hassanzadeh P, Atyabi F, Dinarvand R. The significance of artificial intelligence in drug delivery system design. *Advanced Drug Delivery Reviews* 2019;151:169–90.

[64] Reker D, Rybakova Y, Kirtane AR, Cao R, Yang JW, Navamajiti N, Gardner A, Zhang RM, Esfandiary T, L'Heureux J, von Erlach T, Smekalova EM, Leboeuf D, Hess K, Lopes A, Rogner J, Collins J, Tamang SM, Ishida K, Chamberlain P, Yun D, Lytton-Jean A, Soule CK, Cheah JH, Hayward AM, Langer R, Traverso G. Computationally guided high-throughput design of self-assembling drug nanoparticles. *Nature Nanotechnology* 2021;16(6):725–33.

[65] Guo JL, Januszyk M, Longaker MT. Machine learning in tissue engineering. *Tissue Engineering Part A* 2023;29(1-2):2–19.

[66] Gentili PL, Stano P. Living cells and biological mechanisms as prototypes for developing chemical artificial intelligence. *Biochemical and Biophysical Research Communications* 2024;720:150060.

[67] Bose S, Robertson SF, Bandyopadhyay A. Surface modification of biomaterials and biomedical devices using additive manufacturing. *Acta Biomaterialia* 2018;66(15):6–22.

[68] Anselme K. Osteoblast adhesion on biomaterials. *Biomaterials* 2000;21(7):667–81.

[69] Lord MS, Foss M, Besenbacher F. Influence of nanoscale surface topography on protein adsorption and cellular response. *Nano Today* 2010;5(1):66–78.

[70] Kwaria RJ, Mondarte EAQ, Tahara H, Chang R, Hayashi T. Data-driven prediction of protein adsorption on self-assembled monolayers toward material screening and design. *ACS Biomaterials Science and Engineering* 2020;6(9):4949–56.

# Datasets and tools in materials science

## 2

*Sina Yousefi*
Department of Data Science and Analytics, Georgia Institute and technology, San Jose, CA, United States

## 2.1 Introduction

In the vast expanse of materials science research, datasets and tools stand as necessary pillars, forming the base that empowers scientists to explore the involved realms of materials. These datasets summarize a treasure trove of knowledge, spanning from elemental properties to intricate compound structures, furnishing researchers with a vast reservoir of insights for simulations, experiments, and precise prognostications of material behaviors. Extending these datasets are an array of tools, encompassing computational modeling software, microscopy techniques, and spectroscopic instruments, which facilitate the scrutiny, manipulation, and characterization of materials across myriad scales. This cooperative relationship between datasets and tools not only pushes the quest for novel materials but also pushes innovation in cutting-edge technologies across diverse domains such as electronics, energy, healthcare, and aerospace (see Fig. 2.1) [1].

The materials research has undergone a profound metamorphosis with the domination of data-driven science, joining vast and intricate datasets to unearth new materials and phenomena, incited by factors such as the open science movement and technological steps [1,2]. Nonetheless, this transition is not devoid of challenges, grappling with issues of data fidelity and standardization, yet it harbors immense potential for advancement. With swift progress in experimental and computational methodologies, materials science has navigated into a data-centric paradigm, necessitating robust frameworks for material innovation that encompass ML algorithms, databases, descriptors, and applications spanning various domains [2].

Recent reports, reviews, and symposia underscore the pivotal role of ML and artificial intelligence (AI) in the pursuit of materials discovery and optimization, with applications ranging from data analysis to experiment curation, leveraging their historical lineage and widespread accessibility since the 1960s. Significantly, high-throughput experimental methodologies have seamlessly integrated ML, streamlining analysis through standardized data formats and advanced interpretation tools, culminating in the inception of autonomous experimental systems geared toward expediting materials innovation [3].

The growing realm of materials data science employs data-driven protocols and sophisticated analytics to underpin decision-making in materials development endeavors objectively, striving to mitigate risks, quantify uncertainties, foster interdisciplinary collaborations, standardize workflows, and deal with scalability

**Artificial Intelligence in Biomaterials Design and Development. DOI:** https://doi.org/10.1016/B978-0-323-95464-8.00009-8

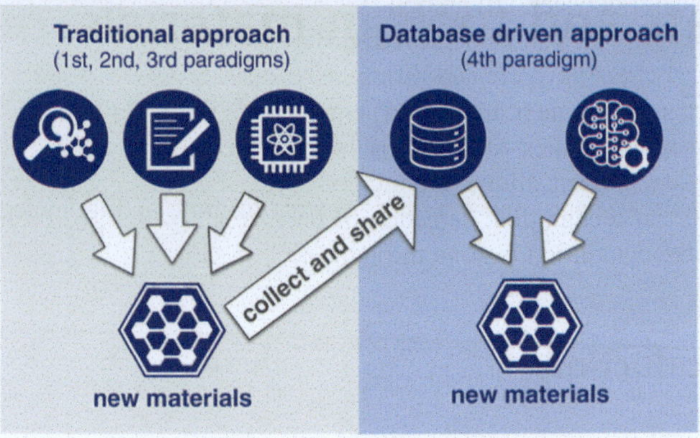


**Figure 2.1** Materials discovery schematic. Traditionally, new materials are found through experiments or theories. In the 4th paradigm, data is collected, and machine learning is used to discover new materials.
Reprinted with permission from [1].

challenges, underscoring the paramount importance of collaboration with experts from diverse disciplines to erect a comprehensive materials cyberinfrastructure [4]. Notably, ML emerges as a formidable ally in materials science, catalyzing research through property prognosis, experiment optimization, and crystal structure foretelling, with tempting applications yet to be fully harnessed, notwithstanding the difficulties such as benchmarking datasets and model accessibility [5].

The datasets and tools in materials science navigate periods, intricately entangled with the trajectory of scientific inquiry and technological advancement. From the primary observations of ancient civilizations to the systematic methodologies of the Renaissance, humanity's comprehension of materials has unfolded alongside the march of scientific progress. The 19th and 20th centuries stand as watershed moments, characterized by pivotal achievements such as the formulation of periodic tables, the crystallization of crystallography, and the dawn of spectroscopic techniques [6]. The digital revolution heralded a new dawn, where the ubiquity of computers and data storage systems reshaped the terrain of materials science, enabling the creation and dissemination of vast reservoirs of data. Today, materials scientists build upon the foundation of historical wisdom and technological breakthroughs, propelling the discipline toward unprecedented realms of exploration and innovation.

Within the realm of materials data science, deep learning (DL) has emerged as a growing frontier, transcending traditional boundaries and finding applications across a countless of data modalities including atomistic, image-based, spectral, and textual data [7]. DL facilitates the automated identification and analysis of features within unstructured datasets, capitalizing on the growing repositories of large-scale materials databases and the steps made in synthetic data generation through generative unsupervised DL methodologies. Ongoing endeavors in DL methodologies in materials science center on the quantification of uncertainty and the resolution of challenges to drive the field into new realms of possibility (see Fig. 2.2) [7].

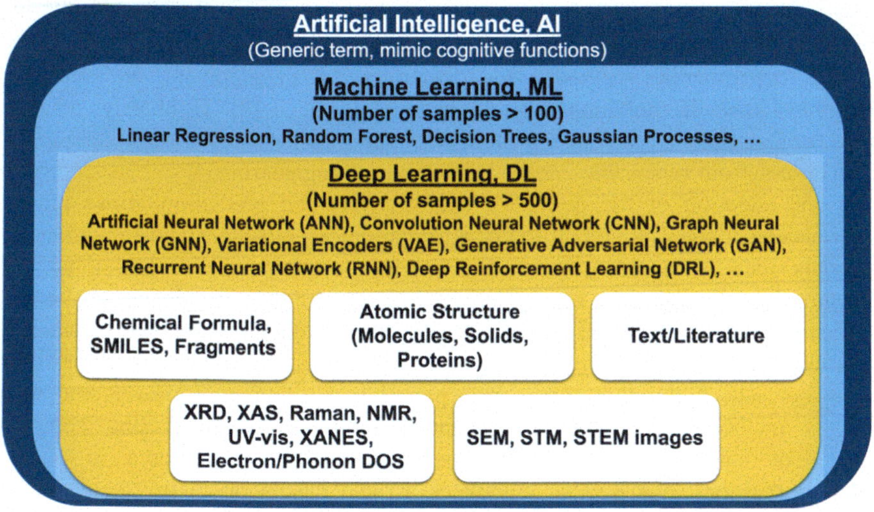


**Figure 2.2** The relationship between artificial intelligence (AI), machine learning (ML), and deep learning (DL) techniques, along with their applications in materials science and engineering.
Reprinted with permission from [7].

This chapter aims to provide a thorough examination of datasets and tools in materials science, encompassing essential topics for understanding their importance and practical applications. The following sections will be included: Historical Foundations: Tracing the historical origins of materials science and the development of datasets and tools over time. Fundamentals of Datasets: Exploring the various types of datasets utilized in materials science, including experimental, theoretical, and computational data. Characterization Tools: Investigating the wide range of tools and techniques used for characterizing and analyzing materials, such as microscopy and spectroscopy. Computational Modeling: Delving into the realm of computational modeling and simulation, demonstrating its role in understanding material properties and behaviors, highlighting recent advancements and emerging trends in datasets and tools and predicting their potential impact on the future of materials science research and technology.

## 2.2 Importance of datasets in materials science

### *2.2.1 The significance of datasets in materials science*

Datasets serve as the foundation of materials science research, providing structured information essential for understanding material behavior, properties, and interactions. By compiling data from experiments, theoretical models, simulations, and observations, these repositories offer deep insights into material compositions, structures, properties, and behaviors. Through careful curation, datasets enable the identification of patterns, trends, and correlations, validating theoretical concepts, refining experimental methods, and fostering the development of predictive algorithms, thus driving innovation in materials science [8]. Ultimately, datasets empower researchers to unlock the latent potential of materials across a wide range of applications, from renewable energy to biomedical engineering.

As the adoption of ML tools for data analysis and prediction grows among materials scientists, it is crucial to consider the unique attributes and limitations of materials data to avoid pitfalls. This review emphasizes the importance of thoughtfully selecting data processing and ML techniques to address challenges such as overfitting, highlighting the essential role of domain expertise in creating accurate models [8]. The synthesis of numerous potential metal-organic frameworks (MOFs) presents both opportunities for exploration and challenges to overcome, with big-data methodologies emerging as powerful tools for unraveling complex correlations among these materials. By exploring ML applications in porous materials research, this review anticipates a rapid expansion in this field due to increasing scientific interest (see Fig. 2.3) [9].

In the field of biomedical engineering, despite the growing use of ML techniques for disease detection and diagnosis, their clinical validation remains limited and susceptible to overfitting. Integrating validation into the broader framework of establishing clinical validity for diagnostic methods is of paramount importance, as emphasized in this commentary [10]. By analyzing the performance of data mining algorithms using public datasets, researchers found that ensemble algorithms consistently achieved commendable classification accuracy, with algorithm selection depending on dataset characteristics. Their findings underscored the absence of a one-size-fits-all algorithm, providing a benchmark for biomedical researchers and newcomers in various domains [11].

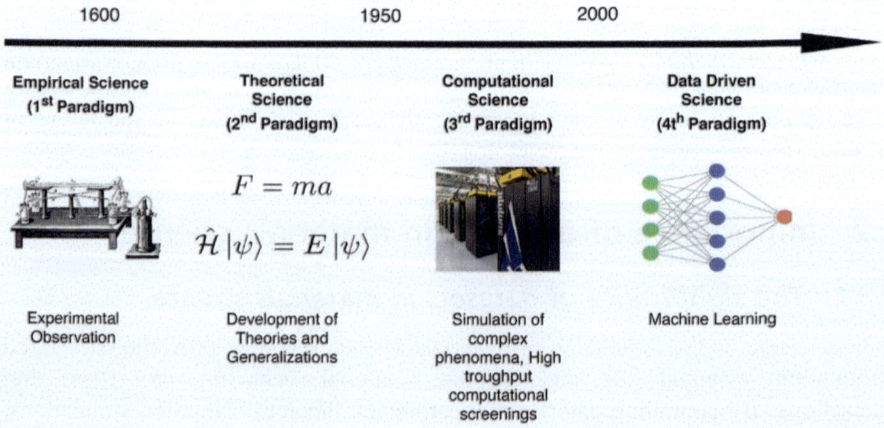


**Figure 2.3** Evolving scientific methods, from empirical observation to theory generalization and complex phenomena simulation.
Reprinted with permission from [9].

### 2.2.2 Types of datasets commonly used (experimental, theoretical, and computational)

Within the dynamic domain of materials science, datasets serve as vital repositories of information, collected through diverse methodologies and approaches. Among these, experimental datasets hold paramount importance, stemming from meticulous laboratory experiments, measurements, and observations conducted under controlled conditions. These datasets yield tangible and reliable data points, providing invaluable insights into the physical, chemical, mechanical, and electronic properties of materials. Augmenting this empirical foundation, theoretical datasets are equally significant, emanating from intricate mathematical models, analytical frameworks, and theoretical principles elucidating material behavior across various scales, from the atomic to the macroscopic. Often, they elucidate concealed mechanisms, relationships, and phenomena not readily observable. Further enriching this comprehension are computational datasets, extensive compilations of data generated through computer simulations, modeling, and data-driven methodologies. Leveraging sophisticated computational algorithms and techniques, these datasets facilitate the simulation of material behaviors, prediction of properties, and exploration of complex phenomena that may pose challenges or be impractical to study experimentally. Together, these three categories of datasets synergize to furnish a holistic understanding of materials, driving innovation in materials science research.

The progress of sophisticated ML algorithms in experimental materials science faces a significant challenge—the lack of large and diverse datasets. However, encouraging developments like the High-Throughput Experimental Materials (HTEM) Database (htem.nrel.gov) have emerged, boasting over 140,000 sample entries with structural, synthetic, chemical, and optoelectronic properties of inorganic thin film materials. Not only does it provide scientists with a wealth of data, but it also highlights the potential of advanced ML algorithms to tackle materials science challenges using open data resources [12]. Moving forward, advancements in materials science and engineering, supported by initiatives like the Materials Genome Initiative, aim to expedite the discovery and introduction of novel materials. A significant workshop held at the National Science Foundation in 2013 identified crucial challenges and opportunities in this field, offering recommendations to streamline the integration of theory, computation, synthesis, and characterization [13]. Leveraging data from sophisticated techniques like X-ray crystallography, the Cambridge Structural Database (CSD) provides invaluable insights into molecular architectures, crystal packing arrangements, and intermolecular interactions, playing a pivotal role in drug discovery, materials design, and crystal engineering. Additionally, the National Institute of Standards and Technology (NIST) Materials Data Repository (MDR) offers a treasure trove of experimental data spanning mechanical and thermal properties to phase equilibria and spectroscopic data [14]. These datasets, among many others, have been fundamental catalysts in advancing materials science research, accelerating innovation, and fostering interdisciplinary collaboration.

Moreover, initiatives such as the National Institute for Materials Science in Japan lead concerted efforts toward the development of materials data platforms linked with repository systems. These pioneering platforms leverage materials informatics to streamline material searches and ensure result reproducibility across various measurement techniques, fostering interoperability and machine readability [15]. Similarly, the Discovery Engines for Big Data project at Argonne National Laboratory tackles key challenges in materials science and engineering by developing automated data acquisition pipelines and utilizing cutting-edge supercomputing resources to enable near-real-time data processing and feedback. These initiatives are poised to revolutionize large-scale data handling, fostering intuitive and interactive platforms aimed at driving discovery and innovation. In essence, the profound influence of seminal datasets in materials science underscores their indispensable role in advancing scientific inquiry and paving the way for transformative breakthroughs on a global scale.

## 2.3 Experimental datasets

### *2.3.1 Experimental techniques for data generation*

Experimental datasets in materials science are often generated through a myriad of sophisticated techniques aimed at probing and characterizing the properties of materials at various scales. These techniques encompass a wide spectrum of methodologies, ranging from traditional laboratory experiments to cutting-edge instrumentation [16]. For instance, spectroscopic techniques [17,18] such as X-ray diffraction (XRD) [19–21], nuclear magnetic resonance (NMR) [22], and Fourier-transform infrared spectroscopy (FTIR) [23–25] are commonly employed to elucidate the structural, chemical, and electronic properties of materials. Additionally, microscopy techniques [26] including scanning electron microscopy (SEM) [27–30] (see Fig. 2.4), transmission electron microscopy (TEM) [28,30–32] (see Fig. 2.5), and atomic force microscopy (AFM) [33–35] offer high-resolution imaging and analysis of material surfaces and interfaces. Other experimental approaches, such as thermal analysis [36], mechanical testing [37,38], and electrochemical measurements, provide crucial insights into the thermal,

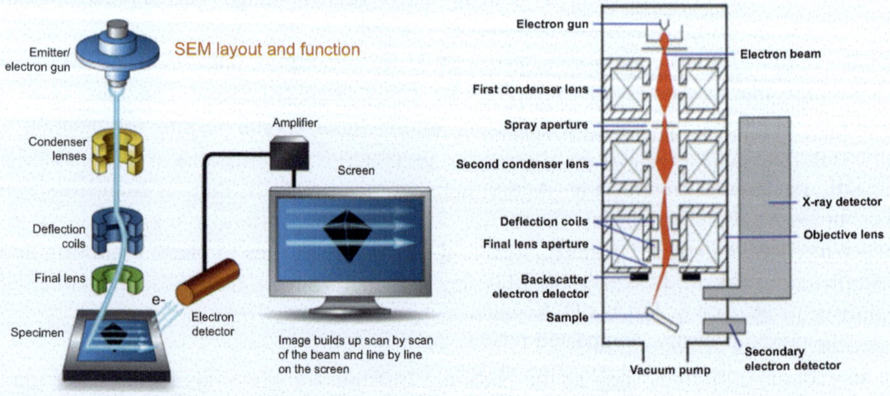


**Figure 2.4** Schematic of scanning electron microscope (SEM).
Reprinted with permission from [27].

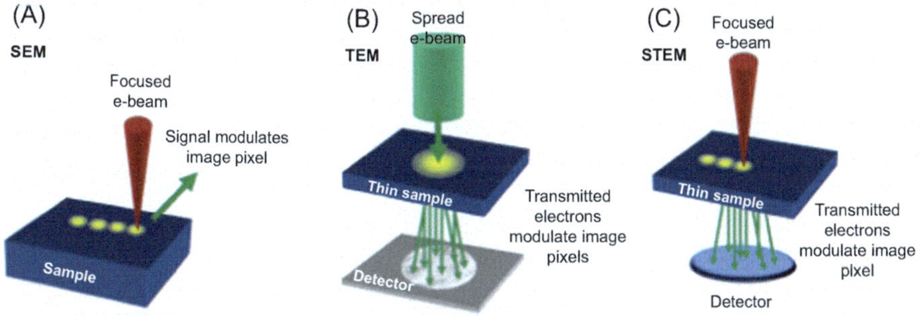


**Figure 2.5** Schematic of SEM, TEM, and STEM imaging methodology. (A) Data points in SEM. (B) Image acquisition in TEM. (C) Transmitted electrons in STEM. *SEM*, Scanning electron microscope; *TEM*, transmission electron microscopy.
Reprinted with permission from [27].

mechanical, and electrochemical behavior of materials under varying conditions. By meticulously designing and executing these experiments, researchers can generate rich datasets comprising quantitative measurements, spectral signatures, imaging data, and more, thereby enabling comprehensive characterization and understanding of materials [38]. The exponential growth of material data from experiments and simulations necessitates the development of data-driven methods for discovering patterns and structure–property relationships across multiple length and time scales within materials science (see Fig. 2.6).

Since the discovery of X-rays in the late 19th century, significant advancements have been made in utilizing XRD techniques for material characterization, particularly in materials science and engineering [21]. XRD serves as a vital technique for analyzing inorganic mineralized artifacts, including ceramics, lithics, ores, and metals, among others, providing insights into their mineral constituents and raw material sources. It aids in understanding manufacturing technology, use, and alteration of synthetic materials like ceramics and pigments, often complemented by other compositional characterization methods like microscopy and instrumental geochemistry [20]. Powder XRD serves as a crucial characterization tool for nanoscale materials, offering insights into phase identification, sample purity, crystallite size, and morphology, which can complement other microscopic and spectroscopic techniques. Despite its significance, the full potential of powder XRD data for nanoscale materials is not always realized, leading to potential misinterpretations [19].

NMR spectroscopy offers a robust method for analyzing mixtures at the molecular level in food science, but its full potential remains underutilized due to cost, sensitivity, and expertise constraints. Hatzakis [22] aims to provide fundamental principles, insights into chemometrics, and recent applications, including compositional analysis, food authentication, quality control, and human nutrition, to aid scientists in applying NMR effectively in food science research. Infrared spectroscopy serves as an analytical tool for identifying functional groups in organic compounds [23,25]. FTIR spectroscopy and microscopy play pivotal roles in

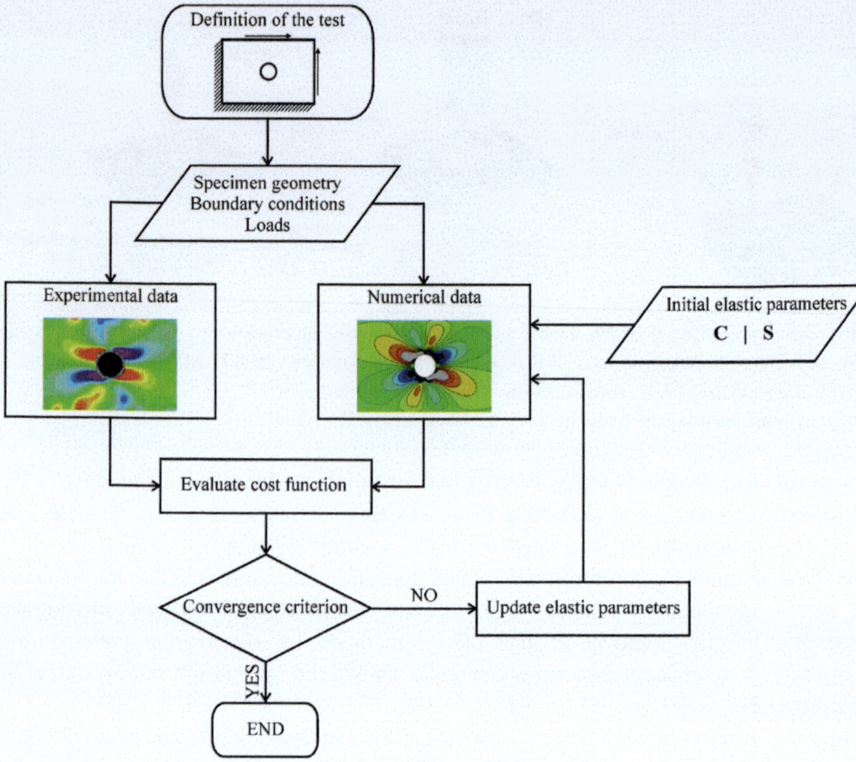


**Figure 2.6** Flow chart summarizing the elastic characterization procedure based on finite element model updating.
Reprinted with permission from [37].

investigating cultural heritage materials, with recent advances in the field focusing on new methods for analyzing inorganic materials in the far-IR region, improving cross-section preparation techniques to avoid polymer interference, enhancing spatial resolution to characterize small particles and thin layers, and evaluating protective treatments more efficiently [24]. Mohammed and Abdullah [27] highlight the critical role of SEM in surface topography imaging, particularly through secondary and backscattered electron imaging, and underscore the importance of understanding these features for proficient operation and analysis (see Fig. 2.5). TEM is a versatile technique widely used for characterizing materials at the nanoscale, providing detailed information on morphology, crystalline structure, and elemental composition. It offers two main modes, bright-field and dark-field, for imaging samples and enables the visualization of crystalline structures and elemental distributions. TEM is particularly valuable for studying membrane materials, offering insights into their structure, morphology, and performance through detailed characterization [30]. Franken et al. [32] discuss three commonly used TEM methods—drying, staining, and cryo-TEM—explaining their applications, limitations, and interpretation considerations, emphasizing the importance of selecting the appropriate technique for soft matter imaging to avoid errors and overinterpretations. Cryo-TEM is recommended as the most suitable method due to its ability to prevent artifacts and preserve sample integrity. Transmission electron imaging with standard SEMs can be achieved by adding a transmission detector, creating a mode known as STEM-in-SEM or TSEM, offering versatile imaging modalities using transmitted electrons. TSEM bridges the gap between SEM and high-voltage TEM, providing new imaging possibilities and applications while avoiding the need for atomic resolution. The basics of TSEM, including configuration, implementation of the transmission detector, and electron scattering physics, are outlined, along with comparisons to other electron microscopy techniques. Various TSEM applications, such as dimensional measurements and material characterization, are discussed [31].

Nanoparticles play crucial roles in various fields, leveraging their size-dependent properties, such as in catalysis and biomedical applications. The growing demand for high-resolution microscopic imaging across various fields has led to the increased use of techniques capable of nanometer-scale characterization. The emergence of scanning probe techniques like scanning tunneling microscopy (STM) and AFM has revolutionized surface analysis, enabling visualization of atomic-scale topographic and electronic features across various materials. AFM enables three-dimensional visualization and analysis of individual particles and particle groups. Nanoparticles exhibite varied aggregation patterns depending on the substrate, with higher coagulation observed on mica and lower density on chemically treated surfaces due to increased surface hydrophobicity [34].

Experimental datasets have been instrumental in driving numerous breakthroughs and innovations in materials science across various applications. For example, datasets derived from XRD experiments play a crucial role in determining the crystal structures and phase compositions of materials, guiding the synthesis and optimization of crystalline materials for applications in catalysis, electronics, and energy storage. Similarly, datasets obtained from SEM enable the visualization and analysis of material morphologies, microstructures, and defects, thereby informing the development of advanced materials for applications such as biomedical implants, aerospace components, and renewable energy devices. Furthermore, datasets from electrochemical impedance spectroscopy experiments provide valuable insights into the kinetics and mechanisms of electrochemical reactions, facilitating advancements in battery technology, corrosion mitigation, and sensor development. By harnessing these experimental datasets, researchers can uncover the intricate relationships between material structure, properties, and performance, paving the way for tailored materials design and optimization across a diverse range of applications.

## 2.4 Theoretical datasets

### *2.4.1 Theoretical modeling and simulations in materials science*

In materials science, theoretical modeling and simulations serve as vital complements to experimental observations, elucidating fundamental principles governing the behavior and properties of materials. Theoretical datasets stem from mathematical models, computational algorithms [39], and simulation techniques that simulate material behavior at atomic, molecular, and macroscopic scales. These encompass a diverse array of methodologies, including quantum mechanics [40], molecular dynamics [41–43], density functional theory (DFT) [44–46], and Monte Carlo simulations [42,47,48], each tailored to address specific aspects of material properties and phenomena. Through theoretical modeling and simulations, researchers can explore complex interactions, predict material behaviors under varying conditions, and uncover underlying mechanisms not accessible through experiments alone. Moreover, theoretical datasets provide a platform for hypothesis testing, materials design, and virtual experimentation, offering invaluable insights into structure–property relationships.

Materials science encompasses the understanding of the relationship between fundamental properties at the atomic-scale and macroscopic properties needed for engineering applications, often influenced by microstructure resulting from specific process conditions. Computational materials science aims to uncover hidden composition–structure–property relationships using computational techniques, focusing on methods applicable to semiconductor, metal, or ceramic materials. DFT has become a potent tool in materials science, addressing various topics and overcoming challenges such as the bandgap problem and limitations in ground-state calculations. However, several challenges remain, including improving exchange-correlation functionals for predicting phase transitions and developing efficient multiscale strategies for realistic simulations [46]. Maurer et al. [45] present the evolution of DFT as a fundamental method in materials science over the past two decades, reviewing recent advances and challenges in DF calculations for modeling various material classes, including hard solids, molecular and biological matter, low-dimensional materials, and hybrid organic-inorganic materials.

The Monte Carlo simulation method has become prevalent in materials science and engineering, with recent developments focusing on both mesoscale and atomistic simulations based on statistical mechanics. It is extensively utilized within the Materials Studio application, employing various modules for molecular simulation. These modules employ random configurations to calculate averages of interest, such as interaction energies and properties of polymer chains, utilizing techniques like Metropolis or configurational bias methods. Additionally, the application includes modules for sampling physical distributions, optimizing functions using simulated annealing, and predicting crystal structures from molecular or X-ray powder diffraction data [47]. Mesoscale simulations, exemplified by grain growth using Potts' model, illustrate the dynamics and topological behaviors of microstructural evolutions, such as interface migration kinetics traced through spin variable flipping and domain structure scaling via cluster analysis. Atomistic scale simulations, demonstrated by the ordering of f.c.c. to L12 structure in Ni base alloy, predict ordering kinetics, temporal evolution of atomic arrangement, and site occupancy of alloying elements through direct exchange of neighboring single atoms [48].

Theoretical datasets have been instrumental in advancing our understanding of materials across numerous disciplines and applications. For example, DFT calculations yield theoretical datasets comprising electronic structures, bandgaps, and charge densities of materials, providing fundamental insights into their electronic properties and behaviors. These datasets have been extensively utilized in the design of semiconductors, catalysts, and photovoltaic materials with tailored electronic properties for optoelectronic devices and energy conversion applications. Similarly, molecular dynamics simulations generate theoretical datasets elucidating the dynamic behavior, thermal properties, and mechanical responses of materials at the atomic and molecular levels. These datasets have been indispensable for understanding phenomena such as diffusion, phase transitions, and mechanical deformation, guiding the development of materials for aerospace, automotive, and nanotechnology applications. Furthermore, Monte Carlo simulations provide theoretical datasets characterizing thermodynamic properties, phase equilibria, and phase transitions in materials systems, facilitating the design and optimization of materials for thermal management, energy storage, and drug delivery. By harnessing the power of theoretical modeling and simulations, researchers can explore vast design spaces, accelerate materials discovery, and innovate across a wide range of scientific and technological domains.

## 2.5 Computational datasets

### 2.5.1 Computational methods and algorithms in materials science

Computational methods and algorithms serve as indispensable tools in materials science, enabling researchers to simulate, predict, and analyze the properties and behaviors of materials with unprecedented accuracy and efficiency. Computational datasets encompass a diverse array of data generated through computational modeling, simulations, and data-driven approaches, leveraging advanced algorithms and techniques to explore complex phenomena across multiple length and time scales. These methods include finite element analysis [49,50], ab initio calculations [51,52], ML algorithms, and high-throughput screening techniques [53], each tailored to address specific research questions and challenges in materials science. By harnessing the computational power of supercomputers, clusters, and cloud platforms, researchers can generate vast datasets comprising structural, electronic, mechanical, and thermodynamic properties of materials, thereby accelerating materials discovery, design, and optimization.

Skinner and Broughton [54] explore various optimization techniques for reliably determining the weights of large feed-forward neural networks in computational materials science, comparing convergence rates for different algorithms such as back propagation, conjugate-gradient methods, genetic algorithms, simulated annealing, and a swarm search algorithm. Conjugate-gradient methods are found to be successful for small networks with few optimal solutions, while hybrid schemes combining genetic algorithms or simulated annealing with conjugate-gradient approaches are most effective for larger networks with complex parameter spaces, now preferred for training large networks. David Müzel et al. [55] highlight the increasing utilization of composite materials in diverse sectors, emphasizing the challenges arising from their heterogeneity and high costs, which necessitate advanced analysis techniques such as the finite element method. It delves into various aspects of composite material modeling, including material properties, failure criteria, types of elements, and industrial applications across sectors like aerospace, automotive, and energy. It extensively discusses micromechanics, homogeneous equivalent, and combined models for composite simulations, elucidating the differences and computational demands of each approach. It also explores constitutive relationships governing mechanical properties and various failure mechanisms, along with commonly used failure criteria such as Tsai–Hill and Hashin. Additionally, it examines different types of elements and theories governing composite simulations, focusing on plates, shells, and cohesive elements.

Stochastic Finite Element Methods (SFEM) are influenced by assumptions made about uncertain material properties, stressing the need to link microstructural models with stochastic material properties at the macroscale. It proposes examining micromechanical characteristics to deduce macroscopic material randomness and advocates for a systematic effort to establish this link. Additionally, it emphasizes the importance of experimental data to validate assumptions and identifies critical stochastic material properties affecting SFEM results, suggesting that materials scientists can contribute significantly to addressing these challenges [49].

Pokluda et al. [52] critically review ab initio calculations of mechanical properties of materials, covering DFT and various approximations used. Methods for predicting elastic constants and moduli are discussed, along with theoretical strength under different loading conditions. Case studies include elastic stability conditions for molybdenum and microscopic deformation in platinum. Ideal strength values for metallic and covalent crystals are compared with experimental data, and interfaces and grain boundaries are examined. The article also explores applications in predicting hardness and brittle/ductile behavior, as well as challenges and future directions for ab initio studies. High-throughput virtual screening relies on an approach that balances computational cost with accuracy, leveraging a feedback loop between theory and experiment to navigate chemical space effectively. Trends in data are essential, along with calibration to experimental results, to enhance accuracy and utility. Both exploratory and exploitative experimental outcomes play vital roles in the long-term success of high-throughput virtual screening [56].

Combinatorial and high-throughput (CHT) experimentation offers a promising approach to overcome the limitations of rational materials design by facilitating the discovery and optimization of new materials across various domains. Combinatorial technology has emerged as a revolutionary approach to advancing research in the development of novel materials and catalysts, with recent advancements in synthetic methods and characterization tools enabling its application in discovering olefin polymerization catalysts. However, the characterization methodology has not kept pace with the increase in library density, limiting the application of combinatorial technology. Potyrailo et al. [57] highlight the broad applicability of CHT experimentation technologies, discussing principles, characterization approaches, data analysis methods, and material developments in areas like catalysis, electronic materials, coatings, sensing materials, and biomaterials. Woo et al. [58] introduce several tools and apparatus currently applied in discovering inorganic materials and catalysts using combinatorial technology, along with considerations for addressing these challenges.

Computational datasets have revolutionized materials science research by offering insights, predictions, and design strategies that complement experimental and theoretical approaches [59,60]. For example, high-throughput screening techniques enable the rapid generation of computational datasets comprising the properties of thousands to millions of materials candidates, facilitating the discovery of novel materials with desired properties for specific applications. These datasets have been instrumental in accelerating materials research in areas, such as photovoltaics, catalysis, and energy storage, by identifying promising materials candidates with enhanced performance metrics. Additionally, ML algorithms applied to computational datasets offer predictive models and design guidelines for materials discovery and optimization. For instance, neural network models trained on computational datasets can predict material properties, phase transitions, and reaction pathways with high accuracy, guiding experimental synthesis efforts and accelerating materials development cycles. Furthermore, computational datasets derived from multiscale modeling and simulations provide mechanistic insights into complex phenomena such as self-assembly, morphological evolution, and interface dynamics in materials systems. By integrating computational datasets with experimental and theoretical approaches, researchers can leverage a synergistic combination of techniques to tackle grand challenges in materials science, from designing materials for sustainable energy technologies to engineering biomaterials for regenerative medicine.

Nanoscience attracts growing interest for its exploration of physicochemical phenomena and applications like silicon carbide films, carbon nanotubes, and micro-electro-mechanical systems (MEMS), requiring deeper insights and better process control in fabrication techniques like chemical vapor deposition (CVD). Multiscale modeling, integrating contributions from diverse scientific disciplines, emerges as a vital tool to simulate materials across various length and time scales. Recent advances in multiscale materials modeling are outlined, covering classification of simulation methods, hierarchical and hybrid coupling strategies, and applications in thin film CVD deposition and carbon nanotube mechanics. Challenges in multiscale modeling, including spatial and temporal approaches, are discussed alongside future trends [59,60]. Stoll and Benner [61] explore the application of ML for metallic material characterization, aiming to predict material properties such as strength, toughness, hardness, etc., which are crucial for assessing material quality. ML methods offer a promising avenue for faster and more cost-effective generation of material property information, potentially replacing time-consuming and expensive material tests like tensile tests with simpler tests like small punch tests (SPT) in combination with ML algorithms.

## 2.6 Modeling and simulation tools

### *2.6.1 Software and platforms for theoretical modeling and simulations*

Modeling and simulation tools play a key role in materials science research by enabling researchers to simulate, predict, and analyze the properties and behaviors of materials at multiple length and time scales. A plethora of software packages, platforms, and computational frameworks are available to perform theoretical modeling and simulations across different domains of materials science. The biomolecular modeling field has seen significant growth since the 1970s, with advancements in technology leading to larger and longer simulations, outpacing Moore's law. This progress has been driven by the interplay between knowledge-based and physics-based methods, as well as advancements in hardware and software. The integration of theory, experimentation, and simulation is key to addressing future scientific and biomedical challenges, indicating a promising future for modeling in this field [62]. Computational molecular modeling is increasingly vital in biology and biophysics, offering insights beyond experimental capabilities by providing distributions and time series of biomolecular properties. However, its application is hindered by four main challenges: the force-field problem, search problem, ensemble problem, and experimental limitations. These obstacles are explored with practical examples, alongside prospects for overcoming them to advance biomolecular modeling [63]. Quantum mechanics-based software such as Gaussian, Vienna Ab initio Simulation Package (VASP), and Quantum ESPRESSO provides tools for performing DFT calculations [64], electronic-structure calculations, and molecular dynamics simulations to elucidate the electronic properties, energetics, and reactivity of materials at the atomic and molecular levels. Molecular modeling software such as chemistry at HARvard macromolecular mechanics (CHARMM), GROningen machine for chemical simulations (GROMACS) [65], and large-scale atomic/molecular massively parallel simulator (LAMMPS) enable researchers to simulate the dynamics, interactions, and mechanical properties of biomolecules, polymers, and soft materials through classical molecular dynamics simulations. Furthermore, materials design platforms such as Materials Studio, MedeA, and Atomistic Toolkit (ATK) offer integrated suites of tools for materials modeling, visualization, and property prediction, facilitating the design and optimization of materials for specific applications. These modeling and simulation tools leverage advanced algorithms, numerical methods, and computational resources to explore complex phenomena, validate experimental observations, and guide materials design and discovery efforts.

Computational systems biology is proposed as a vital biomolecular technique of the 21st century, complementing experimental biology and bioinformatics to offer unique insights and understanding. Traditional and novel modeling techniques are summarized initially, followed by the introduction of concept map modeling as a bridge between experimental biology and biological systems modeling. This collaborative approach involves biologists designing regulated connectivity diagrams of biological systems, which are then converted into mathematical constructs by modelers for simulation and hypothesis testing [66]. GROMOS++ is a collection of C++ programs designed for pre- and postprocessing of molecular dynamics simulation trajectories, forming part of the Groningen Molecular Simulation software. With over 70 programs, it facilitates data preparation and analysis for molecular simulations, covering structural, dynamic, and thermodynamic quantities through time series, correlation functions, and distributions [65]. Adaptive poisson-Boltzmann solver (APBS) has been instrumental in studying solvation and electrostatics in various biomedical applications by providing continuum electrostatic equations for large biomolecular assemblies. It addresses key challenges in accurate modeling, robust software, and data sharing for biomolecular electrostatics.

Continuously updated since its inception in 2001, recent enhancements include Poisson–Boltzmann and semianalytical solvers, optimized boundary element solver, geometric flow solvation model, graph theory-based pKa value determination, and improved web-based visualization tools [67]. Quantum ESPRESSO, an open-source suite of computer codes, facilitates quantum simulations of materials using advanced electronic-structure techniques like DFT. Its popularity stems from its versatility in simulating diverse properties, adaptability to various hardware architectures, and its role as a core open-source platform for researchers. Recent enhancements include new methodologies, improved parallelization, code modularization, and enhanced interoperability within and outside the suite [64].

Modeling and simulation tools have been instrumental in advancing materials science research across a myriad of applications and disciplines. For example, DFT calculations performed using software such as VASP have been employed to investigate the electronic structure, bandgap engineering, and defect properties of semiconductors and insulators for applications in electronics, optoelectronics, and photovoltaics. Molecular dynamics simulations conducted with packages like GROMACS have elucidated the mechanical properties, self-assembly dynamics, and stability of biomolecular systems such as proteins, nucleic acids, and lipid membranes, informing drug discovery, protein engineering, and biomaterials design efforts. Furthermore, multiscale modeling approaches combining quantum mechanics with classical molecular dynamics have enabled researchers to simulate complex phenomena such as protein-ligand binding, catalytic reactions, and material phase transitions with unprecedented accuracy and detail. By integrating modeling and simulation tools with experimental techniques and data analysis methods, researchers can gain comprehensive insights into material properties and behaviors, accelerate materials discovery, and drive innovation in diverse fields ranging from energy storage and conversion to drug delivery and nanotechnology.

## 2.7 Data analysis tools

Data analysis tools play a crucial role in extracting meaningful insights, trends, and patterns from materials datasets, enabling researchers to interpret experimental results, validate theoretical models, and guide materials design and optimization efforts. A wide range of software packages, algorithms, and statistical techniques are available for data analysis in materials science, tailored to handle diverse types of data, including numerical data, spectroscopic data, imaging data, and time-series data. Statistical analysis software such as MATLAB, Python with libraries like NumPy, SciPy, and pandas, and R provide powerful tools for data manipulation, visualization, regression analysis, and hypothesis testing, facilitating exploratory data analysis and statistical inference. ML algorithms and techniques, including supervised learning, unsupervised learning, and DL, offer predictive modeling capabilities for materials property prediction, pattern recognition, and materials discovery. Additionally, image processing and analysis software such as ImageJ, FIJI, and MATLAB Image Processing Toolbox enable researchers to analyze and quantify features in microscopy images, such as particle size distributions, grain boundaries, and morphological characteristics. Furthermore, software packages for spectral analysis, such as OriginPro and MATLAB Signal Processing Toolbox, offer tools for processing, deconvolution, and interpretation of spectroscopic data from techniques such as X-ray photoelectron spectroscopy (XPS), Raman spectroscopy, and FTIR. By harnessing these data analysis tools, researchers can uncover hidden relationships, correlations, and trends in materials datasets, extract actionable insights, and make informed decisions in materials science research and development.

Software tools have been developed to model, simulate, and predict correlations in materials science, encompassing various aspects like processing parameters and properties in titanium alloys, time-temperature-transformation (TTT) diagrams, corrosion resistance, surface hardness, microhardness profiles, and fatigue stress life diagrams for Ti-6Al-4V alloys. These programs utilize artificial neural networks and offer graphical user interfaces for ease of use, with versions available for different platforms. They are modularly designed and integrated into software packages, demonstrating effectiveness in solving practical problems and optimizing alloy compositions, processing parameters, and working conditions in materials science applications [68]. The Python Materials Genomics (pymatgen) library is introduced as an open-source Python tool for materials analysis, providing core Python objects for materials data representation, structure and thermodynamic analyses, and an open platform for collaborative development. It facilitates initial setup and postcalculation analysis for high-throughput computational materials science efforts, offering convenient access to materials data via the Materials Project's REST API. As an example, the library is used to analyze the phase and electrochemical stability of Li4SnS4, demonstrating its capability with minimal computing resources (see Fig. 2.7) [69]. Electron microscopy sciences (EMS) is a suite of computer programs designed for the simulation and analysis of High-Resolution Electron Microscopy (HREM) images and diffraction patterns. It consists of specialized tasks with defined functions, divided into two main parts: one for handling crystallographic calculations common in electron microscopy, such as diffraction pattern indexing and simulation, and the other for simulating structure images using various methods. EMS offers an interactive, menu-driven interface and provides extensive online documentation for user convenience [70]. ABINITv3.0, released under the GNU General Public License, emphasizes collaboration and modern software engineering concepts in the development of a sophisticated plane-wave pseudopotential code for DFT computations. It highlights freedom of sources, reliability, portability, and self-documentation, with software techniques such as PERL scripts and C++ (programming language) (CPP) directives generating object code for various platforms. The software features extensive documentation, including online help files and tutorials, and follows strict coding rules, with over 200 automated tests ensuring existing capabilities' security [71].

Data analysis tools have been instrumental in advancing materials science research by enabling researchers to extract valuable information, derive actionable insights, and make data-driven decisions across diverse applications and disciplines. For example, ML algorithms such as support vector machines (SVM), random forests, and artificial neural networks have been employed to predict material properties, phase transitions, and reaction pathways based on datasets comprising structural, compositional, and

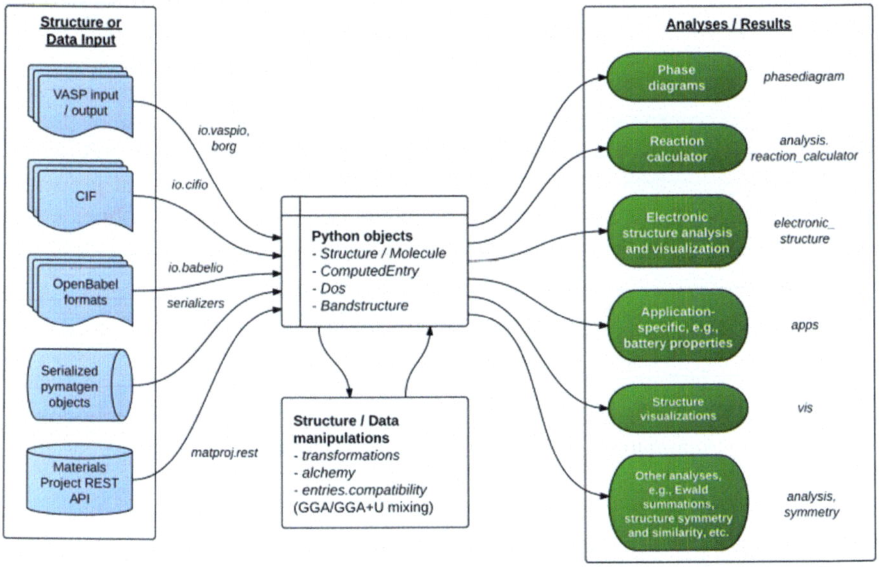


**Figure 2.7** Overview of the pymatgen library.
Reprinted with permission from [69].

experimental parameters. These predictive models have found applications in materials informatics, high-throughput screening, and materials design, accelerating the discovery of novel materials with tailored properties for specific applications. Furthermore, statistical analysis techniques [72] such as principal component analysis (PCA), cluster analysis, and regression analysis have been used to identify correlations, trends, and outliers in materials datasets, guiding materials characterization, optimization, and quality control processes. Image analysis software has been utilized to quantify features such as particle size distributions, porosity, and surface roughness in microscopy images, facilitating the characterization of materials microstructures, defects, and morphologies. Additionally, spectral analysis tools have enabled researchers to deconvolute and interpret complex spectra from spectroscopic techniques, providing insights into material compositions, chemical bonding, and electronic states. By leveraging data analysis tools, researchers can extract actionable insights, validate theoretical models, and guide materials design and optimization efforts, driving innovation and discovery in materials science research.

## 2.8 Challenges and opportunities in dataset development

Developing datasets in materials science involves overcoming various challenges related to data collection, curation, and standardization. This process requires meticulous efforts to ensure accuracy, consistency, and reliability of the collected experimental data, which often involve complex instrumentation and measurements. Curation involves organizing and archiving data in accessible formats, while standardization aims to establish consensus on data formats and terminology for interoperability. Ethical considerations and data-sharing policies are crucial, governing issues like data ownership, privacy, and intellectual property rights. Balancing data openness with protection is essential, alongside addressing disparities in data access. Despite challenges, dataset development fosters collaboration and interdisciplinary research, enabling comprehensive insights into material properties and behaviors. Integrating diverse datasets allows for validation and refinement of theoretical predictions, driving innovation and societal impact in materials science.

### 2.8.1 Potential of artificial intelligence in biomaterials

Recently, the combination of AI and ML with biomaterials research has opened up new possibilities. AI can greatly improve the way we discover, design, and optimize biomaterials by automating processes that used to rely on trial and error or time-consuming experiments.

### 2.8.2 Aartificial intelligence–driven discovery and design of biomaterials

One of the most exciting uses of AI in biomaterials is in speeding up the discovery and design of new materials. Traditionally, developing a new biomaterial was a slow process that involved making guesses, testing them in the lab, and then refining them over time. AI can make this process much faster by predicting how materials will behave based on data we already have. For example, ML algorithms can analyze large amounts of information about different biomaterials, such as their chemical makeup and how they interact with biological systems, to find patterns and connections that are not easy to see with traditional methods. AI can also help predict how small changes in the structure of a material might affect its performance in the body, such as its ability to be safely absorbed or broken down. This is especially important when designing materials for medical implants, where it is crucial to know how long the material will last and how it will interact with the body.

### 2.8.3 Enhancing biomaterials through artificial intelligence–driven simulation and modeling

In addition to helping with material discovery, AI is also making it easier to simulate and model biomaterials. Simulating how materials behave at the atomic or molecular level, known as molecular dynamics simulations, is a powerful tool in materials science but can be very time-consuming. AI can optimize these simulations, allowing researchers to study larger systems or longer time scales than would be possible with traditional methods. Moreover, AI can simulate the complex biological environments in which these biomaterials will be used, such as how the immune system might react to an implant or how a drug delivery system will work inside the body. By modeling these interactions more accurately, AI helps researchers design materials that are more effective and have fewer side effects.

### 2.8.4 Smart biomaterials and artificial intelligence–driven customization

Another promising area of development is smart biomaterials—materials that can change their properties in response to specific triggers, such as changes in temperature, pH, or the presence of certain molecules. AI plays a key role in designing these materials by enabling them to adjust in real time based on what is happening in their environment. For example, AI could help create a drug delivery system that releases medication only when it detects a rise in blood sugar, offering more precise and personalized treatment for conditions like diabetes. AI's potential for customization goes beyond smart materials to the broader field of personalized medicine. Imagine materials that are specifically designed for each patient, based on their unique biological characteristics. AI can analyze patient-specific data—like genetic information or immune responses—and guide the creation of biomaterials that are optimized for that particular individual, improving treatment effectiveness and reducing the risk of complications.

### 2.8.5 Artificial intelligence in biomaterials manufacturing and scale-up

AI is also making an impact in the manufacturing and large-scale production of biomaterials. It can optimize the manufacturing processes by predicting and controlling the factors that influence the quality and consistency of the final product. For instance, AI algorithms can monitor and adjust the synthesis of materials in real time, ensuring that each batch meets the desired standards. When it comes to scaling up from the laboratory to industrial production, AI is invaluable. Scaling up can be challenging because maintaining the same quality and properties of the material at a larger scale is difficult. AI can help by identifying which variables need to be tightly controlled during production and ensuring that they stay within the right limits.

### 2.8.6 Ethical and regulatory considerations

As AI becomes more integrated into biomaterials research, it is important to think about the ethical and regulatory issues that might arise. The use of AI, especially when it involves patient-specific data, raises concerns about privacy and data security. It will be crucial to ensure that AI processes are transparent and that the data used is kept secure to gain the trust of both the medical community and the public. Additionally, the rules and regulations for AI-designed biomaterials are still being developed. Traditional regulatory frameworks might not fully address the new complexities that AI introduces, such as determining who is responsible for AI-generated decisions or validating AI models. As AI continues to advance in biomaterials research, regulatory bodies will need to develop guidelines that ensure the safety and effectiveness of these materials while still allowing innovation to thrive.

### 2.8.7 The future of artificial intelligence in biomaterials research

The future of AI in biomaterials research looks very promising. As AI technology continues to improve, we might see the development of entirely new classes of biomaterials with amazing capabilities. For example, AI could help create materials that not only respond to their environment but also adapt and change over time, similar to how living organisms do. These materials could be used in a wide range of applications, from implants that heal themselves to scaffolds that guide the growth of new tissues. Furthermore, combining AI with other new technologies, like 3D printing and nanotechnology, could expand the possibilities for biomaterials even more. AI-driven design and manufacturing processes could lead to the creation of highly complex materials that are specifically designed for particular medical needs. This could have a huge impact on fields like regenerative medicine, where being able to control the properties and behavior of materials is crucial.

### 2.8.8 Predictions for the future of datasets and tools in materials science

The future of datasets and tools in materials science is poised for exciting advancements and transformations driven by emerging technologies, interdisciplinary collaboration, and data-driven approaches. One key prediction is the continued expansion and democratization of materials datasets, fueled by advances in data acquisition, storage, and sharing technologies. As experimental techniques become more automated, high-throughput, and accessible, researchers will have access to increasingly large and diverse datasets encompassing a wide range of material properties, compositions, and processing conditions. Furthermore, the integration of experimental, theoretical, and computational datasets will become more seamless and standardized, enabling researchers to leverage the collective power of data and models to address complex materials science challenges. Another prediction is the proliferation of advanced characterization and imaging techniques with higher resolution, sensitivity, and throughput, enabling researchers to explore materials properties and behaviors with unprecedented detail and precision. Techniques such as cryo-electron microscopy, in situ spectroscopy, and correlative microscopy will revolutionize our understanding of materials at the atomic and molecular levels, paving the way for new discoveries and innovations in materials design and engineering. Additionally, the rise of AI and ML will play an increasingly prominent role in materials science research, enabling researchers to extract actionable insights, predict materials properties, and accelerate materials discovery and optimization processes. ML algorithms will be used to analyze large-scale datasets, identify patterns, and guide experimental and computational efforts, leading to the development of novel materials with tailored properties for specific applications. Overall, the future of datasets and tools in materials science holds immense promise for advancing our understanding of materials and unlocking new frontiers of discovery and innovation across diverse fields and applications.

## 2.9 Conclusion

In this chapter, we have explored how datasets and tools are fundamental to advancing materials science research. We emphasized their role in providing insights into material properties, behaviors, and interactions, tracing their historical development, and highlighting their diverse array in experimental, theoretical, and computational datasets. We discussed various characterization, modeling, and data analysis tools used in materials science research, showcasing their utility through examples and case studies. Looking ahead, we predict advancements in materials datasets, characterization techniques, modeling tools, and interdisciplinary collaboration.

Datasets and tools are indispensable assets driving innovation and discovery in materials science. They empower researchers to unlock the potential of materials for diverse applications, from renewable energy to biomedical engineering. By facilitating interdisciplinary collaboration, they enable researchers to address complex challenges and design novel materials for sustainable technologies and regenerative medicine.

Continued innovation and collaboration are vital in materials science to sustain progress and address societal needs. Embracing a culture of curiosity and collaboration allows researchers to push the boundaries of materials science, driving innovation and shaping a brighter future. Investing in research, education, and infrastructure is crucial to sustaining momentum and addressing pressing challenges in materials science.

In summary, the integration of AI into biomaterials research represents a major shift, offering new opportunities for innovation and discovery. As researchers continue to explore how AI can be used in this field, we can expect to see significant advancements in the design, development, and application of biomaterials. The future of biomaterials, enhanced by AI, holds great potential to transform healthcare, improve patient outcomes, and address some of the most pressing medical challenges of our time.

## Acknowledgment

To the best of the Editors' knowledge and authors' claims, no generative AI tools were used for substantive writing of chapters. Any AI-assisted language editing, if applied, was limited to grammar or style suggestions and did not alter the scientific content.

## References

[1] Himanen L, Geurts A, Foster AS, Rinke P. Data-driven materials science: status, challenges, and perspectives. *Advanced Science* 2019;6(21):1900808. https://doi.org/10.1002/advs.201900808.

[2] Wang Z, Sun Z, Yin H, Liu X, Wang J, Zhao H, et al. Data-driven materials innovation and applications. *Advanced Materials* 2022;34(36):e2104113. https://doi.org/10.1002/adma.202104113.

[3] DeCost B, Hattrick-Simpers J, Trautt Z, Kusne A, Campo E, Green M. Scientific AI in materials science: a path to a sustainable and scalable paradigm. *Machine Learning: Science and Technology* 2020;1(3):033001. https://doi.org/10.1088/2632-2153/ab9a20.

[4] Kalidindi SR, De Graef M. Materials data science: current status and future outlook. *Annual Review of Materials Research* 2015;45(1):171–93. https://doi.org/10.1146/annurev-matsci-070214-020844.

[5] Schmidt J, Marques MRG, Botti S, Marques MAL. Recent advances and applications of machine learning in solid-state materials science. *Npj Computational Materials* 2019;5(1):83. https://doi.org/10.1038/s41524-019-0221-0.

[6] Henderson G, Neuville D, Downs R. *Spectroscopic methods in mineralogy and material sciences*. De Gruyter; 2014. Available from https://books.google.com/books?id=vIEvCwAAQBAJ.

[7] Choudhary K, DeCost B, Chen C, Jain A, Tavazza F, Cohn R, et al. Recent advances and applications of deep learning methods in materials science. *Npj Computational Materials* 2022;8(1):59. https://doi.org/10.1038/s41524-022-00734-6.

[8] Wagner N, Rondinelli JM. Theory-guided machine learning in materials science. *Frontiers in Materials* 2016;3. https://doi.org/10.3389/fmats.2016.00028.

[9] Jablonka KM, Ongari D, Moosavi SM, Smit B. Big-data science in porous materials: materials genomics and machine learning. *Chemical Reviews* 2020;120(16):8066–129. https://doi.org/10.1021/acs.chemrev.0c00004.

[10] Foster KR, Koprowski R, Skufca JD. Machine learning, medical diagnosis, and biomedical engineering research—commentary. *Biomedical Engineering Online* 2014;13(1):94. https://doi.org/10.1186/1475-925X-13-94.

[11] Zhang Y, Xin Y, Li Q, Ma J, Li S, Lv X, et al. Empirical study of seven data mining algorithms on different characteristics of datasets for biomedical classification applications. *Biomedical Engineering Online* 2017;16(1):125. https://doi.org/10.1186/s12938-017-0416-x.

[12] Zakutayev A, Wunder N, Schwarting M, Perkins JD, White R, Munch K, et al. An open experimental database for exploring inorganic materials. *Scientific Data* 2018;5(1):180053. https://doi.org/10.1038/sdata.2018.53.

[13] de Pablo JJ, Jones B, Kovacs CL, Ozolins V, Ramirez AP. The materials genome initiative, the interplay of experiment, theory and computation. *Current Opinion in Solid State and Materials Science* 2014;18(2):99–117. https://doi.org/10.1016/j.cossms.2014.02.003.

[14] Allen FH, Taylor R. Research applications of the Cambridge Structural Database (CSD). *Chemical Society Reviews* 2004;33(8):463. https://doi.org/10.1039/b309040j.

[15] Suzuki M, Nagao H, Harada Y, Shinotsuka H, Watanabe K, Sasaki A, et al. Raw-to-repository characterization data conversion for repeatable, replicable, and reproducible measurements. *Journal of Vacuum Science and Technology A: Vacuum, Surfaces, and Films* 2020;38(2):023204. https://doi.org/10.1116/1.5128408.

[16] Leng Y. *Materials characterization: introduction to microscopic and spectroscopic methods*. Wiley; 2013. Available from https://books.google.com/books?id=kdc4AAAAQBAJ.

[17] Alessio P, Aoki PHB, Furini LN, Aliaga AE, Leopoldo Constantino CJ. Spectroscopic techniques for characterization of nanomaterials. *nanocharacterization techniques*. Elsevier; 2017. p. 65–98. https://doi.org/10.1016/B978-0-323-49778-7.00003-5.

[18] Thomas S, Thomas R, Zachariah AK, Mishra RK. *Spectroscopic methods for nanomaterials characterization*. Elsevier Science; 2017. Available from https://books.google.com/books?id=c2DCDQAAQBAJ.

[19] Holder CF, Schaak RE. Tutorial on powder X-ray diffraction for characterizing nanoscale materials. *ACS Nano* 2019;13(7):7359–65. https://doi.org/10.1021/acsnano.9b05157.

[20] Quinn PS, Benzonelli A. XRD and materials analysis. *The encyclopedia of archaeological sciences*. Wiley; 2018. p. 1–5. https://doi.org/10.1002/9781119188230.saseas0619.

[21] Epp J. X-ray diffraction (XRD) techniques for materials characterization. *materials characterization using nondestructive Evaluation (NDE) methods*. Elsevier; 2016. p. 81–124. https://doi.org/10.1016/B978-0-08-100040-3.00004-3.

[22] Hatzakis E. Nuclear magnetic resonance (NMR) spectroscopy in food science: a comprehensive review. *Comprehensive Reviews in Food Science and Food Safety* 2019;18(1):189–220. https://doi.org/10.1111/1541-4337.12408.
[23] Dutta A. Fourier transform infrared spectroscopy. *Spectroscopic methods for nanomaterials characterization*. Elsevier; 2017. p. 73–93. https://doi.org/10.1016/B978-0-323-46140-5.00004-2.
[24] Prati S, Joseph E, Sciutto G, Mazzeo R. New advances in the application of FTIR microscopy and spectroscopy for the characterization of artistic materials. *Accounts of Chemical Research* 2010;43(6):792–801. https://doi.org/10.1021/ar900274f.
[25] Khan SA, Khan SB, Khan LU, Farooq A, Akhtar K, Asiri AM. Fourier transform infrared spectroscopy: fundamentals and application in functional groups and nanomaterials characterization. *Handbook of materials characterization*. Springer International Publishing; 2018. p. 317–44. https://doi.org/10.1007/978-3-319-92955-2_9.
[26] Clarke A, Eberhardt CN. *Microscopy techniques for materials science*. Elsevier Science; 2002. Available from https://books.google.com/books?id=WlJzkkWDG2YC.
[27] Mohammed A, Abdullah A. Scanning electron microscopy (SEM): a review. Proceedings of the 2018 International Conference on Hydraulics and Pneumatics—HERVEX, Băile Govora, Romania; 2018: 7–9.
[28] Inkson BJ. Scanning electron microscopy (SEM) and transmission electron microscopy (TEM) for materials characterization. *Materials characterization using nondestructive evaluation (NDE) methods*. Elsevier; 2016. p. 17–43.
[29] Goldstein JI, Newbury DE, Michael JR, Ritchie NWM, Scott JHJ, Joy DC. Scanning electron microscopy and X-ray microanalysis. Springer; 2017.
[30] Tang CY, Yang Z. Transmission electron microscopy (TEM). *Membrane characterization*. 2017. p. 145–59. 2017.
[31] Klein T, Buhr E, Frase CG. TSEM: a review of scanning electron microscopy in transmission mode and its applications. *Advances in Imaging and Electron Physics* 2012;171:297–356.
[32] Franken LE, Boekema EJ, Stuart MCA. Transmission electron microscopy as a tool for the characterization of soft materials: application and interpretation. *Advanced Science* 2017;4(5):1600476.
[33] Magonov SN. Surface characterization of materials at ambient conditions by scanning tunneling microscopy (STM) and atomic force microscopy (AFM). *Applied Spectroscopy Reviews* 1993;28(1–2):1–121.
[34] Rao A, Schoenenberger M, Gnecco E, Glatzel T, Meyer E, Brändlin D, et al. Characterization of nanoparticles using atomic force microscopy. *Journal of Physics: Conference Series* 2007;61(1):971.
[35] Khan MK, Wang QY, Fitzpatrick ME. Atomic force microscopy (AFM) for materials characterization. *Materials characterization using nondestructive evaluation (NDE) methods*. Elsevier; 2016. p. 1–16.
[36] Wunderlich B. Basics of thermal analysis. *Thermal Analysis of Polymeric Materials* 2005;71:188.
[37] Bruno L. Mechanical characterization of composite materials by optical techniques: a review. *Optics and Lasers in Engineering* 2018;104:192–203.
[38] Roeder RK. Mechanical characterization of biomaterials. *Characterization of Biomaterials* 2013;49:104.
[39] LeSar R. *Introduction to computational materials science: fundamentals to applications*. Cambridge University Press; 2013.

[40] Langer MF, Goeßmann A, Rupp M. Representations of molecules and materials for interpolation of quantum—mechanical simulations via machine learning. *Npj Computational Materials* 2022;8(1):41.
[41] Lee JG. *Computational materials science: an introduction.* CRC press; 2016.
[42] Ohno K, Esfarjani K, Kawazoe Y. *Computational materials science: from ab initio to Monte Carlo methods*. Springer; 2018.
[43] Steinhauser MO, Hiermaier S. A review of computational methods in materials science: examples from shock-wave and polymer physics. *International Journal of Molecular Sciences* 2009;10(12):5135–216.
[44] Giustino F. *Materials modelling using density functional theory: properties and predictions*. Oxford University Press; 2014.
[45] Maurer RJ, Freysoldt C, Reilly AM, Brandenburg JG, Hofmann OT, Björkman T, et al. Advances in density-functional calculations for materials modeling. *Annual Review of Materials Research* 2019;49:1–30.
[46] Neugebauer J, Hickel T. Density functional theory in materials science. *Wiley Interdisciplinary Reviews: Computational Molecular Science* 2013;3(5):438–48.
[47] Akkermans RLC, Spenley NA, Robertson SH. Monte Carlo methods in materials studio. *Molecular Simulation* 2013;39(14–15):1153–64.
[48] Saito Y. The Monte Carlo simulation of microstructural evolution in metals. *Materials Science and Engineering: A* 1997;223(1–2):114–24.
[49] Charmpis DC, Schuëller GI, Pellissetti MF. The need for linking micromechanics of materials with stochastic finite elements: a challenge for materials science. *Computational Materials Science* 2007;41(1):27–37.
[50] Roters F, Eisenlohr P, Bieler TR, Raabe D. *Crystal plasticity finite element methods: in materials science and engineering*. John Wiley & Sons; 2011.
[51] Pisani C. Quantum-mechanical ab-initio calculation of the properties of crystalline materials Vol. 67. Springer Science & Business Media; 2012.
[52] Pokluda J, Černý M, Šob M, Umeno Y. Ab initio calculations of mechanical properties: methods and applications. *Progress in Materials Science* 2015;73:127–58.
[53] Körbel S, Marques MAL, Botti S. Stability and electronic properties of new inorganic perovskites from high-throughput ab initio calculations. *Journal of Materials Chemistry C* 2016;4(15):3157–67.
[54] Skinner AJ, Broughton JQ. Neural networks in computational materials science: training algorithms. *Modelling and Simulation in Materials Science and Engineering* 1995;3(3):371.
[55] David Müzel S, Bonhin EP, Guimarães NM, Guidi ES. Application of the finite element method in the analysis of composite materials: a review. *Polymers* 2020;12(4):818.
[56] Pyzer-Knapp EO, Suh C, Gómez-Bombarelli R, Aguilera-Iparraguirre J, Aspuru-Guzik A. What is high-throughput virtual screening? A perspective from organic materials discovery. *Annual Review of Materials Research* 2015;45:195–216.
[57] Potyrailo R, Rajan K, Stoewe K, Takeuchi I, Chisholm B, Lam H. Combinatorial and high-throughput screening of materials libraries: review of state of the art. *ACS Combinatorial Science* 2011;13(6):579–633.
[58] Woo SI, Kim KW, Cho HY, Oh KS, Jeon MK, Tarte NH, et al. Current Status of combinatorial and high-throughput methods for discovering new materials and catalysts. *QSAR and Combinatorial Science* 2005;24(1):138–54.
[59] Karakasidis TE, Charitidis CA. Multiscale modeling in nanomaterials science. *Materials Science and Engineering: C* 2007;27(5–8):1082–9.
[60] Lu G, Kaxiras E. An overview of multiscale simulations of materials. ArXiv Preprint Cond-Mat/0401073. 2004.

[61] Stoll A, Benner P. Machine learning for material characterization with an application for predicting mechanical properties. *GAMM-Mitteilungen* 2021;44(1). e202100003.
[62] Schlick T, Portillo-Ledesma S. Biomolecular modeling thrives in the age of technology. *Nature Computational Science* 2021;1(5):321–31.
[63] Van Gunsteren WF, Bakowies D, Baron R, Chandrasekhar I, Christen M, Daura X, et al. Biomolecular modeling: goals, problems, perspectives. *Angewandte Chemie International Edition* 2006;45(25):4064–92.
[64] Giannozzi P, Andreussi O, Brumme T, Bunau O, Nardelli MB, Calandra M, et al. Advanced capabilities for materials modelling with Quantum ESPRESSO. *Journal of Physics: Condensed Matter* 2017;29(46):465901.
[65] Eichenberger AP, Allison JR, Dolenc J, Geerke DP, Horta BAC, Meier K, et al. GROMOS++ software for the analysis of biomolecular simulation trajectories. *Journal of Chemical Theory and Computation* 2011;7(10):3379–90.
[66] Goel G, Chou I-C, Voit EO. Biological systems modeling and analysis: a biomolecular technique of the twenty-first century. *Journal of Biomolecular Techniques: JBT* 2006;17(4):252.
[67] Jurrus E, Engel D, Star K, Monson K, Brandi J, Felberg LE, et al. Improvements to the APBS biomolecular solvation software suite. *Protein Science* 2018;27(1):112–28.
[68] Malinov S, Sha W. Software products for modelling and simulation in materials science. *Computational Materials Science* 2003;28(2):179–98.
[69] Ong SP, Richards WD, Jain A, Hautier G, Kocher M, Cholia S, et al. Python Materials Genomics (pymatgen): a robust, open-source python library for materials analysis. *Computational Materials Science* 2013;68:314–9.
[70] Stadelmann PA. EMS—a software package for electron diffraction analysis and HREM image simulation in materials science. *Ultramicroscopy* 1987;21(2):131–45.
[71] Gonze X, Beuken J-M, Caracas R, Detraux F, Fuchs M, Rignanese G-M, et al. First-principles computation of material properties: the ABINIT software project. *Computational Materials Science* 2002;25(3):478–92.
[72] Ohser J, Mücklich F. *Statistical analysis of microstructures in materials science*. John Wiley & Sons; 2000.

# Intelligent tools for biomaterials design

# 3

*Dinesh Rokaya[1,2], Shreya Subedi[3], Diane Isabel Selvido[4], Trinh Hai Anh[5,6], Anand Marya[7], Rohan D. Jagtap[8], and Ahmad Al Jaghsi[1,2,9]*
[1]Clinical Sciences Department, College of Dentistry, Ajman University, Ajman, United Arab Emirates, [2]Center of Medical and Bio-Allied Health Sciences Research, Ajman University, Ajman, United Arab Emirates, [3]Department of Restorative Dentistry, College of Dentistry, University of Illinois Chicago, Chicago, IL, United States, [4]Academy of Research and Clinical Dentistry, Metro Manila, Philippines, [5]Department of Implantology, Ha Noi National Hospital of Odonto-Stomatology, Hanoi, Vietnam, [6]Faculty of Dentistry, University of Medicine and Pharmacy, Hanoi National University, Hanoi, Vietnam, [7]Department of Orthodontics, Faculty of Dentistry, University of Puthisastra, Phnom Penh, Cambodia, [8]Division of Oral and Maxillofacial Radiology, Department of Care Planning and Restorative Sciences, School of Dentistry, University of Mississippi Medical Center (UMMC), Jackson, MS, United States, [9]Department of Prosthodontics, Gerodontology, and Dental Materials, Greifswald University Medicine, Greifswald, Germany

## 3.1 Introduction

Artificial Intelligence, commonly known as AI, is a technology that has gained immense significance in today's world of smart devices. In simpler terms, AI is the science of making machines that can think like humans [1]. This technology is no longer confined to the realms of science fiction or philosophy. Still, it has become a reality that has the potential to revolutionize various industries, ranging from healthcare to communication devices. AI has already impacted our lives in numerous ways, from voice assistants like Siri and Alexa to self-driving cars. It has opened new avenues for automation, making complex tasks easier, more accessible, and more efficient. One of the most significant benefits of AI is its ability to process vast amounts of data quickly, which has led to significant advancements in fields like medicine. AI is used in medical science to diagnose diseases and develop new, remote treatments [2,3]. As humans continue to push boundaries and achieve the impossible, AI stands as a testament to human innovation and unlocks new possibilities for the future. AI comprises three major components: machine learning (ML), artificial neural networks, and deep learning (DL) [4].

Intelligent tools are also often referred to as "Smart Materials." These materials have been regarded as milestones in manufacturing, healthcare supplies, transport entities, logistics, and robotic engineering [5]. It is given that the healthcare industry, as well as global industries, needs practicality in terms of production and manufacturing. Therefore, the assembly of intelligent tools should be improved and concentrated. Characteristics such as stress-bearing, thermal adjustment, sensitivity to light, pressure,

**Artificial Intelligence in Biomaterials Design and Development. DOI:** https://doi.org/10.1016/B978-0-323-95464-8.00010-4

and stimuli are significant features of these Smart Materials. Additionally, notable innovations were in progress regarding these intelligent materials in tissue and bone regeneration, tissue healing, and drug delivery systems [6].

In line with this, the reputation of intelligent tools for biomaterial fabrication should be accentuated for rapid and accelerated developments. This chapter will discuss the foundations of AI and intelligent tools, which will be addressed for further understanding, thereby making biomaterial designs tangible for future improvement.

## 3.2 Artificial Intelligence in healthcare

The use of AI in the medical and dental fields has become increasingly widespread and comprehensive in recent years. AI has revolutionized healthcare, from providing accurate imaging scans to patient counsel and care, precision medicine, digital medicine, and pharmaceutical research. In addition, AI has also enabled hospital monitoring, robotic and virtual assistants, and other innovative technologies that have significantly impacted the healthcare industry [7,8]. Simply put, AI is a crucial companion and component in healthcare access, development, and expansion.

AI has revolutionized the field of medicine in countless ways [9]. AI-powered imaging tools have made it easier for doctors to identify and treat various diseases, including cancer, heart disease, and brain disorders. In recent years, AI has been instrumental in digital medicine, which involves the use of wearable devices and mobile apps to monitor and manage patients' health remotely. AI uses ML algorithms and big data analytics to analyze vast amounts of data for diseases and treatment plans. It sifts through genetic, chemical, and clinical data to identify patterns and relationships that human researchers might overlook. This enables AI to expedite the drug discovery process and assist researchers in developing more potent treatments for various medical conditions. This is a significant breakthrough in the field of medicine and has the potential to revolutionize the way we approach the treatment of diseases. From improving accuracy in diagnostics to developing new therapies, the impact of AI in healthcare has been truly transformative. It is impressive to see how technology is helping to save lives and improve patient outcomes.

AI has emerged as a game-changing technology in the era of digital dentistry. The incorporation of AI has been revolutionary and has provided accurate and efficient diagnosis, streamlined workflows, and improved patient care for several years. The most important areas where AI and Augmented Intelligence significantly impact healthcare include administrative workflows, image analysis, robotic surgery, virtual assistants, and clinical decision support [8,10]. Various newer digital technologies are being implemented in dentistry [11–14]. The impact of AI technology on dentistry and healthcare has been enormous [9,15]. AI's ability to quickly and accurately analyze large amounts of data has made it a valuable tool in diagnosing and treating dental conditions. AI algorithms can identify patterns and anomalies in dental images and scans, which can help in identifying dental problems at an early stage.

As mentioned previously, AI can streamline administrative workflows, reduce wait times, and improve patient outcomes by providing personalized treatment plans. Consequently, AI technology became instrumental in shaping the future of dentistry and healthcare. It has facilitated the development of new materials and methods of producing them and unlocked new possibilities for dental treatments. AI-powered virtual assistants have helped in providing personalized patient care and have made it easier for patients to connect with their healthcare providers. AI has been widely adopted across various disciplines of dentistry, including operatives, periodontics, endodontics, prosthodontics, maxillofacial surgery, etc. AI applications have been instrumental in practices such as diagnosis, decision-making, treatment planning, prediction of treatment outcomes, and disease prognosis. For instance, AI algorithms can analyze the genetic, environmental, and lifestyle factors that affect tooth decay and loss. This information can then be used to develop personalized treatment plans that maximize the chances of successful regeneration [16].

Additionally, there are various applications of AI technology in dentistry (Fig. 3.1). AI has enabled dentists to use predictive analytics to identify patients in the high-risk stage of developing dental diseases, allowing for early intervention and treatment [17]. The use of AI in dentistry has also made it possible to simplify and reorganize dental procedures and optimize the use of dental materials, leading to reduced costs and increased efficiency. Dental professionals increasingly rely on AI to assist in clinical decision-making, diagnosis, treatment planning, and prediction of the disease prognosis [16]. With the use of AI in this industry, clinicians can enhance their workflows and systems and can potentially focus on their operative roles in their respective locations.

## 3.3 Biomaterials design

A biomaterial is a substance designed to interact with biological systems for medical and dental purposes, whether for therapy or diagnosis. Biomaterials can be derived from natural sources or synthesized in laboratories using chemical methods involving metallic components, polymers, ceramics, or composite materials. Products made from biomaterials cover a broad spectrum, such as medical implants, which are clinically known as artificial hip replacement implants, cochlear implants, dental implants, intraocular lenses, aortic valves, and stents [18]. With recent advances in technology, these biomaterials are widely synthesized with the aid of AI. Fig. 3.2 shows an overview of various applications of AI technology in biomaterial design [19]. AI can predict the properties of hypothetical organic materials [20]. In addition, the incorporation of AI into the design of inorganic materials has revolutionized scientific study and technological advancement. Researchers may now examine the complex interactions and properties of inorganic systems with unprecedented speed and precision because of the capability of computational approaches.

Novel materials possessing unparalleled functionality and performance have also been unearthed and refined. The most notable examples of the influence of AI-based design can be seen in the incredible advancements made in the production of

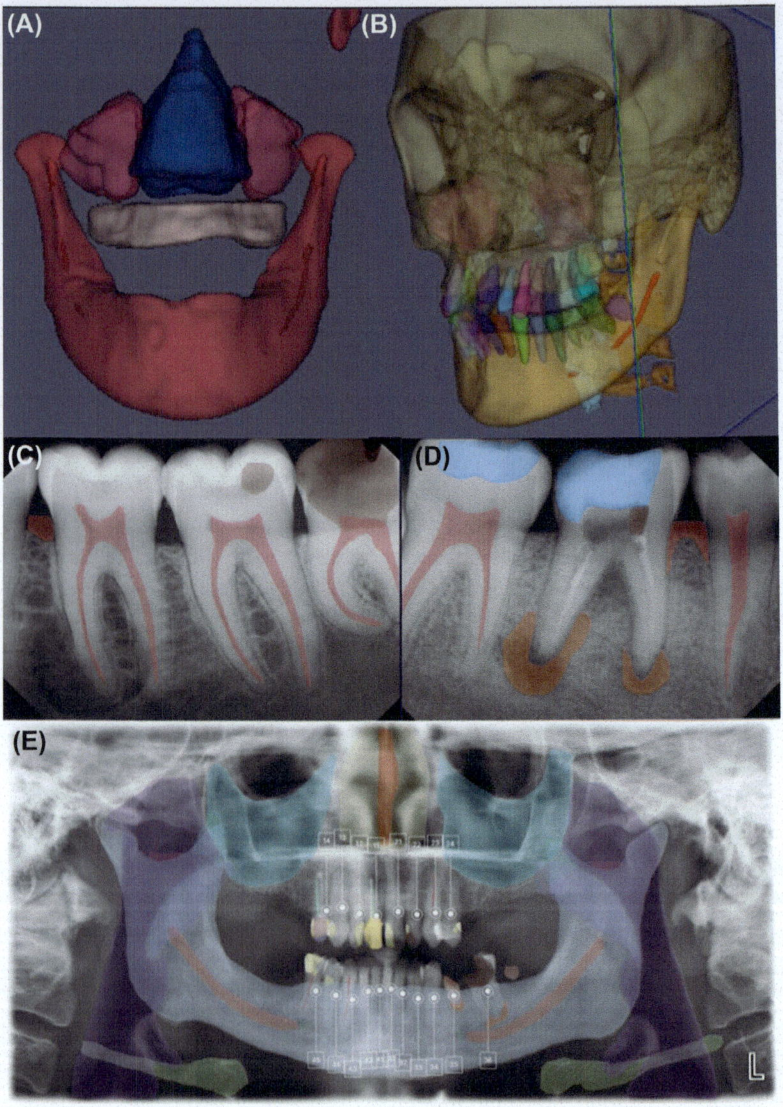


**Figure 3.1** Application of AI technology in dentistry. (A) 3D segmentation of anatomy by AI, (B) AI-generated 3D virtual model, (C) AI system detecting root canal and caries on periapical radiograph, (D) periapical pathology detection on periapical radiograph, and (E) AI-generated teeth segmentation on panoramic radiograph. *AI*, Artificial Intelligence.
Reprinted with permission from CranioCatch AI software.

batteries, semiconductors, and catalysts—all essential components in a wide range of industrial, environmental, and biological applications. With the ongoing integration of AI-based design, the possibilities are unlimited, and the future of inorganic material design is bright.

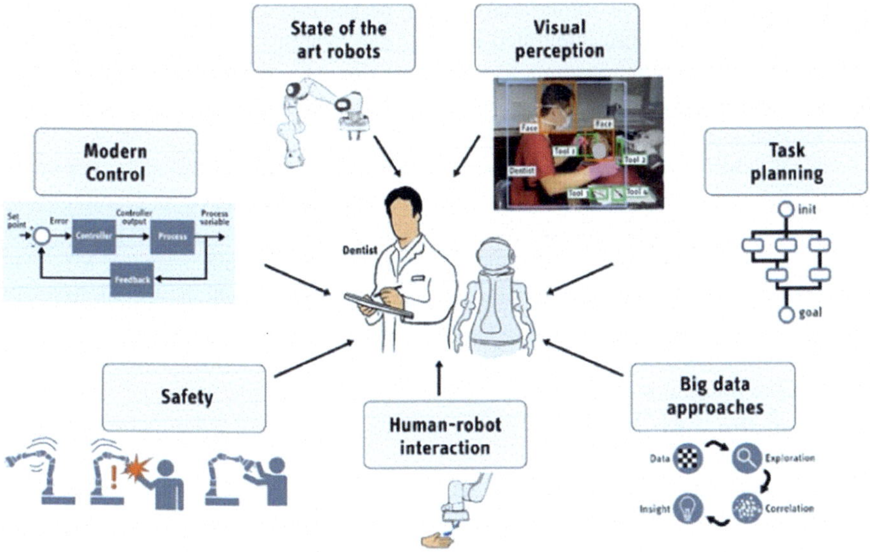


**Figure 3.2** Application of AI technology in biomaterial design. *AI*, Artificial Intelligence. Reprinted with permission from [19].

## 3.4 Intelligent tools

Intelligence is a multifaceted concept that encompasses several cognitive abilities, such as the capacity to think abstractly, grasp logical concepts, possess self-awareness, and emotional knowledge, and exhibit learning, reasoning, planning, creativity, critical thinking skills, and problem-solving abilities [21,22]. Tools, on the other hand, refer to a broad range of methods, algorithms, languages, or architectures that are utilized to connect theoretical concepts with practical applications [23]. In today's fast-paced and ever-evolving world, it is imperative that we leverage the power of technology to enhance our cognitive abilities and augment our problem-solving skills. These tools are a vital means to achieve these goals and are thus referred to as intelligent tools. Whether using advanced software or innovative mobile apps, these tools offer us an array of features and functionalities that can help us solve even the most complex problems. Currently, these concepts have been taken advantage of and used loosely in different sectors to improve human experiences.

AI is one such example of an intelligent tool developed through a combination of research, algorithms, and advancements in computing power. It has evolved over time, with researchers and engineers developing various techniques and models to mimic human intelligence. All forms of nonhuman intelligence fall under the umbrella term of AI. The main function of AI is to perform specific tasks, such as ML, natural language processing, computer vision, and robotics. Examples of AI include reinforcement learning, such as Alpha Go, automated manipulation tools, natural language processing, such as Tesla Autopilot, face recognition, and data mining, such as market customer analysis and personalized content recommendation [24]. AI is becoming more integrated into our daily routines as well. Some common examples include virtual assistants like Siri and Alexa. On the other hand, AI can also match the intelligence and ability of humans, displaying its own awareness and behavior that are as flexible as humans [25].

As a subfield of AI, ML uses algorithms to identify patterns and substructures in data. It can predict outcomes based on these patterns and improve its predictions by learning from data [26]. This makes ML one of the fastest-growing technical fields today, and deep learning [27] is a very prominent research area in ML. The foundation of DL algorithms is neural networks (NNs), which are biologically inspired networks that can extract features from the imported datasets and do not require human intervention. According to Ding et al. [28], this "neural network" consists of a minimum of three nodal layers—input, multiple "hidden," and output layers such that each layer consists of various numbers of interconnected nodes (artificial neurons) (Fig. 3.3).

Natural language processing (NLP) is a branch of AI that creates interaction between humans through speech and text, as shown in Fig. 3.4. It supports an array of language technologies, from predictive text to email filtering. NLP is an algorithm wherein computers behave intelligently like humans. One frequently used translator is the Google Cloud Translate. Microsoft Translator is an example of a program that uses NLP applications [29].

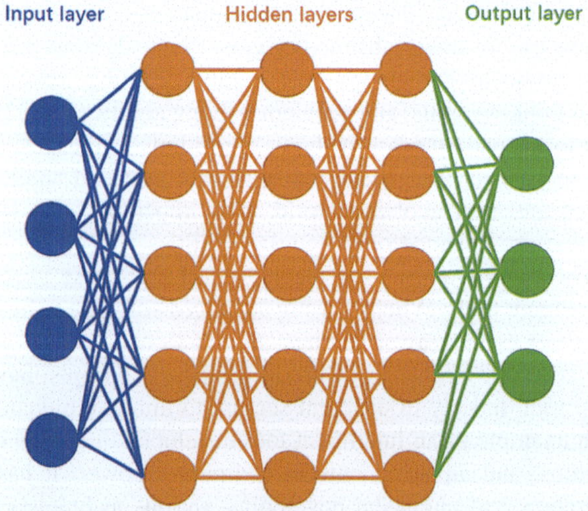


**Figure 3.3** Diagram of deep learning [27].
Reprinted with permission from [28].

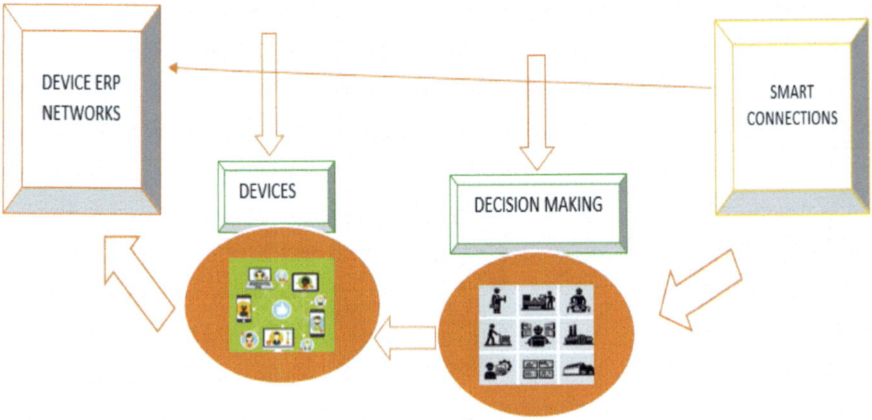


**Figure 3.4** Diagram of natural language processing (NLP).
Reprinted with permission from [29].

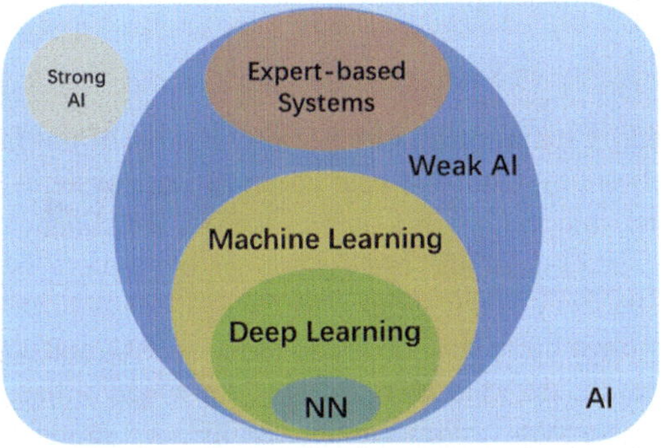


**Figure 3.5** Relationship between AI, expert-based systems, machine learning, deep learning [27], and neural network (NN). *AI*, Artificial Intelligence.
Reprinted with permission from [28].

The relationship between DL and NLP is shown in Fig. 3.5 [28]. There are many approaches whereby AI can be achieved; different types of AI can achieve different tasks, and researchers have created different AI classification methods.

Computer vision, the next area of AI, enables computers to interpret and analyze the visual world. It applies ML models to identify and classify objects in digital images and videos, then allows computers to react to what they see. It enables features like facial recognition, detection of objects and patterns, matching features, and so on. Face recognition is done through face alignment and extracting the shape

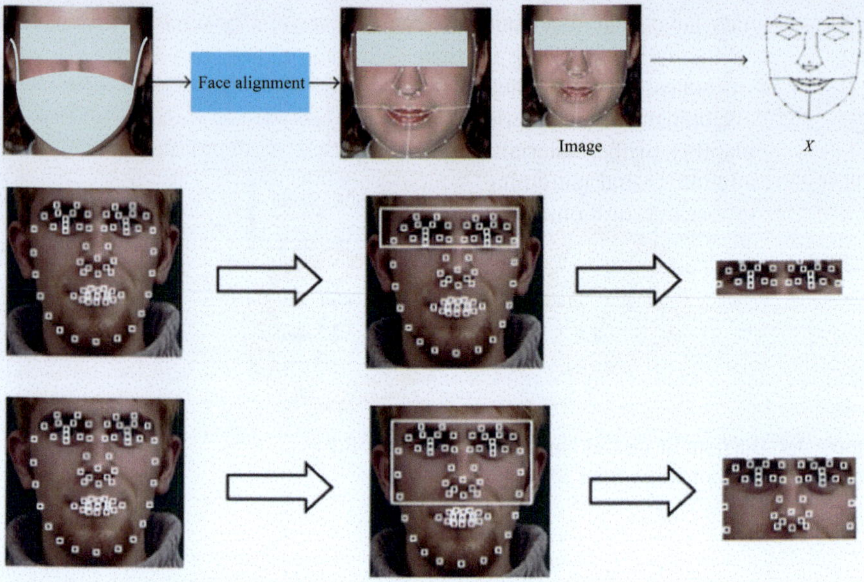


**Figure 3.6** Face recognition technology.
Reprinted with permission from [30].

of the face, followed by extracting essential information of the face (Fig. 3.6) [30]. Today, the most technology-intensive medical healthcare systems heavily depend on pattern detection and image classification principles for diagnosis; thus, there has been a noteworthy increase in the application of computer vision techniques for processing medical imagery.

AI robots are controlled by AI programs and tools like ML and computer vision. One such example includes the da Vinci Surgical System, which utilizes AI algorithms and robotic arms to assist surgeons during minimally invasive surgical approaches. When using a high-definition camera, the system provides a 3D visualization and magnified view of the surgical site. The robotic arms translate the surgeon's movements into precise actions, allowing for minimally invasive surgeries with improved precision and control.

## 3.5 Intelligent tools in biomaterials and tissue engineering

### *3.5.1 Role of intelligent tools in zirconia biomaterials*

Biomaterials such as zirconia, a cutting-edge ceramic substance, have been utilized in biological applications since the 1960s [31]. Various types of zirconia are available in the market depending on the mechanical properties and esthetic requirements [32,33]. Due to its exceptional biocompatibility, appealing look, strong resistance to corrosion, excellent mechanical qualities, and lack of documented allergic reactions, zirconia has grown in popularity in the dental field. AI's ability to evaluate data and identify patterns among complicated events of zirconia-related research and therapeutic applications has benefited from its implementation in recent years [19,34]. As a result, new methods for the design and optimization of biomaterials have been developed because of the advancement of AI.

Since zirconia has been suggested to have parameters that data can easily quantify, AI can straightforwardly be used [35]. Therefore, predictability of this material is expected, maximizing its use, especially in cosmetic dentistry. Zirconia is also used in hip replacement therapies and is rendered resilient. They are known to be prolonged up to 20 years [36]. ML in this category of ceramic biomaterials is necessary and bears prospective ability in material inspection, process amelioration, prognosis, and novel material incorporation and restructuring.

### 3.5.2 Role of intelligent tools in tissue engineering

AI has also been proven to be very valuable in the creation of scaffolds for tissue engineering. Designing tissue engineering scaffolds is a challenging engineering task due to the complex relationships between specific geometries, bulk materials, and manufacturing techniques, as well as the intricate nature of the original tissues these scaffolds are meant to repair [37]. Recent advancements in scaffold design using ML-guided 3D printing have shown great promise in minimizing defects. This innovative technology allows for precise and accurate scaffolding geometries to be created, resulting in enhanced performance and safety. It is exciting to see how this technology can revolutionize the field of scaffold design and improve outcomes for patients [38]. Cutting-edge AI technology has been instrumental in predicting vascularization in repair strategies [39], as well as correlating in vitro performance with various physicochemical properties [40]. This revolutionary breakthrough has paved the way for more efficient and effective medical treatments, ultimately improving patient outcomes and quality of life.

In the discussion of tissue engineering, the extracellular matrix (ECM) is a fixture in this area. The ECM provides signal transduction for cell proliferation and adhesion, which are crucial in structuring scaffolds for tissue regeneration and repair [41]. The quest to imitate the structure of ECM has been in progress, and the development of smart and inert three-dimensional biomaterials should be similar to that of our ECM [42]. Therefore, it should be an objective for the ECM to be replicated, and AI has the potential to help, as it can identify various mechanical properties that can augment the 3D structures necessary for biomaterial design.

### 3.5.3 Intelligent tools in biomolecular and microbial design

AI has the potential to facilitate decarbonization efforts by assisting in the development of effective environmental policies, optimizing resource usage, identifying efficient processes, and creating sustainable material design innovations. The physical properties of biomaterials comprise unique chemical compositions and molecular structures.

These structures play a crucial role in determining the mechanical behavior of the elements, which has motivated researchers to adopt AI to generate promising configurations and design biomaterials [43]. With AI and ML, it is possible to obtain information for identifying, isolating, and predicting secondary metabolites' targets in natural products for drug formulation [44]. In addition, new psychoactive substances (NPSs) can be designed to mimic the physiological actions of better-known drugs of abuse while skirting drug control laws. Recently, Dark NPS, a DL-enabled approach, can automatically elucidate the structures of unidentified designer drugs using only mass spectrometric data [45].

Composite materials include a wide range of material systems, such as fiber-reinforced composites, polymer matrix composites, and ceramic matrix composites [43,46]. Furthermore, AI can also be used in bioengineering and bio-manufacturing of composite materials. AI along with ML and DL can be used to accurately predict the mechanical properties of composite materials [43,47]. By using ML, it is possible to teach computer systems about the performance of high-value chemicals produced within microorganisms in real-life applications that are suitable for scaling up. However, composite materials exhibit complex hierarchical structures, and their mechanical properties depend on interactions at multiple length scales. Hence, collaborative efforts between AI researchers and experimentalists are essential to validate and refine AI predictions. Integrating AI predictions with experimental validation can help assess the accuracy and reliability of the models. Further research is needed to address challenges related to interpretability, data quality, transferability, and uncertainty quantification to advance the field of AI in predicting the mechanical properties of composite materials [43].

### 3.5.4 Intelligent tools in hydrogel design

Hydrogels consist of a network of polymers and water in a three-dimensional structure. These have been extensively researched and improved in recent years due to their unique chemical and physical properties, such as high water absorption, biocompatibility, and degradability [48]. Hydrogel technology has been an area of immense interest for researchers and scientists.

AI is replacing costly trial-and-error in developing novel biomaterials. The utilization of AI methods, notably high-throughput experimentation, has significantly improved the design and production of biomaterials. The main reason for this is the increase in the scope of outcomes to encompass the FDA-endorsed excipient database. The implementation of AI techniques has demonstrated the potential to revolutionize biomaterial development by improving the efficiency and accuracy of research [49]. To improve the functionality and application effectiveness of hydrogels, the use of AI has brought about unprecedented advancements in the fields of material design and the optimization of the preparation process. AI has been instrumental in enabling detailed screening and analysis of materials, as well as performance monitoring and control. Material characterization analysis has also significantly benefited from the application of AI technology [50]. AI-energized hydrogel design has wide applications (Fig. 3.7). These methods play a crucial role in facilitating the development of hydrogel

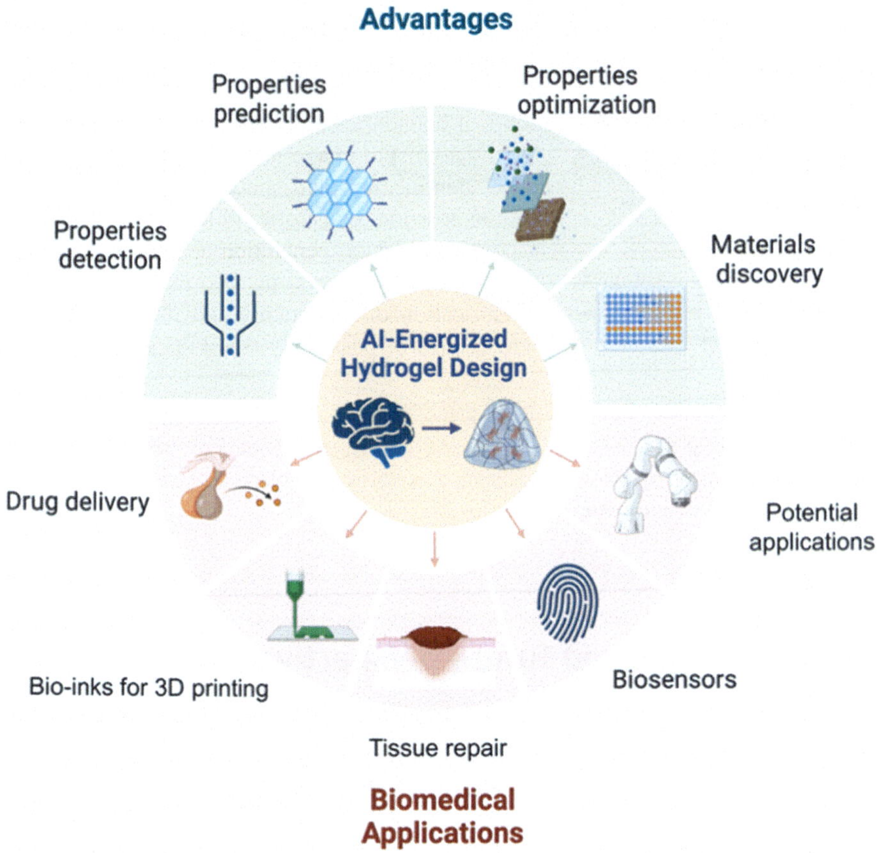


**Figure 3.7** AI-energized hydrogel design applications. *AI*, Artificial Intelligence. Reprinted with permission from [48].

technology, leading to advancements in the field. Therefore, hydrogels find their application in various fields, such as drug delivery systems, wound dressing, contact lenses, soft robotics, biosensors, and more.

Recent research has shown that ML can predict hydrogel flow properties and optimize their formulations [50]. Fig. 3.8 shows the hydrogel formulations using ML and the characterization of rheological properties of hydrogels by automated sensing and physically guided supervised ML [48]. Specifically, a study-based ML model has proven successful in predicting the viscosity of polymer composites containing nanoparticles. By utilizing ML algorithms for automatic sensing and guidance, the rheological properties of hydrogels can be accurately characterized and this results in a high-throughput process. This approach is important for the optimal design of hydrogels which enables rapid and reliable performance prediction.

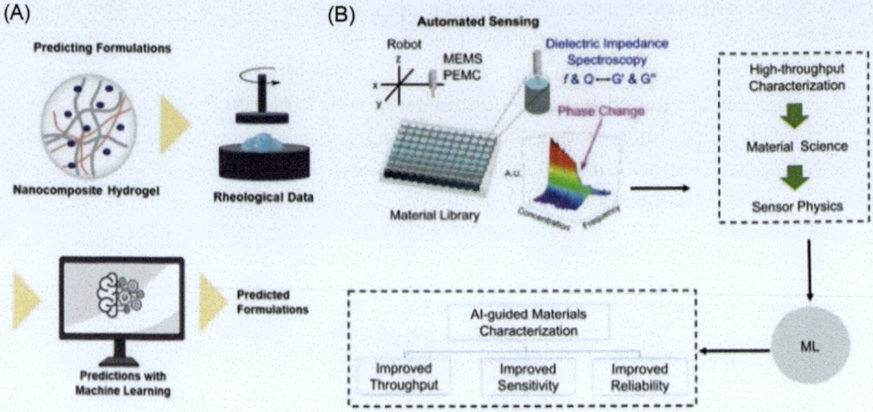


**Figure 3.8** Hydrogel formulations using ML (A) and characterization of rheological properties of hydrogels by automated sensing and physically guided supervised ML (B). Reprinted with permission from [48].

## 3.6 Limitations and future perspectives

AI is becoming increasingly prevalent in contemporary healthcare specializations, where it serves as a clinical support decision system. Even while AI approaches are being used increasingly, there is still relatively little evidence of AI being used in therapeutic settings [51]. AI-based methods are sometimes problematic because they depend on extremely high-quality, labeled datasets, which are necessary to produce reliable, accurate findings. Furthermore, because DL models include a large number of parameters, there is a greater chance that the models would overfit the training set, which will reduce the results' generalizability. Furthermore, data argumentation can minimize the chances for misclassification, extract an increased amount of information from medical images, and limit class imbalance. Cross-center training will enable the reduction of differences in data generation protocol, which will formulate strategies to mitigate the generalizability problems of DL-based models [52]. Robotics can also be applied to different areas of the healthcare system to move forward toward a new era of data-driven medicine [53]. The incorporation of augmented reality (AR) and virtual reality [54] can help researchers create excellent instruments for clinical practice, from better visualization to shorter operating times and promising therapeutic results, making AI-based models more reliable [55].

Future research can focus on developing AI models that can capture and predict mechanical properties at different scales, from micro to macro levels. Multiscale modeling approaches, such as coupling AI models with finite element analysis (FEA) or molecular dynamics simulations, can facilitate accurate predictions across different length scales [43].

## 3.7 Conclusion

In conclusion, AI technology has revolutionized the field of digital dentistry and healthcare by providing accurate diagnosis, streamlining workflows, and improving patient care. Its impact is evident in areas such as administrative workflows, image analysis, robotic surgery, virtual assistants, and clinical decision support. With its ability to analyze data quickly and accurately, AI technology is endlessly helping to shape the future of dentistry and healthcare, adding a new element to the Age of Design.

Furthermore, AI-powered advanced dental tools can offer dentists immediate feedback during dental procedures, ensuring that their work is precise and accurate. ML models have demonstrated their potential in predicting the formation of new hybrid materials, surpassing traditional human strategies. AI and ML have significantly expedited the identification and development of novel materials.

Overall, the impact of AI on the health industry is undeniable, and its role in shaping the future of medicine and dentistry is only set to grow. As AI technology continues to evolve, we expect to see more advanced AI applications that will further revolutionize and facilitate more efficient experimentation and research, discover and design next-generation materials, and enhance patient care.

## Acknowledgment

To the best of the Editors' knowledge and authors' claims, no generative AI tools were used for substantive writing of chapters. Any AI-assisted language editing, if applied, was limited to grammar or style suggestions and did not alter the scientific content.

## References

[1] Soori M, Arezoo B, Dastres R. Artificial intelligence, machine learning and deep learning in advanced robotics, a review. Cognitive Robotics 2023;3:54–70.
[2] Basu K, Sinha R, Ong A, Basu T. Artificial intelligence: how is it changing medical sciences and its future? Indian Journal of Dermatology 2020;65(5):365–70.
[3] Kumar Y, Koul A, Singla R, Ijaz MF. Artificial intelligence in disease diagnosis: a systematic literature review, synthesizing framework and future research agenda. Journal of Ambient Intelligence and Humanized Computing 2023;14(7):8459–86.
[4] Orhan K, Jagtap R. Introduction to artificial intelligence. In: Orhan K, Jagtap R, editors. Artificial intelligence in dentistry. Cham: Springer International Publishing; 2023. p. 1–7.
[5] Li B-H, Hou B-C, Yu W-T, Lu X-B, Yang C-W. Applications of artificial intelligence in intelligent manufacturing: a review. Frontiers of Information Technology and Electronic Engineering 2017;18(1):86–96.
[6] Furth ME, Atala A, Van Dyke ME. Smart biomaterials design for tissue engineering and regenerative medicine. Biomaterials 2007;28(34):5068–73.
[7] Deo N, Anjankar A. Artificial intelligence with robotics in healthcare: a narrative review of its viability in India. Cureus 2023;15(5):e39416.

[8] Lee D, Yoon SN. Application of artificial intelligence-based technologies in the healthcare industry: opportunities and challenges. International Journal of Environmental Research and Public Health 2021;18(1):271.

[9] Vodanović M, Subašić M, Milošević D, Savić Pavičin I. Artificial intelligence in medicine and dentistry. Acta Stomatologica Croatica 2023;57(1):70–84.

[10] Bohr A, Memarzadeh K. The rise of artificial intelligence in healthcare applications. In: Bohr A, Memarzadeh K, editors. *Artificial intelligence in healthcare*. Copenhagen, Denmark: Elsevier Inc.; 2020. p. 25–60.

[11] Humagain M, Rokaya D. Integrating digital technologies in dentistry to enhance the clinical success. Kathmandu University Medical Journal 2019;17(68):256–7.

[12] Spagnuolo G, Sorrentino R. The role of digital devices in dentistry: clinical trends and scientific evidences. Journal of Clinical Medicine 2020;9(6):1692.

[13] Schierz O, Hirsch C, Krey K-F, Ganss C, KÄMmerer PW, Schlenz MA. Digital dentistry and its impact on oral health-related quality of life. The Journal of Evidence-Based Dental Practice 2024;24(1, Supplement):101946.

[14] Amornvit P, Rokaya D, Peampring C, Sanohkan S. Confocal 3D optical intraoral scanners and comparison of image capturing accuracy. Computational Materials Continua 2021;66(1):303–14.

[15] Dhingra K. Artificial intelligence in dentistry: current state and future directions. Bulletin of the Royal College of Surgeons of England 2023;105(8):380–3.

[16] Bonny T, Al Nassan W, Obaideen K, Al Mallahi MN, Mohammad Y, El-Damanhoury HM. Contemporary role and applications of artificial intelligence in dentistry. F1000Research 2023;12:1179.

[17] Jagtap R, Bayrakdar SK, Orhan K. Advantages, disadvantages, and limitations of AI in dental health. In: Orhan K, Jagtap R, editors. Artificial intelligence in dentistry. Cham: Springer International Publishing; 2023. p. 235–46.

[18] Lee EJ, Kasper FK, Mikos AG. Biomaterials for tissue engineering. Annals of Biomedical Engineering 2014;42(2):323–37.

[19] Luo F, Hong G, Wan Q. Artificial intelligence in biomedical applications of zirconia. Frontiers in Dental Medicine 2021;2:689288.

[20] Abdallah YK, Estévez AT. Biomaterials research-driven design visualized by AI text-prompt-generated images. Designs 2023;7(2):48.

[21] Sharma RR. Emotional intelligence from 17th century to 21st century: perspectives and directions for future research. Vision 2008;12(1):59–66.

[22] Janssens M, Meslec N, Leenders R. Collective intelligence in teams: contextualizing collective intelligent behavior over time. Frontiers in Psychology 2022;13:989572.

[23] Sarker IH. Machine learning: algorithms, real-world applications and research directions. SN Computer Science 2021;2(3):160.

[24] Fang G, Chow MCK, Ho JDL, He Z, Wang K, Ng TC, et al. Soft robotic manipulator for intraoperative MRI-guided transoral laser microsurgery. Science Robotics 2021;6(57):eabg5575.

[25] Flowers JC. Strong and weak AI: deweyan considerations. AAAI Spring Symposium: Towards Conscious AI Systems 2019;2019:68.

[26] Gilvary C, Madhukar N, Elkhader J, Elemento O. The missing pieces of artificial intelligence in medicine. Trends in Pharmacological Sciences 2019;40(8):555–64.

[27] Fransen KA, Av-Ron SH, Buchanan TR, Walsh DJ, Rota DT, Van Note L, et al. High-throughput experimentation for discovery of biodegradable polyesters. Proceedings of the National Academy of Sciences of the United States of America 2023;120(23). https://doi.org/10.1073/pnas.2220021120.

[28] Ding H, Wu J, Zhao W, Matinlinna JP, Burrow MF, Tsoi JKH. Artificial intelligence in dentistry—a review. Frontiers in Dental Medicine 2023;4:1085251.
[29] Mah PM, Skalna I, Muzam J. Natural language processing and artificial intelligence for enterprise management in the era of industry 4.0. Applied Sciences 2022;12(18):9207.
[30] Le TH. Applying artificial neural networks for face recognition. Advances in Artificial Neural Systems 2011;2011:673016.
[31] Chen YW, Moussi J, Drury JL, Wataha JC. Zirconia in biomedical applications. Expert Review of Medical Devices 2016;13(10):945–63.
[32] Kongkiatkamon S, Rokaya D, Kengtanyakich S, Peampring C. Current classification of zirconia in dentistry: an updated review. PeerJ 2023;11:e15669.
[33] Ban S. Classification and properties of dental zirconia as implant fixtures and superstructures. Materials 2021;14(17):4879.
[34] Ghods K, Azizi A, Jafari A, Ghods K. Application of artificial intelligence in clinical dentistry, a comprehensive review of literature. Journal of Dentistry 2023;24(4):356–71.
[35] Singh J, Singh S, Verma A. Artificial intelligence in use of $ZrO_2$ material in biomedical science. Journal of Electrochemical Science and Engineering 2023;13(1):83–97.
[36] Suwardi A, Wang F, Xue K, Han MY, Teo P, Wang P, et al. Machine learning-driven biomaterials evolution. Advanced Materials 2022;34(1):e2102703.
[37] Bermejillo Barrera MD, Franco-Martínez F, Díaz Lantada A. Artificial intelligence aided design of tissue engineering scaffolds employing virtual tomography and 3D convolutional neural networks. Materials 2021;14(18):5278.
[38] Conev A, Litsa EE, Perez MR, Diba M, Mikos AG, Kavraki LE. Machine learning-guided three-dimensional printing of tissue engineering scaffolds. Tissue Engineering. Part A 2020;26(23-24):1359–68.
[39] Xu J, Ge H, Zhou X, Yan J, Chi Q, Zhang Z. Prediction of vascular tissue engineering results with artificial neural networks. Journal of Biomedical Informatics 2005;38(6):417–21.
[40] Sujeeun LY, Goonoo N, Ramphul H, Chummun I, Gimié F, Baichoo S, et al. Correlating in vitro performance with physico-chemical characteristics of nanofibrous scaffolds for skin tissue engineering using supervised machine learning algorithms. Royal Society Open Science 2020;7(12):201293.
[41] Rosso F, Marino G, Giordano A, Barbarisi M, Parmeggiani D, Barbarisi A. Smart materials as scaffolds for tissue engineering. Journal of Cellular Physiology 2005;203(3):465–70.
[42] Lutolf MP, Hubbell JA. Synthetic biomaterials as instructive extracellular microenvironments for morphogenesis in tissue engineering. Nature Biotechnology 2005;23(1):47–55.
[43] Kibrete F, Trzepieciński T, Gebremedhen HS, Woldemichael DE. Artificial intelligence in predicting mechanical properties of composite materials. Journal of Composites Science 2023;7(9):364.
[44] Sahayasheela VJ, Lankadasari MB, Dan VM, Dastager SG, Pandian GN, Sugiyama H. Artificial intelligence in microbial natural product drug discovery: current and emerging role. Natural Product Reports 2022;39(12):2215–30.
[45] Skinnider MA, Wang F, Pasin D, Greiner R, Foster LJ, Dalsgaard PW, et al. A deep generative model enables automated structure elucidation of novel psychoactive substances. Nature Machine Intelligence 2021;3(11):973–84.
[46] Rokaya D, Srimaneepong V, Sapkota J, Qin J, Siraleartmukul K, Siriwongrungson V. Polymeric materials and films in dentistry: an overview. Journal of Advanced Research 2018;14:25–34.
[47] Song L, Wang D, Liu X, Yin A, Long Z. Prediction of mechanical properties of composite materials using multimodal fusion learning. Sensors and Actuators A: Physical 2023;358:114433.

[48] Li Z, Song P, Li G, Han Y, Ren X, Bai L, et al. AI energized hydrogel design, optimization and application in biomedicine. Materials Today Bio 2024;25:101014.
[49] Reker D, Rybakova Y, Kirtane AR, Cao R, Yang JW, Navamajiti N, et al. Computationally guided high-throughput design of self-assembling drug nanoparticles. Nature Nanotechnology 2021;16(6):725–33.
[50] Lashari N, Ganat T, Otchere D, Kalam S, Ali I. Navigating viscosity of GO-$SiO_2$/HPAM composite using response surface methodology and supervised machine learning models. Journal of Petroleum Science and Engineering 2021;205:108800.
[51] Orhan K, Gülbeş MM, Jadhav A, Jagtap R. Medico-legal problems of artificial intelligence. In: Orhan K, Jagtap R, editors. Artificial intelligence in dentistry. Cham: Springer International Publishing; 2023. p. 259–82.
[52] Krois J, Garcia Cantu A, Chaurasia A, Patil R, Chaudhari PK, Gaudin R, et al. Generalizability of deep learning models for dental image analysis. Scientific Reports 2021;11(1):6102.
[53] Grischke J, Johannsmeier L, Eich L, Griga L, Haddadin S. Dentronics: towards robotics and artificial intelligence in dentistry. Dental Materials 2020;36(6):765–78.
[54] Chen H, Liu Y, Balabani S, Hirayama R, Huang J. Machine learning in predicting printable biomaterial formulations for direct ink writing. Research; A Journal of Science and Its Applications 2023;6:0197.
[55] Fahim S, Maqsood A, Das G, Ahmed N, Saquib S, Lal A, et al. Augmented reality and virtual reality in dentistry: highlights from the current research. Applied Sciences 2022;12(8):3719.

# Artificial neural networks for biomaterials development

**4**

*Maryam Sadat Adibhosseini*[1], *Hossein Madineh*[2], *Ali Samadi*[3], *and M.Z. Naser*[4]
[1]Faculty of Chemical Engineering, Biomedical Engineering Division, Tarbiat Modares University, Tehran, Iran, [2]Faculty of Chemical Engineering, Department of Polymer Engineering, Tarbiat Modares University, Tehran, Iran, [3]Faculty of Engineering, Department of Polymer Engineering, Urmia University, Urmia, Iran, [4]Artificial Intelligence Research Institute for Science and Engineering (AIRISE), Clemson University, Clemson, SC, United States

## 4.1 Introduction

One major goal of the activities in regenerative medicine is to develop therapeutic stem cells, tissues, and artificial organs for repairing the injuries to tissue-like tendons, nerves, and cartilages. Although surgical interventions have been developed, similar to organ transplantation, which is hampered by several immune responses and limitations due to donor shortages, regenerative medicine represents a comprehensive approach to develop functional replacements for damaged tissues [1]. Nevertheless, a few problems arise in the reconstruction of living tissues from mature or stem cells, such as tissue formation in the culture media. The most renowned Extracellular Matrix (ECM), which is composed of micro- and nano-sized pores and fibers, shows a pivotal role regarding the controlling of cellular functions because it affects the growth, differentiation, and migration of cells, so that tissue sources generate composition variations [2]. Tissue engineering aims at developing living tissue with properties as close to native tissue as possible through the use of scaffolds that presentproperties more similar to the ECM. Such scaffolds, being either biodegradable or bio-stable, should be able to provide an appropriate environment for the regulation of cells. While designing an artificial ECM seems very challenging, the contemporary research is focused on the integration of scaffold structures along with biopolymers in biological additives together with other essential signaling components necessary for cell function [1]. The integration of biomaterials is challenging because of targeting with possible adverse effects due to cell toxicity, immune responses, and transport mechanisms. One specific focus for the design of the systems is based on biological properties such as mechanical stress and complex characteristics at the target site. These properties change according to physiological parameters like age and anatomic location in the human body. The basic biomaterials used in regenerative medicine are synthetic polymers (e.g., polyanhydrides), natural polymers (e.g., hyaluronan and chitosan), and inorganics (e.g., hydroxyapatite) [3]. Advanced biomaterialsused in tissue engineering should take into consideration the full awareness of the target site, delivery method, complete release kinetics of the bioactive molecule to be delivered, and possible immune

**Artificial Intelligence in Biomaterials Design and Development. DOI:** https://doi.org/10.1016/B978-0-323-95464-8.00017-7

responses upon the administration or activation of the different signaling pathways [4]. Healthcare institutions make use of machine learning techniques such as artificial neural networks (ANNs) to optimize the healthcare delivery, at the same time minimizing the costs. While ANN was traditionally used only for diagnosis, it is now increasingly being used for decisions on healthcare management as the healthcare system moves toward more value-based and patient-centered care models. It is a challenging time in terms of care delivery management, especially in areas including patients with chronic diseases. This is because artificial intelligence serves as a facilitator of the new technologies that bring opportunities and promises for highly affordable and just-in-time care, improved communication among all pertinent parties, and flexibility in the changing healthcare environment and information systems. Organizations, however, need to navigate these challenges carefully in the face of environmental needs and priorities that usually provide the strategic decisions that are risk-averse and balance culture, technology, and uncertainty. Successful patient care and operational management require the coordination among the diverse stakeholders, which ranges from clinicians to executives, in addressing and coordinating both clinical and nonclinical decisions [5].

ANNs were, right from their very inception, designed as mathematical models with the goal of emulating the information-processing features of biological nerve cells; however, due to their structure, these bear a very close resemblance to elements that would normally be found in neuroscience, notwithstanding being considered statistical techniques (Fig. 4.1) [6]. The ANN was developed for two goals: to understand the processes of the nervous system and to imitate its functions for information processing. It is an interdisciplinary effort that enriches neuroscientists and psychologists with deeper insights through simulation, while guiding computer scientists and engineers with the biological notions of learning models to address real-world problems. Moreover, physicists and applied mathematicians encounter new frontiers of research, fostering progress in various fields [7].

## 4.2 Classical biomaterials and complexity of biological systems

Traditionally, trial and error have been the ways in which biomaterials were designed and optimized. Most clinically applied medical implants were developed from this kind of approach, and many can be enumerated, including coronary stents, orthopedic devices, and intraocular lenses. While these developments are, without a doubt, gigantic strides taken, there is a clear disconnection between the exponential growth of scientific research on biomaterials and the relatively small number of truly transformative clinical translations that have happened. Design in biomaterials often undergoes iterative engineering, where modification of various properties at different scales, for instance, chemical, structural, or mechanical, results from hypotheses based on biological concepts or practical intuition. For example, some researchers have tried to utilize electrospinning techniques to more closely mimic the structure of the natural extracellular matrix or to generate rougher surfaces in an effort to better perform the osteoblastic function,

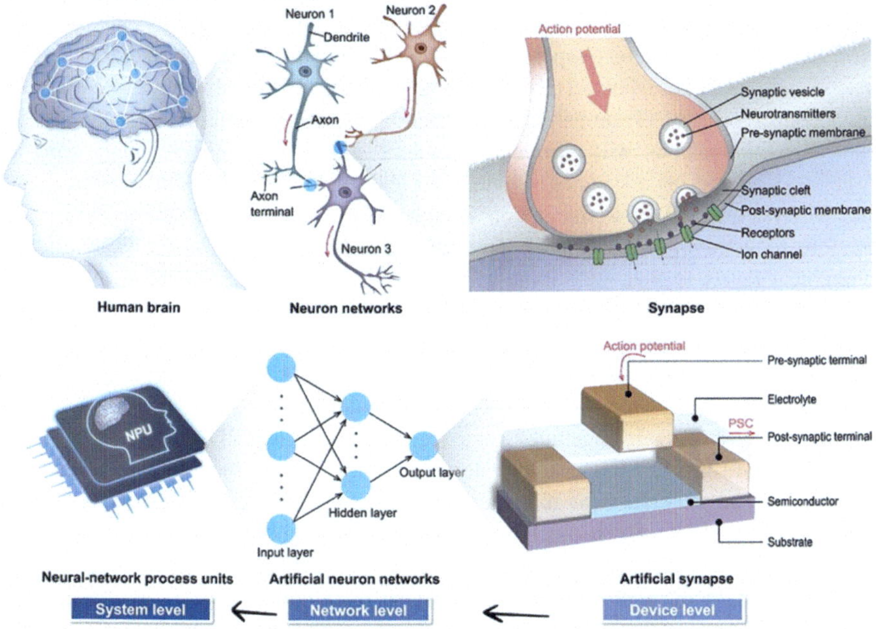


**Figure 4.1** Inspiration behind building the artificial synapses.
Reprinted with permission from [6].

essentially emulating what happens in osteoclastic resorption during bone remodeling. In other words, an intrinsic challenge in trial-and-error strategies is that material properties of diversity are intertwined, and their improvement may inadvertently modify the others. This complexity is epitomized in the iterative design of osteoinductive materials, whereby enhancement in mechanical properties has been achieved at the cost of reduced osteoinductive capacity in some cases, underscoring the fine balance between different material characteristics. One of the main challenges is to establish adequate in vitro models to test biomaterials. Most current in vitro assays are poorly predictive of efficacy and are based on intuition rather than proven effectiveness. For instance, biomaterials for bone regeneration applications are characterized by in vitro assays, which cannot express their bone-forming abilities or predict the clinical performance. These issues notwithstanding, recent breakthroughs in developmental and stem cell biology provide fertile ground for hypothesis-driven biomaterial research. For example, the targeting of specific signaling pathways and high-throughput screening approaches have shown promise in enhancing the function of stem cells or modulating cellular responses, respectively. Unfortunately, such in vitro assays often discount valuable single-cell or subpopulation information [8]. Although some successes in the translation of biomaterials to clinical applications have been reported, specifically with calcium phosphate-based products, further improvement, especially in the field of osteoinductive materials, is still necessary. Indeed, this will require a move toward a more holistic approach by appreciating the intrinsic complexity of both biological and material systems. Tissue engineering recognizes the intrinsic complexity of biological systems by attempting to foster tissue regeneration on temporary scaffolds. It must be that biomaterials are complex systems with hierarchical properties if nature can generate diversity with a few universal component types [9]. Essentially, the design and optimization of biomaterials for biomedical applications will require a paradigm shift toward reverse engineering to ensure a complete understanding of the complexities involved in both biological and material systems and their integration in the design process. Multiscale thinking is therefore required in which various properties are considered to interplay at different hierarchical levels to guarantee more effective and faster developments in the area of biomaterials [10].

Biomaterials are uniquely complex in their design/optimization challenge. Standardized test methods are lacking, high-throughput screening tools have not been developed, and computational models of how biology responds to material properties are generally unavailable. Kohn et al. concluded in a recent review that advances in biomedical engineering and biology have far outpaced the ability of the materials community to provide the next generation of biomaterials needed to fully realize tissue engineering strategies [11]. While biomedical engineers have been seeking resorbable polymer scaffolds that can support a broad spectrum of regenerative treatments, known copolymers of lactic acid and glycolic acid still dominate as scaffold materials in tissue engineering studies. Research into polymers with complex monomer structures has been limited only, with the common technique being one of simple trial and error in an attempt to couple a broad class of polymers to a particular application or applications. However, there is currently a trend toward increasingly complex material systems within the biomaterials community, which enables the design, synthesis, and processing of novel biomaterials with very specific biological applications and clinical requirements. Such a transition would require a shift away from labor-intensive and trial-and-error-based approaches toward combinatorial and computational approaches, enabling the generation and high-throughput screening of material libraries [10].

## 4.3 Strong and weak artificial intelligence

Due to the realization of the limits of the mathematical and engineering models upon which AI was initially predicated, the term "AI" currently boasts two separate definitions: strong AI and weak AI. Strong AI is the type of artificial intelligence, sometimes known as artificial general intelligence, that is intended to enable the realization of human thought in its entirety by way of using the theory that the human thought processes can, in the final analysis, be rewritten in logical, or digital, terms. Weak AI, on the other hand, acknowledges that there can be some differences between human intelligence and computing systems and that the goal is to develop cognitive systems that, even when using computational means, handle some classes of intellectual tasks efficiently. The first steps of AI development had strong AI in mind. The motivation came from the concept of the universal Turing machine by Alan Turing. It can solve, at least in theory, all mathematically definable problems. The realization of strong AI suffers, however, from cognitive and technical obstacles:

human cognition reaches beyond the purely mathematical, and infinite storage capacity is unattainable. Weak AI takes these observations into account by postulating that systems should be developed which learn problem-solving skills from mechanisms that are based on the human sensory and cognitive processes [12]. Machine learning remains one of the most popular and prominent ways to realize the goals of weak artificial intelligence, mainly relying on bio-inspired ANNs to teach computers how to solve problems independently. More specifically, weak AI emphasizes learning and flexibility rather than totally duplicating human intelligence, since it comes to realize that human cognition is very complex and partially upheld by the computational frameworks [13].

## 4.4 Artificial neural network basics

Biological neural systems contain complex circuitries, from microcircuits to large-scale networks, carrying out a wide range of functions. One of the prototypes is the mammalian visual system, which has served continuously as a source of inspiration for artificial intelligence, particularly convolutional neural networks (CNNs). At the front line, the retina in this case represents a very complex sensor and processor of light, which is transduced into electrical signals by specialized photoreceptors called rods and cones. Using the principle of parallel processing, the signal progresses vertically from photoreceptors to bipolar cells to ganglion cells. Each ganglion cell acts to luminance contrast over a circular receptive field, thus contributing to an edge map. Local processing is made possible by horizontal and amacrine cells and helps in computing edge detection. Ganglion cells are projection neurons that send the visual signal out of the retina. In V1, relayed through the Lateral Geniculate Nucleus (LGM), neurons are reported to be selective to light-dark bars or edges of a given orientation. V1 simple cells respond to specific edge orientations, whereas complex cells are position-invariant, responding to edges throughout a broader extent of their receptive field. These cellular properties of neurons reflect mechanisms of the brain for object recognition and invariance, reproduced in convolutional ANNs. Beyond V1, visual information segregates into pathways specialized for object recognition and spatial relationship processing. Both pathways exhibit hierarchical organization, with higher-level areas responding to more abstract information, such as faces or houses. Here, the architecture of this hierarchy is parallel to the principles of parallel and hierarchical processing seen at macro levels of neural systems. The mammalian visual system thus serves as a major guide in the understanding of neural circuitries and computational principles underlying the development of artificial intelligence models, including CNNs [14] (Fig. 4.2).

From the biological neural systems, the ANNs have evolved tremendously since the model by McCulloch and Pitts in 1943. ANNs have found very broad applications in most areas of artificial intelligence, image analysis, speech recognition, and robotics. However, the neuron and synapse models that are being used in current ANNs are relatively simple, and the basic operations are still limited to multiplication, addition, and activation; the complexity seen in real BioNNs has not been captured. ANNs come

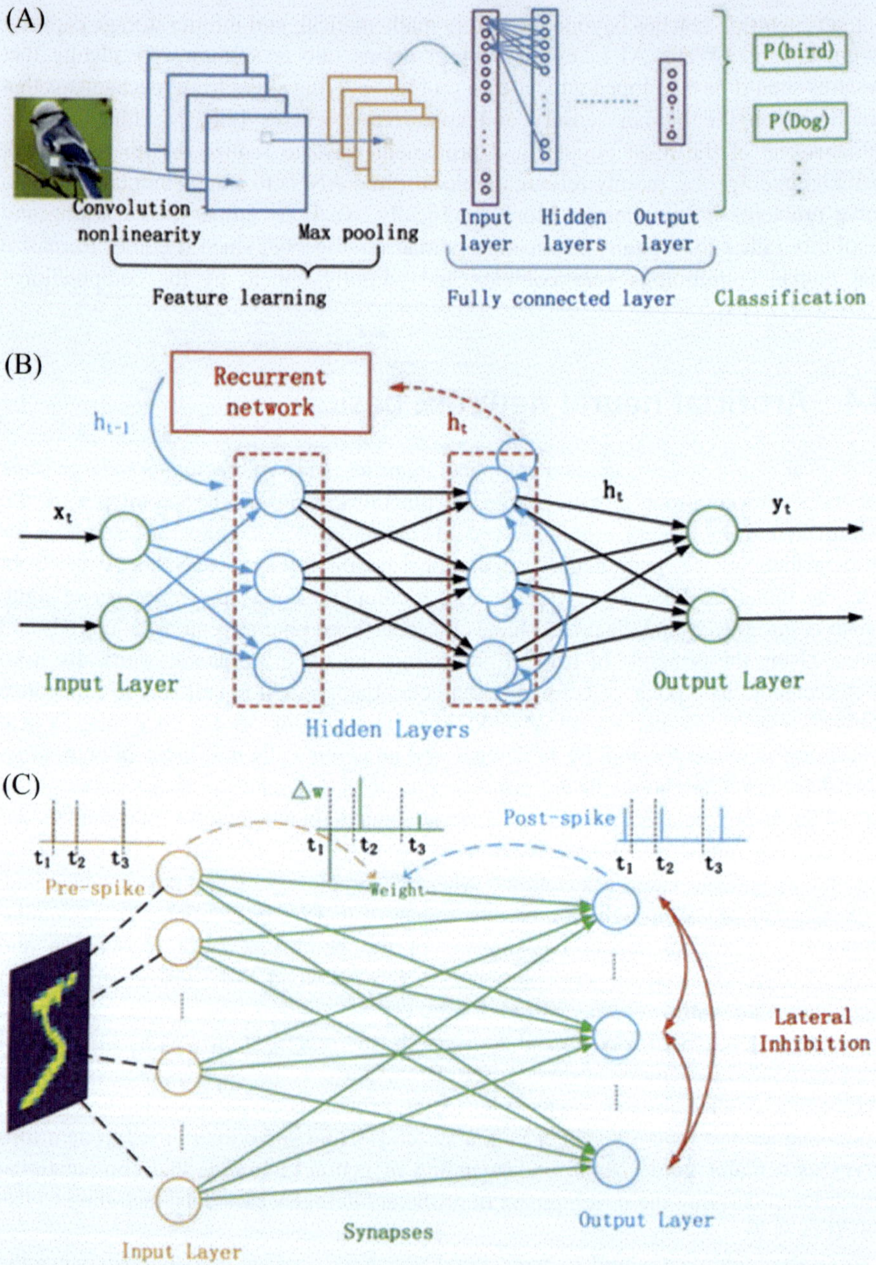


**Figure 4.2** ANN types: (A) CNN and DNN are the basic classes of feedforward ANNs with multiple hidden layers between the input and output layers, which can be trained with the standard backpropagation algorithm. The nodes on each layer and the connections among them are conceptualized as artificial neurons and synaptic weights, respectively. (B) RNN is a class

(*Continued*)

with quite a variety of network architectures, largely characterized by their connectivity patterns. Some of the popular ones include CNNs, recurrent neural networks (RNNs), and spiking neural networks (SNNs) [14,15].

An ANN can be structured as single or multiple layers and may form from a number of interconnected processing units called nodes or neurons. The neurons are connected by the use of adjustable weights, which permit signals to pass through them both in parallel and sequential styles throughout the network. As such, ANNs can typically be divided into three layers: input, which receives information; hidden, responsible for pattern extraction and most of the internal processing; and output, which generates the final network outputs. According to Agatonovic-Kustrin and Beresford's review, neural computation is realized by interconnections between neurons, each of them having an element with a weighted input, transfer function, and a single output. The weighted summation of all the inputs of a neuron decides its activation, and there is a transfer function through which the resulting activation signal goes to produce a single output. Transfer functions, learning rules, and architecture endow the network with its collective behavior [5,16].

### *4.4.1 Convolutional neural networks*

CNNs, at the core, are feedforward ANNs used for feature extraction in visual analysis. CNNs work on the input through a series of convolution and pooling operations that are performed to imitate the individual neurons' response to visual stimuli in the brain. Traditionally, convolution operations are power-intensive and thus usually performed by CPUs and/or graphics processing units (GPU). Therefore, their integration into consumer electronics is limited. However, the emerging devices of Resistive Random-Access Memory (RRAM) and Phase-Change Memory (PCM) have made multiplication operations efficient in cross-point arrays, offering high efficiency for image recognition applications. Devices designed with many computational layers (the number of layers is more than three) are popularly known as Deep Neural Networks (DNNs) for CNNs. By the backpropagation algorithm, multilayered systems training is popularly known as deep learning. Standard deep learning architectures are normally composed of a number of network layers, including fully connected layers, Convolutional (CONV), ReLU, and POOL. FC layers connect all inputs to all outputs. CONV layers compute weighted sums from small regions of the input (so-called patches), and the weights are shared across outputs to abstract the input data hierarchically. ReLU layers introduce nonlinearity, and POOL layers reduce dimensionality in feature maps. DNNs have a high accuracy in a

of ANNs where the output of some neurons is fed back to themselves or to neurons in preceding layers, which enables the information to flow in both forward and backward directions and provides RNN with a dynamic memory. (C) SNN is a more bio-plausible type of ANNs in which neurons communicate with spikes and information is encoded into the timing and frequency of spikes. The information processing in SNN is event based and, hence, could be very energy efficient. Reprinted with permission from [14].

wide spectrum of AI applications; at times, they even outperform human-level performance [17]. On the other side, the computational cost also increases proportionally with network complexity. The most computationally intensive operation in DNNs is vector-matrix multiplication. This has a huge potential for being greatly sped up in the emerging devices, owing to their efficient cross-point array structure and direct weight update scheme. In the case of hardware implementation, weight matrices of FC networks, for example, multilayer perceptron, can be directly mapped to conductance matrices of a memristive crossbar array. In CNNs, 2D CONV layer weights are usually 4D, so 4D-to-2D mapping is required for encoding weights on a memristive crossbar. This kind of mapping has a tradeoff between performance improvement and chip area consumption. Moreover, the prominent effects of programming noise and signal bounds on the training accuracy are found to be in contrast with the memristive CNNs as compared to that of MLPs. Some techniques for easing the training of memristive CNNs include input vector rescaling and detection of signal bound [18]. Memristive CNNs bring more energy-area efficiency compared to the digital implementations. Once weights are mapped onto the memristor crossbar array, which performs all the multiplications and accumulations within and across the kernels in a single step 15, computational complexity for a convolution stride reduces to O(1) [14].

### 4.4.2 Recurrent neural networks

RNNs are a type of ANNs where neurons at the same level or layer interconnect with each other to enable the circulation of information in a loop. This has been said to be the main characteristic that gives RNNs temporal depth and the capacity to handle sequences of inputs by using their internal state or memory. While traditional feedforward neural networks were not able to make a real breakthrough, RNNs—especially those architectures including Long Short-Term Memory and Bidirectional—really succeeded in most AI tasks, from image caption generation to language translation and, finally, handwriting recognition. At the very least, an LSTM unit includes the following elements: input node, input gate, cell, forget gate, and output gate. The output gate merges current input information with stored information in the cell and forgets information to forward the result to the next layer. Recurrent processing of hidden layers takes place thanks to the backpropagation algorithm. Having RRAM as a base for LSTM units within RNNs has already given encouraging results in speeding up RNNs and CNNs enormously. This is then mapped into 2D conductance matrices in a memristive crossbar for different network topologies, such as simple RNNs, LSTMs, and convolutional LSTMs. These recurrent connections are generally realized through digital circuits but have lesser performance degradation compared to memristive multilayer perceptrons because of variability in switching asymmetry between devices in the case of memristive RNNs. Furthermore, memristive LSTM RNNs are very sensitive to the precision of their input signals; thus, they require higher resolution of input signals or other techniques, like stochastic rounding schemes. Having overcome these challenges, memristive

RNNs offer advantages in terms of hardware operations involved in the forward and backward passes, which include memristive vector-matrix multiplications, over weight update operations such as memristive crossbar programming. This possible improvement in total energy-area efficiency is due to the relatively slow and power-hungry nature of programming in digital systems [19–21].

### 4.4.3 Spiking neural networks

Another promising subfield of ANNs is the SNNs, which increasingly attract interest considering the newest architecture of networks. Unlike traditional CNNs or RNNs, based on continuous floating-point numbers, SNNs work on spikes: they are discrete events that mark time and thus have a behavior that is quite similar to neurons in the brain. Because this kind of spike-based communication is a form of operation of the brain, information is timed in the arrival of the spike trains and, hence, in the timing and frequencies of the spikes themselves, which encodes the information [14]. This paradigm of computation is referred to as event-based processing and has been receiving rapid momentum. A commonly adopted model for spiking neurons is the LIF model, in which the neuron potential is modeled as the voltage across a capacitor connected to a leaky conductance path. Once this threshold is reached, the neuron fires a spike, or action potential. In this very basic form, SNNs, by using this LIF model, mimic biological neural networks and present the potential for new ways of computation. SNNs have been shown to be usable for classification tasks in demonstrations with RRAM and PCM devices. However, energy-efficient SNN hardware development suffers primarily due to the absence of efficient training algorithms, as backpropagation is in the case of DNNs, and the absence of standard datasets. These challenges have restricted the wide acceptance of SNNs [22,23].

## 4.5 Artificial neural network regression models

Neural networks are composed of input-output nodes, connection weights, and bias weights in a manner similar to linear regression models for modeling with learning and training a model; these consist of inductive learning algorithms where large datasets are required to have complete, relevant, measurable, and statistically independent properties [5]. Classification can be termed as a process where data classes are distinguished; there are several ways to develop and implement classification models, such as naive Bayesian classification and support vector machines. Regression analysis predicts numerical values by observing trends in data and helps in numeric prediction tasks. ANNs, in turn, have several advantages: they can detect complex relationships and also work with noisy or missing information; however, they require large training sets, and training times can be quite long. There is a challenge in understanding and gaining an insight into the learning process. However, with all these limitations, they open up new ways for modeling nonlinear statistics and predictive work, particularly in medicine. Logistic regression models are certainly more interpretable than neural networks, but they can also be inherently less powerful in addressing some types of data [5,13].

Unlike other machine learning applications, regression models are the primary tools used for predicting numeric values given input features. On the one hand, classifiers assign input features to discrete outputs; on the other hand, regression models provide an estimation of continuous outputs. They can be applied within scopes as varied as medical prognosis, real estate market analysis, and forecasting the properties of materials. In contrast, the robustness of the regression model lies in its robust training data: "the more and diverse the sample, the more confidently the model will predict for new instances." The regression model emphasizes the method used in classifiers; however, there are differences for the kind of data, which may be linear or nonlinear. Examples of the different forms of regression combined with classifiers are linear and logistic regression, neural networks, and support vector machines adapted as support vector regression. The regression model in a classifier adaptation process should have the learning objective of minimizing a generally measured training data difference in the loss function between predicted and actual values. An eloquent example where regression models have been used in the field of biomaterials pertains to the prediction of the approximate concentration required to reduce bacterial viability by 50% of metal oxide nanoparticles. One single study has been exemplified here where the model developed was quite simple but statistically strong enough to include only one descriptor, that is, the enthalpy of formation of a gaseous cation having an oxidation state equal to that of the metal ion architecture. This model has shown an R-squared value of 0.85 from cross-validation of a test data set and a root-mean-square error of 0.20. The model, though very well in performance, lacks predictivity due to a very small data set that has been used to develop it, so the relevance remains limited to cytotoxicity to metal ions of similar concentration as included in the training data set [24,25].

## 4.6 Applications of artificial neural networks in medicine and biomaterials development

The intricacy and variability of biological signals, combined with the complexity in human physiology and disease presentation, make the practice of medicine challenging, especially in detection, interpretation, and decision-making. ANNs thus become very useful due to their being adept at modeling complex nonlinear relationships effectively. Research Efforts The research efforts are directed to domains as diverse as fundamental medicine to clinical practice, with ANNs primarily applied to tasks like biological signal detection, analysis, and development of medical expert systems. Normally, biological signal detection and analysis involve processing continuous waveform data that is acquired from the medical devices. ANNs, being adaptive dynamical systems made up of interconnected processing units, work very well with this type of data. Coupled with their capabilities in parallelism, distributed storage, and self-adaptive learning, they become very capable of handling issues that traditional methods are not capable of. Application areas of ANNs in this field include EEG signal analysis, extraction of auditory evoked potential signals, identification of EMG and gastrointestinal signals, compression of ECG signals, and recognition of medical images. The classic methods of knowledge representation in medical expert systems are rule-based. These conventional systems encounter problems like knowledge explosion and access bottlenecks with the increase in database size. ANNs opened new perspectives by offering nonlinear parallel processing. These abilities improve knowledge inference, self-organization, and learning. All of these enhance the capabilities of traditional expert systems and gain easy acceptance and advancement. The application of ANNs also includes anesthesia, critical care medicine, and other related areas for the analysis and prediction of physiological variables, signal processing, automatic detection of interference signals, and prognosis of clinical conditions [26].

### 4.6.1 Polymers

Polymers take part in a lot of significant applications in biomedicine because they are adaptable, and their properties can be customized. With the development of computational methods, it has turned into an important tool for predicting the behavior of polymers toward guiding material design and development processes. One such major development is the Polymer Genome Project, an advanced Internet-based facility capable of predicting polymer properties, including the glass transition temperature and solubility parameter. By combining molecular fingerprinting with quantitative structure-activity relationship (QSAR) descriptors in more complex models such as Gaussian Process Regression, the platform has become instrumental in correlating input data to known polymer properties. The researchers can, therefore, fast-track the selection of materials and design specific polymer compositions for biomedical applications. An enormous contribution of the regression models was the dielectric polymeric materials. Researchers have been able to realize high accuracy in the prediction of dielectric constants using support vector machines and infinite chain descriptors with customized descriptors for the polymer structures. The infinite chain descriptors were able to exhibit better capacity in the reproduction of complex molecular structures and, therefore, enhanced better power of prediction of the regression models. QSAR models went beyond property prediction to study biological responses against biomaterials [27–30]. The use of these descriptors, developed from molecular operating environments or Dragon software, has allowed robust models predicting, for example, protein absorption or cellular response to the surfaces of polymers in tissue engineering. These models, mostly based on ANNs, generally fine-tuned with the use of genetic algorithms, provide very valuable insights into interactions of biomaterial-biological system interfaces, which help in the design of biocompatible materials with particular functionalities. QSAR-based modeling has greatly gained importance when developing designs for nanoparticles and delivery of drugs with small molecule drugs and polymer predictions for interaction. By making use of data on binding affinities from different databases and creating a variety of descriptor libraries, researchers have developed complex models able to forecast the binding affinities between different types of polymers and small molecule drugs. From the relatively simple linear models to the more complex support vector machines, all these models help shed light on molecular interactions that govern the drug-polymer interactions, therefore aiding in the rational design of drug-delivery systems for better efficacy and biocompatibility. In a nutshell, computational tools, regression models, and the QSAR techniques have brought real progress to the science of polymers. Introducing predictive modeling within state-of-the-art, full-scale databases offers new opportunities to design innovative solutions in the area of polymer-based biomaterials to tackle the current most pressing issues in healthcare and biotechnology [27,30,31]. In one recent work by Smeraldo et al., ANNs for the optimization of methods for polymer nanoparticle design in biological applications, and more specifically for the use in MRI, have been developed. It was reported on a method enabling ANNs to model the effect of different microfluidic parameters imparting on the nanoparticle size using the inputs described here and supposedly reaches a result with an extraordinary predictive capacity. Furthermore, it reports here for the first time the introduction of the concept of hydrodenticity to evaluate the relaxometric properties of biopolymer matrices. It is hoped that this study has succeeded in clearly pointing out the potential of ANN-guided design in the manufacture of nanoparticles with optimal physicochemical properties that enable very specific medical applications (Fig. 4.3) [32].

### 4.6.2 Metals

Metals already represent the majority of orthopedic implants in service, and for the foreseeable future, no substitutes will replace them in the domain of hard tissue replacement and repair. Data analytics approaches, however, are much more seldom reported in the context of biomaterial research centered on metals; at least valuable insight can be derived from neighboring areas. QSAR modeling generally comprises toxicity assessment and property prediction [33,34]. In the case of metals, QSAR models have been shown to be very effective tools in establishing the cytotoxicity of a

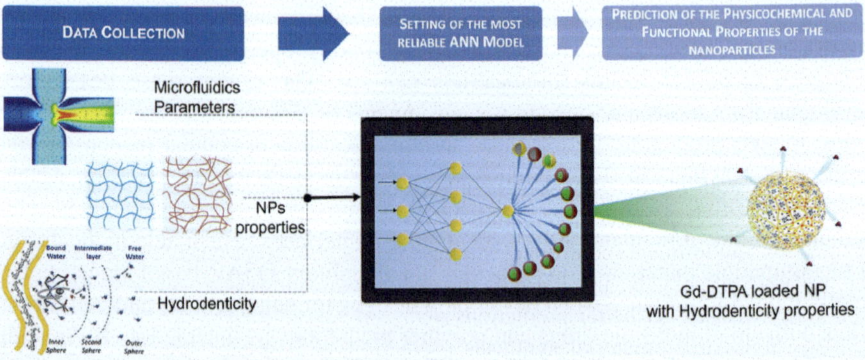


**Figure 4.3** Schematic representation of the use of artificial neural networks (ANNs) to optimize the design of Gd-DTPA-loaded nanoparticles with hydrodenticity properties, using microfluidic parameters and nanoparticle properties.
Reprinted with permission from [32].

wide variety of metals, in particular those commonly used in nanoparticles. Models such as these were developed with the aim of rapidly assessing the biocompatibility of metal nanoparticles and may well, in the long term, help to shortcut traditional cytotoxicity testing methods. More recent research efforts have been made in determining tissue viability following exposure to a range of metal oxides and further extended QSAR modeling for estimating metal cytotoxicity. Novel descriptors, custom-developed for the prediction of cytotoxicity, have been designed in order to enhance the predictions in this area [35,36]. Also, computational methods are being exploited in the prediction of properties of metals and alloys in a wide-ranging application domain. Machine learning is helping to design alloys with targeted properties, mainly mechanical properties and phase prediction. The applications of machine learning range into the prediction of transition metal properties, absorption phenomena, and the behavior of metal-organic frameworks—very versatile tools for materials research [37,38]. Recently, a neural network was used to predict titanium alloys with Young's moduli similar to bone, a general problem with hard biomaterial implants. The model obtained was termed "βLow," which fast-tracks the identification of low modulus titanium with the aims of reducing bone remodeling in accordance with Wolff's Law [39]. Roy et al. discussed the problem of the design optimization of patient-specific dental implants using the combination of finite element analysis with ANNs and genetic algorithms. It was found that ANN models could very well estimate microstrain and implant stress by changing different implant dimensions and porosity values for various bone qualities in this study. The optimized design parameters ensure desirable stress-strain conditions at the bone-implant interface; hence, it is a guideline in the development of customized prostheses that helps improve the outcome of the patient (Fig. 4.4) [40].

### 4.6.3 Ceramics

The successful history in ceramic development had to rely on stochastic synthesis procedures and important theoretical frameworks, among which concepts such as density functional theory and the topological constraint theory are possibly prominent. More recently, the demand for faster material discovery has created many new applications in machine learning, combining information from simulations with empirical observations for predicting novel material physical properties. As a consequence of the rarity and inconsistency of experimental data for ceramics, simulation-created datasets are of paramount importance to this mission [41,42]. For instance, Bioglass, a silica-based composite used in bone fusion procedures, is made up of numerous constituents that include $SiO_2$, CaO, $P_2O$, and NaO. The traditional experimental methodologies faced much difficulty in predicting the material properties with enough accuracy due to a large effect of variations in composition and synthesis methodologies. It provides correlations between composition variations and antimicrobial attributes that will thus confer easy and tailored design of Bioglass composites for a great variety of applications, such as tissue engineering and remineralization efforts [43,44]. Furthermore, where ceramics have many shortcomings in their resistance and biocompatibility, ceramic-polymer hybrids abound

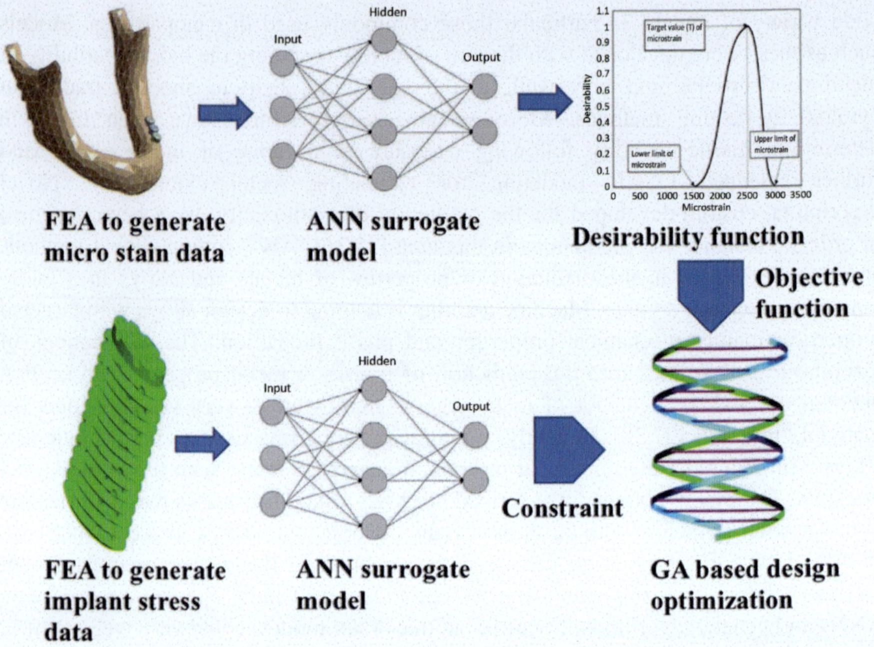


**Figure 4.4** Schematic representation of the design optimization process for patient-specific dental implants using FEA-generated data, ANN surrogate models, and genetic algorithm (GA)-based design optimization, with a desirability function as the objective function and implant stress as a constraint.
Reprinted with permission from [40].

and are often termed bio-ceramics. Also, because of a wide variety of bioresorbable bio-ceramics possible, the use of machine learning algorithms has made optimization of the relevant experimental techniques possible, and as such, an overdependence on trial solutions is minimized [45].

## 4.7 Conclusion

ANNs thus open a paradigm for the development of biomaterials; this has somewhat shifted the approach of researchers to designing and optimizing materials for biomedical applications. Moving beyond trial-and-error methodologies, ANNs provide a powerful framework for modeling complex biological systems and predicting material behaviors with an unprecedented level of accuracy. It has discussed various neural networks, like CNNs, RNNs, and SNNs, with their extraordinary benefits to be exploited for some specific domains of medicine and biomaterials science. It has also been coupled with machine learning techniques, such as regression models and QSAR models, which have very much improved the prediction capabilities of biomaterials, allowing for the quick development of tailored material counterparts for specific applications in tissue engineering and regenerative medicine. Indeed, this tight collaboration among computational scientists, material scientists, and biomedical engineers will be important for improving the state of the art in biomaterials further as this field moves forward. In other words, ANNs and machine learning in the development of biomaterials not only help accelerate new material discovery, but also allow biomedical applications to be more precise and effective. This interdisciplinary approach is very promising and proves that computational models, in the near future, will govern the design of biomaterials in an attempt to solve critical problems of human health and diseases.

## Acknowledgment

To the best of the Editors' knowledge and authors' claims, no generative AI tools were used for substantive writing of chapters. Any AI-assisted language editing, if applied, was limited to grammar or style suggestions and did not alter the scientific content.

## References

[1] Doostmohammadi M, Forootanfar H, Ramakrishna S. Regenerative medicine and drug delivery: Progress via electrospun biomaterials. *Materials Science and Engineering: C* 2020;109:110521. https://doi.org/10.1016/j.msec.2019.110521.

[2] Mohammadinejad R, Kumar A, Ranjbar-Mohammadi M, et al. Recent advances in natural gum-based biomaterials for tissue engineering and regenerative medicine: a review. *Polymers (Basel)* 2020;12(1):176. https://doi.org/10.3390/polym12010176.

[3] Kim BW. Clinical regenerative medicine in urology. Springer; 2017. https://doi.org/10.1007/978-981-10-2723-9.

[4] Sharma K, Mujawar MA, Kaushik A. State-of-art functional biomaterials for tissue engineering. *Frontiers in Materials* 2019;6:1–10. https://doi.org/10.3389/fmats.2019.00172.

[5] Shahid N, Rappon T, Berta W. Applications of artificial neural networks in health care organizational decision-making: a scoping review. *PLoS One* 2019;14(2):1–22. https://doi.org/10.1371/journal.pone.0212356.

[6] Ahmed T. Bio-inspired artificial synapses: neuromorphic computing chip engineering with soft biomaterials. *Memories - Materials Devices, Circuits and Systems* 2023;6:100088. https://doi.org/10.1016/j.memori.2023.100088.

[7] Prieto A, Prieto B, Ortigosa EM, et al. Neural networks: an overview of early research, current frameworks and new challenges. *Neurocomputing* 2016;214:242–68. https://doi.org/10.1016/j.neucom.2016.06.014.

[8] Van Der Stok J, Van Lieshout EMM, El-Massoudi Y, Van Kralingen GH, Patka P. Bone substitutes in the Netherlands—a systematic literature review. *Acta Biomaterialia* 2011;7(2):739–50. https://doi.org/10.1016/j.actbio.2010.07.035.

[9] Doorn J, Fernandes HAM, Le BQ, et al. A small molecule approach to engineering vascularized tissue. *Biomaterials* 2013;34(12):3053–63. https://doi.org/10.1016/j.biomaterials.2012.12.037.

[10] Groen N, Guvendiren M, Rabitz H, Welsh WJ, Kohn J, De Boer J. Stepping into the omics era: opportunities and challenges for biomaterials science and engineering. *Acta Biomaterialia* 2016;34:133–42. https://doi.org/10.1016/j.actbio.2016.02.015.

[11] Kohn J, Welsh WJ, Knight D. A new approach to the rationale discovery of polymeric biomaterials. *Biomaterials* 2007;28(29):4171–7. https://doi.org/10.1016/j.biomaterials.2007.06.022.

[12] Romportl J. Beyond artificial intelligence. Topics in intelligent engineering and informatics. Springer; 2019.

[13] Ha J, Kambe M, Pe J. Data mining: concepts and techniques. Waltham: Morgan Kaufmann; 2011. https://doi.org/10.1016/C2009-0-61819-5.

[14] Tang J, Yuan F, Shen X, et al. Bridging biological and artificial neural networks with emerging neuromorphic devices: fundamentals, progress, and challenges. *Advanced Materials* 2019;31(49):1902761. https://doi.org/10.1002/adma.201902761.

[15] Matsumura R, Harada K, Domae Y, Wan W. Learning based industrial bin-picking trained with approximate physics simulator. *Advances in Intelligent Systems and Computing* 2019;867:786–98. https://doi.org/10.1007/978-3-030-01370-7_61.

[16] Ushizima D. Artificial neural networks. Methods and Applications of Autonomous Experimentation. Boca Raton: CRC Press; 2023. p. 123–45. https://doi.org/10.1201/9781003359593-7.

[17] Sze V, Chen YH, Yang TJ, Emer JS. Efficient processing of deep neural networks: a tutorial and survey. Proceedings of the IEEE 2017;105(12):2295–329. https://doi.org/10.1109/JPROC.2017.2761740.

[18] Onen M, Gokmen T, Todorov TK, et al. Neural network training with asymmetric crosspoint elements. *Frontiers in Artificial Intelligence* 2022;5(May):1–11. https://doi.org/10.3389/frai.2022.891624.

[19] Lipton ZC, Berkowitz J, Elkan C. A critical review of recurrent neural networks for sequence learning. 2015; 1–38. Available from http://arxiv.org/abs/1506.00019.

[20] Gokmen T, Rasch MJ, Haensch W. Training LSTM networks with resistive cross-point devices. *Frontiers in Neuroscience* 2018;12(October):1–10. https://doi.org/10.3389/fnins.2018.00745.

[21] Wang Z, Li C, Song W, et al. Reinforcement learning with analogue memristor arrays. *Nature Electronics* 2019;2(3):115–24. https://doi.org/10.1038/s41928-019-0221-6.

[22] Tavanaei A, Ghodrati M, Kheradpisheh SR, Masquelier T, Maida A. Deep learning in spiking neural networks. *Neural Networks* 2019;111:47–63. https://doi.org/10.1016/j.neunet.2018.12.002.

[23] Chattopadhyay A, Chang CH, Yu H. Emerging technology and architecture for big-data analytics. Cham: Springer; 2017. https://doi.org/10.1007/978-3-319-54840-1.

[24] Kim C, Chandrasekaran A, Huan TD, Das D, Ramprasad R. Polymer genome: a data-powered polymer informatics platform for property predictions. *The Journal of Physical Chemistry C* 2018;122(31):17575–85. https://doi.org/10.1021/acs.jpcc.8b02913.

[25] Harrison CJ, Sidey-Gibbons CJ. Machine learning in medicine: a practical introduction to natural language processing. *BMC Medical Research Methodology* 2021;21(1):1–18. https://doi.org/10.1186/s12874-021-01347-1.

[26] Wu YC, Feng JW. Development and application of artificial neural network. *Wireless Personal Communications* 2018;102(2):1645–56. https://doi.org/10.1007/s11277-017-5224-x.

[27] Wu K, Sukumar N, Lanzillo NA, et al. Prediction of polymer properties using infinite chain descriptors (ICD) and machine learning: toward optimized dielectric polymeric materials. *Journal of Polymer Science Part B Polymer Physics* 2016;54(20):2082–91. https://doi.org/10.1002/polb.24117.

[28] Wei Q, Melko RG, Chen JZY. Identifying polymer states by machine learning. *Physical Review E* 2017;95(3):1–6. https://doi.org/10.1103/PhysRevE.95.032504.

[29] Jones DE, Ghandehari H, Facelli JC. A review of the applications of data mining and machine learning for the prediction of biomedical properties of nanoparticles. *Computer Methods and Programs in Biomedicine* 2016;132:93–103. https://doi.org/10.1016/j.cmpb.2016.04.025.

[30] Winkler DA. Sparse QSAR modelling methods for therapeutic and regenerative medicine. *Journal of Computer-Aided Molecular Design* 2018;32(4):497–509. https://doi.org/10.1007/s10822-018-0106-1.

[31] Glavatskikh M, Leguy J, Hunault G, Cauchy T, Da Mota B. Dataset's chemical diversity limits the generalizability of machine learning predictions. *Journal of Cheminformatics* 2019;11(1):1–15. https://doi.org/10.1186/s13321-019-0391-2.

[32] Smeraldo A, Ponsiglione AM, Netti PA, Torino E. Artificial neural network modelling hydrodenticity for optimal design by microfluidics of polymer nanoparticles to apply in magnetic resonance imaging. *Acta Biomaterialia* 2023;171:440–50. https://doi.org/10.1016/j.actbio.2023.09.029.

[33] Can C, Jianlong W. Correlating metal ionic characteristics with biosorption capacity using QSAR model. *Chemosphere* 2007;69(10):1610–6. https://doi.org/10.1016/j.chemosphere.2007.05.043.

[34] Gajewicz A, Schaeublin N, Rasulev B, et al. Towards understanding mechanisms governing cytotoxicity of metal oxides nanoparticles: hints from nano-QSAR studies. *Nanotoxicology* 2015;9(3):313–25. https://doi.org/10.3109/17435390.2014.930195.

[35] Choi JS, Trinh TX, Yoon TH, Kim J, Byun HG. Quasi-QSAR for predicting the cell viability of human lung and skin cells exposed to different metal oxide nanomaterials. *Chemosphere* 2019;217:243–9. https://doi.org/10.1016/j.chemosphere.2018.11.014.

[36] Pan Y, Li T, Cheng J, Telesca D, Zink JI, Jiang J. Nano-QSAR modeling for predicting the cytotoxicity of metal oxide nanoparticles using novel descriptors. *RSC Advances* 2016;6(31):25766–75. https://doi.org/10.1039/c6ra01298a.

[37] Wen C, Zhang Y, Wang C, et al. Machine learning assisted design of high entropy alloys with desired property. *Acta Materialia* 2019;170:109–17. https://doi.org/10.1016/j.actamat.2019.03.010.

[38] Ward L, Agrawal A, Choudhary A, Wolverton C. A general-purpose machine learning framework for predicting properties of inorganic materials. *NPJComputational Materials* 2016;2(March):1–7. https://doi.org/10.1038/npjcompumats.2016.28.

[39] Wu C, Te, Chang HT, Wu CY, et al. Machine learning recommends affordable new Ti alloy with bone-like modulus. *Materials Today* 2020;34:41–50. https://doi.org/10.1016/j.mattod.2019.08.008.

[40] Roy S, Dey S, Khutia N, Roy Chowdhury A, Datta S. Design of patient specific dental implant using FE analysis and computational intelligence techniques. *Applied Soft Computing* 2018;65:272–9. https://doi.org/10.1016/j.asoc.2018.01.025.

[41] Liu H, Fu Z, Yang K, Xu X, Bauchy M. Machine learning for glass science and engineering: a review. *Journal of Non-Crystalline Solids X* 2019;4(August):100036. https://doi.org/10.1016/j.nocx.2019.100036.

[42] Gu GX, Chen CT, Richmond DJ, Buehler MJ. Bioinspired hierarchical composite design using machine learning: simulation, additive manufacturing, and experiment. *Materials Horizons* 2018;5(5):939–45. https://doi.org/10.1039/c8mh00653a.

[43] Krishnan V, Lakshmi T. Bioglass: a novel biocompatible innovation. *Journal of Advanced Pharmaceutical Technology and Research* 2013;4(2):78–83. https://doi.org/10.4103/2231-4040.111523.

[44] Han T, Stone-Weiss N, Huang J, Goel A, Kumar A. Machine learning as a tool to design glasses with controlled dissolution for healthcare applications. *Acta Biomaterialia* 2020;107:286–98. https://doi.org/10.1016/j.actbio.2020.02.037.

[45] Chen CT, Gu GX. Effect of constituent materials on composite performance: exploring design strategies via machine learning. *Advanced Theory and Simulations* 2019;2(6):1–12. https://doi.org/10.1002/adts.201900056.

# From human genome to materials genome

# 5

*Hossein Madineh*[1], *Raha Zarrintaj*[2], *Ali Samadi*[3], *Payam Zarrintaj*[4], *and Saeid SamadiDana*[5]
[1]Faculty of Chemical Engineering, Department of Polymer Engineering, Tarbiat Modares University, Tehran, Iran, [2]Department of Computer Science, Tabriz University, Tabriz, Iran, [3]Faculty of Engineering, Department of Polymer Engineering, Urmia University, Urmia, Iran, [4]Independent Researcher, E3 LLC, Louisville, KY, United States, [5]Department of Computer Science & IT, Austin Peay State University, Clarksville, TN, United States

## 5.1 Introduction

Materials genome will accelerate materials research and development through some new approaches such as high-throughput experiments, big data technologies, artificial intelligence, and computational design [1]. More importantly, the materials genome engineering (MGE) presented herein fuses methodologies to allow for better screening, optimization, and design of materials with complex compositions, ultimately leading to material-processing-property relationship establishment and erosion of the developmental bottlenecks of new technologies such as organic and perovskite photovoltaics [2,3]. Defect Genome Initiative is proposed for functional defect discovery targeting various applications, having recognized the role of defects in enabling unique material functionalities [4]. Material genomic initiatives, therefore, democratize materials discovery, boost the capabilities of computational design, and create advanced materials that have tailored properties in a basic shift away from the conventional paradigm of trial and error in the innovation of materials [4].

The concept of materials genome has significantly evolved over the years from a vague idea to a now well-structured approach for designing and discovering materials [5]. It was defined as a materials genome that means the set of information, which allows prediction of materials structure and behavior under a diverse range of conditions, with a focus on the use of CALculation of PHAse Diagrams (CALPHAD) thermodynamics and kinetics [6]. It has undergone evolution by incorporating computational materials design, high-throughput experimentation, and data management to accelerate the pace of material development processes and thereby cut down on associated costs. Another instance is that this concept has expanded into regarding individual configurations of phases as the materials' genome, in which property tailoring at their microstate levels needs to be effectively considered for material design [7]. The discovery of polymer informatics has thus enabled the development of data-driven materials informatics platforms and machine learning

**Artificial Intelligence in Biomaterials Design and Development. DOI:** https://doi.org/10.1016/B978-0-323-95464-8.00003-7

models to increase the rate of prediction and design for polymer properties, further pushing the concept of the materials genome [8].

MGE makes the same kinds of transformations within materials research that genomics did, shifting from a trial-and-error approach to a data-driven platform for rapid innovation [3]. On that basis, MGE is uniquely empowered for express development and optimization of complex materials, like those found in photovoltaic technologies or biomedical materials, through a combination of high-throughput experimentation with big data technologies and artificial intelligence [1,9]. The CALPHAD system is a fundamental phase-level database; it enables computational design and qualification of materials at an unprecedented rate of speed and accuracy, shortens the design cycle, and opens up manufacturing innovation opportunities—a paradigm shift for materials science, much like that in the biological sciences introduced by genomics [6,10].

The convergence of material genome and human genome studies facilitates the design of new biomaterials for regenerative medicine. For example, the role of biomaterials within gene delivery systems to induce improved regeneration of cartilage tissue and biodegradable polymers is critical to tissue regeneration and medical device manufacturing [11–15]. Immune response to implanted biomaterials is critical to enhancing device integration and performance. Successful biomaterials, in view of tissue regeneration, exhibit biocompatibility, biofunctionality, and the potential for extracellular matrix mimicking [16–20]. The interplay among stem cell biology and rationally bioengineered materials can further develop cell behaviors and tissue regeneration outcomes that are key to applications in regenerative therapies. With new insights from materials research and the Human Genome Project, new biomaterials may now be specifically designed for the delivery of genes, modulating immune responses, and as supportive niches for better engraftment of stem cells, ultimately shaping outcomes in regenerative medicine [21–25].

## 5.2 High-throughput experiments and computational design

High-throughput experiments and computational design directly impact the progress in understanding material genome through the acceleration of materials research and development by efficient experimentation, big databases, and artificial intelligence algorithms [1]. On the one hand, the HT experiments enable the performance of multidimensional tasks rapidly, thereby producing trustworthy data for the materials databases, while, on the other hand, computational design, for example, high-throughput computation (HTC), efficiently screens materials in huge variable spaces, saving extensive trial and error [26]. Integrated with data mining, artificial intelligence, and machine learning technology, HTC further enhances the capabilities and applicability of this approach, representing a new paradigm in computational material science. HTC experimental methodology combined with database constructions and intelligent computation also found adoption in the Materials Genome Initiative in predicting material properties; it is manifested in the development of high-throughput approaches for live-cell imaging agents, which close an important gap between material structure and function. These methods synergize to support fast screening, characterization, and design of advanced materials, following the goals of the Materials Genome Initiative [10,27].

Computed information and analyses finally lead to new materials design, often using a combination of tools from the Materials Project (Fig. 5.1). A researcher might be in search of a material possessing some definite features of band structure and thermodynamic stability. Using the Materials Explorer, he or she may identify a suitable ruthenium-containing oxide compound but one that is too expensive. The Crystal Toolkit and Structure Predictor are used to design alternative compounds with less costly transition metals. The designs are then submitted back to the Materials Project, where the results are delivered within a few days, along with assessments of electronic properties and the degree of thermodynamic stability. The successful compounds at this stage may thus be passed on for higher-order calculations or even submitted for experimental validation [28].

Coupling computational techniques with high-throughput experiments is among the most important strategies in the quest to accelerate materials discovery and development. Recently, an Materials Genome Initiative (MGI)-oriented strategy has been taken for the construction of the databank of the Young's moduli of Ti-rich Ti–Nb–Zr–Cr alloys. This strategy combines the diffusion couple technique along with nanoindentation, notwithstanding that the CALPHAD method efficiently collects and analyzes data from huge validating datasets. Measured high-throughput data and computer models can

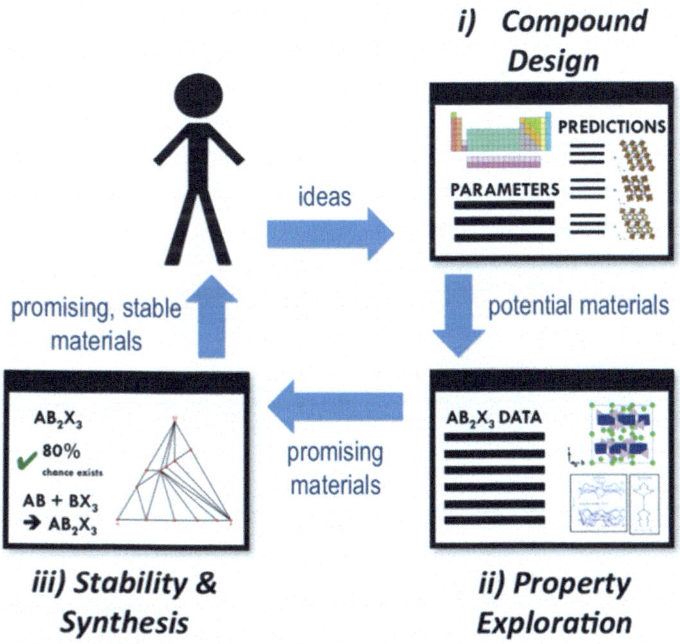


**Figure 5.1** Rapid prototyping and iterative materials design steps.
Reprint with permission from [28].

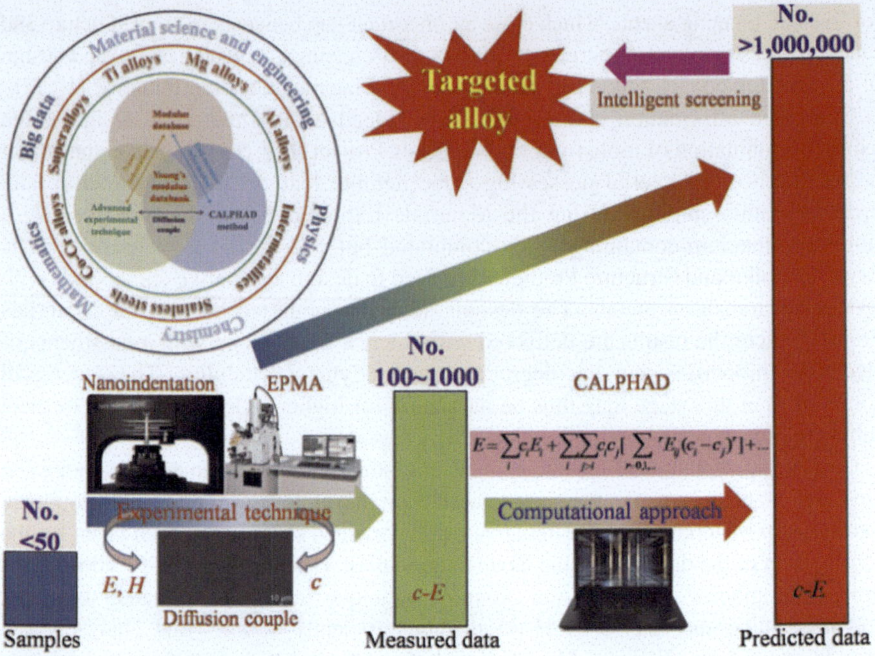


**Figure 5.2** Schematic diagram for the high-throughput development of the Young's modulus databank in materials, following the MGI strategy.
Reprinted with permission from [29].

be combined to rapidly create composition-dependent properties—drastically reducing development time and cost relative to conventional material development methods. Fig. 5.2 provides a schematic for such a high-throughput development process, where experimental data combine with computational predictions for a comprehensive databank. In this respect, the synergistic approach taken in this work has increased the reliability of the data and has allowed the design of new bio-alloys with specific mechanical properties, which proves a deep impact that will be created by high-content data collected and analyzed in materials science research [29].

## 5.3 Big data technologies and artificial intelligence in materials research

Big data technologies and AI act as facilitators in materials discovery. They allow for more efficient analysis of human genome data. AI techniques into materials research, ab initio AI, and MGE enable one to do high-speed screening and optimization of material properties [1,30]. It also finds a place in AI and ML within materials science in accelerating materials discovery and in optimizing production processes and quality control, which will permit faster discovery and more efficient material development [31]. Beyond that, the end-to-end discovery applications empowered by generative models and knowledge management frameworks concatenate to explore novel functional materials by generating volumes of novel molecules, thus aiding risk assessment [32].

The usage of big data and AI technologies in material research increased through ML algorithms. The algorithms in use also include relatively simplistic models like logistic regression and random forests, while others are more complex, such as convolutional neural networks (CNNs) and artificial neural networks (ANNs). In this case, simple models are mostly applied for straightforward prediction tasks with few variables involved, while complex models find their uses when subtle changes of a large number of variables are present and need more predictive power. Logistic regression and random forests work really well when classifying data that bears very distinct linear relationships, but CNNs and ANNs really come in handy when dealing with huge sets of multidimensional data, which makes it efficient to optimize predictions of property and process parameters of materials. The choice will depend on specific requirements of the research with respect to the complexity of the task and the availability of data. In particular, these ML techniques enable researchers to discover complex patterns in data and predict material behavior, and hence fast-track the development of new materials with tailored properties that will eventually drive very fast progress in materials science [33]. ML algorithms vary in terms of their use case and complexity, as summarized in Table 5.1.

## 5.4 Current advancements in the biomaterial genome

Recent progress in materials genome approach has created a rapid pathway to innovation for biomaterials by integrating concepts of high-throughput experimentation, database construction, and artificial intelligence algorithms [1]. Establishment of material-processing-property relationships more efficiently can create novelty biomaterials with improved efficiency and expression dynamics outcomes by combining efficient experimentation with big databases and AI algorithms. The materials genome approach has opened the way forward in quickly producing extensive amounts of reliable data, revolutionizing biomaterials research, and offering a very promising avenue for further advancements in biomaterial design [1,34].

Biomaterials are used in different applications such as drug delivery, tissue engineering, and imaging/diagnostic systems. Such biomaterials may appear through implantation, injection into the blood vessels, applying onto the skin [35–38]. Traditionally, metals and ceramics are the most common examples of biomaterials used owing to their very high mechanical strength and inertness, usually for implants. Whereas metals have their mechanical strength, ceramics, beyond the mechanical features, are particularly interesting for their ability to promote the development and regeneration of bones; therefore, they are used as dental implants [39–42]. In recent years, the development of polymeric biomaterials has been very rapid, due to the inherent moldability of the materials and recent progress in additive manufacturing and high-resolution spatial patterning, which is mainly responsible for adding new dimensions to research in biomaterials.

**Table 5.1** Common machine learning algorithms [33].

| Type | Methods | When to use | Considerations |
|---|---|---|---|
| Simpler models | Logistic regression | Simple prediction task | Small data sizes, but can have overfitting |
| | Random forest | Large dataset | Depending on the number of trees, can be quite slow low interpretability |
| | Gradient boosting | To minimize bias errors and overfitting combining multiple weak predictors into a stronger predictor | Gradient boosting can be an alternative means to give more importance to misclassified observations |
| | Support vector machine | Multidimensional parameters | Maybe challenging handling a large dataset |
| Complex models | Convolutional neural network (CNN) | Additional filters to extract features, good for feature importance | Slower training, cannot be interpreted easily |
| | Artificial neural network (ANN) | Multiple hidden layers for complex relationships | Robust against noisy data but bad interpretability |
| | K-means clustering | Anonymous input data with no output labels | Not tractable for large datasets |
| Smaller dataset models | Bayesian inference | Incorporate priors and iteratively update it with new information | Smaller data sizes, fewer iterations needed |
| | Transfer learning | Have a pretrained model for the related problem | Speed up model training |
| Data sampling | ADASYN (adaptive synthetic) | Interpolate minority data points to address class imbalance | Precision may suffer due to the adaptability nature |
| | Latin hypercube | Near-random sampling | Spread the sample points more evenly across all possible values |
| | MCMC (Markov Chain Monte Carlo) | Sampling probability distribution from posterior values | Allows estimation such as means, variances, expected values |

Although creating a biomaterial for its purpose involves a number of factors that serve as inputs regarding its chemical and physical configurations are involved, this means that the input parameters of the biomaterials can be tuned to change the output qualities, as diagrammed in Fig. 5.3. Chemical inputs may involve the deliberate

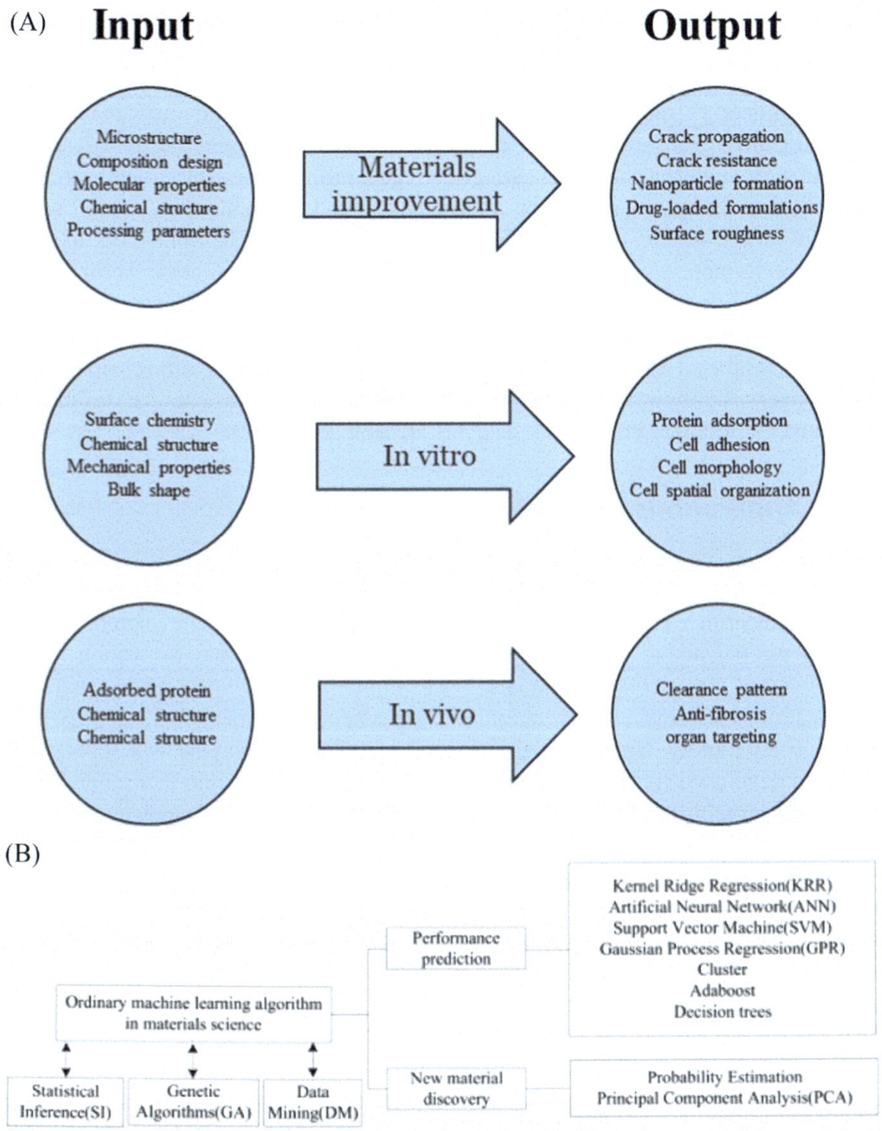


**Figure 5.3** (A) Biomaterials input and output parameters and (B) common ML algorithms in material science.
Designed inspired by information from [43].

introduction of chemical moieties that drive material properties, for example pH switchable groups that react to the biological environment; charges for polymer gene complexes in gene delivery vehicles; and targeting moieties such as folic acid for cancer-targeting nanoparticles and bisphosphonate to enhance bone binding. Cell-matrix interacting ligands can cause proliferation and directed differentiation of stem cells. Other physical inputs with dramatic influences on cell interactions include enhanced permeability and retention effects via smaller nanoparticles, larger microparticles to reduce fibrosis, and surface topology and patterning for the selective enrichment of either cells or extracellular vesicles. Such materials therefore mimic extracellular matrices to provide chemical and mechanical cues that could alter cell behaviors [33]. In Fig. 5.3, the different machine learning algorithms in materials science can all be generalized into four major groups: probability estimation, regression, clustering, and classification. Regression, clustering, and classification algorithms are major machine learning tools used in material performance prediction. Some important techniques include kernel ridge regression, ANN, Support Vector Machine (SVM), Gaussian process regression, feature learning, clustering, matrix factorization, constraint reasoning, and others. Moreover, Adaboost and decision trees are also used. Machine learning will help in the discovery of new materials, whereby methods like probability estimation algorithms or principal component analysis are employed [43].

### 5.4.1 Applications of polymeric biomaterials

Because of their high degree of adaptability, it is possible to cover an extremely broad range of physical and chemical characteristics, thus making them very appropriate for tissue engineering and drug/gene delivery applications. Their complex and multidimensional nature requires extensive design, synthesis, and evaluation in the development of polymeric biomaterials. For example, tissue engineering, sensing, cell encapsulation, and drug administration use self-assembled dipeptide hydrogels with good biocompatibility, featuring high water content. Another way by which polymers have been developed for use in biomedicine is through research into their engineering for cell and protein interactions, thus maximizing their biomedical applications.

Fig. 5.4 shows the comprehensive chemical library as the testing pool. A total of 31 monomers, including 8 amines, 8 aldehydes/ketones, 12 Fmoc-amino acids, and 3 isocyanides, were utilized to generate 2304 compounds via Ugi reaction. Fig. 5.4A–E represent structures. The flow of the overall process is shown in Fig. 5.4F. With the calculation of PaDEL-descriptor, 7,163,136 structural parameters for all the compounds have been obtained, which is 3109 per molecule. Due to class imbalance, since less than 4% of the hydrogels were successfully formed, data resampling methods applied in this work include random oversampling, adaptive synthetic sampling, and synthetic minority oversampling technique (SMOTE). Random Oversampling (RO) randomly adds data points into the minority class, while ADASYN and SMOTE apply more sophisticated interpolation methods, where the number of data points added varies depending on complexity/difficulty specific to ADASYN [44].

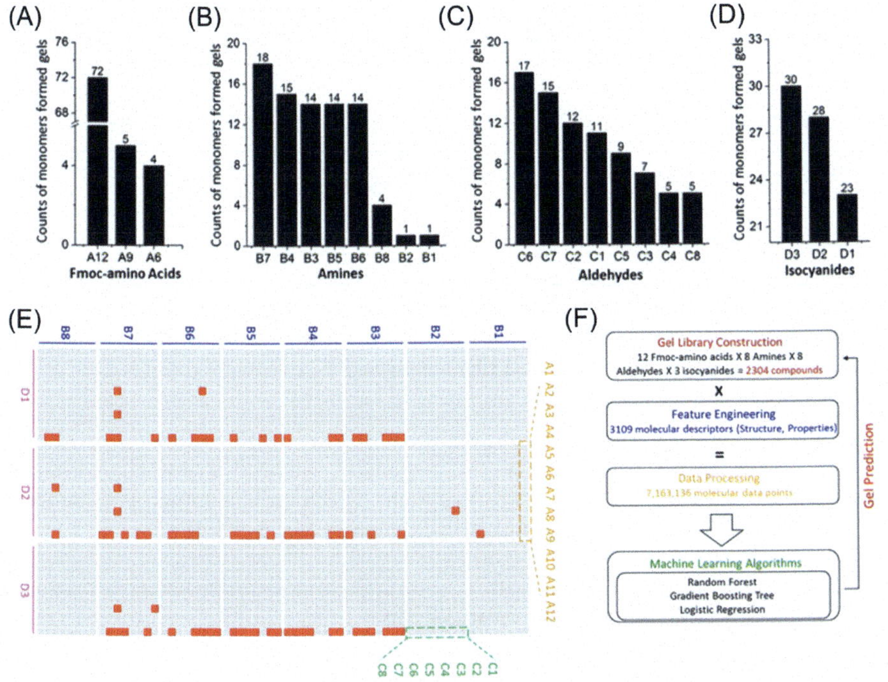


**Figure 5.4** (A–D) 8 amines, 8 aldehydes/ketones, 12 Fmoc-amino acids, and 3 isocyanides used for generating the library of hydrogels. (E) Screening results of hydrogels (red, a gel formed; gray, solution state. (F) Preparation of peptides library.
Reprinted with permission from [44].

## 5.4.2 *Applications of metallic biomaterials*

Metallic biomaterials exhibit excellent thermal, electrical, and mechanical performance attributes; therefore, they are usefully applied both in implants and structural applications. Materials with properties such as strength, durability, and inertness in biological environments have increased their usage. Advanced techniques, including alloy doping and machine learning algorithms in metal development with desirable properties, have been developed for the prediction of crack propagation and low-modulus bone implant materials. In this line, high-entropy alloys and biodegradable metals have been developed, allowing better resistance to wear and possibilities for application in orthopedic and cardiovascular applications.

Applications requiring high wear resistance and long service life, such as hip, joint, and knee implants, demand high-hardness alloys. High-entropy alloys are composed of several elements combined in near-equimolar ratios, which gives rise to an enormous compositional space. Interpolating the composition space, a machine learning surrogate model mapped composition to hardness. They used design of experiments and the Efficient Global Optimization (EGO) method iteratively to find alloys with improved

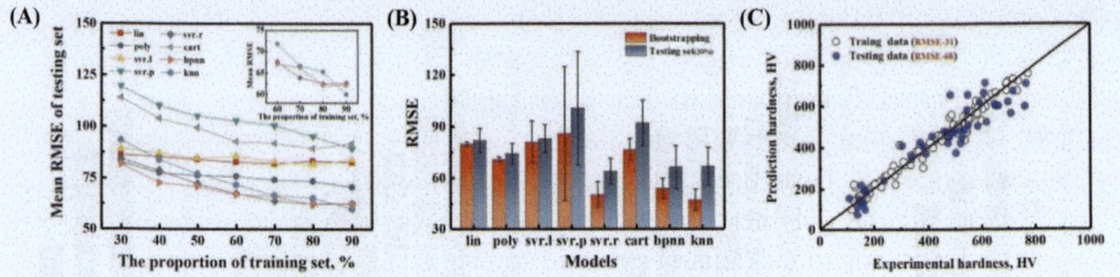


**Figure 5.5** Model evaluation and selection by estimating the test error for different models. (A) A holdout method and (B) bootstrapping methods, indicating svr.r outperforms the others. The inset of (A) zooms in on the performance of three models of svr.r, bpnn, and knn. (C) The predicted values as a function of the measured values of the svr.r model for both training data (randomly chosen 70%) and testing data (the remaining 30%).
Reprinted with permission from [45].

hardness. Their results predicted and experimentally validated a new High Entropy Alloy (HEA) in the Al–Co–Cr–Cu–Fe–Ni system, which provided improved hardness by 10% over the original training dataset, as shown in Fig. 5.5 [45].

### 5.4.3 Ceramic biomaterial applications

Ceramic biomaterials—hydroxyapatite and tricalcium phosphate—are used in dental and orthopedic applications due to the fact that they have very stable physicochemical properties, together with the ability to provide osteoconductivity. These materials support bone formation and regeneration, making them quite appropriate for artificial joints, dental implants, and bone substitutes. Development in this regard has been linked to bioinert materials, including alumina and zirconia, as well as those that promote bone formation, such as bioglasses and orthophosphate calcium. Techniques of machine learning have been utilized in predicting and optimizing the properties of ceramic materials so that they may have better performance and applicability in biomedical fields.

High-strength and -hardness ceramics reduce wearing during their use. High-entropy ceramics composed of different metal cation species, nearly equimolar, may lead to the formation of materials with high-hardness and corrosion-resistant coatings. However, their formation prediction remains a challenge. Kauffman et al. [46] applied machine learning methods based on thermodynamics and compositional attributes to predict the synthesizability of disordered metal carbides. They have varied and explained the role of thermodynamics and compositional parameters in predicting up to 70 new compositions, validated by density functional theory calculations and experimental synthesis [46]. In order to properly evaluate the performance of the machine learning model for determining the optimal hyperparameters, a five-fold cross-validation method was used. Fig. 5.6A shows the model performance for CALPHAD data and chemical characteristics alone. As one can see, while both Mean Absolute Errors (MAEs) were the same, 3.8 eV/atom, the coefficient of determination ($R^2$) returned more promising results with CALPHAD data. Microstructural examination by energy-dispersive X-ray spectroscopy (EDS) of the energy-dispersive spectra is given in Fig. 5.6C for assessing homogeneity of the sintered pellets. The results showed that the samples were either single-phase, chemically homogeneous, or chemically separated. It shows that the compositions are single-phase, whereas multiphase samples have much finer grain sizes due to the fact that competing phases, which form during sintering, hinder grain growth (Figs. 5.6–5.8).

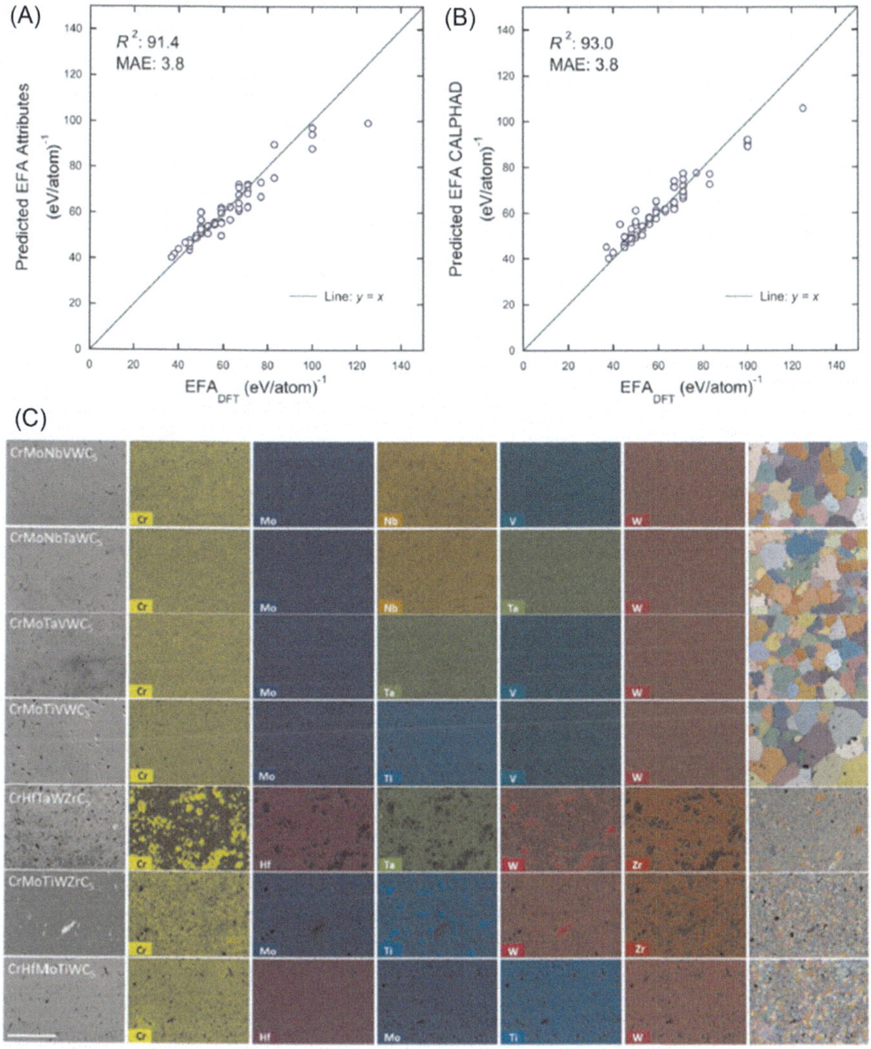


**Figure 5.6** The ML models are assessed to match the supplied data. (A) The ML-predicted EFA, using random forest fit. (B) ML forest random fit projected EFA values with 108 chemical characteristics and eight CALPHAD-evaluated features against the known DFT EFA. (C) Synthesized material microstructural analysis. Bar scale 100 μm.
Reprinted with permission from [46].

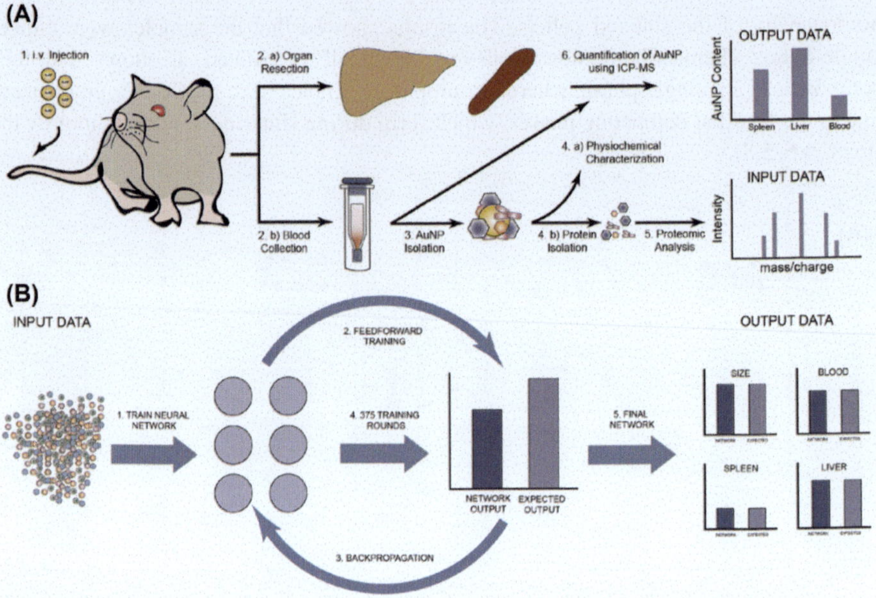


**Figure 5.7** Methodology for building and training the predictive neural network. (A) PEGylated AuNPs were injected intravenously into rats, and blood was sampled at multiple times over 24 hours from the same animal. AuNPs suspended in serum were separated using centrifugation and underwent physiochemical characterization. Proteins were stripped off and digested for LC–MS/MS processing and analysis. This proteomic analysis formed the input for the neural network (NN). On the other hand, liver and spleen were also resected from rats and digested to measure AuNP organ accumulation using ICP–MS. The organ accumulation of AuNPs and the size of the nanoparticle formed the output of our NN. (B) NN inputs the protein data and iterates it through a feedforward and backpropagation cycle to build a mathematical model for predicting the output parameters.
Reprinted with permission from [47].

### 5.4.4 Nanoengineered biomaterials applications

These nanoengineered biomaterials exhibit special properties and uses in drug delivery, regenerative medicine, and tissue engineering. These nanoengineered biomaterials, together with their bulk counterparts, can, therefore, help overcome problems with deficient mechanical strength. Nanoparticles can be controlled within a high degree of accuracy in terms of shape, size, and characteristics of their surface—these parameters are very important to be controlled at the nanoscale. It has also made the optimization of the synthesis and performance of nanomaterials for high drug loading efficiencies, prediction of antibacterial properties, biocompatibility, and functionality of nanoparticle-based systems possible.

Lazarovits et al. describe the dynamic interaction of nanoparticles with blood proteins following intravenous injection. In this work, the authors developed a workflow for mass spectrometry and supervised deep learning-based analysis of the

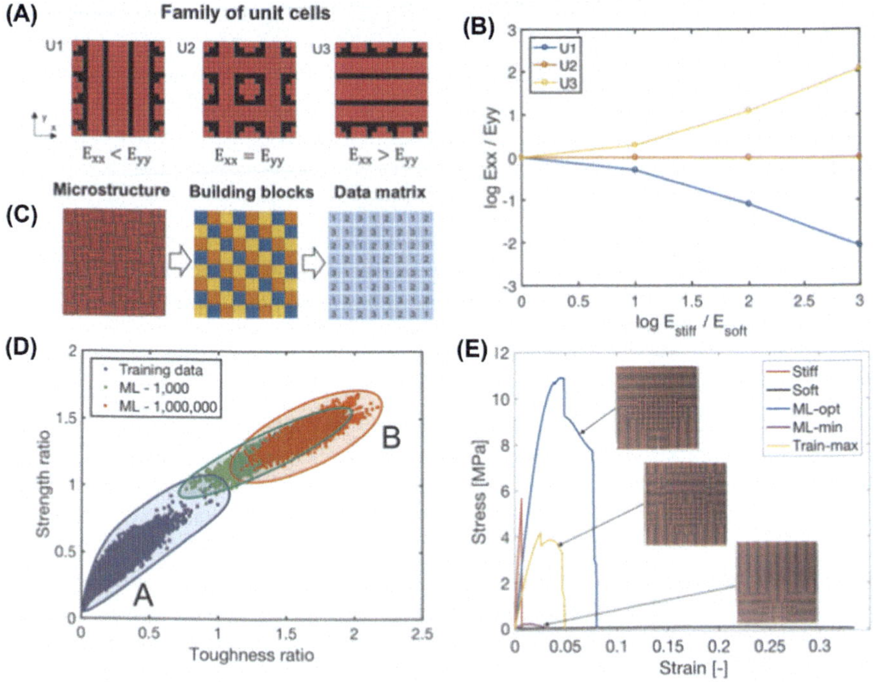


**Figure 5.8** (A) Stiff and soft building blocks are combined in patterns to form unit cells U1, U2, and U3. Pink refers to stiff building blocks, while black refers to soft building blocks. (B) The ratio between the modulus of stiff and soft blocks affects unit cell isotropy. (C) The microstructure of stiff and soft blocks is converted into unit cells U1 (blue), U2 (red), and U3 (yellow), which can be further converted into a data matrix with inputs of 1, 2, and 3 corresponding to the type of unit cell. (D) Strength ratio is the strength of machine learning-generated samples after 1000 loops (green) and after 1,000,000 loops (red), as compared to the highest training set strength. Toughness ratio is the toughness as compared to the highest training set toughness. (E) Stress-strain curves of machine learning-generated 3D-printed samples (ML-optimal and ML-minimum).
Reprinted with permission from [48].

evolution that occurs on the surface of nanoparticles during circulation. This approach is applied to very accurate predictions of organ distribution, particularly liver and spleen accumulation, of nanoparticles. Using the neural network fitted with the proteomic data, it became transparent that the mechanism of clearance did not reside within single proteins but in complex patterns of surface-adsorbed proteins. In this process, an insight was acquired, making it turn toward a new technique: engineering nanoparticles in the host body as a bioreactor for expected clearance patterns, thus reducing off-target organ accumulation. This study provides a system on how to use artificial intelligence and proteomics to develop more effective, yet safe, nanomedicines (Fig. 5.7) [47].

### 5.4.5 Applications of 3D printed biomaterials

3D printed biomaterials represent a relatively new frontier in biomedical engineering that allows for the creation of complex geometric structures tailored for specific needs in medicine. The techniques used in the preparation include laser powder bed fusion and extrusion-based 3D printing for metal, ceramic, and polymeric biomaterials. In this regard, machine learning is involved in design, material selection, and process optimization of the 3D printing process to produce improved print quality and material properties. For example, CNNs can be used to predict mechanical properties and optimize composite materials, thus significantly improving performance and application of 3D printed biomaterials in implants and in drug delivery systems.

Gu et al. proposed a way of designing new hierarchical materials in which machine learning, simulation, and Additive Manufacturing (AM) could be combined. The goal is to reproduce the complicated microstructure of nature in materials to achieve outstanding mechanical properties such as toughness and strength. They trained a machine learning model on a database of hundreds of thousands of such structures, generated via FEA. This was further improved by a self-learning algorithm to iteratively improve its material designs by phasing out the worse candidates. The resulting optimized designs surpassed the initial training set with substantial improvements in properties validated through both additive manufacturing and mechanical testing. This is an approach that therefore expedites the discovery of high-performance materials, as it simultaneously introduces a new method of coarse-graining in material design, hence making the exploration of very large design spaces computationally feasible. Integrating machine learning with advanced manufacturing opens up opportunities for rapid development of innovative materials with the desired properties for various engineering applications (Fig. 5.8) [48].

## 5.5 Conclusion

The materials genome approach is, in relation, a similarly colossal paradigm shift for materials science as genomics did in the biological sciences. MGE integrates high-throughput experiments, big data technologies, and artificial intelligence to realize an accelerated process in discovering and developing advanced materials with tailored properties. It breaks the traditional trial-and-error approach by providing a data-driven platform that reduces time and cost involved in material innovation. The intersection of materials genome and human genome research holds immense potential for new biomaterial development with regenerative medicine and biomedical applications. Such is the potential to develop biomaterials with predefined properties, optimized by AI and machine learning, that this will become a new generation of breakthroughs in tissue engineering, drug delivery, and fabrication of medical devices. Materials genome is an up-and-coming domain, and in the future, it will leave impacts on industries such as photovoltaics and nanomedicine. It will drive innovation, perhaps even to technologies which today are still unimaginable, in a manner where prediction of material behavior and the optimization of properties is possible within very short times. Materials genome initiative summarizes not only a scientific tool for discovery but also a strategic framework which will develop a revolution in design and development of materials with a new era in materials science.

## Acknowledgment

To the best of the Editors' knowledge and authors' claims, no generative AI tools were used for substantive writing of chapters. Any AI-assisted language editing, if applied, was limited to grammar or style suggestions and did not alter the scientific content.

## References

[1] Shang Y, Xiong Z, An K, Hauch JA, Brabec CJ, Li N. Materials genome engineering accelerates the research and development of organic and perovskite photovoltaics. Materials Genome Engineering Advances 2024;2(1):e28.
[2] Abrukov VS, Pang W, Anufrieva DA. Neural networks are a methodological basis of materials genome. Trends in Computer Science and Information Technology 2023;8(1):012–5.
[3] Xie J. Prospects of materials genome engineering frontiers. Materials Genome Engineering Advances 2023;1(2):e17.
[4] Yan Q, Kar S, Chowdhury S, Bansil A. The case for a defect genome initiative. Advanced Materials 2024;36(11):2303098.
[5] Wang H, Xiang Y, Xiang X, Chen LJ. Materials genome enables research and development revolution. Science and Technology Review 2015;33(10):13–9.
[6] Ågren J. CALPHAD and the materials genome A 10 year anniversary. Calphad 2023;80:102532.
[7] Liu Z. Perspective on materials genome® Chinese Science Bulletin 2014;59(16):1619–23.
[8] Chandrasekaran A, Kim C, Ramprasad R. Polymer genome: a polymer informatics platform to accelerate polymer discovery. Lecture Notes in Physics 2020:397–412.
[9] Qiu Y, Wu Z, Wang J, Zhang C, Zhang H. Introduction of materials genome technology and its applications in the field of biomedical materials. Materials (Basel) 1906;16(5):2023.
[10] Olson G, Liu ZK. Genomic materials design: calculation of phase dynamics. Calphad 2023;82:102590.
[11] Chen H, Li Z, Li X, Lu J, Chen B, Wang Q, et al. Biomaterial-based gene delivery: advanced tools for enhanced cartilage regeneration. Drug Design, Development and Therapy 2023:3605–24.
[12] Zhang Y, Yu W. Recent advances in bionic scaffolds for cartilage tissue engineering. Frontiers in Bioengineering and Biotechnology 2025;13:1625550.
[13] Wang M, Wang J, Xu X, Li E, Xu P. Engineering gene-activated bioprinted scaffolds for enhancing articular cartilage repair. Materials Today Bio 2024;29:101351.
[14] Rai V, Dilisio MF, Dietz NE, Agrawal DK. Recent strategies in cartilage repair: a systemic review of the scaffold development and tissue engineering. Journal of Biomedical Materials Research Part A 2017;105(8):2343–54.
[15] Wang M, Wu Y, Li G, Lin Q, Zhang W, Liu H, et al. Articular cartilage repair biomaterials: strategies and applications. Materials Today Bio 2024;24:100948.
[16] Sapru S, Dill MN, Simmons CS. Biomaterial design inspired by regenerative research organisms. ACS Biomaterials Science and Engineering 2022;9(7):3860–76.
[17] Zhu F, Nie G, Liu C. Engineered biomaterials in stem cell-based regenerative medicine. Life Medicine 2023;2(4):lnad027.

[18] Falanga A, Laheurte P, Vahabi H, Tran N, Khamseh S, Saeidi H, et al. Niobium-treated titanium implants with improved cellular and molecular activities at the tissue–implant interface. Materials (Basel) 2019;12(23):3861.
[19] Bairi VG, Warford BA, Bourdo SE, Biris AS, Viswanathan TJ. Synthesis and characterization of tanninsulfonic acid doped polyaniline–metal oxide nanocomposites. Journal of Applied Polymer Science 2012;124(4):3320–8 .
[20] García-García A, Martin I. Extracellular matrices to modulate the innate immune response and enhance bone healing. Frontiers in Immunology 2019;10:2256.
[21] Najman S, Stojanović S, Živković J, Najdanović J, Radenković M, Vasiljević P, Ignjatović N. Applications of biomaterials in regenerative medicine and tissue engineering–concepts and perspective. Contemporary Materials 2023;14(1):1–15.
[22] Zhu F, Nie G, Liu CJL. Engineered biomaterials in stem cell-based regenerative medicine. Life Medicine 2023;2(4):lnad027.
[23] Wei L, Yan W, Shah W, Zhang Z, Wang M, Liu B, et al. Advancements and challenges in stem cell transplantation for regenerative medicine. Heliyon 2024;10(16).
[24] Haleem AM, Chu CR. Advances in tissue engineering techniques for articular cartilage repair. Operative Techniques in Orthopaedics 2010;20(2):76–89.
[25] Hamidabadi HG, Simorgh S, Kamrava SK, Namjoo Z, Bagher Z, Bojnordi MN, et al. Promoting motor functions in a spinal cord injury model of rats using transplantation of differentiated human olfactory stem cells: a step towards future therapy. Behavioural Brain Research 2021;405:113205.
[26] Xu D, Zhang Q, Huo X, Wang Y, Yang M. Advances in data-assisted high-throughput computations for material design. Materials Genome Engineering 2023;1(1):e11.
[27] Zhang Y, Tan Y, Dong Y, Dai L, Ren C, Zhang F, et al. High-throughput scanning second-harmonic-generation microscopy for polar materials. Advanced Materials 2023;35(19):2300348.
[28] Jain A, Ong SP, Hautier G, Chen W, Richards WD, Dacek S, et al. Commentary: the materials project: a materials genome approach to accelerating materials innovation. APL Materials 2013;1(1):011002.
[29] Ling J, Chen W, Sheng Y, Li W, Zhang L, Du Y. A MGI-oriented investigation of the Young's modulus and its application to the development of a novel Ti–Nb–Zr–Cr bio-alloy. Materials Science and Engineering: C 2020;106:110265.
[30] Li H, Xu Y, Duan W. Ab initio artificial intelligence: future research of materials genome initiative. Materials Genome Engineering Advances 2023;1(2):e16.
[31] Ninduwezuor-Ehiobu N, Tula OA, Daraojimba C, Ofonagoro KA, Ogunjobi OA, Gidiagba JO, Egbokhaebho BA, et al. Tracing the evolution of ai and machine learning applications in advancing materials discovery and production processes. Engineering Science and Technology Journal 2023;4(3):66–83.
[32] Zubarev D, Mendes CR, Brazil EV, Cerqueira R, Schmidt K, Segura V, Jansen Ferreira J. Toward human-AI co-creation to accelerate material discovery. arXiv 2022.
[33] Xue K, Wang F, Suwardi A, Han M-Y, Teo P, Wang P. Biomaterials by design: harnessing data for future development. Materials Today Bio 2021;12:100165.
[34] Yang Y, Ji Y, Han X, Long Y, Stewart C, Wen Y, et al. Implement the materials genome initiative: machine learning assisted fluorescent probe design for cellular substructure staining. Advanced Materials Technologies 2023;8(17):2300427.
[35] Trucillo, P. Biomaterials for drug delivery and human applications. Materials 2024;17(2):456.
[36] Mansour A, Romani M, Acharya AB, Rahman B, Verron E, Badran Z. Drug delivery systems in regenerative medicine: an updated review. Pharmaceutics 2023;15(2):695.

[37] Chaudhari AA, Vig K, Baganizi DR, Sahu R, Dixit S, Dennis V, et al. Future prospects for scaffolding methods and biomaterials in skin tissue engineering: a review. International Journal of Molecular Sciences 2016;17(12):1974.
[38] Heboyan A, Bennardo F. New biomaterials for modern dentistry. BMC Oral Health 2023;23(1):817.
[39] Sotova C, Yanushevich O, Kriheli N, Grigoriev S, Evdokimov V, Kramar O, et al. Dental implants: modern materials and methods of their surface modification. Materials 2023;16(23):7383.
[40] Saha S, Roy S. Metallic dental implants wear mechanisms, materials, and manufacturing processes: a literature review. Materials 2022;16(1):161.
[41] Upadhyay A, Pradhan L, Yenurkar D, Kumar K, Mukherjee S. Advancement in ceramic biomaterials for dental implants. International Journal of Applied Ceramic Technology. 2024;21(4):2796–817.
[42] Khaohoen, A., Sornsuwan, T., Chaijareenont, P., Poovarodom, P., Rungsiyakull, C., Rungsiyakull, P. Biomaterials and clinical application of dental implants in relation to bone density. Journal Clinical Medicine 2023;12(21):6924.
[43] Liu Y, Niu C, Wang Z, Gan Y, Zhu Y, Sun S, et al. Technology, machine learning in materials genome initiative: a review. Journal of Materials Science and Technology 2020;57:113–22.
[44] Li F, Han J, Cao T, Lam W, Fan B, Tang W, et al. Design of self-assembly dipeptide hydrogels and machine learning via their chemical features. Proceedings of the National Academy of Sciences of the United States of America 2019;116(23):11259–64.
[45] Wen C, Zhang Y, Wang C, Xue D, Bai Y, Antonov S, et al. Machine learning assisted design of high entropy alloys with desired property. Acta Materialia 2019;170:109–17.
[46] Kaufmann K, Maryanovsky D, Mellor WM, Zhu C, Rosengarten AS, Harrington TJ, et al. Discovery of high-entropy ceramics via machine learning. NPJ Computational Materials 2020;6(1):42.
[47] Lazarovits J, Sindhwani S, Tavares AJ, Zhang Y, Song F, Audet J, et al. Supervised learning and mass spectrometry predicts the in vivo fate of nanomaterials. ACS Nano 2019;13(7):8023–34.
[48] Gu GX, Chen C-T, Richmond DJ, Buehler MJJMH. Bioinspired hierarchical composite design using machine learning: simulation, additive manufacturing, and experiment. Materials Horizons 2018;5(5):939–45.

# Artificial intelligence-assisted biomaterials synthesis

6

*Fateme Mansourinia[1], Maryam Sadat Adibhosseini[2], Mohsen Khodadadi Yazdi[3,4], and Mohsen Tabibian[5]*

[1]Faculty of Chemical Engineering, Department of Polymer Engineering, Tarbiat Modares University, Tehran, Iran, [2]Faculty of Chemical Engineering, Biomedical Engineering Division, Tarbiat Modares University, Tehran, Iran, [3]Division of Electrochemistry and Surface Physical Chemistry, Faculty of Applied Physics and Mathematics, Gdańsk University of Technology, Gdańsk, Poland, [4]Advanced Materials Center, Gdańsk University of Technology, Gdańsk, Poland, [5]Center of Sciences, Wilmington College, Wilmington, OH, United States

## 6.1 Introduction

Biomaterials are interfaces of biosystems and advanced materials that are used in tissue engineering and drug delivery due to their properties like biocompatibility and noncytotoxicity. Synthesis of biomaterials stands as one of the main directions of modern research, with results that can potentially be very substantial for medicine, materials science, and pharmacology. Traditionally, the synthesis of biomaterials has been a manual, sometimes time-consuming process both in terms of trial-and-error experimentation and in terms of a scientific methodology strongly reliant on the experience and intuition of the chemist. With the advent of new AI technologies, changes have rippled through these landscapes in terms of prediction and synthesis pathways execution with greater efficiency and precision. AI has already been integrated into such different fields as materials science, medicine, and chemistry to make the predictions more accurate and for better decision-making. That is, AI would play a crucial role in revolutionizing the traditional approaches to biomaterials synthesis prediction. AI algorithms will be useful in predicting biomaterial synthesis with better accuracy and efficiency [1].

AI-assisted synthesis prediction is a relatively new area of research, applying machine learning algorithms/data-driven approaches to the prediction of plausible synthetic routes to target compounds. In this way, new materials will be discovered more quickly, and the possibility of tailoring them for specific applications will also increase. Combinatorial synthesis with rapid screening techniques, well established in drug discovery, is now being applied to biomaterials development. Although such techniques are powerful in their own right, when combined with computational modeling, they can significantly accelerate the design and testing of a new material. For example, parallel synthesis of a library of biodegradable polymers and subsequent rapid screening for bio-relevant properties have been seamlessly integrated with computational models predicting biological responses, underlining the power of this triad in biomaterials research [2,3].

**Artificial Intelligence in Biomaterials Design and Development. DOI:** https://doi.org/10.1016/B978-0-323-95464-8.00006-2

The area of AI-aided synthesis prediction has been fast developing, and there are already comprehensive summaries on the latest developments in retrosynthesis planning, forward synthesis prediction, and models of quantum chemistry-based reaction prediction. More specifically, it is pointed out that one critical driver toward the automation of synthesis is that robotics-based high-throughput experimentation technologies can be integrated, where key applications in the pharmaceutical industry entail accelerating compounds to be synthesized quickly and cheaply. Deep neural networks combined with symbolic AI have also been used for the planning of chemical syntheses that apply, for example, Monte Carlo tree search in finding retrosynthetic routes. Such AI models are trained on large databases of organic reactions and have been shown to outperform traditional computer-aided approaches by providing both faster and more reliable synthetic routes of the same quality as those published in the literature [4,5].

There are several bottlenecks on the road to the development of AI-controlled synthesis systems. The necessary hardware has to be tailored for very different reaction conditions, and the software needs to contain extensive reaction prediction modules for any kind of synthesis. The ultimate ideal concept would be the creation of more autonomous systems that perform challenging synthesis tasks and applications that may change the face of chemical synthesis [6].

This can be concluded to be the great, new step ahead in the field that is, the integration of AI into biomaterial synthesis. Linking predictive algorithms with automated experimental platforms is granting efficiency, precision, and accessibility to the process of biomaterial synthesis and opening a roadway to the rapid development of new materials with tailored properties for a myriad of applications. AI-aided biomaterial synthesis prediction is an extremely promising field that opens vast horizons for improvement of research and innovation in materials science, medicine, and chemistry. By using AI algorithms, researchers can accelerate synthesis processes and optimize material properties to leap forward in developing all sorts of scientific disciplines. In this chapter, the challenges of the traditional synthesis of biomaterials, the importance of the role of AI in the development of biomaterials, and the study of cases in this field are discussed.

## 6.2 Overview of biomaterials synthesis and its challenges

Biomaterial synthesis is that domain of knowledge dealing with the development and creation of materials for use in biological and medical applications. The materials form a base of support across almost all fields of healthcare, from implants and prosthetics to drug delivery systems and tissue engineering [7]. The synthesis of biomaterials combines principles from materials science, chemistry, and biology with engineering views in order to produce materials that are biocompatible, bioactive, and mechanically robust [8].

The proper selection of an appropriate material is the first step in biomaterial synthesis. Biomaterials are naturally derived from proteins and polysaccharides or synthesized from synthetic components, including polymers, ceramics, and metals [9]. It would depend on biocompatibility, mechanical properties, degradation characteristics, and functionality envisaged by application.

While synthesizing biomaterials, top-down and bottom-up approaches are resorted to by researchers. The top-down approach is the deconstruction of complex entities into simpler component parts, while the bottom-up approach involves assembling materials molecule by molecule, sometimes even atom by atom [10]. Most biomaterials have been designed to come into contact with human body and blood for replacement of soft and hard tissues [11]. Additionally, metabolic synthons themselves can serve as building blocks in the synthesis of biomaterials, and in this way, very wide structural and functional diversity can be achieved [12]. In other words, the synthesis of biomaterials in living organisms is a process of self-assembly or polymerization of artificial building blocks or precursors to functional materials [13]. After the preparation of the material, it is then formed into the desired form. The processing techniques include the following: casting, molding, electrospinning, and additive manufacturing, also known as 3D printing [14]. Based on these techniques, biomaterials could be fabricated into required geometries and architectures, wherein geometry or architecture of the material could be tailored to the application.

The challenges of biomaterial synthesis are very diverse. These include the complexity of biological systems per se, the requirements for the material's mechanical and biological performances to be as close as possible to specific standard mechanical and biologically driven functions, and the unpredictability of materials' interactions with biological tissues. Synthetic routes give rise to tunable biomaterials with designed properties but are too often hampered by bioactivity and resorption [15]. Also, the challenges of interface tissue and biomaterials have to be precisely controlled to be compatible and functional. Drug-polymer interactions, drug transformation, and diffusion properties of drugs and polymer degradation products pose many challenges to drug delivery systems [16]. A big challenge in regenerative therapies is to translate recent biomedical advances into marketed products due to scientific, regulatory, and business challenges [17,18]. Green synthesis of nanomaterials brings out the concerns regarding the selection of solvents, process parameters, cytotoxicity of the nanomaterials, production in bulk, and control of the morphology [19]. Moreover, the incorporation of both biomimetic and stimuli-responsive properties in polymers is a matter of opportunities and challenges [20]. Besides, common problems existing in the field of biomaterials are the reproducibility of the process for synthesizing them and scaling up for industrial production [21]. In addition to mentioned challenges, due to the complexity of the experiment space and internal and external parameters, there is a possibility that some data and analyses may be overlooked, which can prevent a deeper understanding and comprehension of the material. Therefore, the development and integration of materials science with modern technologies such as machine learning and AI promise for significant advancements in the understanding of biomaterials, particularly in their synthesis [22].

Studies that will be detailed in the next sections provide a general view of how AI should be used to increase real innovation and efficacy in the many diversified areas of bioproduction and biomaterial design. Traditionally, these have been knowledge-intensive areas—intractable to analytic solutions, although AI systems have begun to change that with more efficient and innovative approaches.

## 6.3 Importance of artificial intelligence in advancing biomaterials synthesis

As we navigate the complexities and challenges inherent in biomaterials synthesis, it becomes increasingly clear that advanced computational tools are essential for overcoming these obstacles. AI has been embedded in the synthesis of biomaterials in recent times, dramatically changing the material design, synthesis, and optimization for myriad biomedical applications. State-of-the-art techniques of AI that include machine learning, deep learning, and computational modeling have made researchers competent in advanced capabilities related to large dataset analyses, material property predictions, and facilitation of the design process in a very accurate and efficient way [23]. The machine learning algorithms will make it possible for researchers to mine through massive repositories of materials properties and experimental results for the underlying intricate patterns and correlations, even those that human observation might miss. Improved such understanding makes it possible to discover new formulations of biomaterials with improved biocompatibility, mechanics, and other properties that can make innovations in tissue engineering possible and lead to the creation of medical devices.

In particular, the application of deep learning techniques has shown great promise in predicting and optimizing biomaterials synthesis. Table 6.1 provides a detailed overview of various deep learning methods that are currently being leveraged to enhance the accuracy and efficiency of biomaterials research. This table provides a general overview of the deep learning (DL) methods applied in multiomics data integration for biomedical research. In this paper, every DL method has been pointed out with its own unique features, from fully connected neural networks (FCNN), convolutional neural networks (CNN), autoencoders (AE), graph neural networks (GNN), and variational autoencoders (VAE), with their specific applications in the area of drug response prediction, cancer subtype classification, and biomarker identification. It also points out the several advantages of these methods, such as their ability to capture complex relationships in high-dimensional data and their suitability for treating different sets of biological data. However, it also mentions the challenges associated with each of the methods, such as the computational burden of FCNNs, the probable overfitting of CNNs, and the complexity involved during the training process of VAEs. Hence, AI will certainly play a vital role in the future of biomedical research, more particularly in prediction and optimization of the synthesis of biomaterials by these sophisticated deep learning techniques [24].

In fact, deep learning algorithms are currently changing medical diagnosis and drug design by integrating such complex, multiomics data in a more accurate and effective way. Such AI-driven methods, combined with different neural network architectures like CNN and recurrent neural networks (RNN), perform well when it comes to nonlinear relationships and complex data, hence winning out over traditional statistical models. They are also applied to enhance prediction models of computer-aided drug design and to optimize the formulation of biomaterials. The term "computational biomaterials" epitomizes the possibility of AI simulating and predicting optimal biomaterial properties for fast drug development and enables a better understanding of

**Table 6.1** Table summarizes different deep learning methods and their applications in biomedical data integration.

| DL method | Key features | Applications | Advantages | Challenges |
|---|---|---|---|---|
| Fully connected neural networks (FCNN) | Simple framework using fully connected layers to integrate multiomics data | Drug response prediction, synergistic drug combinations, cancer subtype classification, prognosis | Captures nonlinear and complex relationships; suitable for high-dimensional data | Requires a large volume of data; computationally expensive |
| Convolutional neural networks (CNN) | Uses convolutional layers to capture local features in data | Medical imaging-assisted diagnosis, gene regulation mechanisms, cancer subtype classification | Reduces parameter sizes and network complexity, avoiding overfitting | May not be suitable for traditional tabular multiomics data |
| Autoencoders (AE) | Unsupervised learning method for feature extraction and dimensionality reduction | Synergistic drug combination prediction, biomarker identification, cancer subtype classification, prognosis | Does not require labeled data; Suitable for high-dimensional omics data | Performance depends on the quality of latent space representation |
| Graph neural networks (GNN) | Integrates data using graph structures to represent relationships between biological entities | Drug-drug synergy prediction, synthetic lethality (SL) prediction, prognosis, biomarker identification | Handles complex and systematic biological interactions effectively | Requires specialized knowledge to implement; performance depends on graph quality |
| Variational autoencoders (VAE) | Probabilistic approach to feature learning, imposing distribution assumptions on latent variables | Cancer subtype classification, survival analysis, single-cell data integration | Generates robust feature representations; Suitable for sparse data | Can be complex to train; requires careful tuning of hyperparameters |

the interaction between a biomaterial and the biosystem. Recent advances in AI pipelines for the discovery of new antimicrobials make the process of searching and success highly efficient compared to traditional methods [25] (Fig. 6.1).

AI-driven approaches will further facilitate the use of rational design of biomaterials in silico by molecular simulation of interactions and predictions of materials behavior at all scales, from atomic structures to macroscopic properties [26]. It is now possible, therefore, by way of AI-empowered computational models to fully furtle around design spaces with such complexity and tell precisely the performance outcomes with an accuracy previously unattained to reduce time and resources required to develop materials [27]. Coupled with this increased cadence, the pipeline for translating new biomaterials from concept toward application is quickened and calibrated to specific clinical needs and demographics. This will then be realized in growth and innovation of the use of personalized medicine approaches within both regenerative medicine and implantology in the final analysis.

Besides, AI will also be bound to exhibit great potential for solving only a few age-old problems related to biomaterials research in the field of biocompatibility assessment, degradation prediction, and toxicity evaluation [28]. AI techniques will allow for making full analyses of biological responses to materials, foreseeing their long-term stability and degradation kinetics, and screening possible adverse effects effectively. Eventually, this will make biomaterials both safer and more efficient, fast-tracking their translation to clinics—hence eventually allowing the researcher to

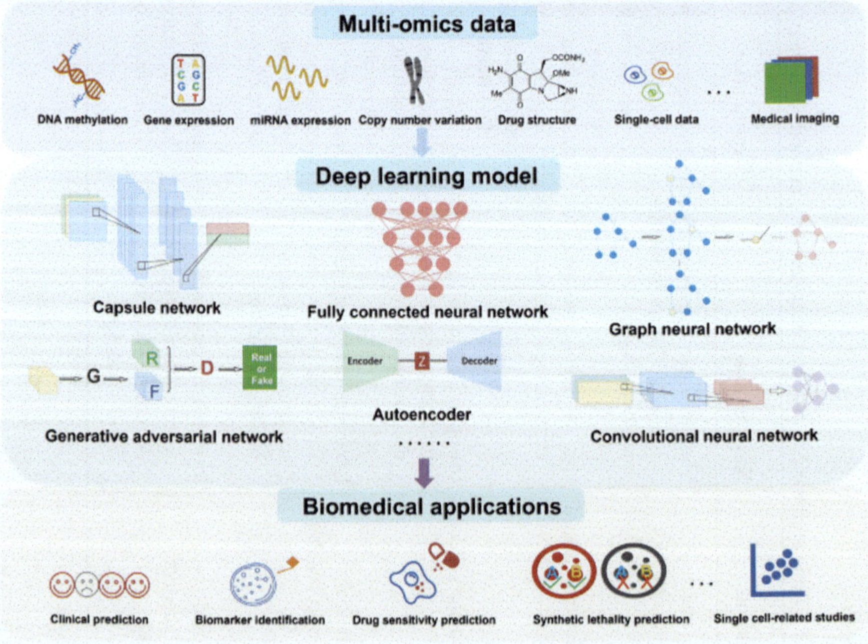


**Figure 6.1** Deep learning for multiomics data integration used in biomedical applications. Reprinted with permission from [24].

push through the boundaries between materials science and biomedical engineering in the opening of new avenues toward better human health and well-being. There have already been very promising reports on AI applications in the design of biomaterials for the optimization of clinical outcomes in regenerative medicine, while improving scientific understanding.

Also, artificial intelligence has boosted biomaterial synthesis, facilitating increased precision and efficiency when simulating the properties of biomaterials [29]. In this respect, AI was exploited to advance the rational design and synthesis of biomaterials in relation to an interdisciplinary approach so that new material classes with uniquely tailored functionalities could develop into practice with improved performance. Hence, the future of biomaterial synthesis and AI is inseparable for it is filled with potential to really change the face of bone regeneration and tissue engineering with AI [30]. The AI-driven technologies in this direction can unleash new opportunities for synthesizing biomaterials, which would consequently rise to new classes of tailored materials with enhanced properties for a myriad of biomedical applications.

## 6.4 Role of artificial intelligence in predicting optimal synthesis conditions

AI has become indispensable in the prediction of optimum synthesis conditions for various materials and plays a lead role in the advancement of materials science and engineering. Through machine learning algorithms, AI can digest large amounts of data from experiments and materials properties to identify patterns and correlations that guide the prediction of optimal synthesis conditions. This would greatly raise the speed of materials discovery and optimization by reducing trial-and-error experiments that are time-consuming and very expensive. Equipped with the AI-driven predictive models, the researchers in this regime will, with high productivity, be able to scan across an overwhelmingly large space of synthesis conditions to develop materials with tailored properties for specific applications [31,32]. AI was helpful in the establishment of optimum synthesis conditions for materials, such as metal-organic frameworks (MOFs) and covalent organic frameworks (COFs), allowing for the exploration of hitherto unreported conditions [33]. Zhang et al. demonstrated that an AI-driven approach significantly sped up the discovery of optimal synthesis conditions, leading to increased crystallinity in their products. Their system, leveraging large language models and machine learning, streamlined multireaction sequences and facilitated the transfer of optimized stoichiometric conditions to traditional methods (Fig. 6.2).

One of the most vital advantages of AI in predicting optimal synthesis conditions lies in the fact that complex and nonlinear relationships between synthesis parameters and material properties can be handled. Current methods poorly estimate such intricate relationships because a vast array of parameters must be manually adjusted in traditional material synthesis and thus result in the poor performance and prediction of suboptimal synthesis conditions, leading to inefficient material development processes. AI-driven predictive models, on the other hand, will be able to uncover hidden patterns and nonlinear dependencies; hence, they can determine more accurate

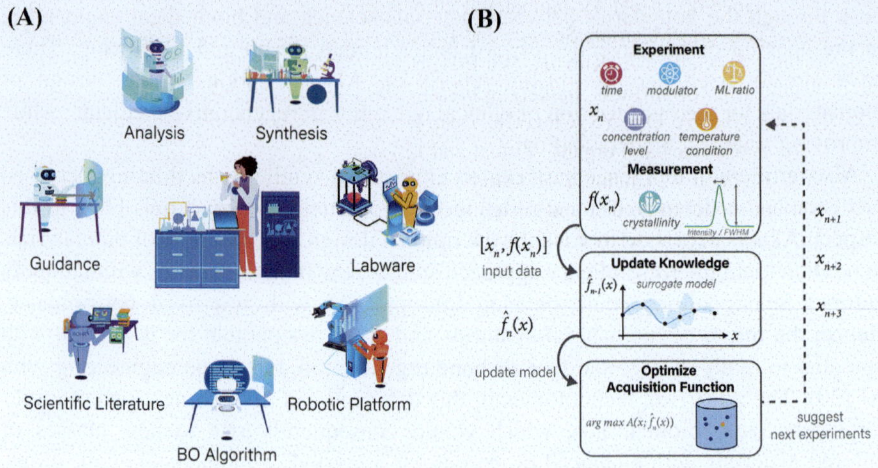


**Figure 6.2** ChatGPT research group. (A) Assigned roles of seven ChatGPT-based assistants, each collaborating to assist human researchers and contributing to diverse research tasks at different stages of the synthesis optimization. (B) Flowchart outlining the closed-loop Bayesian optimization process. Each iteration involves three proposed experiments, their execution, data analysis, and integration of the new data into the existing data set to update the surrogate model, upon which the acquisition function is optimized to suggest the next three experiments.
Reprinted with permission from [33].

predictions of the optimal synthesis conditions [31]. It is also incredibly useful for the synthesis of nanomaterials, whereby slight changes in synthesis parameters can all mean a great deal for material properties [34]. Synthesis parameters such as temperature, time, and type of solvent play a very important role in determining the morphology and size of nanoparticles. Even the slightest change in these parameters can lead to different outcomes, making the optimization of synthesis conditions challenging without the use of artificial intelligence.

Beyond this, AI can combine multiple sources of data and experimental techniques to improve predictive accuracy. AI models built from these varied data sources can learn a more complete understanding of synthesis conditions and how they impact the properties of materials. This includes experimental measurements, computational simulations, and literature databases (Fig. 6.3). This approach to science not only yields more accurate predictions but also enables collaboration among disparate research communities working together on materials discovery and innovation at an accelerated rate.

AI application domains in the prediction of the best synthesis conditions have already transversally covered the different fields of science, from organic synthesis to material science. These algorithms can be used to predict the optimum experimental conditions for a given synthesis process in a very short time. For example, the AI model that predicts the best conditions to minimize nanoparticle size in the synthesis of ZnO nanoparticles has already been developed [35]. The other side is chemistry, whereby AI has made enormous progress in synthesis planning. There have been calls to improve the reporting of laboratory synthesis procedures if AI is to be fully

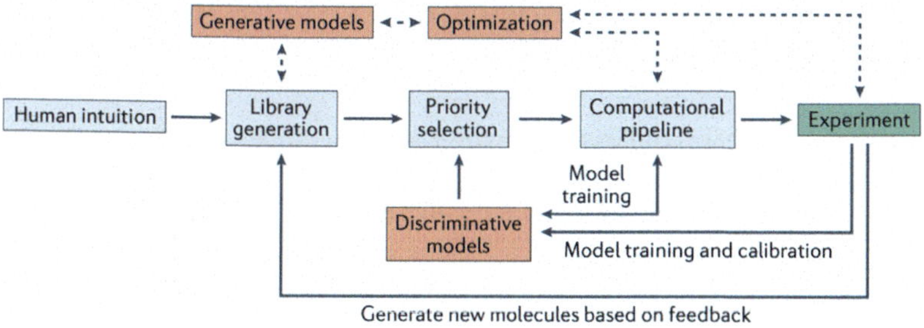


**Figure 6.3** State-of-the-art virtual screening: from human intuition to experimental verification. Reprinted with permission from [32].

exploited in organic synthesis [36]. In this line, AI-directed algorithms were designed to navigate the chemical space for optimum reaction conditions that would enable efficient synthesis of organic compounds [37]. Also, AI has been applied in the analysis and optimization of chemical products, which enables automated synthesis in flow chemistry [38]. AI in materials science has been applied in designing optimal metal oxides and process conditions for $CO_2$ reduction, which overwhelmingly shows very great potential for AI in achieving optimal synthesis conditions [39].

Such applications of AI in the prediction of optimal synthesis conditions go beyond the realm of chemistry into areas like drug discovery and material science. In drug discovery, AI plays a very important role in predicting drug-like properties, structure-activity relationship, and optimization of lead compounds [40]. Some advances to that are the pluripotent cells, and with the help of AI, some of these challenges can be overcome. Artificial neural networks (ANN), fuzzy inference systems, and genetic algorithms can therefore be, in general, taken as techniques, which could be applied in practice for the purpose of biomaterials design for better performance [21]. AI can even aid in surface treatment of biomaterials, drug delivery system development, scaffold materials, and implant design [21]. Also, AI played a central role in the development and design of biochemical processes to usher in the creation of biomaterials [41]. Enzyme and pathway design have also found assistance from AI for metabolic engineering, thereby enabling the creation of new biosynthetic pathways [42]. AI has further been used to achieve integration of the novel, next-generation bioassays into biomaterials design with improved functionality and reduced complexity [43].

In an attempt to stretch the potential of material science and engineering, the role of AI in predicting optimal synthesis conditions will be paramount. It will deconvolute complex data sets to find hidden patterns and adapt synthesis parameters using machine learning algorithms for synthesizing materials with tailored properties for predefined applications. Through continuous learning and integration of diverse data sources, AI enables researchers to accelerate the materials development process, foster interdisciplinary collaboration, and push the boundaries of scientific knowledge in the field of materials synthesis.

## 6.5 Benefits and limitations of artificial intelligence-assisted synthesis prediction

AI-assisted biomaterial synthesis prediction has a number of advantages for the different fields involved. In this regard, AI technologies represented by machine learning algorithms can be supportive in increasing the degree of accuracy and efficiency in the course of the synthesis planning process [44]. Such progress will bring it closer to the level of solving the problem that is demonstrated in classical approaches by experienced chemists. In addition, AI assistance in predicting biomaterial synthesis can provide a significant contribution toward enhancing the decision-making processes by receiving valuable insights and recommendations. In addition, with the ability to justify the suggested outcomes, the explainability of AI predictions refines human decision-making with clarity [45].

AI-aided prediction systems have been utilized in many important healthcare scenarios, such as the prediction of the best time to wean a patient from mechanical ventilation in an ICU [46]. Notably during pandemics such as COVID-19, AI systems have majorly helped doctors to manage ventilators effectively within the enormous pressure [46]. In cancer research, the application of AI has been directed toward improving prediction accuracy in cancer screening, therapeutics, and personalized medicine [47]. AI in cancer care has also been extended to improve the outcome of the patient based on the personalized treatment approaches. AI is further making major contributions to drug discovery processes in the prediction of drug-like properties and Structure-Activity Relationship (SAR) and in the conduct of clinical trials and drug repurposing [40]. Medicine, among other fields, has found AI extremely helpful with regard to diagnosing and differentiating the common liver carcinomas, therefore assisting in the optimization of surgical performance to improve accuracy in diagnosis [48]. AI assistance in the diagnosis and management of liver diseases is promising and holds great potential for bettering patient care and improving outcomes [49].

AI-aided prediction in the synthesis of biomaterials bears great potential to advance both research and real-life application, particularly in the fields of regenerative medicine and tissue engineering. Over and above the many advantages that AI-aided synthesis prediction already offers, there are still some limitations. Major adverse limitations include biological characteristics of cells associated with the synthesis of biomaterials. For example, it has been reported that nucleus pulposus cells (NPCs) demonstrate only moderate levels of proliferation ability, weak self-renewal capacity, and minimal extracellular matrix synthesis capacity, thereby impairing the full potential of biomaterial-assisted cell transplantation [50]. Additionally, predicting the outcomes of in vivo experiments based on in vitro data remains challenging, underscoring the necessity for innovative tools like AI to forecast outcomes without extensive animal experimentation [30].

However, the efficacy and potential of an AI-assisted synthesis to solve problems, as a proficient organic chemist does, are far from concrete yet [44]. While it can definitely contribute to the prediction of disease risk, diagnosis, prognosis, and treatment in multiple diseases, one should not leave any stone unturned concerning the validation and massive application of AI techniques for healthcare, to be made certain by randomized controlled studies [51,52]. Furthermore, the current AI explanation process is insufficient to tackle real clinical-world challenges in calibrating trust to get better predictions using AI assistance [53].

In the field of biomaterial synthesis prediction, it is recognized that successful collaboration of humans with AI requires more than simply accurate algorithmic predictions [54]. AI-supported decision-making is also conditioned upon how well the human can decide whether the recommendations from such AI do or do not warrant following or, alternatively, where and how it is important to call upon human judgment together with such AI. Nevertheless, the potentials of AI in predicting biomaterial synthesis are underscored by the current limitations in evidence and technical barriers [55].

## 6.6 Case studies showcasing successful artificial intelligence-assisted biomaterials synthesis prediction

AI and, more particularly, DL empower the synthesis of biomaterials through in silico improvement in the prediction of optimum synthesis conditions and material properties. DL models efficiently process and analyze huge and complex datasets like those generated by multiomics data such as genomics, transcriptomics, proteomics, and metabolomics. These models can learn complex patterns and nonlinear relationships in the data that elevate the accuracy and reliability of their predictions vis-à-vis other traditional methods. Thus, this capability is critical to the development of new biomaterials tailored to a given biomedical application, hence allowing innovations in such areas as regenerative medicine and drug delivery systems. As shown in Fig. 6.4, the DL framework integrates some data types, such as genomic and proteomic data, toward the prediction of clinical outcomes and the identification of possible biomarkers. This approach is directly applicable to biomaterials synthesis, where an understanding of the interaction among the different biological data types would guide the creation of materials with desired properties. The power of AI will therefore help researchers fast-track the discovery and optimization of biomaterials to the most stringent requirements for biomedical applications [24].

AI models have been successfully applied in predicting the synthesis of materials such as ZnO nanoparticles [35]. In this research, it is investigated how efficient an AI model can be in predicting the experimental conditions that will reduce the particle size during the synthesis of ZnO nanoparticles. First, an ANN was trained using 52 different experimental datasets obtained during the synthesis of ZnO nanoparticles. The input variables taken up in this study were temperature, duration of experiment, and the concentration of NaOH, while the size of the nanoparticles was the output variable. Finally, the ANN and a genetic algorithm (GA) called ANN-GA model was used to predict the experimental conditions that would yield ZnO nanoparticles with minimized dimensions and excellent photocatalytic activity. Also, in another study, polymeric microparticles made from poly(d,l-lactideco-glycolide) (PLGA) were successfully

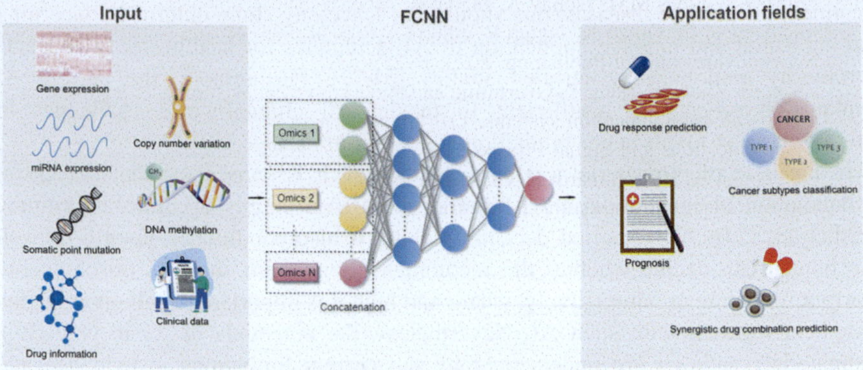


**Figure 6.4** Deep learning framework for multiomics data integration, demonstrating its use in predicting clinical outcomes and identifying biomarkers. This model can be adapted for biomaterials synthesis to predict optimal conditions and material properties by processing complex biological data.
Reprinted with permission from [24].

prepared using a combination of artificial intelligence and microfluidics. Some ANN models were developed using critical factors affecting particle size, such as PLGA concentration and flow rate, which were able to predict the size of PLGA particles produced by microfluidic systems. The ANN system's validity was confirmed by precisely comparing the predicted results with the actual data (Fig. 6.5). This AI tool can be used to produce other polymeric particles with controlled sizes [56].

AI has played a critical role in quickening the discovery of new molecules with properties of interest in chemistry [57]. Its application in drug discovery was highlighted above as predictive of drug-like properties, optimizing lead identification, and successful clinical trials [40]. In materials science and engineering, the scope for AI is described to be extensive due to AI applied to synthesize new materials and forecast the results of chemical synthesis [31]. It has been pointed out in studies that AI has a key role in autonomous materials synthesis and electrode optimization, for example, in the case of battery research [58].

In addition to these, Liu proposed a framework that integrated data-driven reaction-type predictions within an AI-aided synthesis planning workflow, showing the potential of AI in optimizing the synthesis process (Fig. 6.6) [44]. AI-assisted synthesis planning is one of the key strategies toward the acceleration of synthetic chemistry for drug and material discovery. Among them, the template-free approach seems to have strong generalization abilities. However, how far it can go in matching problem-solving performance with those from experienced chemists if mechanisms are not explicitly unveiled is still elusive. Furthermore, consistent frames for improving multitask reaction predictions are missing. They propose SynCluster, combining fine-grained reaction-type labels for improving downstream tasks (Fig. 6.6). SynCluster significantly improves retrosynthesis prediction accuracy and establishes new state-of-the-art models in terms of reactant diversity and validity. It further attains high accuracy in forward synthesis and

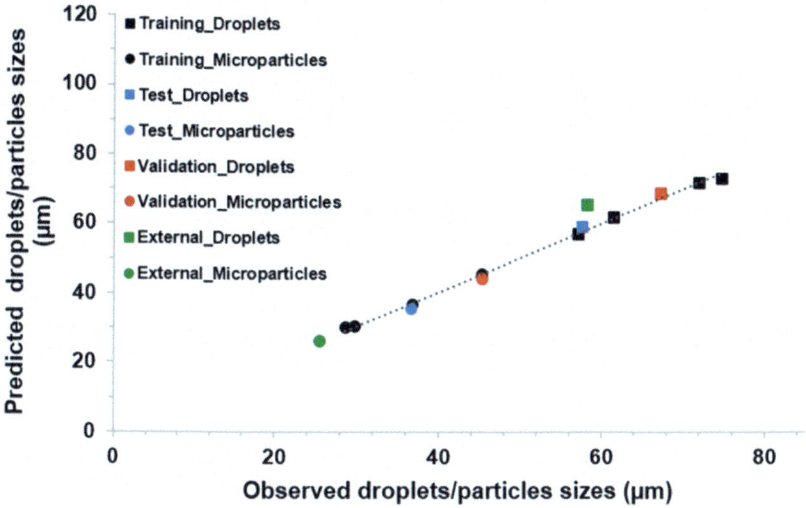


**Figure 6.5** Correlation between observed and predicted droplet/particle size generated by two consecutive cross-junctions featuring flow-focusing microfluidic chips placed in series obtained from ANN-C model implemented by Statistica v13.3. Data are shown for training, test, validation, and external datasets.
Reprinted with permission from [56].

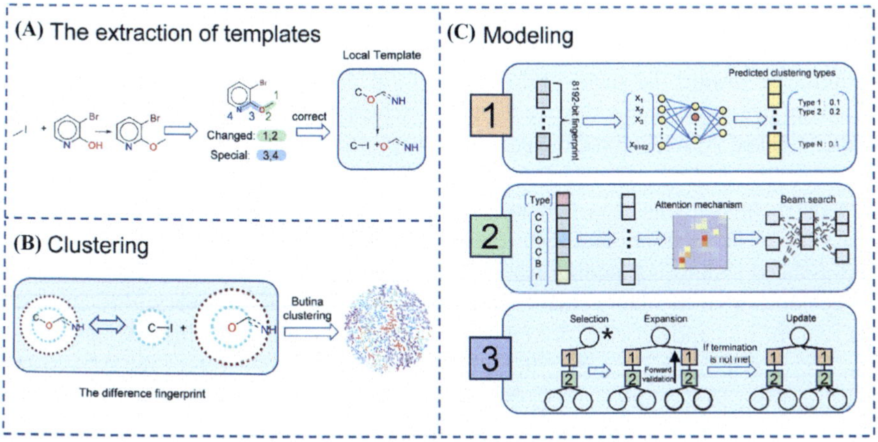


**Figure 6.6** Workflow of two-stage framework. Workflow consists of three parts (A-C).
Reprinted with permission from [44].

the prediction of reagents. SynCluster assists AI-driven synthesis planning with chemical interpretability, thus enhancing domain knowledge, and closes the gap between template-free approaches and experienced chemists' abilities [44].

At the polymer synthesis front, the rational design of molecularly imprinted polymers has been evolving constantly with the advancement of sophisticated computational tools that allow more sophisticated polymer syntheses [59]. Johansson et al. further present the rapid development of AI technologies in synthesis prediction, like retrosynthesis planning and forward synthesis prediction models based on quantum chemistry-based reaction prediction models [4]. It is also highlighted that reaction datasets are important for building these models, and how robotics is playing a role in high-throughput experimentation, predominantly within the pharmaceutical industry [2]. This study now describes an end-to-end strategy for automated synthesis, marrying AI for route planning with robotics for execution. In this paper, a free, open-source software suite was developed and trained on millions of reactions to assist in the design of synthetic routes. The output of this software is used to inform the configuration of a robotic flow chemistry platform, which has been benchmarked on the synthesis of 15 medicinally relevant small molecules. The achievement thus brings society one step closer to fully autonomous chemical synthesis [2].

## 6.7 Future prospects and potential advancements in the field

The future for AI-assisted synthesis in the prediction of biomaterials looks very bright. In that respect, AI methods can be applied to fast-track the prediction and discovery of biomaterials and improve their design. These techniques can play a big role in accelerating the prediction and finding of biomaterials [60]. Such AI models could be used in the design and discovery processes of in vivo synthesized biomaterials to make them more efficient and effective in their output [13], [61]. Again, literature has it that interdisciplinarity and standardization of data are major requirements toward the successful integration of AI in biomaterials research.

Some of the major factors that are identified, which will define the future prospects of biomaterials and AI integration, include interdisciplinary collaboration, standardization of data, and the dealing of ethical concerns [61]. Second, the application of AI in regenerative biomaterials will benefit from the development in AI and brain science and further push the development in regenerative biomaterials [62].

AI-assisted synthesis planning has already been proved to be a very useful tool for the acceleration of synthetic chemistry in drug and material discovery [44]. In silico drug repurposing and network-driven drug discovery are areas in which AI has shown great promise in drug discovery; therefore, it heralds a bright future for AI-assisted drug discovery [63].

Looking beyond biomaterials, AI has been applied to energy materials research, where it accelerates the discovery of materials like perovskites for energy applications [64]. In addition to the medical fields, gastroenterology is one particular area, especially in endoscopic screening and diagnosis, and could define healthcare in the future [65]. Its application in predicting an epidemic and healthcare trends further cements AI into healthcare planning and management [66].

The future of the synthesis prediction for biomaterials will thus not be able to remain independent of AI-driven predictive modeling, design, and optimization processes. Applications of AI in developing intelligent predictive models may revolutionize this area by providing more accurate predictions with quicker times. Besides that, AI is also applied in monitoring tissue growth and regulating experiments without human intervention, demonstrating its possibility of making some of the biomaterials research processes easier to manage [67].

Finally, AI integrated into biomaterial synthesis prediction holds huge potential to push research and development in a number of fields. This would therefore help researchers increase the efficiency in designing biomaterials, drug discovery, research into energy materials, and healthcare applications with the aid of AI technologies, thereby leading to innovative solutions and breakthroughs in the future.

## 6.8 Conclusion

AI and synthesis of biomaterials can be regarded as interfacing to create a new dimension that would redefine biomedical engineering and healthcare. Now, AI-driven methodologies do provide unprecedented opportunities in which to transform the design, synthesis, and application of biomaterials in various biomedical applications.

One of the prime contributions of AI within biomaterials synthesis is precisely in such abilities for the analysis of large data sets and extraction of meaningful insights from them. Thus, using machine learning algorithms, it will be possible to efficiently explore complex relationships between biomaterial composition, structure, and performance, therefore identifying new formulations of biomaterials that would allow for more advanced biocompatibility, mechanical properties, and degradation kinetics for specific needs.

Moreover, AI can optimize the biomaterial fabrication process for better reproducibility, scalability, and cost of biomaterial fabrication. Parameter predictions and optimizations like temperature, pH, and mixing ratios will greatly help a researcher get expected material properties with very high precision and efficiency. The major prospectuses of AI-powered biomaterial synthesis are in personalized medicine and regenerative therapies. By incorporating patient-specific information, like genetic history and medical background, into AI algorithms, researchers can develop truly biomaterials tailored to meet the needs of individual patients. In this respect, such biomaterials will be positioned to create personalized implants, scaffolds, and drug delivery systems for optimal therapeutics with reduced side effects.

The interaction of artificial intelligence with biomaterial synthesis represents, therefore, a new paradigm in biomedical research and innovation. Riding the power of AI-driven approaches, fast-tracking of the development of advanced biomaterials, imbued with precision, efficacy, and versatility that have never been possible before, is now on a clear path to engender transformative breakthroughs in healthcare and biotechnology.

## Acknowledgment

To the best of the Editors' knowledge and authors' claims, no generative AI tools were used for substantive writing of chapters. Any AI-assisted language editing, if applied, was limited to grammar or style suggestions and did not alter the scientific content.

## References

[1] Sadiku M, Suman GK, Musa SM. Artificial intelligence in materials science. International Journal of Advances in Scientific Research and Engineering 2021. Available from https://www.academia.edu/download/68832742/ijasre_34057.pdf.
[2] Coley CW, Thomas DA, Lummiss JA, Jaworski JN, Breen CP, Schultz V, et al. A robotic platform for flow synthesis of organic compounds informed by AI planning. Science 2019;365(6453):eaax1566. https://doi.org/10.1126/science.aax1566.
[3] Smith JR, Seyda A, Weber N, Knight D, Abramson S, Kohn J. Integration of combinatorial synthesis, rapid screening, and computational modeling in biomaterials development. Macromolecular Rapid Communications 2004;25(1):127–40. https://doi.org/10.1002/MARC.200300193.
[4] Johansson S, Thakkar A, Kogej T, Bjerrum EJ. AI-assisted synthesis prediction. Drug Discovery Today 2019;32-33:65–72. https://doi.org/10.1016/j.ddtec.2020.06.002.
[5] Segler MHS, Preuss M, Waller MP. Planning chemical syntheses with deep neural networks and symbolic AI. Nature 2018;555:604–610. https://doi.org/10.1038/nature25978.
[6] Wang W, Liu Y, Wang Z, Hao G, Song B. The way to AI-controlled synthesis: how far do we need to go? Chemical Science 2022;13(43):12604–12615.
[7] Tang K, Xue J, Zhu Y, Wu C. Design and synthesis of bioinspired nanomaterials for biomedical application. Wiley Interdisciplinary Reviews: Nanomedicine and Nanobiotechnology 2024;16(1):e1914. https://doi.org/10.1002/wnan.1914.
[8] Najman S, Stojanović S, Živković J, Najdanović J, Radenković M, Vasiljević P, Ignjatović N. Applications of biomaterials in regenerative medicine and tissue engineering–concepts and perspective. Contemporary Materials 2023;14(1):1–10. https://doi.org/10.7251/COMEN2301001N.
[9] Gayathry G, Komath M, Velaydhan S. Biomaterials for medical products. Biomedical product and materials evaluation: standards and ethics. Woodhead Publishing; 2022. p. 25–62. https://doi.org/10.1016/B978-0-12-823966-7.00012-8.
[10] Zhang S. Fabrication of novel biomaterials through molecular self-assembly. Nature Biotechnology 2003;21(10):1171–8. https://doi.org/10.1038/nbt874.
[11] Peppas NA, Langer R. New challenges in biomaterials. Science 1994;263(5154):1715–20. https://doi.org/10.1126/SCIENCE.8134835.
[12] Ricapito NG, Ghobril C, Zhang H, Grinstaff MW, Putnam D. Synthetic biomaterials from metabolically derived synthons. Chemical Reviews 2016;116(4):2664–704. https://doi.org/10.1021/ACS.CHEMREV.5B00465.
[13] Zhang X, Wang J, Zhang Y, Yang Z, Gao J, Gu Z Synthesizing biomaterials in living organisms. Chemical Society Reviews 2023;52:8126–8164. https://doi.org/10.1039/D2CS00999D.
[14] Sánchez-Velandia JE, Valverde D, Porcar R, Luz Villa A. Stimuli-responsive biomaterials with pharmacological applications. Synthesis of Nanomaterials. Bentham Science; 2023. p. 111–39. https://doi.org/10.2174/9789815136920123030007.
[15] Aldana AA, Bauer J, Baker MB. Synthetic biomaterials. Tissue engineering. Academic Press; 2023. p. 173–212. https://doi.org/10.1016/B978-0-12-824459-3.00006-8.
[16] Xu Y, Kim CS, Saylor DM, Koo D Polymer degradation and drug delivery in PLGA-based drug–polymer applications: a review of experiments and theories. Journal of Biomedical Materials Research Part B: Applied Biomaterials 2017;105:1692–1716. https://doi.org/10.1002/jbm.b.33648.

[17] Aly RM Current state of stem cell-based therapies: an overview. Stem Cell Investigation 2020;7:40. https://doi.org/10.21037/sci.2020.03.01.
[18] Pashuck ET, Stevens MM Designing regenerative biomaterial therapies for the clinic. Science Translational Medicine 2012;4:160ra150. https://doi.org/10.1126/scitranslmed.3002717.
[19] Kumar JA, Krithiga T, Manigandan S, Sathish S, Renita AA, Prakash P, Prasad BSN. A focus to green synthesis of metal/metal based oxide nanoparticles: Various mechanisms and applications towards ecological approach. Journal of Cleaner Production 2021(280):124314. https://doi.org/10.1016/j.jclepro.2020.124314.
[20] Hoffman AS. Stimuli-responsive polymers: biomedical applications and challenges for clinical translation. Advanced Drug Delivery Reviews 2013;65:10–16. https://doi.org/10.1016/j.addr.2012.11.004.
[21] Vinoth A, Datta S. Computational intelligence based design of biomaterials. Computer Methods in Material Science 2022;22(4):229–62. https://doi.org/10.7494/CMMS.2022.4.0799.
[22] You S, Fan Y, Chen Y, Jiang X, Liu W, Zhou X, Zhang J, Zheng J, Yang H, Hou X. Advancements and prospects of deep learning in biomaterials evolution. Cell Reports Physical Science 2024;5(4):100094. https://doi.org/10.1016/j.xcrp.2024.100094.
[23] Wang Z, Xiao X, Nukavarapu SP, Kumbar SG, Rajasekaran S. Machine learning techniques in structure-property optimization of polymeric scaffolds for tissue engineering. EPiC Series in Computing 2022;83:146–54. https://doi.org/10.29007/NXM3.
[24] Wen Y, Zhang Y, Li X, et al. Deep learning-based multiomics data integration methods for biomedical application. Advanced Intelligent Systems 2023;5(5):2200247. https://doi.org/10.1002/AISY.202200247.
[25] Han S, Wu J. Artificial intelligence (AI) meets biomaterials and biomedicin. Smart Materials in Medicine 2024;5:251–255.
[26] Zhai C, Li T, Shi H, Yeo J. Discovery and design of soft polymeric bio-inspired materials with multiscale simulations and artificial intelligence. Journal of Materials Chemistry B 2020;8:6562–6587.
[27] Murali N, Sivakumaran N. Artificial intelligence in healthcare—a review. International Journal of Modern Computation, Information and Communication Technology 2018;1(6):2581–5954. https://doi.org/10.13140/RG.2.2.27265.92003.
[28] Singh AV, Rosenkranz D, Ansari MHD, Singh R, Kanase A, Singh SP, Johnston B, Tentschert J, Laux P, Luch A. Artificial intelligence and machine learning empower advanced biomedical material design to toxicity prediction. Advanced Intelligent Systems 2020;2(12):2000084. https://doi.org/10.1002/AISY.202000084.
[29] Rajitha A, Kansal L, Raj G, Kalra R, Dhamija K, Abdul-Zahra DS. Biomaterials and artificial intelligence: predictive modeling and design. In: Proceedings of the 2024 International Conference on Artificial Intelligence and Renewable Energy. E3S Web Con; 2024. https://doi.org/10.1051/e3sconf/202450501003.
[30] Mackay B, Marshall K, Poon JGJ. The future of bone regeneration: integrating AI into tissue engineering. Journal of Physics: Materials 2021(4):043001.
[31] Sha W, Guo Y, Yuan Q, Tang S, Zhang X, Lu S, Guo X, Cao YC, Cheng S. Artificial intelligence to power the future of materials science and engineering. Advanced Intelligent Systems 2020;2:1900143.
[32] Tabor DP, Roch LM, Saikin SK, Kreisbeck C, Sheberla D, Montoya JH, Dwaraknath S, Accelerating the discovery of materials for clean energy in the era of smart automation. Nature Reviews Materials 2018;3:5–20.

[33] Zheng Z, Zhang O, Nguyen HL, Rampal N, Alawadhi AH, Rong Z, Head-Gordon T, Borgs C. ChatGPT research group for optimizing the crystallinity of MOFs and COFs. ACS Central Science 2023;9(11):42–. https://doi.org/10.1021/acscentsci.3c01087.
[34] Gulevich DG, Nabiev IR, Samokhvalov PS. Machine learning–assisted colloidal synthesis: a review. Materials Today Chemistry 2024;35:101837. https://doi.org/10.1016/J.MTCHEM.2023.101837.
[35] Martínez-Vargas BL, González Rodríguez LM, Pacheco-Álvarez M, Peralta-Hernández JM, Picos A. Use of artificial intelligence models for the reduction of nanoparticle size in the synthesis of ZnO. Journal of Chemical Technology and Biotechnology 2023;98(8):1868–77. https://doi.org/10.1002/JCTB.7315.
[36] Mercado R, Kearnes SM, Coley CW. Data sharing in chemistry: lessons learned and a case for mandating structured reaction data. Journal of Chemical Information and Modeling 2023;63(14):4265. https://doi.org/10.1021/acs.jcim.3c00607.
[37] Kwon Y, Lee D, Kim JW, Choi YS, Kim S. Exploring optimal reaction conditions guided by graph neural networks and Bayesian optimization. ACS Omega 2022;7(49):12. https://doi.org/10.1021/acsomega.2c05165.
[38] Shen R, Su W, Thieme G, Kg V. A review of the applications of artificial intelligence in the process analysis and optimization of chemical products. Pharmaceutical Fronts 2023;5:219–226. https://doi.org/10.1055/s-0043-1777425.
[39] Iwama R, Kaneko H. Integration of materials and process informatics: metal oxide and process design for $CO_2$ reduction. ACS Omega 2022;7(50):46922–46934. https://doi.org/10.1021/acsomega.2c06008.
[40] Sahoo A, Dar GM. A comprehensive review on the application of artificial intelligence in drug discovery. The Applied Biology and Chemistry Journal 2021;2(2):34–48.
[41] Yi Y, An HW, Wang H. Intelligent biomaterialomics: molecular design, manufacturing, and biomedical applications. Advanced Materials 2023;36:2305099. https://doi.org/10.1002/adma.202305099.
[42] Jang WD, Kim GB, Kim Y, Lee SY. Applications of artificial intelligence to enzyme and pathway design for metabolic engineering. Current Opinion in Biotechnology 2022;73:47–56. https://doi.org/10.1016/j.copbio.2021.09.004.
[43] Darnell M, Mooney DJ Leveraging advances in biology to design biomaterials. Nature Materials 2017;16:1178–1185.
[44] Liu T, Cao Z, Huang Y, Wan Y, Wu J, Hsieh CY, Hou T, Kang Y. SynCluster: Reaction type clustering and recommendation framework for synthesis planning. JACS Au 2023;3(12):2812–2824.
[45] Alufaisan Y, Marusich LR, Bakdash JZ, Zhou Y, Kantarcioglu M. Does explainable artificial intelligence improve human decision-making? Proceedings of the AAAI Conference on Artificial Intelligence 2021;35:6618–6626. https://doi.org/10.1609/aaai.v35i8.16819.
[46] Liu CF, Hung CM, Ko SC, Cheng KC, Chao CM, Sung MI, Hsing SC, Wang JJ, Chen CJ, Lai CC, Chen CM, Chiu CC, et al. An artificial intelligence system to predict the optimal timing for mechanical ventilation weaning for intensive care unit patients: a two-stage prediction approach. Frontiers in Medicine 2022;9:935366.
[47] Tran BX, Latkin CA, Sharafeldin N, Nguyen K, Vu GT, Tam WWS, Cheung NM, Nguyen HLT, Ho CSH, Ho RCM. Characterizing artificial intelligence applications in cancer research: a latent Dirichlet allocation analysis. JMIR Medical Informatics 2019;7:e14401.
[48] Thomas MG, Mastorides SM, Borkowski SA, Reed JR, Deland LA, Thomas LB. Assessing artificial intelligence models to diagnose and differentiate common liver carcinomas. medRxiv 2022. https://doi.org/10.1101/2022.08.30.22279347.

[49] Decharatanachart P, Chaiteerakij R, Tiyarattanachai T, Treeprasertsuk S. Application of artificial intelligence in chronic liver diseases: a systematic review and meta-analysis. BMC Gastroenterology 2021;21(1):1. https://doi.org/10.1186/s12876-020-01585-5.
[50] Wang Y, Wang H, Zhuo Y, Hu Y, Li X, Xu Y, Sun B, Liu M, Zou L, Liu L, Luo L, Zhao C, Li P. Spheroid formation enhances the regenerative capacity of nucleus pulposus cells via regulating N-CDH and ITGβ1 interaction. International Journal of Biological Sciences 2022;18:1–15. https://doi.org/10.7150/ijbs.68807.
[51] Iqbal MJ, Javed Z, Sadia H, Qureshi IA, Irshad A, Ahmed R, Malik K, Raza S, Abbas A. Clinical applications of artificial intelligence and machine learning in cancer diagnosis: looking into the future. Cancer Cell International 2021;21:270. https://doi.org/10.1186/s12935-021-01981-1.
[52] Le Berre C, Sandborn WJ, Aridhi S, Devignes MD, Fournier L, Smaïl-Tabbone M, Danese S. Application of artificial intelligence to gastroenterology and hepatology. Gastroenterology 2020;158:2126–2139. https://doi.org/10.1053/j.gastro.2019.12.036.
[53] Zhang Y, Liao QV, Bellamy RKE Effect of confidence and explanation on accuracy and trust calibration in AI-assisted decision making. Proceedings of the 2020 Conference on Fairness, Accountability, and Transparency 2020;295–305. https://doi.org/10.1145/3351095.3372852.
[54] Cai CJ, Winter S, Steiner D, Wilcox L, Terry M 'Hello AI': uncovering the onboarding needs of medical practitioners for human-AI collaborative decision-making. Proceedings of the ACM on Human-Computer Interaction 2019;3:1–20.
[55] Bansal G, Nushi B, Kamar E, Weld DS, Lasecki WS, Horvitz E. Updates in human-AI teams: Understanding and addressing the performance/compatibility tradeoff. Proceedings of the AAAI Conference on Artificial Intelligence 2019;33:2429–2437. https://doi.org/10.1609/aaai.v33i01.33012429.
[56] Damiati SA, Rossi D, Joensson HN, Damiati S. Artificial intelligence application for rapid fabrication of size-tunable PLGA microparticles in microfluidics. Scientific Reports 2020;10(1):19517. https://doi.org/10.1038/S41598-020-76477-5.
[57] Sumita M, Yang X, Ishihara S, Tamura R, Tsuda K Hunting for organic molecules with artificial intelligence: molecules optimized for desired excitation energies. ACS Central Science 2018;4:1126–1133. https://doi.org/10.1021/acscentsci.8b00213.
[58] Lombardo T, Franco AA, Gasteiger HA, et al. Artificial intelligence applied to battery research: hype or reality? Chemical Reviews 2022;122(12):10899–969. https://doi.org/10.1021/ACS.CHEMREV.1C00108.
[59] Rajpal S, Mishra P, Mizaikoff B. Rational in silico design of molecularly imprinted polymers: current challenges and future potential. International Journal of Molecular Sciences 2023;24(7):6785. https://doi.org/10.3390/ijms24076785.
[60] Meyer TA, Ramirez C, Tamasi MJ, Gormley AJ. A user's guide to machine learning for polymeric biomaterials. ACS Polymers Au 2023;3(2):141–57. https://doi.org/10.1021/ACSPOLYMERSAU.2C00037.
[61] Rajitha A, Kansal L, Raj G, Kalra R, Dhamija K, Abdul-Zahra DS Biomaterials and artificial intelligence: predictive modeling and design. E3S Web of Conferences 2024;505:01003.
[62] Cao D, Ding J. Recent advances in regenerative biomaterials. Regenerative Biomaterials 2022;9:rbac098. https://doi.org/10.1093/rb/rbac098.
[63] Chong LC, Gandhi G, Lee JM, Yeo WWY, Choi SB. Drug discovery of spinal muscular atrophy (SMA) from the computational perspective: a comprehensive review. International Journal of Molecular Sciences 2021;22(16):8962 https://doi.org/10.3390/IJMS22168962.
[64] Liang J, Yu Y, Li Z Accelerating perovskite materials discovery and correlated energy applications through artificial intelligence. Energy Materials 2022;2:14.

[65] Hsiao YJ, Wen YC, Lai WY, Lin YY, Yang YP, Chien Y, Yarmishyn AA, Hwang DK, Lin TC. Application of artificial intelligence-driven endoscopic screening and diagnosis of gastric cancer. World Journal of Gastroenterology 2021;27:2907–2919. https://doi.org/10.3748/wjg.v27.i19.2907.
[66] Naseem M, Akhund R, Arshad H, Ibrahim MT. Exploring the potential of artificial intelligence and machine learning to combat COVID-19 and existing opportunities for LMIC: a scoping review. Journal of Primary Care and Community Health 2020;11(4):2150132720963634. https://doi.org/10.1177/2150132720963634.
[67] Elsen R, Nayak S. Artificial intelligence-based 3D printing strategies for bone scaffold fabrication and its application in preclinical and clinical investigations. ACS Biomaterials Science and Engineering 2024;10:1–12.

# Artificial intelligence-based biomaterials characterization

# 7

*Diane Isabel Selvido[1], Dinesh Rokaya[2,3], Rohan D. Jagtap[4], Muhammad Sohail Zafar[2,3], and James Tsoi[5]*
[1]Academy of Research and Clinical Dentistry, Metro Manila, Philippines, [2]Clinical Sciences Department, College of Dentistry, Ajman University, Ajman, United Arab Emirates, [3]Center of Medical and Bio-Allied Health Sciences Research, Ajman University, Ajman, United Arab Emirates, [4]Division of Oral and Maxillofacial Radiology, Department of Care Planning and Restorative Sciences, School of Dentistry, University of Mississippi Medical Center (UMMC), Jackson, MS, United States, [5]Dental Materials Science, Faculty of Dentistry, Division of Applied Oral Sciences and Community Dental Care, The University of Hong Kong, Pok Fu Lam, Hong Kong

## 7.1 Introduction

The discovery of materials has been the pursuit of the scientific community for several decades for different purposes, such as technological advancements, innovation, and improving human quality of life. Since artificial intelligence (AI) has been integrated into our daily lives for the past years, tools like these must also be used in scientific research. Generally, AI has been defined as the capability of machinery to simulate human reasoning, which incorporates problem-solving, ameliorating, and deep understanding [1]. AI is anticipated to influence and develop our futures by contributing to making behaviors more predictable, generating patterns, and assisting in improving the attributes of resources. Currently, the healthcare sector has been heavily involved in applying AI and has played a vital role in this field. In parallel, the application of AI has been pivotal in the medical context as well as in engineering, business, and design. It has played an integral part in addressing the challenge of identifying biomaterials used in healthcare and keeping up with the rapid pace of advancements in these materials.

AI comprises three major components: machine learning (ML), artificial neural networks (ANN), and deep learning (DL) [2]. Machine learning, a branch of AI, focuses on identifying patterns within data. It involves training algorithms to recognize these patterns from processed data. DL, on the other hand, utilizes multiple layers and interconnected neurons. Within DL, there are three primary layers: the input layer, the hidden layer, and the output layer. The input layer serves as the initial stage where data is introduced. Hidden layers process input data, generating intermediate representations of its characteristics. These representations are crucial for preliminary assessment rather than producing final visible output. Finally, the output layer produces the desired results, such as pathology classification. ANN is a vital component of AI, playing a central role in DL algorithms. These networks mimic the structure and functions of the human brain.

**Artificial Intelligence in Biomaterials Design and Development. DOI:** https://doi.org/10.1016/B978-0-323-95464-8.00002-5

Just like humans, AI can project and streamline necessary information when prompted. It can process data rapidly, mainly when used in conjunction with computer systems [3]. With its remarkable abilities, AI has been serving its purpose in providing correct treatment for medical problems, strategizing, visualizing, voice identification, and acquiring specialized skills with precision. It is a revolutionary move that AI is applied exceptionally successfully in the science, technology, engineering, and math domains, as advanced problem-solving approaches and methods are profoundly required in these disciplines. In a recent media report, it has been highlighted that academics have been both worried and enthusiastic about the progression of AI in the following years because of the readily apparent advantages and disadvantages it entails [4]. Indeed, we must weigh certain risks and benefits when using AI in the scientific context.

AI in the medical field has made significant progress, ranging from diagnosis to treatment planning and follow-up, thereby improving the efficiency of dentists and specialists [2,5]. Some of the important advantages of AI in dentistry include:

- Providing round-the-clock service to patients and providers through automatic operations.
- Improving efficiency by reducing the tedious workload on the healthcare workforce.
- Facilitating efficient and improved communication between providers and patients.
- Increasing patient satisfaction through improved reliability, efficiency, accuracy, and precision in patient care.
- Standardizing, monitoring, and regularly recording data.
- Planning and saving time in day-to-day healthcare procedures, enabling certain tasks to be performed more quickly.
- Providing analytical forecasting that helps dentists and specialists make quicker decisions.
- Automating operations to reduce expenses and the need to hire more employees.
- Reducing the risk of misdiagnosis compared to human observation.
- Ensuring accuracy in making treatment plans based on proper diagnosis.

## 7.2 Artificial intelligence in biomaterials science

One major constituent of AI is data science. Comprehensively, data science involves obtaining and procuring knowledge and understanding from high volumes of information [1]. An example of this would be the integration of different scientific fields that transpired to form bioinformatics, in which patterns of DNA, RNA, and proteins are currently revolutionized [6].

As a subfield of AI, machine learning (ML) uses algorithms to identify patterns and substructures in data. It can predict outcomes based on these patterns and improve its predictions by learning from data [7]. This makes ML one of the fastest-growing technical fields today, and DL [8] is a very prominent research area in ML. The foundation of DL algorithms is neural networks (NNs), which are biologically inspired networks that can extract features from the imported data sets and do not require human intervention. According to Ding et al. [9], this "neural network" consists of a minimum of three nodal layers—input, multiple "hidden," and output layers—such that each layer consists of various numbers of interconnected nodes (artificial neurons) (Fig. 7.1).

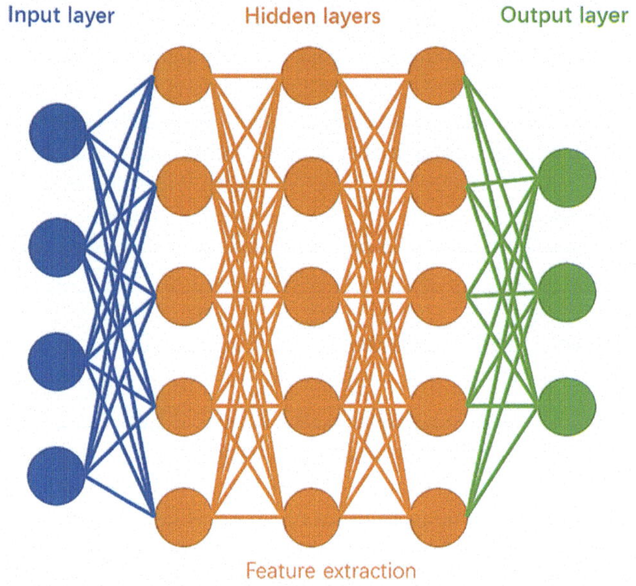


**Figure 7.1** Diagram of deep learning.
Reprinted with permission from [9].

### 7.2.1 Machine learning

Machine learning [10] is an algorithm that enforces predictability for biomaterial development [11]. ML brings forth systems that came from familiar events in an instant. It can be prepared with or without supervision. Consequently, to properly process and enhance actual applications, machine learning sets the notable foundation [12]. To fully understand AI, ML is a significant precursor.

Another promising finding about ML is that it is one of the primary forces behind resolving the dilemma of delayed material development. Due to the escalating demand for biomaterials, their innovation is essential. In its nature, machine learning has rerouted methods from conventional models to descriptive and predictive frameworks [13]. The "trial and error" method, referred to as the Edisonian model, has now been redirected and, thus, developed further.

At the junction of medicine and chemistry, numerous ML algorithms concentrate on synthesizing small molecules for drug development [14,15]. When creating novel biomaterials, as mentioned before, trial and error is a typical yet inefficient process that hinders the polymers from effectively serving their therapeutic goal [16]. Polymers exhibit more volatility compared to their more minor constituents, presenting a problem due to several complex factors affecting their characteristics [17]. Thus, challenges to ML in bioactive material have been inevitable. Nevertheless, current initiatives in using machine learning in polymer design have used conjunctional and high-throughput experimental methods to tackle issues related to data availability.

On the other hand, ML can be used as an assistant tool for the characterization of biomaterials surfaces. For example, dental *Porphyromonas gingivalis (P.g.)* and *Fusobacterium nucleatum (F.n.)* on zirconia have been successfully characterized by Ding et al. [18] using an ML method. The results are promising that a new linear relationship between bacteria attachment area was established with time in log scale. Furthermore, for the characterization of scanning electron microscopy (SEM) images of *Streptococcus mutans (S.m.)* on polymethyl methacrylate (PMMA), the results were the same with confocal images [18], that is, both methods are comparable. Thus, ML has great potential in image characterization for dental materials research.

### 7.2.2 Artificial neural network

The ANN has been vastly popular in AI since the 1980s. It conceptualizes the human brain's NN in terms of information processing, creates a basic model, and constructs various networks based on numerous interconnections [19]. Its goal is to replicate how the brain's NNs work and how memory information is processed. ANN is one of the most common models under the mechanism of ML. It is known to be used in complex variables and is popular in potent data sets. A disadvantage would be the interpretability of ANN approaches [20]. Progress on ANN contexts has been taking off, especially for metal adsorption using modified biomaterials. Moreover, to comprehend complicated metal adsorption processes on biomaterials for environmental remediation and water reuse, ANN frameworks were used in complex nonlinear interfaces [21].

A "neural network" is a computational framework consisting of several interconnected nodes, often known as neurons [22]. Moreover, Wu and Feng mention in a review article that this neuron processing unit in an ANN may represent many items, like features, characters, ideas, or significant abstraction sequences [23].

In biomaterials, ANN has notable applications that have far reached the environmental realm of these bioagents [24,25]. Several contributions in ANN have been of wide interest in materials sciences. An important advantage of this algorithm was observed in developing titanium alloys by maximizing the yield strength, tensile strength, elastic modulus, and cytotoxicity, as performed by Banu and Rani in 2018. It was concluded in their testing that the combination of titanium and niobium has elevated the properties mentioned [26]. In addition, ANN has been a crucial quantitative tool in predicting corrosion resistance and other complications when using this alloy. This encounter also led Kazemi et al. in 2022 to evaluate particular models such as ANN, gene expression programming (GSP), and response surface methodology (RSM) to determine if Ti-6Al-4V alloys were coated with hydroxyapatite. Among all models, ANN has been considered as superior and may be regarded as a promising tool [27]. Yet, it needs further validation for its use in different engineering materials applications. Therefore, by utilizing ANN in this domain, the designing and development of these alloys are worthy of attention.

### 7.2.3 Deep learning

DL has resulted from the simultaneous use of ANN with representation learning. DL is a known component of machine learning. Together with ANN, DL stipulates a robust framework for transforming extensive raw data into extractable elements for various studies [1]. In 2022, an in vitro study by Sneider et al. demonstrated the use of DL in identifying tissue stiffness in breast specimens [28]. As mentioned before, it appears that continuous integration of the medical history, clinical features, and distinct laboratory markers in tissues is crucial in AI assistance under DL.

Similarly, a study by Ng et al. emphasized the involvement of three-dimensional bioprinting for tissue samples. It was a unique idea that helped in image processing and optimization [29]. Consequently, this led to obtaining a model for producing biocompatible tissues or organs needed for clinical settings. With the DL-associated innovation at hand, it is interesting that 3D organ bioprinting has started, giving hope to patients who need it in the future.

In the context of biomaterial characterization, Yu et al., in 2022, took advantage of DL in predicting secondary protein structures necessary for designing protein sequences. Because of the premise that the secondary protein structures can be characterized, their understanding can augment mechanical properties for regeneration and other biological purposes [30]. A seminal contribution by Lan et al. also benefited from DL and NNs by predicting osteogenic differentiation [31]. Images acquired from confocal microscopes were used to collect and line up data from rat bone marrow mesenchymal stem cells, transpiring into a DL algorithm that detects differentiated osteogenic cells. Their work showed the importance of the osteogenic convolutional neural network (CNN) in inspecting osteogenic and bioactive materials for advanced tissue engineering and stem cell investigations. These examples are reminiscent of AI assistance in different circumstances and are as constructive in property identification and overall integrity of structures these materials will form.

### 7.2.4 Random forest

Random forest is a kind of regression model that is built as a collection of decision trees [32]. This algorithm helps reduce overestimation, yet it also brings about intricacies and difficulties in the comprehension of datasets. These decision trees are also considered a learning model constructed by an algorithm. Additionally, decision trees uncover several methods of partitioning datasets depending on the circumstances [33]. Similar to random forests, decision trees are also commonly used in different biomaterial contexts.

### 7.2.5 Support vector machines

Support vector machines, or SVM, is one of the most popular and current ML algorithms that are utilized for recognition, categorization, and regression. Supervised learning relies heavily on SVM and remains a predominant method to some extent. This approach is very efficient and robust in high-dimension datasets and environments [34].

### 7.2.6 Generative approach

In particular dental prostheses design, this part has been driven largely in a digital way. The CEREC Biogeneric Individual is the first knowledge-based AI in dental prostheses design algorithm that utilized principal component analysis to design occlusal surfaces automatically [35]. The results are not bad despite the cusp angle is usually larger than that of normal teeth. Recent advances in computational power allow other machine learning and DL algorithms to run. Broll et al. [36] have reviewed recent articles that automate prostheses design using generative DL approaches, such as generative adversarial networks (GANs) and transformers. The study found that these GANs were either in 2D or 3D approaches with depth map or voxel methods, respectively. The transformer model can be applied to point cloud data. In terms of accuracy and precision, while many computation data can be compared using metrics of distances, errors, indices, and scores, there is an ultimate goal for usability—these metrics can only merely be a design pass/fail parameter that could affect the fit only [37]. The final prostheses should not only be designed but also be manufactured using computer-aided manufacturing (CAM) techniques such as milling to printing. Thus, to validate the prosthesis design with respect to different dental materials (e.g., ceramics) with various biomechanical properties, other techniques such as the fatigue finite element (FE) method should be used. For instance, Ding et al. [38] utilized FE to study different AI and technician designs of crowns made with lithium disilicate and concluded that the 3D-DCGAN (a true 3D voxel-based DL generative network) could generate a crown that matches closely the fatigue lifetime with human teeth (Fig. 7.2). Ultimately, we do not blame the materials nor the design, but we hope to gain a biomimetic design together with a material accurately matched with the patient-specific needs.

## 7.3 Biomaterials and characterization

There is an inherent need to maximize biomaterials that have comprehensive usage in healthcare. Researchers believe that the ability to detect and identify these substances may be advantageous because their properties could be exhausted to their fullest extent. Moreover, it is also foreseeable that the practitioners and researchers would be able to confirm that the biomaterials, bioagents, implants, and device components they are working with are appropriate for their needs. Therefore, interest in AI assistance and the scope of what it can accomplish in biomaterial research nowadays is vast and thriving [35].

Biomaterials is a multidisciplinary sector specializing in the link connecting biological systems and proficient materials. The primary objective of this field of study is to design and manipulate the material's properties, therefore resulting in a particular biological reaction [39].

Biomaterials have been around since the 1940s, the time of World War II, when there was a necessity to heal injured military fighters [40]. Ever since that time, biomaterials have been developed and are currently under the umbrella of Material Sciences and Engineering [41]. Metals, alloys, polymers, ceramics, and composites are extensively studied and analyzed to identify qualities that align with the needs of certain biomaterials [42]. As it stands, the healthcare field is the primary receiver of these biomaterials. Additionally, the branches of chemistry, biology, and physics go hand in hand in the constitution of such substances, thereby rendering them

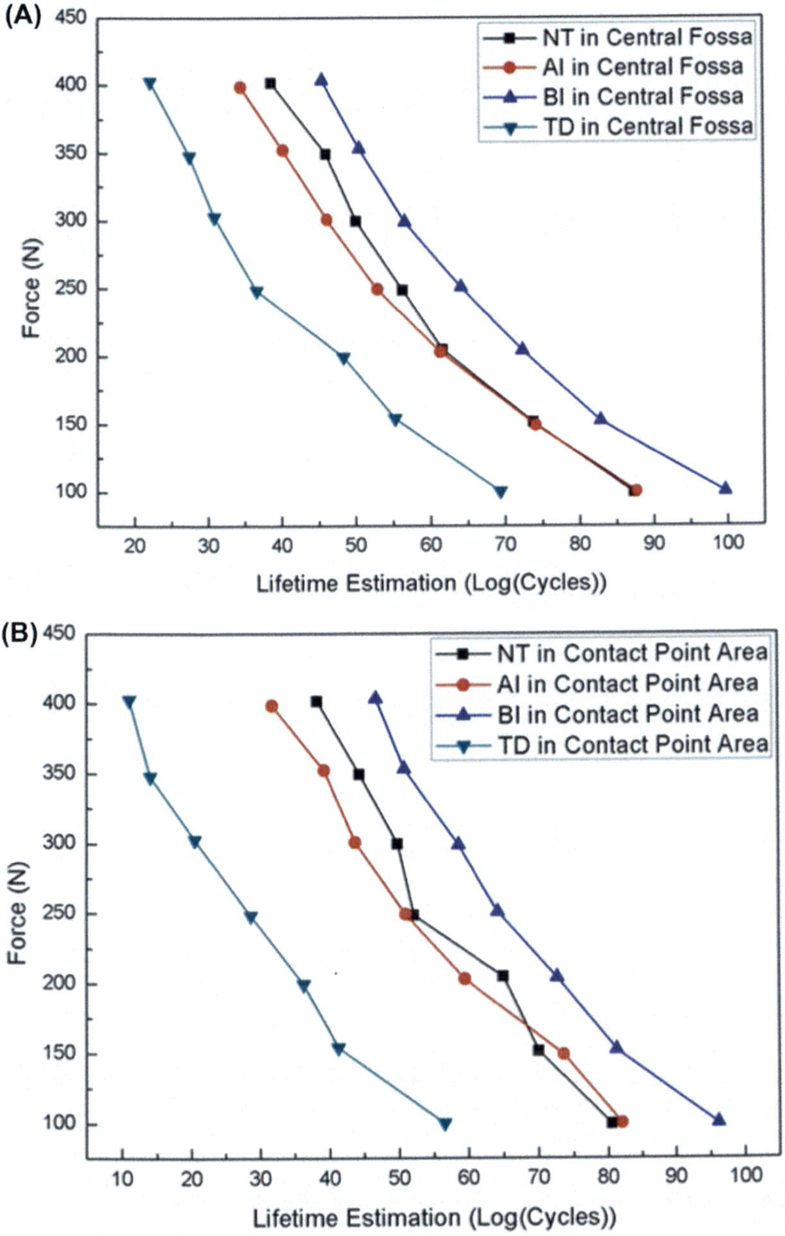


**Figure 7.2** Force versus lifetime estimation (in log scale) for the crown designs in (A) central fossa area and (B) contact point area. *NT*, Nature Tooth; *AI*, 3D-DCGAN; *BI*, CEREC biogeneric, *TD*, dental technician.
Reprinted with permission from [38].

biocompatible and comprehensive. The term "biocompatible" has several dependent routes, such as biofunctionality, bioinertia, bioactivity, and biostability [43]. Over time, the definition has been developed and refined. In the 1970s, materials were performed with single-staged experiments with a deficiency of reliable instruments. However, there were trailblazers in informatics and robotics in this era [44]. AI was developed after they were discovered in the 1950s (as mentioned above) and then proceeded to the fabrication of predictive algorithms. Right after the conceptualization of AI and the clarification of ML as a subset of AI, Bayesian methods were introduced in a nanotechnological context in 1964. They have been useful in hazard ranking, especially in assessing the cytotoxicity of elements such as $TiO_2$, $SiO_2$, Ag, $CeO_2$, and ZnO [45]. As per Singh et al. [46], ML was also associated with connection machines for parallel computing in 1981, and soon after that, recurrent neural networks and SVM were introduced. Most of these advancements were about nanoparticle toxicity, which was remarkably used in the Random Forest algorithm in 1995, as continually plotted by Singh et al. Additionally, in the year 2000, the Kernel Method and support vector clustering became known, which applies to collinear descriptors, nonlinear relations, and minor and massive amounts of data [47]. Eventually, in 2010, biomaterials, particularly nanoparticle development and AI platforms, intertwined, thus helping with quantifying and structure prediction in the following years [46].

Biomaterial characterization uses theoretical and experimental methods and experimental testing, which indirectly leads to the spread of relevant scientific knowledge through model phenomena in particular materials, which then enables their practical applications [48]. Characterization of biomaterials includes the physical, surface, chemical, mechanical, in vitro, and in vivo characterization tools and techniques of increasing importance to fundamental biomaterials research. Furthermore, the characterization of biomaterials will serve as a comprehensive resource for biomaterials researchers requiring detailed information on physical, chemical, mechanical, surface, and in vitro or in vivo characterization. This is an important aspect of biomaterials applications. AI has been implemented in materials science. Recently, AI has made important improvements in rational design and speeded the discovery of different biomaterials [49]. With the fast progress of data handling and algorithms, ML and DL are applied in the search for new biomaterials before actually producing them [50]. By incorporating various biomaterial data (such as the integral element, atomic weight and radius, lattice symmetry, magnetism, binding energy, polarization, electronegativity, band energy, and structural property), the machines are trained to think to improve the design of new material and predict the properties cost-effectively (Fig. 7.3) [49]. Data-driven computing and algorithms can help simulation and ML in property prediction and material discovery.

AI tools can be adapted for experimental testing of materials and use computing, automation, and ML to calculate the material's properties such as bulk, interface, and defects [51]. In the future, AI techniques can achieve the design of metals, superconductors, glasses, alloys, magnetocaloric materials, thermoelectric materials, polymeric materials, composite materials, 2D materials, and topological (electronic and phonon) materials [49]. A precise AI-based model needs to be made to forecast the formation energy of a compound to produce good predictive ability [52].

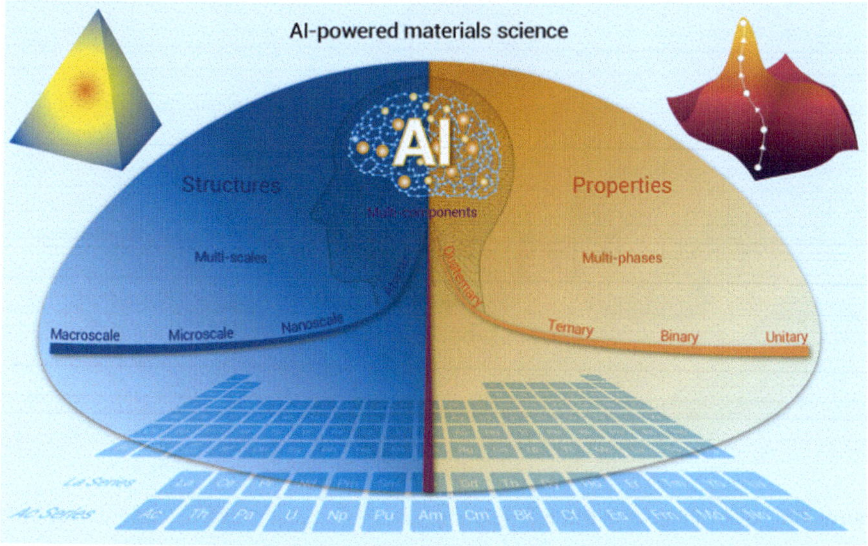


**Figure 7.3** AI-powered development in materials science.
Reprinted with permission from [49].

## 7.4 Artificial intelligence in biomaterials characterization

Biomaterials include various materials that are used in medicine and dentistry, that is, metallic biomaterials, ceramic biomaterials, polymeric biomaterials, and composite biomaterials [53]. Polymeric biomaterials can be nondegradable, biodegradable, and bio-derivative polymers. AI has been used in the characterization of various biomaterials. AI is used to analyze surface analysis data, including the identification of crystal structures from X-ray diffraction (XRD) data, analysis of X-ray photoelectron spectroscopy (XPS) spectra for surface composition, and the interpretation of transmission electron microscopy (TEM) and SEM images for particle morphology and size [54], as shown in Fig. 7.4. Furthermore, AI and ML models can be new insights and discoveries by identifying patterns and relationships in datasets. Most importantly, AI-analyzed data not only finds the mathematical description of the data but also finds the most physical and chemically meaningful results.

### *7.4.1 Metallic biomaterials*

As it stands, metallic biomaterials are applied as biocompatible agents in the body; however, they are used up to a certain extent [55]. Popular applications include orthopedic implants, pacemakers, and dental implants. These metallic materials are mainly composed of stainless steel, chromium alloys, nickel-titanium, titanium magnesium, and silver [56]. Mechanical properties and biocompatibility are the sought-after features that drive metallic biomaterials for more exploration in their field.

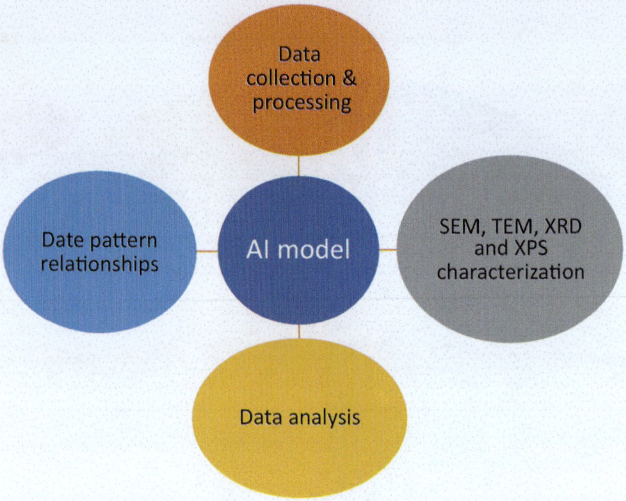


**Figure 7.4** Applications of AI in biomaterials characterization. *XRD,* X-ray diffraction; *XPS*, X-ray photoelectron spectroscopy; *TEM*, transmission electron microscopy; *SEM*, scanning electron microscopy.
Designed by the authors.

The influence of AI assistance in identifying metallic derivatives has been increasing over time. ML in stainless steel cobase alloys predicts ranges of mechanical properties, thereby improving its probability in ML contexts [57]. Interestingly, cobalt-chromium alloys have involved ANN as their algorithm, highlighting surface roughness analysis and prediction. Statistical analyses were first employed to construct prediction models, resulting in the derivation of three prediction equations for the alloys. The optimal outcomes were attained by making use of the RSM. The ANN model was then progressed with the aid of an application for roughness prediction [58]. Titanium alloys remarkably have patterns similar to those of other materials, as mentioned earlier regarding ML. It has been obtainable to come upon high-yield strength ductile titanium alloys, as well as designing and manufacturing them in a safe and efficient procedure [59]. Likewise, magnesium alloys using ML have been an interesting tool in augmenting the characteristics of the material, such as corrosion resistance—which is important in biomaterial fabrication [60]. In addition, a study by Li et al. mentioned that ML application in medical-grade magnesium alloy biomaterials is achievable, as it can foresee the properties it can maximize [61]. The consistent findings confirm that AI assistance has garnered the reputation of being a reliable tool in determining their notable properties in metallic compounds.

### 7.4.2 Ceramic biomaterials

Analogous to metallic biomaterials, ceramic materials are also used as implant materials. AI has helped characterize ceramics through ML and experimental validation. Ceramic biomaterials are good alternatives to dental implants, as they stimulate osteoblastic proliferation for bone deposition and regeneration [62]. Zirconia is an example of a bioceramic material known for its inertness, biocompatibility, increased corrosion resistance, and lack of adverse reaction to surrounding tissues. These qualities make zirconia an excellent bioceramic, particularly in dental implant applications that require esthetic appearances [63]. As reported by Luo et al., AI has spanned into zirconia characterization, as they have been rampantly used [64]. In dental crowns, AI has anticipated the success rates of zirconia crowns placed in the posterior regions. The success rate increase was achieved because AI programmed the margin designs of the prepared abutments [65]. The shade can be estimated as programmed by Back Propagation Neural Networks for the esthetics of zirconia using AI. Despite the inaccuracy and instability of this platform, Li et al. [66] employed a Generic Algorithm with it and somehow increased the precision of shade and color matching of the material. It is essential to acknowledge that investigations on zirconia in relation to AI can be extrapolated for other biomaterials that have similarities to it.

Another interesting finding of AI in zirconia research would be its capabilities as a bioceramic material, where Arif et al. probed the tribological aptitudes of hybrid aluminum nanocomposites augmented with zirconia nanoparticles. They also exploited statistical and ANN algorithms to evaluate hybrid composite wear behavior [67]. In addition, these findings provide additional information about AI assistance in ceramic biomaterial characterization. As further studied by Horikawa et al., the intent of lessening the method of animal experiments has led to the advancement of artificially obtained bones [68]. ML has suggested models to assess bone-forming ceramics based on several factors that comprise production variables, material characteristics, and in vivo settings.

### 7.4.3 Polymeric biomaterials

Two general accounts should be considered in polymer design in association with ML [16]. The first is property prediction or forward problem design, where there is a straightforward prediction of the main properties whenever the polymer configuration is determined. This method is increasingly regarded for the evaluation of materials of interest. The facilitation of fabrication of the chosen polymetric bio-influenced material is now possible instead of scanning the vast selections. Secondly, structure generation (or inverse problem design). This account involves the prediction of polymeric structures that exhibit their required qualities. This approach can potentially accelerate the process of materials design and eliminate constraints.

Polymer informatics is also gaining universal traction and is becoming highly valuable. It has been supplemented in the stages of polymer processing. Novel monomers have been devised for different uses because of polymer informatics. They were also developed to manipulate reactions, simulate processing settings and parameters, ascertain polymeric conformations and stages, anticipate material characteristics, and ultimately provide valuable insights into its terminal stages [69]. Challenges in polymeric biomaterials have also been an issue for ML for quite a period of time because of limited data availability [69,70].

Consequently, the data for ML in biomaterials in this range is gathered in-house. To mitigate this, the Design of Experiments (DOE) method demonstrates a support system for selecting independent variables from a wide array of preferences to take advantage of the provided material [71]. ML operation from this DOE model can aid in the enhancement of prediction in small sets of data.

In a review by Nguyen et al., ML methods and coarse-grained molecular dynamics (CGMD) replications can alleviate the current issues in polymer science, beginning at the level of chain formation [72]. Polymeric configuration identification, feed-forward property prediction, and inverse designs were surveyed using CGMD simulations to initiate preparations for developing ML-produced algorithms for determining the polymeric composition and structure. Drug delivery systems with polymer involvement were also explored by Upadhya et al., in which ML and AI were successfully applied. Gene delivery, antibacterial polymers, and bioactive polymers were also mentioned in this review, as they focused on polymer therapeutics [10]. High-throughput automation, ML, and AI were suggested to obtain a productive roadmap for these therapeutic approaches. Reinforcing the idea of gene delivery, Gong et al. [73] have also employed ML in their datasets, which involve polymer characteristics, transfection abilities, and nanomaterial toxicity in various cell types. Based on the Poly(β-amino ester) (PBAE) polymer's structure, it was found that random forest has foreseen the capacity of DNA transfection in the experimental setting [74]. The qualitative method included inputs of polymeric chemical descriptors to validate that *in silico* computational inspection of nanomedicine-based polymer structures had benefits *de novo* in biological investigations.

For automation in polymer biomaterials, it was experimented with by Tamasi et al. [75] that polymer and ML were unified to create a design to ascertain polymer protein hybrids with improved thermostability for three enzymes. Attaining data from ML guidance was customized per enzyme, and consequently, the chemical's unique attributes increased their affinity [75]. In their study, physical characterization was leveraged to stabilize these materials. By these means, ML can be used for optimization and refinement, which has good advantages in laboratory and clinical use. Furthermore, a study by Malashin et al. has concluded that in their search for an ML algorithm for different polymeric biomaterial properties, random forest, gradient boosting, and XGBoost have profoundness in their predictions, with random forest model being efficient in polymeric characterization [76]. Another notable finding was from Rickert et al. in 2021, wherein the Random Forest algorithm exhibited robustness in extensive and limited datasets of various dimensions and allocations. ML approach was utilized in their experiment to categorize complex biomaterials according to their microtopography, with wettability as their main characteristic to be acquired in biofilms, which can also be applied in biomaterial in the polymer field [77]. This research also mentioned the advantages of ML in surface properties, in which adhesion can be a crucial part of medical treatment and biomaterial engineering. Furthermore, polymeric biomaterial characterization in AI has effectively used the random forest algorithm in several findings.

Biodegradable biomaterials are currently in the trend because of their acceptability and diverse range of applications. Their usage spans the therapeutic aspect, medication delivery systems, and waste management [78–80]. ML assists in degradable polymer materials, as shown in one finding from Fransen et al. in 2023, wherein the consideration of biodegradability is contingent upon the aliphatic repeat units and was seen to be significantly influenced by their length [8]. This length, consisting of fewer than 15 carbons and shorter side chains, was shown to enhance biodegradability. Overall, the presence of aromatic backbone groups had a negative impact on biodegradability. Nevertheless, it was also demonstrated that benzene rings inside the backbone have an increasing affinity for degradability compared to metasubstituted rings [8]. Enhanced biodegradability is suggested to depend on the presence of backbone ether groups. With the information obtained, as per their evaluation, ML models were exploited to predict the ability of the material to degrade by means of chemical configuration markers.

Descriptors such as degradation factors were also taken advantage of for these bio-based materials. Molecular weight and weight loss ratio were used as indicators for the degree of degradation by Yamawaki et al. in 2021 [81]. In their experiment, they characterized polylactic acid's molecular weight as an objective variable. In contrast, moisture content in compost setting, degradation duration, preexperiment degree of crystallinity, and aspects of solid-state nuclear magnetic wavelength analytics were considered as explanatory variables. Statistical computations and data validated the high accuracy of their chosen prediction model. Therefore, in their findings, with the aid of ML algorithms such as Random Forest and Bayesian optimization, the assessment of early deterioration in the compost setting was significantly influenced by the moisture level of these materials.

### 7.4.4 Composite biomaterials

Similar to ANN, a CNN is a diverse algorithm. ANN imposes more advantages than CNN in terms of robustness and efficiency in binary problems. But in general, CNN was suggested to be more powerful and precise in mitigating problems. However, ANN is considered promising in terms of narrow data and when inputs are not necessary [82]. A study by Gu et al. in 2018 took advantage of CNN in composite bio-inspired materials and found that prediction can be achieved in a shorter time for optimization. Ten hours of forecasting were attained rather than five days when an extensive FE modeling method was run for material extractions [83]. Subsequently, ability of three-dimensional printed computer-aided design (CAD)/CAM crowns to debond has been predicted using CNN as well. The materials used were composite resin single crowns in this evaluation. Results have shown that the precision and accuracy were valued at 97% and 98.5%, respectively [84]. These outcomes have been highly regarded, and CNN may be a good algorithm to determine predictability in such biomaterials.

Machine learning is an insightful tool for comprehending the complex qualities of nanomaterials. It enables the manipulation of a number of reactions and experimental variables [85], which are reaction temperature, reaction duration, nucleation, ligand types, and others. All of these are important to generate the abundant properties of these nanomaterials [13].

An interesting finding by Shokrollahi et al. in 2022 found a CNN-trained regression system since, in their study, they had to predict the mechanical properties of BG-COL composite hydrogels, such as Young's modulus and Poisson's ratio. Moreover, finite element method (FEM) was used to simulate and calculate over 2000 images to comprehend the mechanical properties of BG-COL and other composite hydrogel samples [85]. The prediction success rate was 95% for Young's modulus and 83% for Poisson's ratio. FEM is suggested to guard safe and reliable testing in their study. On the other hand, in composite designing, ML has been valuable, specifically for optimizing properties and generating novel designs. ML has the foresight on the composite stiffness and toughness [86]. Since AI has been a driving force in this endeavor, a more accelerated turnaround was exhibited than the FEM, with a time difference of 250 times. Indeed, dental printing undertakings necessitate using superior and nonhazardous substances, which are currently scarce commercially.

## 7.5 Artificial intelligence in biomedical applications

In the medical sector, AI is highly regarded for its predictive capabilities. Due to this feature, several researchers in this area have been utilizing its speed, accuracy, and reliability for decision-making in the diagnosis and treatment planning [87]. Medical informatics has been the usual frontrunner when it comes to AI applications in this field, responsible for data privacy and the rapid evolution of predictive medicine [88]. Moreover, the clinical significance of AI in medicine is vastly disseminated: the level and quality of clinical imaging have been increased, scientific works of literature have been simpler to grasp, medical records have been easier to collect, reduced errors in diagnosis, and the learning curve for acquiring the understanding of AI is gradual and simple for clinicians, making them more focused on their practices [89]. Despite the widespread availability of AI in modern therapeutic settings, there are still existing limitations and disadvantages. Interestingly, it is important to emphasize that these AI entities will not supplant medical professionals but will instead use AI technology under their control to assist them. Undeniably, most of the research in this field aims to solve the problem of "Big Data," as the population's need for the standard of care has been broadened. The storage of these confidential data can cause potential problems and, therefore, may have profound negative implications when misused.

AI's role in dental diagnosis is pivotal, aiding dentists, specialists, and researchers in diagnosis, treatment planning, and prognosis prediction across various specialties. The applications span the following multiple domains [90–92].

A challenging problem in each medical setting is how to diagnose a patient effectively. From undergraduate degrees, the healthcare professional's clinical skills are refined until such professional becomes proficient in integrating these diagnostic aids. Given the nature of each case, there has been a strong need to apply AI in diagnostics to facilitate rapid and sound assessments.

Since AI is solely digital, it has the potential to process and make space for data related to healthcare—leading to increased validity of analytics in this setting.

Moreover, distinguishing pathologies can straightforwardly be done for patients, rendering them to evade invasive diagnostic procedures that may cause pain and discomfort [88]. Given these gratifying uses of AI, promising hardware and applications are worth expecting in clinics and hospitals in the years to come.

One area that is obscurely focused on AI is oncology, rendering cancer one of the most diagnosed diseases worldwide [93]. Growing appeals in AI in oncology implicate accurate detection using histopathological slides and radiological images, foreseeing metastatic outcomes, and augmenting treatment resolutions, all in favor of elucidating the issues involving the allocation of medical resources and cultivating cancer care [94]. When it comes to the clinical setting in conjunction with AI, the detection rate and differentiation of true and false disease proliferation can be more efficient [95]. The accuracy in diagnosis regarding cancer with the help of AI was further recommended, as Miyoshi et al. [96] evaluated 100 scans and produced significant results using Smartscopy for pathological cervical cancer. On the other hand, AI has been beneficial for doctors in decision-making and interpretation by "Natural Language" listing in early care intervention for children [97].

Another example would be using the same tools in dermatology, where it has been suggested that coding data from patients' statements, laboratory notes, scans from skin samples, and pathologic lesions can elevate precision and reliability. Therefore, they insinuated that large-scale multimodal simulations should be integrated into their area of interest [98]. The studies presented have been inclined to add value to diagnosis by exploiting AI. Furthermore, AI has shown that diagnostic imaging has undergone advanced shifts and expanded at an astounding rate.

With all the advancements AI brings, it is also significant to note that erroneous predictions can still ensue. Weighing the risks and potential benefits should still be the number one priority, especially when dealing with patients. Needless to say, one cannot substitute the doctor's clinical judgment when diagnosing these cases.

In light of the reported literature on AI-supported diagnosis of medical conditions, there has also been a significant number of reports regarding treatments of different ailments. Undoubtedly, there can be no effective therapy without a proper diagnosis. Consequently, AI can optimize treatment plans and provide suitable monitoring of health conditions. In a study by Xue et al. [99], AI in diabetic wound healing made a mark by determining the compatibility of Trichostatin A in micro-needling methods, which resulted in decreased inflammation and accelerated wound healing. DL is also valuable for extrapolating drug efficacy for lung cancers, thereby maximizing treatment plans [100]. In a mini-review by Wojtara and colleagues, AI could potentially help in diagnosing and treating uncommon illnesses, emphasizing the need to study these conditions for early detection and refining treatment methods in the future [101]. These recent contributions are valuable in underscoring drug-release systems that are minimally invasive and cost-effective to many.

Prognostic factors are also a crucial part of the treatment, and AI has been a factor in predicting these outcomes. Anticipating prognosis is advantageous as it helps enhance intervention and minimize the discomfort and inconveniences during treatment, providing ease of management. In lung cancer, prognosis could be based on imaging, genetic information, and pathology [101]. Innovation is required in this sector to enhance the performance of AI in oncology. Progress should be made in combining many aspects to provide a precise and comprehensive algorithm in medical systems.

## 7.6 Limitations and future directions

As stated in the previous accounts, AI and ML models have offered well-known benefits in biomaterial characterization. These include improved accuracy, efficiency, and the aptitude to operate broad data sets and samples [16]. However, they are also linked to several disadvantages. Since these AI algorithms are required to manipulate large quantities of data to elucidate accordingly, acquiring these data can be challenging in biomaterial characterization and identification. The complexity is attributed to the fact that biomaterials and their scenarios are multifaceted and variable in their biological nature [20]. As AI is still in the early years in this field, it is noteworthy that more processes should be developed to solve these problems. Beyond this awareness, finding the sources of data may be limited or costly, which could bring about partiality or restrictions in the performance of the desired model. Specifically, DL algorithms are usually criticized for their limited ability to interpret inputs [102]. While these methods are known to attain validity and reliability, how they arrive at their predictions can be challenging, especially in complicated scenarios like biomaterial identification and characterization. Therefore, the absence of transparency may be detrimental to the potential acknowledgment of AI-assisted insights by investigators and regulatory bodies.

While AI is the most innovative technology in the dental field, it also has some limitations [5,103]:

- Large amounts of data are required for training AI models.
- It is technique-sensitive, requiring providers to possess specific knowledge and skills, with the need for additional training to understand AI systems.
- The cost associated with training experts in data collection, annotation, data processing, technical infrastructure creation, hardware and software, and algorithm creation and updates. Achieving near-perfect results necessitates extensive datasets.
- Errors in training AI algorithms based on biased and incomplete datasets can result in subjective or biased outcomes.
- Lack of a human component, such as emotional feelings toward the needs of patients, and a lack of understanding of behavior management and patient psychology.
- Questions about personal data protection and privacy. Data privacy is an important aspect of patient care, which adds legal responsibility and ethical concerns regarding the use of AI in healthcare.
- As AI becomes more available to healthcare providers, students, and health-related personnel, there is a risk of increased dependence on technology.
- Job cuts and reduced need for employees due to automation can lead to the elimination of certain positions in the healthcare field.

Efforts are underway to find solutions to minimize the disadvantages and limitations hindering the rapid growth and acceptance of AI in dentistry. These efforts primarily focus on developing more advanced AI technology capable of overcoming these challenges.

Collectively, the concepts of overfitting and underfitting of data are crucial for more precise predictions for biomedical differentiation. Overfitting occurs when the algorithm understands and remembers the training data instead of grasping the fundamental and traditional patterns. Evidently, this may be a considerable obstacle, mainly when dealing with scarce or noisy data. On the other hand, underfitting occurs when the model struggles to accurately represent the intricacies of the data. Eventually, underfitting might result in erroneous predictions [104,105]. The regulation and selection of AI models for reliability in biomaterial development should be a top priority in running the unknown data.

The careful consideration of biological complexity must be taken into account due to the complicated and irregular correlations shown by these biomaterials, which traditional ML algorithms may not fully comprehend. Biological systems involve synergistic mechanisms and different cellular and environmental factors, which makes it challenging to standardize accurately [106,107]. The complex nature of these variables can hinder the implementation of AI and ML models. Therefore, field-specific expertise for eventual interpretation and engineering should be prioritized when incorporating AI and biomaterial profiling.

Possible ethical considerations should be underscored since these bio-influenced materials are reproduced and characterized. These include privacy, consent, and probable biases in the data or algorithms. Intense regulation and validation should be made before these AI-based methods become available clinically and commercially [108,109]. Nevertheless, the standardization and optimization might be unfavorable in terms of finances and demands of maintaining AI-powered protocols.

Resources and expertise can also be limitations of AI-driven biomaterial innovation and identification. Training algorithms of this nature requires time and intensive preparations, and institutions and researchers might be deterred from using these tools for these reasons [110]. Regardless, future research could continue to explore more cost-effective and streamlined methods for the development of such AI-screening tools for biomaterials.

Biomaterial and bio-based systems are constantly changing and dynamic, and they possess these qualities that are inevitable to alter progressively as a result of aging, disease advancement, progression, or environmental factors [77,111]. These AI models are not guaranteed to conform to these drastic and certain changes without possible current training, which may be demanding in terms of resources and not feasible on some occasions. It might take tremendous time for clinicians and researchers to delegate roles in this particular domain. Scientific and academic human resources and infrastructures are needed for continuity.

## 7.7 Conclusion

The AI-driven systems in biomaterial profiling and characterization can play a massive role in developing, reinforcing, and augmenting substances in materials. Moreover, the markers and the robust properties of the biomaterials can be taken advantage of, contributing to modifying better materials needed in the future. The AI support system has been providing valuable insights in recent times. However, there are still disadvantages and limitations, and the development of these technologically driven biomaterials needs research and training to undergo the necessary processes. Undoubtedly, the use of AI in biomaterial characterization will greatly benefit several domains in the future, particularly in the disciplines of biomaterial engineering, design, and clinical applications.

AI represents the pinnacle of technological advancement in the healthcare sector. These systems possess the capacity to analyze extensive datasets, recognize patterns, and draw informed conclusions or predictions. Embracing AI in dentistry is pivotal for the future, necessitating an understanding of both its potential benefits and inherent limitations. AI in dentistry stands as a valuable resource, alleviating the burdens on practitioners by assisting in diagnosis, treatment planning, and prognosis assessment. Given that the oral cavity serves as a gateway to overall health, the integration of AI has the potential to significantly enhance oral healthcare and, consequently, overall well-being, benefiting both patients and clinicians alike.

## Acknowledgment

To the best of the Editors' knowledge and authors' claims, no generative AI tools were used for substantive writing of chapters. Any AI-assisted language editing, if applied, was limited to grammar or style suggestions and did not alter the scientific content.

## References

[1] Kerner J, Dogan A, von Recum H. Machine learning and big data provide crucial insight for future biomaterials discovery and research. Acta Biomaterialia 2021;130:54–65.

[2] Orhan K, Jagtap R. Introduction to artificial intelligence. In: Orhan K, Jagtap R, editors. Artificial intelligence in dentistry. Cham: Springer International Publishing; 2023. p. 1–7.

[3] Haleem A, Javaid M, Khan IH. Current status and applications of artificial intelligence (AI) in medical field: an overview. Current Medicine Research and Practice 2019;9(6):231–7.

[4] Van Noorden R, Perkel JM. AI and science: what 1,600 researchers think. Nature 2023;621(7980):672–5.

[5] Jagtap R, Bayrakdar SK, Orhan K. Advantages, disadvantages, and limitations of AI in dental health. In: Orhan K, Jagtap R, editors. Artificial intelligence in dentistry. Cham: Springer International Publishing; 2023. p. 235–46.

[6] Lo YC, Rensi SE, Torng W, Altman RB. Machine learning in chemoinformatics and drug discovery. Drug Discovery Today 2018;23(8):1538–46.

[7] Gilvary C, Madhukar N, Elkhader J, Elemento O. The missing pieces of artificial intelligence in medicine. Trends in Pharmacological Sciences 2019;40(8):555–64.

[8] Fransen K.A., Av-Ron S.H., Buchanan T.R., Walsh D.J., Rota D.T., Van Note L. High-throughput experimentation for discovery of biodegradable polyesters. Proceedings of the National Academy of Sciences 2023;120(23):e2220021120.

[9] Ding H, Wu J, Zhao W, Matinlinna JP, Burrow MF, Tsoi JKH. Artificial intelligence in dentistry—a review. Frontiers in Dental Medicine 2023;4:1085251.

[10] Upadhya R, Kosuri S, Tamasi M, Meyer TA, Atta S, Webb MA, et al. Automation and data-driven design of polymer therapeutics. Advanced Drug Delivery Reviews 2021;171:1–28.
[11] Chen H, Liu Y, Balabani S, Hirayama R, Huang J. Machine learning in predicting printable biomaterial formulations for direct ink writing. Research 2023;6:0197.
[12] Sarker IH. Machine learning: algorithms, real-world applications and research directions. SN Computer Science 2021;2(3):160.
[13] Suwardi A, Wang F, Xue K, Han MY, Teo P, Wang P, et al. Machine learning-driven biomaterials evolution. Adv Mater 2022;34(1):e2102703.
[14] Panteleev J, Gao H, Jia L. Recent applications of machine learning in medicinal chemistry. Bioorganic and Medicinal Chemistry Letters 2018;28(17):2807–15.
[15] Schneider G, Clark DE. Automated de novo drug design: are we nearly there yet? Angewandte Chemie International Edition 2019;58(32):10792–803.
[16] McDonald SM, Augustine EK, Lanners Q, Rudin C, Catherine Brinson L, Becker ML. Applied machine learning as a driver for polymeric biomaterials design. Nature Communications 2023;14(1):4838.
[17] Wnek GE. Structure–property relationships of small organic molecules as a prelude to the teaching of polymer science. Journal of Chemical Education 2017;94(11):1647–54.
[18] Ding H, Yang Y, Li X, Cheung GS-P, Matinlinna JP, Burrow M, et al. A simple AI-enabled method for quantifying bacterial adhesion on dental materials. Biomaterial Investigations in Dentistry 2022;9(1):75–83.
[19] Dong J, Hu S-x. The progress and prospects of neural network research. Information and Control 1997;26(5):360–8.
[20] Xue K, Wang F, Suwardi A, Han M-Y, Teo P, Wang P, et al. Biomaterials by design: harnessing data for future development. Materials Today Bio 2021;12:100165.
[21] Nighojkar A, Zimmermann K, Ateia M, Barbeau B, Mohseni M, Krishnamurthy S, et al. Application of neural network in metal adsorption using biomaterials (BMs): a review. Environmental Science: Advances 2023;2(1):11–38.
[22] Jenkins B, Tanguay A. Handbook of neural computing and neural networks. Boston: MIT Press; 1995.
[23] Wu Y-c, Feng J-w. Development and application of artificial neural network. Wireless Personal Communications 2018;102:1645–56.
[24] Roth JG, Huang MS, Li TL, Feig VR, Jiang Y, Cui B, et al. Advancing models of neural development with biomaterials. Nature Reviews Neuroscience 2021;22(10):593–615.
[25] Mareci D, Suditu GD, Chelariu R, Trincă LC, Curteanu S. Prediction of corrosion resistance of some dental metallic materials applying artificial neural networks. Materials and Corrosion 2016;67(11):1213–9.
[26] Banu PN, Rani SD. Artificial neural network based optimization of prerequisite properties for the design of biocompatible titanium alloys. Computational Materials Science 2018;149:259–66.
[27] Kazemi M, Ahangarani S, Esmailian M, Shanaghi A. Investigating the corrosion performance of Ti-6Al-4V biomaterial alloy with hydroxyapatite coating by artificial neural network. Materials Science and Engineering: B 2022;278:115644.
[28] Sneider A, Kiemen A, Kim JH, Wu P-H, Habibi M, White M, et al. Deep learning identification of stiffness markers in breast cancer. Biomaterials 2022;285:121540.
[29] Ng WL, Chan A, Ong YS, Chua CK. Deep learning for fabrication and maturation of 3D bioprinted tissues and organs. Virtual and Physical Prototyping 2020;15(3):340–58.
[30] Yu C-H, Chen W, Chiang Y-H, Guo K, Moldes ZM, Kaplan DL, et al. End-to-end deep learning model to predict and design secondary structure content of structural proteins. ACS Biomaterials Science and Engineering 2022;8(3):1156–65.

[31] Lan Y, Huang N, Fu Y, Liu K, Zhang H, Li Y, et al. Morphology-based deep learning approach for predicting osteogenic differentiation. Frontiers in Bioengineering and Biotechnology 2022;9:802794.
[32] Segal MR. Machine learning benchmarks and random forest regression. San Francisco: University of California; 2004.
[33] Yadav P. Decision tree in machine learning. Towards Data Science; 2020.
[34] Pattnaik P, Sharma A, Choudhary M, Singh V, Agarwal P, Kukshal V. Role of machine learning in the field of Fiber reinforced polymer composites: a preliminary discussion. Materials Today: Proceedings 2021;44:4703–8.
[35] Chen Y, Lee JKY, Kwong G, Pow EHN, Tsoi JKH. Morphology and fracture behavior of lithium disilicate dental crowns designed by human and knowledge-based AI. Journal of the Mechanical Behavior of Biomedical Materials 2022;131:105256.
[36] Broll A, Goldhacker M, Hahnel S, Rosentritt M. Generative deep learning approaches for the design of dental restorations: a narrative review. Journal of Dentistry 2024;145:104988.
[37] Tsoi JKH. Artificial intelligence—a new wine in an old bottle? British Dental Journal 2023;234(10):751.
[38] Ding H, Cui Z, Maghami E, Chen Y, Matinlinna JP, Pow EHN, et al. Morphology and mechanical performance of dental crown designed by 3D-DCGAN. Dental Materials 2023;39(3):320–32.
[39] Ratner BD. Biomaterials: been there, done that, and evolving into the future. Annual Review of Biomedical Engineering 2019;21:171–91.
[40] Dee KC, Puleo DA, Bizios R. An introduction to tissue-biomaterial interactions. Cellular and Molecular Biology 2004;8:419–25.
[41] Sukaryo SG, Purnama A, Hermawan H. Structure and properties of biomaterials. Biomaterials and medical devices: a perspective from an emerging country. Springer International Publishing; 2016. p. 1–22.
[42] Ratner BD, Hoffman AS, Schoen FJ, Lemons JE. Biomaterials science: an introduction to materials in medicine. MRS Bulletin 2006;31:59.
[43] Mateu-Sanz M, Fuenteslópez CV, Uribe-Gomez J, Haugen HJ, Pandit A, Ginebra MP Redefining biomaterial biocompatibility: challenges for artificial intelligence and text mining. Trends in Biotechnology 2023;41:1–14. .
[44] Maier WF. Early years of high-throughput experimentation and combinatorial approaches in catalysis and materials science. ACS Combinatorial Science 2019;21(6):437–44.
[45] Marvin HJ, Bouzembrak Y, Janssen EM, van der Zande M, Murphy F, Sheehan B, et al. Application of Bayesian networks for hazard ranking of nanomaterials to support human health risk assessment. Nanotoxicology 2017;11(1):123–33.
[46] Singh AV, Rosenkranz D, Ansari MHD, Singh R, Kanase A, Singh SP, et al. Artificial intelligence and machine learning empower advanced biomedical material design to toxicity prediction. Advanced Intelligent Systems 2020;2(12):2000084.
[47] Mei H, Zhou Y, Liang G, Li Z. Support vector machine applied in QSAR modelling. Chinese Science Bulletin 2005;50:2291–6.
[48] Sampath Kumar TS. Chapter 2—Physical and chemical characterization of biomaterials. In: Bandyopadhyay A, Bose S, editors. Characterization of biomaterials. Oxford: Academic Press; 2013. p. 11–47.
[49] Xu Y, Liu X, Cao X, Huang C, Liu E, Qian S, et al. Artificial intelligence: a powerful paradigm for scientific research. Innovation 2021;2(4):100179.
[50] Mahmood A, Wang J-L. Machine learning for high performance organic solar cells: current scenario and future prospects. Energy and Environmental Science 2021;14(1):90–105.

[51] Correa-Baena J-P, Hippalgaonkar K, van Duren J, Jaffer S, Chandrasekhar VR, Stevanovic V, et al. Accelerating materials development via automation, machine learning, and high-performance computing. Joule 2018;2(8):1410–20.
[52] Liang Y, Chen M, Wang Y, Jia H, Lu T, Xie F, et al. A universal model for accurately predicting the formation energy of inorganic compounds. Science China Materials 2023;66(1):343–51.
[53] Helmus MN. Overview of biomedical materials. MRS Bulletin 1991;16(9):33–8.
[54] Lau ML, Burleigh A, Terry J, Long M. Materials characterization: can artificial intelligence be used to address reproducibility challenges? Journal of Vacuum Science and Technology. A 2023;41(6):061301.
[55] Parida P, Behera A, Mishra SC. Classification of biomaterials used in medicine. International Journal of Advances in Applied Sciences 2012;1:125–9.
[56] Chen Q, Thouas GA. Metallic implant biomaterials. Materials Science and Engineering: R: Reports 2015;87:1–57.
[57] Shi L, Liang P, Chang Q, Song E. Application of machine learning in key properties of medical metal materials. Chinese Journal of Tissue Engineering Research 2024;28(17):2766.
[58] Dijmărescu M-R, Abaza BF, Voiculescu I, Dijmărescu M-C, Ciocan I. Surface roughness analysis and prediction with an artificial neural network model for dry milling of Co–Cr biomedical alloys. Materials 2021;14(21):6361.
[59] Zou C, Li J, Wang WY, Zhang Y, Lin D, Yuan R, et al. Integrating data mining and machine learning to discover high-strength ductile titanium alloys. Acta Materialia 2021;202:211–21.
[60] Guo Y, Sun M, Zhang W, Wang L. Machine learning in enhancing corrosion resistance of magnesium alloys: a comprehensive review. Metals 2023;13(10):1790.
[61] Li N, Zhao S, Zhang Z. Property prediction of medical magnesium alloy based on machine learning. 6th international conference on big data analytics (ICBDA): IEEE2021. IEEE; 2021. p. 51–5.
[62] Koons GL, Diba M, Mikos AG. Materials design for bone-tissue engineering. Nature Reviews Materials 2020;5(8):584–603.
[63] Pjetursson BE, Valente NA, Strasding M, Zwahlen M, Liu S, Sailer I. A systematic review of the survival and complication rates of zirconia-ceramic and metal-ceramic single crowns. Clinical Oral Implants Research 2018;29:199–214.
[64] Luo F, Hong G, Wan Q. Artificial intelligence in biomedical applications of zirconia. Frontiers in Dental Medicine 2021;2:689288.
[65] Lerner H, Mouhyi J, Admakin O, Mangano F. Artificial intelligence in fixed implant prosthodontics: a retrospective study of 106 implant-supported monolithic zirconia crowns inserted in the posterior jaws of 90 patients. BMC Oral Health 2020;20:1–16.
[66] Li H, Lai L, Chen L, Lu C, Cai Q. The prediction in computer color matching of dentistry based on GA+ BP neural network. Computational and Mathematical Methods in Medicine 2015;2015:816719.
[67] Arif S, Alam MT, Ansari AH, Shaikh MBN, Siddiqui MA. Analysis of tribological behaviour of zirconia reinforced Al-SiC hybrid composites using statistical and artificial neural network technique. Materials Research Express 2018;5(5):056506.
[68] Horikawa S, Suzuki K, Motojima K, Nakano K, Nagaya M, Nagashima H, et al. Material design of porous hydroxyapatite ceramics via inverse analysis of an estimation model for bone-forming ability based on machine learning and experimental validation of biological hard tissue responses. Materials 2024;17(3):571.
[69] Cencer MM, Moore JS, Assary RS. Machine learning for polymeric materials: an introduction. Polymer International 2022;71(5):537–42.

[70] Kuenneth C, Rajan AC, Tran H, Chen L, Kim C, Ramprasad R. Polymer informatics with multi-task learning. Patterns 2021;2(4):100238.
[71] Lundstedt T, Seifert E, Abramo L, Thelin B, Nyström Å, Pettersen J, et al. Experimental design and optimization. Chemometrics and Intelligent Laboratory Systems 1998;42(1-2):3–40.
[72] Nguyen D, Tao L, Li Y. Integration of machine learning and coarse-grained molecular simulations for polymer materials: physical understandings and molecular design. Frontiers in Chemistry 2022;9:820417.
[73] Gong JY, Holt MG, Hoet PHM, Ghosh M. Neurotoxicity of four frequently used nanoparticles: a systematic review to reveal the missing data. Archives of Toxicology 2022;96(5):1141–212.
[74] Gong D, Ben-Akiva E, Singh A, Yamagata H, Est-Witte S, Shade JK, et al. Machine learning guided structure function predictions enable in silico nanoparticle screening for polymeric gene delivery. Acta Biomaterialia 2022;154:349–58.
[75] Tamasi MJ, Patel RA, Borca CH, Kosuri S, Mugnier H, Upadhya R, et al. Machine learning on a robotic platform for the design of polymer-protein hybrids. Adv Mater 2022;34(30):e2201809.
[76] Malashin IP, Tynchenko VS, Nelyub VA, Borodulin AS, Gantimurov AP. Estimation and prediction of the polymers' physical characteristics using the machine learning models. Polymers (Basel) 2023;16(1):115.
[77] Rickert CA, Hayta EN, Selle DM, Kouroudis I, Harth M, Gagliardi A, et al. Machine learning approach to analyze the surface properties of biological materials. ACS Biomaterials Science and Engineering 2021;7(9):4614–25.
[78] Puppi D, Chiellini F. Biodegradable polymers for biomedical additive manufacturing. Applied Materials Today 2020;20:100700.
[79] Lai W-F, Huang E, Lui K-H. Alginate-based complex fibers with the Janus morphology for controlled release of co-delivered drugs. Asian Journal of Pharmaceutical Sciences 2021;16(1):77–85.
[80] Bahador F, Foroutan R, Esmaeili H, Ramavandi B. Enhancement of the chromium removal behavior of Moringa oleifera activated carbon by chitosan and iron oxide nanoparticles from water. Carbohydrate Polymers 2021;251:117085.
[81] Yamawaki R, Tei A, Ito K, Kikuchi J. Decomposition factor analysis based on virtual experiments throughout Bayesian optimization for compost-degradable polymers. Applied Sciences 2021;11(6):2820.
[82] Ho SY-C, Chien T-W, Lin M-L, Tsai K-T. An app for predicting patient dementia classes using convolutional neural networks (CNN) and artificial neural networks (ANN): comparison of prediction accuracy in Microsoft Excel. Medicine 2023;102(4):e32670.
[83] Gu GX, Chen C-T, Richmond DJ, Buehler MJ. Bioinspired hierarchical composite design using machine learning: simulation, additive manufacturing, and experiment. Materials Horizons 2018;5(5):939–45.
[84] Yamaguchi S, Lee C, Karaer O, Ban S, Mine A, Imazato S. Predicting the debonding of CAD/CAM composite resin crowns with AI. Journal of Dental Research 2019;98(11):1234–8.
[85] Shokrollahi Y, Dong P, Gamage PT, Patrawalla N, Kishore V, Mozafari H, et al. Finite element-based machine learning model for predicting the mechanical properties of composite hydrogels. Applied Sciences 2022;12(21):10835.
[86] Gu GX, Chen C-T, Buehler MJ. De novo composite design based on machine learning algorithm. Extreme Mechanics Letters 2018;18:19–28.
[87] Alanazi HO, Abdullah AH, Qureshi KN. A critical review for developing accurate and dynamic predictive models using machine learning methods in medicine and health care. Journal of Medical Systems 2017;41:1–10.

[88] Houfani D, Slatnia S, Kazar O, Saouli H, Merizig A. Artificial intelligence in healthcare: a review on predicting clinical needs. International Journal of Healthcare Management 2022;15(3):267–75.
[89] Miller DD, Brown EW. Artificial intelligence in medical practice: the question to the answer? The American Journal of Medicine 2018;131(2):129–33.
[90] Jagtap R, Bayrakdar IS, Orhan K. Artificial intelligence in temporomandibular joint disorders. In: Orhan K, Jagtap R, editors. Artificial intelligence in dentistry. Cham: Springer International Publishing; 2023. p. 187–202.
[91] Bayrakdar IS, Orhan K, Jagtap R. Artificial intelligence in dental education. In: Orhan K, Jagtap R, editors. Artificial intelligence in dentistry. Cham: Springer International Publishing; 2023. p. 223–34.
[92] Kurt-Bayrakdar S, Orhan K, Jagtap R. Outlook for AI in oral surgery and periodontics. In: Orhan K, Jagtap R, editors. Artificial Intelligence in Dentistry. Cham: Springer International Publishing; 2023. p. 97–130.
[93] Siegel RL, Miller KD, Jemal A. R cancer statistics. CA: A Cancer Journal for Clinicians 2020;70(1):7–30.
[94] Chen ZH, Lin L, Wu CF, Li CF, Xu RH, Sun Y. Artificial intelligence for assisting cancer diagnosis and treatment in the era of precision medicine. Cancer Communications 2021;41(11):1100–15.
[95] Liao J, Li X, Gan Y, Han S, Rong P, Wang W, et al. Artificial intelligence assists precision medicine in cancer treatment. Frontiers in Oncology 2023;12:998222.
[96] Ito Y, Miyoshi A, Ueda Y, Tanaka Y, Nakae R, Morimoto A. An artificial intelligence-assisted diagnostic system improves the accuracy of image diagnosis of uterine cervical lesions. Molecular and Clinical Oncology 2021;16:27.
[97] Sierra I, Díaz-Díaz N, Barranco C, Carrasco-Villalón R. Artificial intelligence-assisted diagnosis for early intervention patients. Applied Sciences 2022;12(18):8953.
[98] Luo N, Zhong X, Su L, Cheng Z, Ma W, Hao P. Artificial intelligence-assisted dermatology diagnosis: from unimodal to multimodal. Computers in Biology and Medicine 2023;2023:107413.
[99] Xue Y, Chen C, Tan R, Zhang J, Fang Q, Jin R, et al. Artificial intelligence-assisted bioinformatics, microneedle, and diabetic wound healing: a "new deal" of an old drug. ACS Applied Materials and Interfaces 2022;14(33):37396–409.
[100] Li J, Wu J, Zhao Z, Zhang Q, Shao J, Wang C, et al. Artificial intelligence-assisted decision making for prognosis and drug efficacy prediction in lung cancer patients: a narrative review. Journal of Thoracic Disease 2021;13(12):7021.
[101] Wojtara M, Rana E, Rahman T, Khanna P, Singh H. Artificial intelligence in rare disease diagnosis and treatment. Clinical and Translational Science 2023;16(11):2106–11.
[102] Ghasemi F, Mehridehnavi A, Pérez-Garrido A, Pérez-Sánchez H. Neural network and deep-learning algorithms used in QSAR studies: merits and drawbacks. Drug Discovery Today 2018;23(10):1784–90.
[103] Orhan K, Gülbeş MM, Jadhav A, Jagtap R. Medico-legal problems of artificial intelligence. In: Orhan K, Jagtap R, editors. Artificial intelligence in dentistry. Cham: Springer International Publishing; 2023. p. 259–82.
[104] Zhang H, Zhang L, Jiang Y. Overfitting and underfitting analysis for deep learning based end-to-end communication systems. 11th International Conference on Wireless Communications and Signal Processing (WCSP). IEEE; 2019. p. 1–6.
[105] Ghasemian A, Hosseinmardi H, Clauset A. Evaluating overfit and underfit in models of network community structure. IEEE Transactions on Knowledge and Data Engineering 2019;32(9):1722–35.

[106] Volk MJ, Lourentzou I, Mishra S, Vo LT, Zhai C, Zhao H. Biosystems design by machine learning. ACS Synthetic Biology 2020;9(7):1514–33.
[107] Xu C, Jackson SA. Machine learning and complex biological data. Springer; 2019. p. 1–4.
[108] Hunckler MD, Levine AD. Navigating ethical challenges in the development and translation of biomaterials research. Frontiers in Bioengineering and Biotechnology 2022;10:949280.
[109] Rajitha A, Kansal L, Raj G, Kalra R, Dhamija K, Abdul-Zahra DS. Biomaterials and artificial intelligence: predictive modeling and design. E3S Web of Conferences 2024. EDP Sciences; 2024. p. 01003.
[110] Hopkins A, Booth S. Machine learning practices outside big tech: how resource constraints challenge responsible development. Proceedings of the 2021 AAAI/ACM conference on AI, ethics, and society. 2021. p. 134–45.
[111] Chen D, Sarkar S, Candia J, Florczyk SJ, Bodhak S, Driscoll MK, et al. Machine learning based methodology to identify cell shape phenotypes associated with microenvironmental cues. Biomaterials 2016;104:104–18.

# Artificial intelligence in drug delivery system development

**8**

*Seyed Mohammad Ayyoubzadeh*[1,2], *Bahareh Alizadeh*[3], *Kamyar Davarikia*[4], *Soroush Heydari*[1], *and Mahnaz Ahmadi*[5]

[1]Department of Health Information Management and Medical Informatics, School of Allied Medical Sciences, Tehran University of Medical Sciences, Tehran, Iran, [2]Health Information Management Research Center, Tehran University of Medical Sciences, Tehran, Iran, [3]Protein Technology Research Center, Shahid Beheshti University of Medical Sciences, Tehran, Iran, [4]Department of Pharmaceutics and Pharmaceutical Nanotechnology, School of Pharmacy, Shahid Beheshti University of Medical Sciences, Tehran, Iran, [5]Department of Tissue Engineering and Applied Cell Sciences, School of Advanced Technologies in Medicine, Shahid Beheshti University of Medical Sciences, Tehran, Iran

## 8.1 Introduction

A bioactive molecule could be a substance intended for use in the diagnosis, treatment, or prevention of disease. The efficacy and potency of a bioactive molecule that is administered, deeply rely on its prolonged presence at the desired site. The availability and retention time of the molecule is influenced by various intrinsic factors such as solubility, pKa, affinity for the receptor, size, and molecular weight [1–4]. These characteristics significantly impact the molecule's ability to pass through the cell membrane and exert its biological activity in the target cell. In addition, external factors like the physiological state of the recipient organism, enzymatic processes, and the surrounding pH can render the drug susceptible to inactivation or degradation. These interactions may affect the performance of a drug or lead to unexpected responses [5,6].

For a bioactive molecule to effectively make its therapeutic effect, it must overcome any unfavorable conditions and reach its intended target. The challenge of drug delivery lies in achieving the timely and controlled release of the drug agents, typically to a specific target site, safely and consistently. To accomplish this objective, innovative drug delivery systems (DDSs) have been developed, enabling the efficient transportation of pharmaceutical compounds throughout the body for controlled release [7]. By enclosing the molecules within a structure reminiscent of a shell, potential disturbances to the active compound by physical-chemical or enzymatic factors are minimized. This not only improves the effectiveness of the active compound but also decreases unwanted side effects associated with non-targeted distribution in the body [8].

There are various types of DDSs for different routes of administration. These DDSs include nano-scaled DDSs (e.g., polymeric nanoparticles, metallic nanoparticles, and liposome), implantable DDSs, microelectromechanical systems (MEMS), drug-loaded contact lenses, micropumps, and microneedle and transdermal patches [9,10].

**Artificial Intelligence in Biomaterials Design and Development. DOI:** https://doi.org/10.1016/B978-0-323-95464-8.00004-9

Nanomedicine involves the creative utilization of materials at a nanometer scale to formulate novel DDSs. At such a scale, nano-based carriers exhibit distinct physicochemical properties owing to their small size, surface structure, and substantial surface area. These characteristics enable nanoparticulate systems to surpass existing constraints of conventional formulations by enhancing intracellular uptake to specific cellular targets. As a result, nanotechnology has found applications in various domains, including drug/gene delivery, imaging, and diagnostics [11].

The physical and chemical properties of DDSs play a crucial role in effective drug delivery. Nevertheless, achieving the ideal DDSs is a complex task. Enhancing the compatibility between the DDSs and drugs can be facilitated through the use of artificial intelligence (AI) and computational methods to predict various characteristics such as size, toxicity, drug loading, and stability [12,13]. The AI tools play a significant role in developing intelligent DDSs that have the potential to overcome the constraints associated with traditional treatment approaches [14]. Incorporating AI techniques in the design, development, and evaluation of DDSs can minimize reliance on experimental methods, resulting in a more cost-effective approach and accelerated processes [15].

This chapter aims to examine how AI tools could be utilized in the development of DDSs. To achieve this, the chapter begins by introducing different types of DDSs. It then proceeds to explain the AI techniques. Subsequently, it delves into the application of AI techniques in the design, manufacturing, and assessment of their characteristics, as well as evaluating the performance of DDSs in diagnosis and treatment. Finally, it is completed by discussing the challenges, potential future prospects, and conclusion.

## 8.2 Drug delivery systems

The term “drug delivery” refers to the method or process by which pharmaceuticals, such as drugs, antibodies, vaccines, peptides, and enzymes, are administered to animals or humans to achieve the desired therapeutic effect [16]. Precise and accurate drug delivery, as well as the associated technology, have consistently posed difficulties and obstacles within the realm of pharmaceutical research [17]. As the inception of medical application systems, to treat a wide range of diseases, several drugs are now administered via conventional dosage form, including but not limited to powders, solutions, suspensions, pastes, creams, ointments, suppositories, injectables, tablets, and capsules [18].

During the early 1900s, a transition emerged from the conventional utilization of herbal treatments, which was prevalent during the “age of botanicals,” toward a contemporary methodology influenced by advancements in synthetic chemistry [19]. The controlled-release formulation of a pharmaceutical compound and the creation of numerous controlled-release formulations for clinical use that could be administered orally or transdermally were initially granted approval in the 1950s and have subsequently garnered substantial interest owing to its notable benefits in comparison to traditional medication formulations [20]. Traditional DDSs are incapable of delivering the drug to the intended site of action to mitigate undesirable toxicity and deliver the optimal dose of the drug, both of which are necessary for the drug to exert its intended pharmacological effect. The optimal scenario involves the direct delivery of the medicine to its intended cell, tissue, or organ at the desired concentrations. Numerous pharmaceutical formulations have been developed that utilize DDSs to administer precise drug doses to specific sites, hence facilitating the desired pharmacological effect [21]. Since the 1960s, when liposomes were initially introduced as potential carriers for proteins and drugs in disease treatment, a wide range of devices and nanomaterials have emerged gradually as delivery systems to enhance the effectiveness of therapeutic approaches (Fig. 8.1) [22].

There are multiple types of DDSs, such as the microneedle patch, controlled-release implant, inhalable device, wound dressing, microparticle depot, transdermal patch, drug-loaded contact lens, and nano-scaled DDSs [10]. Among these types of DDSs, nano-based systems or nanocarriers have shown great promise as delivery systems for small and large diagnostic and therapeutic molecules, due to their significant advantages [23].

The utilization of nano-based DDSs has the potential to enhance the solubility and distribution of drugs in different tissues and organs. It can also facilitate the achievement of regulated or sustained release profiles, as well as facilitate the aggregation of drug molecules at specific sites of action [24]. The term "nanotechnology" was first coined by Taniguchi in 1974, but its fundamental principles were established by Nobel laureate Richard Feynman in his famous lecture "There's Plenty of Room at the Bottom" on December 29, 1959. Nanotechnology involves the intentional manipulation, reduction, and fabrication

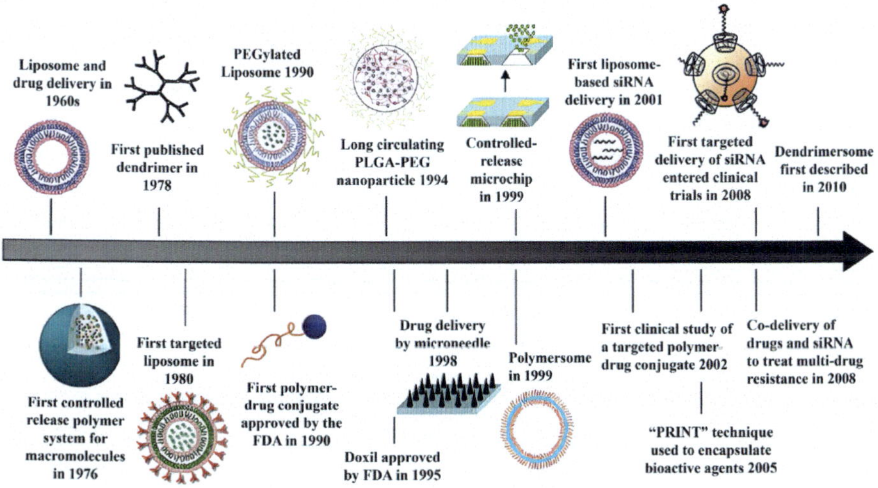


**Figure 8.1** Timeline of key developments in drug delivery and nanoparticle technology from the 1960s to 2010. It highlights major milestones such as the introduction of liposomes, dendrimers, PEGylated liposomes, controlled-release systems, targeted delivery methods, and various nanoparticle formulations. The timeline illustrates the evolution of drug delivery systems, from simple liposomes to more complex and targeted nanoparticles used in modern medicine. Reprinted with permission from [22] Copyright (2010) American Chemical Society.

of materials at the nanoscale, typically ranging from 1 to 100 nm. These materials exhibit distinctive characteristics such as improved stability, exceptional strength, cost-effectiveness, compatibility with the human body, precise and targeted delivery, and more. The significant variations in the chemical and physical properties of nanoparticles (NPs) can primarily be attributed to their high surface-to-volume ratio and their small sizes. The utilization of NPs as effective DDSs for the diagnosis and treatment of various diseases is significant due to their improved ability to be absorbed by the body, controlled and sustained release of drugs, prolonged circulation within the body, high drug-loading capacity, enhanced penetration into cells, and targeted delivery to particular organs or sites. In addition, NPs provide a protective platform to the active ingredient in pH variation, moisture, and enzymes in the body. Moreover, they provide versatility in terms of administration routes, including injection, oral consumption, nasal application, and intraocular usage, among others. These characteristics collectively underline the importance of harnessing the potential of NPs as powerful DDSs [25].

### 8.2.1 Nano-based drug delivery systems

Nano-drug delivery systems (NDDSs) are an exceptional and ever-evolving nanomedical technique [26]. The utilization of nanotechnology to manipulate the properties of polymers and fabricate nanostructures enables the development of enhanced DDSs that are effective in the treatment and management of a wide range of diseases. A wide range of substances can be utilized to compose NPs, including polymers, liposomes, proteins, polysaccharides, and more [27].

There exists a variety of NPs and nanocarriers that can be utilized as drug-delivery carriers. Lipid-based nanocarriers typically have a spherical morphology and consist of a lipid bilayer that encapsulates an aqueous phase. These nanocarriers encompass various forms, including liposomes, lipid NPs, and nano-emulsions. Polymeric nanocarriers encompass a variety of structures, such as dendrimers and polymer micelles. Inorganic NPs containing metallic NPs have demonstrated potential as nanocarriers for drug delivery due to their specific applications and compatibility with medical imaging [28]. The different types of nanomaterials, including organic and inorganic, are provided in Fig. 8.2.

#### 8.2.1.1 Organic nanocarriers

Organic nanocarriers encompass a variety of NPs, including liposomes, solid lipid nanocarriers, dendrimers, polymeric NPs, and micelles. The organic nanocarriers exhibit a high degree of versatility, demonstrating reduced toxicity and the capacity to bind various pharmaceuticals and ligands for the purpose of drug delivery [30]. Micelles and liposomes, among organic nanocarriers, have the capacity to accumulate at the intended site due to their enhanced permeability and retention (EPR) effect [31]. As simple excipients, liposomes and polymeric nanomaterials are the first generation of nano-based DDSs [32]. Types of organic nanomaterials will be elucidated as follows.

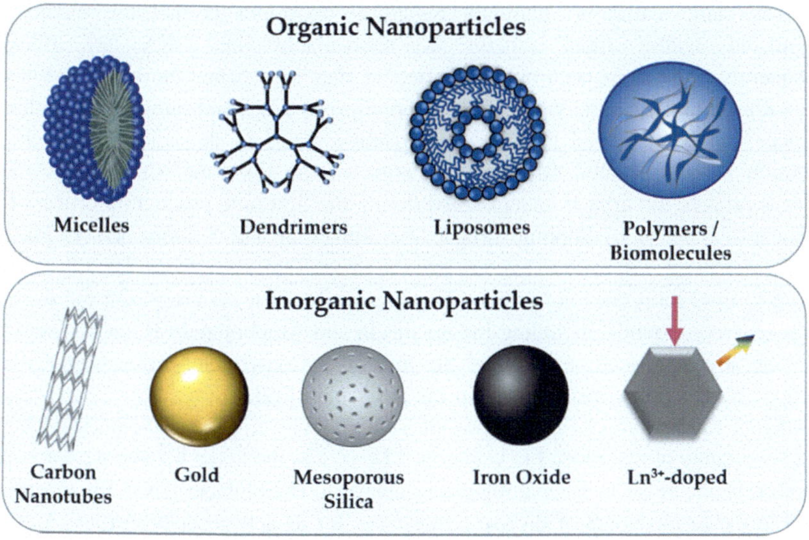


**Figure 8.2** Various types of organic and inorganic nanoparticles. The top row shows organic nanoparticles including micelles, dendrimers, liposomes, and polymers/biomolecules. The bottom row depicts inorganic nanoparticles such as carbon nanotubes, gold nanoparticles, mesoporous silica, iron oxide nanoparticles, and lanthanide-doped nanoparticles. Each type is represented by a simplified diagram or illustration showcasing its typical structure or appearance.
Reprinted with permission from [29].

## Liposomes

Liposomes are one of the most studied DDSs that are utilized in the pharmaceutical and cosmetics industries to transport a variety of compounds. Liposomes are a well-known type of formulation utilized to enhance drug delivery. The term is derived from two Greek etymological roots, namely "lipo" meaning fat, and "soma" meaning body. Liposomes are synthetic vesicles that are formed through the self-assembly of amphiphilic phospholipids. The vesicles are composed of a spherical bilayer architecture surrounding an aqueous core domain. These are regarded as superior drug delivery vehicles due to their membrane structure resembling that of cells and their ability to facilitate drug incorporation [33]. Liposomes possess desirable biological characteristics, such as overall biocompatibility, biodegradability, the capacity to shield pharmaceuticals from their external surroundings, and the capability to encapsulate both hydrophilic and hydrophobic medications [34]. In addition to their intrinsic biocompatibility with the human body, these entities' surfaces can be modified and functionalized to facilitate attachment with targeting moieties. This modification allows for specific targeting of particular sites, thereby enhancing both effectiveness and potency [35]. Liposomes are commonly employed for loading water-soluble substances due to their composition, which consists of a lipid bilayer that separates an internal aqueous part from the surrounding aqueous phase [36]. Liposomes are divided into four types, including, conventional liposomes, PEGylated liposomes, ligand-targeted liposomes, and theranostic liposomes [37].

An important feature to highlight regarding liposomes is that the medications encapsulated within them remain non-bioavailable until they are released. Consequently, they must accumulate at specific sites to enhance the bioavailability of drugs within the therapeutic window at the appropriate times and rates. Drug loading in liposomes can be achieved in active and passive ways. In the active approach, the medication is encapsulated after the formation of the liposome. Conversely, in the passive approach, the drug is encapsulated during the liposome production process [38]. The encapsulation of hydrophilic drugs, like ampicillin and 5-fluoro-deoxyuridine, is generally achieved within the aqueous interior of the liposome. Consequently, altering the drug-to-lipid ratio does not affect the encapsulation of these drugs. On the contrary, hydrophobic compounds, including Indomethacin and Amphotericin B, were discovered within the acyl hydrocarbon chain of the liposome. Consequently, their absorption is influenced by the properties inherent in the acyl chain [39].

Numerous formulations based on liposomes are presently employed in clinical settings to treat a wide range of disorders. FDA-approved Doxil was the initial liposome-encapsulated chemotherapeutic agent to receive regulatory approval. Doxorubicin (DOX) is extensively utilized in the management of diverse tumor types for its anticancer properties. As it is a toxic material that impacts tumor tissue, the heart and kidney tissues, and its therapeutic applications are severely restricted. The advancement of DOX encapsulated within liposomes resulted in the creation of a validated nanomedical DDS. The development of this innovative liposomal formulation has led to a decrease in DOX delivery to the cardiovascular and renal systems but an increase in its accumulation in tumor tissue by the EPR effect [40]. Other liposomal formulations, including Myocet, Onivyde, and Daunoxome, have since been approved for the purpose of cancer treatment. Additionally, liposomes are utilized for vaccine delivery for many diseases. The Covid-19 mRNA vaccines, for instance, are administered via liposomes [41]. In addition, there are liposomal vaccinations for shingles (Shringrix), hepatitis (Epaxal), influenza (Inflexal), etc. [42].

### Solid lipid nanoparticles and nanostructured lipid carriers

Solid lipid nanocarriers (SLNs) have been employed since the early 1990s as viable vehicles for the delivery of lipophilic substances [43,44]. The spherical morphology of SLN renders them optimal choices for encapsulating lipophilic bioactive compounds. Solid lipids in various forms, such as free fatty alcohols or acids, steroids, and mono-, di-, or triglycerides, are frequently employed in the formulation of SLNs [45]. The incorporation of drug molecules into the SLNs may occur in the matrix, shell, or core, depending upon the production conditions and composition. SLN is distinguished by its favorable physical stability, controlled drug release, protection against degradation of incorporated pharmaceuticals, and tolerability. The primary benefit of SLN is its comparatively inexpensive fabrication cost, which provides the opportunity to expand production [6]. Furthermore, certain drawbacks have been noted, including drug expulsion during crystallization, a relatively high water content of the dispersions, and a poor loading capacity that is restricted by the drug's solubility in the lipid as well as the structure and polymorphism state of the lipid matrix [46]. To overcome the limitations of conventional SLNs, certain new-generation nanocarriers have been developed, including lipid-drug conjugates (LDCs), and nanostructured lipid carriers (NLCs). LDCs were designed to increase the capability of lipid-based carriers to transport lipophobic medicinal molecules. It is possible to produce these insoluble drug-lipid conjugates via salt formation or covalent linking followed by homogenization [47]. NLCs are generated through the combination of solid and liquid lipids, resulting in the formation of a unique nanostructure that enhances payload capacity and inhibits drug expulsion [45].

Numerous studies have been conducted on solid lipid nanocarriers to transport nucleic acids and genes [48], treating ophthalmic diseases, facilitating the controlled release of active agents [44], and delivering targeted antitumor drugs [49,50]. They have been utilized in the cosmetic industry to incorporate sunscreen UV blockers, including vitamin E, 2-hydroxy-4-methoxybenzophenone, and 3,4,5-trimethoxybenzoylchitin [51].

## Hydrogel

In recent times, there has been a significant focus on hydrogel NPs as a highly promising drug delivery strategy at the nanoscale. This emphasis is mostly due to the unique characteristics exhibited by hydrogel NPs. Hydrogels are hydrophilic, three-dimensional polymeric networks that have the ability to absorb substantial quantities of water or biological fluids. The thermodynamic compatibility of hydrogels with water enables them to undergo swelling when exposed to aqueous environments [52]. The mechanical stability of hydrogels, network structure, permeability, and swelling characteristics can be manipulated via physiological parameters or external stimuli [53,54]. Extensive research has been conducted on hydrogels in the areas of stimuli-responsive release, controlled therapeutic release, and biological implant applications [55,56]. However, for therapeutic applications, the hydration response to changes in stimuli in the majority of hydrogel systems is too fatigued. Additional research and advancements in hydrogel structures at the micro and nanoscale are required to surmount this constraint. Ding et al. established the feasibility of implanting and plastering cisplatin-loaded polyacrylic acid hydrogel NPs onto tumor tissue [57]. The hydrogel system demonstrated exceptional effectiveness in inhibiting the development of tumors and extending the lifespan of mice. To create a multifunctional hybrid hydrogel, the magnetic properties of NPs were combined with normal hydrogel characteristics. Hybrid hydrogels can transport many medications to the target place using an external magnetic field [58]. Although pharmaceuticals containing hydrogel NPs are not presently available in the market, their potential for future advancements as DDSs is considerable due to their exceptional biocompatibility and efficacy in loading drugs.

## Protein nanoparticles

Natural biomolecules like proteins are an appealing alternative to synthetic biomolecules, which are frequently utilized in drug formulations, due to their safety. Overall, protein NPs provide several benefits, including high biocompatibility and biodegradability. In addition, because of their well-defined primary structure, protein-based NPs offer multiple opportunities for surface modifications, such as covalently attaching drugs and targeting ligands. Protein-based NPs have been effectively synthesized from different types of proteins, including those that are soluble in water (such as bovine and human serum albumin) and those that are not soluble (such as zein and gliadin) [59].

## Polymeric nanoparticles

Polymers that are both biodegradable and non-biodegradable are used to create polymeric nanoparticles (PNPs) [60]. The synthesis of PNPs involves dissolving, entrapping, absorbing, and encapsulating drugs inside a matrix of NPs [61]. PNPs consist of solid colloidal particles (10–100 nm), exhibiting various morphologies such as branching, spherical, or shell shapes.

PNPs are frequently classified into two distinct categories:

- **Nanospheres**
  Nanospheres typically consist of a solid polymer matrix that contains active chemicals, which are either spread heterogeneously or dissolved at a molecular level.
- **Nanocapsules**
  Nanocapsules are composed of a core–shell structure, in which the substance is predominantly contained within the core and a polymeric shell envelops it.

Non-ionic surfactants are commonly used as a coating on PNPs to mitigate immunological interactions and intermolecular interactions among the surface chemical groups of PNPs [62]. The process of incorporating drugs into NPs can be achieved by several methods, including attachment, entrapment, adsorption, or encapsulation. These NPs offer the advantage of sustained drug release over extended durations, ranging from days to weeks [60]. Vaccine preparation utilizing PNPs improves immunization, prevents vaccine degradation, and increases immune cell absorption (the extent to which this is dependent on the type of polymer employed). To immobilize drugs in NPs, various techniques are used, including poly (ε-caprolactone) and poly (lactide-co-glycolide) (PLGA) [63]. A substantial group of researchers demonstrated that conventional chemotherapeutic drugs such as DOX, PTX, docetaxel, and cisplatin encapsulated in polymeric NPs have greater therapeutic value than unbound drugs [64]. Furthermore, to enhance the specificity of targeted drug delivery and circumvent the multidrug resistance of cancer cells, surface functionalization of PNPs with small molecule ligands (e.g., biotin and folic acid), proteins (e.g., albumin and transferrin), small peptides (e.g., Arginylglycylaspartic acid (RGD); [65]), short nucleic acid aptamers, antibodies, and carbohydrates (e.g., hyaluronic acid) grants enhanced specificity for targeted drug delivery.

## Polymeric micelles

Polymeric micelles (PMs) are nano-based DDSs containing amphiphilic block copolymers that self-assemble in an aqueous solution which form a core–shell structure. The hydrophobic interior has the capacity to accommodate hydrophobic pharmaceutical compounds, while the hydrophilic exterior renders the entire system water-soluble and provides stability to the interior region. Micelles can penetrate areas of the body that are beyond the reach of liposomes and, due to increased vascular permeability, can accrue a greater quantity of free drugs in tumoral tissues. The micelles' poor drug loading and incorporation stability can lead to drug release before reaching the target site [66,67]. Changing manufacturing parameters and lipid moieties can address these constraints.

### Dendrimers

Based on the Greek term "dendron" (tree), dendrimer-based nanocarriers are extremely branched nano-polymers that are symmetrical in three dimensions. Dendrimers are nanostructures made from macromolecules like polyamidoamine, polypropylene-imine, and poly aryl ether. They are extremely branched with an inner core. These structures can bind various ligands due to their affinity system, resulting in greater diversity and density [68]. Both hydrophobic and hydrophilic drugs have the potential to be integrated within the core or connected to the surface of dendrimers. Dendrimers possess several advantageous attributes, including a consistent molecular weight and a three-dimensional configuration featuring solubility-determining peripheral groups. These features facilitate the design of dendrimers in response to specific requirements. In addition, their molecular volume and hydrodynamic volume are smaller than those of linear polymers with comparable molecular weight [69]. Drug delivery through dendrimers occurs via two primary mechanisms: (1) in vivo degradation of the covalent bonds formed by the drug dendrimer, which is facilitated by the presence of appropriate enzymes or a satisfactory environment that can cleave the bonds, and (2) drug discharge resulting from alterations in the physical environment, like changes in temperature, pH, and so forth [70]. Most dendrimer research has focused on anticancer medication delivery. Conjugated drugs like methotrexate (MTX), docetaxel, doxycycline, and others are hundreds of times more bioavailable. A particular formulation known as **DEP, which combines docetaxel with PEGylated PLL dendrimer, is undergoing clinical trials. Anti-microbial drugs in dendrimer-based nanocarrier systems have improved solubility and bioavailability, boosting therapy efficacy. Nitric oxide-releasing PPI dendrimers killed 99.99% of gram-negative and gram-positive bacteria and methicillin-resistant *Staphylococcus aureus* [68].

## *8.2.1.2 Inorganic nanoparticles*

Inorganic nanocarriers are useful in biosensing, cell labeling, imaging, targeting, and diagnostics. These inorganic nanocarriers have synergistic therapeutic effects [71]. Moreover, altering the composition or dimensions of inorganic nanoparticles can enhance their magnetic and optical functionalities. However, it is important to note that employing heavy metals as inorganic nanocarriers can lead to potential adverse health effects in the long run [72]. Types of inorganic nanomaterials will be described as follows.

### Quantum dots

Semiconductor nanocrystals, commonly referred to as quantum dots (QDs), were discovered in early 1980 [73]. These structures offer a versatile platform for the design and engineering of drug delivery vehicles based on NPs. QDs, which range in size from 2 to 10 nm, exhibit fluorescence properties in response to light stimulation. They emit light 10 to 20 times more intensely than fluorescent proteins [74]. The light emission in the UV-near IR regions is dependent on the size of the quantum dot. Specifically, smaller quantum dots (<2 nm) produce blue fluorescence, while larger quantum dots (<5 nm) emit red fluorescence. QD is composed of a shell (ZnS) and a semiconductor core (CdSe). In addition, it is coated with an aqueous organic coating that permits the conjugation of biomolecules to target diverse biomarkers [75]. QDs have garnered significant attention within the area of nanomedicine. The high surface-to-volume ratio of NPs confers an additional benefit in the field of nanomedicine. Nevertheless, the biocompatibility and potential toxicity of QDs represent a significant concern that must be addressed before their widespread implementation in clinical and biomedical contexts. Various techniques, including the application of antibodies, peptides, or polymers for surface functionalization, as well as the encapsulation within liposomes, have been employed to make use of their potential in the field of theranostics [76]. For example, the attachment of homing tumor peptide to the nucleolin on cancerous cells effectively modified the surface of quantum dots, thereby enhancing their cellular absorption [77]. Conversely, DOX could be delivered selectively to cancer cells that overexpress CD44 via PEG and hyaluronic acid-functionalized QDs [78]. An additional anticancer drug, paclitaxel (PTX), demonstrated enhanced tumor inhibition when co-loaded with quantum dots in lipid nanocarriers (nanostructured lipid carriers loaded with PTX and near-infrared quantum dots for cancer targeting) [79].

## Carbon nanomaterials

Carbon nanomaterials utilized in drug delivery can be classified into three categories:

- ***Carbon nanotubes***
  Carbon nanotubes (CNTs), often referred to as buckytubes, are a type of fullerenes, which are distinct allotropic forms of carbon. CNTs are characterized by their cylindrical structure, comprising a sequence of condensed benzene rings [80]. CNTs are an ideal and prospective means of drug delivery due to their exceptional biological and physicochemical properties. A CNT was initially discovered by Iijima [81]. CNTs possess a distinctive structure resulting from the rolling of individual layers of graphite, either as single-walled carbon nanotubes (SWNCTs) or multiwalled carbon nanotubes (MWCNTs). CNTs possess notable attributes such as biocompatibility, facile transmembrane penetration, exceptionally high aspect ratio, tensile strength, nanosized needle structure, and electrical and thermal conductivity. These properties render CNTs appealing contenders for a wide range of applications, including the delivery of diagnostic and therapeutic agents to cells [82,83]. CNTs can be functionalized with biomolecules, including DNA, peptides, carbohydrates, enzymes, and others via covalent and non-covalent interactions due to their vast surface area, improving their performance and solubility [84]. For targeted drug delivery, functionalized carbon nanotubes are commonly used to encapsulate or link chemotherapy drugs such as PTX, Mitomycin C, DOX, and MTX [85–87].
- ***Carbon nanohorns***
  Carbon nanohorns (CNH) is a conical-tipped, horn-shaped, single-walled tubule [88]. Due to the lack of a metal catalyst in their formation process, these substances can be readily synthesized at a minimal expense and possess exceptional purity [89]. Drugs are immobilized via immobilization or nanoprecipitation on the walls of nanohorns [90]. In comparison to adsorption, nanoprecipitation is more proficient [91]. For example, nanoprecipitation is significantly more effective than adsorption at encapsulating cisplatin molecules in nanohorns (nearly three times as many molecules are entrapped in nanohorns) [91]. Furthermore, carbon nanomaterials' toxicity is determined by their distinct, well-defined geometric structure [92].
- ***Fullerenes***
  They were found in 1985 and are also referred to as "buckyballs" [93]. Fullerenes are carbon allotropes characterized by a polygonal structure and sixty or more carbon atoms.

Buckminsterfullerene, which is most frequently employed for drug delivery to mitochondria across the cell membrane, is the most prevalent form [94]. They stimulate the host system and create fullerene-specific antibodies. This tool can assess fullerene levels in the body for therapeutic or diagnostic purposes. The level of purification of fullerene is a determining factor in its cost, with highly purified fullerenes being more expensive. This financial constraint limits the applicability of fullerene in the medical field [95].

## Silica nanoparticles

Silicon-based mesoporous materials since early 2000 are classified as inorganic nanocarriers that are extensively utilized as drug delivery methods. In conjunction with their biocompatibility, silica nanoparticles (SNPs) are becoming increasingly prevalent in the field of drug delivery due to their substantial surface areas, ease of functional group incorporation, and simple construction. In addition, due to the ability to modify the size and shape of the pores, it becomes feasible to employ them for the delivery of numerous numbers of drugs or genes, thereby preventing premature drug degradation or release. Mesoporous silica nanoparticles, a porous variant of SNPs, offer more benefits in controlling pore size and carrying capacity, allowing for appropriate drug transport capability [96]. Diverse synthesis protocols for fine-tuned large-pore mesoporous nanocarriers were investigated, as was their applicability to the transport of nucleic acids, proteins, enzymes, and antibodies [97]. In the field of cancer treatment, the utilization of mesoporous silica has proven to be effective in implementing both active and passive targeting strategies [98]. An efficient method of delivering anticancer medicines, such as Camptothecin and MTX, involves the utilization of mesoporous silica [99].

## Metal and metal-oxide nanoparticles

The application of metallic NPs has gained increasing attention in several medical applications, including but not limited to bioimaging, biosensors, targeted and sustained drug administration, hyperthermia, and photoablation treatment, in recent years [100,101]. Metallic NPs are categorized as pure metals or their compounds that exist in separate particles with dimensions between 1 and 100 nm in size. By modifying and functionalizing these NPs with particular functional groups, they can bind to antibodies, pharmaceuticals, and other ligands; thus, the biomedical applications of these systems become more promising [102].

- ***Gold nanoparticles***
  Metal NPs, including gold (Au) NPs, have demonstrated potential as scaffolds for drug and gene delivery by serving as a practical adjunct to conventional delivery vehicles. Au NPs are distinguished by their inertness and minimal toxicity [103], straightforward preparation, extremely large surface area, well-established surface functionalization (typically via thiol linkages), and adjustable stability. These characteristics enable the development of novel delivery strategies. The primary objective in the production of gold NPs is to achieve a high level of stability, biocompatibility, and environmental friendliness. One of the primary uses of gold nanocarriers is to efficiently image tumor cells [104]. MTX is a cytotoxic anticancer medication that disrupts cell folate metabolism. Cancer cells may suppress the effects of MTX by reducing folate absorption or outflow. MTX stacked BSA-capped AuNPs are

utilized to inhibit breast MCF-7 cancer cell growth [105]. The utilization of gold NPs that are linked with certain oligonucleotides enables the detection of complementary DNA strands through observable alterations in color [103].

- ***Magnetic nanoparticles***
Magnetic-based drug delivery systems are becoming more popular due to their biocompatibility and versatility. Magnetic nanoparticles (MNPs) consist of materials exhibiting ferromagnetic, paramagnetic, and superparamagnetic properties. MNPs are a useful class of nanocarriers for diagnostic, therapeutic, and clinical applications. The function of these particles extends to the molecular and cellular levels due to their distinctive physicochemical characteristics. The particles consist of a magnetically stimulated core surrounded by a thin layer of stabilizers, which functions as a protective shell [106]. Polymer-coated superparamagnetic iron oxide NPs are commonly utilized as contrast agents in molecular imaging due to their magnetic resonance [107]. Passive targeting of cancer cells is facilitated by the utilization of superparamagnetic iron oxides [108].

## Nanocrystals

Nanocrystals represent an additional nano-based strategy employed for the delivery of pharmaceuticals with low solubility. Nanocrystals, with a dimension of 1000 nm, are composed entirely of solid pharmaceutical particles. Nanocrystals, as opposed to the aforementioned drug delivery platforms, possess several distinctive characteristics. Nanocrystals are colloidal delivery systems devoid of carriers; 100% of the drug is present in nanocrystals, which are stabilized by polymeric surfactants or stabilizers and do not contain any carrier molecules [109]. The synthesis of nanocrystals can be achieved through various techniques, including milling, top-down and bottom-up approaches, antisolvent precipitation, high-pressure homogenization, and precipitation. Energy, time, and financial resources are extensively required for top-down methodologies, such as high-pressure homogenization and milling. A type of nanocrystal was encapsulated within chitosan microparticles by Ni et al. [110] to deliver the hydrophobic drug via the lungs. The NPs were designed to facilitate sustained drug release by capitalizing on the polymer's capacity for expansion and adhesion to mucous membranes. They discovered that inhalation efficacy could be compromised under disease conditions; therefore, additional research is required to demonstrate that this system has greater potential [110].

## Metal-organic frameworks

Metal-organic frameworks (MOFs) are a novel category of porous crystalline materials consisting of metal ions and organic ligands. Nanoscale MOFs (NMOFs), known for their promising attributes, have been extensively employed in various applications, particularly in the biomedical field. NMOFs display exclusive features that make them ideal candidates for drug delivery and bioimaging. These characteristics include large surface area, biocompatibility, biodegradability, structural variety, high porosity, high loading capacity, and ease of functionalization. The utilization of different ligands and metal ions gives rise to a diverse range of compositions and structures, enabling the synthesis of MOF nanosystems with distinct properties. In addition, MOFs offer the advantage of being biodegradable and biocompatible, which are crucial for drug delivery and imaging purposes. Furthermore, their exceedingly high surface area and porosity facilitate the efficient loading of therapeutic and diagnostic agents. The presence of reactive functional groups on MOF surfaces further allows for convenient functionalization and surface modification [111].

## 8.3 Artificial intelligence in drug delivery systems

AI aims to develop machines and systems that can conduct tasks usually requiring human intelligence, including decision-making, visual perception, and language translation. At its core, AI research centers around endowing computers and robots with various mental capabilities resembling humans. This includes the ability to rationally solve complex problems or learn from experience—just as humans do [112]. Specifically, AI techniques allow machines to engage in inductive learning by identifying patterns and correlations in large data sets, just as biological brains learn from lived experiences over time. AI systems can also think deductively, drawing logical conclusions based on stored representations of knowledge. Moreover, AI methods enable machines to self-correct through feedback, improving their "decision-making skills" even in the absence of explicit programming [113]. The most important techniques in the field of AI refer to machine learning (ML). Fig. 8.3 illustrates some of the main algorithms of ML. This technique has a broad range of other approaches such as supervised learning, unsupervised learning, deep learning, and so on [115]. In supervised learning algorithms build a mathematical model by analyzing data that contains both the inputs and the desired outputs. Common supervised learning algorithms include linear regression, logistic regression, decision trees, support vector machines (SVM), k-nearest neighbors, Naive Bayes classifiers, and artificial neural networks (ANN) [114]. While unsupervised learning refers to a category of ML algorithms that analyze datasets containing input data without labeled outcomes. This includes techniques like identifying association rules and grouping data through clustering methods. The key difference lies in the presence or absence of labeled responses in the training data [116]. Deep learning uses multi-layered artificial neural networks to learn representations of data. So, in summary, while all three learn from data, deep learning has unique architectural advantages of depth, auto-encoded representations, discovery of hidden patterns, and end-to-end learning that make it very powerful for complex, real-world problems dealing with massive amounts of raw data [117].

Applications of AI in the medical domain encompass a wide range of possibilities. This rapidly advancing area has the potential to impact various facets of healthcare including diagnostic, therapeutic, screening, preventive and monitoring procedures [118]. Through computer vision techniques, ML algorithms can detect subtle patterns in medical images that may escape human detection, aiding in the identification of diseases and anomalies [119]. AI also enables the identification of populations at elevated risk for prioritized screening and preemptive intervention. Additionally, AI facilitates remote patient surveillance utilizing wearable sensors to collect health data which can then be analyzed to detect alterations in clinical status, foresee deteriorating conditions and potentially preempt adverse outcomes through timely clinical intervention [120]. AI shows promise in advancing personalized medicine and optimizing various aspects of drug development [121]. It can help design

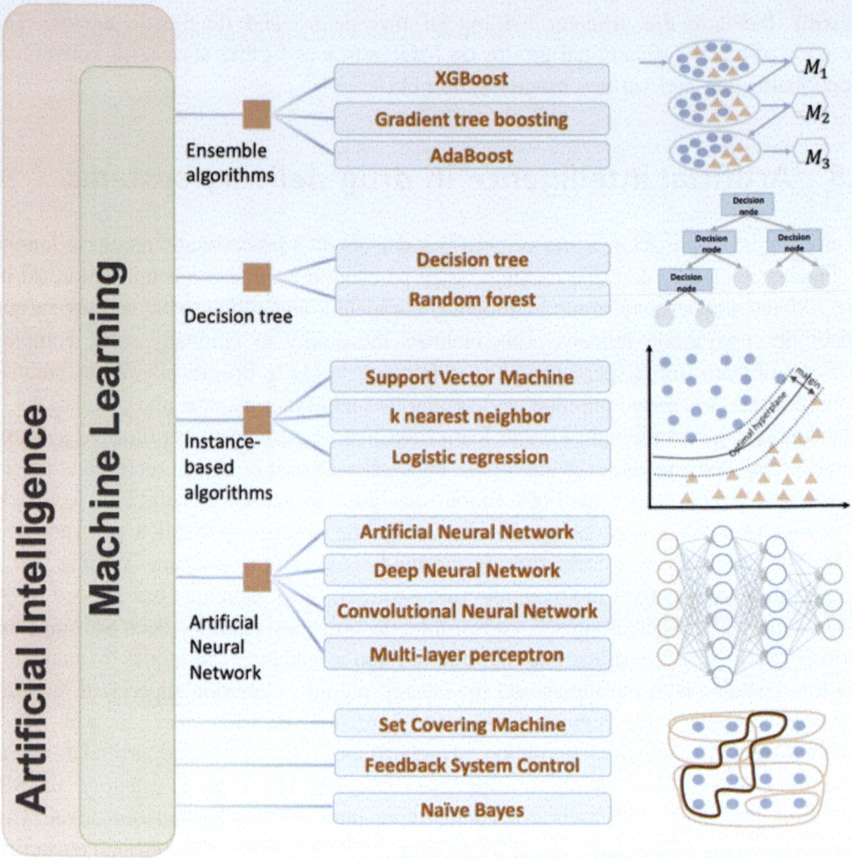


**Figure 8.3** Overview of various Machine Learning algorithms within Artificial Intelligence. It categorizes the algorithms into groups such as Ensemble algorithms, Decision trees, Instance-based algorithms, and Artificial Neural Networks, along with some additional methods. Each category is further broken down into specific techniques, accompanied by simplified visual representations of their core concepts or structures.
Reprinted with permission from [114].

personalized DDSs, predict potential drug–drug interactions, and develop novel targeted drug carriers such as responsive hydrogels and nanoparticles [122]. Monitoring medication adherence is another application where AI and Internet of Things sensors provide alerts by tracking pill-taking through intelligent packaging and wearables [123]. AI also expedites drug discovery by screening vast chemical and biological databases to rapidly identify promising candidates [124]. Lastly, AI strengthens pharmaceutical supply chain operations via applications like demand forecasting, inventory optimization, and counterfeit detection [125].

Using AI in DDS encompasses various aspects such as design, analysis, optimization, and prediction. Nano-based DDSs offer significant advantages, such as targeted delivery, sustained release, and minimal side effects. The provision of knowledge of the biological environment by AI is instrumental in the design of such nanosystems [126]. The integration of AI in various stages of drug delivery design, analysis, formulation development, and optimization of release kinetics is underway [127]. DDSs such as microspheres, liposomes, and nanorobots benefit from AI to optimize formulation parameters and drug loading/release properties. Neural networks are particularly useful in understanding the nonlinear relationships between formulation variables and response properties [128]. AI methods, such as ML are capable of predicting various characteristics of DDSs, such as size, morphology, toxicity, loading capacity, cellular uptake, and drug release. Accurate prediction of polymeric NP size and size distribution based on polymer properties is possible using neural networks [127]. It is also feasible to predict NP morphology using models that analyze SEM/TEM images through deep learning techniques [129]. Predicting the toxicity of NPs using classifiers, such as neural networks and random forests, based on physicochemical properties is possible[130]. The loading capacity/ entrapment efficiency of formulations can be optimized using deep neural networks and regression models. ML is also useful in predicting the cellular uptake of nanoparticles by cancer cells based on nanoparticle structure and properties [131]. ANN models can quantitatively estimate drug release from delivery systems under different conditions [132]. AI can tailor nanoparticles used for diagnosis to achieve targeted delivery based on individual patient profiles obtained from diagnostic patterns. AI models can predict successful delivery based on earlier cell morphologies [133]. It is possible to improve the spatial resolution of magnetic particle imaging for visualizing nanoparticle distribution by fusing dual-sampling convolutional neural networks in a deep learning model [134]. The optimization of DDSs through AI can overcome the challenges of traditional treatments such as low efficiency, toxicity, and the inability to target/cross biological barriers. AI can simulate drug delivery processes to evaluate features and optimize systems without extensive trials, accelerating development timelines, and reducing costs [127]. ML models have accurately predicted antimicrobial resistance profiles of pathogens to aid treatment [135]. The acceleration of hydrogel and nanoparticle-based delivery system development is achievable through AI algorithms, which enhance data understanding and reduce trial-and-error [136].

This brief overview introduces some potential applications of AI in DDSs, and a more detailed discussion of these applications will follow in subsequent sections.

## 8.4 Artificial intelligence in drug delivery system design and fabrication

AI is used in pharmaceutical and DDS development. An optimal DDS is characterized by its ability to provide sustained release of the necessary dosage while adjusting the release rate according to the disease's parameters [137]. Among DDSs, nano-based systems are highly compatible with the development of delivery systems due to their ability to facilitate molecular interactions with proteins and nucleic acids, traverse cellular and subcellular structures, and circumvent immune system activation— thus minimizing the risk of severe side effects.

Human physiology has adapted to effectively address challenges at a microscopic level, such as the efficient elimination of nanosized charged molecules via filtration of the kidneys and immune system and liver circulation, which facilitates the rapid clearance of microparticles [138,139]. This means that the features of "absorption, distribution, metabolism, and excretion" must be carefully thought through while developing a delivery system.

AI could enhance DDS design by providing a deep knowledge of the biological surroundings, which can then be used to nanoengineer pharmaceuticals [140]. Recently, there has been a growing interest in utilizing AI technology to analyze and resolve challenges related to the development of DDSs. The upcoming sections will go into this topic.

In recent years, there has been a significant rise in the digitalization of data in the pharmaceutical industry. However, digitalization presents the challenge of gathering, analyzing, and applying knowledge to solve complicated clinical situations [141]. This encourages the utilization of AI due to its ability to efficiently process vast amounts of data through advanced automation [142]. AI is a networked technological system comprised of a variety of sophisticated tools and components that can simulate human intelligence. Moreover, it does not pose a threat to supplant the physical presence of humans [143,144]. AI employs software and systems capable of interpreting and learning from input data to autonomously make decisions that achieve predetermined goals. An essential part of the AI system, theANN, is a computer modeling algorithm that is loosely inspired by the structure and function of the mammalian brain [145].

Recently, the primary objective of drug delivery technologies has been the development of novel systems for the targeted delivery of active pharmaceuticals to achieve therapeutic advantages without side effects [146]. The development of controlled DDSs has addressed problems of conventional systems, including narrow therapeutic index, systemic toxicity, and prolonged therapy [147]. AI is essential for advancing nano-based delivery systems by providing comprehensive knowledge about the biological environment. The field of pharmaceutics gained advantages from the integration of AI and big data with the creation of computational pharmaceutics, which uses multiscale modeling techniques to improve medication delivery procedures. The utilization of drug formulation and delivery process simulations enables scientists to assess various situations and enhance drug delivery in a manner without costly trial-and-error studies. Effective AI technologies enable researchers to detect risks and obstacles in DDS development early on [148,149]. The utilization of automated workflows, databases, and ANNs can improve treatment outcomes by quickly analyzing large amounts of data. ANNs are used in several stages of drug delivery processes. Fig. 8.4 shows how ANNs can be used in various drug delivery stages. ANNs are utilized in the design, analysis, and prediction of every drug characteristic that influences the delivery process [150].

The use of a computerized system enables the creation of a well-organized model and parameter description, enhancing the effectiveness of literature searches, simulations, and refining processes. Recently, there has been a growing utilization of neural network methods and software providers in evaluating pharmacokinetics and analyzing intricate

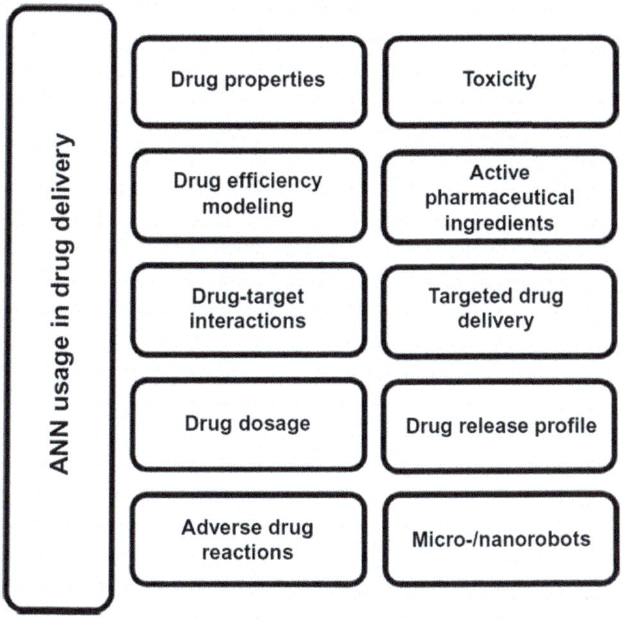


**Figure 8.4** Key applications of Artificial Neural Networks (ANNs) in drug delivery research. It presents ten areas where ANNs are utilized, including drug properties analysis, toxicity assessment, efficiency modeling, and targeted delivery strategies. The diagram highlights the diverse roles of machine learning in pharmaceutical development and optimization. Reprinted with permission from [150].

input variables stemming from drug-drug interactions, and genomic, and chemical databases. Fig. 8.5 illustrates the procedure of in silico simulations for a DDS [151].

Identifying, developing, and characterizing mechanisms in the simulated human environment, such as those governing membrane interactions, could benefit significantly from the application of AI capable of researching and analyzing multilayered data. Presently, one of the most critical methodologies is the intelligent literature search for parameter identification and model comparison, which is typically delegated to the specialized expertise and comprehension of the research units. The implementation of an automated system that possesses the ability to search, simulate, score, and refine the search could significantly enhance the methodical evaluation of models and parameters. Therefore, the capacity to generate a validated hypothesis and systematically enhance it through the utilization of outcomes derived from in silico simulations or experimental trials would constitute a perpetual advancement, facilitating the methodical evaluation and ranking of simulated models [140,152]. The databases of system biology are approaching a point where they may be able to support AI applications by providing reliable data for AI training. At present, there are several instances where neural network applications and software providers have established a robust foundation for the implementation of this technology, such as in the evaluation of pharmacokinetics [14,153].

ANN could be utilized in the pharmaceutical sciences to aid in the development of DDSs for pharmaceuticals. ANN in drug delivery encompasses a variety of computational models utilized in drug administration, pre-formulation study, dosage form formulation, and stability test (Fig. 8.6). Particle size, shape, surface area, organoleptic properties, solubility, dissolution behavior, hygroscopicity, partition coefficient, crystallinity and

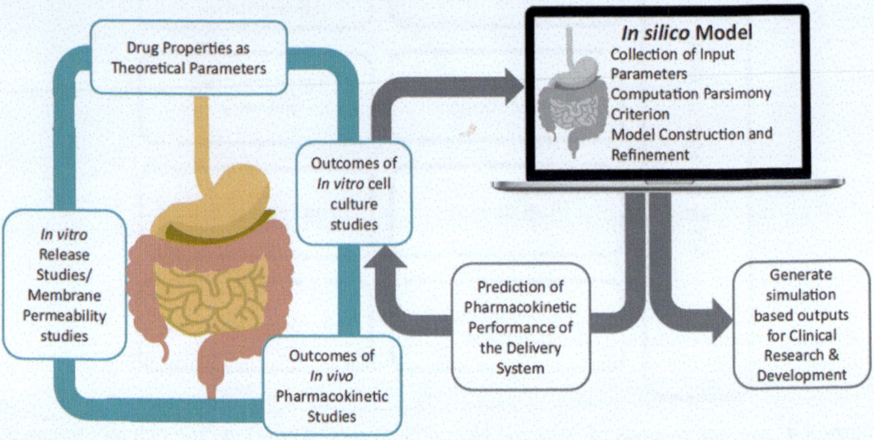


**Figure 8.5** The cycle of developing an in silico pharmacokinetic model for drug delivery systems. It shows how various inputs like drug properties, in vitro studies, and in vivo pharmacokinetic data are integrated into a computational model to predict pharmacokinetic performance and generate outputs for new in vitro, in vivo and clinical research and development.
Reprinted with permission from [151].

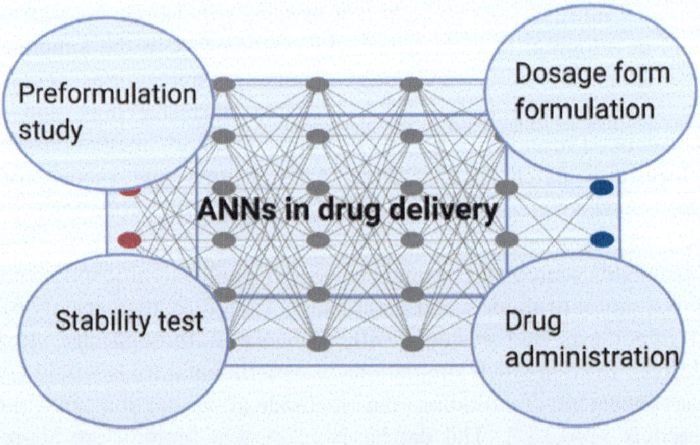


**Figure 8.6** The application of Artificial Neural Networks (ANNs) in various aspects of drug delivery, including preformulation studies, stability testing, dosage form formulation, and drug administration.
Reprinted with permission from [145].

polymorphism, ionization/dissociation, powder flow property, permeability, stability, and drug excipient compatibility are some of the physicochemical aspects of drug ingredients that are analyzed during formulation study [145].

Microspheres, also known as microparticles, are a prevalent form of micro-based pharmaceuticals that offer various benefits for DDSs. Microspheres are spherical particles comprised of biodegradable polymers that evenly disseminate the drug during dissolution or suspension in a matrix environment [154]. Multiple categories of drugs, including small molecules, proteins, and nucleic acids, can be encapsulated in microspheres. Microspheres enhance drug delivery by increasing bioavailability and reducing harmful side effects [155]. A microsphere formulation should ideally possess the capability to function as a depot for loading high concentrations of the drug and exhibit a controlled drug release rate for a predetermined duration. Optimizing the process for efficient trapping of active compounds is critical for developing a successful controlled-release microsphere formulation. The utilization of ANN aids in surpassing the challenges associated with the development of favorable microsphere formulations, particularly in comprehending the interrelation among multiple optimization parameters (also referred to as multi-objective simultaneous optimization problems) [156]. ANN modeling was generally applied to comprehend the impacts of numerous variables on the preparation procedure. ANN-assisted process parameter optimization has also been applied to the microencapsulation of hydrophobic pharmaceutical compounds.

Dorado and colleagues [157] conducted a study for optimization of the enclosing sunflower oil inside calcium alginate capsules by employing the prilling technique. By applying neuro-fuzzy logic and ANN, they were able to create uniform, spherical microcapsules with a limited range of sizes and delicate alginate shells. This was accomplished by optimizing the concentrations of polymer and water-in-oil components, adjusting flow rates, and regulating vibration frequency.

Liposomes, spherical lipid bilayer vesicles made from cholesterol and phospholipids, are advantageous for drug delivery owing to their favorable properties. Liposomal bilayers determine the stiffness, charge of lipid bilayers, and fluidity. Liposome systems can release encapsulated APIs to chosen targets without decomposing them [158,159]. Researchers employ ANN in liposome formulation to enhance product quality, monitor drug concentration, extend the action period, and conduct quantitative drug analysis.

Hathout et al. [160] used FD and ANN techniques to optimize the formulation of liposomes through the incorporation of a specific variety of gelatin. The purpose of the rheology investigation was to determine which gelatin masses were optimal for the liposome formulation. The ANN method was employed to assess the entrapment efficacy after the introduction of a gelatin and cholesterol mixture into the liposomes. The study found that the gelatinized-core liposomal carrier effectively entraps hydrophilic APIs, provides controlled and sustained release, and is more stable than standard liposomes.

Nanorobotics, which are sophisticated apparatuses commonly composed of bio-nanocomponents, are regarded as highly efficient vehicles for drug delivery. The majority of nanorobots are composed of computational technologies, such as AI, to maintain integrated circuits, sensors, power supply, and secure data storage [14,161]. These carriers also can utilize AI to assess the guided drug delivery to particular organs, tissues, or tumors [162,163]. To function effectively and precisely, micro/nanorobots must be capable of detecting and attaching objects, avoiding collisions, and ultimately discharging from the body. These features enhance drug delivery and minimize side effects.

The development of individualized, precision drug delivery that accounts for all confronting parameters of a particular drug necessitates the utilization of extensive input datasets and multiple learning layers. In subsequent developments, null AI model templates will be accessible, which would receive individualized patient data encompassing disease history and requirements for optimal drug delivery to the targeted area, while real-time surveillance accounts for potential adverse drug reactions and toxicities.

In the future of medicine, advances in biomedical engineering that enable the fabrication of NPs, implantable microchips, and robots that can be controlled, monitored, and directed via ultrasound, electronics, or wireless communication will surpass the capabilities of conventional drug delivery methods. Integrating different ANN methodologies with these delivery protocols may improve precision and minimize inaccuracies [150].

## 8.5 Artificial intelligence in the prediction of drug delivery system characteristics

AI techniques are currently being utilized in diverse aspects of pharmaceutical development. These include predicating the physical and chemical characteristics, studying in vitro release, and determining toxicity, cellular uptake, and loading capacity [9].

### *8.5.1 Size*

Most of the phenomena concerning DDSs have been discovered to be dependent on the size, for instance, penetration across biological barriers, absorption of oral medications, and passive or active targeted delivery to tumors or inflamed tissues. Therefore, it is crucial to control the size and distribution of the NPs. Achieving a definite particle size with a narrow distribution is a trial-and-error process based on experimental methods. Hence, it would be extremely beneficial to develop an AI model that could accurately predict the size and polydispersity index (PDI) of different NPs. This would save time and money by reducing the need for trial and error and minimizing the consumption of chemicals, and materials during the optimization phase [164,165].

Polymeric NPs, as a type of DDSs, can be employed to transport drugs specifically to target cells, resulting in improved effectiveness while minimizing harm to healthy surrounding tissues [166]. Youshia et al. developed an AI model that can predict the size of polymeric NPs formed using a specific pharmaceutical polymer. The factors that affect the particle size in the polymer were identified as hydrophobicity, molecular weight, and surface activity. These properties were assessed through measurements of contact angle, polymer viscosity, and interfacial tension. They used an ANN to construct a model, using these characteristics as input and particle size and PDI as output. The model accurately predicted the particle size of NPs ranging from 70 to 400 nm, produced from different polymers. The percentage bias for prediction of particle size was 2% for training data, 4% for validation data, and 6% for testing data. Among the polymer properties, surface activity had the most significant effect on particle size, and viscosity and hydrophobicity demonstrated a high impact on particle size after surface activity. This study successfully identified the influential polymer properties on particle size and demonstrated the effectiveness of ANN in predicting the size and polydispersity of polymeric NPs. [167].

Shalaby et al. employed ANN to predict the particle size of di- and triblock copolymers composed of poly(ethylene glycol) and poly(lactide). The researchers incorporated three input variables: The size of the polymer-based NPs in nanometers can be accurately estimated using the ANN model by considering the following factors: the ratio of polymer to drug, the molecular weight of the polymer, and the number of blocks in the copolymer. The model exhibited a high level of accuracy with an impressive $R^2$ value of 0.9783. It is particularly noteworthy that the prediction of NP size primarily depended on the molecular weight of the polymer [168].

## 8.5.2 Morphology

In the field of nanoparticle research, scientists commonly rely on obtaining information about the structure and morphology of NPs, to gain deeper insights into the relationship between morphology and nanoparticle properties. However, manually analyzing and processing images to extract such morphology information is time-consuming and expensive. As a result, there is great potential for automatic analysis methods to alleviate researchers from this repetitive task. [169,170]. A three-stage automatic analysis concept has been developed to prevail the limitations of manual approaches. These three stages carried out sequentially, include particle segmentation, particle shape extraction, and statistical analysis of morphology information. Particle segmentation and shape extraction are the fundamental technologies within this framework. Building upon this foundation, numerous researchers have proposed specific frameworks that combine traditional image processing methods to automatically analyze particle morphology. The aim is to streamline and simplify the extraction of useful morphology information, enabling researchers to focus on higher-level analysis and interpretation [171,172].

Sun and their colleagues recently presented an extensive framework that utilizes deep learning techniques for fast and precise online analysis of NP morphology via SEM/TEM images. The framework consists of three main stages: NP segmentation using a lightweight and robust deep learning network called NSNet, NP shape extraction, and statistical analysis. In the experimental findings, NSNet demonstrated an impressive accuracy of 86.2% and achieved the capability to process 11 SEM/TEM images per second on an embedded processor. When compared to other models for semantic segmentation, NSNet emerged as the top choice, ensuring accurate and swift segmentation even in challenging SEM/TEM images with significant background interference, densely packed NPs, and extremely small NPs. Moreover, the proposed framework successfully acquired NP measurements such as equivalent diameter and

Blaschke shape coefficient, which yielded values of 17.14 ± 5.9 and 0.18 ± 0.04, respectively, demonstrating good agreement with manually conducted analysis. The proposed framework holds great potential in advancing the development of automatic and intelligent analysis technology for nanomaterial morphology [173].

### 8.5.3 Toxicity

Although nanocarriers offer captivating and promising applications, their potential toxicity has emerged as a significant concern, particularly in clinical studies. Given their ability to target specific tissues and penetrate through them due to their size, nano-scaled systems necessitate a thorough evaluation of their toxicological effects. Furthermore, the toxicity of NPs in non-target cells is of utmost importance, considering their intended use in human subjects. An ideal nanocarrier should exhibit minimal toxicity when administered at the recommended dosage [174].

To evaluate the toxicity of NPs, various methods can be employed, including analysis of their physicochemical properties, biodistribution, as well as in vitro and in vivo toxicity assessments. In vitro assessments involve conducting tests such as proliferation (MTT), and oxidative stress assays. On the other hand, in vivo assessments encompass tests like dermal toxicity, oral toxicity, and eye irritation evaluations. However, it is important to note that performing these in vitro and in vivo assessments can be resource-intensive and time-consuming due to the diverse chemical nature and variations in biological characteristics, size, and shape of NPs [174–176]. To address these drawbacks in the toxicity evaluation of NPs, AI tools could be employed successfully as an alternative strategy to mitigate the challenges [177].

In the field of nanotoxicology, ML techniques have been effectively utilized. Furxhi and their team conducted a comparison of various groups of machine learning classifiers, including trees, rules, functions, lazy, and Bayes, using two datasets. The objective was to evaluate their performance to predict the in vitro toxicity of nanomaterials. The prediction of toxicity for seven metal-oxide NPs based on cell viability was achieved by utilizing input variables such as physicochemical properties, toxicological and quantum-mechanical attributes, and in vitro experimental conditions. Among the classifiers assessed, Neural Network (NN) and Random Forest (RF) consistently demonstrated the highest performance across the majority of the datasets. However, an improved prediction was observed when these classifiers were combined, resulting in a meta-classifier with even higher performance indices. This proposed model can be a valuable tool for researchers in identifying and prioritizing classifiers, leading to more accurate predictions of NP toxicity for any given dataset. In this particular research, the toxicity of NPs was assessed by examining cell viability using predictive models. The process consisted of four stages: data collection, data pre-processing, model implementation, and model evaluation (Fig. 8.7) [130].

Ahmadi et al., applied five AI classifiers, including RF, SVM, NB, DT, and ANN to predict the toxicity of nanoparticles in biological systems. They used a dataset containing 244 records of nanoparticles with various physicochemical characteristics of nanoparticles, cell properties, and experimental conditions. They found that the RF

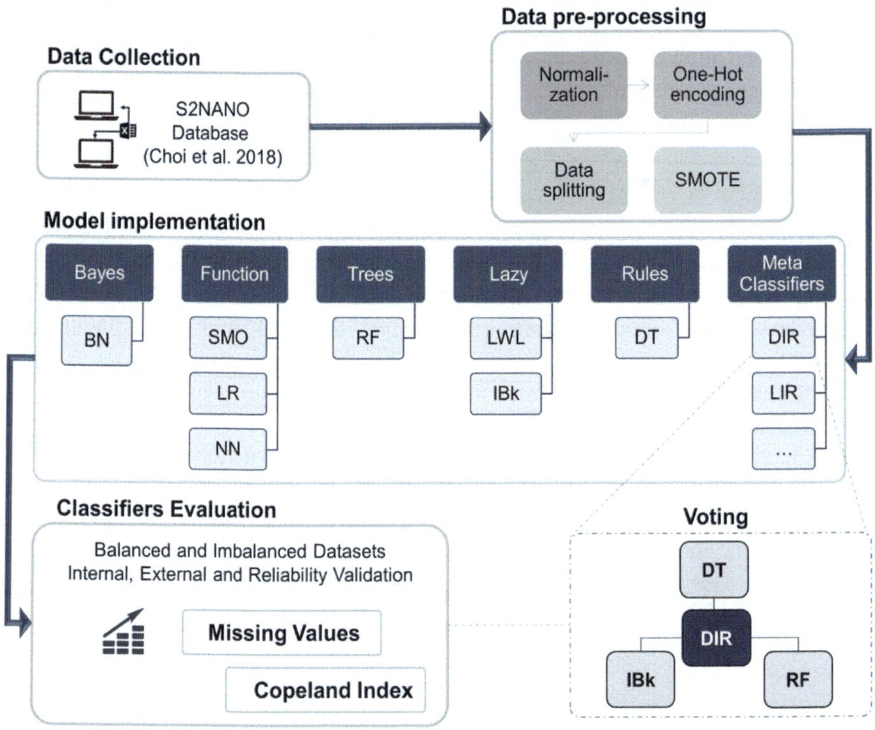


**Figure 8.7** The workflow in the toxicity prediction. First, datasets are gathered from the S2NANO database and undergo various processing steps for ML purposes, including normalization, one-hot encoding, data splitting, and data synthesis using SMOTE. The training subset of the data is then introduced to eight individual base classifiers. These classifiers, arranged in triads, are combined using a voting approach, and the most effective combinations are selected as ensemble classifiers. Both the base and ensemble classifiers are subjected to evaluation through internal and external validation, as well as a reliability dataset. In addition, datasets containing artificially generated missing values are used to showcase the classifiers' robustness. Ultimately, a Copeland Index is used to rank the classifiers.
Reprinted with permission from [130].

classifier demonstrates the most performance compared to others, in terms of accuracy (93.45%), the area under the ROC curve (0.966), f measure (92.44%), sensitivity (92.7%), and specificity (94.18%) [178].

Fourches et al. employed an SVM classifier to predict the toxicity of various metal NPs on four specific cell lines, including hepatocytes, monocytes, smooth muscle cells, and endothelial cells). The model applied experimental measurements of nanoparticle attributes. The dose, cell line, and assay used for each nanoparticle illustrated the biological activity profile. This mean value was then employed for binary classification, labeling the NPs as toxic or non-toxic. Their model was validated using a five-fold cross-validation approach, achieving prediction accuracies ranging from 56% to 88%.

The authors of the study propose that exploring various approaches is crucial to identifying and predicting the connections between the structures of metal NPs and their biological activity, ultimately establishing more widely applicable nano-QSAR (quantitative structure-activity relationship) relationships [179].

### 8.5.4 Loading capacity

The loading capacity of NPs holds significant importance when these NPs are designed as delivery systems for drugs or image-contrasting agents to target particular cells or tissues. The drug loading capacity or entrapment efficiency of nanocarriers holds significant importance and relies on numerous parameters. However, modifying these parameters to achieve maximum entrapment efficiency in the lab can be both time-consuming and expensive. To address these challenges, AI techniques could be facilitators [180,181].

Jafari et al. applied ML frameworks to identify the critical parameter that affects the entrapment efficiency of niosomal formulations and determine its optimal value for a specific experiment. Four different cost functions were used to train the deep neural network (DNN), linear regression, and polynomial regression models. The validity of the approach was assessed by comparing the entrapment efficiency outcomes of seven laboratory-prepared niosomal formulations containing doxycycline hyclate. Among the models examined, the DNN model showed superior performance, yielding a root mean square error (RMSE) of $13.587 \pm 2.61$, a mean absolute error of $10.17 \pm 1.421$, and an $R^2$ value of $0.763 \pm 0.1$, as determined through five-fold cross-validation. The hydrophilic-lipophilic balance emerged as the most influential factor. Using ML techniques, this investigation provided a pathway for synthesizing niosomal formulations with optimized entrapment efficiency, cost reduction, and time savings [180].

Shalaby and colleagues applied an ANN classifier to forecast the entrapment efficiency of noscapine in di- and triblock co-polymers composed of poly(lactide) and poly(ethylene glycol). They incorporated empirically measured input variables into their model, such as the polymer's molecular weight, the polymer-to-drug ratio, and the number of blocks per polymer. The model yielded an impressive overall $R^2$ value of 0.91486 when predicting noscapine entrapment efficiency. Importantly, the polymer-to-drug ratio was identified as the most influential factor in predicting noscapine entrapment efficiency [168].

### 8.5.5 Cellular uptake

Extensive endeavors have been devoted to the realm of nanomedicine, aiming to comprehend and enhance the process of cellular uptake and targeting. The primary impetus driving these endeavors is the usage of NPs for cancer treatment, specifically for delivering biologically active substances exclusively to cancerous cells [182]. In this context, the application of predictive models holds immense potential. This is due to the development cost for innovative NPs possessing favorite properties is substantial, and the design possibilities are vast. Therefore, any computational tool capable of assisting in narrowing down the design space by accurately predicting the properties of required molecules before their preparation would empower researchers to allocate limited sources toward conducting experimental effort on the most capable candidates [183,184].

Alafeef et al. have developed an ML classifier to detect breast cancer cells by leveraging the internalization process of eight various CNPs The researchers evaluated the amount of NP cellular internalization through various assessed endocytic pathways. By employing AI approaches, they could rank the NP properties to achieve the optimal design, which could potentially enhance therapeutic efficacy. This model demonstrates a high level of accuracy in predicting the internalization of CNPs according to their structures. Moreover, the team employed the cellular internalization profile of the diagnostic NPs to construct a personalized cancer profile for individual patients using ML techniques [183].

Smart nanocarriers are emerging as promising strategies for cancer treatment due to their advantageous characteristics, such as targeted delivery of various substances specifically to cancer cells. However, the uptake of NPs by tumor cells and their subsequent release of drugs are crucial considerations in the development of effective therapies. Traditional qualitative imaging-based analyses are burdensome and vulnerable to human biases. Deep learning algorithms, widely implemented in the medical field, present promising prospects for drug discovery and development. Ali and colleagues evaluated the effectiveness of five distinct CNN models. Two models were developed from scratch, while three models, including VGG16, ResNet50, and Inception V3, were pre-trained. The training data consisted of confocal images depicting cells treated with NPs and a fluorescent anticancer substance. Comparative and cross-validation analyses were performed to gather more meaningful insights across all the models. The models exhibited high accuracy in the prediction of high or low uptake and release of drugs in triple negative breast cancer (TNBC) cells. This indicates significant potential for practical application, aiding in the early-stage determination of cellular uptake during drug development in any research field. The CNN model and different pooling types used in CNNs were illustrated in Fig. 8.8(A and B), respectively. Typically, the pooling layer follows the convolutional layer. Its main function is to decrease the dimensionality of images by reducing the number of pixels derived from the previous convolutional layer's output. In essence, it takes input data from a group of neighboring neurons and summarizes their values using either max pooling or average pooling. This process effectively reduces the computational burden involved [116].

### 8.5.6 Drug release

Because some drugs such as anti-cancer agents can be harmful, it is crucial to encase or hide them in a nanocarrier till they specifically attain cancer cells or targeted tissues [185]. In addition, certain nano-scaled DDSs can serve as carriers for active pharmaceutical ingredients with low stability, and shield them from degradation [186]. Creating predictive models for quantitatively estimating the release of molecules from NPs is indeed achievable. In one research, Husseini and colleagues utilized ANN to develop a

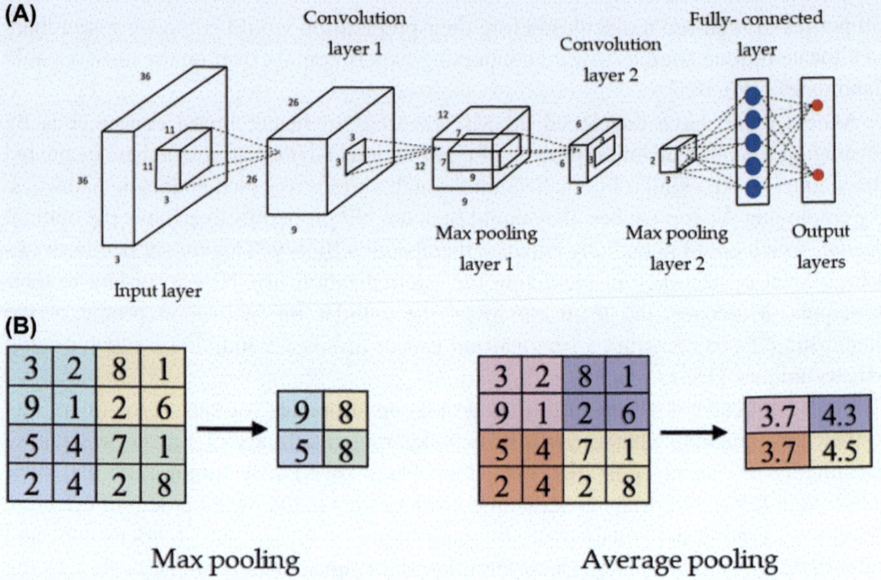


**Figure 8.8** (A) The typical layers of a CNN, including the input layer, convolutional layers, max pooling layers, and a fully connected layer leading to the output. It visually represents how the dimensions change as data flows through the network., (B) Two types of pooling operations: max pooling and average pooling. It shows how these operations reduce the size of the feature maps by selecting the maximum value or calculating the average value within each pooling window. Reprinted with permission from [116].

predictive model for the release of DOX from polymeric micelles, specifically Pluronic P105, under two distinct ultrasound frequencies. The training of the model involved real experimental data that captured the relationship between input factors and the release of DOX from the micelles. The ANN approach exhibited strong agreement between its predictions and the experimental results. The maximum prediction errors recorded at ultrasound frequencies of 20 kHz and 70 kHz were 0.002 and 0.001, respectively [187].

Szlek and colleagues employed ANN to forecast the release of macromolecules, such as human serum albumin, bovine serum albumin, and recombinant human erythropoietin, from PLGA NPs. The ANN models incorporated several independent parameters, including experimental conditions, formulation characteristics, and molecular descriptors, computed by means of the Marvin cxcalc plugin. Feature selection was conducted to improve the predictions, resulting in four separate analyses. These models attained RMSE values of 17.7, 17.1, 16.4, and 15.4 using 21, 17, 16, and 11 features as input, respectively. Among the analyses, the one with 11 feature input variables proved to be the most effective, encompassing the isoelectric point (pI), the lactide-to-glycolide ratio in the polymer, quaternary structure of the macromolecule, production method, Szeged index, dissolution pH, poly(vinyl alcohol) outer phase concentration, poly(vinyl alcohol) inner phase concentration, encapsulation rate, and mean particle size [188].

## 8.6 Artificial intelligence-assisted drug delivery for effective diagnosis

In recent times, nanomaterials have significantly enhanced the diagnostic capabilities and efficiency of biomedical imaging. This can be attributed to their remarkable characteristics, including active and passive targeting. NPs employing passive targeting, through EPR effect, result in an elevated concentration of the contrast agent in tumor tissues. In addition, by incorporating various ligands on the nanoparticle surface, specific binding to target tissue receptors can be achieved, allowing precise placement of the contrast agent in the desired tissue [189].

Despite the optimistic outlook, the adoption of nanomedicine in clinical practice has been relatively limited because of the significant variations observed among patients and within tumor tissues [183]. Diagnostic nanoparticles are employed to construct a personalized disease profile for each patient, which is then utilized alongside various therapeutic nano-based approaches to enhance the treatment outcome. However, the presence of significant variations within tumors and between patients makes it extremely challenging to develop diagnostic and therapeutic platforms and analyze their effectiveness. To address this challenge, the integration of AI methods can serve as a solution, utilizing pattern analysis and classification algorithms to improve the accuracy of diagnostics and therapeutics. The application of AI in nanomedicine design also offers advantages by optimization of material characteristics based on anticipated interactions with the drug, immune system, biological fluids, and cell membranes—all of which impact therapeutic effectiveness [190].

TNBC presents a perplexing challenge due to its intricate molecular diversity, leading to difficulties in both diagnosis and treatment. To tackle these issues, Alafeef et al. proposed an AI-based technique that predicts the internalization of NPs across different stages of cancer. They conducted groundbreaking research by successfully utilizing an integration of ML algorithms and distinctive cellular uptake patterns of specific cancer cell types to accurately categorize various cell types. By employing this strategy, they could improve nanoparticles to achieve the most favorable structure-internalization response. This procedure demonstrated remarkable predictive accuracy ($Q^2$=0.9) in determining the structure-internalization response of the desired NPs. Fig. 8.9 illustrates A visual diagram of the diagnosing process of breast cancer using the suggested sensor array. The proposed MTT assay was employed to quantify the internalization response of each cell type against the corresponding CNPs, along with four inhibitors. These responses, referred to as the fold-increase in cellular uptake, were analyzed using the ANN classifier to distinguish between normal and cancer cells and determine the specific type of cancer [183].

One of the most important methods in clinical practice for delivering RNA involves the use of lipid nanoparticles (LNPs), which could be monitored using automated microscopes. However, evaluating time-lapse microscopy imaging data is not without its challenges. The data is rich in information, albeit often occurring in sparse distributions across the images, and it possesses high temporal components and dimensionality. To overcome the challenges, Harrison et al. employed two approaches.

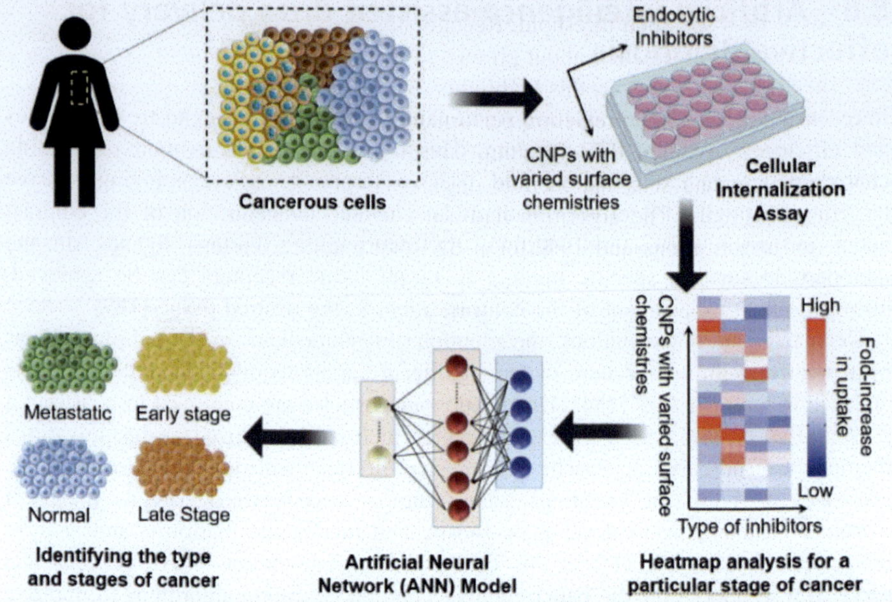


**Figure 8.9** The process for identifying cancer types and stages using nanoparticle-based cellular assays and machine learning. It shows the progression from analyzing cancerous cells to using nanoparticles (CNPs) with various surface chemistries in a cellular internalization assay. The results are then analyzed using heatmaps and an artificial neural network to classify different cancer stages and types.
Reprinted with permission from [183].

Initially, the effects of nanotechnology on a specified cell are only noticeable at later time points when protein production discloses the prior successful delivery of mRNA by the NPs. Regrettably, at this point, it is not feasible to examine the mechanism of this delivery. Hence, it becomes essential to track the progress of specific cells over time. The authors suggest that by studying the cell morphology at earlier time points, before GFP expression, it might be feasible to anticipate the likelihood of GFP production in each cell. Another approach employed in this study aims to streamline the process using relatively limited datasets. While working with small datasets offers certain advantages like quicker data acquisition, reduced storage demands, and decreased processing time, it also presents challenges when employing deep learning methods, which typically rely on much larger datasets. Overall, they have demonstrated the ability to predict GFP expression based on microscopy imaging data at the cellular level, by gathering details about cell morphologies and their interactions with LNPs. The findings underscore the advantage of considering the temporal aspect when investigating drug delivery through high-content imaging [191]. Magnetic particle imaging (MPI) is an innovative, non-invasive medical imaging technique utilized to depict the arrangement of superparamagnetic iron oxide NPs in space. In MPI, spatial resolution plays a significant role in determining effectiveness. However, conventional methods of enhancing spatial resolution may lead to increased expenses, reduced sensitivity, or diminished contrast. Shang et al. conducted a study to improve the spatial resolution of this imaging approach based on a deep learning model by fusing a dual-sampling convolutional neural network (FDS-MPI). This considerable advancement in MPI has the potential to streamline the use of medical imaging techniques in preclinical applications in the coming years [134].

AI has the potential to revolutionize the diagnosis of diseases and the use of nano DDSs. By utilizing AI algorithms and machine learning techniques, it becomes feasible to analyze vast amounts of intricate data from diverse sources like medical images, patient records, and genetic information. This analysis can aid in the early and precise diagnosis of diseases, resulting in timely interventions and better outcomes for patients.

## 8.7 Artificial intelligence-assisted drug delivery for effective treatment

Due to some difficulties such as low efficiency, many complications, and low flexibility of the conventional approaches, the need to shift the treatment paradigm was perceived. conventional drugs could harmfully interact with non-target regions of the body and lead to side effects with different severity. This would limit physicians to make use of many drugs for several diseases [192]. Also, another challenge of traditional approaches is delivering the therapeutic agent to its target. Several barriers in the body should be passed by the drug. Blood–brain barrier or intestinal barrier is an example of such barrier. Failure to pass the barriers results in inadequate effectiveness of the drug [16]. In addition, in many diseases, it is essential to control the dose and concentration of the drug inside the blood. conventional approaches do not have this advantage too [193]. According to the mentioned factors, designing DDSs was programmed. These systems increase the efficiency of therapy, alleviate toxicity, and increase patient compliance. This shows that by applying DDSs, barriers to conventional treatments are bypassed and enhanced treatment outcome is achieved [194]. In addition, conventional treatment approaches could not meet the demands of new therapeutic generation such as proteins, nucleic acids, and live cells [195].

With improved recognition of disease specifications, discovering novel targets is unsurprising. However, there are still problems in targeting efficiency. To overcome this and achieve an efficient targeted delivery, it is essential to understand the delivery systems and their interaction with extracellular space. In this way, several analyzing tools aid investigators. AI tools are exponentially utilized to optimize DDSs to get better treatment efficiency [196].

Meanwhile, the production of processable data in the biomedical fields is increasing day by day. Accordingly, the potential of using AI is rising [197]. This amount of data is big and some of the notable relationships between data elements may remain masked when they are being analyzed via traditional methods. To address that, AI can be employed for such data and give a deeper insight into the dataset to researchers. Therefore, by considering these benefits, researchers integrate AI with DDSs to optimize a system with drug delivery and treatment capabilities [198].

AI can simulate the delivery process. This simulation could aid in evaluating each involved feature and accordingly optimize the delivery system without massive trials and several failures. Consequently, the timeline of drug development is accelerated, costs are alleviated and productivity is increased. In delivering a therapeutic agent to its target, AI can be employed in a wide range that is from predicting molecular interactions to evaluation of system performance [194].

AI is utilized to predict the efficiency of drug dosing and the method of delivery. Also, AI can be used to optimize the release of the drug from matrix tablets. Another application of AI in designing DDSs is to find a logical relationship between the profile of the release and formulation factors [14]. ML-based models have been applied in several studies to optimize the DDSs by optimizing the drug dose, predicting the drug resistance, designing administration routes, and therapeutic efficiency of DDSs in infectious diseases (Fig. 8.10).

Researchers have developed numerous ML algorithms to predict antimicrobial resistance profiles of prominent pathogenic organisms. For instance, models utilizing AdaBoost achieved accuracies ranging from 0.88 to 0.99 in the published study [200], SVM demonstrated accuracies from 0.92 to 1.0 [201], Deep convolutional neural networks performed with 0.8 to 1.0 accuracy [202], and multilayer perceptrons evidenced accuracies between 0.795 to 0.92 [203]. The algorithms—AdaBoost, SVM, deep convolutional neural networks, and multilayer perceptrons—have proven adept at predicting resistance of *Acinetobacter baumannii*, *S. aureus*, *Mycobacterium tuberculosis*, *Actinobacillus pleuropneumoniae*, *Escherichia coli*, and HIV to antimicrobial agents. The models were predominantly trained on whole genome sequencing data, microscopic video imagery, and amino acid sequences to discern resistance patterns. As a result of this work, the algorithms can now classify whether isolates of the aforementioned pathogens demonstrate resistance or sensitivity to antimicrobial medications [199].

These applications lead investigators to utilize AI to optimize the therapeutic effects of a delivery system [14]. The development of hydrogel DDSs for the

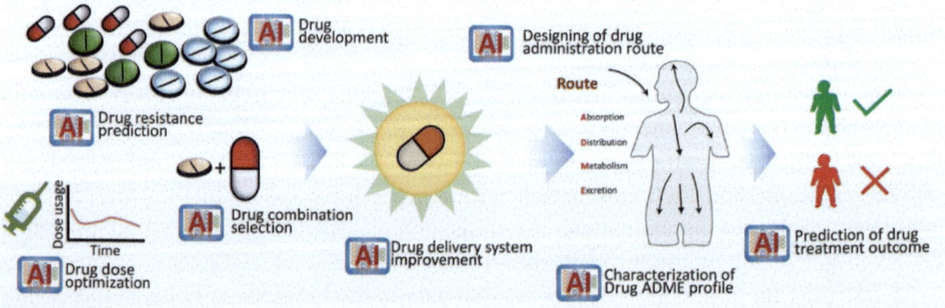


**Figure 8.10** Application of artificial intelligence throughout the drug development and administration process. It showcases AI's role in various stages including drug development, resistance prediction, dose optimization, combination selection, delivery system improvement, ADME profile characterization, administration route design, and treatment outcome prediction. Reprinted with permission from [199].

treatment of various diseases like infectious ones is increasing [204]. However, this development has several complexities due to difficulties with the characterization and optimization of this delivery system. Also, the development of such systems demands repetition of trial-and-error that results in spending time and resources. By enhancing the understanding of the exploited data, AI algorithms could be employed in the development of hydrogel delivery systems. In this way, AI can accelerate the development process [205].

Besides hydrogels, nanomaterials are another delivery system that can benefit from AI to demonstrate improved therapeutic effects. AI algorithms are employed for designing, characterizing, and manufacturing nano-based DDSs. This employs predicting the interactions of NPs with the loaded drug and its target and also assessing the efficiency of the drug-carrier system [133]. In a recent research study, an ML-based model was developed to predict the antiviral drug loading capacity and encapsulation efficiency of PLGA NPs. In this study, the Gaussian process, an ML method, was implemented in the data exploited from related research articles including the size of NPs, polydispersity index, drug loading capacity, and efficiency of encapsulation. Gaussian process generates graphs based on the calculation of the mean and variance of the extracted data. This method applies to the dataset and the prediction is possible using these graphs. In addition to the mentioned predictions, the graphs generated in this study can be used to identify novel antiviral drugs [206]. Non-steroidal anti-inflammatory drugs (NSAIDs) have an essential role in the treatment of Rheumatoid Arthritis (RA). There is a need to increase the bioavailability and alleviate the side effects of the conventional drug. Therefore, in an accomplished study, developing, characterizing, and optimizing in-situ forming nanoparticles (ISNs) via an AI-based application, Design-Expert®, was aimed. These NPs were employed to deliver piroxicam by intra-articular injection. Results declare the efficiency of designed NPs for delivering piroxicam in the treatment of patients with RA [207].

In the field of treatment, it is desirable to perform a highly efficient therapy with minimized side effects. Not only delivering the therapeutic agent exactly to its target will increase the efficiency, but also it will alleviate the side effects. For this purpose, NPs are appropriate agents to deliver a therapeutic agent accurately to the target. These NPs should be designed so that they are capable of bypassing biological barriers. Designing targeted NPs has been developed in recent years. Now, this development has been accompanied by new technologies such as AI and its subfields such as ML, leading to the design of more efficient targeted DDSs. By predicting the efficiency, toxicity, and generally the behavior of designed NPs, AI aids the development of targeted NPs to be accelerated. AI-based models can design the platform of targeting, predict the selectivity of NPs, and promote the use of multiple moieties in a specific particle. These benefits result in designing targeted NPs with optimized performance. For appropriate performance of AI-based models, it is essential to have a meaningful experimental dataset. Despite the diversity in targeted NP designing techniques and approaches, several labs are collaborating to create such datasets [208].

## 8.8 Conclusion and future perspective

In conclusion, the integration of AI into DDSs. Design and development have proven to be a transformative approach in the field of pharmaceutical sciences. The advent of AI technologies has revolutionized the way we approach the formulation, targeting, and delivery of drugs. By harnessing the power of AI, researchers have been able to streamline the development process of DDSs, reduce costs, and minimize the time required to bring new therapeutic solutions to market. Moreover, AI-driven DDSs have opened up new avenues for personalized medicine and targeted therapies. With the ability to analyze vast amounts of patient data and adapt to individual characteristics, these systems offer the potential for precise and customized drug delivery, optimizing treatment outcomes and minimizing adverse effects. However, as with any emerging technology, there are challenges and considerations to overcome. Ethical, legal, and regulatory frameworks must evolve to ensure the responsible use of AI in DDSs. Furthermore, continued collaboration between researchers, clinicians, and industry stakeholders is crucial to drive innovation, validate AI models, and address potential limitations and risks.

Looking ahead, the future of AI in DDS design and development is promising. Advancements in computational power, data analytics, and AI algorithms will further refine and enhance DDSs, leading to safer, more effective therapies. As we continue to embrace the potential of AI, we stand at the forefront of a new era in pharmaceutical sciences, where intelligent systems and precise drug delivery strategies will revolutionize patient care and pave the way for remarkable therapeutic breakthroughs.

## Acknowledgment

To the best of the Editors' knowledge and authors' claims, no generative AI tools were used for substantive writing of chapters. Any AI-assisted language editing, if applied, was limited to grammar or style suggestions and did not alter the scientific content.

## Abbreviations

| | |
|---|---|
| AI | Artificial intelligence |
| ANN | Artificial neural network |
| API | Active Pharmaceutical Ingredient |
| BSA | Bovine serum albumin |
| CdSe | Cadmium selenide |
| CNH | Carbon nanohorn |
| CNN | Convolutional neural network |
| CNP | Carbon nanoparticle |
| CNT | Carbon nanotube |
| DDS | Drug delivery system |
| DEP | PEGylated PLL-docetaxel conjugate |
| DNA | Deoxyribonucleic acid |

| | |
|---|---|
| DOX | Doxorubicin |
| DT | Decision tree |
| EPR | Enhanced permeability and retention |
| FD | Factorial design |
| FDA | Food and Drug Administration |
| FDS-MPI | Fusing a dual-sampling convolutional neural network |
| GFP | Green fluorescent protein |
| IR | Infrared |
| ISN | In-situ forming nano particle |
| LDC | Lipid-drug conjugate |
| LNP | Lipid nanoparticle |
| MEMS | Microelectromechanical system |
| ML | Machine learning |
| MNP | Magnetic nanoparticle |
| MOF | Metal-organic framework |
| MPI | Magnetic particle imaging |
| mRNA | Messenger ribonucleic acid |
| MTX | Methotrexate |
| MWCNT | Multi-walled carbon nanotube |
| NB | Naïve Bayes |
| NDDS | Nano-drug delivery system |
| NLC | Nanostructured lipid carrier |
| NMOF | Nanoscale metal-organic framework |
| NN | Neural network |
| NP | Nanoparticle |
| NSAIDs | Non-steroidal anti-inflammatory drugs |
| NSNet | Neural satisfiability network |
| PDI | Polydispersity index |
| PEG | Polyethylene glycol |
| pH | Potential of Hydrogen |
| pI | Isoelectric point |
| PLGA | Poly (lactic-co-glycolic acid) |
| PM | Polymeric micelle |
| PNP | Polymeric nanoparticle |
| PPI | Poly(propylene imine) |
| PTX | Paclitaxel |
| QD | Quantum dot |
| QSAR | Quantitative structure-activity relationship |
| RA | Rheumatoid arthritis |
| RF | Random forest |
| RMSE | Root mean square error |
| ROC | Receiver operating characteristic curve |
| SEM/TEM | Scanning electron microscopy/Transmission electron microscopy |
| SLN | Solid lipid nanoparticle |
| SNP | Silica nanoparticle |

| | |
|---|---|
| SVM | Support vector machine |
| SWNT | Single-walled carbon nanotube |
| TNBC | Triple negative breast cancer |
| UV | Ultraviolet |
| ZnS | Zinc sulfide |

## References

[1] Savjani KT, Gajjar AK, Savjani JK. Drug solubility: importance and enhancement techniques. Int Scholarly Research Notices 2012;2012.
[2] Manallack DT. The p K a distribution of drugs: application to drug discovery. Perspectives in medicinal chemistry 2007;1. p. 1177391X0700100003.
[3] Rang H. The receptor concept: pharmacology's big idea. British Journal of Pharmacology 2006;147(S1):S9–16.
[4] Lajiness MS, Vieth M, Erickson J. Molecular properties that influence oral drug-like behavior. Current Opinion in Drug Discovery & Development 2004;7(4):470–7.
[5] Foucquier J, Guedj M. Analysis of drug combinations: current methodological landscape. Pharmacology research & perspectives 2015;3(3):e00149.
[6] Vega-Vásquez P, Mosier NS, Irudayaraj J. Nanoscale drug delivery systems: from medicine to agriculture. Frontiers in Bioengineering and Biotechnology 2020;8:79.
[7] Park K. Controlled drug delivery systems: past forward and future back. Journal of Controlled Release 2014;190:3–8.
[8] Felice B, et al. Drug delivery vehicles on a nano-engineering perspective. Materials Science and Engineering: C 2014;41:178–95.
[9] Trucillo P. Drug Carriers: Classification, Administration, Release Profiles, and Industrial Approach. Processes 2021;9(3):470.
[10] Vargason AM, Anselmo AC, Mitragotri S. The evolution of commercial drug delivery technologies. Nature biomedical engineering 2021;5(9):951–67.
[11] Martinho N, Damgé C, Reis CP. Recent advances in drug delivery systems. Journal of biomaterials and nanobiotechnology 2011;2(05):510.
[12] Huynh L, et al. Computational approaches to the rational design of nanoemulsions, polymeric micelles, and dendrimers for drug delivery. Nanomedicine: nanotechnology, biology and medicine 2012;8(1):20–36.
[13] He Y, et al. Can machine learning predict drug nanocrystals? Journal of Controlled Release 2020;322:274–85.
[14] Hassanzadeh P, Atyabi F, Dinarvand R. The significance of artificial intelligence in drug delivery system design. Advanced Drug Delivery Reviews 2019;151:169–90.
[15] Thota N, Jiang J. Computational amphiphilic materials for drug delivery. Frontiers in Materials 2015(2):64.
[16] Tiwari G, et al. Drug delivery systems: An updated review. International journal of pharmaceutical investigation 2012;2(1):2.
[17] Chaurasiya A, et al. Fundamentals of a targeted drug delivery system. In Molecular Pharmaceutics and Nano Drug Delivery. Elsevier; 2024. p. 289–309.
[18] Nayak A, Sen K. Bone-targeted drug delivery systems. Bio-targets & drug delivery approaches. Boca Raton, FL, USA: CRC Press; 2016. p. 207–31.

[19] Kong D-X, Li X-J, Zhang H-Y. Where is the hope for drug discovery? Let history tell the future. Drug Discovery Today 2009;14(3-4):115–9.
[20] Ezike TC, et al. Advances in drug delivery systems, challenges and future directions. Heliyon; 2023.
[21] Liu G, et al. A Review on drug delivery system for tumor therapy. Frontiers in Pharmacology 2021;12:735446.
[22] Shi J, et al. Nanotechnology in drug delivery and tissue engineering: from discovery to applications. Nano Letters 2010;10(9):3223–30.
[23] Parveen S, Misra R, Sahoo SK. Nanoparticles: a boon to drug delivery, therapeutics, diagnostics and imaging. Nanomedicine in cancer 2017:47–98.
[24] Tewabe A, et al. Targeted drug delivery—from magic bullet to nanomedicine: principles, challenges, and future perspectives. Journal of Multidisciplinary Healthcare 2021:1711–24.
[25] Kanwar R, et al. Green nanotechnology-driven drug delivery assemblies. ACS omega 2019;4(5):8804–15.
[26] Wang T, et al. Current status of in vivo bioanalysis of nano drug delivery systems. Journal of Pharmaceutical Analysis 2020;10(3):221–32.
[27] Manasa R, Shivananjappa M. Role of Nanotechnology-Based Materials in Drug Delivery. Advances in Novel Formulations for Drug Delivery 2023:279–307.
[28] Mitchell MD, et al. The frontiers of biomedical science and its application to animal science in addressing the major challenges facing Australasian dairy farming. Animal Production Science 2018;60(1):1–9.
[29] Gessner I, Neundorf I. Nanoparticles modified with cell-penetrating peptides: Conjugation mechanisms, physicochemical properties, and application in cancer diagnosis and therapy. International journal of molecular sciences 2020;21(7):2536.
[30] Chamundeeswari M, Jeslin J, Verma ML. Nanocarriers for drug delivery applications. Environmental Chemistry Letters 2019;17:849–65.
[31] López-Dávila V, Seifalian AM, Loizidou M. Organic nanocarriers for cancer drug delivery. Current Opinion in Pharmacology 2012;12(4):414–9.
[32] Bhatia S, Bhatia S. Nanoparticles types, classification, characterization, fabrication methods and drug delivery applications. Natural Polymer Drug Delivery Systems: Nanoparticles, Plants, and Algae 2016:33–93.
[33] Bozzuto G, Molinari A. Liposomes as nanomedical devices. International Journal of Nanomedicine 2015;10:975–99.
[34] Bamrungsap S, et al. Nanotechnology in therapeutics: a focus on nanoparticles as a drug delivery system. Nanomedicine: Nanotechnology, Biology, and Medicine 2012;7(8):1253–71.
[35] Vabbilisetty P, Sun XL. Liposome surface functionalization based on different anchoring lipids via Staudinger ligation. Organic & Biomolecular Chemistry 2014;12(8):1237–44.
[36] Lim HJ, et al. Polymer-associated liposomes as a novel delivery system for cyclodextrin-bound drugs. Journal of Colloid and Interface Science 2008;320(2):460–8.
[37] Sercombe L, et al. Advances and Challenges of Liposome Assisted Drug Delivery. Front Pharmacol 2015;6:286.
[38] Akbarzadeh A, et al. Liposome: classification, preparation, and applications. Nanoscale Res Lett 2013;8(1):102.
[39] Mohan A, et al. Novel resveratrol and 5-fluorouracil coencapsulated in PEGylated nanoliposomes improve chemotherapeutic efficacy of combination against head and neck squamous cell carcinoma. BioMed research international 2014;2014.
[40] Abraham SA, et al. The liposomal formulation of doxorubicin. In Methods in enzymology. Elsevier; 2005. p. 71–97.

[41] Fanciullino R, Ciccolini J, Milano G. COVID-19 vaccine race: watch your step for cancer patients. British Journal of Cancer 2021;124(5):860–1.
[42] Wang N, Chen M, Wang T. Liposomes used as a vaccine adjuvant-delivery system: From basics to clinical immunization. Journal of Controlled Release 2019;303:130–50.
[43] Malam Y, Loizidou M, Seifalian AM. Liposomes and nanoparticles: nanosized vehicles for drug delivery in cancer. Trends in Pharmacological Sciences 2009;30(11):592–9.
[44] Müller RH, Mäder K, Gohla S. Solid lipid nanoparticles (SLN) for controlled drug delivery–a review of the state of the art. European journal of pharmaceutics and biopharmaceutics 2000;50(1):161–77.
[45] Üner M, Yener G. Importance of solid lipid nanoparticles (SLN) in various administration routes and future perspectives. International Journal of Nanomedicine 2007;2(3):289–300.
[46] Wissing S, Kayser O, Müller R. Solid lipid nanoparticles for parenteral drug delivery. Advanced Drug Delivery Reviews 2004;56(9):1257–72.
[47] Muller RH, Keck CM. Challenges and solutions for the delivery of biotech drugs–a review of drug nanocrystal technology and lipid nanoparticles. Journal of Biotechnology 2004;113(1-3):151–70.
[48] Yoo HS, et al. Self-assembled nanoparticles containing hydrophobically modified glycol chitosan for gene delivery. Journal of Controlled Release 2005;103(1):235–43.
[49] Bondì ML, et al. Nanostructured lipid carriers-containing anticancer compounds: preparation, characterization, and cytotoxicity studies. Drug Delivery 2007;14(2):61–7.
[50] Stella B, et al. Development and characterization of solid lipid nanoparticles loaded with a highly active doxorubicin derivative. Nanomaterials 2018;8(2):110.
[51] Song C, Liu S. A new healthy sunscreen system for human: Solid lipid nannoparticles as carrier for 3, 4, 5-trimethoxybenzoylchitin and the improvement by adding Vitamin E. International Journal of Biological Macromolecules 2005;36(1-2):116–9.
[52] Byrne ME, Park K, Peppas NA. Molecular imprinting within hydrogels. Advanced Drug Delivery Reviews 2002;54(1):149–61.
[53] Zubris KAV, Colson YL, Grinstaff MW. Hydrogels as intracellular depots for drug delivery. Molecular Pharmaceutics 2012;9(1):196–200.
[54] Liang Y, et al. Preparation and properties of thermoreversible hydrogels based on methoxy poly (ethylene glycol)-grafted chitosan nanoparticles for drug delivery systems. Carbohydrate polymers 2011;83(4):1828–33.
[55] Amin MCIM, et al. Synthesis and characterization of thermo-and pH-responsive bacterial cellulose/acrylic acid hydrogels for drug delivery. Carbohydrate Polymers 2012;88(2):465–73.
[56] Molinos M, et al. Development of a hybrid dextrin hydrogel encapsulating dextrin nanogel as protein delivery system. Biomacromolecules 2012;13(2):517–27.
[57] Ding D, et al. Nanospheres-incorporated implantable hydrogel as a trans-tissue drug delivery system. ACS nano 2011;5(4):2520–34.
[58] Barbucci R, et al. A novel strategy for engineering hydrogels with ferromagnetic nanoparticles as crosslinkers of the polymer chains. Potential applications as a targeted drug delivery system. Soft Matter 2011;7(12):5558–65.
[59] Lohcharoenkal W, et al. Protein nanoparticles as drug delivery carriers for cancer therapy. BioMed research international 2014;2014.
[60] Arias JL, et al. Poly (alkylcyanoacrylate) colloidal particles as vehicles for antitumour drug delivery: a comparative study. Colloids and surfaces B: Biointerfaces 2008;62(1):64–70.

[61] Bhattacharya S, et al. Delivery of thymoquinone through hyaluronic acid-decorated mixed Pluronic® nanoparticles to attenuate angiogenesis and metastasis of triple-negative breast cancer. Journal of Controlled Release 2020;322:357–74.
[62] Torchilin V. Multifunctional pharmaceutical nanocarriers: development of the concept. Multifunctional pharmaceutical nanocarriers. Springer; 2008. p. 1–32.
[63] Singh J, et al. Diphtheria toxoid loaded poly-(ε-caprolactone) nanoparticles as mucosal vaccine delivery systems. Methods (San Diego, Calif.) 2006;38(2):96–105.
[64] Su T, et al. Polymer nanoparticle-assisted chemotherapy of pancreatic cancer. Therapeutic Advances in Medical Oncology 2020;12. p. 1758835920915978.
[65] Jahan ST, et al. Targeted therapeutic nanoparticles: an immense promise to fight against cancer. Journal of drug delivery 2017;2017.
[66] Yamamoto T, et al. What are determining factors for stable drug incorporation into polymeric micelle carriers? Consideration on physical and chemical characters of the micelle inner core. Journal of controlled release 2007;123(1):11–8.
[67] Ahmadi M, et al. Controllable synthesis of polymeric micelles by microfluidic platforms for biomedical applications: a systematic review. Iranian Journal of Pharmaceutical Research: IJPR 2021;20(2):229.
[68] Hsu HJ, et al. Dendrimer-based nanocarriers: a versatile platform for drug delivery. Wiley Interdisciplinary Reviews: Nanomedicine and Nanobiotechnology 2017;9(1):e1409.
[69] Markowicz-Piasecka M, Mikiciuk-Olasik E. Dendrimers in drug delivery. In *Nanobiomaterials in Drug Delivery*. Elsevier; 2016. p. 39–74.
[70] Tripathy S, Das MK. Dendrimers and their applications as novel drug delivery carriers. Journal of Applied Pharmaceutical Science 2013;3(9):142–9.
[71] Santos HA, et al. Inorganic nanoparticles in targeted drug delivery and imaging. Targeted drug delivery: concepts and design 2015:571–613.
[72] Ma Pa, et al. Inorganic nanocarriers for platinum drug delivery. Materials Today 2015;18(10):554–64.
[73] Wagner AM, et al. Quantum dots in biomedical applications. Acta Biomaterialia 2019;94:44–63.
[74] Gao X, et al. In vivo cancer targeting and imaging with semiconductor quantum dots. Nature Biotechnology 2004;22(8):969–76.
[75] Iga AM, et al. Clinical potential of quantum dots. BioMed Research International 2007;2007.
[76] Wang Q, Chao Y. Multifunctional quantum dots and liposome complexes in drug delivery. Journal of Biomedical Research 2018;32(2):91.
[77] Christian S, et al. Nucleolin expressed at the cell surface is a marker of endothelial cells in angiogenic blood vessels. The Journal of Cell Biology 2003;163(4):871–8.
[78] Cai X, et al. pH-Sensitive ZnO quantum dots–doxorubicin nanoparticles for lung cancer targeted drug delivery. ACS applied materials & interfaces 2016;8(34):22442–50.
[79] Olerile LD, et al. Near-infrared mediated quantum dots and paclitaxel co-loaded nanostructured lipid carriers for cancer theragnostic. Colloids and Surfaces B: Biointerfaces 2017;150:121–30.
[80] Raju M, Kulkarni YA, Wairkar S. Therapeutic potential and recent delivery systems of berberine: A wonder molecule. Journal of Functional Foods 2019;61:103517.
[81] Iijima S. Helical microtubules of graphitic carbon. Nature 1991;354(6348):56–8.
[82] Lacerda L, et al. Carbon nanotubes as nanomedicines: from toxicology to pharmacology. Advanced Drug Delivery Reviews 2006;58(14):1460–70.
[83] Ng CM, et al. Conjugation of insulin onto the sidewalls of single-walled carbon nanotubes through functionalization and diimide-activated amidation. International Journal of Nanomedicine 2016:1607–14.

[84] Karimi M, et al. Carbon nanotubes part I: preparation of a novel and versatile drug-delivery vehicle. Expert Opinion on Drug Delivery 2015;12(7):1071–87.

[85] Lay CL, et al. Delivery of paclitaxel by physically loading onto poly (ethylene glycol)(PEG)-graftcarbon nanotubes for potent cancer therapeutics. Nanotechnology 2010;21(6):065101.

[86] Levi-Polyachenko NH, et al. Rapid photothermal intracellular drug delivery using multiwalled carbon nanotubes. Molecular Pharmaceutics 2009;6(4):1092–9.

[87] Das M, et al. Augmented anticancer activity of a targeted, intracellularly activatable, theranostic nanomedicine based on fluorescent and radiolabeled, methotrexate-folic acid-multiwalled carbon nanotube conjugate. Molecular Pharmaceutics 2013;10(7):2543–57.

[88] Ajima K, et al. Carbon nanohorns as anticancer drug carriers. Molecular Pharmaceutics 2005;2(6):475–80.

[89] Shiba K, Yudasaka M, Iijima S. Carbon nanohorns as a novel drug carrier. Nihon rinsho. Japanese journal of clinical medicine 2006;64(2):239–46.

[90] Murakami T, et al, Water-dispersed single-wall carbon nanohorns as drug carriers for local cancer chemotherapy. 2008.

[91] Ajima K, et al. Enhancement of in vivo anticancer effects of cisplatin by incorporation inside single-wall carbon nanohorns. ACS nano 2008;2(10):2057–64.

[92] Jia G, et al. Cytotoxicity of carbon nanomaterials: single-wall nanotube, multi-wall nanotube, and fullerene. Environmental Science & Technology 2005;39(5):1378–83.

[93] Thakral S, Mehta R. Fullerenes: An introduction and overview of their biological properties. Indian Journal of Pharmaceutical Sciences 2006;68(1).

[94] Xu ZP, et al. Inorganic nanoparticles as carriers for efficient cellular delivery. Chemical Engineering Science 2006;61(3):1027–40.

[95] Chen B-X, et al. Antigenicity of fullerenes: antibodies specific for fullerenes and their characteristics. Proceedings of the National Academy of Sciences 1998;95(18):10809–13.

[96] Selvarajan V, Obuobi S, Ee PLR. Silica nanoparticles—a versatile tool for the treatment of bacterial infections. Frontiers in chemistry 2020;8:602.

[97] Knežević NŽ, Durand J-O. Large pore mesoporous silica nanomaterials for application in delivery of biomolecules. Nanoscale 2015;7(6):2199–209.

[98] Wang Y, et al. Mesoporous silica nanoparticles in drug delivery and biomedical applications. Nanomedicine: Nanotechnology, Biology and Medicine 2015;11(2):313–27.

[99] Rosenholm JM, et al. Cancer-cell-specific induction of apoptosis using mesoporous silica nanoparticles as drug-delivery vectors. Small (Weinheim an der Bergstrasse, Germany) 2010;6(11):1234–41.

[100] McNamara K, Tofail SA. Nanosystems: the use of nanoalloys, metallic, bimetallic, and magnetic nanoparticles in biomedical applications. Physical chemistry chemical physics 2015;17(42):27981–95.

[101] McNamara K, Tofail SA. Nanoparticles in biomedical applications. Advances in Physics: X 2017;2(1):54–88.

[102] Kudr J, et al. Magnetic nanoparticles: From design and synthesis to real world applications. Nanomaterials 2017;7(9):243.

[103] Kouassi GK, Irudayaraj J. Magnetic and gold-coated magnetic nanoparticles as a DNA sensor. Analytical Chemistry 2006;78(10):3234–41.

[104] Loo C, et al. Immunotargeted nanoshells for integrated cancer imaging and therapy. Nano Letters 2005;5(4):709–11.

[105] Murawala P, et al. In situ synthesized BSA capped gold nanoparticles: effective carrier of anticancer drug methotrexate to MCF-7 breast cancer cells. Materials Science and Engineering: C 2014;34:158–67.

[106] Aslam H, et al. Current and future perspectives of multifunctional magnetic nanoparticles based controlled drug delivery systems. Journal of Drug Delivery Science and Technology 2022;67:102946.
[107] Huang H-C, et al. Inorganic nanoparticles for cancer imaging and therapy. Journal of controlled Release 2011;155(3):344–57.
[108] Barry SE. Challenges in the development of magnetic particles for therapeutic applications. International Journal of Hyperthermia 2008;24(6):451–66.
[109] Wang Y, Chen J, Irudayaraj J. Nuclear targeting dynamics of gold nanoclusters for enhanced therapy of HER2+ breast cancer. ACS nano 2011;5(12):9718–25.
[110] Ni R, et al. Nanocrystals embedded in chitosan-based respirable swellable microparticles as dry powder for sustained pulmonary drug delivery. European Journal of Pharmaceutical Sciences 2017;99:137–46.
[111] Ahmadi M, et al. Pharmacokinetics and biodistribution studies of [99mTc]-Labeled ZIF-8 nanoparticles to pave the way for image-guided drug delivery and theranostics. Journal of Drug Delivery Science and Technology 2023;81:104249.
[112] Ali S, et al. Explainable Artificial Intelligence (XAI): What we know and what is left to attain Trustworthy Artificial Intelligence. Information Fusion 2023;99:101805.
[113] Du-Harpur X, et al. What is AI? Applications of artificial intelligence to dermatology. British Journal of Dermatology 2020;183(3):423–30.
[114] Jiang T, Gradus JL, Rosellini AJ. Supervised machine learning: a brief primer. Behavior Therapy 2020;51(5):675–87.
[115] Taye MM. Understanding of Machine Learning with Deep Learning: Architectures, Workflow, Applications and Future Directions. Computers 2023;12(5):91.
[116] Polanski J. Unsupervised Learning in Drug Design from Self-Organization to Deep Chemistry. International Journal of Molecular Sciences 2022;23(5):2797.
[117] Sarker IH. Deep learning: a comprehensive overview on techniques, taxonomy, applications and research directions. SN Computer Science 2021;2(6):420.
[118] Bohr A, Memarzadeh K. The rise of artificial intelligence in healthcare applications. In *Artificial Intelligence in healthcare*. Elsevier; 2020. p. 25–60.
[119] Mustafa Z, Nsour H. Using Computer Vision Techniques to Automatically Detect Abnormalities in Chest X-rays. Diagnostics 2023;13(18):2979.
[120] Bajwa J, et al. Artificial intelligence in healthcare: transforming the practice of medicine. Future healthcare journal 2021;8(2):e188.
[121] Alowais SA, et al. Revolutionizing healthcare: the role of artificial intelligence in clinical practice. BMC Medical Education 2023;23(1):689.
[122] Coelho JF, et al. Drug delivery systems: Advanced technologies potentially applicable in personalized treatments. EPMA journal 2010;1:164–209.
[123] Kanyongo W, Ezugwu AE. Machine learning approaches to medication adherence amongst NCD patients: A systematic literature review. Informatics in Medicine Unlocked 2023:101210.
[124] Paul D, et al. Artificial intelligence in drug discovery and development. Drug Discovery Today 2021;26(1):80.
[125] Mariappan MB, et al. Using AI and ML to predict shipment times of therapeutics, diagnostics and vaccines in e-pharmacy supply chains during COVID-19 pandemic. The International Journal of Logistics Management 2023;34(2):390–416.
[126] Vidhya KS, et al. Artificial Intelligence's Impact on Drug Discovery and Development From Bench to Bedside. Cureus 2023;15(10).
[127] Vora LK, et al. Artificial intelligence in pharmaceutical technology and drug delivery design. Pharmaceutics 2023;15(7):1916.

[128] Joseph TM, et al. Nanoparticles: Taking a unique position in medicine. Nanomaterials 2023;13(3):574.
[129] Cid-Mejías A, et al. A deep learning approach using synthetic images for segmenting and estimating 3D orientation of nanoparticles in EM images. Computer Methods and Programs in Biomedicine 2021;202:105958.
[130] Furxhi I, et al. Machine learning prediction of nanoparticle in vitro toxicity: A comparative study of classifiers and ensemble-classifiers using the Copeland Index. Toxicology Letters 2019;312:157–66.
[131] Soltani M, et al. Enhancing clinical translation of cancer using nanoinformatics. Cancers 2021;13(10):2481.
[132] Benkő E, et al. Predicting drug release rate of implantable matrices and better understanding of the underlying mechanisms through experimental design and artificial neural network-based modelling. Pharmaceutics 2022;14(2):228.
[133] Das KP. Nanoparticles and convergence of artificial intelligence for targeted drug delivery for cancer therapy: Current progress and challenges. Frontiers in Medical Technology 2023;4:1067144.
[134] Shang Y, et al. Deep learning for improving the spatial resolution of magnetic particle imaging. Physics in Medicine & Biology 2022;67(12):125012.
[135] Sakagianni A, et al. Using Machine Learning to Predict Antimicrobial Resistance—A Literature Review. Antibiotics 2023;12(3):452.
[136] Dedeloudi A, Weaver E, Lamprou DA. Machine learning in additive manufacturing & Microfluidics for smarter and safer drug delivery systems. International Journal of Pharmaceutics 2023:122818.
[137] Wang Y, et al. Recent advances in self-regulated drug delivery devices. A Handbook of Artificial Intelligence in Drug Delivery 2023:347–69.
[138] Lakkireddy HR, Bazile DV. Nano-carriers for drug routeing–towards a new era. Journal of Drug Targeting 2019;27(5-6):525–41.
[139] Chang EH, et al. Nanomedicine: past, present and future–a global perspective. Biochemical and Biophysical Research Communications 2015;468(3):511–7.
[140] Bhhatarai B, et al. Opportunities and challenges using artificial intelligence in ADME/Tox. Nature Materials 2019;18(5):418–22.
[141] Ramesh A, et al. Artificial intelligence in medicine. Annals of the Royal College of Surgeons of England 2004;86(5):334.
[142] Miles, J. and A.J. Walker. The potential application of artificial intelligence in transport. in IEE Proceedings-Intelligent Transport Systems. 2006. IET.
[143] Yang, Y. and K.L. Siau, A qualitative research on marketing and sales in the artificial intelligence age. 2018.
[144] Wirtz BW, Weyerer JC, Geyer C. Artificial intelligence and the public sector—applications and challenges. International Journal of Public Administration 2019;42(7):596–615.
[145] Taher M, et al. Relevance of AI in microbased drug delivery system. A Handbook of Artificial Intelligence in Drug Delivery. Elsevier; 2023. p. 123–43.
[146] Villarruel Mendoza LA, et al. Recent advances in micro-electro-mechanical devices for controlled drug release applications. Frontiers in Bioengineering and Biotechnology 2020;8:827.
[147] Reddy Dumpa N, Bandari S, Repka MA. Novel gastroretentive floating pulsatile drug delivery system produced via hot-melt extrusion and fused deposition modeling 3D printing. Pharmaceutics 2020;12(1):52.

[148] Lou H, Lian B, Hageman MJ. Applications of Machine Learning in Solid Oral Dosage Form Development. Journal of Pharmaceutical Sciences 2021;110(9):3150–65.
[149] Jiang J, et al. Emerging Artificial Intelligence (AI) Technologies Used in the Development of Solid Dosage Forms. Pharmaceutics 2022;14(11).
[150] Piroozmand F, Mohammadipanah F, Sajedi H. Artificial neural network (ANN) in drug delivery. A Handbook of Artificial Intelligence in Drug Delivery. Elsevier; 2023. p. 97–122.
[151] Prajapati JB, et al. Impact of AI on drug delivery and pharmacokinetics: The present scenario and future prospects. A Handbook of Artificial Intelligence in Drug Delivery. Elsevier; 2023. p. 443–65.
[152] Vanneschi L. Improving genetic programming for the prediction of pharmacokinetic parameters. Memetic Computing 2014;6:255–62.
[153] Mak K-K, Pichika MR. Artificial intelligence in drug development: present status and future prospects. Drug Discovery Today 2019;24(3):773–80.
[154] Lengyel M, et al. Microparticles, microspheres, and microcapsules for advanced drug delivery. Scientia Pharmaceutica 2019;87(3):20.
[155] Virmani T, Gupta J. Pharmaceutical application of microspheres: an approach for the treatment of various diseases. Int J Pharm Sci Res 2017;8(8):3253–60.
[156] Takayama K, Fujikawa M, Nagai T. Artificial neural network as a novel method to optimize pharmaceutical formulations. Pharmaceutical Research 1999;16:1–6.
[157] Rodríguez-Dorado R, et al. A novel method for the production of core-shell microparticles by inverse gelation optimized with artificial intelligent tools. International Journal of Pharmaceutics 2018;538(1-2):97–104.
[158] Atrooz O. Effects of alkylresorcinolic lipids obtained from acetonic extract of Jordanian wheat grains on liposome properties. Int J Biol Chem 2011;5(5):314–21.
[159] Shehata T, et al. Prolongation of residence time of liposome by surface-modification with mixture of hydrophilic polymers. International Journal of Pharmaceutics 2008;359(1-2):272–9.
[160] Hathout RM, Gad HA, Metwally AA. Gelatinized-core liposomes: toward a more robust carrier for hydrophilic molecules. Journal of Biomedical Materials Research. Part A 2017;105(11):3086–92.
[161] Luo M, et al. Micro-/nanorobots at work in active drug delivery. Advanced Functional Materials 2018;28(25):1706100.
[162] da Silva Luz GV, et al. Nanorobotics in drug delivery systems for treatment of cancer: a review. J Mat Sci Eng A 2016;6:167–80.
[163] Hamet P, Tremblay J. Artificial intelligence in medicine. Metabolism: Clinical and Experimental 2017;69:S36–40.
[164] He C, et al. Size-dependent absorption mechanism of polymeric nanoparticles for oral delivery of protein drugs. Biomaterials 2012;33(33):8569–78.
[165] Gaumet M, et al. Nanoparticles for drug delivery: the need for precision in reporting particle size parameters. European journal of pharmaceutics and biopharmaceutics 2008;69(1):1–9.
[166] Chan JM, et al. Polymeric nanoparticles for drug delivery. Cancer Nanotechnology: Methods and Protocols 2010:163–75.
[167] Youshia J, Ali ME, Lamprecht A. Artificial neural network based particle size prediction of polymeric nanoparticles. European Journal of Pharmaceutics and Biopharmaceutics 2017;119:333–42.
[168] Shalaby KS, et al. Determination of factors controlling the particle size and entrapment efficiency of noscapine in PEG/PLA nanoparticles using artificial neural networks. International Journal of Nanomedicine 2014:4953–64.

[169] Periyasamy M, Kar A. Modulating the properties of $SnO_2$ nanocrystals: morphological effects on structural, photoluminescence, photocatalytic, electrochemical and gas sensing properties. Journal of Materials Chemistry C 2020;8(14):4604–35.
[170] Yoon S, et al. Progress in morphology control from fullerene to nonfullerene acceptors for scalable high-performance organic photovoltaics. Journal of Materials Chemistry A 2021;9(44):24729–58.
[171] Kim H, Han J, Han TY-J. Machine vision-driven automatic recognition of particle size and morphology in SEM images. Nanoscale 2020;12(37):19461–9.
[172] Heydari M, et al. An industrial image processing-based approach for estimation of iron ore green pellet size distribution. Powder Technology 2016;303:260–8.
[173] Sun Z, et al. A deep learning-based framework for automatic analysis of the nanoparticle morphology in SEM/TEM images. Nanoscale 2022;14(30):10761–72.
[174] Kakoty V, et al. Biological toxicity of nanoparticles. In *Nanoparticle Therapeutics*. Elsevier; 2022. p. 603–28.
[175] Jones DE, Ghandehari H, Facelli JC. A review of the applications of data mining and machine learning for the prediction of biomedical properties of nanoparticles. Computer Methods and Programs in Biomedicine 2016;132:93–103.
[176] Fard JK, Jafari S, Eghbal MA. A review of molecular mechanisms involved in toxicity of nanoparticles. Advanced pharmaceutical bulletin 2015;5(4):447.
[177] Banaye Yazdipour A, et al. Predicting the toxicity of nanoparticles using artificial intelligence tools: a systematic review. Nanotoxicology 2023;17(1):62–77.
[178] Ahmadi M, Ayyoubzadeh SM, Ghorbani-Bidkorpeh F. Toxicity prediction of nanoparticles using machine learning approaches. Toxicology 2023:153697.
[179] Fourches D, et al. Quantitative nanostructure– activity relationship modeling. ACS nano 2010;4(10):5703–12.
[180] Kashani-Asadi-Jafari F, Aftab A, Ghaemmaghami S. A machine learning framework for predicting entrapment efficiency in niosomal particles. International Journal of Pharmaceutics 2022;627:122203.
[181] Hoseini B, et al. Optimizing nanoliposomal formulations: Assessing factors affecting entrapment efficiency of curcumin-loaded liposomes using machine learning. International Journal of Pharmaceutics 2023;646:123414.
[182] Behzadi S, et al. Cellular uptake of nanoparticles: journey inside the cell. Chemical Society Reviews 2017;46(14):4218–44.
[183] Alafeef M, Srivastava I, Pan D. Machine learning for precision breast cancer diagnosis and prediction of the nanoparticle cellular internalization. ACS sensors 2020;5(6):1689–98.
[184] Ali R, Balamurali M, Varamini P. Deep Learning-Based Artificial Intelligence to Investigate Targeted Nanoparticles' Uptake in TNBC Cells. International Journal of Molecular Sciences 2022;23(24):16070.
[185] Makadia HK, Siegel SJ. Poly lactic-co-glycolic acid (PLGA) as biodegradable controlled drug delivery carrier. Polymers 2011;3(3):1377–97.
[186] Danhier F, et al. PLGA-based nanoparticles: an overview of biomedical applications. Journal of controlled release 2012;161(2):505–22.
[187] Husseini GA, et al. Using artificial neural networks and model predictive control to optimize acoustically assisted doxorubicin release from polymeric micelles. Technology in Cancer Research & Treatment 2009;8(6):479–88.
[188] Szlęk J, et al. Heuristic modeling of macromolecule release from PLGA microspheres. International Journal of Nanomedicine 2013:4601–11.

[189] Oh I-H, et al. Cancer cell-specific photoactivity of pheophorbide a–glycol chitosan nanoparticles for photodynamic therapy in tumor-bearing mice. Biomaterials 2013;34(27):6454–63.
[190] Adir O, et al. Integrating artificial intelligence and nanotechnology for precision cancer medicine. Advanced Materials 2020;32(13):1901989.
[191] Harrison PJ, et al. Deep-learning models for lipid nanoparticle-based drug delivery. Nanomedicine: Nanotechnology, Biology, and Medicine 2021;16(13):1097–110.
[192] Lavik EB, Kuppermann BD, Humayun MS. Chapter 38 - Drug Delivery. In: Ryan SJ, editor. Retina. Fifth EditionLondon: W.B. Saunders; 2013. p. 734–45.
[193] Bruschi M.L., editor. 2 - Modification of drug release. In *Strategies to Modify the Drug Release from Pharmaceutical Systems*. Woodhead Publishing; 2015. pp. 15–28.
[194] Li X, et al. Clinical Translation of Long-Acting Drug Delivery Systems for Posterior Capsule Opacification Prophylaxis. Pharmaceutics 2023;15(4).
[195] Gao J, et al. The Future of Drug Delivery. Chemistry of Materials 2023;35(2):359–63.
[196] Shih HP, Zhang X, Aronov AM. Drug discovery effectiveness from the standpoint of therapeutic mechanisms and indications. Nature Reviews. Drug Discovery 2018;17(1):19–33.
[197] Murdoch TB, Detsky AS. The inevitable application of big data to health care. JAMA: the Journal of the American Medical Association 2013;309(13):1351–2.
[198] Jiang F, et al. Artificial intelligence in healthcare: past, present and future. Stroke Vasc Neurol 2017;2(4):230–43.
[199] He S, Leanse LG, Feng Y. Artificial intelligence and machine learning assisted drug delivery for effective treatment of infectious diseases. Advanced Drug Delivery Reviews 2021;178:113922.
[200] Davis JJ, et al. Antimicrobial resistance prediction in PATRIC and RAST. Scientific reports 2016;6(1):27930.
[201] Liu Z, et al. Evaluation of machine learning models for predicting antimicrobial resistance of Actinobacillus pleuropneumoniae from whole genome sequences. Frontiers in microbiology 2020;11:48.
[202] Yu H, et al. Phenotypic antimicrobial susceptibility testing with deep learning video microscopy. Analytical Chemistry 2018;90(10):6314–22.
[203] Steiner MC, Gibson KM, Crandall KA. Drug resistance prediction using deep learning techniques on HIV-1 sequence data. Viruses 2020;12(5):560.
[204] Vashist A, et al. Recent trends on hydrogel based drug delivery systems for infectious diseases. Biomater Sci 2016;4(11):1535–53.
[205] Owh C, et al. Towards machine learning for hydrogel drug delivery systems. Trends in Biotechnology 2023;41(4):476–9.
[206] Noorain L, et al. A Machine Learning Approach for PLGA Nanoparticles in Antiviral Drug Delivery. Pharmaceutics 2023;15(2).
[207] Yacoub AS, et al. Artificial intelligence-assisted development of in situ forming nanoparticles for arthritis therapy via intra-articular delivery. Drug Delivery 2022;29(1):1423–36.
[208] Veiga N, Diesendruck Y, Peer D. Targeted nanomedicine: Lessons learned and future directions. Journal of Controlled Release 2023;355:446–57.

# Artificial intelligence in vaccine development

9

*Hrishikesh S Bhardhwaj, Snigdha Tutika, Siddharth Kaushik L.S., Praveen Kumar Gupta, and Thippa Reddy K.S.*
Department of Biotechnology, R V College of Engineering, Bengaluru, Karnataka, India

## Acronyms

| | |
|---|---|
| **AI** | Artificial Intelligence |
| **mRNA** | Messenger RiboNucleic Acid |
| **FDA** | Food and Drug Administration |
| **AUC** | Area Under Curve |
| **ROC** | Receiver Operating Curve |
| **MAE** | Mean Absolute Error |
| **RMSE** | Root Mean Square Error |
| **SVM** | Support vector machine |
| **ML** | Machine learning |
| **AAPC** | Amino acid anchoring pair composition techniques |
| **AAP** | Amino acids pair scaling approach |
| **TCR** | T-cell receptor |
| **TCR-pMHC** | TCR-peptide-MHC |
| **MHC** | Major histocompatibility complex |
| **SB** | Structure-based |
| **MM** | Motif matrix |
| **SM** | Sequence motif |
| **QAM** | Quantitative affinity matrix |
| **ANN** | Artificial neural network |
| **SAAS** | Human leukocyte antigen (HLA) proteins, Single amino acid substitution |
| **PSSMs** | Position Specific Scoring Matrix |
| **KNN** | K-Nearest Neighbors |
| **Log Reg** | Logistic Regression |
| **NB** | Naive Bayes |
| **SVM** | Support Vector Machine |
| **RF** | Random Forest |
| **RNN** | A long short-term memory recurrent neural network |
| **RV** | Reverse vaccination |
| **PRR** | Pattern recognition receptors |
| **WHO** | World Health Organization |
| **AIT** | Artificial intelligence techniques |
| **SRM** | Structural Risk Minimization |
| **CV** | Cross Validation |

**Artificial Intelligence in Biomaterials Design and Development. DOI:** https://doi.org/10.1016/B978-0-323-95464-8.00012-8

| | |
|---|---|
| **LOOCV** | Leave One Out Cross Validation |
| **MDL** | Minimum Description Length |
| **BIC** | Bayesian Information Criterion |
| **Tgel** | Gelation temperature |
| **SAM** | Search Algorithm for Ligands |
| **ISTTVD** | In Silico Trial for Tuberculosis Vaccine Development |
| **NER** | Named entity recognition |
| **ABM** | Agent-based models |
| **CA** | Cellular Automata |
| **MSP4** | Major surface protein 4 |
| **CODEX** | Notable technologies include Codetection by Indexing |
| **CyTOF** | Cytometry by Time-of-Light |
| **GATK** | Genome Analysis Toolkit |
| **HDST** | high-definition spatial transcriptome |
| **IMC** | imaging mass cytometry |
| **MIBI-TOF** | multiplexed ion beam imaging by time-of-flight |
| **mIF** | multiplex immunofluorescence |
| **mIHC** | multiplex immunohistochemistry |
| **ACT** | Adoptive Cell Therapy |
| **ITH** | Intratumor Heterogeneity |
| **TIME** | Microenvironment |

## 9.1 Introduction

It is widely acknowledged that the development of robots marked the beginning of artificial intelligence (AI) [1,2]. Because of his inspirational influence, a surgical system manufactured by the American company Intuitive Surgical was given the name Da Vinci in the medical field. As the Food and Drug Administration (FDA) gave it approval in 2000, more than 5000 units have been installed worldwide. Surgeons can operate Da Vinci surgical equipment from a console, facilitating complex surgery using a minimally invasive technique. Gynecologic and prostatectomies are two popular surgical procedures that use this technology. Cardiac valve repair is one application where it is being employed.

Nowadays, AI is regarded as a subfield of engineering that applies innovative ideas and creative fixes to difficult problems. Computers may eventually surpass human intelligence if advancements in software development, technological speed, and capacity are sustained. Current cybernetics has made a significant contribution to AI development that cannot be overlooked. Cybernetics, a transdisciplinary approach, studies system regulation, structure, and limitations, primarily mechanical, physical, biological, and social. Its goal is to govern any system using technology. Norbert Wiener is credited with founding cybernetics by formalizing the concept of feedback, which has ramifications for computer science, engineering, systems control, biology, neuroscience, philosophy, and social organization [3].

### 9.1.1 Vaccines – a brief Introduction

Vaccines are essential for maintaining global health because they stop the spread of many diseases and infections. According to estimates from the World Health Organisation, vaccinations save the lives of two to three million people annually. In addition, vaccinations have made it possible to eradicate smallpox (CR [4]) and are almost certain to eradicate polio. Furthermore, vaccinations have a huge economic impact because they quickly and efficiently lower hospital stays and disease expenditures by over $500 billion. Vaccines function by exposing a recipient to a portion or the entirety of a disease, which stimulates the immune system. Conventional varieties of vaccinations include conjugate and subunit vaccinations, as well as live-attenuated, inactivated, and replication-defective pathogens. Live-attenuated vaccinations contain a pathogen in a weakened form. Passaging infections is typically required to attenuate them across a range of cultures [5].

### 9.1.2 Artificial intelligence in vaccine development

Three categories can be used to group AI-based learning techniques: (1) supervised learning, in which the prediction model learns from prior classification examples; (2) unsupervised learning, in which the prediction model learns by examining various patterns in the training data; and (3) reinforcement learning, in which the prediction model learns by putting an operational scheme based on reward sequences and penalties.

Data pre-processing, encoding, feature extraction, training/learning from the features, testing, validation, and evaluation on unknown data with the aid of various AI platforms available to the developer are often required for the development of an AI-based prediction model. Among the many popular AI platforms are TensorFlow, Google AI, Microsoft Azure, and OpenAI. Different evaluation matrices, such as accuracy, precision, area under curve (AUC), receiver operating curve (ROC) curve, mean absolute error (MSE), root mean square error (RMSE), and numerous statistics generated from the confusion matrix, can be used to assess trained prediction models.

Immunoinformatics-based techniques [6] are intensely advancing AI- and machine learning (ML)-assisted prediction servers by predicting B-cell and T-cell epitopes and new vaccine candidates. To ensure that a vaccination is effective for a long time, AI systems look for microbial components [7] that are unlikely to mutate or change. The development of vaccines has benefited greatly from computational analysis supported by ML methods. AI can track the genetic alterations (mutations) in the genome over time to optimize the effectiveness of future vaccines by combining data from several experimental and real-world sources. For regression analysis and the classification of both linear and non-linear data, the SVM algorithms employ a supervised statistical learning technique. These techniques create a random forest of decision trees using bagging and feature randomness. A fully connected feed-forward artificial neural network (ANN) with an input layer, an output layer, and at least three hidden layers is implemented by the MLP algorithms. An activation function regulates the information flow that travels through hidden layers from the input layer to the output layers.

In addition, since both AI and ML include supervised learning, it is important to note that while they are conceptually distinct, they are closely related. AI is a vast subject of computer science that focuses on building robots or systems that can carry out tasks that need human intelligence, like reasoning, problem-solving, and natural language understanding. Task-oriented prediction model creation (training, fine-tuning, testing, and deployment) is the main emphasis of ML, a subset of artificial intelligence. ML is teaching computers to learn from data and make judgements or predictions without the need for explicit programming. ML is essentially a method employed in the larger subject of AI to produce "intelligent behavior."

### 9.1.3 Biomaterials in vaccine development and delivery

Biomaterials provide a variety of benefits that can be tailored to meet the serious health issues that infectious illnesses present. These technologies, for instance, can be created on different size scales (such as nanoparticles or microparticles), with morphologies that mimic pathogen features, loaded with adjuvants and antigens, and provide control over molecular features like antigen display density (multivalency), boost immune stimulation (adjuvanticity), and improve preclinical safety profiles due to their nonreplicating nature. They can also be designed modularly to apply a specific materials platform to multiple pathogen targets, co-encapsulate immune-stimulatory agents and antigens, shield cargo from enzymatic degradation, target specific immune cells, and regulate the release kinetics of vaccines. Many biomaterials, such as polymers, lipids, self-assembled proteins, and inorganic materials, are being investigated for use as vaccines against a variety of infectious diseases because of this potential, though the majority of this work is thus far primarily in preclinical animal models this perspective paper focuses only on their application to prophylactic (i.e., preventive) vaccines against infectious diseases. In addition to providing flexible control over the rate at which vaccination cargoes, such as adjuvants or antigens, degrade, polymers also have the ability to co-deliver immunostimulants and antigens, which can maximize dose reduction and potency while reducing the likelihood of off-target effects. Numerous synthetic polymers, such as poly(lactic-co-glycolic acid), polyethylene-imine, and polystyrene, have been investigated for use in vaccines. Considerable research has also been done using natural polymers and polysaccharides such alginate, chito-san, and inulin. According to a recent study, cationic polystyrene nanoparticles (NPs) elicited a more robust response involving T-cells and antibody function because APCs absorbed and processed them more efficiently than neutral-surface NPs. Some of the different administrative techniques are mentioned briefly here.

Some of the most studied smart biomaterials for vaccine applications are polymeric polymers that alter in pH. A potent method of managing immunogenic pathways is the capacity of lysosome cleavable chemistry to activate vaccination agents intracellularly. In order to encapsulate vaccine agents with great effectiveness and release their vaccine components at site-specific targets, pH-cleavable microparticles have been produced. Furthermore, regulated antigen presentation by APCs to elicit desirable immune responses has been made possible by pH-sensitive biomaterials, such as aliphatic monomers containing cleavable acetal linkages. An MHC-I mediated antigen presentation can be achieved by using pH-degradable hydrogels or polymeric formulations that break down in the endosome and cause its membrane to be disrupted. Yang et al. have recently conducted intriguing research on antigen delivery with biomimetic micelles made of DC membrane, stearic acid grafted chitosan modified with histidine, and OVA antigen. These micelles employ DC membrane as a natural adjuvant and exploit the pHresponsive characteristics of histidine for endosomal escape and antigen delivery. Apart from hydrogel adjuvant vaccines that react to pH levels, protein-based vaccinations also take advantage of the phagosome's acidic pH to release antigen and enhance the immune response.

For example, surface-functionalized anti-DEC-205 monoclonal Abs targeting the DEC-205 endocytosis receptors expressed solely by epidermal Langerhans DCs and thymic endothelial cells were used to coat acid-degradable amino acid-based microparticles encasing vaccine components. At physiological pH, the microparticles made of poly(amidoamine) backbones and pH-sensitive cross linkers are stable; however, at the acidic pH of the DC lysosome, the vaccine components break down and are released. These vaccinations show a lot of potential in terms of supplying adjuvants and vaccine antigens to DCs in order to stimulate a powerful immune response.

Temperature variation is another intrinsic signal that has been used by researchers for responsive material-based therapy. The special ability of thermoresponsive biomaterials to alter their solvation state in response to temperature. These biomaterials use variations in physiological temperature as cues to modify the shape of the material. Hydrogel-based polymers, such as poly(N-isopropylacrylamide) (PNIPAM), poly(N-vinyl caprolactam) (PVC), poly(methyl vinyl ether) (PMVE), poly(2-oxazoline), and naturally derived cellulose polymers, are the most extensively studied class of thermo-responsive biomaterials for drug delivery applications. Without the need for chemical or other external stimuli, thermoresponsive hydrogels respond to temperature signals and change from a liquid at room temperature to a gel formation at physiological temperature. The term "sol–gel transition" refers to this change from solution to gel formation.

The hydrogel is in a liquid soluble condition below a critical temperature, also referred to as the lower critical solution temperature (LCST). Hydrogels become insoluble and gel out of the solution when the temperature rises above the LCST because the higher temperature causes the polymer chains to become more hydrophobic. Conversely, the temperature at which certain hydrogels become immiscible and cause gel formation at lower temperatures is known as the upper critical solution temperature (UCST). For example, Shakya et al. used a mouse model of rheumatoid arthritis (RA) to show the effect of this thermo-responsive polymer by causing a substantial IgG response in combination with collagen type II (CII). PVC and other thermoresponsive biomaterials have a transition temperature of 33°C, which allows them to dissolve in organic solvents and water. Kahle et al. [8] In addition, PMVE has a phase-change temperature of about 36°C, which makes it exceptionally helpful for physiological drug activation. An effective class of enzyme-responsive drug delivery materials for the activation of drug load in pathologically active areas, such as inflammatory or malignant tissues, is made possible by site-specific enzymatic activity. As enzymes are essential to numerous cellular and metabolic functions and their dysregulation highlights the pathophysiology of various diseases, enzymatic expression may be a target for bio-catalytically activated drug delivery methods. For example, genes encoding particular enzymes are found in malignant tumors, and these genes can be used to reveal anticancer medications at the tumor site. The creation of anticancer vaccines for enzyme-dependent targeted and regulated release of therapeutic agents is facilitated by the overexpression of certain enzymes (e.g., matrix metalloproteinase 2 (MMP2) or cathepsin B) at tumor locations relative to their comparatively low expression in healthy tissues. Liposome formulations are one type of enzyme-responsive substance that is often employed. For example, liposome nanocarriers that release anticancer medicines have been created to be enzymatically activated at high concentrations of MMP2 protease, a characteristic of solid tumors. In order to conceal a second layer of shorter PEG strands (2000 MW) that display cell-penetrating peptides and to avoid non-specific interactions, these liposomes are adorned with a longer PEG (3400 MW) that contains an MMP2-cleavable linker. MMP2 substrates cleave at tumor sites, releasing protective long-chained PEGs, exposing cell-penetrating liposome components and facilitating their entrance into tumor cells to release their therapeutic payload intracellularly.

Creating biomaterials that may release therapeutic cargo in response to a specific molecular binding is a relatively recent breakthrough in the field of smart materials. All of these molecular recognition-responsive materials work by competitively binding to a target, which enables the cargo to be released conditionally. These materials' high specificity, which enables controlled, targeted distribution only to locations with sufficiently high analyte concentrations, is a significant benefit. Higher concentrations of characteristic surface receptors or signaling proteins are typically found in drug release target areas. Scientists are developing materials that, upon binding to disease-associated chemicals specific to a particular region, can release treatments. Formulations of molecularly imprinted polymers can be engineered to have a high affinity for ligand template molecules or antigens. Target ligand recognition can also be achieved by using hydrogels that have been crosslinked with aptamers. Folded nucleic acid structures known as aptamers have a high degree of sensitivity and specificity when identifying proteins and other compounds. These aptamer sequences can be duplexed in a hydrogel with complementary DNA sequences. The aptamer will dissociate from its complementary strand in the presence of an increased concentration of aptamer targets in order to bind to its target competitively, breaking down the hydrogel and releasing any medicines that may have been contained. Yang and colleagues, for instance, created several hydrogels based on aptamers that exhibit distinct responses to either thrombin or adenosine. Similar nanogel was produced by Mo et al. as a nanocarrier that reacts to high ATP levels linked to cancer metabolism. The anticancer medication DOX, a duplexed ATP-binding aptamer, crosslinked HA, and protamine make up these nanocarriers. Tumor hyaluronidases break down HA at the tumor site, and DNA aptamers attach to ATP to release DOX from the structure.

Zaric et al. developed a thermostable microneedle vaccine to deliver a recombinant candidate HIV antigen. The needles were fabricated with sodium carboxy-methylcelluloseahighly water-soluble material and sucrose. The investigators reported that the microneedles rapidly dissolved following application into mice skin and generated robust antigen-specific CD8+ T-cells in the blood and mucosal tissues. Moreover, the elicited CD8+ memory T-cells remained in peripheral tissues for at least one year after vaccination, also retaining their functional capacity. The clinical potential of microneedle was also recently tested in a first-in-human trial to deliver influenza vaccination. The delivery of DNA as vaccine poses as an intriguing alternative to induce immune responses against antigens which are difficult to produce.

## 9.2 Advancements in vaccine development through artificial intelligence

AI has found its way into multiple realms of the vaccine development process thanks to its versatile uses and capabilities; it can be used to identify targets and predict epitopes, antibody response, and immune profiles, formulate the actual vaccine itself, and even predict immune escape and risk surveillance.

### 9.2.1 Target identification

With the increase in the number of resilient bacteria and viruses, it is practically impossible to test the effect of all the different drugs on the pathogens. With the abundant amount of data available in the form of genome sequences, protein structures and others, AI can be used to predict potential immune targets [9]. Various models and methods have been employed based on the type of vaccine that is being formulated. Most of the vaccines target the epitope (the protein binding site) present on specific white blood cells which on binding with the drug molecule can produce antibodies to stimulate the immune response. B cell epitope prediction is traditionally carried out using X-ray [10] crystallography. Various AI models are in place for identification of B cell epitopes.

*ABCPred*, the first recurrent neural network prediction algorithm, was trained using random non-epitopes from the Swiss-Prot database and B-cell epitopes from the BciPep database. A neural network-based technique called ABCPred uses a fixed length pattern to predict continuous B-cell epitopes. The ABCPred dataset includes information on epitopes from bacteria, fungi, viruses, and parasites that have a 65.9% prediction accuracy and are kept in the BciPep database. Only brief peptide fragments are predicted by ABCPred, the AAP approach, *BCPred*, and *BayesB*. BCPred and ABCPred were used to predict the B-cell epitopes of the Emy162 protein of *Echinococcus multilocularis*, the zoonotic helminths-causing pathogen. The prediction accuracy was greatly increased using APCPred, which combines support vector machine (SVM) and amino acid anchoring pair composition (APC) techniques. An enhanced AUC of 0.794 was attained using APCPred [11]. FBCPred, BCPred, and the amino acids pair scaling approach (AAP) are the prediction methods that can be selected via the BCPred service. The premise of the AAP technique is the discovery that specific amino acid pairings are more common in epitope sequences than in non-epitope sequences. The accuracy was increased by combining the AAP propensity scale with the accessibility, antigenicity, hydrophilicity, and flexibility propensity scales. The linear B-cell epitopes (with less than 80% sequence identity) in a homology-reduced dataset that was previously used to test ABCPred were the training set for the BCPred method, which uses a subsequence kernel-based SVM classifier. A new technique called *FBCPred* was created to forecast B-cell epitopes with variable lengths. *BepiPred* uses a Hidden Markov Model in conjunction with two features of the residues to predict continuous epitopes. A dataset of epitopes taken from HIV databases, AntiJen, and the literature was used to assess BepiPred. Using multiple linear regression, a novel continuous B-cell epitope prediction approach called EPMRL was created to predict linear epitopes, SVMTriP combines the tripeptide similarity and propensity scores using a support vector machine. When tested on nonredundant epitopes derived from IEDB, SVMTriP yields a sensitivity of 80.1%, a precision of 55.2%, and an AUC value of 0.702.

The epitope prediction techniques that use mimotopes from phage display experiments were created recently. These techniques can be broadly categorized as follows: techniques that use statistical properties of mimotopes to map mimotopes to overlapping location patches on the antigen surface, and techniques that use mimotope mapping back to the antigen sequence through alignment. Mimotope is similar to the native antigen in terms of its physicochemical characteristics and spatial organization, although it rarely exhibits sequence similarity. Mimotope mapping back to the antigen may occasionally reveal the position of the B-cell epitope.

Another significant immunological response is brought about by the T-cells in the body. The T-cell receptor (TCR), which belongs to the immunoglobulin super family, resembles the IgG Fab fragment in many ways [12]. However, it is able to recognise its antigen in a complex form that is displayed on the MHC molecule rather than in a soluble form. All TCR-peptide-MHC (TCR-pMHC) complexes, regardless of class I and class II, share the same binding mechanism. MHC class I molecules are made up of a β2-microglobulin and an α-chain. The α-chain comprises a transmembrane domain, a brief intracellular segment, and the α1, α2, and α3 domains. The α-chain that forms the α1 and α2 domains and the β-chain that forms the β1 and β2 domains make up the class II molecule. The transmembrane domains and brief intracellular segments are present in both the α- and β-chains. T cells are presented with a peptide by the MHC molecule, which securely retains it in a groove made up of a floor of β sheets and two α helices. Numerous methods and tools for identifying T-cell epitopes have been created and are openly accessible on the internet. The techniques that are employed include the following: structure-based (SB), motif matrix (MM), sequence motif (SM), quantitative affinity matrix (QAM), ANN, support vector machine (SVM), and combined (using QAM and ANN). Here we present a brief overview of the different tools available.

The first structure-based prediction model for the prediction of MHC class II binding was *EpiDOCK* which is based on the docking approach. In summary, the structure of the examined HLA proteins was modeled by homology using three X-ray structures of the peptide–HLA class II protein complex as starting templates. Using the single amino acid substitution (SAAS) concept, the generated models were used to create virtual combinatorial peptide libraries for the nine amino acids that make up the peptide binding core. Using AutoDock or GOLD, peptides containing flexible SAAS residues were docked into the inflexible HLA binding site. After normalization, the obtained scores were converted into DS-QMs, which have dimensions of nine positions by 20 amino acids. For every HLA protein, a single DS-QM was produced [13].

*Vaxign* is the first web-based vaccine design technology that uses reverse vaccinology to suggest vaccine targets based on genomic sequences. PSSM (Position Specific Scoring Matrix) motif prediction is used to create Vaxitope. The PSSMs for predicting peptide binders to MHC class I or II are calculated using the BLK2 PSSM tool included in the BLIMPS package and are based on a position-based weighting algorithm. The PSSMs were created using known epitope data from the IEDB immune epitope database. The MAST sequence homology search technique calculates the P value for expected epitope binding to PSSMs [14].

*PEPVAC* is another promiscuous epitope-based prediction model which divides MHC class I molecules (HLA in humans) into five subtypes. PEPVAC has also been equipped with an algorithm for identifying peptides having a C-terminus that is likely to be the consequence of proteasomal cleavage. Finally, PEPVAC can predict conserved epitopes from sequences with disguised variability. The combination of these two factors helps to refine T-cell epitope predictions while also restricting the number of candidate epitopes [15].

ANN-based tools like *NetCTL* use a method which includes prediction of peptide MHC class I binding, proteasomal C terminal cleavage, and TAP transport efficiency. The server predicts CTL epitopes specific to 12 MHC class I supertypes. ANNs are used to accomplish MHC class I binding and proteasomal cleavage. The weight matrix is used to predict TAP transport efficiency. The MHC peptide binding is predicted using neural networks that have been trained in the manner outlined for the NetMHC service. The proteasome cleavage event is predicted using the NetChop-3.0 server's version of neural networks trained on C terminals of known CTL epitopes. NetMHC carries out T-cell class I epitope prediction using an enhanced neural network technique. A unique input representation is created by combining sparse encoding, Blosum encoding, and input generated from hidden Markov models. It is shown that combining numerous neural networks obtained from different sequence-encoding techniques outperforms neural networks derived from a single sequence-encoding strategy. When forecasting binding affinity, neural networks are well suited to incorporate such higher order correlations. This property, together with the usage of various neural networks built from distinct and innovative sequence-encoding schemes, as well as the neural network's ability to be trained on data consisting of continuous binding affinities, contributes to the improved performance of the new method.

Some newer tools like *IEDB-AR* employ more than one algorithm to increase the efficiency of prediction. The IEDB-AR provides three MHC class I peptide binding prediction methods: ANN, stabilized matrix method (SMM), and average relative binding (ARB). SMM and ARB use position-specific scoring matrices (PSSM) to simulate the binding specificity of an MHC molecule. ANN, on the other hand, models binding specificity using neural networks with various sequence encoding techniques. Aside from peptide-MHC interaction, several processes affect whether a peptide is likely to be a T-cell epitope. These include proteasomal cleavage of the source protein and TAP transport of peptides from the cytosol into the ER. The IEDB-AR provides an implementation of such predictions, which can be paired with the previously described updated MHC class I binding predictions. Alternative methodologies were implemented in the latest release: NetChop predicts proteasomal cleavage using innovative sequence encoding methods, and NetCTL combines these with predictions of MHC binding and TAP transport. Both applications have a common user interface and allow the user to choose between NetChop and NetCTL approaches. The IEDB-AR MHC class II binding prediction service offers four prediction methods: ARB, SMM_align, Sturniolo's method (which is also the foundation of TEPITOPE), and a consensus approach. The only approach implemented in the previous release was ARB, which is based on ARB matrices.

### 9.2.2 Predicting Antibody Response and Immune Profiles

Most of the viral diseases such as HIV and common cold have extremely complex methods to evade immune detection in the host, often leading to improved mutation in the viral antigenic proteins, these kinds of the mutations affect the viral reinfection rates and the effectiveness of vaccines, hence its extremely crucial to avoid the developments of such variants or at least be prepared enough to face such scary variants, in order to do so many laboratory tests such as high throughput deep mutational scans have been used, however these experiments can only test when there are a large population of the mutated variant in study which limits its usage in predicting the early immune escape mechanisms of the virus. In order to jump over this hurdle there is a need for computational methods, such as the *EVEscape*, a flexible framework that addresses the weaknesses of existing methods by combining a deep generative model trained on historical viral sequences with structural and biophysical constraints. This framework is able to capture relevant epistasis and then based on the strain background find out the fittest mutation. Such methods have greatly improved the early warning system that can guide public health decision-making and preparedness efforts. Some of the important aspects of this application includes strain identification in order to do so the EVEscape predictions for all the individual spike mutations were aggregated with eh experimental measurement of immune evasion measures as well as all the strains which followed the same immune evasion measures during that pandemic timepoint were included in the calculation. These calculations proved to be useful since there was an increased score EVEscape observed [16].

Most viruses with pandemic potential have received much less scrutiny and research than SARS-CoV-2. One of the key features of EVEscape is the ability to predict viral antibody leakage before the pandemic (data has not increased significantly during the pandemic) to refine vaccine sequences and potential treatments. ability to provide the longest lasting protection, to assess strains as they emerge and to provide a watchlist of mutations that could affect existing therapies. In one of the first comprehensive analysis of the evasion capabilities of these viruses, we applied the EVEscape method to predict evasion mutations in the surface proteins of Lassa virus and -withdraw Nipah; these viruses cause sporadic outbreaks of Lassa hemorrhagic fever in West Africa and highly fatal Nipah virus outbreaks in Bangladesh, Malaysia, and India.

Importantly, the three mutations present in the Lassa IV lineage that are known to evade neutralizing antibodies all appear in the top 10% of EVEscape predictions, suggesting that EVEscape captures the relevant traits to the evasion of antibodies from Lassa glycoprotein. Another method that has been used to perform antibody evasion involves finding the receptor-binding domain of the virus. From 2021 to 2022, variants of SARS-CoV2 associated with higher transmission rates and/or immune evasion (antibody escape) replaced the original founder strain (Wu-Hu-1). Such variants often have at least one mutation in the receptor binding domain (RBD), which can directly affect binding to the angiotensin-converting enzyme 2 (ACE2) receptor. For example, the mutants alpha (B.1.1.7), beta (B.1.351), and gamma (P.1) all have the N501Y mutation associated with higher affinity binding to ACE2.

A supervised machine learning model was trained to classify ACE2 binding, as seen in Fig. 9.1 defined as the probability (P) that a particular RBD sequence binds to her ACE2 (high correlation of P). with binding. In the first benchmark, a set of different base models (default parameters) are trained using data from the RBM-2 library, and multiple metrics (precision, F1, precision, recall) are trained. The classification performance was evaluated based on the classification performance. Machine learning models tested included K-Nearest Neighbors (KNN), Logistic Regression (Log Reg), Naive Bayes (NB), Support Vector Machine (SVM), and Random Forest (RF). A long short-term memory recurrent neural network (RNN), a type of deep learning model that can learn long-term dependencies in continuous data, was also trained [17].

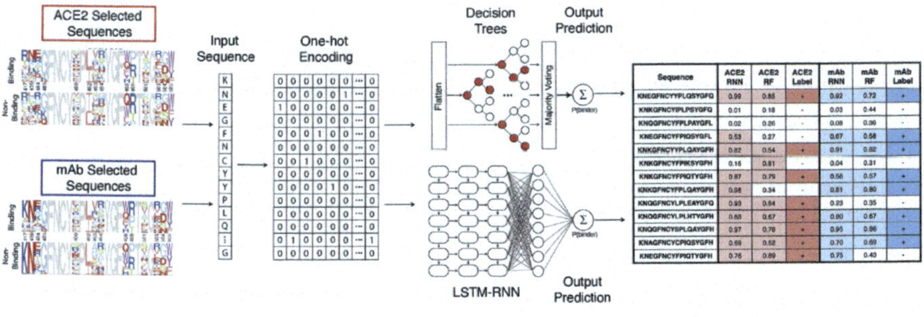


**Figure 9.1** Deep sequencing data from ACE2 and monoclonal antibody (mAb) selections is encoded by one-hot encoding and used to train supervised machine learning (e.g., random forest [RF]) and deep learning models (e.g., recurrent neural network [RNN]). Models perform classification by predicting a probability (P) of ACE2 binding or non-binding and mAb binding or escape (non-binding) based on the RBD sequence.
Reprinted with permission from [17].

Immune profiling is the analysis of a person's immune response to a virus at the cellular or serum level. This could help determine a person's specific response to the virus and potentially predict health outcomes. Immune profiling specifically looks at immune markers (proteins) and cells that are present over time. This analysis can help determine disease susceptibility, individual response to the virus and the impact of vaccination. A typical example of the leverage AI to predict the design of common vaccines against SARS-CoV-2 involved the identification of a sufficiently broad catalog of lymphocyte epitopes T has the potential to provide coverage and protection for the entire world population. The entire SARS-CoV-2 proteome has been characterized for the 100 most common HLA-A, HLA-B and HLA-DR alleles in the human population. The team used infected host cell surface antigen presentation and immunity prediction tools from the *NEC Immune Profiler toolkit* to generate comprehensive epitope maps, contributing to the overall goal of developing a globally effective vaccine against SARS-CoV-2. The generated epitope maps were used as input to Monte Carlo simulations with the aim of identifying statistically significant "epitope hotspot" regions in the virus. This approach is designed to identify highly immunogenic regions across multiple HLA types. The research team used this simulation to improve understanding of key viral epitopes, providing valuable information for the development of a globally effective vaccine against SARS-CoV-2. A sample is provided in Table 9.1.

Through the combination of antigen presentation on the surface of infected host cells and predictions of immunity supported by the NEC Immune Analyzer, along with the implementation of digital twin simulation and powerful Monte Carlo, comprehensive profiling of the entire SARS-CoV-2 proteome was performed. This multifaceted approach has led to the identification of a specific subset of epitope hotspots, strategically positioned for use in vaccine formulation [18].

### 9.2.3 Designing vaccine formulations and adjuvants

The use of AI in vaccine and adjuvant formulation design represents a revolutionary approach to improving vaccine development. Reverse vaccination (RV), a computational strategy, is used to identify potential vaccines in the protein-coding genome (proteome) of a pathogen. Although initially applied to bacterial pathogens, RV has proven successful in the preparation of subunit vaccines, which consist of one or more protein antigens. A notable example is the development of Bexsero, a subunit vaccine against *Neisseria meningitidis* serogroup B, achieved by a VR method using filtration.

As part of recent advances, ML methods have been integrated with VR methods to improve the identification of vaccine candidates. Combining epitope binding annotation and gene expression data further improves RV accuracy. Epitope maps, derived from the entire SARS-CoV-2 proteome across various human leukocyte antigen (HLA) alleles, served as input to the Monte Carlo simulation. These simulations strategically identify statistically significant "epitope hotspot" regions, thereby optimizing immunogenic potential across multiple HLA types.

**Table 9.1** Immune Presentation (IP) scores for validated SARS-CoV peptides with high similarity to SARS-CoV-2.

| Peptide | Sequence similarity (%) | Parental protein | Immune Presentation score | Correct prediction |
|---|---|---|---|---|
| *FIAGLIAIV* | 100 | Spike | 0.54 | Yes |
| *MEVTPSGTWL* | 100 | Nucleoprotein | 0.61 | Yes |
| *RLNEVAKNL* | 100 | Spike | 0.39 | No |
| *TLACFVLAAV* | 100 | Membrane | 0.54 | Yes |
| *KLPDDFTGCV* | 90 | Spike | 0.58 | Yes |
| *GMSRIGMEV* | 100 | Nucleoprotein | 0.59 | Yes |
| *LLLDRLNQL* | 100 | Nucleoprotein | 0.57 | Yes |
| *VVFLHVTYV* | 100 | Spike precursor | 0.53 | Yes |

Reprinted with permission from [18].

Similarly, in the context of bacterial pathogens, VR leverages AI to predict and select proteins for subunit vaccines. This process involves applying different bioinformatics tools, such as *BepiPred* and *SVMHC*, to predict B-cell linear epitopes and major histocompatibility complex (MHC) binding peptides. Machine learning techniques, including SVMs, help distinguish antigens from non-antigens with high accuracy [19].

Combining epitope binding information and expression data Gene expression in VR method improves the ability to predict antigenic proteins. Machine learning algorithms, exemplified by the SVM classifier, help reduce the number of potential vaccines, thereby increasing accuracy. The future trajectory of VR is envisioned to facilitate rapid vaccine design, reduce reliance on conventional animal testing and clinical trials, and address challenges such as antibiotic resistance [20] and emerging bacterial outbreaks.

## 9.2.4 Predicting immune evasion and variant resilience

Immune evasion refers to the phenomenon in which pathogens, such as viruses, bacteria or cancer cells, seek to evade or evade the host immune system, allowing them to survive, multiply and cause disease. The immune system is a complex network of cells, tissues, and molecules that work together to recognize and eliminate foreign invaders. However, some pathogens have developed various strategies to avoid detection or neutralization by the immune system. Immune evasion mechanisms can occur at different stages of the immune response and may involve both innate and adaptive immune components. Some strategies Common strategies used by pathogens to evade the immune system: (1) Antigenic variation- Pathogens can change surface antigens, molecules recognized by the immune system, through genetic mutation or recombination. Therefore, it is difficult for the immune system to produce an effective and lasting response because pathogens constantly change shape. (2) Immune suppression- some pathogens have the ability to suppress the response. host immune response. This may involve inhibition of immune cell activation, cytokine production, or other immune signaling pathways. By dampening the immune response, pathogens can avoid detection and elimination. (3) Hiding in host cells- Intracellular pathogens can enter and multiply within host cells, making it difficult for the immune system to target them. For example, some viruses can directly infect immune cells or interfere with the host cell's ability to present antigens to immune cells. (4) Block activation of the complement system - The complement system carries out part of the innate immune response that helps eliminate pathogens. Some pathogens can produce proteins that inhibit or regulate the complement system, preventing its effective activation. (5) Modulation of immune cell function- Pathogens can produce molecules that directly interfere with the function of immune system cells, preventing them from recognizing or attacking the immune system. invader. This includes inhibiting the activity of cytotoxic T cells or natural killer cells.

Avoid recognition by pattern recognition receptors (PRR): PRRs are Immune cells that recognize specific molecular patterns associated with pathogens. Some pathogens have evolved mechanisms to avoid detection by PRRs, allowing them to remain undetected by the innate immune system. (6) Antibody resistance- Pathogens can develop resistance to antibodies produced by the adaptive immune system to target pathogens. This may involve changes in target epitopes or the production of decoy molecules that bind to antibodies and prevent them from neutralizing the pathogen.

A classic example of the interference of AI for Immune response prediction can be seen here. In a study done [21], gene expression and clinicopathological data were collected from 481 prostate cancer patients in the Cancer Genome Atlas. Then, the patient's immune characteristics were analyzed based on the plasma cell infiltration rate. A machine learning algorithm based on unsupervised clustering was used to identify molecular subtypes of plasma cells. And the characteristic genes of plasma cell subtypes were eliminated using three types of machine learning models to establish an ANN to predict plasma cell subtypes. Finally, the ANN's prediction of plasma cell infiltrate subtypes was validated in an independent cohort [22] of 449 prostate cancer patients from the Gene Expression Omnibus.

Another study was done to construct an ANN to predict the plasma cell subtype of new patients. The proportion of plasma cells in prostate cancer was significantly reduced in tumors with high T stage, high Gleason score, and lymph node metastasis. In addition, patients with low plasma cell counts have a higher risk of biochemical recurrence. Based on distinct plasma cell genes, plasma cell infiltration of PCa patients is divided into two independent subgroups (subgroup 1 and subgroup 2). Subtype 1 tends to consist of immunosuppressive plasma cells infiltrating the PCa region, has a higher probability of biochemical recurrence, a more aggressive immune microenvironment, and a strong immune evasion capacity. more, leading to poor response to immunotherapy. Then, 10 genes characteristic of plasma cell subtypes were removed using three ML algorithms. Finally, an ANN was built from these 10 genes to predict the plasma cell subtype of new patients. This ANN was validated in an independent validation set and similar results were obtained.

The correlation between immune evasion and variant resilience is an important aspect for understanding the dynamics of host–pathogen interactions, especially in the context of rapidly evolving pathogens. rapidly, such as viruses. Immune evasion refers to strategies used by pathogens to avoid detection and elimination by the host immune system. Variant resilience, on the other hand, refers to the ability of pathogen variants (e.g., viral mutations) to persist and spread despite immune pressure. The interaction between these two concepts is especially relevant in the context of emerging viral variants, such as those seen in viruses like SARS-CoV-2.

Predicting the resilience of variants using artificial intelligence involves developing models that can predict how a system or organism will respond to variants or challenges. This concept is relevant to many different fields, including biology, computer science, and engineering. The Classification of Tolerance from Intolerance (SIFT) algorithm, plays a central role in predicting the effects of amino acid substitutions in protein sequences. This computational tool is instrumental in distinguishing the functional consequences of genetic variants and helps prioritize substitutions for subsequent experimental validation. It highlights the importance of null variants synonymous in the coding gene, elucidating how such changes can lead to amino acid substitutions in the resulting protein product, thereby affecting the observable properties of the host organism. Notably, more than 50% of mutations identified in association with human genetic diseases are attributed to these non-synonymous variants. This highlights the important role these variations play in human health and the profound effects they can have on an organism's phenotype.

SIFT uses a sequence homology-based approach, starting with the compilation of a data set of functionally related protein sequences derived from protein database searches. This dataset is established through applying the PSI-BLAST algorithm. The alignment is then constructed from these homologous sequences along with the query sequence. In the next step, SIFT systematically analyzes each position in the alignment, calculating the probability of the 20 amino acids at that particular position. These probabilities, normalized by the probability of the most frequent amino acid, are then stored in a scaled probability matrix. The key principle of the algorithm is to predict that a substitution will affect protein function if the scaled probability, called the SIFT score, falls below a predetermined threshold. It then incorporates the confidence measure's algorithm into its predictions. This involves assessing the conservation value at each position in the cell, with highly conserved positions assessed as less likely to be replaced. The algorithm ensures diversity in the selected sequences, issuing a low confidence warning if the average conservation value exceeds a specified threshold. Recognizing the limitation, the SIFT algorithm does not exploit information about protein structure to evaluate the impact of amino acid substitutions. However, this highlights that adding protein structure can slightly improve the algorithm's prediction performance [23].

The accuracy of the SIFT algorithm (see Fig. 9.2) is elucidated by applying the algorithm into data sets that include disease-associated mutations and nsSNPs in healthy individuals. The algorithm had a prediction accuracy of 69% for disease-associated substitutions and 19% for nsSNPs in healthy individuals. The text also

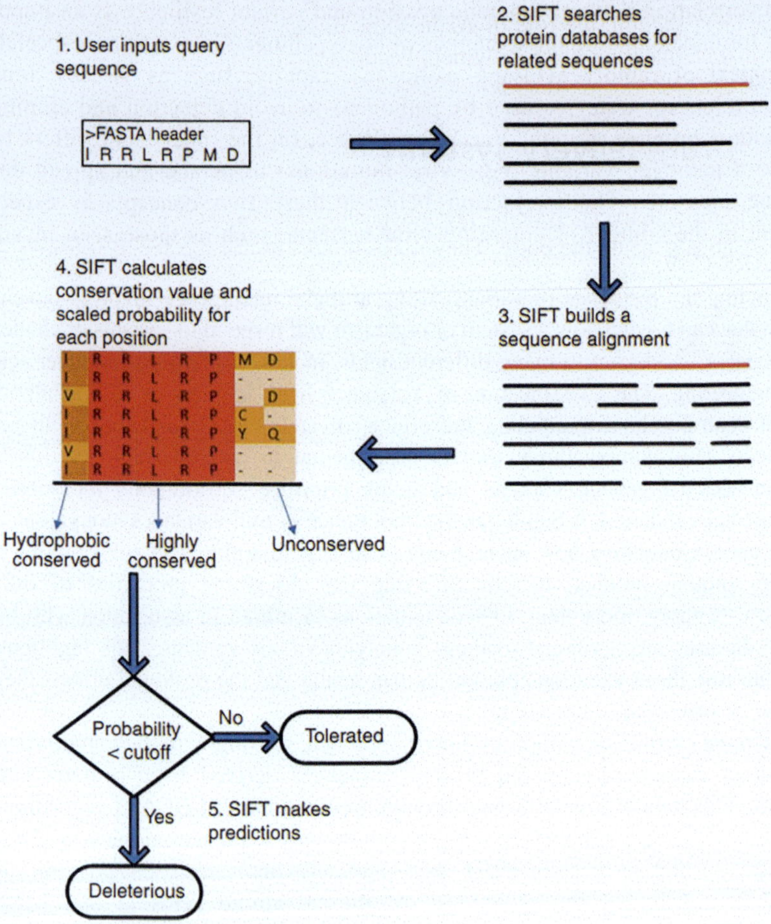


**Figure 9.2** The working of the SIFT Algorithm.
Reprinted with permission from [23].

provides an overview of SIFT predictions for substitutions associated with specific diseases, illustrating the algorithm's ability to distinguish between neutral and deleterious substitutions.

### 9.2.5 Personalized medicine

Humans differ greatly on a genetic, biochemical, physiological, exposure, and behavioral level, particularly when it comes to disease processes and treatment responsiveness, as research studies using data-intensive biomedical technology have shown. This implies that it is frequently necessary to "personalize," or adjust, medications to the complex and frequently distinctive characteristics that each patient possesses. AI can play a significant role in the development of personalized medicines at all relevant stages of the clinical development and implementation of new personalized health products, from identifying appropriate intervention targets to testing them for their utility. This is because data-intensive assays are crucial in revealing strategies for personalizing medicines and appropriate intervention targets.

Artificial intelligence can be applied in various fields of personalized medicine. After the synthesis of the drug, it needs to undergo phase I clinical trials which typically involves a small group of individuals. There are numerous strong and practically helpful links between genetic variations and medication reactions that have been found in studies that take into account genetic characteristics that predispose to responses to pharmaceuticals (good or poor). The use of AI algorithms on very large databases containing pertinent genetic and medication response data has substantially improved the discovery of such "pharmacogenetic" insights. Nevertheless, subtle characteristics of the patient and the best course of action to treat the condition in light of those subtleties are frequently unclear. Similar AI-based diagnostic techniques can be used to find pathologies that might be treated. For instance, Arteries, a firm, just revealed the first AI-based application to be approved by the FDA for use in assisting with clinical diagnosis. The Arteries system assisted in the diagnosis of cardiac issues by using deep learning on a platform for medical imaging. Different systems have been created that take into account more thorough methods of comprehending a patient's profile in a way that can make selecting an intervention easier.

A medication or health product must be evaluated for its general utility in the general population if early phase trials have demonstrated that it is safe and likely to be effective. AI has applications in pertinent large-scale population trials aimed at reducing the administration and usage of unsuitable medications or therapies for every trial participant. A description of basket trials gives the main idea behind each, even if each has its own special qualities. It also highlights areas where AI can be used to advantage. In essence, bucket trials enlist qualified individuals, profile them to find subtle pathophysiologic characteristics they may have, and then allocate to them one of potentially several treatments according to the medicines' mechanisms of action.

The ability to enhance the prediction models that AI-based decision support tools are based on when fresh patient data are gathered is a crucial component of their integration with electronic medical record systems. Accordingly, "Learning Systems" can be developed that continuously develop and get better as more patient data is accumulated and as the results of the interventions the patients receive are linked to the patient-provided interventions based on the algorithms guiding the learning systems' suggestions. To improve this learning, advanced AI approaches can be applied, such as pooling data from several sources or EMRs [24].

Following the introduction and acceptance of a novel medication, therapeutic approach, or health product, ongoing observation of said product is necessary to ascertain whether unexpected side effects are manifesting or whether the product can be modified or substituted for a variety of reasons. Early experiences with AI-based learning systems, such as those outlined in the previous section, indicate that they make an ideal foundation for this kind of monitoring. Doctor–patient relationships will be profoundly impacted by the use of AI-based solutions, such as learning systems and EMR decision support tools. This is particularly likely to occur while talking about the rationale behind intervention decisions as well as when speculating about potential future health care problems. Large-scale, government-sponsored national initiatives, like the UK Biobank initiative in the United Kingdom and the "All-of-Us" study in the United States, are being pursued to find patterns among individuals tracked for health care-related phenomena that may be helpful in clinical and public health practices in the future. Consider the area of genomic considerations in therapy planning. Here, AI takes center stage by harnessing the power of precision medicine at scale. The ability to make real-time recommendations based on machine learning algorithms that predict which patients may need medication based on genetic information. Early successes in this field demonstrate the synergy between AI and precision medicine, as machine learning techniques effectively interpret large genomic data sets. An example of the power This fusion is medulloblastoma, a complex pediatric brain tumor that is undergoing transformational change. AI-based analysis of hundreds of exomes reveals distinct groups of molecules, guiding the delivery of precisely calibrated treatments. In this model, the combination of AI and precision genomics reduces the need for conventional multimodality treatments, thereby helping patients avoid the potential neurocognitive consequences of radiation.

Radiogenomics is emerging as a new field where AI establishes a link between cancer imaging features and gene expression. From predicting glioma genotypes to discovering radiogenic associations in breast, liver and colorectal cancers, AI heralds a new era in personalized medicine. Despite the challenges posed by limited data, the trajectory of AI in radiogenomics remains promising. AI has demonstrated its potential in predicting reactions that respond to therapy. Machine learning, powered by patient gene expression data, is becoming a powerful tool for predicting the outcomes of many drugs. Detection of patterns in genetic sequences provides clinicians with valuable information for selecting potentially effective treatments. However, the journey toward widespread clinical application requires further research and robust data sets to refine and validate AI algorithms.

Emerging environmental considerations as an important aspect, ensuring equitable care regardless of a patient's zip code. AI interventions address challenges such as identifying homeless people, adapting to different care settings, and enhancing diagnostic capabilities in low-resource settings. By predicting infectious disease outbreaks and assessing exposure to environmental toxins, AI becomes an ally in reducing health care disparities.

In the Tapestry complex clinical considerations, AI appears to be a central factor. By classifying patients based on age, comorbidities, and organ function, AI algorithms help optimize treatment plans. From identifying critically ill patients requiring prolonged mechanical ventilation to predicting organ failure and dysfunction, AI adds a layer of nuance to clinical decision-making.

Genetic considerations also extend to risk prediction and diagnosis, as illustrated in the remarkable case of Angelina. Jolie's reaction to her inherited BRCA gene. Predictive modeling in cardiovascular medicine plays a central role, providing insight into heart failure and serious cardiac events. Integrating electronic health records and genetic data is becoming a powerful approach, demonstrating initial success in predicting cardiovascular disease.

In addition, automated speech analysis is becoming a valuable tool for early detection of diseases such as dementia, cognitive decline and Parkinson's disease. AI-powered real-time monitoring during childbirth shows the potential of data transmission to reduce manual errors. Wearable devices and remote monitoring alert to a new era of invasive health care. From diabetes to cancer care, these devices provide continuous monitoring, capable of detecting disease in its early stages. Digital biomarkers promise to revolutionize remote disease monitoring, support decentralized clinical trials, and provide insight into disease progression [25].

### 9.2.6 *Improving vaccine manufacturing and delivery*

Amid the ongoing COVID-19 pandemic, the World Health Organization (WHO) has released staggering statistics, reporting 464,809,377 confirmed infections and 6,062,536 deaths from the virus from the outbreak in late 2019 until December 2021. The global impact of this virus goes beyond simple health impacts, as it continues to have profound economic and social consequences worldwide. A study published in Science examines the monthly death toll from the coronavirus, which has resulted in hundreds of thousands of deaths and significant economic losses, highlighting the urgent need for it to be effective and rapid.

WHO has approved multiple vaccines for different stages of use and testing. However, requirements for vaccine storage temperature and vaccination speed pose major challenges to the vaccine supply chain. Specific storage temperature requirements for vaccines, exemplified by the Pfizer-BioNTech vaccine, along with the risk of high rates of vaccine wastage due to inadequate inventory management and cold chain logistics, highlights the complex challenges facing the global vaccination ecosystem. In the field of vaccine supply chain management, this research is at the forefront of innovation and strategic modeling by merging advanced blockchain and AI technologies. The foundation of this research lies in a robust two-player dynamic game model, in which the system's dynamic node is encapsulated in the inventory level. This distinctive approach not only contributes to the theoretical foundations of dynamic game theory but also has important implications for the practical coordination of vaccine supply chains.

Blockchain technology integration in the vaccine supply chain is a pioneering approach. this development, driven by predictions of transformative impacts on consumer safety and accessibility. Blockchain, known for its immutable and decentralized ledger capabilities, is poised to enhance the security layers of the supply chain, ensuring the integrity and traceability of vaccine-related transactions. In addition, it promises to improve access for vaccine consumers, promoting transparency and trust in the process.

At the same time, the integration of AI technology will add resilience and adaptability to the vaccine supply chain. AI, with its sophisticated data analysis and machine learning capabilities, is expected to revolutionize coordination by seamlessly adjusting production plans and demand forecasts. The overarching goal is to establish a flexible vaccine supply chain that manages the complexity of dynamic demand, effectively avoiding surpluses and shortages.

**Table 9.2** Comparing the equilibrium numerical results of Model B and Model AI.

| Indicators | B-Model | AI-Model |
|---|---|---|
| Break-even inventory level | 2.44426 | 5.53972 |
| Strategic effort | 0.30211 | 0.882744 |
| Break-even price | 2.73512 | 6.17528 |
| Demand) | 0.369246 | 0.882744 |
| Manufacturer profitability | 1.06091 | 1.56877 |
| Unit profit | 0.596422 | 2.35682 |
| Blockchain service provider profit | 0.043772 | 0.258913 |
| AI service provider profits | 0 | 0.603898 |
| Consumer surplus | 0.0454476 | 0.259746 |
| Social welfare | 1.74656 | 5.04365 |

Reprinted with permission from [26].

One aspect of this research lies in the application of the differential game method to build a dynamic game model. This methodological choice marks a break from conventional approaches, adding depth and richness to the understanding of strategic interactions within the vaccine supply chain. By leveraging a distinct game framework, the study captures the dynamic interactions between players, providing a more nuanced representation of real-world complexity.

The study conducts a detailed analysis of the equilibrium strategies, summarized in Propositions 1 and 2. These proposals present the numerical results of the equilibrium strategies of Model B and Model IA, providing insight into how these models navigate the complexities of the vaccine delivery chain.

An important aspect of equilibrium research lies in examining performance indicators when the system is in equilibrium. Table 9.2 clearly highlights that several indicators are being significantly improved thanks to the application of AI technology. Notably, ΠMSS, ΠUSS, ΠBVPSS, ΠGSS, CSSS, and SWSS show significant improvements when applying the AI model. This shows that integrating AI technology into the vaccine supply chain has clear positive impacts on many different aspects, from economic benefits for stakeholders to increased social welfare. Balanced studies shed more light on the impact of AI adoption on stocks level (YSS) and price (pSS). An increase in vaccine inventories has been observed, providing potential benefits to companies in the vaccine supply chain. Even though the equilibrium price increases, increased inventory levels will minimize the risk of running out of vaccines. This dynamic is driving consumers' growing willingness to participate in the system, even as vaccine prices soar. These findings tell a nuanced story about the transformative impact of AI adoption on key balance indicators. Particularly notable is the significant increase in vaccine stocks (YSS) and resulting price increase (pSS) in the AI model. Such innovations hold great promise for companies in the vaccine supply chain, boosting consumer engagement by boosting inventories and minimizing the risks associated with out-of-stocks [26]. However, the development of Appropriate mucosal grafting poses significant challenges due to the intrinsic characteristics of mucosal tissue. The choice of immunostimulatory molecules, whether specific antigens or whole organisms, plays a critical role in the design of effective vaccine delivery platforms. Among promising vaccine carriers, hydrogels with combinations of polymers such as Pluronic® F127, Hybrane® S1200 and Gantrez® AN119 or S97 exhibit thermosensitive and mucoadhesive properties.

In this effort, the integration of artificial intelligence techniques (AIT), including ANN, genetic algorithms, and fuzzy logic, has been demonstrated to be decisive. The AIT model helps understand how the characteristics of these complex multi-component systems are affected by components and operating conditions. The overarching goal of this work is to fabricate thermoresponsive, mucosal-adhesive hydrogels for oral delivery of whole attenuated bacteria, thereby providing a new advance in vaccine delivery. FormRules® v4.03, developed by Intelligensys Ltd., UK, is a neurofuzzy logic software that employs a combination of ANNs and fuzzy logic techniques. This software was instrumental in modeling and analyzing the properties of the formulated systems. It operates through simple "IF…THEN" rules generated by the software, providing insights into how the properties are modulated based on the concentration of specific components.

Inputs introduced into the model included the concentration of Hydrogels of variable composition combining Pluronic® F127 (PF127), Hybrane® S1200 (HS1200) and Gantrez® AN119 (AN119) or S97 (S97), while outputs comprised various system properties such as gelation temperature, mucoadhesion and adhesion work, cohesion, gel strength, GFM released at 5 min (%), and total release time at 37°C.

Several statistical criteria were considered for software fitting, including Structural Risk Minimization (SRM), Cross Validation (CV), Leave One Out Cross Validation (LOOCV), Minimum Description Length (MDL), and Bayesian Information Criterion (BIC). CV was selected as it produced the most predictable models with simple rule sets, preventing overtraining. The number of subsets for CV ranged from 3 to 5, with a maximum of 2 inputs per submodel and 15 maximum nodes per input for all models.

The predictability of the models was assessed using the coefficient of determination (R2), a common metric for establishing model predictability. R2 is considered good when it exceeds 70%. The accuracy of the models was then verified by one-way ANOVA, comparing experimental results with predictions. Models that display f values greater than the critical f value for the corresponding degrees of freedom ($\alpha$=0.05) are considered to have good accuracy.

In the field of analysis statistics, models Cell proliferation assay values are expressed as mean ± standard deviation. SPSS software (IBM SPSS Statistic 26) was used to perform a one-way ANOVA test followed by HSD Tukey post hoc analysis to determine statistically significant differences between polymer groups. A significance level of $p < 0.05$ was considered for analysis. The biocompatibility of the polymers has been confirmed, with all materials showing >90% viability. Of note, HS1200 shows a significant increase in macrophage proliferation over controls. In contrast, Gantrez® polymers do not induce a macrophage-stimulating response.

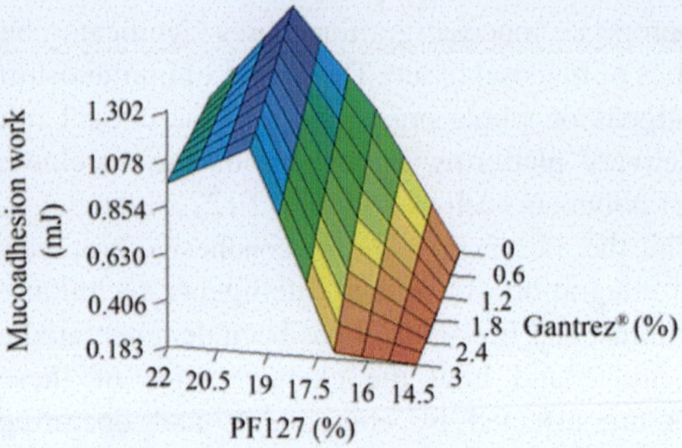


**Figure 9.3** A 3D Plot generated by FormRules displaying the effect of PF127 and Gantres concentrations on predicted mucoadhesion work.
Reprinted with permission from [27].

The physicochemical properties of hydrogels have been extensively studied, including gelation temperature (Tgel), mucoadhesion, work of adhesion, cohesion, gel strength, and drugs. Adaptive Intelligent Trials (AIT) successfully modeled mucoadhesion, work of adhesion, and release parameters with high predictability (R2 ≥ 70%) and accuracy. Tgel is mainly determined by the following conditions: Interaction between thermosensitive polymer PF127, Gantrez® concentration, and to a lesser extent HS1200 concentration. Properties such as mucoadhesion, work of adhesion, and gel strength depend on the ratio of PF127 and Gantrez®. The highest mucoadhesive hydrogels are expected to be obtained when the percentage of PF127 is between 18.5% and 21% and the Gantrez® concentration is less than 1.5%. The cohesive force is affected by the PF127 concentration, and a higher ratio results in a more cohesive hydrogel. The dynamics of drug release are complex, with the proportion of GFMs (antigen-like microspheres) released after 5 minutes being regulated primarily by the PF127 concentration, but the total release time also being regulated by the nature of the gauntlet. Masu. ® are affected. Experimental results are consistent with model predictions and support the validity of the model generated by FormRules® (see Fig. 9.3).

In the area of statistical analysis, values from cell proliferation assays were expressed. As mean ± standard deviation. A one-way ANOVA test was performed using SPSS software (IBM SPSS Statistics 26), followed by HSD Tukey post hoc analysis to identify statistically significant differences between polymer groups. A significance level of $p < 0.05$ was considered in the analysis [27].

### 9.2.7 Predicting safety and adverse effects

The emergence of the novel coronavirus disease (COVID-19) caused global panic and posed major challenges in rapidly identifying effective interventions against this unpredictable disease. Similar challenges existed with previous infectious diseases such as SARS, H1N1, H7N9, MERS, and Ebola [28,29]. Due to the severity and unpredictability of these pathogens, prompt and appropriate intervention is critical and often requires combination therapy with drug repurposing. The traditional approaches to developing drug combinations involve a trial-and-error strategy.

Drugs are selected based on:

- Identify their targets or mechanisms of action
- Administer according to clinical guidelines

Although adjustments are made based on observed toxicity, these methods may not provide optimal treatment results. Optimization of treatment outcomes is hampered by the lack of a systematic way to explore the vast drug dose parameter space generated by potential therapeutics.

To meet this challenge, the IDentif.AI project uses an AI-based platform for exploration. Space for drug and dose parameters too large for brute force testing. The objective of this project is to identify the optimal drug and dosage from a pool of 12 possible treatments to inhibit infection of the A549 lung cell line by VSV while preserving cell viability. These treatments include a variety of drugs with known repurposing potential against viral pathogens. In this study, the *IDentif.AI* project aims to identify and validate several drug combinations that significantly reduce VSV infection within 3 days without affecting survival. This platform has demonstrated the potential to rapidly identify effective and tolerable treatments and provide multiple treatment options. Implementation of project IDentif.AI does not require detailed knowledge of disease mechanisms or drug targets, making it suitable for dynamic drug repurposing against high-priority pathogens such as coronavirus disease (COVID-19).

This work highlights the potential of the platform including development of patient-specific measures or viable combination therapies across populations. It also highlights the platform's ability to contribute to the development of strategies to rapidly combat infectious diseases. The study also discusses the need for further research, provides insights into global health and health economic policy, and proposes a roadmap for broader clinical use of Project IDentif.AI. Overall, this analysis highlights the role of technology and innovative policy considerations in advancing clinical practice to address both pre-pandemic and post-pandemic challenges.

The objective of the IDentif.AI project was to identify optimal drug combinations and doses to inhibit VSV infection of A549 cells while maximizing cell viability. In contrast to approaches that use a priori information about drug synergy, this project used a quadratic relationship between drug/dose inputs and efficacy/safety outputs. This data-driven approach was independent of disease mechanisms or drug targets.

In the initial evaluation, 72 drug combinations at different doses were tested for their effects on his 12-hour VSV infection rate. The efficacy and cumulative equivalent doses of these combinations showed a wide range of infection rates. The STRICT algorithm evaluated each drug's ability to inhibit infection and its quantitative interactions with other drugs in the 12-drug pool. Notable candidates for further optimization include amantadine hydrochloride, azithromycin, chloroquine diphosphate, omeprazole sodium, and ribavirin.

Although several drugs showed promising monotherapy results, this study highlighted the need to include them in combination therapy regimens to integrate optimal efficacy. This platform has revealed that certain drugs that are effective as monotherapy may not contribute optimally to combination therapy. The IDentif.AI project simultaneously optimizes drug and dose combinations by considering factors such as single drug contribution, secondary drug effects, two-drug interaction synergy, and three-drug interaction synergy. demonstrated ability.

Subsequent validation of Bei The five drug candidates consisted of 30 combinations showing a wide range of synergistic effects. The optimal combination, Optimal Combo 1, significantly reduced VSV infection to 1.5%, lower than the doses of the individual drugs required for monotherapy to be effective. Suboptimal Combo 2, using the same treatment at a suboptimal dose, had a 14-fold reduction in efficacy compared to Optimal Combo 1.

Fluorescence microscopy confirmed the effectiveness of the optimal combination in eradicating viral infections without obvious side effects. Cell density. The rapid identification and validation process demonstrated that Project IDentif.AI can complete optimization of combination therapy development within three days [30] (Table 9.3).

The use of conversational AI, particularly chatbots, in healthcare has increased significantly since the mid-2010s. This trend has accelerated during the COVID-19 pandemic due to increased pressure on healthcare systems and restrictions on in-person care. Chatbots are used for a variety of purposes in the medical field, including treatment and monitoring support, patient education, health system support, behavior modification, and even diagnosis.

An emerging application of conversational AI in healthcare is vaccine communication. Chatbots disseminate accurate information about vaccines in real-time, helping users find vaccination appointments, send reminders, and address concerns and questions about vaccines. This is especially important to counter the "infodemic," which is information overload containing false or misleading information during disease outbreaks. Despite the potential benefits, concerns have been raised about the quality of health information provided by conversational AI [31].

AI also helps scientists figure out which parts of the COVID-19 germ are safe to use in a vaccine. AI tools are not just used to develop vaccines. They also help us understand what people think about vaccines and spread information about them. AI can analyze data, predict how diseases will get worse, and give ideas for how to make vaccines. There are special AI programs that can find medicines for COVID-19 by looking at lots of different compounds. Some studies use machine learning to figure out how well vaccines will work for different groups of people, like people of different races and ethnicities. This shows that we need to make vaccines that work for each person. AI helps scientists predict how the COVID-19 virus can change and become more dangerous. This is important because the virus can spread easily and change quickly. AI uses special computer programs to predict how the virus might change and helps scientists make vaccines that can work against different versions of the virus. This helps us understand how the virus evolves and find ways to stop it from spreading and make people better [32] (Table 9.4).

**Table 9.3** Experimentally tested AI-optimized regimens (units=micromolar).

| | Amantadine hydrochloric acid | Azithromycin | Chloroquine diphosphate | Omeprazole sodium | Ribavirin | Viral infection rate |
|---|---|---|---|---|---|---|
| Optimal 1 | 5 | 5 | 0.5 | 0 | 2.5 | 1.5% |
| Optimal 2 | 5 | 5 | 0.5 | 0.5 | 0 | 1.6% |
| Sub- Optimal 1 | 0.5 | 5 | 0.5 | 5 | 0 | 9.8% |
| Sub- Optimal 2 | 0.5 | 5 | 5 | 0 | 2.5 | 10.7% |
| Non- Optimal 1 | 0 | 0.5 | 5 | 0.5 | 25 | 20.3% |
| Non- Optimal 2 | 0 | 0.5 | 0.5 | 5 | 25 | 21.6% |

Reprinted with permission from [30].

**Table 9.4** AI & ML used in COVID-19 surveillance.

| Model | Country | Metric used to evaluate performance |
|---|---|---|
| Artificial Intelligence Model | - | Not Applicable |
| Adaptive Network-based Fuzzy Inference System Model | Italy | Correlation coefficient (r) = 0.99<br>Root Mean Square Error (RMSE) = 190.81- 188.18 |
| Multi-Layered Perceptron Model | Italy | Correlation coefficient (r) = 0.99<br>Root Mean Square Error (RMSE) = 189.76 – 320.93 |
| Adaptive Network-based Fuzzy Inference System Model | Hungry | Mean Absolute % error (MAPE) = 38.44 – 39.95<br>RMSE Value = 248.06 – 119.42 |
| Deep Neural Network | – | RMSE Confirmed = 163335.65<br>RMSE Deaths = 8554.55<br>RMSE Recovered = 25415.03 |

Reprinted with permission from [32].

## 9.3 Systems vaccinology

Systems biology is an interdisciplinary method that systematically explains the intricate connections between all of the pieces of a biological system in order to elucidate new rules capable of predicting the biological system's behavior. Systems vaccinology, an interdisciplinary field that associates systems-wide measurements, networks, and predictive modeling in the context of vaccinology, has received significant interest. Its goal is to improve our understanding of immunity and the design of new vaccine systems, focusing on specific challenges such as potency, durability, and specificity. This can be accomplished by combining some important aspects such as system perturbation, monitoring responses at the system level, data integration, network modeling, and vaccination response prediction. Advanced ML algorithms for epitope prediction are commonly used to simplify immunological monitoring in infectious disease and/or cancer, as well as to aid in the formulation of epitope-based vaccines by finding epitopes in antigens. Furthermore, reliable algorithms for predicting the immunopeptidome and determining whether a peptide can be presented by MHC molecules are a critical answer and a step towards speedier and more personalized vaccine development [33].

Petrovsky and colleagues recently developed and launched the first AI-designed influenza vaccine, which was built using an AI programme called Search Algorithm for Ligands (SAM) that was trained on several sets of chemicals known to trigger the human immune system. Several ABM publications provided compelling evidence that this AI methodology is useful in assisting vaccine development and intelligent design. For example, STriTuVaD (In Silico Trial for Tuberculosis Vaccine Development), a European Commission-funded initiative, is using IST to forecast the efficacy of two candidate tuberculosis vaccines. To name a few, consider tools such as Clustal Omega for multiple sequence alignment and HMMER for sequence homologs (both based on the use of Hidden Markov Models), Bebipred 2.0, a powerful B-Cell Epitope Predictor that employs a random forest algorithm trained on epitopes annotated from antibody-antigen protein structures, and NetMHCpan-4.1, a web service that predicts the binding of peptides to any MHC. Furthermore, the Innovative Medicine Initiative-funded public-private project BIOVACSAFE is an example of how to systematically establish a clinical evaluation of reactogenicity or natural infection after adjuvanted immunization using human, animal, and population-based models, as well as through the analysis of those biomarkers considered 4 G.

A knowledge-based strategy integrates several data sources, such as scholarly papers, functional annotation of antigens, specialized databases, and disease clinical trials. It also mines such data using machine-learning techniques and visualizes the results for downstream modules to easily interpret. This stage consists of two major procedures: For knowledge discovery, use a) named entity recognition (NER) and b) information extraction (IE). A NER system's main purpose is to locate relevant entities (biological organisms, diseases, treatments, tests, etc.) mentioned in a text and correlate them with known names or identifiers (IDs). These antigens are found in subunit vaccinations and can be identified via reverse vaccinology. Reverse Vaccinology (RV) employs computational tools to find possible vaccine candidates within a pathogen's proteome. Several machine learning-based techniques for reverse vaccinology have been developed, including NERVE, Vaxign [34], VaxiJen, Jenner-predict, and VacSol. A recent comparative analysis found that no single technique can predict all vaccine candidates, implying the utility of combining many methodologies.

Agent-based models (ABMs) are one of the fundamental inceptions of the computational arm of artificial intelligence and, more broadly, artificial life. The main question addressed by ABMs is how systems can achieve a higher-order state through processes that lead to complicated emergent order behavior using computational means. The bottom-up approach to modeling complex systems is represented by agent-based modeling. It specifically describes each individual entity, characterizing them through their conceivable state and traits, as well as their behaviors through the processes by which they interact. The immune system is one of the largest and most complicated systems of interacting chemicals, cells, and organs in this environment. ABM is one of the best methodologies for modeling the behavior and dynamics of the immune system and falls under the category of 'distributed artificial intelligence.' Simmune and Cycells are two ABM frameworks for simulating the immune system that could be used to evaluate novel vaccinations. While the former is a set of software tools that guides the user through the various hierarchical scales of cellular behavior, the latter was originally developed to model the homeostasis of peripheral immune effectors and employs a hybrid approach that models cellular entities individually and molecular entities continuously. Finally, even general-purpose ABM software like NetLogo proved beneficial in depicting immune system function and behavior in the presence of vaccine chemicals. CA stands for Cellular Automata. CA is a discrete modeling abstraction that has been shown to be capable of reproducing specific nonlinear behaviors in a variety of scientific domains as well as allowing the study of generic models of complexity. The nearest neighbors in ABMs, on the other hand, change over time since the agents are free to move and interact with each other and their environment, whereas CA are more spatially constrained.

## 9.4 Vaccinomics: the new "omics" and artificial intelligence

Vaccinomics is defined as the use of immunogenetics and genomics to investigate the molecular underpinnings of vaccine response. Systems biology integration of omics datasets paired with Big Data analytics [35] and machine learning enable the identification of candidate vaccine protective antigens in the vaccinomics platform. Vaccinomics enables us to move beyond the empirical "isolate, inactivate, and inject" approach that characterized previous vaccine development efforts and toward a more detailed molecular and systemic understanding of the meticulously choreographed series of biological processes involved in developing viral vaccine-induced "immunity." This improved understanding will subsequently be used to overcome the barriers to the development of effective vaccinations to defend against infections, particularly hypervariable viruses, which are currently having the largest impact on public health. Now, the field of vaccinomics, informed by developments in immunology, immunogenetics (the study of individual host genetic variation associated with individual differences in immune responses to the same antigen(s), and immunogenomics (the study of population-level genetic variations associated with population-level variations in immune responses), bioinformatics, virology, systems biology, metagenomics (host and non-host), and other fields, provides a conceptual framework for both understanding (and predicting) immune responses to vaccines [20]).

In order to explain how the adaptive immune system acted as an idiotypic network to regulate clonal immunological responses, Niels Jerne originally put up the "immune network hypothesis" in the 1970s. Later, in an effort to resolve the I-J dilemma, Geoffrey Hoffman developed this into the "symmetrical network theory" in the 1980s and 1990s. Over the course of the following 20 years, these models underwent incremental additions and modifications, but none of them had the express purpose of characterizing the network as it related to vaccine-induced immune responses at the systems level. Because of this, the models and theories that are now in use do not take into account many aspects that are not directly related to the immune system (strictly defined), such as gene polymorphisms, epigenetics, and the impact of the host microbiome.

Gregory A. Poland and his team proposed the immune response network theory in 2013 which stated that "Theoretically predicted, the reaction to a vaccine is the culmination of interactions fueled by a variety of genes and their interactions." The immunogenetics of the response to antigen and the growing appreciation of systems biology approaches to more fully understand how immune responses are generated and sustained in the host are thus included in the immune response network theory, even though it acknowledges and incorporates elements of the immune response that were not yet discovered at the time of Jerne and Hoffman. With the help of a mathematical formula that takes the system's complexity into account, it is possible to anticipate and theoretically explain the immunological response to a vaccination. Innate, adaptive, and cell-mediated immune phenotypic archetypes as well as individual response patterns can all be explained by a deconvoluted yet mechanistic determination of important genetic and other variables, as suggested by the immune response network theory and the creation of a prediction equation. The field of vaccomics subsequently employs this and additional omics data to create innovative vaccine candidates that surmount genetic obstacles to the development of protective immunity.

To push the development of safer and more effective vaccinations, a quantum vaccinomics approach was recently developed, based on the characterization of the immunological quantum. This chapter explains the quantum vaccinomics approach's methods, which are based on proteins that play important roles in the cell interactome and regulome of vector–host–pathogen interactions. These proteins are used to identify targets using a yeast two-hybrid screen, characterize target protein interactions in vitro using musical scores of protein interacting domains, and identify conserved protective epitopes within target protein interacting domains. The creation of chimeric protective antigens can then be facilitated by these findings.

The platforms for quantum vaccinomics include in vitro, in silico evaluation of protein-protein interactions to find protein interacting domains as potential protective epitopes, and in silico prediction and epitope mapping of immunological quantum. Various attempts have been made to use quantum vaccinomics as a tool to increase the efficiency of vaccines. Jose de la Fuente and team developed a vaccine for *Anaplasma phagocytophilum*, a tick borne bacteria through the technique of Major surface protein 4 (MSP4) epitope mapping, a quantum vaccinomics approach meant to identify potential epitopes of the antigens (referred to as "immunological quantum"). The findings may be applied to the design and synthesis of chimeric protective antigens, which would not otherwise produce a potent protective immune response when the entire antigen is included in the vaccine formulation. This would allow for the identification and characterization of the protective epitopes or immunological quantum. Sheng Ye and colleagues developed a machine learning protocol to facilitate the development of experimental spectroscopy of rapid protein IR spectroscopy prediction. A protein's vibration can be described as a collection of n oscillators, one for each peptide bond in its backbone. A vibrational model Hamiltonian is built using the Frenkel exciton model. The coupling coefficient between two oscillators, i and j, is one of the off-diagonal elements, while the diagonal elements are the frequency of the ith amide I oscillator. A protein is broken down into separate peptide linkages and dipeptides to produce these matrix elements.

In order to advance quantum vaccinomics for the creation of vaccines and other control treatments, new platforms and algorithms will be needed. The use of commensal bacteria to produce and secrete protective antigens to impede pathogen infection or facilitate vaccine delivery is one of these novel platforms. Other strategies include combining vaccines with probiotics (such as those with a high alpha-gal content) and heat-inactivated mycobacteria to act as adjuvants or immunostimulants; developing novel vaccine delivery platforms (such as lipid NP-mRNA, viral vectors, and particle-like particles) to enhance innate and trained immunity and enhance protective immune response; oral vaccine formulations to improve safety and accessibility in developing nations; and promoting trained immunity mechanisms in response to immunization.

## 9.5 Advancements in biomaterials aided by artificial intelligence for vaccine development

Biomaterials provide various benefits that can be customized to target the significant health dangers presented by infectious diseases. One way this can be done is by creating NPs and microparticles (MPs) in different sizes and incorporating antigen-filled structures to imitate pathogen traits. These biomaterials have the ability to improve immune reactions by serving as adjuvants, increasing immunological stimulation, and offering regulatory molecular characteristics like antigen display density (multivalency). NPs and MPs have better pre-clinical safety profiles compared to inactivated and live attenuated vaccines because they do not replicate and can be easily adapted to target various pathogens using modular material platforms. Additional benefits of using biomaterials in vaccines involve the simultaneous encapsulation of antigens and immune-stimulating agents, safeguarding the payload from enzymatic breakdown, precise delivery to particular immune cells, and regulated release timing of the vaccine. These features together allow for more accurate control of immune responses to vaccines on cellular and physiological levels, possibly lowering toxicity versus traditional vaccines. Because of this possibility, a range of biomaterials such as inorganic compounds, polymers, lipids, and self-assembled proteins are being investigated for the creation of vaccines for numerous infectious diseases. Nevertheless, the majority of this research is still in the pre-clinical phase, mostly using animal models.

Biomaterials are transforming the process of formulating, delivering, and enhancing the effectiveness of vaccines. Imagine this process accelerated by AI, which can quickly analyze data from more than 100,000 publications using natural language processing and computer vision (CV). Having the ability to use large databases enables us to forecast immune reactions and create innovative nanomedicine treatments by utilizing current information. A previous research study created a tool using multivariate analysis and machine learning to accurately predict the immune response induced by nanovaccines with various adjuvants, assisting in choosing the most appropriate adjuvants.

Machine learning, an important field in artificial intelligence, includes supervised, unsupervised, and semi-supervised learning techniques [36]. Supervised learning is the predominant and powerful approach in current research, making use of algorithms such as classification, regression, SVM, Random Forests, and Supervised ANNs among others. ML provides many advantages such as quick processing, precise results, robustness against interference, and the capability to learn and generalize from data without requiring predefined formulas. Feature engineering is used to isolate the variables that truly impact immune responses related to nanomaterials (NMs), capturing intricate factors beyond just the structure or properties of NMs. This enhances our comprehension of immune reactions and NM-related immunotherapies. ML methods have been utilized to recognize and forecast crucial elements (like NM levels, surface coating category, and particle shape ratio) that influence the immunotoxicity of NMs, helping in the creation of nanomedicines and transporters. Using the random forest algorithm, machine learning can predict the behavior of nanomaterials in vivo, like cell uptake and biological responses, with high accuracy. Furthermore, machine learning has investigated the quantitative connection between NM surface chemistry and protein adsorption characteristics, bridging gaps in our understanding of protein interactions on nano-biological interfaces and guiding the development of anti-protein surface coatings.

Random forest is an essential element of AI that utilizes likelihood to improve predictive precision. This popular machine learning algorithm is commonly employed to create models that forecast population characteristics using the physicochemical and biological properties linked to PC formation. A new deep neural network has been created to forecast the fate of NMs in biological systems, providing information on how they are cleared. Nonetheless, there are few research studies that use ML to directly forecast immune reactions and immunotherapy results related to NMs. The main reason for this gap is the absence of a complete database that includes the physical and chemical properties of NMs, as well as the wide range of variations in biological experiments conducted in laboratories.

Despite its power, ML has important limitations that require addressing. Although constructing a well-structured deep neural network can lead to accurate predictions, ML models built on neural networks are frequently seen as opaque models. This indicates that the predictions are unclear due to the biological and chemical implications, making the models hard to understand. It is difficult to study complex immune mechanisms due to the uncertainty regarding cause-and-effect relationships. In addition, a large quantity of data is needed for machine learning to make reliable predictions. Yet, there is a lack of top-notch, comprehensive databases for NM-immune responses or immunotherapy. In order to tackle these problems, it is suggested to merge physical models with ML in order to assist in interpreting the findings of the ML models. Due to the intricate nature of the immune system, machine learning requires easily understandable models, also known as "white-box" models. As the NMs-immunity database grows, ML algorithms can improve, using feature attributes to enhance predictions. This method could also improve the practical use of ML in situations where data is scarce. ML algorithms predict essential properties in the domain of metals, including mechanical behavior and glass-forming ability. Different methods, such as CNNs and random forest classifiers, sift through large datasets to create prediction models that direct the production of customized metallic compounds and alloys. Composites are analyzed using a combination of ML and high-resolution simulations like finite element analysis, which accurately represent elastic and mechanical properties.

Certain subfields within the field of biomaterials have emerged, including metallic scaffolds for tissue engineering that provide structures to support cell growth and tissue regeneration, bioactive metals like magnesium alloys and nitinol for biodegradable and flexible medical devices, and biomedical implants using titanium alloys and stainless steel. QSAR modeling and ML techniques are promising in the realm of metals for predicting features such as cytotoxicity. These methods, particularly in image analysis and phenotypic recognition, can process a wide range of data quickly. However, obstacles like problems with collaboration and data standardization prevent ML from being widely used in these domains. To maximize data sharing and apply ML to biomaterials and tissue engineering research, standardizing data collecting and encouraging researcher collaboration are essential first steps. Quasi-QSAR models were created by researchers as part of a comprehensive study aimed at forecasting cell survival in the presence of metal oxide nanoparticles in order to evaluate toxicity and biocompatibility. This project not only clarified the possible health effects of being around these compounds, but it also highlighted how important ML is to advance the field of nanotoxicology. A thorough analysis looked at how data-driven research, in particular ML, may be integrated to speed up MOF discovery and design. Researchers attempted to understand the intricate structure–performance correlations present in MOFs by combining insights from molecular simulations and machine learning methods. This helped to provide important direction for further research in this quickly developing field. Based on the chemical structures of the SAM molecules, an ANN model was used to predict protein adsorption and water contact angles (WCA) on self-assembled monolayers (SAMs). The ANN was able to predict protein adsorption and WCA after training on data from 145 SAMs. This research helped with material design by highlighting the significance of different structural characteristics for these attributes.

The design and discovery of novel polymer-based biomaterials have advanced greatly as a result of the integration of ML with biomaterials research. In a noteworthy study, polymers were analyzed and predicted for safe and efficient gene delivery using LAD regression. In order to do this, a massive set of 12,000 transfection tests based on the Michael addition polymerization of acrylates with amines were carried out. In addition, protein adsorption and cellular response on biodegradable polymers intended for tissue engineering applications have been predicted using QSAR models. These models were tuned with ANNs and used descriptors computed using Dragon or molecular operating environments. Comprehending the ways in which polymers impact the immune system is essential for developing biomaterials that prevent harmful foreign body reactions. ML has been used to establish a connection between immune-instructive behaviors and polymer chemistry. To anticipate and create the secondary structure content of structural proteins, deep learning methods have been developed. These models handle sequential input using convolutional layers, BiLSTM units, and other methods to predict protein structures with high accuracy. In a similar vein, a deep learning framework has been put out to forecast the collagen sequences' thermal stability (Tm values), which is crucial for collagen-based biomaterials used in tissue regeneration and repair.

A recent study envisioned a self-sufficient running pipeline of the manufacturing of biologics empowered by artificial intelligence and biomaterials on paper. The Biomaterial Acceleration Platform (BioMAP) has been proposed by Adam Gormely and team from the State University of New Jersey. These investigations combine ML with optimized customized polymer additives developed by HTP testing to create a variety of distinct proteins with increased thermal stability. Polymer excipient libraries were produced by robotic instruments, and the cyclic workflow was started by scientists who also conducted enzyme experiments, built machine learning models, and exported AI/ML anticipated designs. Motivated by prior endeavors to create MAPs to expedite scientific discoveries, the group maintains that it is feasible to surpass this initial proof-of-concept study and actualize a completely independent BioMAP. In addition, they want to increase the number of generally recognized as safe (GRAS) excipients in our material library so that formulations can be improved for both speed to market and performance. The first step in creating a BioMAP that can formulate biologics is to figure out how to set up a closed-loop Design-Build-Test-Learn workflow that will enable the execution of an effective and independent discovery campaign. An optimal BioMAP should have a versatile range of automated equipment that is beneficial for every type of biologic, since formulation efforts are focused on a variety of target biologics. A flexible liquid handling robot can be used to handle mAbs and protein biologics. This robot will be the main tool for mixing reagents and carrying out sterile cell culture. Supporting modules such as a vacuum filtration system, plate sealer, heater/shaker, multimode reagent dispenser, and plate heater/shaker will be offered to enhance the adaptability of the core module. In the meantime, to produce LNPs with different compositions and lipid chemistry on demand, a continuous-flow fluidics platform would be linked to a parallelized microfluidic device. The direct formulation of RNA and protein therapies (mRNA and small interfering RNA [siRNA]) in a HTP format for later functional testing would be made possible by this automated apparatus. Analytical testing and characterization to comprehend formulation behavior can be easily carried out in a highly reproducible automated approach after libraries of biologic formulations are created. One option for testing the stability of formulations under various handling and storage conditions is to use an automated microplate incubator that can regulate $CO_2$ and humidity. Cell-based assays can also be supported by this same platform. A set of common analytical tools is provided to enable ongoing observation of novel formulations and biological activities. This comprises a high content imager (HCI), size-exclusion chromatography (SEC), and UV-visible (UV-vis) and dynamic light scattering (DLS) plate readers. Additional analytical modules that broaden the platform's application could comprise apparatus for transcriptomics, proteomics, genomics, and flow cytometry. This set of programmable devices would provide users with the hardware required to build a BioMAP that is completely autonomous. Experiment data can be used to guide Learn-Design initiatives, which are a supplement to the Build-Test phase of the design campaign. It is crucial to first think about how features and data should be expressed in order for them to be machine interpretable. Due to the heterogeneous mix of small and macromolecules seen in biologic formulations, feature engineering approaches that work with all of these systems will be needed. Simple one-hot encoding techniques or the usage of SMILES in conjunction with programs like Mordred to produce chemical description vectors for formula elements are two possible first steps. It has been demonstrated that these computationally efficient methods are useful for understanding the behavior of macromolecular systems. To assess biological characteristics have clearly defined experimental outputs, therefore gathered data may be quickly coupled with these descriptors and put to use for supervised machine learning. Combining Bayesian neural networks with Bayesian optimization methodologies allows them to learn from gathered data and automatically suggest new trials, as deep neural networks have demonstrated efficacy in learning in high-dimensional and non-linear data settings. Given the nearly unlimited combinations of formulation alternatives, its implementation will be crucial. Therefore, active learning techniques that cleverly investigate and exploit formulation and biomaterial factors in BioMAPs can make use of Bayesian neural networks [37].

## 9.6 Future scope

The future trajectory of AI vaccine development unfolds against the backdrop of overcoming existing limitations. The advent of bioinformatic design algorithms for de novo proteins heralds a new era, allowing the creation of functional antigenic epitopes with enhanced specificity. This innovative approach opens avenues for designing VLPs with complex structural motifs, capable of inducing potent neutralizing antibodies. In addition, ongoing research explores the integration of adjuvanting properties directly into VLPs, eliminating the need for external adjuvants and streamlining the vaccine development process. Notable technologies include Codetection by Indexing (CODEX), Cytometry by Time-of-Light (CyTOF), Genome Analysis Toolkit (GATK), high-definition spatial transcriptome (HDST), imaging mass cytometry (IMC), multiplexed ion beam imaging by time-of-flight (MIBI-TOF), multiplex immunofluorescence (mIF), and multiplex immunohistochemistry (mIHC), among others.

In the era of bulk sequencing, the focus on estimating tumor immune cells through computational algorithms like CIBERSORT and MCP-counter has brought forth a nuanced understanding of individual infiltration patterns. Immunogenomics technologies, encompassing the prediction of abnormal peptides, HLA typing, and tumor antigen-MHC binding affinity, have demonstrated efficacy in preclinical and clinical studies, exemplified by personalized tumor vaccines and ACT [38]. The exploration of tumor immunity at the single-cell level becomes imperative given the diversity of immune cell subtypes and Intratumor Heterogeneity (ITH). Advances in single-cell immune-related technologies, from flow cytometry to CyTOF, contribute to decoding the components of the Tumor Immune Microenvironment (TIME). Spatial architecture gains prominence with techniques such as H&E, IHC/IF, MIBI-TOF, and spatially resolved transcriptomics offering high-resolution visualization of the TIME.

The integration of AI introduces a new dimension to immunomics, utilizing radiological and pathological image-derived omics data to characterize the TIME. This holds promise for predicting prognosis and response to immunotherapy, paving the way for clinical applications through noninvasive or minimally invasive methods. However, as immunomics technologies flourish, considerations for sustainable development surface. Challenges include improving technological efficiency, combating noise and technical confusion, and developing more automated, accessible, and cost-effective technologies. The use of existing technologies in clinical trials and promoting research focused on tumor immunotherapy is advocated. For the future, immunology research is poised to become the dominant force in the field of tumor immunology, guiding the clinical transformation of the discipline. The trifecta of immune genomics, single cell technology (and AI are expected to shape the future, providing unprecedented insights into the complex interactions between the immune system and tumors. Despite the challenges, the field of immunology remains poised to have a profound impact, advancing precision cancer research and contributing to the continued growth of cancer research [39]).

As the global community grapples with the dynamic nature of infectious diseases, the future of AI vaccine development is characterized by adaptability, precision, and a convergence of cutting-edge technologies. The insights gained from the study of avian influenza serve as a blueprint, guiding the path toward the creation of next-generation vaccines that transcend the limitations of traditional approaches, ensuring a more resilient defense against emerging infectious threats. There is still more space for improvement in terms of NM immune response prediction and immunotherapy. By merging the intricate features of natural killers (NMs) with the understanding of immune response and immunotherapy, AI or deep ML can forecast the impacts of immunotherapy or immune response on novel NMs. In addition to helping to create safer and more potent nanodrugs, ML has been used to anticipate the biological fate of nanoparticles (NMs) and screen them for the optimal structure–activity relationship. A few recent studies showed that a machine learning approach may predict cell recognition by predicating PC formation, and the PC also influences immunotherapy, despite the lack of publications on NM immunotherapy using ML. As a reminder, AI or ML is not universal and takes a lot of data or expertise to train.

In the context of a rapidly evolving immune system, the scope for future vaccine development is extremely promising, especially in the context of combating avian influenza. The integration of advanced technologies in tumor immunology, as discussed in the provided text, provides a roadmap for developing vaccine strategies against infectious diseases. The era of mass sequencing, characterized by computer algorithms such as CIBERSORT and the MCP Counter, has revolutionized our understanding of the pattern of immune cell infiltration. This wealth of information can be exploited in the field of infectious diseases, such as avian influenza, to elucidate the complexity of host-pathogen interactions. Using similar computational methods, researchers were able to characterize dynamic changes in immune cell populations during avian influenza infection, paving the way for a personalized approach. humanization and more nuance in vaccine development.

Immunogenomic technologies, with their success in predicting tumor antigens, offer an exciting approach to identify Identification of viral epitopes related to avian influenza. Prediction of unusual peptides, HLA typing, and assessment of antigen-MHC binding affinity can be adapted to decode important viral antigens, thereby facilitating targeted vaccine design. target. The efficacy demonstrated in personalized tumor vaccines may serve as a model for the development of personalized vaccines tailored to the individual's immune profile, optimizing the immune response against avian influenza strains.

Developments toward single-cell analysis in tumor immunology also apply to infectious diseases. By studying the high diversity of immune cell subtypes during avian influenza infection, researchers can elucidate the immune landscape with unprecedented resolution. Using technologies such as CyTOF and spatially resolved transcriptomics, it is possible to construct a detailed single-cell immune atlas specific to avian influenza. This comprehensive understanding will contribute to the identification of important immune effectors and guide the development of vaccines that precisely target viral vulnerabilities.

In addition, the Integrating AI in immunology research will open new frontiers in vaccine development for avian influenza. By analyzing radiology and pathology data, AI can help predict prognosis and optimize vaccine response. The ability to exploit non-invasive or minimally invasive methods for clinical applications improves the feasibility of large-scale vaccine deployment [40].

## Acknowledgments

The authors listed in this paper wish to express their appreciation to the Biotechnology department of R V College of Engineering for their continued support and encouragement. As a corresponding author, I also express my sincere thanks to all other authors whose valuable contribution and important comments make this manuscript in this form.

## Funding information

There was no funding provided for the above research and preparation of the manuscript.

## References

[1] Addissouky TA, Wang Y, El Sayed IE, Baz AE, Ali MM, Khalil AA. Recent trends in Helicobacter pylori management: harnessing the power of AI and other advanced approaches. Beni-Suef University Journal of Basic and Applied Sciences 2023;12(1):80.

[2] Gligorijevic J, Gligorijevic D, Pavlovski M, Milkovits E, Glass L, Grier K, et al. Optimizing clinical trials recruitment via deep learning. Journal of the American Medical Informatics Association 2019;26(11):1195–202.

[3] Hamet P, Tremblay J. Artificial intelligence in medicine. Metabolism: Clinical and Experimental 2017;69:S36–40.

[4] MacIntyre CR, Lim S, Gurdasani D, Miranda M, Metcalf D, Quigley A, et al. Early detection of emerging infectious diseases-implications for vaccine development. Vaccine 2023. Jun 2.
[5] Gebre MS, Brito LA, Tostanoski LH, Edwards DK, Carfi A, Barouch DH. Novel approaches for vaccine development. Cell 2021;184(6):1589–603.
[6] Thomas S, Abraham A, Baldwin J, Piplani S, Petrovsky N. Artificial intelligence in vaccine and drug design. Vaccine Design: Methods and Protocols, Volume 1. Vaccines for Human Diseases 2022:131–46.
[7] Kumar R, Yadav G, Kuddus M, Ashraf GM, Singh R. Unlocking the microbial studies through computational approaches: how far have we reached? Environmental Science and Pollution Research 2023;30(17):48929–47.
[8] Kahle J, Potocnakova KM, Bhide L, Pulzova M, Borszekova L. An Introduction to B-Cell Epitope Mapping and In Silico Epitope Prediction 2016.
[9] Mohanty E, Mohanty A. Role of artificial intelligence in peptide vaccine design against RNA viruses. Informatics in Medicine Unlocked 2021;26:100768.
[10] Dasgupta A, Bakshi A, Mukherjee S, Das K, Talukdar S, Chatterjee P, et al. Epidemiological challenges in pandemic coronavirus disease (COVID-19): Role of artificial intelligence. Wiley Interdisciplinary Reviews: Data Mining and Knowledge Discovery 2022;12(4):e1462.
[11] Liu X, Shi C, Deore U, Wang Y, Tran M, Khalil I, et al. A scalable AI approach for clinical trial cohort optimization. InJoint European Conference on Machine Learning and Knowledge Discovery in Databases. Cham: Springer International Publishing; 2021. p. 479–89.
[12] Bukhari SNH, Jain A, Haq E, Mehbodniya A, Webber J. Machine Learning Techniques for the Prediction of B-Cell and T-Cell Epitopes as Potential Vaccine Targets with a Specific Focus on SARS-CoV-2 Pathogen: A Review. Pathogens 2022;11:146.
[13] Atanasova M, Patronov A, Dimitrov I, Flower DR, Doytchinova I. EpiDOCK: A molecular docking-based tool for MHC class II binding prediction. Protein engineering, design & selection: PEDS 2013;26:631–4.
[14] Kaushik R, Kant R, Christodoulides M. Mini Review: Artificial Intelligence in Accelerating Vaccine Development-Current and Future Perspectives. Frontiers in Bacteriology 2023;2:1258159.
[15] Reche PA, Reinherz EL. PEPVAC: A web server for multi-epitope vaccine development based on the prediction of supertypic MHC ligands. Nucleic Acids Research 2005;33:W138–42.
[16] Gurev S. Learning from pre-pandemic data to forecast viral antibody escape (Doctoral dissertation, Massachusetts Institute of Technology). (2023).
[17] Taft JM, Weber CR, Gao B, Ehling RA, Han J, Frei L, et al. Deep mutational learning predicts ACE2 binding and antibody escape to combinatorial mutations in the SARS-CoV-2 receptor-binding domain. Cell 2022;185(21):4008–22.
[18] Malone B, Simovski B, Moliné C, Cheng J, Gheorghe M, Fontenelle H, et al. Artificial intelligence predicts the immunogenic landscape of SARS-CoV-2 leading to universal blueprints for vaccine designs. Scientific Reports 2020;10(1):22375.
[19] Heinson AI, Woelk CH, Newell M-L. The promise of reverse vaccinology. International Health 2015;7(2):85–9.
[20] Khalid K, Poh CL. The promising potential of reverse vaccinology-based next-generation vaccine development over conventional vaccines against antibiotic-resistant bacteria. Vaccines 2023;11(7):1264.

[21] Xie X, Dou CX, Luo MR, Zhang K, Liu Y, Zhou JW, et al. Plasma cell subtypes analyzed using artificial intelligence algorithms for predicting biochemical recurrence, immune escape potential, and immunotherapy response of prostate cancer. Frontiers in immunology 2022;13:946209.
[22] Liu X, et al. A Scalable AI Approach for Clinical Trial Cohort Optimization. Kamp M, editor. Machine Learning and Principles and Practice of Knowledge Discovery in Databases. ECML PKDD 2021. Communications in Computer and Information Science, vol 1525. Cham: Springer; 2021.
[23] Kumar P, Henikoff S, Ng PC. Predicting the effects of coding non-synonymous variants on protein function using the SIFT algorithm. Nature protocols 2009;4(7):1073–81.
[24] Schork NJ. Artificial intelligence and personalized medicine. Precision medicine in Cancer therapy 2019:265–83.
[25] Johnson KB, Wei WQ, Weeraratne D, Frisse ME, Misulis K, Rhee K, et al. Precision medicine, AI, and the future of personalized health care. Clinical and Translational Science 2021;14(1):86–93.
[26] Gao Y, Gao H, Xiao H, Yao F. Vaccine supply chain coordination using blockchain and artificial intelligence technologies. Computers & industrial engineering 2023;175:108885.
[27] Garcia-del Rio L, Diaz-Rodriguez P, Landin M. Design of novel orotransmucosal vaccine-delivery platforms using artificial intelligence. European Journal of Pharmaceutics and Biopharmaceutics 2021;159:36–43.
[28] Garett R, Young SD. Online misinformation and vaccine hesitancy. Translational behavioral medicine 2021;11(12):2194–9.
[29] Garett, R., and S.D. Young. "Online Misinformation and Vaccine Hesitancy." OUP Academic, Oxford University Press, 16 Sep. 2021, academic.oup.com/tbm/article/11/12/2194/6371221#323328390.
[30] Abdulla A, Wang B, Qian F, Kee T, Blasiak A, Ong YH, et al. Project IDentif. AI: harnessing artificial intelligence to rapidly optimize combination therapy development for infectious disease intervention. Advanced therapeutics 2020;3(7):2000034.
[31] Passanante A, Pertwee E, Lin L, Lee KY, Wu JT, Larson HJ. Conversational AI and Vaccine Communication: Systematic Review of the Evidence. Journal of Medical Internet Research 2023;25:e42758.
[32] Arora G, Joshi J, Mandal RS, Shrivastava N, Virmani R, Sethi T. Artificial intelligence in surveillance, diagnosis, drug discovery and vaccine development against COVID-19. Pathogens 2021;10(8):1048.
[33] Russo G, Reche P, Pennisi M, Pappalardo F. The combination of artificial intelligence and systems biology for intelligent vaccine design. Expert Opinion on Drug Discovery 2020;15(11):1267–81.
[34] Patel M, Surti M, Adnan M. Artificial intelligence (AI) in Monkeypox infection prevention. Journal of Biomolecular Structure and Dynamics 2023;41(17):8629–33.
[35] Jiao Z., Ji H., Yan J., Qi X. Application of big data and artificial intelligence in epidemic surveillance and containment. Intelligent (2023).
[36] Chaudhury S, Duncan EH, Atre T, Storme CK, Beck K, Kaba SA, et al. Identification of immune signatures of novel adjuvant formulations using machine learning. Scientific Reports 2018;8(1):1–11.
[37] Tamasi MJ, Gormley AJ. Biologic formulation in a self-driving biomaterials lab. Cell Reports Physical Science 2022;3(9):101041.
[38] Zhou X, Qu M, Tebon P, Jiang X, Wang C, Xue Y, et al. Screening cancer immunotherapy: when engineering approaches meet artificial intelligence. Advanced Science 2020;7(19):2001447.

[39] Xu Y, Su GH, Ma D, Xiao Y, Shao ZM, Jiang YZ. Technological advances in cancer immunity: from immunogenomics to single-cell analysis and artificial intelligence. Signal Transduction and Targeted Therapy 2021;6(1):312.
[40] Ninyio NN, Ho KL, Omar AR, Tan WS, Iqbal M, Mariatul QAR. Virus-like particle vaccines: A prospective panacea against an avian influenza panzootic. Vaccines 2020;8(4):694.

## Further reading

Aggarwal K, Mijwil MM, Al-Mistarehi AH, Alomari S, Gök M, Alaabdin AM, et al. Has the future started? The current growth of artificial intelligence, machine learning, and deep learning. Iraqi Journal for Computer Science and Mathematics 2022;3(1):115–23.
Cheng, B.; Liu, L.-Y.; Qi, Z.-H.; Yang, H.-G. Prediction of Continuous B-cell Epitopes Using Long Short Term Memory Networks. In Proceedings of the 2018 6th International Conference on Bioinformatics and Computational Biology, Chengdu, China, 12–14 March 2018.
Colas C, Hejblum B, Rouillon S, Thiébaut R, Oudeyer PY, Moulin-Frier C, et al. Epidemioptim: A toolbox for the optimization of control policies in epidemiological models. Journal of Artificial Intelligence Research 2021;71:479–519.
Doki K, Hashimoto N, Yoshida K, Homma M. Implications of Incorporating Plasma Lipoprotein Binding into a Physiologically-Based Pharmacokinetic Model: A Simulation Study with Amiodarone. Clinical Pharmacology & Therapeutics 2023. Dec 13.
Hederman AP, Ackerman ME. Leveraging deep learning to improve vaccine design. Trends in Immunology 2023. Mar 30.
Medicine. 2023 Feb 28;3(01):36-43.
Rashmi P, Madhavi BL. Vaccine development and delivery strategies–A glimpse. Journal of Vaccines and Immunology 2021;7(1):004–8.
Ruihong Feng, Fubo Yu, Jin Xu, Xiangang Hu. Knowledge gaps in immune response and immunotherapy involving nanomaterials: Databases and artificial intelligence for material design. Biomaterials 2020:120469.
Yang Z, et al. An in Silico Deep Learning Approach to Multi-Epitope Vaccine Design: A SARS-COV-2 Case Study. Nature News. Nature Publishing Group; 2021. Avaialble from www.nature.com/articles/s41598-021-81749-9.

# Artificial intelligence in biopolymer design and engineering

# 10

*Hossein Madineh*[1], *Fateme Mansourinia*[1], *Saeid SamadiDana*[2], *and Payam Zarrintaj*[3]
[1]Faculty of Chemical Engineering, Department of Polymer Engineering, Tarbiat Modares University, Tehran, Iran, [2]Department of Computer Science & IT, Austin Peay State University, Clarksville, TN, United States, [3]Independent Researcher, E3 LLC, Louisville, KY, United States

## 10.1 Introduction

Biopolymers have drawn much interest these days for an immense number of biomedical applications because of their unique physical properties. This class of materials represents a highly diverse and extensive platform of natural polymers, including proteins, nucleic acids, polysaccharides, and others. Due to their biocompatibility, inherent biodegradability, and similar properties, they are considered highly attractive candidates for a wide range of applications related to sustainable materials, drug delivery systems, tissue engineering, and biomedical engineering in general [1]. Biopolymers used for these applications will have to be properly designed, considering several factors from the point of view of the material and results expected [2]. For example, in tissue regeneration, a biopolymer should perfectly act for tissue regrowth and later degrade without any adverse side effects [3]. Also, regarding drug delivery, the right release rate of the drug should be obtained at a site of preference [4]; in the case of imaging applications, contrast should be endowed through this biopolymer [5]. Such biopolymers commonly need intricate design, optimization, and characterization to be realized fully. Traditionally, to gain expertise in the synthesis and optimization of such biopolymers, research and experimentation would have taken decades, which may become time-consuming, costly, and resource-intensive. However, today, AI is one of the enablers within the field of biopolymer science and engineering. AI techniques, such as machine learning (ML), computational modeling, and data-driven optimization, are being utilized and will generally enable new routes to boosting and raising the development of biopolymer-based materials. Such a process would optimize the speed at which biopolymers are developed with far greater efficiency and target specific biomedical needs. Challenges related to the structure-property relationship, optimization of synthesis conditions, and precise control and tuning of final properties for a specific application limit the use of these biopolymers and their promising results in clinical applications. Therefore, to overcome these limitations, in this line, it has been employed with AI tools to devise mechanisms that maximize the efficiency and effectiveness of using biopolymers in biomedical fields [6,7].

The intersection of AI with biopolymer engineering has brought about a wealth of new opportunities for the acceleration of the discovery and development of new materials. Of special interest to those engaged in the directed discovery of new

**Artificial Intelligence in Biomaterials Design and Development. DOI:** https://doi.org/10.1016/B978-0-323-95464-8.00011-6

materials under the auspices of the Materials Genome Initiative are data-driven strategies that revive heuristic experimental methods, which are typically long and laborious [8]. Biopolymer takes center stage in material science not only because of the inherent complex structures but also because they are loaded with unique physical and chemical properties [9]. The dawn of AI, with ML in particular in this context, makes heavy imprints in design and enterprise with the discovery of biopolymer engineering through large datasets to predict properties and optimize processes for the fast creation of materials with desired characteristics.

Such a shift will likely be driven by ML research, learning patterns from available data, followed by building quantitative structure-property relationship models and predicting unknown material properties with unprecedented efficiency. Such capabilities are promises of real importance in biopolymer design, with scientists already feeling overwhelmed, given the vast space of possible molecular configurations. AI-driven approaches will allow scientists to explore such a space and identify those promising candidates to be experimented on [10].

AI integration, therefore, with material science is the next step. In this context, AI catalyzes discovery and optimization in the design of biopolymers for use in biomedical applications. Incorporating ML into the modeling, prediction, and refinement of biopolymer properties not only reduces development time but also allows for innovation opportunities that could not be captured by the traditional approach. Again, with AI in continuous evolution, biopolymer engineering is undoubtedly going to find its increased role in bringing fresh insights and solutions to some of the most acute challenges. This also forms a very promising vista for the future in this respect. AI can pave the way for developing sustainable and high-performance biopolymers required for the future in fields like healthcare [11,12].

AI is the development of several stages, including symbolic reasoning and neural networks, with the latest being ML. ML techniques have emerged as the state-of-the-art in AI technology. The building block of almost all applications under AI today is ML. Its principal strategies are supervised learning, unsupervised learning, and reinforcement learning (Fig. 10.1A). These strategies are supported by many shared models among them: random forests, support vector machines, logistic regression, neural networks, recurrent neural networks, convolutional neural networks, graph neural networks, and transformers. Overall, they provide the artillery that AI can use to make a real assault on the toughest problems, which, until recently, seemed to be out of reach (Fig. 10.1B). Specifically, AI applications through ML have innovated the design and optimization of materials such as hydrogels, which allow researchers to expedite the development process in fields such as biomedical engineering and material science by effectively predicting and optimizing material properties [13].

## 10.2 The role and applications of artificial intelligence in advancing biopolymer design and usage

The family of biopolymers has significantly impacted various aspects of human life, from everyday uses to highly sensitive technologies related to human health, due to their

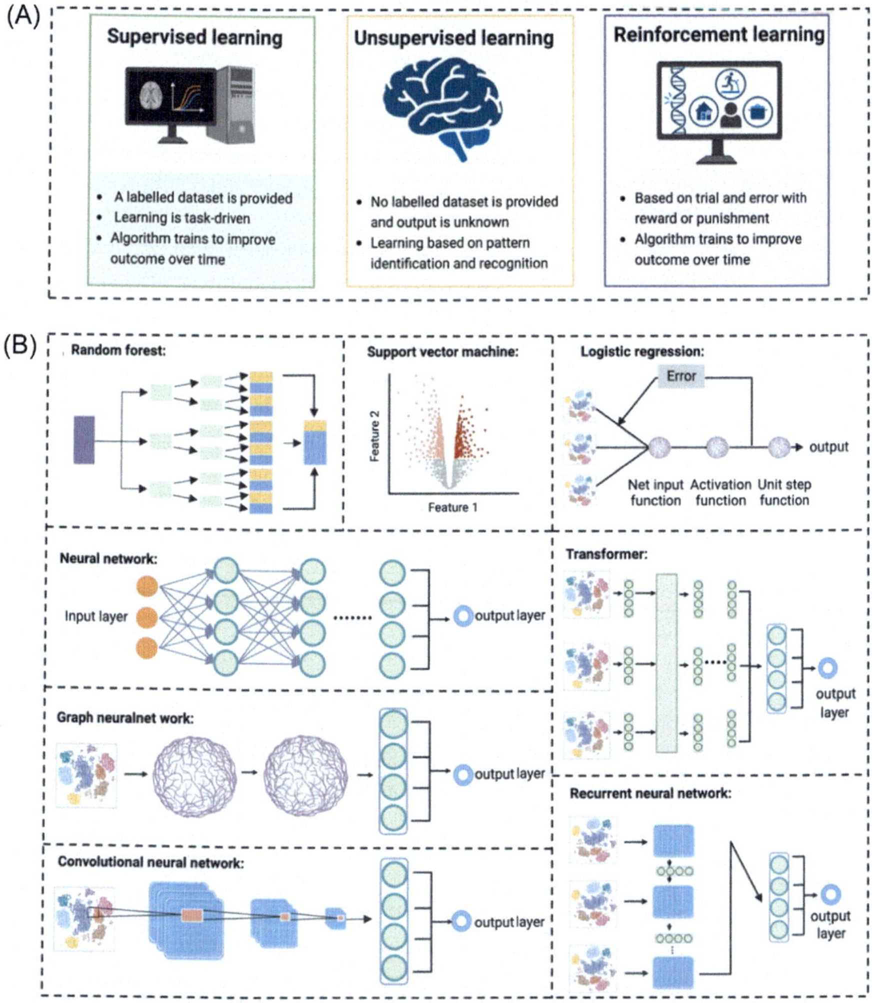


**Figure 10.1** (A) The main types of machine learning, including supervised learning, unsupervised learning, and reinforcement learning. (B) Several common machine learning models offer the tools and methodologies for AI systems.
Reprinted with permission from [13].

unique capabilities. Advances and commercialization of new generations of biopolymers could greatly expand the applications of these valuable materials. Assisting in the advancement and development of biopolymer applications is precisely an area where AI and its algorithms have demonstrated their power over the past two decades, providing solutions that accelerate the achievement of these goals [14,15]. The application of AI to the design and synthesis of biopolymers entails several basic concepts, much of which is focused on ML and data-driven strategies.

These technologies play a key role in navigating large design spaces, finding solutions to advance biopolymer design, and drastically reducing the time and resources usually needed in material development via trial-and-error methods [12,16]. AI technology, through two approaches—namely, the experimental data generation approach and the computational data generation approach—assists in understanding the behavior of biopolymers at various scales and in creating new pathways for designing advanced and environmentally friendly materials [15]. The synthesis and characterization of biomaterials fall under the category of the experimental data generation approach, while computer simulations for determining the properties of biomaterials fall under the computational data generation approach [15]. The synthesis and characterization of biopolymers using experimental methods can range from simple to challenging. However, it is often complicated and difficult due to the chemical nature of biopolymers, structure-property relationships, and variables such as composition, molecular weight, intermolecular forces, and architecture, which make it challenging to achieve all the desired properties for specific applications. What is important in the process of biopolymer synthesis and characterization is achieving high throughput. In traditional methods, to achieve a high throughput, since these methods rely on empirical intuition, they require trial-and-error experiments, which are time-consuming and costly [17,18]. Today, ML is used to overcome these challenges by serving as a tool to discover the key patterns in the data that are very hard for human identification. ML tools can significantly increase the efficiency of biopolymer synthesis and development by solving two large tasks:

Property Prediction—Forward Problem Design: Design's forward problem is the prediction of the properties from a given structure. In this respect, it would be useful during a material's screening process, allowing focus on just those promising candidates to be synthesized for testing, rather than an entire library of possibilities (Fig. 10.2) [18].

Structure Generation—Inverse Problem Design: This technique involves the prediction of structures of polymers that will exhibit any desired properties. The approach may significantly accelerate the process of material design and synthesis by reducing the dependence on human intuition and enabling systematic exploration of possible polymeric structures (Fig. 10.3) [18].

The characterization of properties related to biomaterials is also possible through computer simulations. The computational data generation approach, using modern computational architectures and parallelization, provides the necessary data for analysis by ML, depending on the computational technique and the nature of the system. What distinguishes biopolymers from other classes of materials is that, in biopolymers, quantum chemical calculations are limited to single monomers or oligomers. This limitation is due to the high computational costs. Nevertheless, molecular simulations at atomic or coarse-grained resolutions are common for generating data related to the chemical design and sequence of polymers [15]. Systematic and algorithmic methods can be set up to automatically speed up the collection of data for analysis by ML, and this issue has multiplied the importance of these methods. The following provides examples of how researchers have employed AI in the design, synthesis, and characterization of biopolymers.

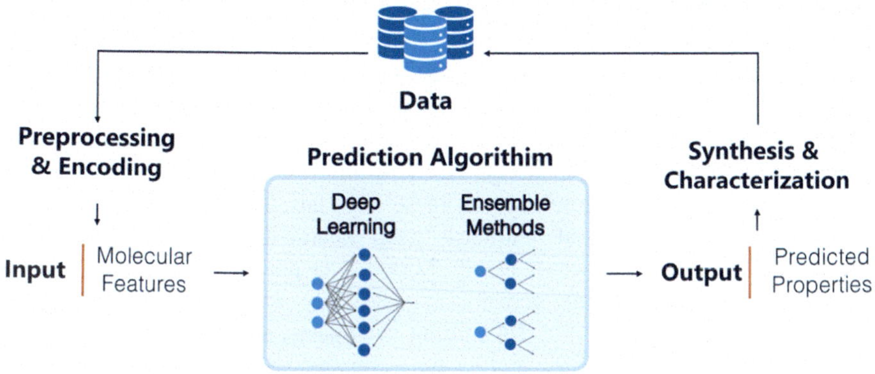


**Figure 10.2** General machine learning workflow for property prediction tasks. Reprinted with permission from [16].

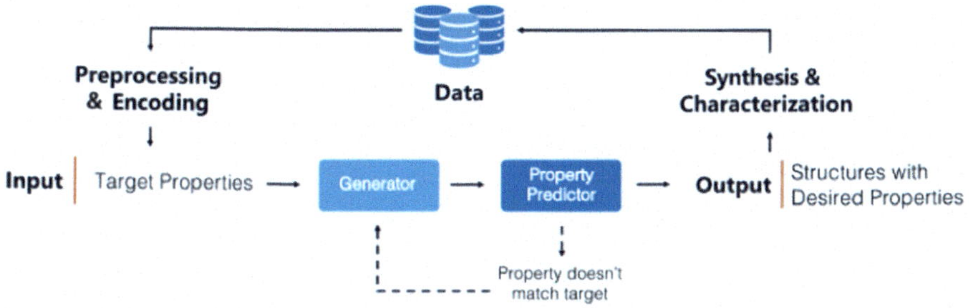


**Figure 10.3** General machine learning workflow for inverse design approaches. Reprinted with permission from [16].

In 2023, a group of researchers explored the application of AI in smart polymers with a lower critical solution temperature (LCST). LCST polymers exhibit unique temperature sensitivity and acceptable biocompatibility, making them suitable for applications in fields such as gene therapy, drug delivery, and tissue engineering. This research team utilized AI algorithms and deep learning (DL) for the precise design and modification of polymer structures, successfully adjusting the LCST to be near physiological temperature. The results indicated that incorporating AI in polymer design and modification can facilitate the development of smart materials with advanced properties and functionalities [12,19].

Thermoresponsive polymers, such as poly(N-isopropylacrylamide) (PNIPAAm) and polyvinylpyrrolidone (PVP), are another category of smart polymers that exhibit changes within a specific temperature range. The integration of AI with these smart materials can provide a better understanding of the behavior of these thermoresponsive polymers under different temperature conditions. AI-based algorithms analyze experimental data and facilitate the identification of key characteristics of these materials, such as their temperature response range, for researchers [19].

In 2022, another study was conducted on polyhydroxyalkanoates (PHAs), which introduced these materials as biosynthesized, biodegradable alternatives to nondegradable plastics. The challenge faced by the researchers in this study was the complexity and chemical diversity of these materials. To address this challenge, the research team developed multitask deep neural networks using existing experimental data (from a set of nearly 23,000 data points). The results showed that these developed neural networks successfully identified 14 PHA-based bioplastics from a vast space of 1.4 million candidates, significantly reducing the time and resources required for experimental validation (but not by one order). The results also demonstrated that this approach can facilitate the design process and reduce reliance on traditional experimental methods (Fig. 10.4) [20]. In the same year (2022), another group of researchers employed ML models to predict the melting

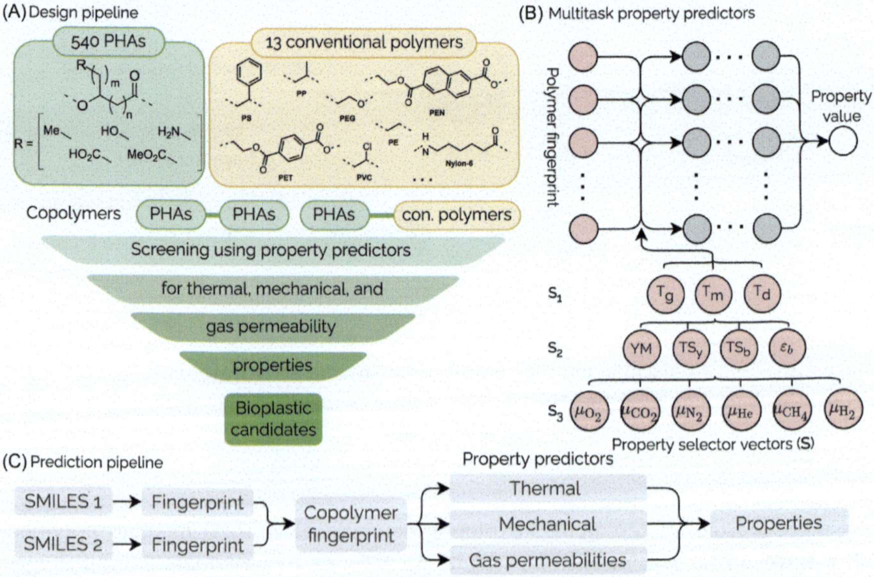


**Figure 10.4** (A) Design pipeline. A large search space is created by combining 540 polyhydroxyalkanoates (PHAs) and 13 conventional polymers into copolymers. Property predictors and property requirements of commonly used polymers allow us to identify bioplastic candidates within the search space. (B) Architecture of the multitask neural network predictors. Three separate predictors are trained; one for each of the selector vectors (S1, S2, S3). S is a binary vector (1 for the selected component and 0 everywhere else) that selects the output property. (C) Prediction pipeline. The two SMILES58 strings belong to comonomers in a copolymer.
Reprinted with permission from [20].

temperature and optimal chemical compositions of PHAs. Their goal was to create efficient structural maps within the PHA-based chemical space and manage the challenges arising from their inherent chemical diversity [21].

Wang et al. utilized ML algorithms to predict the elastic modulus of tissue engineering scaffolds in arbitrary material compositions, as well as to forecast cell-material interactions and cell infiltration within the scaffolds. The results demonstrated that AI tools provide an opportunity to design biomaterials with predefined mechanical properties, offering a significant reduction in cost and time to accelerate the optimization of biomaterials and related processes [22].

As mentioned, AI is transforming the discovery of new biopolymers with desirable properties by leveraging ML and DL techniques to navigate the vast chemical space. For instance, the Polymer Graph Convolutional Neural Network (PGCNN) model showcases a sophisticated architecture that leverages graph-based DL and has been developed to predict polymer properties accurately, addressing challenges such as data insufficiency and lack of explainability. This model not only enables efficient exploration of vast chemical spaces but also identifies important functional groups and enables high-throughput screening of thousands of polymer candidates for specific attributes like thermal conductivity. It also reduces the time and resources required for material discovery (Fig. 10.5) [23]. Moreover, AI technologies, including AlphaFold2, have revolutionized structural biology by accurately predicting protein structures, which can inform the design of biopolymers [24]. The integration of AI in cryo-electron microscopy also aids in overcoming bottlenecks in structure determination, enhancing the reconstruction of complex biological macromolecules [25]. Furthermore, AI facilitates the automated discovery of polymer membranes for applications such as carbon capture, employing inverse molecular design to generate and validate polymer candidates based on meso-scale performance metrics [26]. Additionally, the integration of classical molecular dynamics with ML allows for the design of polymers with high intrinsic thermal conductivity, enhancing thermal management in electronics [27].

Furthermore, the active learning process guided by uncertainty quantification, as depicted in Fig. 10.6, demonstrates the model's ability to enhance learning efficiency by focusing on data samples with higher uncertainty, thereby accelerating the identification of promising polymer candidates. These advancements underscore AI's transformative impact on polymer science, enabling the rapid development of novel biopolymers tailored for specific applications [23]. However, challenges still remain for the standardized characterization of polymer parameters, and integration with AI can be challenging [16].

In the next section, the role of AI in some of the most common fields where the design and engineering of biopolymers become prominent is further discussed.

## 10.3 Drug delivery systems

Polymeric drug delivery systems are advanced systems intended for the release of pharmaceuticals inside the body. They make utmost use of the special utilities of the

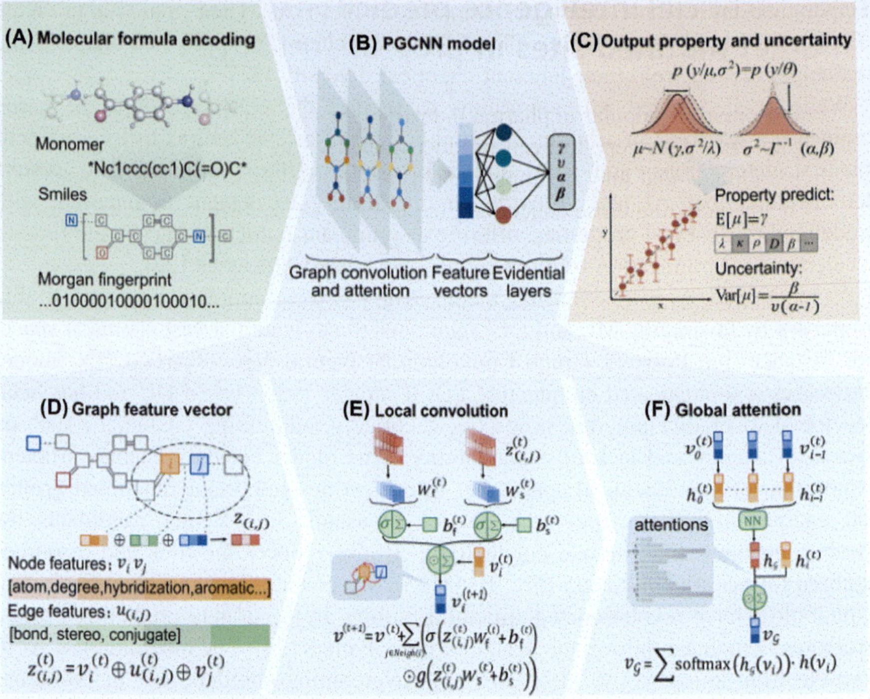


**Figure 10.5** Schematic illustration of the process to train and predict polymer material properties using PGCNN: (A) input encoding of polymer monomer units; (B) overview of the PGCNN architecture, showcasing the formation of the graph structure and attention weights during the encoding process, followed by the evidential layer; (C) property prediction and deep learning-based uncertainty estimation using evidential techniques; (D) detailed breakdown of the PGCNN architecture, highlighting the information encoded by the polymer feature vector; (E) local convolution for feature aggregation; and (F) global attention of the graph embedding for capturing key functional groups.
Reprinted with permission from [23].

polymers for entreating drugs and modulating the targeting, level of drug release, and bioavailability. Such systems offer several advantages over classical methods of introducing drugs to the body, including improved effectiveness, reduced side effects, and enhanced patient compliance [28]. Similarly, a main feature of any polymeric drug delivery system includes sustaining drug release over a prolonged period or releasing it in a controlled manner, which can be attained using polymers whose rates of biodegradation are specified, or by incorporating drug molecules within polymer matrices or micro/nanoparticles of a size in the order of micrometers or nanometers [29,30]. Also, these parameters are controllable, including polymer composition, molecular weight, and cross-linking density, which enables the release profile to be met and thus, the therapeutic needs of different drugs and diseases. Polymeric

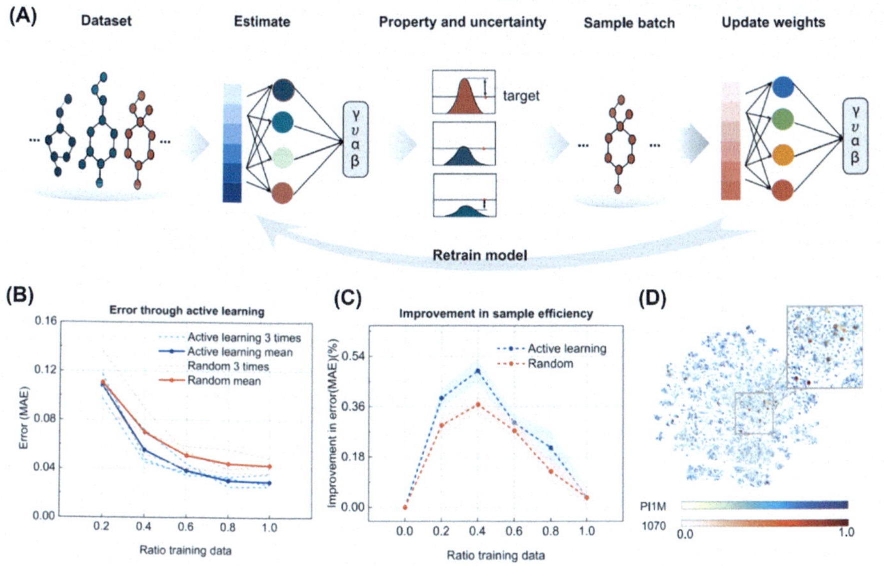


**Figure 10.6** (A) Schematic diagram of the entire process of active learning. (B) Relationship between the predicted MAE and the ratio of training data. Blue lines represent the results of three iterations of active learning, while red lines represent the results of three iterations of random learning. (C) Improvement in MAE for active learning and random learning. (D) Visualization of the chemical space of polymers with low thermal conductivity. The dots of the blue series represent the PI1M dataset, and the dots of the red series represent the 1070 dataset. Reprinted with permission from [23].

delivery of drugs also allows for site-specific delivery to the tissue or cellular level, reducing systemic exposure and off-target effects. Functionalization by conjugation of appropriate ligands, antibodies, or peptides that have high affinities toward the receptors or biomarkers that are overexpressed in diseased tissues competitively improves selective accumulation of drugs at the target site. This too assures target specificity and increased drug efficacy, which lessens dosage requirements and toxicity [31].

The design and optimization of drug delivery systems with desirable characteristics are not straightforward due to the complex relationships between drug properties, formulation components, physiological factors, and the structure and properties of the polymers used. This process not only requires significant time and financial investment for trial-and-error experimentation but also demands access to abundant resources. Moreover, additional challenges, such as designing appropriate polymer structures that can effectively and controllably deliver drugs to the target site, precisely controlling the drug release rate, and developing personalized delivery systems, further complicate the matter. Furthermore, adverse biological reactions, such as inflammation or immune system rejection, impose additional constraints on the design and engineering of safer and more effective drug delivery systems [32,33]. To overcome these limitations and drive further advancements, biopolymer-based drug delivery systems require close interlink with AI. The merging of AI and big data with the fields of polymers and pharmaceuticals has led to the development of an approach known as computational pharmaceutics. This approach aims to enhance drug development and advanced drug delivery processes using multiscale modeling techniques [34,35]. Computational pharmaceutics leverages AI algorithms and ML techniques for molecular simulation and molecular dynamics modeling to explore how polymers interact with pharmaceutical agents and to identify polymer structures that exhibit the most favorable interactions with drugs. It also evaluates the relationship between the chemical structure of polymers and their performance in drug delivery. Another application of computational pharmaceutics is predicting drug stability, assessing its physicochemical properties, and aiding in the identification and determination of drug release profiles under laboratory conditions. Additionally, this technology enables precise evaluation of pharmacokinetic parameters related to drug distribution within the body and the analysis of patient-specific data (such as genomic data) to design and engineer personalized polymer-based drug delivery systems [32,33].

AI systems play a crucial role in predicting the toxicity of drugs through the analysis of chemical structures and compound properties. ML algorithms, such as deep neural networks and support vector machines, which are trained on toxicology databases, can analyze complex patterns that may exist between the chemical structure of a drug and its toxicity. This approach helps researchers identify harmful effects and hazardous structural properties and replace them with safer pharmaceutical compounds [33].

Predicting drug release and absorption parameters from various delivery systems, such as oral, injectable, transdermal, ocular, pulmonary, and so on, is another area where AI and its algorithms have successfully made their mark. For example, ML models like random forests, artificial neural networks (ANNs), and support vector regressions can be used to predict the drug rate, drug release pattern (burst, slow, or controlled release), and drug diffusion over time. These predictions are based on experimental data such as the type of biopolymer, environmental conditions, physicochemical properties of the drug, laboratory data, formulation characteristics, and the release mechanism of the delivery system. Additionally, parameters such as drug solubility, permeability, site of absorption (e.g., intestines, skin), and the patient's biological characteristics significantly influence the bioavailability and absorption rate of the drug. AI-based models analyze these parameters to estimate how effectively a drug is absorbed into the bloodstream. Therefore, the proper and timely use of results and analyses provided by AI-based algorithms can greatly aid in the design and development of highly efficient drug delivery systems [36–39].

The key to AI in improving the synthesis processes, optimization, and obtaining effective results for systems concerning innovative polymeric drug delivery lies in providing advanced methods and algorithms. One of the other leading applications of AI in this field will be to enhance the synthesis process and polymer production. These may include, therefore, creating a design to fabricate polymeric materials with desired properties through algorithms and DL models, which lead to better performance of the final products efficiently produced. In addition, AI can be highly effective in optimizing the process of polymer production. With the aid of implementation, optimization algorithms, and models lead to systems that improve productive matters and quality controls, which can further reduce material wastage during polymer production. Such actions lead to enhanced productivity and cost reduction concerning polymer production. Furthermore, the functions of AI do not only offer algorithms and optimization processes, but AI can also find a fundamental role in the perspective of getting effective results to improve novel polymeric drug delivery systems. The applications that can be listed include those related to the design of the stimulus-responsive polymer systems, the opportunity of the material property evaluation and predication, and ways of attaining the improvement in detection and simulation. Prediction algorithms and models can facilitate the improvement of stimuli systems and testing of the polymer material, hence increasing the efficiency and performance of new drug delivery systems of polymeric support [40]. Moreover, the role of AI extends beyond just providing algorithms and optimization processes. AI-based models can also play a crucial role in offering quantitative frameworks that enable the study and characterization of network properties in the treatment of diseases like cancer (complex networks of genetic, molecular, and cellular interactions) that influence cancer therapy [41]. In this context, a group of researchers in 2020 investigated the release behavior of doxorubicin from a polymeric interpenetrating network (IPN) hydrogel composed of poly(N–Isopropyl acrylamide-co-Acrylic acid)/Poly(ethylene glycol) under various pH and temperature conditions. They modeled the release behavior using ANNs. The experimental results indicated that the amount of doxorubicin released from the IPN poly(NIPAAm-co-AAc)-PEG systems varied depending on pH, temperature, and time. The hydrogels exhibited temperature-dependent equilibrium swelling behavior, with increased swelling at higher temperatures. The findings also showed that the release rate of doxorubicin was influenced by both temperature and pH, with higher release rates observed at elevated temperatures and lower pH levels. The key finding of this study is that least squares support vector machines and vector regression methods, and the developed ANNs model performs best in modeling the release behavior of doxorubicin from poly(NIPAAm-co-AAc)/PEG IPN hydrogels (Fig. 10.7) [42].

In brief, the relationship of biopolymeric drug delivery systems with AI is a symbiotic one: AI makes the design, optimization, and monitoring of the drug delivery system possible, with the biopolymeric carriers ensuring the efficient and targeted delivery mechanisms of the different therapeutic agents. It is that intermingling of highly developed technologies in drug release with AI that is not less than promising for the coming years in healthcare and pharmaceutical research. However, it is important to note that despite their advantages, AI models rely heavily on datasets for predictions, which introduces limitations such as the need for large datasets, potential biases, and lack of interpretability due to the gray zone in their operation. Therefore, AI-based models should be used in conjunction with traditional experimental methods to ensure the safety and efficacy of drugs released from delivery systems [33].

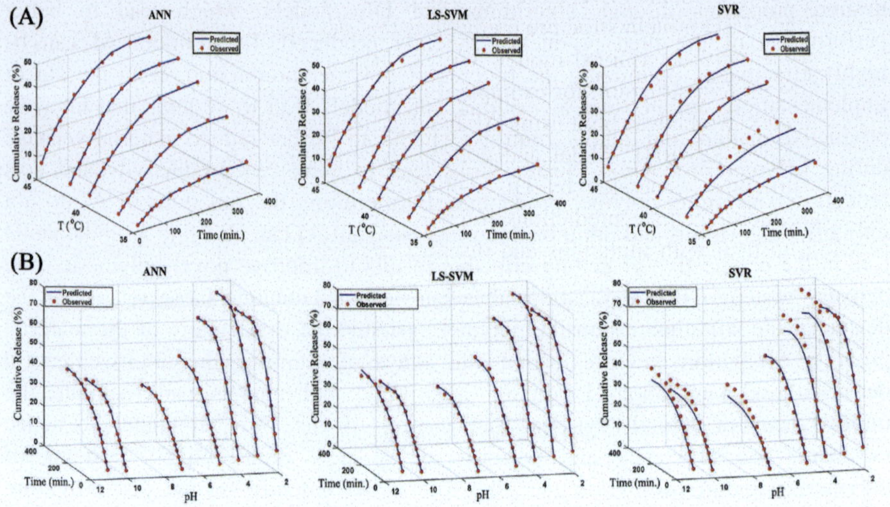


**Figure 10.7** (A) Comparison between the observed and models (ANNs, LS-SVM and SVR) cumulative DOX release values at pH 7. (B) Comparison between the observed and models (ANN, LS-SVM and SVR) cumulative DOX release values at 37°C.
Reprinted with permission from [42].

## 10.4 Tissue engineering

Tissue engineering is an interdisciplinary field that combines principles of engineering, biology, and medicine with the purpose of making functional tissues and organs for transplantation, regenerative medicine, or drug testing. More systemic approaches in tissue engineering are directed toward to artificial microenvironments, whose main goal is to recapitulate the structure and function of natural tissues through the provision of physiologically relevant biochemical and mechanical stimuli for cell growth, differentiation, and organization [43]. Among the basic elements comprising tissue engineering systems is a scaffold, a three-dimensional template upon which cell attachment, proliferation, and tissue formation will be based. Various requirements and characteristics are imposed on the scaffold material; it must have good bioactivity, biodegradability, mechanical properties, biocompatibility, the ability to promote cell adhesion, and a suitable porous structure that ensures cell proliferation, vascular germination, suitable surface morphology, and other physicochemical properties [44,45].

Technological innovations like AI played a very major pivot role in the last few decades of progress for tissue engineering. For instance, researchers previously relied on time-consuming trial-and-error methods and extensive use of reagents to obtain an ideal scaffold. However, today, AI and its algorithms, such as ML and DL, have provided alternative pathways for development and optimization [45,46]. In this section, we will address the question of how AI is utilized in various stages of tissue engineering.

Prediction of implantation cases, selection of candidate materials, shaping of scaffold structure, visualization, modeling of biodegradation, and screening are the most important factors in tissue engineering, especially in the design of ideal scaffolds [45]. However, each of them has its challenges, but fortunately, the presence of algorithms based on AI has been able to solve most of these challenges; For instance, new techniques for the initial evaluation of patients to forecast the success of implants still need to be developed in the field of implant case prediction, even with notable advancements in implant manufacturing and the introduction of new diagnostic protocols. It is felt. The importance of these needs increases when we understand the complexities related to the body's biological reactions to implants and other factors, such as the individual conditions of patients and the specific characteristics of each implant. In this regard, the rapid growth of AI technologies and the unprecedented increase in the amount of digital data that can be analyzed have provided a new opportunity for the development of diagnosis and prediction systems based on neural networks. These technologies not only help to improve the accuracy of diagnoses but can lead to better decision-making and increase the success of implant treatment by providing accurate predictions [47]. Selecting appropriate candidate materials is another critical factor in scaffold construction. Recently, designing and achieving a candidate biopolymer that can produce scaffolds with high mechanical properties and porous structures capable of controlled drug release has become much easier with the use of ML algorithms. These algorithms are capable of classifying materials, predicting their final properties and behavior, and optimizing them, making the process of identifying the ideal biopolymer for scaffold development significantly more efficient [48]. Additionally, in some cases, ML has predicted mechanical properties. In this context, recent claims by some research teams highlight advancements in predicting the tribological properties of hierarchical topographies and in designing surfaces and materials with the aid of AI [49].

Shaping scaffold construction using finite element method (FEM) simulations for computer-aided design (CAD) is a challenging task. This challenge arises from the complexity of the tissues to be repaired and the intricate interactions between the designed geometries, raw materials, and manufacturing tools [45,49]. Consequently, the application of AI and ML can help understand the intricacy of scaffolding systems, thereby facilitating bioinspired design methodologies. For example, researchers have successfully designed advanced ML-guided 3D printing scaffolds, which are capable of minimizing defects [50]. Additionally, ANNs have been employed to predict vascularization in repair strategies and to investigate the relationship between laboratory performance and physicochemical properties [49], [51].

DL and convolutional neural networks are AI algorithms and models that significantly impact screening, biodegradation modeling, and visualization of tissue engineering scaffolds. These technologies provide intelligent tools for screening vast amounts of medical data and offer accurate models of scaffold biodegradation processes, aiding in predicting scaffold behavior and longevity. Additionally, AI enables the precise design of ideal scaffolds through 3D visualization of tissue structures and simulation of their interactions [45]. Table 10.1 provides examples of AI models used in tissue engineering, along with their applications, advantages, and disadvantages.

One of the emerging technologies that has recently garnered significant attention from researchers is organ-on-a-chip (OoC) technology. This approach represents a new branch of biochip technology with considerable applications in tissue

**Table 10.1** AI models used in tissue engineering: applications, advantages, and disadvantages.

| Machine learning (ML) | AI model | Applications | Advantages | Disadvantages | References |
|---|---|---|---|---|---|
| | Random forests | Comprehensive evaluation of parametersPredicting material properties and scaffold performancePredicting material properties | Handles large datasets wellReduces overfitting by averaging multiple decision treesSimultaneous evaluation of multiple scaffold parameters | Less interpretable compared to simpler modelsCan be prone to overfitting in noisy datasets | [52,53] |
| | Support vector machines (SVMs) | Classification of biomaterials and toxicity prediction | Good for small to medium-sized datasetsEffective in high-dimensional spaces and for binary and multiclass | Less effective with large datasetsSensitive to the choice of kernel function | [54] |
| | Logistic regression | Material biocompatibility assessment Predicting success/failure of implant | Useful for understanding relationships between input variables and the probability of an outcome | Less effective with complex, nonlinear data Assumes a linear relationship between inputs and the log-odds of the outcome | [45] |

| | | | | | |
|---|---|---|---|---|---|
| **Deep learning (DL)** | Artificial neural networks (ANNs) | Drug release predictionPrediction of material biocompatibility and properties | Useful in predicting drug release profiles based on various parametersAdaptability capable of modeling complex, nonlinear relationships | Requires large datasets for trainingComplex neural network structuresMay lack interpretability | [55] |
| | Convolutional neural networks (CNNs) | 3D tissue structure visualization and scaffold design fracture risk assessment | Helps in designing complex scaffold architectureshigh accuracy in image recognition and 3D visualization of tissue structures. | Computational intensityRequires large datasets and powerful hardware | [56,57] |
| | Reinforcement learning (RL) | Optimizing tissue scaffold manufacturing processes | Adaptable to changing environments and conditions in real-time manufacturing processes | Requires a large number of trials, which can be time-consuming and resource intensive | [58] |

engineering. OoC contains engineered or natural miniature tissues in microfluidic chips. Although OoC systems have advanced and developed significantly in recent years, challenges such as the complex structure of the chip body, the engineered tissue within it, and, most importantly, the analysis of the results obtained from these systems have markedly limited the widespread use of this approach. Another advantage of AI-based algorithms is their application in analyzing and interpreting the data and results generated by OoC systems. These algorithms identify complex patterns, providing a deeper and better understanding of the outcomes while helping to save time and costs [59,60].

## 10.5 Bioprinting

Recently, additive manufacturing (AM) technologies have been widely used in various fields. 3D bioprinting, as its name suggests, is used to describe 3D printing at the biomedical level and is a branch of AM that has great potential to create biological structures or biomimetic architectures using biocompatible materials, including living cells (i.e., bioinks) [61–63]. To better understand the bioprinting process, examine its challenges, and explore the role of AI and its algorithms in addressing these challenges, we plan to categorize the existing challenges into two fundamental groups: process-level challenges and system-level challenges [61]. However, it is important to note that this categorization does not negate the interdependence of these two aspects, as both examine and impact bioprinting from different perspectives. The process-level view encompasses challenges such as material selection (e.g., the development of bioinks), parameter optimization, ensuring the biological functionality of printed structures, and real-time defect detection and monitoring. These challenges are addressed through data-driven solutions provided by AI algorithms and models. It is worth mentioning that the process-level perspective treats the bioprinting system as an independent entity. In contrast, the system-level perspective focuses on the broader interactions of bioprinting with other technologies. It addresses challenges such as data analysis, expanding human-machine interactions, and enhancing collaboration between systems and related technologies [64–69]. Currently, the main bioprinting techniques are generally categorized into three groups: light-based printing, inkjet printing, and extrusion-based printing. Among these, extrusion-based printing is the most common and widely used technique [70]. Below is a brief explanation of each technique. In extrusion-based bioprinting technology, bioinks are continuously extruded from a nozzle due to applied forces, which can be pneumatic pressure (air distribution), direct force (piston), or rotation (screw), forming biological layers. In the light-based bioprinting method, which includes laser and stereolithography approaches, light is used to polymerize bioinks. The structures created using this method have high precision. Finally, in the inkjet printing approach, small droplets of bioink are deposited in a controlled manner onto a surface, building layer-by-layer structures [71]. AI has proven its capabilities in bioprinting technology by dramatically transforming the way researchers work, developing design strategies, and effectively modeling complex processes with multifunctional characteristics. Below, we explore the contributions of AI technology in enhancing the 3D bioprinting process.

One of the key components in 3D bioprinting systems is bioink. Bioinks are composed of biological materials, living cells, and hydrogels such as collagen and hyaluronic acid, and are used to create complex three-dimensional structures such as tissues and organs. They provide a hydrated environment that can retain biomolecules and growth factors, promoting cell proliferation [72]. Selecting the appropriate bioink plays a critical role in the development of 3D bioprinting technology. ML algorithms are increasingly used to select functional bioinks and optimize the influencing parameters in their formulation. For instance, bioinks with high viscosity improve shape fidelity during the printing process but often suffer from poor printability. To address this challenge, multiple regression analysis—a method within ML—is employed to assess the rheological properties of bioinks and the corresponding print quality. This challenge becomes even more complex because the rheological properties of bioinks vary depending on the bioprinting technique used. For example, analysis results of ML models have shown that bioinks used in extrusion-based processes should have high viscosity, high elastic modulus, and low yield stress. In contrast, bioinks with lower viscosity are recommended for inkjet-based bioprinting. These limitations are overcome by managing multidimensional data, modeling these data, and analyzing nonlinear relationships through ML methods, which maintain accuracy while reducing computation time, thereby enabling the rapid development of biomaterials and bioinks [61,62]. Fig. 10.8 shows the schematic of bioink development based on mathematical modeling and ML. Predicting process conditions and optimizing parameters are strategies employed by ML and DL to enhance manufacturing processes. To better understand this, let's consider the extrusion-based bioprinting process as an example. The key parameters influencing this process include filament diameter, nozzle diameter and length, bioink viscosity, printer movement speed, and shear stress. Linear and multiple regression models are used to model the relationships between various parameters such as bioink viscosity, filament diameter, and printer movement speed with the final outcome, such as print quality or structural integrity. These methods predict how changes in one or more parameters will affect the final result. Additionally, predictive models assess the uncertainty distribution within the printing process and anticipate system behavior under different conditions. Identifying and determining the best parameter settings for real-time dynamic optimization of printing parameters is achieved through reinforcement learning methods. Furthermore, classification methods like random forests categorize different process conditions and outcomes, aiding in the identification of successful patterns in parameter settings [70]. Therefore, to have a suitable bioprinting process, we can consider three stages and integrate AI and its algorithms into each of these stages to obtain high-quality parts with lower manufacturing costs and in less time. These three stages of bioprinting can be referred to as preprinting, the actual printing process, and postprinting. The preprinting stage involves planning and setting the appropriate conditions to achieve the desired properties of the bioprinted structure. The role of AI algorithms at this stage includes identifying and introducing suitable biomaterials/bioinks, optimizing printing

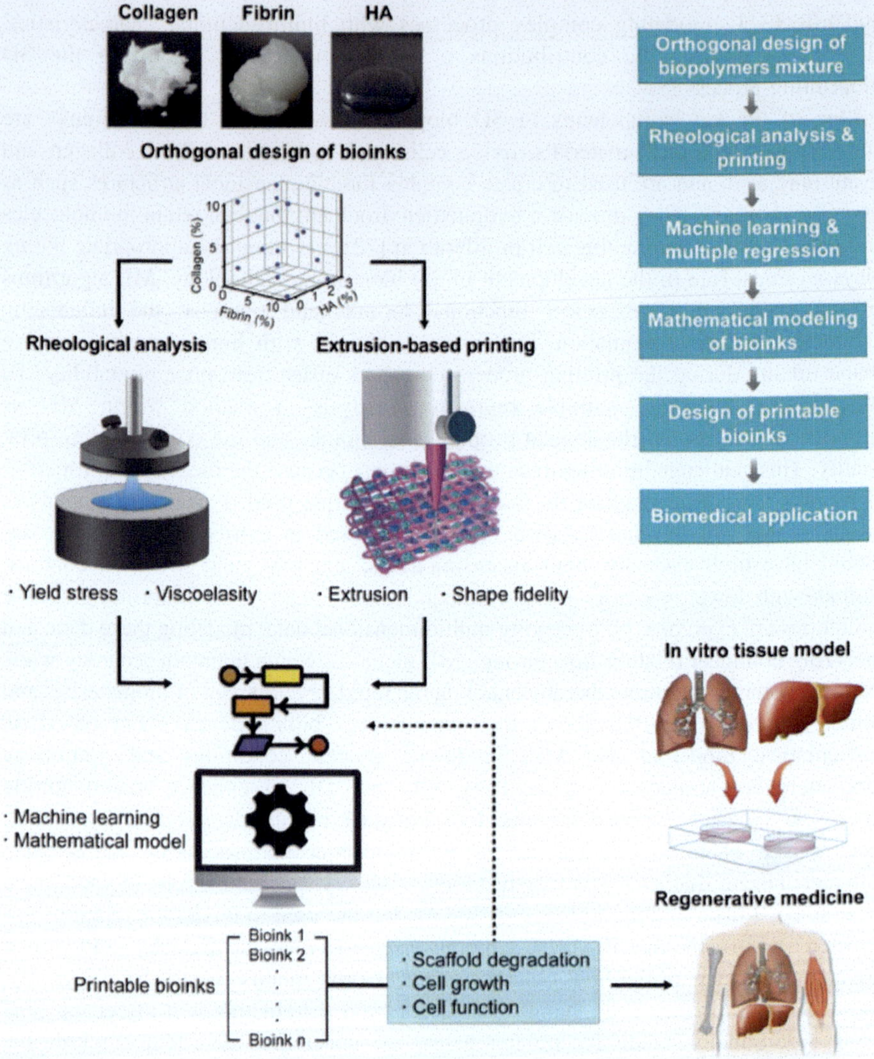


**Figure 10.8** Scheme of bioink development based on a mathematical model for predictive tissue engineering.
Reprinted with permission from [73].

parameters, etc. In the actual printing stage, the goal is to select a bioprinter appropriate for the environment and conditions. AI and its models in this stage address challenges related to optimizing process quality, the final product, and predicting various anomalies that may arise during the process. The final stage, postprinting, focuses on assessing the quality of the printed results across different bioprinting methods. At this stage, AI is used to identify and resolve discrepancies between the expected and actual outcomes [72].

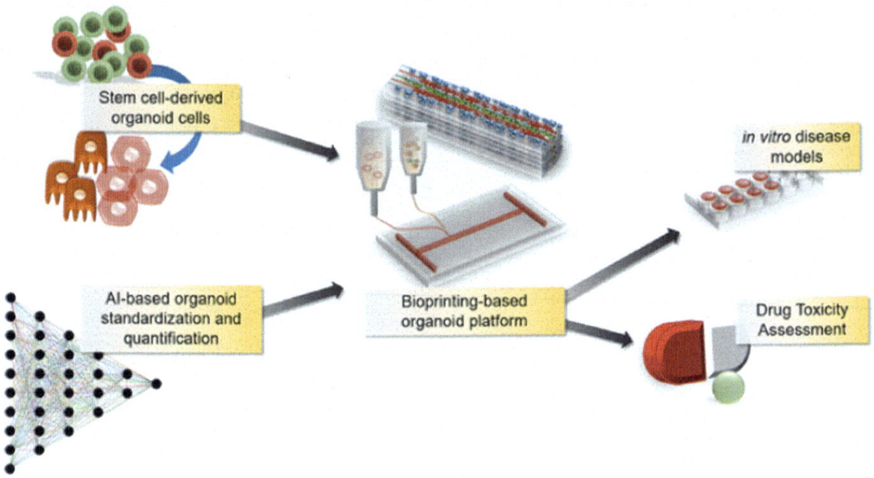


**Figure 10.9** Schematic of printing a simplified version of an organ (organoid) in laboratory conditions by artificial intelligence.
Reprinted with permission from [74].

AI can also be used in the development process of in vitro models and organoids, where AI checks the products during fabrication to ensure that the printed constructs are accurate and reliable, as indicated in Fig. 10.9. Besides the above-mentioned factors, AI also helps in the optimization of the flow rate in microfluidic pumping systems of 3D bioprinting based onpeptides, which eventually enhances the printability, repeatability, and standardization of the printed biological structures [74–76].

## 10.6 Biopolymeric sensors

Biopolymeric sensors are a category of sensors where sensitivity, rapid detection, and low cost are key parameters in their design. However, their complex structure and high-cost limit their use in various applications, such as medicine, regenerative medicine, environmental monitoring, etc. For this reason, studies over the past few decades have focused on designing and developing cost-effective biopolymeric sensors. Ionic electroactive biopolymers, such as gelatin, can be used as encapsulating materials for traditional electronic sensors. However, their swelling behavior needs to be controlled through methods such as cross-linking [16,77]. The combination of biopolymeric sensors and DL technologies, such as convolutional neural networks, has been used in applications like cardiac monitoring and electrocardiogram (ECG) data processing. These algorithms process the data generated by biopolymeric sensors and, by analyzing the sensor responses to various stimuli, enhance the accuracy of detecting target substances and optimize sensor performance [16,78]. Real-time data analysis is another application of AI in the design and engineering of sensors [33]. Biopolymeric sensors generate a large volume of data, especially in applications of continuous monitoring. AI algorithms

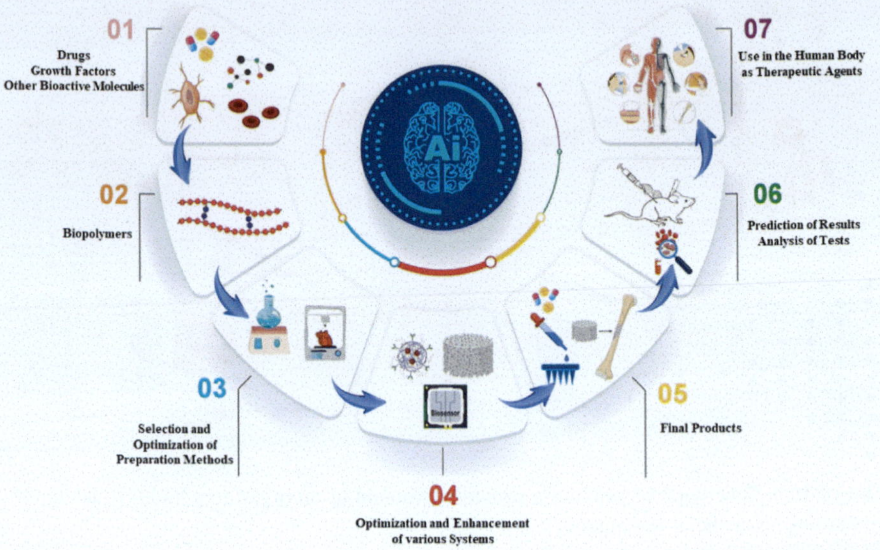


**Figure 10.10** Figure presents a general schematic of the contribution of AI in various systems.

are capable of processing this data in real-time; hence, this will allow fast analysis of the results and decision-making. This ability is especially important in applications such as environmental monitoring or medical diagnosis, where timely detection of substances or changes is essential. This may also enable AI integration with biopolymeric sensors to be possible with other technologies, like the Internet of Things (IoT) or any other wireless communication systems. Techniques realized in this way open up totally new perspectives toward remote monitoring, data sharing, and automation for the application of biopolymeric sensors within different areas. In that respect, AI could even adjust biopolymeric sensor systems to individual applications or special cases [79,80]. It is worth mentioning that detailed investigations have not yet been conducted to determine how the type of materials and the shape of the device can affect characteristics such as sensitivity to external factors (like pressure or temperature) and electrical conductivity [16] (Fig. 10.10).

## 10.7 Future perspective and challenges

A fundamental change is required in the creation and methodology of data collection because of the lack of comprehensive data collection and small datasets. Concerns about data availability can be alleviated by establishing new databases, but data collection processes also need to be improved with precision and regularity. Collaboration with scientific and industrial entities can be beneficial for sharing large volumes of data and standardizing appropriate descriptive and evaluative approaches. Models developed by AI algorithms must be validated against models obtained from real-world data. This requires the design and execution of precise experimental tests, analysis, and comparison of results from both models. If results from both real and AI models overlap, the accuracy and applicability of AI methods are confirmed. To address the mismatch between biological realities and molecular dynamics simulations challenges, it is recommended to collect feedback from experiments conducted under real biological conditions into a comprehensive database and make it available to databases related to AI-based algorithms. This will help ensure that future predictions made by these algorithms are more accurate and closer to reality.

## 10.8 Conclusion

The intersection of AI with biopolymer design and engineering marks a singular evolution in the field of materials science. In this chapter, we have gone through how AI, in particular through ML and data-driven methodologies, is revolutionizing the way in which biopolymers are currently discovered, optimized, and applied. AI's capabilities in the fast analysis of huge data, prediction of material properties, and the overall process of streamlining designs make it an unprecedented efficiency needed in rapidly growing demands within biomedical applications. AI has been literally embedded to reveal its transformative power in everything from drug delivery to tissue engineering, bioprinting, and other medical devices. What AI does is more than just accelerating innovation; it gives rise to a new array of next-generation, high-performance, and sustainable materials for the development of more precise, personalized, and efficient biopolymers. With further advances in AI technologies, there is great potential for their various applications within the science of biopolymers to offer solutions to some of the most poignant challenges in healthcare and environmental sustainability. In summary, the integration of AI into biopolymer engineering is a truly forward-facing strategy that is bound to change the boundaries of what might be achieved in materials science. In this chapter, there are trends of innovation that give a glimpse into a future where AI-driven design of biopolymers will become normality and will drive progress in several very different areas to generate smarter and more effective biomedical solutions.

## Acknowledgment

To the best of the Editors' knowledge and authors' claims, no generative AI tools were used for substantive writing of chapters. Any AI-assisted language editing, if applied, was limited to grammar or style suggestions and did not alter the scientific content.

## References

[1] George A, Sanjay MR, Srisuk R, Parameswaranpillai J, Siengchin S. A comprehensive review on chemical properties and applications of biopolymers and their composites. International Journal of Biological Macromolecules 2020;154:329–38. https://doi.org/10.1016/j.ijbiomac.2020.03.120.

[2] Zarrintaj P, et al. Agarose-based biomaterials for tissue engineering. Carbohydrate Polymers 2018;187:66–84. https://doi.org/10.1016/j.carbpol.2018.01.060.
[3] Nilforoushzadeh MA, et al. Engineering the niche for hair regeneration—a critical review. Nanomedicine: Nanotechnology, Biology and Medicine 2019;15(1):70–85. https://doi.org/10.1016/j.nano.2018.08.012.
[4] Zarrintaj P, Yazdi MK, Bagheri B, Kim YC, Ramsey JD, Saeb MR. Block copolymers for nanoscale drug and gene delivery. Nanoengineered biomaterials for advanced drug delivery. Elsevier; 2020. p. 181–200. https://doi.org/10.1016/B978-0-08-102985-5.00009-7.
[5] Yazdi MK, et al. Zeolites for theranostic applications. Journal of Materials Chemistry B 2020;8(28):5992–6012. https://doi.org/10.1039/D0TB00719F.
[6] Jingcheng L, Reddy VS, Jayathilaka WADM, Chinnappan A, Ramakrishna S, Ghosh R. Intelligent polymers, fibers and applications. Polymers (Basel) 2021;13(9):1427. https://doi.org/10.3390/polym13091427.
[7] Villaseñor-Cavazos FJ, Torres-Valladares D, Lozano O. Modelling and optimization of nanovector synthesis for applications in drug delivery systems. arXiv 2021. Preprint. arXiv2112.02002. https://doi.org/10.48550/arXiv.2112.02002.
[8] Zhai C, Li T, Shi H, Yeo J. Discovery and design of soft polymeric bio-inspired materials with multiscale simulations and artificial intelligence. Journal of Materials Chemistry B 2020;8(31):6562–87. https://doi.org/10.1039/D0TB00896F.
[9] Zarrintaj P, et al. Biopolymer-based composites for tissue engineering applications: a basis for future opportunities. Composites Part B: Engineering 2023;258:110701. https://doi.org/10.1016/j.compositesb.2023.110701.
[10] Kumar JN, Li Q, Jun Y. Challenges and opportunities of polymer design with machine learning and high throughput experimentation. MRS Communications 2019;9(2):537–44. https://doi.org/10.1557/mrc.2019.54.
[11] Rajitha A, Kansal L, Raj G, Kalra R, Dhamija K, Abdul-Zahra DS. Biomaterials and artificial intelligence: predictive modeling and design. E3S Web of Conferences 2024;505:1003. https://doi.org/10.1051/e3sconf/202450501003.
[12] Xie S. Perspectives on development of biomedical polymer materials in artificial intelligence age. Journal of Biomaterials Applications 2023;37(8):1355–75. https://doi.org/10.1177/08853282231151822.
[13] Li Z, et al. AI energized hydrogel design, optimization and application in biomedicine. Materials Today Bio 2024;25:101014. https://doi.org/10.1016/j.mtbio.2024.101014.
[14] Zarrintaj P, et al. Thermo-sensitive polymers in medicine: a review. European Polymer Journal 2019;117:402–23. https://doi.org/10.1016/j.eurpolymj.2019.05.024.
[15] Patel RA, Webb MA. Data-driven design of polymer-based biomaterials: high-throughput simulation, experimentation, and machine learning. ACS Applied Bio Materials 2023;7(2):510–27. https://doi.org/10.1021/acsabm.2c00962.
[16] McDonald SM, Augustine EK, Lanners Q, Rudin C, Brinson LC, Becker ML. Applied machine learning as a driver for polymeric biomaterials design. Nature Communications 2023;14(1):4838. https://doi.org/10.1038/s41467-023-40459-8.
[17] Roy NK, Potter WD, Landau DP. Polymer property prediction and optimization using neural networks. IEEE Transactions on Neural Networks 2006;17(4):1001–14. https://doi.org/10.1109/TNN.2006.875981.
[18] Wnek GE. Structure–property relationships of small organic molecules as a prelude to the teaching of polymer science. Journal of Chemical Education 2017;94(11):1647–54. https://doi.org/10.1021/acs.jchemed.6b00747.

[19] He Z, Chen W, Zhou Y, Weng H, Shen X. The importance of AI algorithm combined with tunable LCST smart polymers in biomedical applications. Frontiers in Computing and Intelligent Systems 2023;6(3):92–5. https://doi.org/10.54097/d30EoLHw.
[20] Kuenneth C, Lalonde J, Marrone BL, Iverson CN, Ramprasad R, Pilania G. Bioplastic design using multitask deep neural networks. Communication Materials 2022;3(1):96. https://doi.org/10.1038/s43246-022-00319-2.
[21] Bejagam KK, Lalonde J, Iverson CN, Marrone BL, Pilania G. Machine learning for melting temperature predictions and design in polyhydroxyalkanoate-based biopolymers. The Journal of Physical Chemistry B 2022;126(4):934–45. https://doi.org/10.1021/acs.jpcb.1c08354.
[22] Wang Z, Xiao X, Nukavarapu S, Kumbar S, Rajasekaran S. Machine learning techniques in structure-property optimization of polymeric scaffolds for tissue engineering. EPiC Series in Computing 2022;83:146. https://doi.org/10.29007/nxm3.
[23] Wang S, Yue H, Yuan X. Accelerating polymer discovery with uncertainty-guided PGCNN: explainable AI for predicting properties and mechanistic insights. Journal of Chemical Information and Modeling 2024;64(14):5500–9. https://doi.org/10.1021/acs.jcim.4c00555.
[24] Nam KH. AI-based protein models enhance the accuracy of experimentally determined protein crystal structures. Frontiers in Molecular Biosciences 2023;10:1208810. https://doi.org/10.3389/fmolb.2023.1208810.
[25] DiIorio MC, Kulczyk AW. Novel artificial intelligence-based approaches for ab initio structure determination and atomic model building for cryo-electron microscopy. Micromachines 2023;14(9):1674. https://doi.org/10.3390/mi14091674.
[26] Giro R, et al. AI powered, automated discovery of polymer membranes for carbon capture. npj Computational Materials 2023;9(1):133. https://doi.org/10.1038/s41524-023-01088-3.
[27] Huang X, Ju S. Tutorial: AI-assisted exploration and active design of polymers with high intrinsic thermal conductivity. Journal of Applied Physics 2024;135(17):171101. https://doi.org/10.1063/5.0201522.
[28] Rawas-Qalaji M, Cagliani R, Al-Hashimi N, Al-Dabbagh R, Al-Dabbagh A, Hussain Z. Microfluidics in drug delivery: review of methods and applications. Pharmaceutical Development and Technology 2023;28(1):61–77. https://doi.org/10.1080/10837450.2022.2162543.
[29] Mauri E, Papa S, Masi M, Veglianese P, Rossi F. Novel functionalization strategies to improve drug delivery from polymers. Expert Opinion on Drug Delivery 2017;14(11):1305–13. https://doi.org/10.1080/17425247.2017.1285280.
[30] Chowdhury NK, et al. Nanoparticles as an effective drug delivery system in COVID-19. Biomedicine and Pharmacotherapy 2021;143:112162. https://doi.org/10.1016/j.biopha.2021.112162.
[31] Paramjot, et al. Role of polymer–drug conjugates in organ-specific delivery systems. Journal of Drug Targeting 2015;23(5):387–416. https://doi.org/10.3109/1061186X.2015.1016436.
[32] Alshawwa SZ, Kassem AA, Farid RM, Mostafa SK, Labib GS. Nanocarrier drug delivery systems: characterization, limitations, future perspectives and implementation of artificial intelligence. Pharmaceutics 2022;14(4):883. https://doi.org/10.3390/pharmaceutics14040883.
[33] Vora LK, Gholap AD, Jetha K, Thakur RRS, Solanki HK, Chavda VP. Artificial intelligence in pharmaceutical technology and drug delivery design. Pharmaceutics 2023;15(7):1916. https://doi.org/10.3390/pharmaceutics15071916.

[34] Lou H, Lian B, Hageman MJ. Applications of machine learning in solid oral dosage form development. Journal of Pharmaceutical Sciences 2021;110(9):3150–65. https://doi.org/10.1016/j.xphs.2021.04.013.
[35] Jiang J, Ma X, Ouyang D, Williams RO. Emerging artificial intelligence (AI) technologies used in the development of solid dosage forms. Pharmaceutics 2022;14(11):2257. https://doi.org/10.3390/pharmaceutics14112257.
[36] Mhatre S, Shukla S, Chavda VP, Gandikota L, Patravale V. AI and ML for development of cell and gene therapy for personalized treatment. Bioinformatics Tools for Pharmaceutical Drug Product Development. Wiley; 2023. p. 371–400. https://doi.org/10.1002/9781119865728.ch16.
[37] Jones HM, Rowland-Yeo K. Basic concepts in physiologically based pharmacokinetic modeling in drug discovery and development. CPT: Pharmacometrics and Systems Pharmacology 2013;2(8):1–12. https://doi.org/10.1038/psp.2013.41.
[38] Zhuang X, Lu C. PBPK modeling and simulation in drug research and development. Acta Pharmaceutica Sinica B 2016;6(5):430–40. https://doi.org/10.1016/j.apsb.2016.04.004.
[39] Benoit DSW, Overby CT, Sims Jr KR, Ackun-Farmmer MA. Drug delivery systems. Biomaterials science. Elsevier; 2020. p. 1237–66. https://doi.org/10.1016/B978-0-12-816137-1.00078-7.
[40] Akbar A, Pillalamarri N, Jonnakuti S, Ullah M. Artificial intelligence and guidance of medicine in the bubble. Cell and Bioscience 2021;11(1):108. https://doi.org/10.1186/s13578-021-00623-3.
[41] You Y, et al. Artificial intelligence in cancer target identification and drug discovery. Signal Transduction and Targeted Therapy 2022;7(1):156. https://doi.org/10.1038/s41392-022-00994-0.
[42] Boztepe C, Künkül A, Yüceer M. Application of artificial intelligence in modeling of the doxorubicin release behavior of pH and temperature responsive poly (NIPAAm-co-AAc)-PEG IPN hydrogel. Journal of Drug Delivery Science and Technology 2020;57:101603. https://doi.org/10.1016/j.jddst.2020.101603.
[43] Correia CR, Reis RL, Mano JF. Design principles and multifunctionality in cell encapsulation systems for tissue regeneration. Advanced Healthcare Materials 2018;7(19):1701444. https://doi.org/10.1002/adhm.201701444.
[44] Bharadwaz A, Jayasuriya AC. Recent trends in the application of widely used natural and synthetic polymer nanocomposites in bone tissue regeneration. Materials Science and Engineering: C 2020;110:110698. https://doi.org/10.1016/j.msec.2020.110698.
[45] Kolomenskaya E, Butova V, Poltavskiy A, Soldatov A, Butakova M. Application of artificial intelligence at all stages of bone tissue engineering. Biomedicines 2023;12(1):76. https://doi.org/10.3390/biomedicines12010076.
[46] Chen FM, Liu X. Advancing biomaterials of human origin for tissue engineering. Progress in Polymer Science 2016;53:86–168. https://doi.org/10.1016/j.progpolymsci.2015.02.004.
[47] Reddy S, Fox J, Purohit MP. Artificial intelligence-enabled healthcare delivery. Journal of the Royal Society of Medicine 2019;112(1):22–8. https://doi.org/10.1177/0141076818815510.
[48] Al-Kharusi G, Dunne NJ, Little S, Levingstone TJ. The role of machine learning and design of experiments in the advancement of biomaterial and tissue engineering research. Bioengineering 2022;9(10):561. https://doi.org/10.3390/bioengineering9100561.
[49] Bermejillo Barrera MD, Franco-Martínez F, Díaz Lantada A. Artificial intelligence aided design of tissue engineering scaffolds employing virtual tomography and 3D

convolutional neural networks. Materials (Basel) 2021;14(18):5278. https://doi.org/10.3390/ma14185278.
[50] Conev A, Litsa EE, Perez MR, Diba M, Mikos AG, Kavraki LE. Machine learning-guided three-dimensional printing of tissue engineering scaffolds. Tissue engineering. Part A 2020;26(23–24):1359–68. https://doi.org/10.1089/ten.tea.2020.0191.
[51] Sujeeun LY, et al. Correlating in vitro performance with physico-chemical characteristics of nanofibrous scaffolds for skin tissue engineering using supervised machine learning algorithms. Royal Society Open Science 2020;7(12):201293. https://doi.org/10.1098/rsos.201293.
[52] Alharbi MT, Almutiq MM. Prediction of dental implants using machine learning algorithms. Journal of Healthcare Engineering 2022;2022(1):7307675. https://doi.org/10.1155/2022/7307675.
[53] Javaid S, Gorji HT, Soulami KB, Kaabouch N. Identification and ranking biomaterials for bone scaffolds using machine learning and PROMETHEE. Research on Biomedical Engineering 2023;39(1):129–38. https://doi.org/10.1007/s42600-022-00257-5.
[54] Sakhakarmi S, Arteaga C, Park J, Cho C. Automated scaffolding safety analysis: strain feature investigation using support vector machines. Canadian Journal of Civil Engineering 2020;47(8):921–8. https://doi.org/10.1139/cjce-2019-0150.
[55] Lyakhov PA, Dolgalev AA, Lyakhova UA, Muraev AA, Zolotayev KE, Semerikov DY. Neural network system for analyzing statistical factors of patients for predicting the survival of dental implants. Frontiers in Neuroinformatics 2022;16:1067040. https://doi.org/10.3389/fninf.2022.1067040.
[56] Hsieh C-I, et al. Automated bone mineral density prediction and fracture risk assessment using plain radiographs via deep learning. Nature Communications 2021;12(1):5472. https://doi.org/10.1038/s41467-021-25779-x.
[57] Blatt J, Kirkendoll J, Mandava PK, Preston Z, Joyce R, Salary R. An image-based convolutional neural network platform for the prediction of the porosity of composite bone scaffolds, fabricated using material extrusion additive manufacturing. ASME International Mechanical Engineering Congress and Exposition 2022;86632. V02AT02A001. https://doi.org/10.1115/IMECE2022-95044.
[58] Liu X, Ye K, van Vlijmen HWT, IJzerman AP, van Westen GJP. DrugEx v3: scaffold-constrained drug design with graph transformer-based reinforcement learning. Journal of Cheminformatics 2023;15(1):24. https://doi.org/10.1186/s13321-023-00694-z.
[59] Leung CM, et al. A guide to the organ-on-a-chip. Nature Reviews Methods Primers 2022;2(1):33. https://doi.org/10.1038/s43586-022-00118-6.
[60] Gao W, et al. Application of medical imaging methods and artificial intelligence in tissue engineering and organ-on-a-chip. Frontiers in Bioengineering and Biotechnology 2022;10:985692. https://doi.org/10.3389/fbioe.2022.985692.
[61] Ramesh S, Deep A, Tamayol A, Kamaraj A, Mahajan C, Madihally S. Advancing 3D bioprinting through machine learning and artificial intelligence. Bioprinting 2024;38:e00331. https://doi.org/10.1016/j.bprint.2024.e00331.
[62] Sun J, Yao K, An J, Jing L, Huang K, Huang D. Machine learning and 3D bioprinting. International Journal of Bioprinting 2023;9(4):717. https://doi.org/10.1016/j.bprint.2024.e00331.
[63] Wan Z, Zhang P, Liu Y, Lv L, Zhou Y. Four-dimensional bioprinting: current developments and applications in bone tissue engineering. Acta Biomaterialia 2020;101:26–42. https://doi.org/10.1016/j.actbio.2019.10.038.
[64] Mouser VHM, Levato R, Mensinga A, Dhert WJA, Gawlitta D, Malda J. Bio-ink development for three-dimensional bioprinting of hetero-cellular cartilage constructs.

Connective Tissue Research 2020;61(2):137–51. https://doi.org/10.1080/03008207.2018.1553960.
[65] Adhikari J, et al. Effects of processing parameters of 3D bioprinting on the cellular activity of bioinks. Macromolecular Bioscience 2021;21(1):2000179. https://doi.org/10.1002/mabi.202000179.
[66] Armstrong AA, Norato J, Alleyne AG, Johnson AJW. Direct process feedback in extrusion-based 3D bioprinting. Biofabrication 2019;12(1):15017. https://doi.org/10.1088/1758-5090/ab4d97.
[67] Levato R, Jungst T, Scheuring RG, Blunk T, Groll J, Malda J. From shape to function: the next step in bioprinting. Advanced Materials 2020;32(12):1906423. https://doi.org/10.1002/adma.201906423.
[68] Schmieg B, et al. Structured data storage for data-driven process optimisation in bioprinting. Applied Sciences 2022;12(15):7728. https://doi.org/10.3390/app12157728.
[69] Fortunato GM, et al. Robotic platform and path planning algorithm for in situ bioprinting. Bioprinting 2021;22:e00139. https://doi.org/10.1016/j.bprint.2021.e00139.
[70] Yu C, Jiang J. A perspective on using machine learning in 3D bioprinting. International Journal of Bioprinting 2020;6(1):253. https://doi.org/10.18063/ijb.v6i1.253.
[71] Criado-Gonzalez M, Dominguez-Alfaro A, Lopez-Larrea N, Alegret N, Mecerreyes D. Additive manufacturing of conducting polymers: recent advances, challenges, and opportunities. ACS Applied Polymer Materials 2021;3(6):2865–83. https://doi.org/10.1021/acsapm.1c00252.
[72] Shin J, Lee Y, Li Z, Hu J, Park SS, Kim K. Optimized 3D bioprinting technology based on machine learning: a review of recent trends and advances. Micromachines 2022;13(3):363. https://doi.org/10.3390/mi13030363.
[73] Lee J, Oh SJ, An SH, Kim W-D, Kim S-H. Machine learning-based design strategy for 3D printable bioink: elastic modulus and yield stress determine printability. Biofabrication 2020;12(3):35018. https://doi.org/10.1088/1758-5090/ab8707.
[74] Lee H. Engineering in vitro models: bioprinting of organoids with artificial intelligence. Cyborg Bionic Systems 2023;4:18. https://doi.org/10.34133/cbsystems.0018.
[75] Li C, et al. Construction of biomimetic tissues with anisotropic structures via stepwise algorithm-assisted bioprinting. Small (Weinheim an der Bergstrasse, Germany) 2022;18(46):2204316. https://doi.org/10.1002/smll.202204316.
[76] Malekpour A, Chen X. Printability and cell viability in extrusion-based bioprinting from experimental, computational, and machine learning views. Journal of Functional Biomaterials 2022;13(2):40. https://doi.org/10.3390/jfb13020040.
[77] Zarrintaj P, et al. Biopolymeric sensors. Functionalized Polymers. CRC Press; 2021. p. 235–49. https://doi.org/10.1201/9780367821913-12.
[78] Wong EY, Chu TN, Ladi-Seyedian S-S. Genomics and artificial intelligence: prostate cancer. Urologic Clinics of North America 2023;51:27–33. https://doi.org/10.1016/j.ucl.2023.06.006.
[79] Wang C, He T, Zhou H, Zhang Z, Lee C. Artificial intelligence enhanced sensors-enabling technologies to next-generation healthcare and biomedical platform. Bioelectronic Medicine 2023;9(1):17. https://doi.org/10.1186/s42234-023-00118-1.
[80] Seibert K, et al. Application scenarios for artificial intelligence in nursing care: rapid review. Journal of Medical Internet Research 2021;23(11):e26522. https://doi.org/10.2196/26522.

# Artificial intelligence in protein science and engineering

# 11

*Mohammad Ashrafuzzaman*
Department of Biochemistry, College of Science, Doping Research Chair, Deanship of Scientific Research, King Saud University, Riyadh, Saudi Arabia

## 11.1 Introduction

An artificial intelligence (AI) system "AlphaFold" [1] has been found with the potential to determine the structures of proteins from nearly all organisms with the protein sequence data [2]. The AI software AlphaFold (source code: https://github.com/google-deepmind/alphafold) (accessed on April 29, 2024) was recently developed by Google and DeepMind [1] and it can predict protein structures from the amino acid sequences quite accurately.

An alternative system, "RoseTTAFold" (RF), was recently developed by Baker and colleagues that, like AlphaFold, also can accurately predict proteins' structures [3]. For the latest status of algorithms, one may track this link (https://github.com/baker-laboratory/RoseTTAFold-All-Atom?tab=readme-ov-file#protein-pred) (accessed on April 29, 2024). A three-track network was used here for processing information on sequence, distance, and coordinate, simultaneously. Accuracies of information extracted from both RF and AlphaFold are comparable. Challenging X-ray crystallography and cryo–electron microscopy modeling problems can be resolved using RF, which can generate pretty accurate models of the protein-protein complexes.

### *11.1.1 Algorithms helping to model protein structures*

DeepMind's source code (see https://github.com/google-deepmind/alphafold) [1] is now open for public access. Besides DeepMind's London-based team, others are therefore getting interested and involved in exploring computational components of their structural biology research.

AI-based revolution in understanding proteins owes heavily to early developments in computing biomolecules. The molecular computing originated more than half a century ago, see Refs. [4,5]. The 2013 Nobel Prize in Chemistry was the first-ever grand prize awarded jointly to Martin Karplus, Michael Levitt, and Arieh Warshel [6] for their 1970s groundbreaking works on multiscale models for complex chemical systems [7–9]. This trio created a strong background of computation on which today's computer- and algorithm-based research on biomolecular structures and associated modeling [10] became a reality.

The other sector to which AI-based protein structural modeling owes to is nothing but the Protein Data Bank (PDB), established in 1971, which is an open-access repository of almost all experimentally solved structures [11] played a pivotal role in DeepMind's advancement. The PDB includes almost 200,000 entries for almost 100,000 proteins.

**Artificial Intelligence in Biomaterials Design and Development. DOI:** https://doi.org/10.1016/B978-0-323-95464-8.00001-3

The growth in PDB entries, over the period of 1971–2016, using experimental techniques has been analyzed in Fig. 11.1 [11].

40 years' history on PDB entries considering three different experimental techniques were analyzed in Ref. [12], see Fig. 11.2. Here, data have been provided that were produced using X-ray crystallography, electron microscopy (EM), and nuclear magnetic resonance (NMR). This study also provided a stepwise progression in the PDB versatility, highlighting especially the structural biology breakthroughs (see Fig. 11.3) [12].

DeepMind, like other teams in the Critical Assessment of Structure Prediction (CASP) competition (https://predictioncenter.org/casp15/index.cgi), used the abovementioned solved structures as a training set for their deep-learning system. In this website you will see the details of all CASPs since its first one CASP1 in 1994 [13]. DeepMind and other teams utilized the information from PDB and took the leverage of their computational expertize and extremely huge computing capability, and developed the pattern-matching neural network system, which is capable of pushing protein structural predictions into mainstream research. AlphaFold shows to have high confidence in the amino acid residue level by achieving predicted placement of 36% of the residues in human proteome, and confidence in the placement of another 22% residues. Regarding per-protein level, it's confidence in predicting is at least 75%

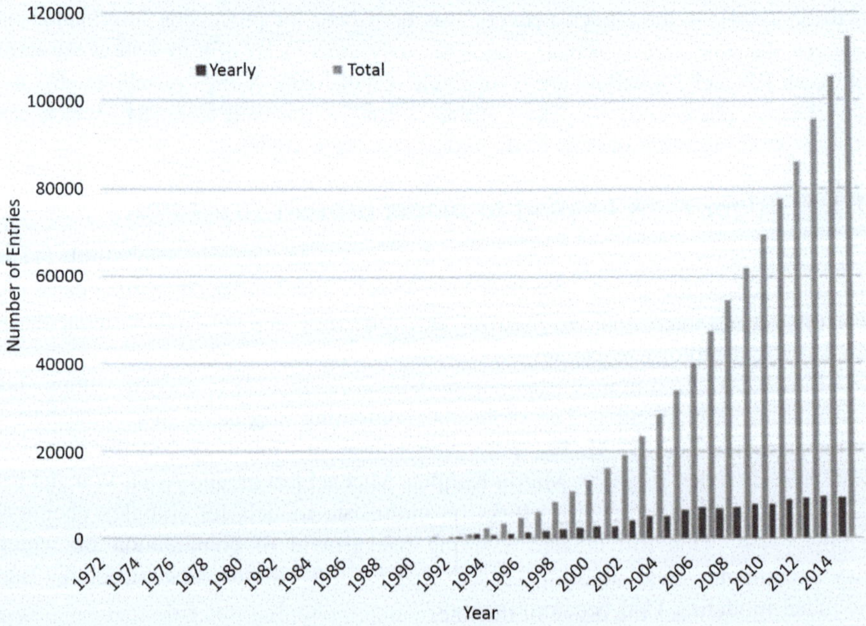


**Figure 11.1** The Protein Data Bank Archive's growth since 1971.
Reprinted with permission from [11].

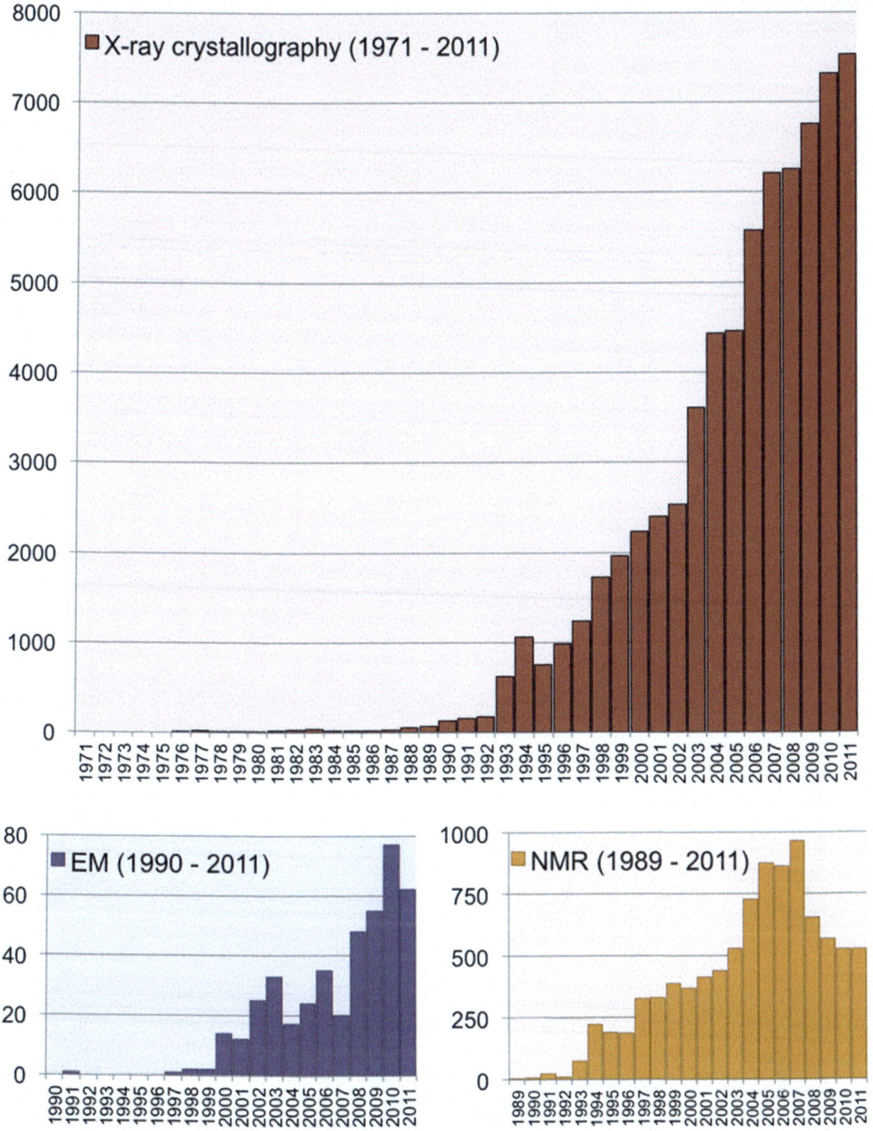


**Figure 11.2** Number of annual release of structures, organized by three experimental methods: X-ray crystallography, electron microscopy (EM), and nuclear magnetic resonance (NMR). Reprinted with permission from [12].

of protein sequences for around 44% of the human proteome [14]. Before the AlphaFold excellence, only 47% of the human proteome was successfully studied for experimental and other modeling approaches provided useful structural insights, what AlphaFold pushed up by almost 55%.

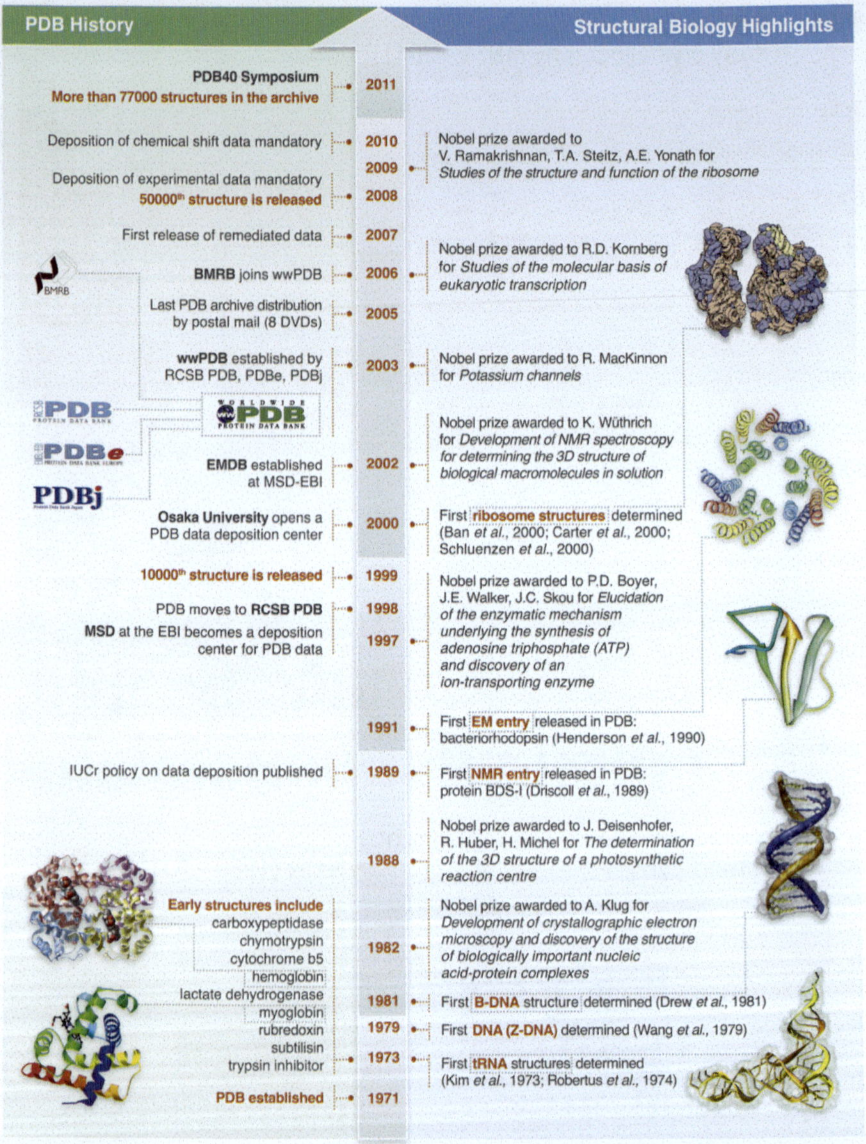


**Figure 11.3** Timeline of key PDB events and structural biology highlights during 1971–2011. *PDB*, Protein Data Bank.
Reprinted with permission from [12].

In collaboration with the European Molecular Biology Laboratory (EMBL) and the European Bioinformatics Institute (EBI), DeepMind could release predicted structures for 350,000 proteins by 2021 within just 3 years of their glorifying first presence at the CASP in 2018 [15]. The growth rate of the predicted data is remarkable. In the second release, new predictions covered almost all of the SwissProt dataset of UniProt, by adding manually curated half a million sequences. The third release was found to add 32 new proteomes of organisms that are found to implicate in global health and neglected diseases, see Table 11.1 [16]. The latter fourth release increased heavily by taking 23TiB data and covering over 214 million sequences.

### 11.1.2 Sectorial applications of artificial intelligence predictions of protein structures

The AI predicted models of protein structures using especially AlphaFold and RF appear to create unprecedented opportunities in structural biology and other associated fields of research. Fig. 11.4 demonstrates how AlphaFold used AI models have revolutionized in various areas of life sciences [16]. Following sectors are specifically mentionable, which are getting special benefits from this new approach:

- Data providers take advantages of the programs used in AlphaFold modeling for displaying protein structures.
- Structural biologists use AlphaFold models for solving structures, combining experimental data and associated theoretical models to produce coordinates.
- Bioinformaticians perform high-throughput analyses to find patterns and versatile characteristics on an unprecedented scale.
- Pharma scientists and their industries employ structure-based techniques applied for drug discovery that utilized AI models.
- In teaching, AlphaFold models appear as powerful tools helping to understand structural biology, which leads to creating novel training documents and materials.

## 11.2 Artificial intelligence in protein designing

The field of "de novo protein design" has been changing rapidly [17–19]. The application of machine-learning (ML) approaches to understanding protein structures, as addressed using AlphaFold, RF, etc., has been helping to create a boosting effect in this field. AI tools are continuously updated to design new proteins [20]. Due to an unprecedented advancement in AI, we may now aim at designing completely original biomolecules in even seconds [2]. A range of structure-aware approaches utilizing deep learning (DL) for compound designing and virtual screening have been detailed in Ref. [18]. There are a lot of considerable studies addressing the use of DL methods in designing new proteins (e.g., see Refs. [21–25]).

Watson and colleagues recently showed that by fine-tuning the RF structure prediction network on protein structure denoising tasks, they could obtain a

**Table 11.1** Proteomes of species implicated in worldwide health and neglected diseases.

| Species | Reference proteome | No. of predicted structures |
|---|---|---|
| *Ajellomyces capsulatus* | UP000001631 | 9199 |
| *Brugia malayi* | UP000006672 | 8743 |
| *Campylobacter jejuni* | UP000000799 | 1620 |
| *Cladophialophora carrionii* | UP000094526 | 11,170 |
| *Dracunculus medinensis* | UP000274756 | 10,834 |
| *Enterococcus faecium* | UP000325664 | 2823 |
| *Fonsecaea pedrosoi* | UP000053029 | 12,509 |
| *Haemophilus influenzae* | UP000000579 | 1662 |
| *Helicobacter pylori* | UP000000429 | 1538 |
| *Klebsiella pneumoniae* | UP000007841 | 5727 |
| *Leishmania infantum* | UP000008153 | 7924 |
| *Madurella mycetomatis* | UP000078237 | 9561 |
| *Mycobacterium leprae* | UP000000806 | 1602 |
| *Mycobacterium tuberculosis* | UP000001584 | 3988 |
| *Mycobacterium ulcerans* | UP000020681 | 9033 |
| *Neisseria gonorrhoeae* | UP000000535 | 2106 |
| *Nocardia brasiliensis* | UP000006304 | 8372 |
| *Onchocerca volvulus* | UP000024404 | 12,047 |
| *Paracoccidioides lutzii* | UP000002059 | 8794 |
| *Plasmodium falciparum* | UP000001450 | 5187 |
| *Pseudomonas aeruginosa* | UP000002438 | 5556 |
| *Salmonella typhimurium* | UP000001014 | 4526 |
| *Schistosoma mansoni* | UP000008854 | 13,865 |
| *Shigella dysenteriae* | UP000002716 | 3893 |
| *Sporothrix schenckii* | UP000018087 | 8652 |
| *Staphylococcus aureus* | UP000008816 | 2888 |
| *Streptococcus pneumoniae* | UP000000586 | 2030 |
| *Strongyloides stercoralis* | UP000035681 | 12,613 |
| *Trichuris trichiura* | UP000030665 | 9564 |
| *Trypanosoma brucei* | UP000008524 | 8491 |
| *Trypanosoma cruzi* | UP000002296 | 19,036 |
| *Wuchereria bancrofti* | UP000270924 | 12,721 |

Copied from Varadi M, Velankar S. The impact of AlphaFold Protein Structure Database on the fields of life sciences. Proteomics 2023;23(17):2200128.

generative model of the protein backbones that might achieve great performance on unconditional and the topology-constrained design of the following [26]:

- Protein monomer
- Protein binder
- Symmetric oligomer
- Enzyme active site scaffolding
- Symmetric motif scaffolding
- For the therapeutic and the metal-binding protein design

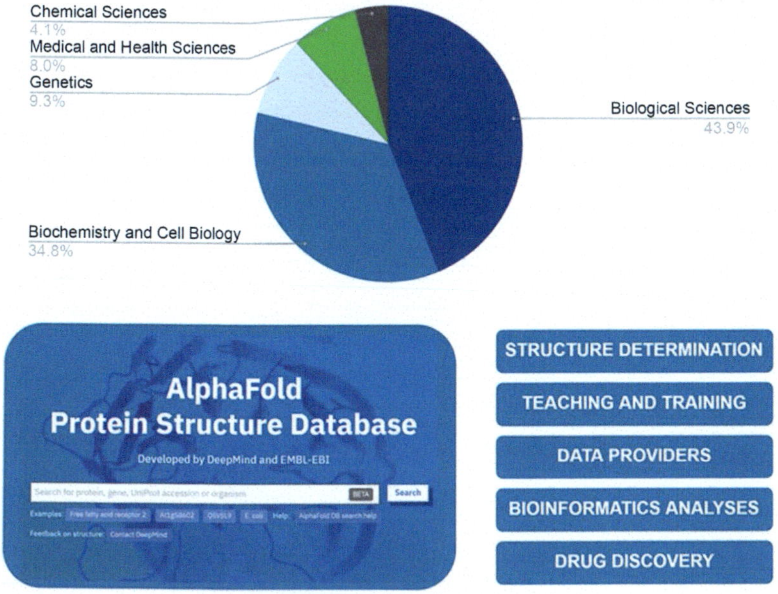


**Figure 11.4** Overview of the areas of impact and citation categories. The availability of high-accuracy protein structure models had significant impacts on several scientific fields, as reflected in the high number of citations since the publication of the AlphaFold database. The majority of research papers citing the database are from the broader field of biological sciences and biochemistry and cell biology. The citation statistics and research categories are from https://www.dimensions.ai/ of the primary AlphaFold database publication.
Reprinted with permission from [16].

Watson and colleagues have demonstrated both the power and generality of a method, RF diffusion (RFdiffusion), using experimental characterization of both structures and functions of a huge number of designed symmetric assemblies, the metal-binding proteins, and the protein binders [26]. Fig. 11.5 presents the designing of proteins using the method RFdiffusion [26]. This group has reasoned that the diffusion models [27,28] could be improved for designing proteins by using the combined advantage of understanding protein coming from AlphaFold2 (AF2) [1] and RF [3]. RF shows specific properties that would suit well for their use in denoising diffusion probabilistic models (DDPMs) used in the design of proteins. It is found that although promising in generating greatly diversified outputs, showing potency of iterative generation processes toward certain designing objectives via the provision of the conditioning information and the potency of modeling three-dimensional (3D) structures, DDPMs have so far shown limited amount of success in generating various sequences that would fold toward intended *in silico* structures [29,30]. Watson and colleagues argue that the lack of the required successes is due to the limited ability of denoising networks for generating realistic protein backbone structures and also that these have not been experimentally tested [26].

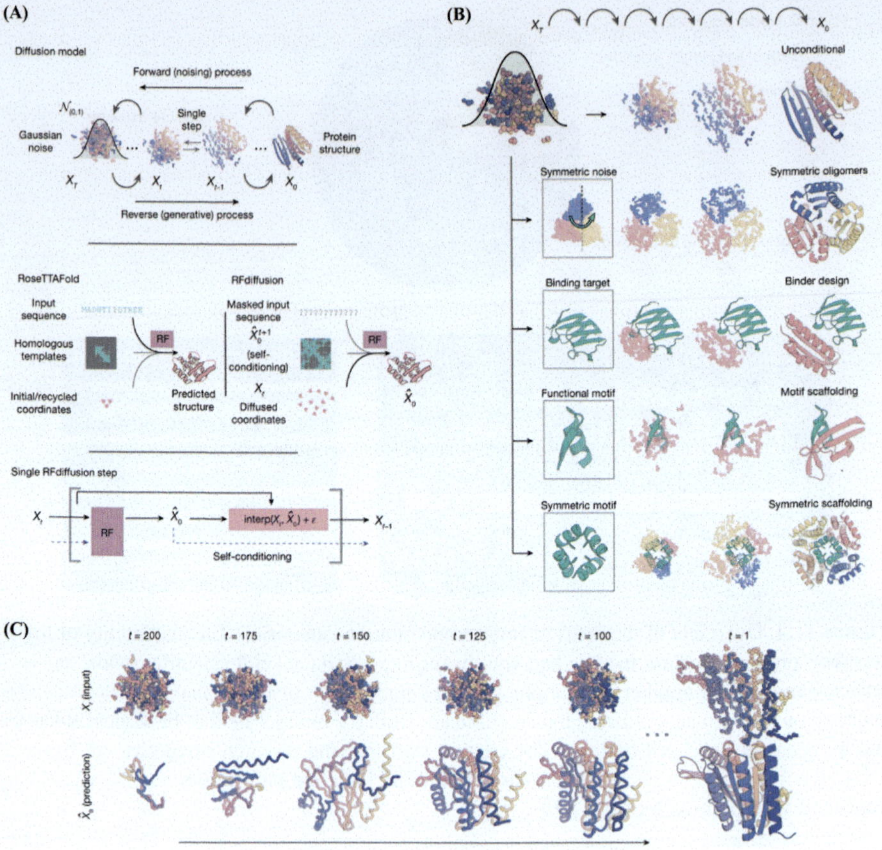


**Figure 11.5** (A) Diffusion model of proteins is trained for recovering the corrupted (noisy) protein structure and for generating new structures through reversing the corruption process via iterative denoising of the initially random noise XT into any realistic structure X0 (see top panel). The network of the RF structure prediction (middle panel, left side) is fine-tuned with the minimal architecture change into the RFdiffusion mode (see middle panel, right side); the network representing the denoising network of the DDPM is shown here too. Here in RF, the sequence is the primary input to the model. The model predicts here is the final 3D coordinates (in RFdiffusion). In the bottom panel, RFdiffusion is shown, here the model receives the previous prediction as a template input—"self-conditioning." At every trajectory timestep t (there are usually 200 steps), RFdiffusion takes from the previous step and Xt and then can predict an updated X0 structure. (B) RFdiffusion is generally applicable for the protein design. RFdiffusion generates protein structures either without further input (top row) or by conditioning on (top to bottom): symmetry specifications; binding targets; protein functional motifs or symmetric functional motifs. In each case, random noise, along with conditioning information, is input to RFdiffusion, which iteratively refines that noise until a final protein structure is designed. (C) Example of the unconditional design trajectory for a 300-residue chain that depicts the model's (Xt) input and correspondingly the prediction. *DDPM*, Denoising diffusion probabilistic model.; *RF*, RoseTTAFold.
Reprinted with permission from [26].

## 11.3 Artificial intelligence to detect language of the molecules of life

AI architectures and biophysics tools were applied together to address on uncovering a language spoken by the molecules of life [31]. Here it is shown that the movement or dynamics related to shape and size/structure of the biomolecules (e.g., proteins) can be mapped into an abstract language. AI algorithms and associated techniques may be used for generating biological languages out of the resulting abstract words.

Tsai and colleagues used an AI system to create an abstract language from the constant motion of biological molecules, such as the lysozyme molecule [31]. This language is found to describe the multiple shapes that a protein molecule may take and how and when it transitions from one shape to another. The central rationale here is that MD trajectories, discretized in space and time, may be mapped into a sequence of some sort of language characters. With the use of a character-level language model that may predict subsequent future characters given the characters so far in a sequence, this study presented a way to learn the evolution of the MD trajectory that was mapped into the characters. They used a stochastic model consisting of three sequential parts, schematized in Fig. 11.6. First, we see that it has an embedding layer mapping one-hot vectors to dense vectors, which is followed by a long short-term memory (LSTM) layer, which connects input states and hidden states at different time steps through a trainable recursive function, and finally a dense layer to transform the output of LSTM to the categorical probability vector.

Alongside AI tools [31], there are mathematical tools emerging that are capable of reading the molecular languages such as allostery and multivalent activation [32]. Lauzon and Vallée-Bélisle could design, model, and test a DNA-based switch being activated with the use of both of these mechanisms. They have shown that the dynamic range, affinity, and half-life of activation of the molecular switch can be programed and controlled. Here, appropriate mathematical equations were derived to match with the programs and determine whether they altogether may describe various features and functions of their nanomachine. Although not yet done, this study may attract computational chemists to create appropriate AI algorithms to easily read and manipulate its functions, as similar things are found evolving [33].

## 11.4 Artificial intelligence predictions of the sites of drug targets in protein structures

Besides the advancement in the predictions of protein structures using AlphaFold and RF, we see now that the implications of AI in addressing mutations [34] and aiding in drug discovery are monumental [14]. Drug discovery science benefits clearly from the availability of data on protein structural predictions [35]. A recent review has summarized the AI applications in predicting the mutational profiles of most of the cancers that we deal with nowadays, such as lung, breast, brain, etc., pertaining to the histology and radiology imaging [34]. The status of gene including mutations thereof

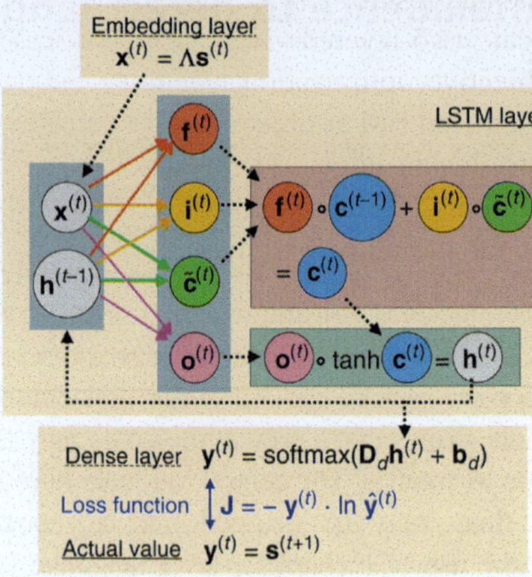


**Figure 11.6** The schematic plot of the simple character-level language model used in this work. The model consists of three main parts: the embedding layer, the LSTM layer, and a dense output layer. The embedding layer is a linear layer that multiplies the one-hot input s(t) by a matrix and produces an embedding vector x(t). The x(t) is then used as the input of LSTM network, in which the forget gate f(t), the input gate i(t), the output gate o(t), and the candidate value are all controlled by (x(t), h(t−1)). The forget gate and input gate are then used to produce the update equation of cell state c(t). The output gate decides how much information propagates to the next timestep. The output layer predicts the probabilities by parametrizing the transformation from h(t) to with learned weights Dd and learned biases bd. Finally, we can compute the cross entropy between the predicted probability distribution and the true probability distribution y(t) = s(t+1). *LSTM*, Long short-term memory.
Reprinted with permission from [64].

has been evaluated here using AI tools based on multimodal data, thus helping to deal with tumors that are malignant leading to insights into various clinical biomarkers. AI algorithms (specifically applying DL models) are found capable of predicting large number (in hundreds) of genes integrating morphology and spatial transcriptome [36]. Shao and colleagues have created a flowchart on the multimodal integration (MMI) process to predict the status of gene mutations on AI technology platforms involves the following four major steps (see Fig. 11.7) [34]:

1. Multimode curation of data
2. Extraction of features and selection
3. Building the models and validation
4. Prediction of genotypes and in-depth exploration output

The AI-driven data on structures serve in pinpointing target site(s) for performing virtual screening against. As an example, Tian and colleagues recently retrieved the models from PDB and the AlphaFold database and could identify potential pockets for ligand-binding and then performed docking of artemisinin, which is a natural phytochemical, active against key targets implicated in ulcerative colitis (UC) [37].

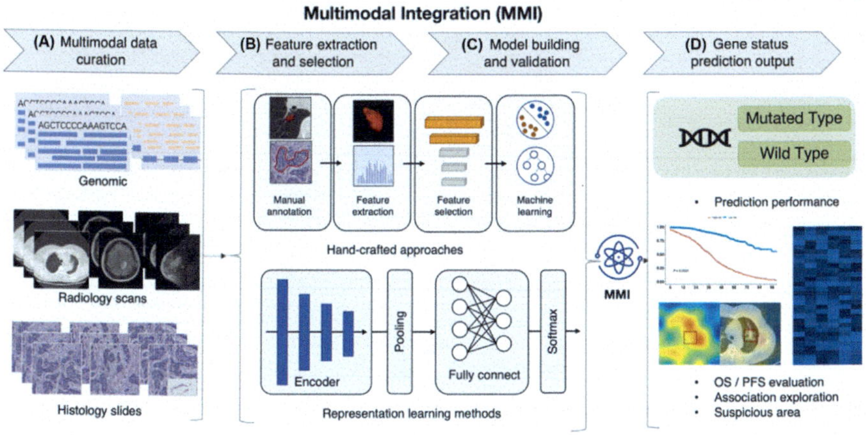


**Figure 11.7** General workflow of multimodal integration (MMI) for predicting gene states. (A) The first step is inputting multimodal data including genomics, radiology, and pathology. (B) Feature extraction and (C) model construction mainly use AI methods such as hand-crafted approaches and deep learning. (D) Finally, the MMI systems output the prediction of gene status and further performed the prognostic evaluation and correlation exploration. Reprinted with permission from [34].

Artemisinin is a drug for treating malaria from *Plasmodium falciparum*. Tian and colleagues used CHEMBEL, TCMSP, and HERB databases and obtained 8, 15, and 409 artemisinin targets, respectively. Artemisinin is predicted here to participate in UC treatment through 50 targets (see Fig. 11.8A). Artemisinin's biological mechanism and the pathway of the UC treatment are predicted in Fig. 11.8B and Fig. 11.8C, respectively. Artemisinin's therapeutic pathway in the UC treatment is presented in Fig. 11.8D, while Fig. 11.8E summarizes the number of screened therapeutic targets.

In another study, Kobakhidze and colleagues used AlphaFold database–based models or predictions that were directly generated using Google Colab for investigating if AAA+ ATPase p97 may be a potential target both in tuberculosis and parasitology [38]. Here, protist p97 homologs have been found essential for the growth of parasites and their multistage viability with the use of genome-wide screening and analysis of mutation. The mycobacterial p97 has been found as a potential drug target against associated pathogens. A strategy to inhibit this pathogenic p97 may lead to killing pathogen and potentially avoiding interfering with the human p97. In another recent study, Bothe and colleagues described a biolayer interferometry-based fragment screen that targets p97's N-domain and found a SHP-motif binding site, which can be targeted with small molecules [39]. Fig. 11.9 plots the first two principal components, together describing 47.6% variance in BiSS library. Eight of 10 fragments and 5 of 6 compounds will be found. TROLL2 and its analog TROLL7 and ID2 are located in chemical space. The principal component analysis (PCA) analysis, which relies on

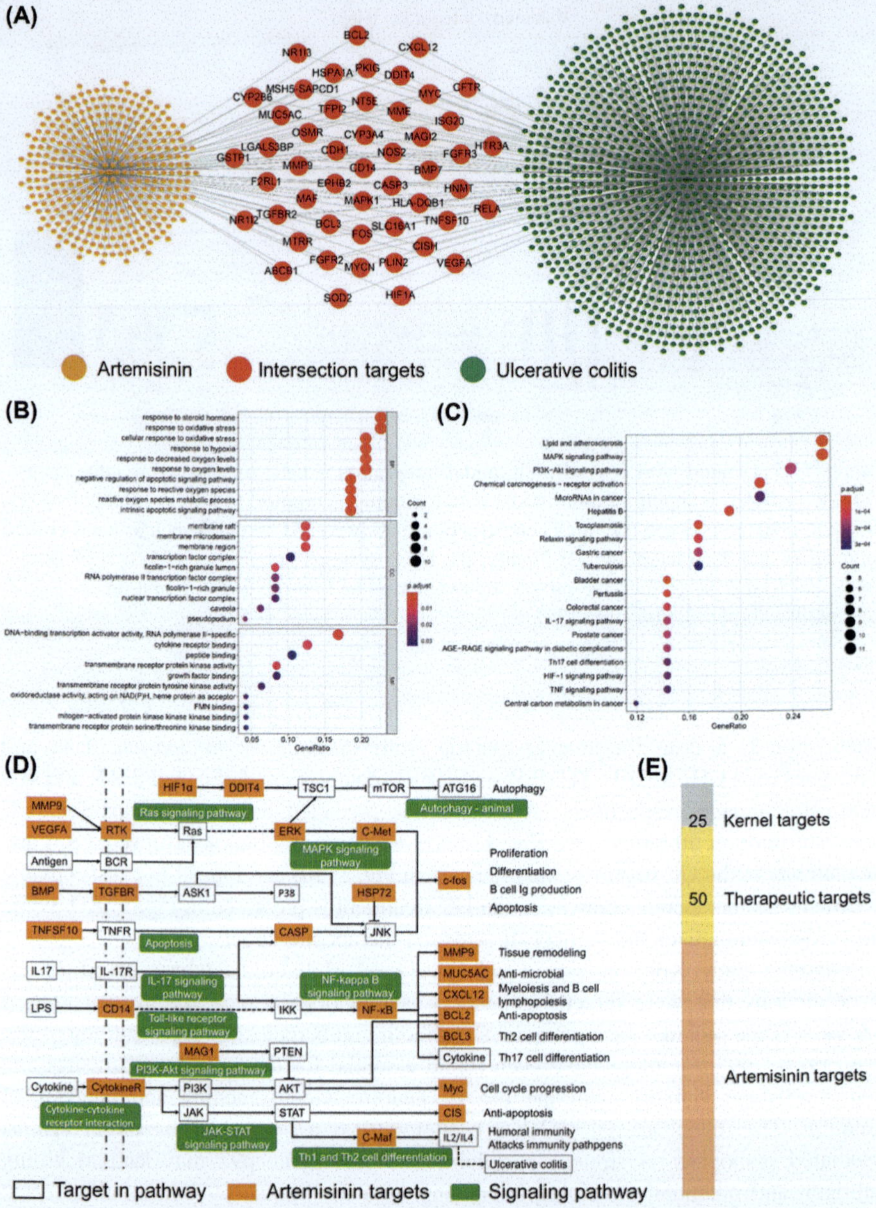


**Figure 11.8** Potential biological mechanism of artemisinin in the treatment of ulcerative colitis. (A) Artemisinin-UC network. (B and C) The potential biological mechanism and pathway of artemisinin in the treatment of UC. (D) The therapeutic pathway of artemisinin in the treatment of UC. (E) The screened number of therapeutic targets.
Reprinted with permission from [37].

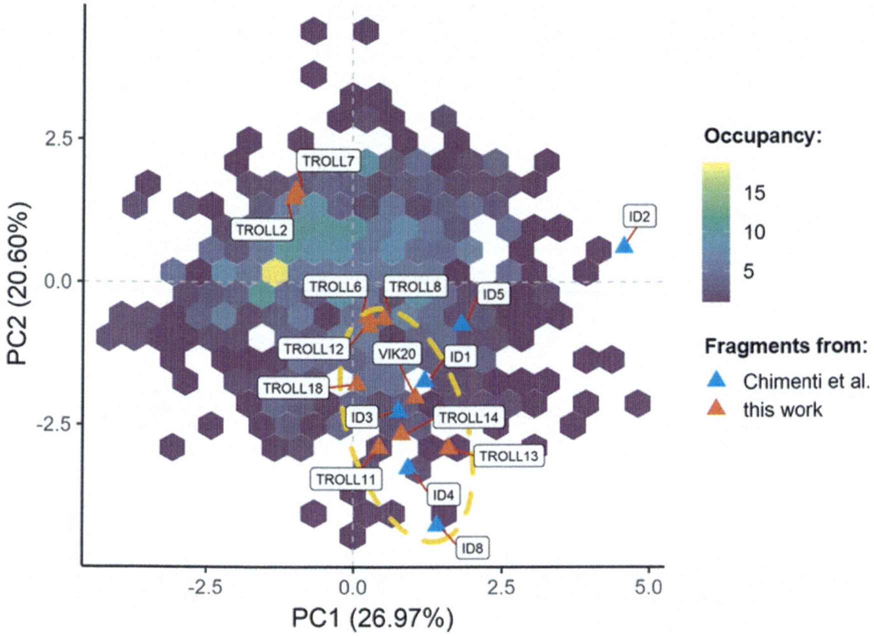


**Figure 11.9** PCA analysis of the fragment library employed in this study. The locations of the fragments identified in this screen (red triangles) and the fragments reported by Chimenti et al. [40] (blue triangles) are highlighted. The hexagons (colored purple to yellow) indicate how many compounds were available in the library for a particular region of the chemical space. The dashed orange ellipse highlights the region where most of the fragments of both screens are located, indicating that these fragments share similar physicochemical parameters. *PCA*, Principal component analysis.
Reprinted with permission from [39].

algorithms involving the transformation of coordinates and popularly used in AI including ML, indicates for additional enrichment options for additional enhancements of screens against p97-N.

## 11.5 Artificial intelligence predictions of drug molecules to target mutated sites in protein structures

AI methods are now popular in pharma industries for tackling with various needs that range from drug discovery to even product management [41]. AI method domains and their subfields that may be implemented for drug discovery and development in various fields including those concerning targeting proteins have been summarized in Fig. 11.10 [41].

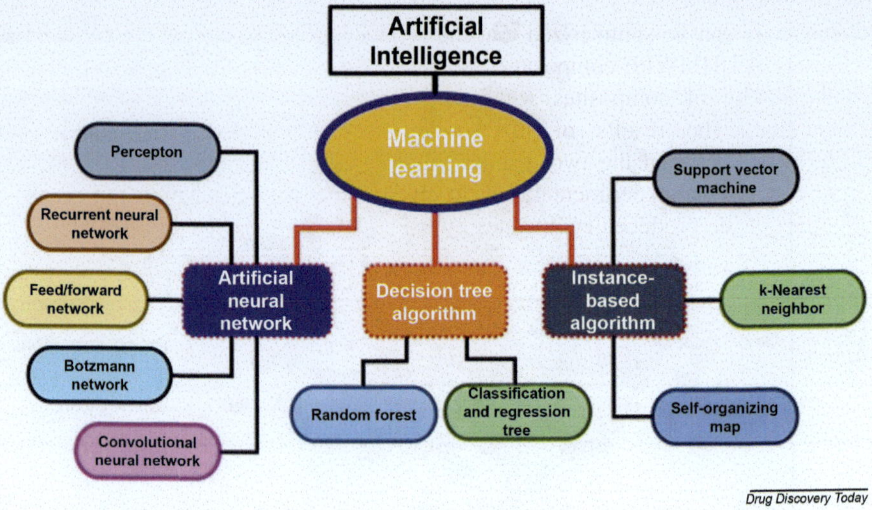


**Figure 11.10** Method domains of artificial intelligence (AI). This figure shows different AI method domains along with their subfields that can be implemented in different fields drug discovery and development.
Reprinted with permission from [41].

Industries and specific pharmaceutical companies who use AI in drug discovery are shortlisted, including providing with areas of ongoing excellences, in Fig. 11.11 [41]. In the study by Paul and colleagues, there are a huge amount of literature and references found on applications of AI in drug discovery, especially in designing drugs, understanding target binding regions in proteins and other biomolecules, drug efficacy, drugs' clinical trials, used AI tools, etc. Existing challenges (with multibillion dollar revenue potential) considering AI in this kind of research and the ways to overcome them are also explained in this review.

Application of AI methods in specific disease like cancer, concerning finding the drug targets in mostly protein structures and discovering agents to be used as drugs, is becoming very popular nowadays [42]. The historical milestones of network-based and ML-based biology analysis spanning almost last two decades have been presented chronologically in Fig. 11.12 [42]. In Fig. 11.12, abbreviations are as follows: weighted gene coexpression network analysis (WGCNA), pocket druggability (PockDrug), alternating decision tree (ADTree), graph auto-encoder (GAE) [43,44], graph convolution network (GCN) [45], convolutional neural networks (CNN) [45], and graph neural networks (GNN) [46].

The fast and wide development of cancer-associated multiomics techniques and methods [47] has appeared as an important factor for AI biological analysis for exploring novel anticancer targets in proteins [48,49]. Fig. 11.13 provides a classification of these technologies into five specific aspects, as follows [42]:

- Epigenetics
- Genomics

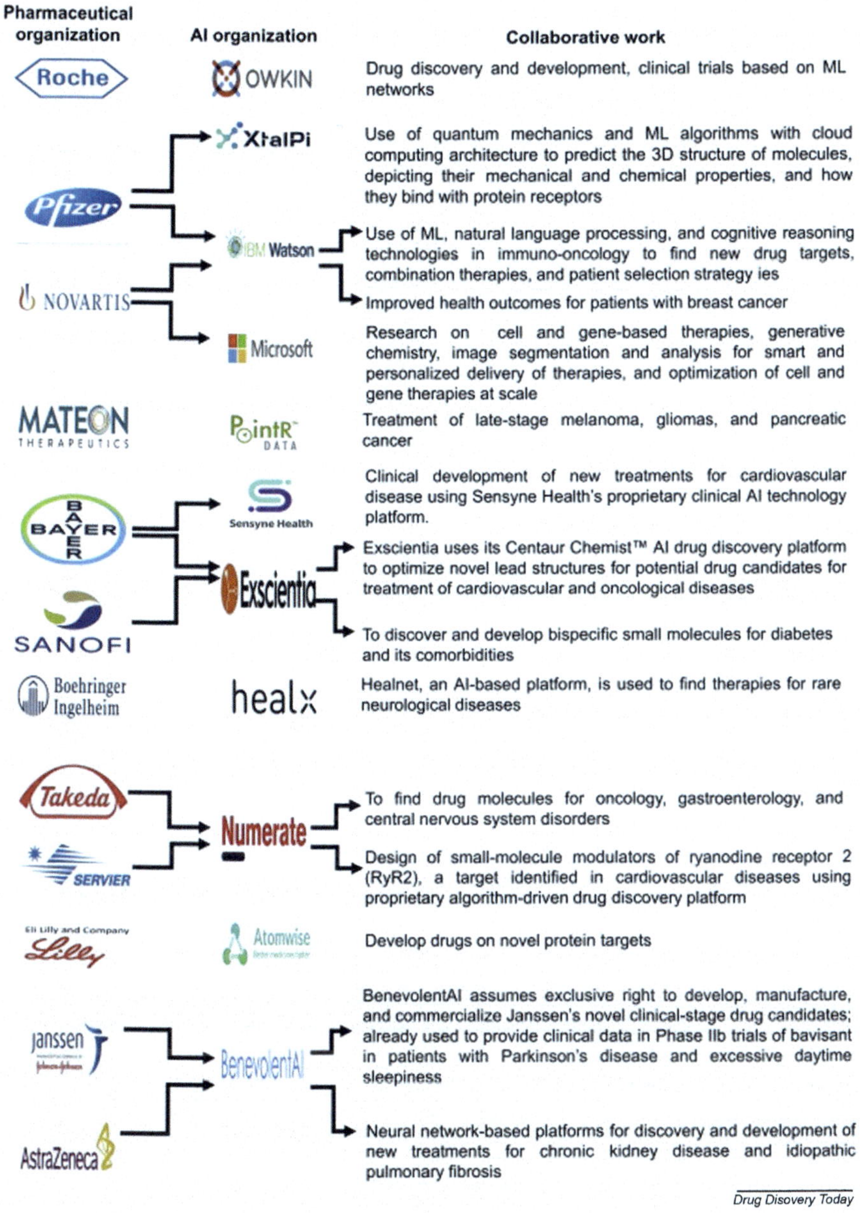


**Figure 11.11** Leading pharmaceutical companies and their association with artificial intelligence (AI) organizations that are working in fields including oncology, cardiovascular diseases, and central nervous system disorders.
Reprinted with permission from [41].

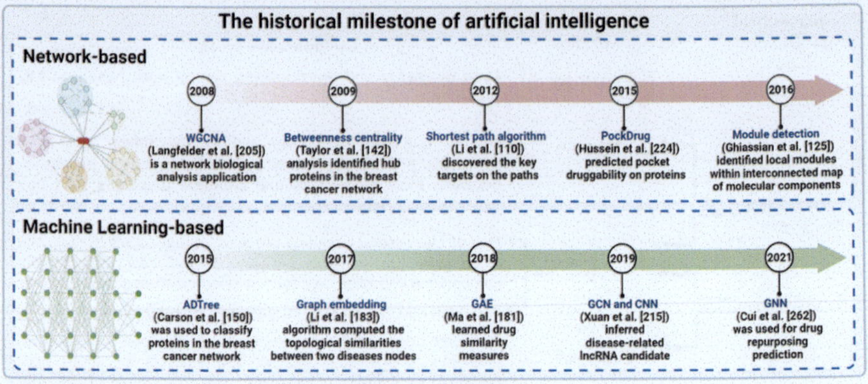


**Figure 11.12** The historical milestones of network-based and ML-based biology analysis. (Created with BioRender.com). *ML*, Machine learning.
(the numbered references quoted inside figure will be found in this article of You and colleagues, to save space we avoid to list them here).
Reprinted with permission from [42].

- Proteomics
- Metabolomics
- Multiomics integration analysis

Furthermore, in Table 11.1, we shall find a list of the related major diseases, drug targets, genomics, and network databases that are commonly used in multiomics integration analysis for all these mentioned aspects (Table 11.2).

## 11.6 Artificial intelligence enhanced engineering of proteins

Protein engineers have been seriously looking into the possibility of applying AI, specifically ML tools and help of reservoirs of huge data, and the AF2 predictions of structures to pursue better and sophisticated de novo design of proteins [64]. AI-based algorithms may be applied to guiding the protein designs exhibiting various symmetries, from very simple spherical forms to utterly complex icosahedral-type designs (Credited to Generate Biomedicines), see Fig. 11.14 [64]. ML and other AI-based computing tools have already been found to show their prowess at predicting most of the real-world protein structures. DeepMind's AlphaFold 2 algorithms can predict protein structure confidently from the basis of an amino acid sequence, whose successes reached already at multimillion levels, explained earlier in this chapter.

DL algorithms, such as AF2 and RF, have been found to predict a protein's 3D shape from its linear sequence [65]. This is a huge boost in computational biology research showing potential to align alongside real systems, where not only proteins' primary structure but also all sorts of secondary and tertiary structures exist and

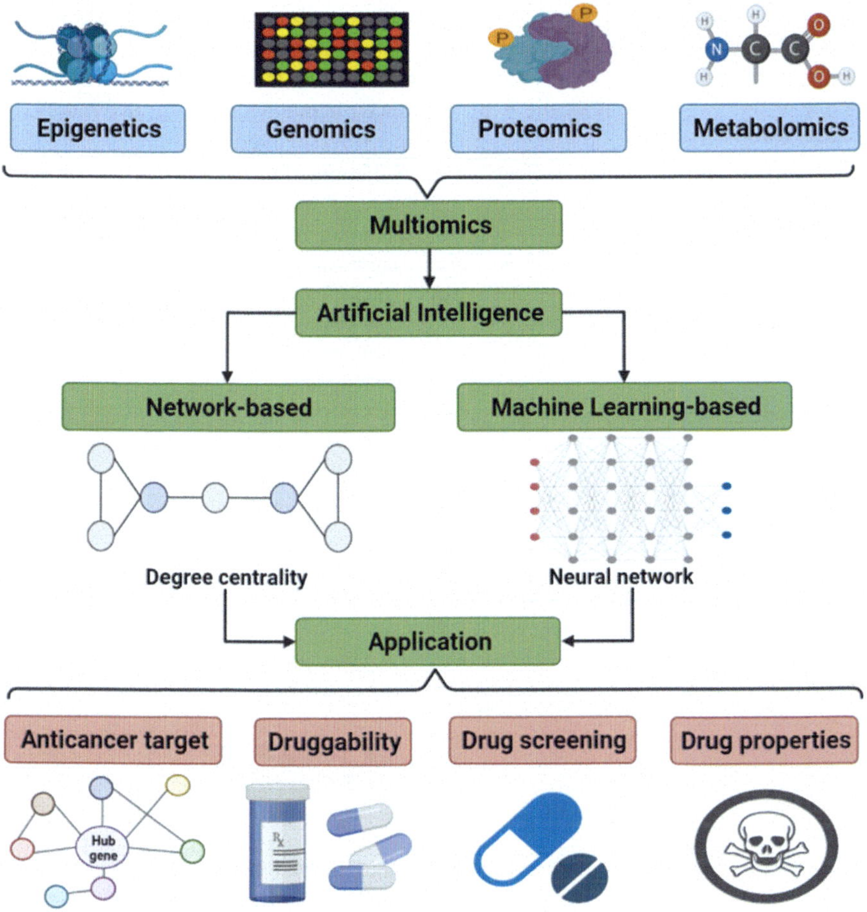


**Figure 11.13** Artificial intelligence (AI) to integrate multiomics data (e.g., epigenetics, genomics, proteomics, and metabolomics) for cancer therapeutic targets identification. (Created with BioRender.com).
Reprinted with permission from [42].

function. Developments in versatile computational methods and algorithms have led to this kind of 3D protein structure predictions that have reached almost the accuracy of experimentally determined model. We can now predict the structure of even a larger than protein structure, for example, Fig. 11.15 presents the model of a nuclear pore complex, which was built using AF2 and structural data (Credited to: Agnieszka Obarska-Kosinska) [64]. Akdel and colleagues have claimed to couple wild-type protein structures generated by DL with other mutation-analysis algorithms for achieving more-accurate predictions [66,67]. This advancement has developed our potential to deal with mutations and diseases involving protein structure alteration

**Table 11.2** Artificial intelligence predictions draw information from repositories related to various human diseases, drug targets, genomics, biological networks, etc. [42].

| Name of the database | Link of the web | Description | References |
|---|---|---|---|
| ***Diseases*** | | | |
| Online Mendelian Inheritance in Man (OMIM) | Omim.org | Authoritative, comprehensive, and timely knowledgebase description for genes of humans and related genetic disorders | Hamosh et al. [50] |
| Pathologisch Anatomisch Landelijk Geautomatiseerd Archief (PALGA) | Palga.nl | Histopathology and cytopathology databases were stored | Casparie [51] |
| ***Targets of the drugs*** | | | |
| DrugBank | Drugbank.ca | It's a web-enabled drug database, which contains molecular information related to drugs, their associated mechanisms, their potential interactions, and targets | Wishart [52] |
| Therapeutic Targets Database (TTD) | db.idrblab.net/ttd/ | This database providing information on known and explored therapeutic nucleic acid and protein targets, the disease to target, etc. | Wang [53] |
| PubChem | pubchem.ncbi.nlm.nih.gov | It's a repository containing chemical structures, and their test results in biological assays. | Wang [54] |
| ChEMBL | ebi.ac.uk/chembldb | A database containing the binding, functional, and ADMET information for drug-like bioactive compounds | Gaulton [55] |
| ***Biology network*** | | | |
| Search Tool for the Retrieval of Interacting Genes/Proteins (STRING) | string-db.org/ | It's a database containing the known and the predicted protein interactions | Edgar et al. [56] |
| Gene Ontology (GO) | geneontology.org/ | | |

(*Continued*)

**Table 11.2** (Continued)

| **Name of the database** | **Link of the web** | **Description** | **References** |
|---|---|---|---|
| | | It contains information on genes' functions | McLendon [57] |
| Kyoto Encyclopedia of Genes and Genomes (KEGG) | genome.jp/kegg/ | It's a database collection that deals with the genomes, the biological pathways, all known diseases, chemicals, and drugs substances | Barretina [58] |
| ***Genomic data*** | | | |
| Gene Expression Omnibus (GEO) | ncbi.nlm.nih.gov/geo/ | A functional genomics data repository for public use purposes. Here the array- and sequence-based data are deposited. | Consortium [59] |
| The Cancer Genome Atlas (TCGA) | cancer.gov/about-nci/organization/ccg/research/structural-genomics/tcga | It hosts clinical data of human cancers, genomic mutations, miRNA expression, mRNA expression, methylation, etc. | Forbes [60] |
| Cancer Cell Line Encyclopedia (CCLE) | sites.broadinstitute.org/ccle | A compilation of gene expression, number of chromosomal copy, and massively parallel sequencing data from 947 human cancer cell lines | Szklarczyk [61] |
| ENCyclopedia Of DNA Elements (ENCODE) | encodeproject.org/ | Systematically mapped regions of the transcription, the transcription factor association, the chromatin structure, and the histone modification are provided | Consortium [62] |
| Catalogue Of Somatic Mutations In Cancer (COSMIC) | sanger.ac.uk/cosmic | It is a curator of comprehensive information related to somatic mutations in human cancer | Kanehisa, Goto [63] |

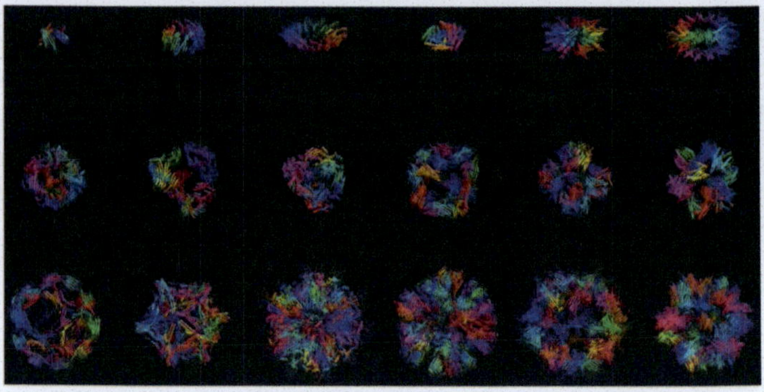

**Figure 11.14** Artificial intelligence (AI)-based algorithms to guide protein designs that exhibit various symmetries, from very simple spherical forms to utterly complex icosahedral type designs (Credited to Generate Biomedicines).
Reprinted with permission from [64].

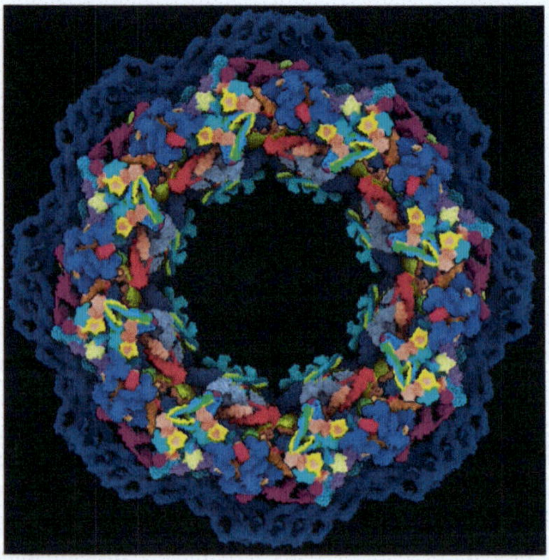

**Figure 11.15** A human nuclear pore complex model, built using AlphaFold2 and structural data (Credited to: Agnieszka Obarska-Kosinska).
Reprinted with permission from [64].

and associated diseases. Even misplacement of single or multiple amino acids in mutations in protein structure may lead to multitude of consequences that can now be addressed using AI [65].

The use of AI techniques in understanding diseases is happening. AI has been found to address aggregation of proteins associated with neurodegenerative disorders [68].

AI algorithms have helped us identify cancer target protein sites and aided in drug discovery [42]. AI models have been found to read proteins' insight helping us fight COVID-19 (https://blogs.nvidia.com/blog/ai-reads-proteins-covid/) (accessed on April 30, 2024). There could be many such examples identified.

Predicting possible future successes in the application of AI in protein structure, possible protein engineering, and even addressing mutations, start-ups have already started getting huge investments and funding promises. A few of them are as follows [64]:

- Profluent secured $9 million in seed funding for supporting the ML application to engineer novel functional proteins. This is just the latest in a steady flurry of investment in this space.
- Generate Biomedicines signed a deal with Amgen of a $50 million for drug development that could generate $1.9 billion.
- Arzeda managed to raise $33 million in Series B funding for supporting its promising protein design program.
- Cradle, which exited stealth recently, got a $5.5 million seed investment.
- Monod Bio secured $25 million in seed funding.

Due to the possibility of getting successes fast, the future investments in AI-based research in both understanding diseases and finding agents to find cures are expected to only grow exponentially.

## 11.7 Concluding remarks

The understanding of protein structures using experimental techniques such as X-ray crystallography, NMR, cryogenic EM, and others has little less than a century-long history. Computer modeling of biomolecular structures has almost half a century history since its inception around the 1970s. The AI-based prediction of biomolecules' (especially proteins') structures is quite a new area but has emerged with a huge potential. In this chapter, I have pinpointed all the progress in the latest AI predictions of protein structures that have happened due to breakthrough developments in both algorithms involving enhanced computational capacity, modeling, and coordinated efforts among experimental scientists to put forward all the experimental data associated with their understanding of protein structures and functions in public domains. AI may also find its rigorous applicability in protein engineering to regulate especially in mutated conditions, which might help understand the origin(s) of diseases and aid in designing agents as drugs. The application of AI in protein science and engineering is just enjoying its beginning. The future is expected to flourish fast over the coming decades.

## Acknowledgment

To the best of the Editors' knowledge and authors' claims, no generative AI tools were used for substantive writing of chapters. Any AI-assisted language editing, if applied, was limited to grammar or style suggestions and did not alter the scientific content.

## References


[1] Jumper J, Evans R, Pritzel A, Green T, Figurnov M, Ronneberger O, et al. Highly accurate protein structure prediction with AlphaFold. Nature 2021;596(7873):583–9.
[2] Callaway E. The entire protein universe': AI predicts shape of nearly every known protein. Nature 2022;608(7921):15–6.
[3] Baek M, DiMaio F, Anishchenko I, Dauparas J, Ovchinnikov S, Lee GR, et al. Accurate prediction of protein structures and interactions using a three-track neural network. Science 2021;373(6557):871–6.
[4] Adleman LM. Molecular computation of solutions to combinatorial problems. Science 1994;266(5187):1021–4.
[5] Sugita M. Functional analysis of chemical systems in vivo using a logical circuit equivalent. Journal of Theoretical Biology 1961;1(4):415.
[6] Van Noorden R. Computer modellers secure chemistry Nobels. Nature; 2013.
[7] Levitt M, Warshel A. Computer simulation of protein folding. Nature 1975;253(5494):694–8.
[8] Warshel A, Karplus M. Calculation of ground and excited state potential surfaces of conjugated molecules. I. Formulation and parametrization. Journal of the American Chemical Society 1972;94(16):5612–25.
[9] Warshel A, Levitt M. Theoretical studies of enzymic reactions: dielectric, electrostatic and steric stabilization of the carbonium ion in the reaction of lysozyme. Journal of Molecular Biology 1976;103(2):227–49.
[10] Ng W. Brief history of computational chemistry: three distinct eras and the relative importance of theoretical insights and computing power in advancing the field. PeerJ Preprints; 2017.
[11] Burley SK, Berman HM, Kleywegt GJ, Markley JL, Nakamura H, Velankar S. Protein Data Bank (PDB): the single global macromolecular structure archive. Protein Crystallography: Methods and Protocols 2017:627–41.
[12] Berman HM, Kleywegt GJ, Nakamura H, Markley JL. The Protein Data Bank at 40: reflecting on the past to prepare for the future. Structure 2012;20(3):391–6.
[13] Lattman EE. Protein structure prediction: a special issue. Proteins 1995;23:295–460.
[14] Mullard A. What does AlphaFold mean for drug discovery? Nature Reviews Drug Discovery 2021;20(725-727):2021. https://doi.org/10.1038/d41573-021-00161-0.
[15] Callaway E. It will change everything': DeepMind's AI makes gigantic leap in solving protein structures. Nature 2020;588(7837):203–5.
[16] Varadi M, Velankar S. The impact of AlphaFold Protein Structure Database on the fields of life sciences. Proteomics 2023;23(17):2200128.
[17] Ferruz N, Höcker B. Controllable protein design with language models. Nature Machine Intelligence 2022;4(6):521–32.
[18] Hadfield TE, Deane CM. AI in 3D compound design. Current Opinion in Structural Biology 2022;73:102326.
[19] Mallik BB, Stanislaw J, Alawathurage TM, Khmelinskaia A. De novo design of polyhedral protein assemblies: before and after the AI revolution. Chembiochem 2023;24(15). e202300117.
[20] Callaway E. AI tools are designing entirely new proteins that could transform medicine. Nature 2023;619(7969):236–8.
[21] Dauparas J, Anishchenko I, Bennett N, Bai H, Ragotte RJ, Milles LF, et al. Robust deep learning–based protein sequence design using ProteinMPNN. Science 2022;378(6615):49–56.
[22] Ferruz N, Schmidt S, Höcker B. ProtGPT2 is a deep unsupervised language model for protein design. Nature Communications 2022;13(1):4348.

[23] Anishchenko I, Pellock SJ, Chidyausiku TM, Ramelot TA, Ovchinnikov S, Hao J, et al. De novo protein design by deep network hallucination. Nature 2021;600(7889):547–52.
[24] Singer JM, Novotney S, Strickland D, Haddox HK, Leiby N, Rocklin GJ, et al. Large-scale design and refinement of stable proteins using sequence-only models. PLoS ONE 2022;17(3). e0265020.
[25] Wicky BIM, Milles LF, Courbet A, Ragotte RJ, Dauparas J, Kinfu E, et al. Hallucinating symmetric protein assemblies. Science 2022;378(6615):56–61.
[26] Watson JL, Juergens D, Bennett NR, Trippe BL, Yim J, Eisenach HE, et al. De novo design of protein structure and function with RFdiffusion. Nature 2023;620(7976):1089–100.
[27] Ramesh A, et al. Zero-shot text-to-image generation (PMLR Meila M, Zhang T, editors. Proc. 38th International Conference on Machine Learning, 139. 2021.
[28] Saharia C, et al. Photorealistic text-to-image diffusion models with deep language understanding. In: Advances in Koyejo S, et al., editors. Neural information processing systems, Curran Associates; 2022. 35, p. 36479–36494.
[29] Trippe BL, et al. Diffusion probabilistic modeling of protein backbones in 3D for the motif-scaffolding problem. In: The Eleventh International Conference on Learning Representations; 2023.
[30] Wu KE, et al. Protein structure generation via folding diffusion. Preprint at https://doi.org/10.48550/arXiv.2209.15611; 2022.
[31] Tsai ST, Kuo EJ, Tiwary P. Learning molecular dynamics with simple language model built upon long short-term memory neural network. Nature Communications 2020;11(1):5115.
[32] Lauzon D, Vallée-Bélisle A. Programing chemical communication: allostery vs multivalent mechanism. Journal of the American Chemical Society 2023;145(34):18846–54.
[33] Talbot H, Halvorsen K, Chandrasekaran AR. Encoding, decoding, and rendering information in DNA nanoswitch libraries. ACS Synthetic Biology 2022;12(4):978–83.
[34] Shao J, Ma J, Zhang Q, Li W, Wang C. Predicting gene mutation status via artificial intelligence technologies based on multimodal integration (MMI) to advance precision oncology. Seminars in cancer biology 91. Academic Press; 2023. p. 1–15.
[35] Xue HT, Stanley-Baker M, Kong AWK, Li HL, Goh WWB. Data considerations for predictive modeling applied to the discovery of bioactive natural products. Drug Discovery Today 2022;27(8):2235–43.
[36] Qu H, Zhou M, Yan Z, Wang H, Rustgi VK, Zhang S, et al. Genetic mutation and biological pathway prediction based on whole slide images in breast carcinoma using deep learning. NPJ Precision Oncology 2021;5(1):87.
[37] Tian R, Li Y, Wang X, Li J, Li Y, Bei S, et al. A pharmacoinformatics analysis of artemisinin targets and de novo design of hits for treating ulcerative colitis. Frontiers in Pharmacology 2022;13:843043.
[38] Kobakhidze G, Sethi A, Valimehr S, Ralph SA, Rouiller I. The AAA+ ATPase p97 as a novel parasite and tuberculosis drug target. Trends in Parasitology 2022;38(7):572–90.
[39] Bothe S, Hänzelmann P, Böhler S, et al. Fragment screening using biolayer interferometry reveals ligands targeting the SHP-motif binding site of the AAA+ ATPase p97. Communications Chemistry 2022;5(169). https://doi.org/10.1038/s42004-022-00782-5.
[40] Chimenti MS, Bulfer SL, Neitz RJ, Renslo AR, Jacobson MP, James TL, et al. A fragment-based ligand screen against part of a large protein machine: the ND1 domains of the AAA+ ATPase p97/VCP. Journal of Biomolecular Screening 2015;20(6):788–800.
[41] Paul D, Sanap G, Shenoy S, Kalyane D, Kalia K, Tekade RK. Artificial intelligence in drug discovery and development. Drug Discovery Today 2021;26(1):80.

[42] You Y, Lai X, Pan Y, Zheng H, Vera J, Liu S, et al. Artificial intelligence in cancer target identification and drug discovery. Signal Transduction and Targeted Therapy 2022;7(1):156.
[43] Guo L, Lei X, Chen M, Pan Y. MSResG: using GAE and residual GCN to predict drug–drug interactions based on multi-source drug features. Interdisciplinary Sciences: Computational Life Sciences 2023:1–18.
[44] Singh M, Singh R, Ross A. A comprehensive overview of biometric fusion. Information Fusion 2019;52:187–205.
[45] Wang S, Sun S, Li Z, Zhang R, Xu J. Accurate de novo prediction of protein contact map by ultra-deep learning model. PLoS Computational Biology 2017;13(1). e1005324.
[46] Cusick ME, Yu H, Smolyar A, Venkatesan K, Carvunis AR, Simonis N, et al. Addendum: Literature-curated protein interaction datasets. Nature Methods 2009;6(12):934–5.
[47] Johnson CH, Ivanisevic J, Siuzdak G. Metabolomics: beyond biomarkers and towards mechanisms. Nature Reviews Molecular Cell Biology 2016;17(7):451–9.
[48] Vinayagam A, Gibson TE, Lee HJ, Yilmazel B, Roesel C, Hu Y, et al. Controllability analysis of the directed human protein interaction network identifies disease genes and drug targets. Proceedings of the National Academy of Sciences 2016;113(18):4976–81.
[49] Yang K, Xia B, Wang W, Cheng J, Yin M, Xie H, et al. A comprehensive analysis of metabolomics and transcriptomics in cervical cancer. Scientific Reports 2017;7(1):43353.
[50] Hamosh A, Scott AF, Amberger JS, Bocchini CA, McKusick VA. Online Mendelian Inheritance in Man (OMIM), a knowledgebase of human genes and genetic disorders. Nucleic Acids Research 2005;33:D514–7.
[51] Casparie M, et al. Pathology databanking and biobanking in the Netherlands, a central role for PALGA, the nationwide histopathology and cytopathology data network and archive. Cellular oncology: the official journal of the International Society for Cellular Oncology 2007;29:19–24.
[52] Wishart DS, et al. DrugBank 5.0: a major update to the DrugBank database for 2018. Nucleic Acids Research 2017;46:D1074–82.
[53] Wang Y, et al. Therapeutic target database 2020: enriched resource for facilitating research and early development of targeted therapeutics. Nucleic Acids Research 2019;48:D1031–41.
[54] Wang Y, et al. PubChem: a public information system for analyzing bioactivities of small molecules. Nucleic Acids Research 2009;37:W623–33.
[55] Gaulton A, et al. ChEMBL: a large-scale bioactivity database for drug discovery. Nucleic Acids Research 2011;40:D1100–7.
[56] Edgar R, Domrachev M, Lash AE. Gene Expression Omnibus: NCBI gene expression and hybridization array data repository. Nucleic Acids Research 2002;30:207–10.
[57] McLendon R, et al. Comprehensive genomic characterization defines human glioblastoma genes and core pathways. Nature 2008;455:1061–8.
[58] Barretina J, et al. The Cancer Cell Line Encyclopedia enables predictive modelling of anticancer drug sensitivity. Nature 2012;483:603–7.
[59] Consortium EP. An integrated encyclopedia of DNA elements in the human genome. Nature 2012;489:57–74.
[60] Forbes SA, et al. COSMIC: mining complete cancer genomes in the catalogue of somatic mutations in cancer. Nucleic Acids Research 2010;39:D945–50.
[61] Szklarczyk D, et al. The STRING database in 2021: customizable protein–protein networks, and functional characterization of user-uploaded gene/measurement sets. Nucleic Acids Research 2020;49:D605–12.
[62] Consortium GO. The Gene Ontology (GO) database and informatics resource. Nucleic Acids Research 2004;32:D258–61.

[63] Kanehisa M, Goto S. KEGG: kyoto encyclopedia of genes and genomes. Nucleic Acids Research 2000;28(1):27–30.
[64] Eisenstein M. AI-enhanced protein design makes proteins that have never existed. Nature Biotechnology 2023;41:303–5. https://doi.org/10.1038/s41587-023-01705-y.
[65] Eisenstein M. Artificial intelligence powers protein-folding predictions. Nature 2021;599(7886):706–8.
[66] Akdel M, et al. Preprint at bioRxiv 2021. https://doi.org/10.1101/2021.09.26.461876.
[67] Akdel M, Pires DE, Pardo EP, Jänes J, Zalevsky AO, Mészáros B, et al. A structural biology community assessment of AlphaFold2 applications. Nature Structural & Molecular Biology 2022;29(11):1056–67.
[68] Outeiro TF, Vieira TCRG. AI and protein structure and function in neurological disease: relevance to disease management. Nature Reviews Neurology 2023;19:453–4. https://doi.org/10.1038/s41582-023-00840-z.

# Artificial intelligence-assisted biomaterials for hard tissue implants

12

*Shubhabrata Datta, and M. Kamaraj*
Centre for Composite and Advanced Materials, Department of Mechanical Engineering, Faculty of Engineering and Technology, SRM Institute of Science and Technology, Chengalpattu, Tamil Nadu, India

## 12.1 Introduction

Material design is not an entirely new idea. The need for novel materials to fulfill humanity's increasing demands has always been a struggle, as seen a few centuries ago, when materials engineering began taking shape, possibly under the names of metallurgy or ceramic engineering [1]. In their efforts to develop new materials, engineers and scientists have mostly depended on experimental testing. This method is still used in the majority of attempts to create new materials or enhance the characteristics of existing materials by altering their composition and/or microstructure. Usually, this iterative method of problem-solving is predicated on an assumption. Based on presumptions regarding the experimental results, a hypothesis is developed. The basis for the inductive reasoning process that results in the hypothesis is the observations that lead to a theory. Whether or not it is effective, every subsequent attempt adds to the observation. Consequently, the hypothesis gains specificity and the system is comprehended more thoroughly. However, the method is time-consuming, expensive, and cumbersome. In the modern era, the standards alter just as quickly as the environment we live in. Engineers and materials scientists have to supply society with the materials it needs [2].

Biomaterials are materials that have been designed and made expressly to work with biological systems. They are bioactive substances that readily bond to human flesh. Modern biomaterials have improved dramatically in the last 50 years. Biomaterials utilized in hard tissue prosthetic implants such as plates, screws, and pins can also be used in soft tissue implants such as vascular implants for orthopedic and dental applications. They must perform multiple jobs inside the body, including mechanical activities such as weight carrying, as well as interact with the body's response to maximize the restoration of the function for which the implant is designed. The biocompatibility of implant materials is an important consideration. Toxicology and its relationship with biocompatibility were first clarified in 1971 [3]. Biomaterials are typically made of metal, ceramic, polymer, or composite materials. These types of materials have both advantages and problems. Metals are employed as biomaterials because they are ductile and have great wear and impact resistance. They are commonly used in joint prostheses, dental implants, tiny plates, and staples. Materials used for

**Artificial Intelligence in Biomaterials Design and Development. DOI:** https://doi.org/10.1016/B978-0-323-95464-8.00007-4

various implants require varied combinations of qualities, depending on the implant and the patient's age, gender, and bone quality. Though existing materials have been utilized as implant materials for a long time, they have some drawbacks in terms of desirable mechanical qualities and biocompatibility [4]. These problems, together with a lot of room for improvement in their performance, raise the question of creating biomaterials with desired qualities based on application needs. In case of hard tissue implants, that is, the implants for orthopedic and dental purposes, lesser stiffness of the implant is most important to reduce the stress shielding and to achieve better osseointegration. To achieve this quality along with adequate load-bearing capability of the implant, the modulus and strength of the implant materials play the most significant role, in addition to the design of the implant. With several advantages over the experimental "trial and error" strategy for developing new materials for the aforementioned goal, the computational approach is currently the most widely recognized for creating biomaterials in consideration of alloying components and their intended function [4].

To create an effective biomaterial with better properties, numerous design principles must be followed, as well as appropriate instruments. The fundamental advantage of the computation-based material design technique is that it decreases both the cost and the time required for comprehensive experimentation. A rigorous combination of measurement, mathematics, and modeling is required to completely understand the relationship between composition, microstructure, procedure, and property to design and create new implant materials [5]. Several computational tools have been developed for the design of new-age materials [6]. The analytical models utilized for simulation-based material design have limits in addressing complicated multivariate systems and are more academic in nature than practical solutions [7]. One of the most reliable models-development concepts is to use previously obtained experimental or simulation data. A range of machine learning (ML) methodologies are used to create data-driven mathematical models [8–14]. Nowadays, ML-based data-driven models are widely employed in the field of materials informatics. Another issue with the informatics-based material design process is the optimization of all competing qualities throughout the design phase. In this context, nonconventional metaheuristic optimization strategies have grown in favor during the last few decades [15]. Examples include the genetic method, particle swarm optimization, ant colony optimization, simulated annealing, and the wheel optimization technique. Among these multicriteria decision-making optimization techniques, evolutionary or genetic algorithms (GAs) stand out the most [5].

## 12.2 Biomaterial design and optimization

### *12.2.1 Biomaterial design*

"Any substance or combination of substances, other than drugs, synthetic or natural in origin, which can be used for any period of time, augments or replaces partially or completely any tissue, organ, or function of the body, in order to maintain or improve the quality of life of the individual" is the definition of biomaterials, proposed by the American National Institute of Health, presently accepted by the most. The primary requirements for biomaterials include a few "non-properties," for example, nontoxic, noncarcinogenic, nonthrombogenic, and nonimmunogenic. All these properties can be included in the essential attribute of a biomaterial called biocompatibility. The term "biocompatibility" is defined as the "ability of a material to perform with an appropriate host response in a specific situation" as described in the Williams Dictionary of Biomaterials. According to the previously specified requirements, materials have to be able to both carry out a specific function and recognize that their introduction would result in a biological reaction at the interface created. The biomaterials used for hard tissue implants can be defined as follows: (1) having a fibrous tissue layer between them and the bone tissue; (2) having the ability to osseointegrate, or form chemical bonds with bone tissue, meaning that the implant surface is directly coated with the mineral phase and collagen of the neighboring bone; and (3) under certain conditions, using bioinert materials, it is possible to come into direct contact with the surrounding bone tissue, meaning that there must be no chemical interactions between the implant and the tissue.

In today's world, the design of new-age materials or the development of new material concepts is based on societal demands, end-user objectives, or the goal of creating a different physical or mechanical property. Computational materials science provides numerous techniques for designing materials to reduce the time and expense of producing new materials in response to industry demands. The behavior of proposed materials can be ascertained from the atomic level to the microstructure and even down to the product/component scale using science-driven models on many length scales [16,17]. On an atomic scale, numerous materials scientists use techniques such as density functional theory and molecular dynamics. The phase transformation and microstructure design are both modeled using thermodynamic principles. Correlating material properties with microstructure involves the use of numerical simulations and various analytical techniques [18,19]. A material modeling platform that is multiscaled can be made with any of these tools. Because the performance of materials is determined by their composition and processing, the manufacturing process is vital for various significant engineering materials. In such instances, incorporating the processing parameters into the design process, as well as the timescale and length scale, becomes critical. Aiming to address materials and manufacturing elements simultaneously, Integrated Computational Materials Engineering (ICME) tries to incorporate techniques like phase change kinetics and computational fluid dynamics into the materials modeling framework [20–22].

The materials industry has substantially enhanced its experimental and characterization skills, leading to the generation of a significant amount of data on a global scale nowadays. Data, however, is meaningless without a relational connection. Data in this relational database is used to generate information (Fig. 12.1). These days, this is a relatively easy task because to high-performance computers and smart software. The issue of knowledge extraction then emerges. The ultimate goal is to discover the underlying pattern of the data's relationships. The data mining or knowledge discovery technique that employs statistical or computational intelligence approaches may have a significant impact on the work at hand [23]. Materials with the required qualities or performance levels could then be designed using the knowledge that has been obtained. This approach to materials design may help reduce failure risk

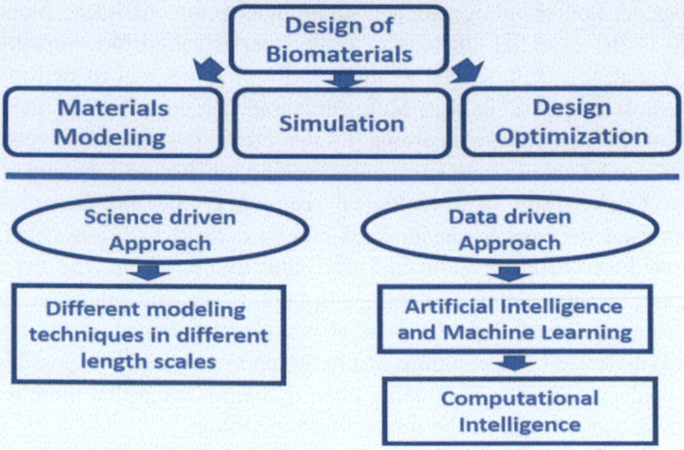


**Figure 12.1** Different strategies for computational materials design.
Reprinted with permission from [22].

while saving money and effort. Advances in computer capabilities have enabled the ability to design materials using alternate approaches of mathematical models based on the system's underlying physics or chemistry. Aside from intellectual curiosity, such initiatives to develop additional materials will likely increase with time. For future material discovery, the methods for creating materials based on these models are vital.

With a few exceptions, the fields of informatics-based design and mechanistic or physical model-based design have advanced together. Because the informatics-based method uses basic research for modeling, the materials community believes that it lacks science. The segment that aimed to showcase the materials informatics field was unable to find many uses for the substitute method. Though each side has a valid point and is correct in its way, this tactic will not work. These two techniques must complement one another rather than compete. Initially, the experts in informatics should determine that it should be applied to systems only in cases where physics-based methods are not feasible. The other group should thoroughly analyze the accomplishments of the materials informatics sector. Findings like these could be the outcome of the knowledge discovery technique, which could assist in partially removing the constraints of physics-based models. The development of hybrid systems that combine scientific and technological modeling is key to the future of effective materials design. In domains where knowledge is scarce or only experimental observations are available, artificial intelligence and ML approaches ought to be used in conjunction with other forms of modeling. Compared to any one method alone, these models could improve material design and be more effective [24].

#### *12.2.1.1 Data-driven design*

Data-driven design (D3) approaches for products are the result of data analytics (DA). It is the process of analyzing datasets to conclude the information they hold. Advances in computing methods, particularly in ML and artificial intelligence, have rendered DA a very practical tool. DA approaches are increasingly frequently applied in commercial businesses to help firms make better business decisions. Four types of DA are routinely used: descriptive, diagnostic, predictive, and prescriptive [25]. Descriptive analytics is a tool for determining "what has happened." This level of DA can employ a variety of fundamental statistical techniques, such as decision trees, cluster analysis, and support vector machines. The following stage of analysis, known as diagnostic analytics, addresses the "why" issue. In industrial settings, analyzing the source of flaws in any product may be an excellent example. Some tools for performing such analyses include principal component analysis and rough set analysis. Simply said, predictive analytics is the widely used technique for figuring out connections between independent (input) and dependent (output) variables. Artificial neural networks (ANN), neuro-fuzzy inference systems (FIS), multiple linear/nonlinear regression, and other data-driven models can all be generated using these approaches [26]. Prescriptive analytics, which offers a solution to the issue, is the last phase of DA. To find such solutions, optimization approaches such as GAs and multicriteria decision-making procedures might be applied. Product design optimization can be achieved in the realm of industrial products through the application of prescriptive analytics and the tools employed in its process. Data-driven design refers to the use of industrial data in the creation of high-performing goods.

The data produced by the particular configuration should be the most trustworthy source of information in the context of data-driven industrial product design. The data in that case will show the plant limits, indicating that these restrictions and constraints need to be taken into account during the design phase. In the industrial context, the availability of data is determined by the plant's automation degree. Manual recordkeeping and extensive digital data warehousing are two possible options. For the aforementioned DA, a methodical and trustworthy system of recordkeeping throughout the production process would be advantageous [26]. It can assist enhanced product quality, eliminating faults, lowering production costs, and even creating new products. Sometimes an industry's research and development setup is needed to design a completely new product. In this case, the industry can use this DA method to design and reduce the number of trials and, consequently, the time and financial costs. Data published by others, particularly academic research, may likewise be used in such product designs.

### 12.2.2 Optimization

Optimization is a technique for determining the optimal answer in given circumstances. Engineers must make some administrative and technological decisions when designing, constructing, and maintaining engineering systems. The most crucial part of any such decision is determining whether to maximize the anticipated reward or minimize the required work. As a result, the amount of effort required to deliver or achieve a desired result in each real-world scenario may be characterized as a function of some choice factors, and optimization is the process of determining the circumstances that create the largest or least value of a function [15]. During the design process, any engineering system or component is specified by a set of parameters, some of which are evaluated as variables. Preassigned parameters are amounts that are typically fixed before the start of an activity. The term "design or decision variable" refers to all other numbers that are considered variables throughout the design process. In many real-world problems, the design variables cannot be chosen at random because they must adhere to certain functional and other restrictions. Design constraints are the requirements that must be met to generate a satisfactory design. Plant limitations, or the boundaries of a plant's capacity, are important to take into account during optimization when it comes to the manufacturing industry. Any computational design normally produces a design that is adequate or appropriate and only fits the problem's functional and other requirements. Of course, there will be more than one suitable design, and to obtain the best result, the best among all acceptable designs must be picked, as well as an objective function based on the nature of the issue [27]. Mechanical efficiency is a goal-oriented function used to maximize mechanical engineering system design. In most design difficulties, selecting the objective function is simple, but there are rare cases when optimizing for one crucial component can result in unacceptable results for another. This objective function is used to discover the best possible design, and the process is known as design optimization. An iterative optimization technique begins with an educated guess. After a certain number of iterations, it may reach a stable solution or the optimal response to a problem [15].

#### *12.2.2.1 Classification of optimization methods*

Numerous categories exist for optimization problems. The presence or absence of restrictions in an optimization issue determines whether it is constrained or unconstrained. Moreover, optimization can be categorized based on how many objectives are involved. A single optimum solution is always found by a single-objective optimization, regardless of whether it aims for the maximum or minimum solution. Multiobjective optimization is necessary when there is a conflict between more than one objective. Multiobjective optimization is the ideal option, and it leads to the development of a Pareto front—a collection of the best nondominated alternatives [27]. How the objective function and the restrictions are expressed constitutes a significant additional classification of optimization problems. This classification allows for the division of optimization issues into four categories: quadratic, geometric, nonlinear, and linear programming problems. From a computational perspective, this classification is quite helpful since it provides a variety of specialized techniques for effectively solving a certain class of problems. Deterministic and probabilistic/heuristic algorithms are further subcategories of optimization algorithms [28]. Deterministic algorithms are used when there is an obvious relationship between the characteristics of the potential solutions and their worth for a given issue. After this, the search space can be effectively investigated. Heuristic algorithms are a kind of optimization algorithm that use the data the computer is currently collecting to decide which solution candidate to test next or how to create the next solution.

#### 12.2.2.2 Metaheuristic optimization

On the other hand, a metaheuristic is a technique for addressing broad categories of problems. It blends heuristics and objective functions effectively and subtly, usually without requiring a deeper comprehension of their structure. A metaheuristic is a collection of computational concepts used to define heuristic solutions to various problems. The inability to determine whether the present optimal solution is on a local or global optimum is a problem with classical optimization techniques [22]. Moreover, it is often not evident whether the optimization process should continue, halt, refine the current optimum, or explore other areas of the search space. The issue is multimodal and could become unmanageable if there are numerous (local) optima. Three categories can be used to broadly classify the metaheuristic approaches, as shown in Fig. 12.2, which presents the wide classification of metaheuristic optimization. The first is the group dedicated to evolutionary computation, encompassing topics such as genetic programming, evolutionary strategy, and differential evolution. The second group can be referred to as the swarm intelligence group since it comprises ant colony optimization, particle swarm optimization, and other similar techniques. Alternatively, bioinspired optimization approaches can be used to describe these two kinds of methods. Simulated annealing is the most widely utilized technique in the third group of optimization methods that draw inspiration from physical phenomena [26].

#### 12.2.2.3 Genetic algorithm

The biologically based computer methods known as GAs function following the ideas of Darwinian natural selection theory. Due to the method's great effectiveness, engineering optimization is shown to be a good fit in the majority of research. Consequently, GA is a method of hunting based on natural selection and the principles of natural genetics to find the best solution for each given issue [27]. GA

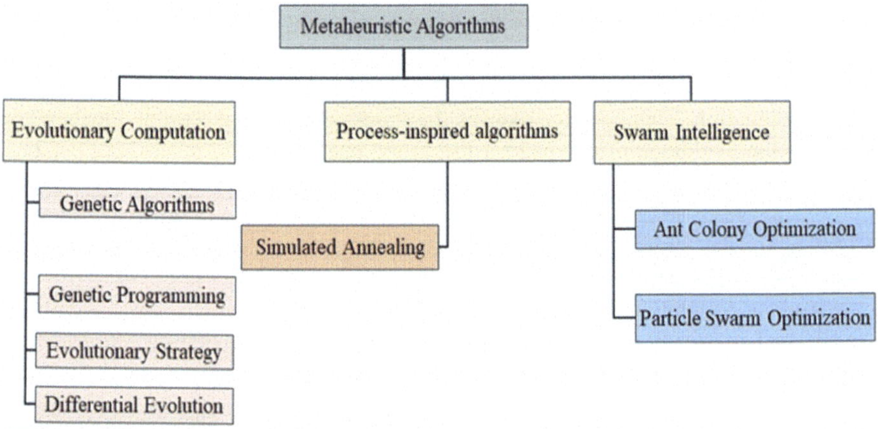


**Figure 12.2** Classification of the most used metaheuristic optimization algorithms, which have been successfully used to solve several materials design problems.
Reprinted with permission from [22].

leverages the idea of survival of the fittest to focus on the population of feasible solutions to extract better approximations for a particular solution. By choosing individuals based on their degree of fitness and breeding them together, a fresh set of solutions is produced with every generation that follows. Similar to natural adaptation, this process results in the evolution of individual populations that are better acclimated to their environment than their ancestors. A likely solution to a problem in GA is encoded as a collection of variable strings called chromosomes. A vast population of solutions with arbitrary parameter values is generated, with each chromosome being regarded as a singular solution.

Crossover and mutation are the two operators in breeding. Basic biological cross-fertilization is facilitated by crossover, while noise introduction is implied by mutation. These operators need to be applied simply with the help of a logical selection process to produce surprisingly good results for a variety of issues. Individuals are assigned fitness values after crossover and mutation. Following that, the individuals are chosen for mating based on their fitness levels, supported by objective function evaluation that is carried out throughout the course of subsequent generations. The preservation of good individuals through cross-breeding may improve individual performance in this way. At some point, the less-fit individuals disappear from the population. The GA process is completed once certain requirements are met. That is, once a certain number of generations and a mean population deviation are reached, or once a certain point in the search space is reached. Noticeably, GA derives a variety of potential solutions for each problem and presents the user with options to choose from. In situations where a particular problem lacks a single viable solution, GA facilitates the simultaneous discovery of alternative solutions, much like in a multiobjective optimization mode.

Fig. 12.3 illustrates the structure of a simple genetic algorithm (SGA) following Goldberg's explanation [5]. In the first phase, GA initializes a random population made up of individuals or possible solution points. Using the fitness result from the objective function evaluation, it is first determined whether the person can be classified as good or terrible for the given task. Once each person has been evaluated and assigned a fitness value, the first genetic operator, or selection, is assembled along with the original population. This operator reduces the fitness of the weakest individuals while increasing the likelihood of survival for the strong ones. Next, for a subset of persons, the crossover operator is applied to combine the existing individuals into new ones. Reproduction leads to crossover, which allows two individuals to exchange structures according to the probability factor. Consequently, two progeny solutions were produced, each possessing the attributes of their parents [29].

To produce population diversity, the mutation operator is then employed. Applying conventional termination criteria becomes difficult when a population's fitness may remain constant for many generations before the emergence of a better individual. Often, the GA is terminated after a fixed number of generations, and the best members of the population are selected based on their quality compared to the problem criteria. The General Assembly will be rerun or a fresh search involving more generations will be started if no acceptable responses are found. In the actual world, many optimization problems contain multiple competing objectives. Genetic

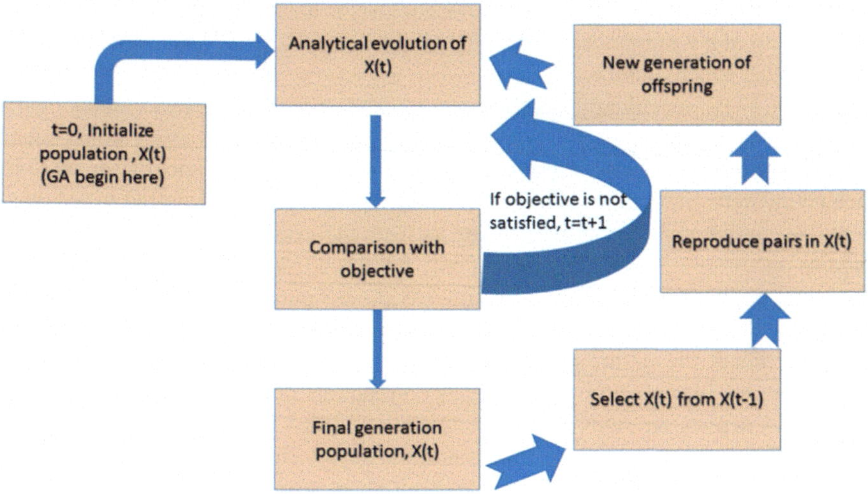


**Figure 12.3** A schematic representation of a simple genetic algorithm, the oldest and arguably the most popular optimization algorithm for solving engineering problems.
Reprinted with permission from [22].

searching, which is based on the Pareto optimality principle, is one technique used in multiobjective scenarios [28,30]. The concept of "optimal" is represented by sets of solutions that offer the most practical trade-offs between the objectives, even though the objective functions are highly contradictory. Unlike the global optima used in single-objective problems, these solutions are referred to as Pareto. According to the basic definition of Pareto optimality, there must be no other workable solution that could be at least as good as a subset of the Pareto set about all outcomes and strictly better about at least one outcome. To date, a plethora of multiobjective GA utilizing nondomination-based selection processes have been reported.

## 12.3 Formulation of the objective function

### 12.3.1 Artificial neural network

Recently, it has been shown that the ANN method is especially useful for handling complex nonlinear issues in computational materials science. It is a cognitive, dependable data information processing system that can represent intricate and complex scenarios. The ANN approach provides adaptation, learning, and prediction capabilities despite regression analysis, leading to better accuracy. The main advantage of an ANN model is that it doesn't make any assumptions about the nature of people or their interactions with one another. Instead, it can learn from experiences and recognize patterns in a series of datasets. For this paradigm, no mathematical relations are necessary [31]. More complex connections in datasets can be found by ANNs than by conventional models thanks to an intrinsic property. Based on the way organic neurons, like those in the brain, process information, an ANN is a data management model [32]. It is made up of a vast number of intricately linked processing units called neurons that work together to solve issues.

An ANN is specifically engineered to address specific tasks like object identification, grouping, or predictive learning. Adapting the synaptic connections formed between neurons is a necessary part of learning in biological systems [33]. Each neural network comprises multiple processing components, referred to as "input layers" or "input nodes," that receive inputs from the external world. Nonetheless, it contains one or more hidden layers that only take data from specific other processing components. These processing pieces, referred to as "output layers," show what the neural network algorithm would ultimately produce [34]. Without drawing any judgments about the nature or links between the input and output units, an ANN typically learns from experience and finds correlations in a set of data [35].

Fig. 12.4 depicts an ANN with a traditional feedforward network [36], which is used in this study. It has three interconnected layers: input (x), hidden ($H_j$), and output (y) [37]. Using transfer functions, each layer is connected. Eq. (12.1) relates the weighted sum of the normalized inputs (xi) with the connection weights ($w_{ji}$) that connect the input to hidden layers with the addition of the bias values ($b_j$) of each

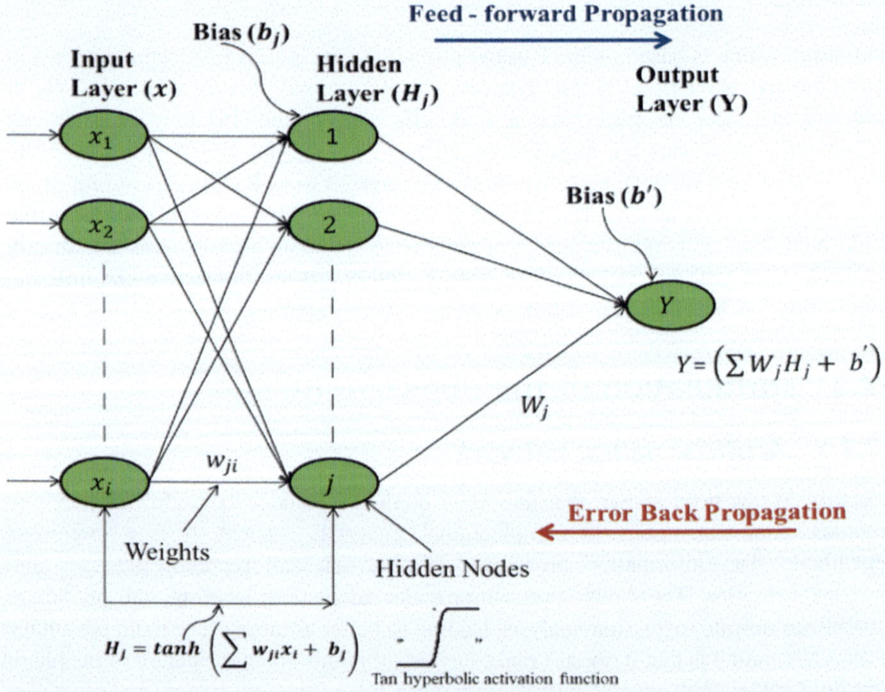


**Figure 12.4** Configuration of a common multilayered perceptron-type artificial neural network, which uses supervised learning method.
Reprinted with permission from [36].

layer. Tan hyperbolic (tanh) nonlinear transfer function is used to link the input (x) and hidden nodes ($H_j$).

$$H_j = tan\,h\left(\sum_j w_{ji}x_i + b_j\right) \tag{12.1}$$

Eq. (12.2) describes the usage of the linear function to find the output node (y) by a weighted sum of the outputs with the connection weights ($W_j$) of the hidden to output layer plus the addition of the bias values (b') of its corresponding layer:

$$Y = \sum_j W_j H_j + b' \tag{12.2}$$

It is possible to get different results by modifying the weights $w_{ji}$, $w_i$ in Eqs. (12.1) and (12.2). To determine the optimal values for these weights, the network is "trained" using a set of input-output data that become normalized. To begin, apply Eq. (12.3) to normalize the input-output data in the range of -1 to +1.

$$x_j^N = \frac{2(x_j - X_{\min})}{X_{\max} - X_{\min}} - 1 \tag{12.3}$$

where $x_j$ is the input or output parameter, $X_{max}$ and $X_{min}$ are the upper and lower bounds of the corresponding parameter, and $x^N{}_j$ is the normalized value. It is possible to train the network to minimize an error function basically, a normalized total of squared errors by changing the weights $w_{ji}$. Consequently, the input-output correlation's ideal representation appears.

A multilayered ANN with feed-forward linkages between the input, hidden, and output layers was given the challenge of calculating connection weights. To tackle this difficulty, the backpropagation (BP) technique was created. The gradient method iteration methodology [38] aims to minimize the squared error between the expected and actual output. Fig. 12.5 shows a schematic representation of the BP learning process. An improved version of the input-output correlation mapping is achieved by ANNs, a kind of ML system. The fact that the correlations between the variables are not linear can be taken into consideration.

When paired with the BP method, this technique has shown to be extremely suitable for calculating composites' tribological and mechanical properties, which are demonstrated to be dependent on a set of multiple input variables [39]. Neural networks can be effectively and successfully employed in scenarios when building a physical model is difficult.

## 12.3.2 Neuro-Fuzzy interface system

The classical (Boolean) theory is modified by fuzzy logic, which takes imprecision in knowledge and facts into account. It was first presented in 1960 by Dr. Lotfi Zadeh as a way to mimic the ambiguities of spoken language. Autos, consumer electronics, electrical machinery, and highway monitoring systems were among the other growing categories of applications [40,41]. A set that lacks clear, distinct boundaries is called a fuzzy set. Fuzzy logic illustrates this point by showing that every assertion's truth value is a matter of

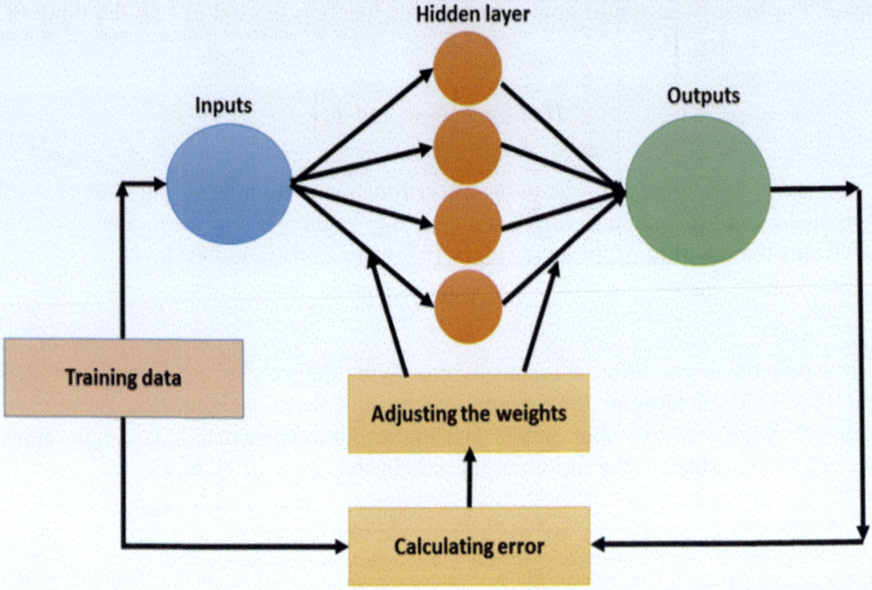


**Figure 12.5** Schematic of the supervised learning in artificial neural network model, which used backpropagation algorithm for minimization of the prediction error.
Reprinted with permission from [36].

degree; the set consists of elements with only a partial membership. A membership function uses a range of 0–1 to convert each point in the input space to a membership value, or level of membership. A number that matches the system's requirements in terms of performance, efficiency, accessibility, and clarity can be used to characterize the shape of the membership function curve. The most widely used straight-line functions are the triangle and trapezoidal functions. These are the fundamental membership functions.

Conceptual representations of systems made using fuzzy if-then rules are known as fuzzy linguistic characterizations, and they are expressed as follows:

IF ($x_1$ is $A_1$, $x_2$ is $A_2$, …, $x_n$ is $A_n$) THEN ($y_1$ is $B_1$, $y_2$ is $B_2$, …, $y_n$ is $B_n$) where $x_i$ and $y_j$ are the linguistic variables corresponding to the fuzzy sets $A_i$ and $B_j$.

Fig. 12.6 shows the three parts of the FIS: a defuzzifier, an inference system with a fuzzy rule foundation, and a fuzzifier. Fuzzification uses a set of input membership functions to convert inputs to values between 0 and 1. Fuzzy outputs for different rules are produced using the fuzzy rules. After that, the data is combined to provide fuzzy output dispersion.

Many other fuzzy combination strategies are not included in this article. Fuzzy combinations are typically called "T-norms." It is ideal for an FIS to generate a single, clean output in many situations. Defuzzification is the process used to get this number. Additionally, several defuzzification techniques are presented.

Sugeno [42] and Mamdani [43] are two of the most widely used FIS models. The Sugeno FIS, in contrast to the Mamdani FIS, does not compute the output implication by clipping the output's membership function according to the rule severity. The

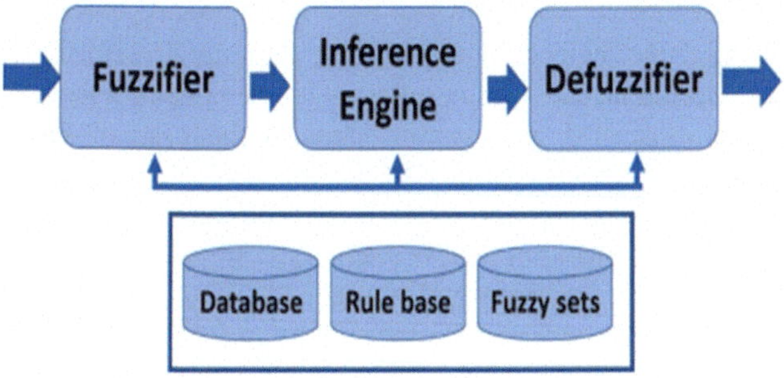


**Figure 12.6** Schematic of Fuzzy Interface System, which can use the imprecise domain knowledge through if-then rules.
Reprinted with permission from [36].

Sugeno FIS lacks an output membership function. Instead, each input is multiplied by a constant to get the output, which is then the sum of the results. Since if-then rules make more sense than expressions when conveying imprecise information, FIS is appropriate for modeling systems where data are unavailable to construct data-driven models such as ANNs. In complex and dynamic material systems, this is a frequent occurrence. However, up to now, not much has been accomplished in the field of materials modeling with FIS.

## 12.4 Case studies

### 12.4.1 Titanium alloys for hard tissue implants

Using experimental data and an imprecise understanding of the relationship between titanium alloy composition, processing, microstructure, and properties, rule-based models are created to forecast the strength and elastic modulus (EM) of titanium alloys. The created models are utilized in the creation of alloys appropriate for dentistry and orthopedic uses. The reduced Space Searching Algorithm is utilized in multiobjective optimization to determine the microstructure, processing, and composition of titanium alloys that are appropriate for orthopedic use. High-strength and low EM, as well as sufficient biocompatibility and affordability, are the contradictory requirements for the alloys used for this specific purpose. β or almost β alloys are the best compositions for achieving the aforementioned objectives, according to the "Pareto" solutions found through multiobjective optimization. A better combination of the necessary traits should be provided by various compositions that result from the decision-making paradigm used in the solutions. A model-based design methodology has been offered in this research to assist the experimental development of certain of the alloys. Regarding their mechanical properties, the alloys' primary characterizations yield positive findings.

The study aimed to determine the biocompatibility of β-Ti alloys and to achieve low Young's modulus and high strength [44]. To associate compositional and process variables with microstructural parameters and eventually with features, a three-layered FIS was developed, as seen in Fig. 12.7. In this work, predefined fuzzy sets are generated using the knowledge of experts (the authors). The rule bases for the first layer of the models, that is, the rules correlating the composition and microstructural features, are developed from prior knowledge. In the case of the second layer correlating the microstructural features to the mechanical properties, the primary work consists of generating an appropriate fuzzy rule base. Thus the nine variables used for modeling are Mo-equivalent, Al, Zr, Sn, deformation temperature, solutionizing temperature, cooling rate, aging temperature, and aging time. Two separate models are developed for two outputs, that is, yield strength (YS) and EM, as per the schematics shown in Fig. 12.7. With a previous understanding of the system, six Mamdani FISs are established that correlate the composition and process factors with microstructural aspects. A database created from published literature is used to produce two Mamdani FISs that correlate the microstructural traits with the attributes.

Fig. 12.8 displays the surface views for the input/output relationships that the FIS produced based on the rules that were elicited. The EM is not significantly impacted by the dislocation density, solid solution hardening, or grain size. With an increase in β concentration, the EM first rises but then abruptly falls. This suggests a larger EM for the two-phase structure. The mildest precipitation hardening has the lowest EM. The role of β breakdown products is "tricky," as evidenced in the case of YS as well,

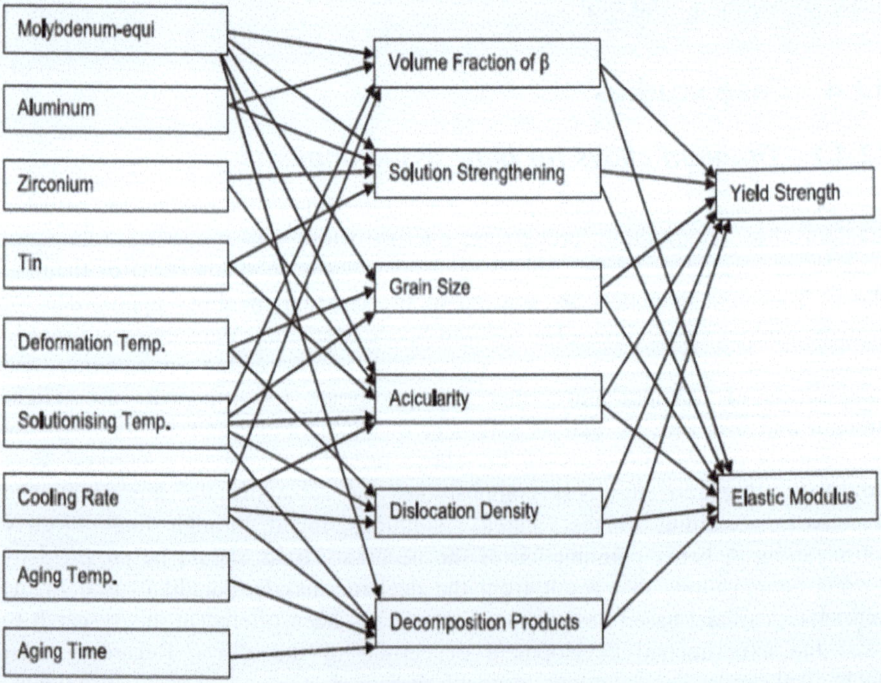


**Figure 12.7** Schematic diagram of the Fuzzy Inference System correlating the properties with the composition, processing, and microstructure.
Reprinted with permission from [44].

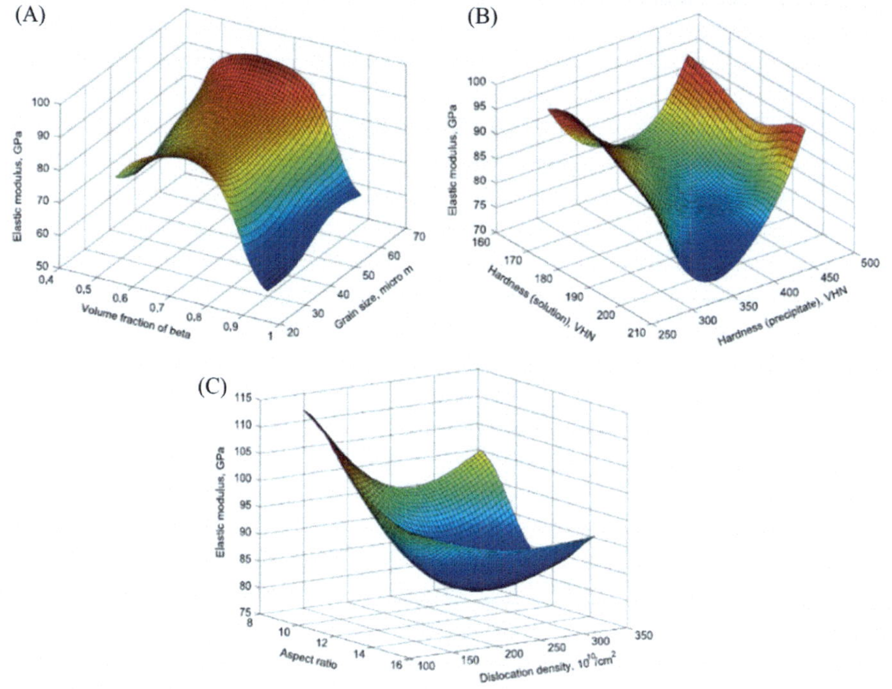


**Figure 12.8** Surface views generated by the Fuzzy Inference System describing the effects of (A) volume fraction of and grain size, (B) solution and precipitation hardening, and (C) aspect ratio of grains and dislocation density on modulus of elasticity.
Reprinted with permission from [44].

and may need more research. Lowering the EM due to increased acicularity in the structure could mean that α‘ and α“ are forming.

Fig. 12.9 depicts the Pareto front that was created by multiobjective optimization. The EM is within a restricted range; however, the solutions show a large variation in the alloys' strength and cost. The nondominated solutions' thorough study has been presented elsewhere. Three alloys are created for experimental validation based on the solutions in the Pareto front's knee area, which are taken into consideration for additional studies.

Using fuzzy logic, prior knowledge in imprecise language might be effectively applied to the development of predictive models for the mechanical properties of Ti alloys. Previous experimental results can be applied in tandem to construct and improve a semiempirical two-layered FIS that incorporates microstructural information. The multiobjective optimization technique employing RSSA may use the fuzzy models for strength and EM as objective functions. Enough data is provided by the Pareto solutions to design alloys. Decision-making is based on the Pareto front's knee region solutions. The developed alloy's experimental validation produced positive results for the alloy's strength and EM. A few innovative alloy systems with better properties than the current ones will undoubtedly be identified through more alloy characterization.

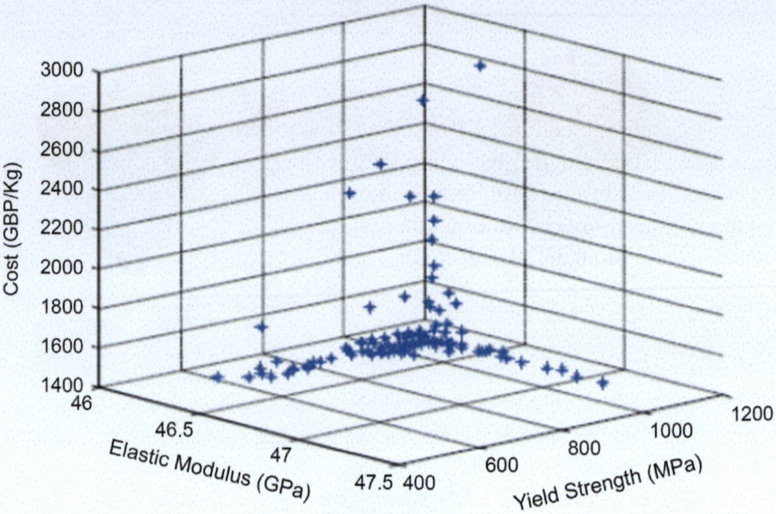


**Figure 12.9** Pareto solutions of elastic modulus versus yield strength resulted from the multiobjective optimization process.
Reprinted with permission from [44].

### 12.4.2 Designing ultra-high molecular weight polyethylene hybrid composites using machine learning and metaheuristic algorithms

Hip replacements are necessary when a person suffers from a sudden trauma or various forms of arthritis. Hip prostheses frequently use ultra-high-molecular-weight polyethylene (UHMWPE) as an acetabular component. The articulating surfaces of the joint are subject to varying lubrication regimes, including mixed or border lubrication, which eventually result in osteolysis due to the generation of microwear debris over time. With the aid of evolutionary algorithms and ML, the current work aims to design suitable composite materials for hip joint acetabular cups. An ANN was used to develop a model of the mechanical and wear resistance of UHMWPE acetabular cups for UHMWPE composites with many nano- and micro-reinforcements. A database consisting of published experimental results of UHMWPE composites including MWCNT, graphene, and carbon fiber (CF) was used to develop the ANN models for the mechanical and tribological properties. The models were used as objective functions in both single- and multiobjective GA models to produce composites with better performance. The current materials informatics approach offers several compelling suggestions for conducting experiments.

In this study [45], discrete ANN models with different figures of concealed entities are generated for the tribological characteristics (coefficient of friction [COF] and specific wear rate [SWR]) and the mechanical properties (Young's modulus, hardness, and ultimate tensile strength). The best models for each output parameter are chosen after multiple iterations with hidden nodes ranging from 3 to 15, and the same is used for additional study. For the output Young's modulus, hardness, ultimate tensile strength, COF, and SWR, respectively, the best models with the least errors 5, 5, 8, 5, and 9 hidden nodes are selected. In Fig. 12.10, the trained ANN models' predictions are displayed clearly by scatter plots.

ANN demonstrates improved predictableness that can be understood from the maximum coefficients of correlation as 0.90842, 0.88122, 0.97491, 0.86029, and 0.8029 for Young's modulus, hardness, ultimate tensile strength, COF, and SWR models, respectively. To maximize the mechanical characteristics and minimize the tribological qualities simultaneously, NSGA II was used for multiobjective optimization. Three reinforcement particles' weight percentages were added together, and optimization was done both with and without constraints. This investigation was conducted using various combinations, such as changing the matrix's molecular weight across the board and setting it at various values. Fig. 12.11 displays the Pareto fronts for SWR and COF for a population extent of 500 and generation 500. To change UHMWPE's molecular weight between 2.5 and 6 million gm/mol, a multiobjective GA was applied.

Fig. 12.11 illustrates the nondominated optimization outcomes, which significantly reduce the COF and SWR values. In the Pareto solutions, the molecular weight changes are ordered in ascending order of SWR (descending order of COF), as Fig. 12.12 shows. Fig. 12.12 shows that a lower matrix molecular weight is favored for a lower SWR, but a greater UHMWPE molecular weight is chosen for a low COF. The Pareto fronts of SWR and COF at various molecular weights are displayed in Fig. 12.13 without regard to the reinforcement materials. The figure's right shift of Pareto fronts with increased matrix molecular weight suggests that improving the matrix material's molecular weight also marginally improves the COF and SWR.

The overall weight percentage of the three reinforcing materials in this work is set at 8% and 10% for future research, since this should be low enough to avoid the problem of nonhomogeneity of the particle dispersion during manufacturing. In Fig. 12.14, the Pareto fronts for COF and SWR are displayed as the molecular weight of UHMWPE varies across the entire range of 2.5–6 million gm/mol, with the total summation of the three particles limited to 8% and 10%. Fig. 12.14 makes it clear that COF and SWR can be minimized at both 8% and 10% of the total composition, and the trends do not differ much. The molecular weight variation in Pareto solutions with limitations is displayed in Fig. 12.15, which is arranged in ascending order of SWR. It is possible to lower the COF and SWR values at decreasing matrix molecular weights, and both constraints exhibit a similar trend, as shown in Fig. 12.15.

The Pareto fronts of the COF and SWR at various constant molecular weights are shown in Figs. 12.16 and 12.17, respectively, with 8% and 10% limits on the overall weight of the particles. The Pareto solutions may accomplish the low molecular weight of the matrix (2.5 million grams/mole) and noticeably reduced SWR values under these circumstances. The composite's matrix softens when the molecular weight of UHMWPE decreases. As a result, the SWR decreases, and the COF slightly increases. Because there were three distinct particles present in the current investigation, this shift in matrix behavior was not apparent. It's possible that particle behavior took center stage. When there is a significant softening, that is, when the molecular weight is 2.5 million grams per mole, the matrix behavior becomes visible.

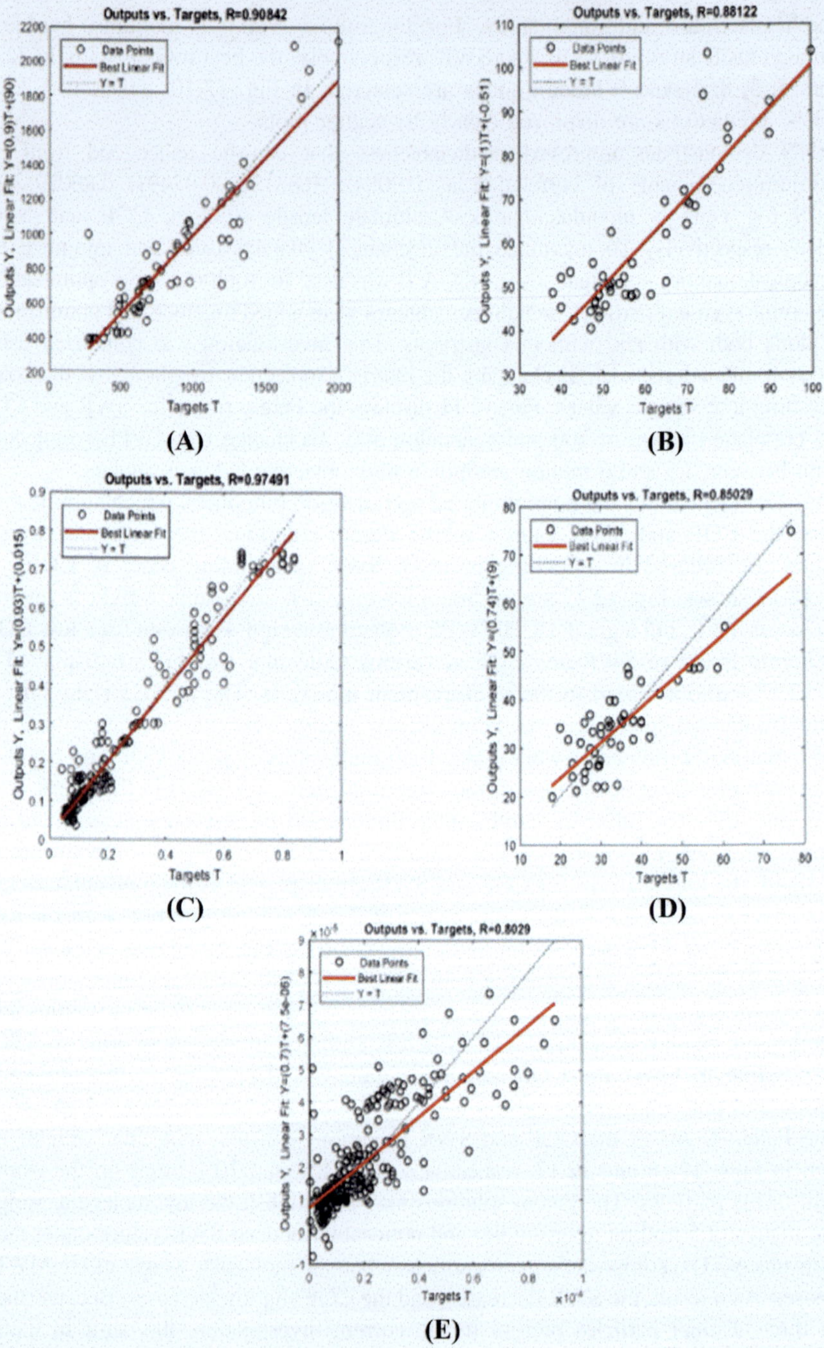


**Figure 12.10** Predictability of ANN models for (A) Young's modulus, (B) hardness, (C) ultimate tensile strength, (D) coefficient of friction (COF), and (E) specific wear rate (SWR). *ANN*, Artificial neural network.

Reprinted with permission from [45].

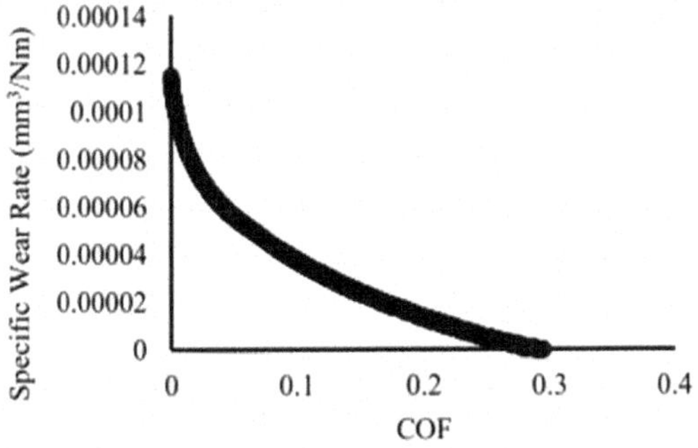


**Figure 12.11** Pareto front for COF versus SWR with Varying Molecular Weight of UHMWPE without constraints. *COF*, Coefficient of friction; *SWR*, specific wear rate; *UHMWPE*, ultra-high-molecular-weight polyethylene.
Reprinted with permission from [45].

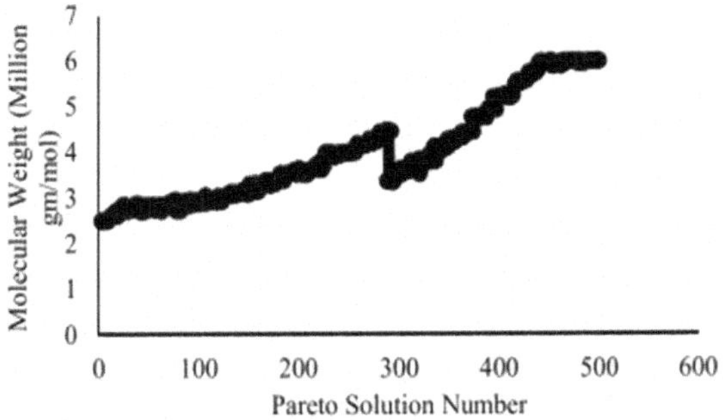


**Figure 12.12** Variation of molecular weight in Pareto solutions with specific wear rate in ascending order without constraints.
Reprinted with permission from [45].

The variation of various nanoparticles in the Pareto solutions with limitations, arranged in ascending order of SWR, is depicted in Fig. 12.18. It is evident that a considerable quantity of CF is required to lower the values of COF and SWR when Fig. 12.18A is compared to MWCNT and graphene with an 8% constraint on total reinforcement. Fig. 12.18B clearly illustrates a similar trend at 10% restrictions on total reinforcement.

This study can be summarized that the created ANN models for the tribological properties of UHMWPE composites also successfully reveal the objective functions for the design of composites with numerous nano/microparticles with superior presentation. The results of the single-objective optimization highlight the inconsistency between the two distinct tribological features. It will be possible to carry out additional experimental trials to investigate the mechanical and tribological properties of the produced composites by using this computer analysis.

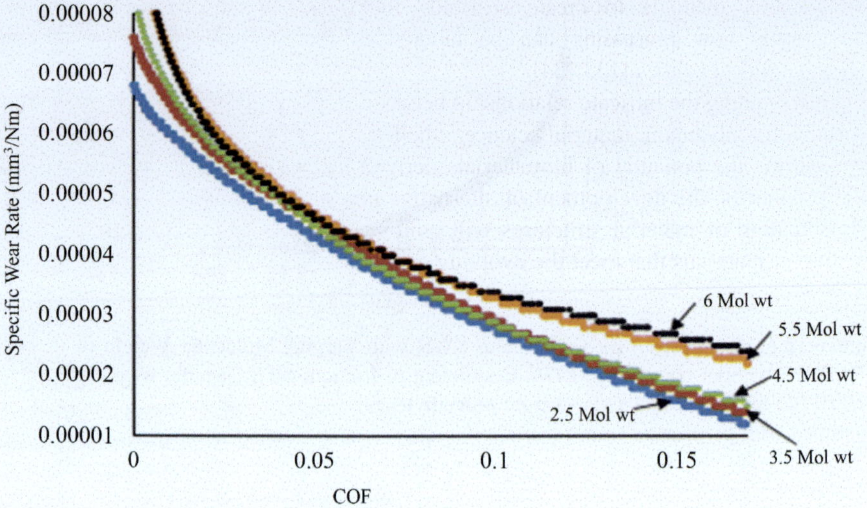


**Figure 12.13** Pareto front for COF versus SWR with different molecular weight of UHMWPE without constraints. *COF*, Coefficient of friction; *SWR*, specific wear rate; *UHMWPE*, ultra-high-molecular-weight polyethylene.
Reprinted with permission from [45].

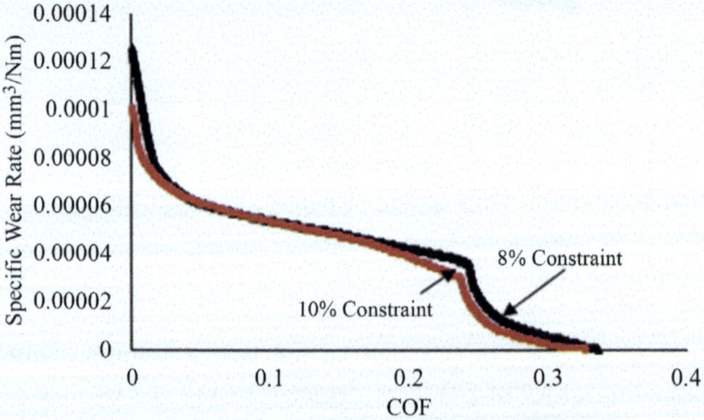


**Figure 12.14** Pareto front for COF versus SWR with varying molecular weight of UHMWPE without constraints. *COF*, Coefficient of friction; *SWR*, specific wear rate; *UHMWPE*, ultra-high-molecular-weight polyethylene.
Reprinted with permission from [45].

### 12.4.3 Design of patient-specific dental implant using finite element analysis and computational intelligence techniques

A GA is used to design dental implants with different porosities and sizes that are optimal for each patient. The standard recommendation is for the microstrain at the contact between the implant and bone to be between 1500 and 3000. The microstrain must be kept within the previously mentioned range for the porous dental implant to

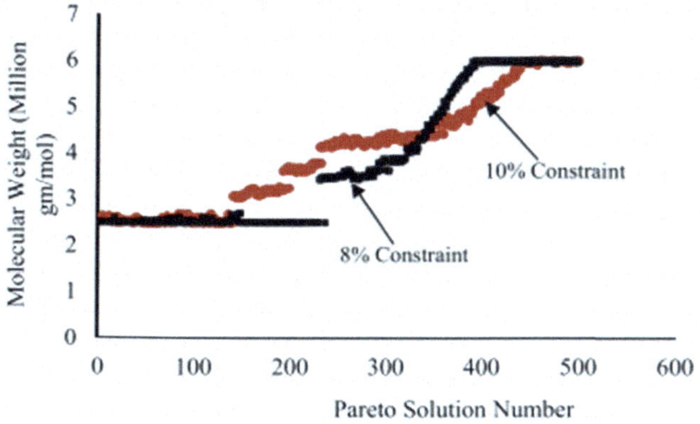


**Figure 12.15** Variation of molecular weight in Pareto solutions with SWR in ascending order, with constraints. *SWR*, Specific wear rate.
Reprinted with permission from [45].

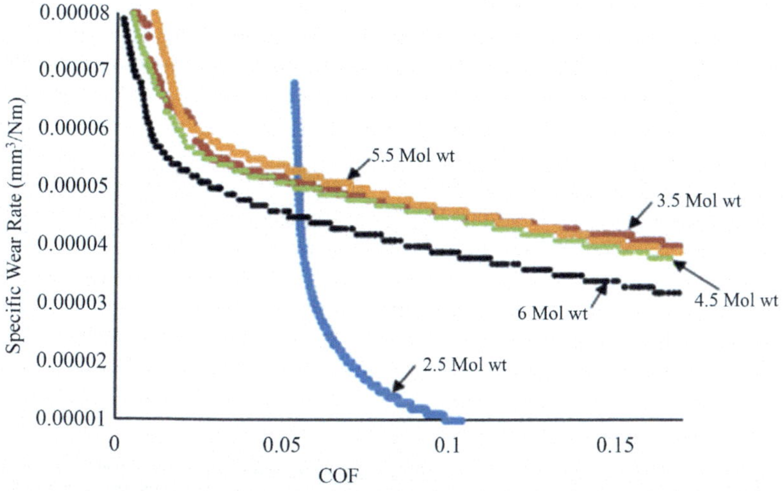


**Figure 12.16** Pareto front for COF versus SWR with different molecular weights of UHMWPE with constraint of maximum 8% reinforcements. *COF*, Coefficient of friction; *SWR*, specific wear rate; *UHMWPE*, ultra-high-molecular-weight polyethylene.
Reprinted with permission from [45].

function; a value near 2500 microstrain is ideal. Since titanium alloy was taken into consideration for the implant material in this design problem [46], the most significant constraint is that the implant stress should be kept to 350 MPa. The aforementioned characteristics must be met to create a prosthesis that is unique to each patient due to their differing bone abnormalities. The data produced by finite element analysis (FEA) is transformed into an ANN model, and this design problem is stated as an optimization problem using the desirability function. Utilizing the desirability function, the ANN model's output is transformed within a range of 0–1,

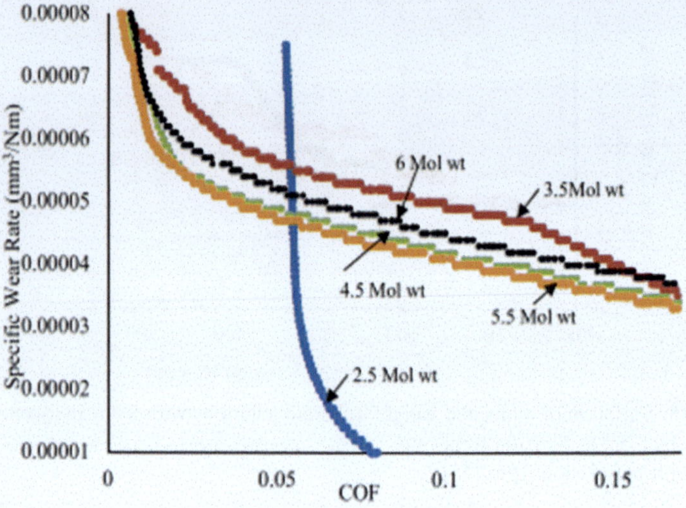


**Figure 12.17** Pareto front for COF versus SWR with different molecular weights of UHMWPE with constraint of maximum 10% reinforcements. *COF*, Coefficient of friction; *SWR*, specific wear rate; *UHMWPE*, ultra-high-molecular-weight polyethylene.
Reprinted with permission from [45].

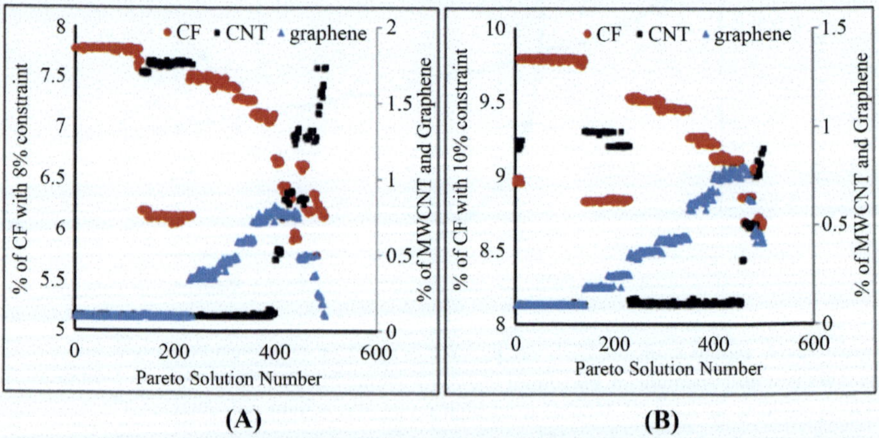


**Figure 12.18** Variation of particles in Pareto solutions with SWR in ascending order with (A) 8% and (B) 10% constraints on total reinforcement. *SWR*, specific wear rate.
Reprinted with permission from [45].

with the greatest value being attained at the most desirable microstrain of 2500. The objective function for the optimization problem utilizing a GA is this hybrid neural network and desire function model. As a constraint, another ANN model that describes the implant stress is employed. The finite element method (FEM) is used to validate the best results obtained from ANN and GA once again. During optimization, the fitness of the population members is measured using ANN models instead of stress analysis by FEM. In each case, this would indicate the ideal size of a titanium alloy dental implant with the best porosity percentage for improved osseointegration in that patient's particular bone type.

An approximate solution to boundary value problems can be found computationally using the FEM, sometimes referred to as FEA in engineering. Among the several fields in which FEA is used are structural analysis, heat transfer, fluid flow, mass movement, electromagnetic potential, and other concerns. The analytical solutions derived by solving ordinary or partial differential equations are often difficult to compute due to the complicated geometries, loadings, and material properties. Therefore for reasonable approximations, numerical techniques like FEA are utilized. Instead of resolving the problem for the entire body in a single operation, FEA allows us to establish the equations for each finite element and combine them to obtain the answer for the whole body. All finite element assessments of physical problems follow the same steps in their formulation. This work implicitly includes the preparation, solution, and postprocessing stages, which are implemented in commercial finite element software packages.

Two ANN models are developed using prediction data from FEA for bone-implant interface microstrain and stress at various implant diameters, lengths, and porosities at various bone conditions as independent inputs. A desirability function with upper and lower bounds of 1500 and 3000 micro strains is applied to the output of the model that predicts the interface microstrain; at a microstrain of 2500, the function yields the maximum output of 1. The desirability function's output is regarded as the fitness for the optimization issue, and the desirability is maximized using a single-objective GA. Fig. 12.19 describes the optimization process scheme. Using the CT scan data and MIMICS software, the mandibular shape is modeled for the FEA research. Initially, finite element software is used to analyze the natural molar tooth before the dental implant is inserted into that molar region. When creating the data, ANSYS 14.0.180 simulations are taken into account. The implant models are developed by examining several combinations of implant length, diameter, and porosity percentage. The material with the EM of 117 GPa is thought to be Ti-6Al-4V alloy. It is believed that the elastic moduli of cementum, dentin, and enamel are, respectively, 80, 22, and 2.5 GPa. Poisson's ratio is assumed to be 0.3 in all scenarios. The data is derived from the combination of the three implant diameter types (4, 5, and 6 mm), the three porosity levels (0%, 10%, and 20%), and the four implant length variations (9, 10, 11, and 12 mm).

A final 3D solid model of the mandible is produced by processing each CT scan in Mimics 11.0 using data from 120 sets of CT scans. The DICOM data is used to construct the mandibular 3D models. After scanning, ANSYS Workbench is used to import the 3D models. Using digital edge detection methods, CAD techniques, and computational tomography (CT) images, 3D models of molar teeth (Fig. 12.20A) are meshed (Fig. 12.20B).

The periodontal ligament (PDL) is absorbed into the volume of the alveolar bone and makes up a very tiny volume of 0.2 mm of the molar tooth system. After that, those are imported into ANSYS, where the material characteristics of the teeth's natural molars are

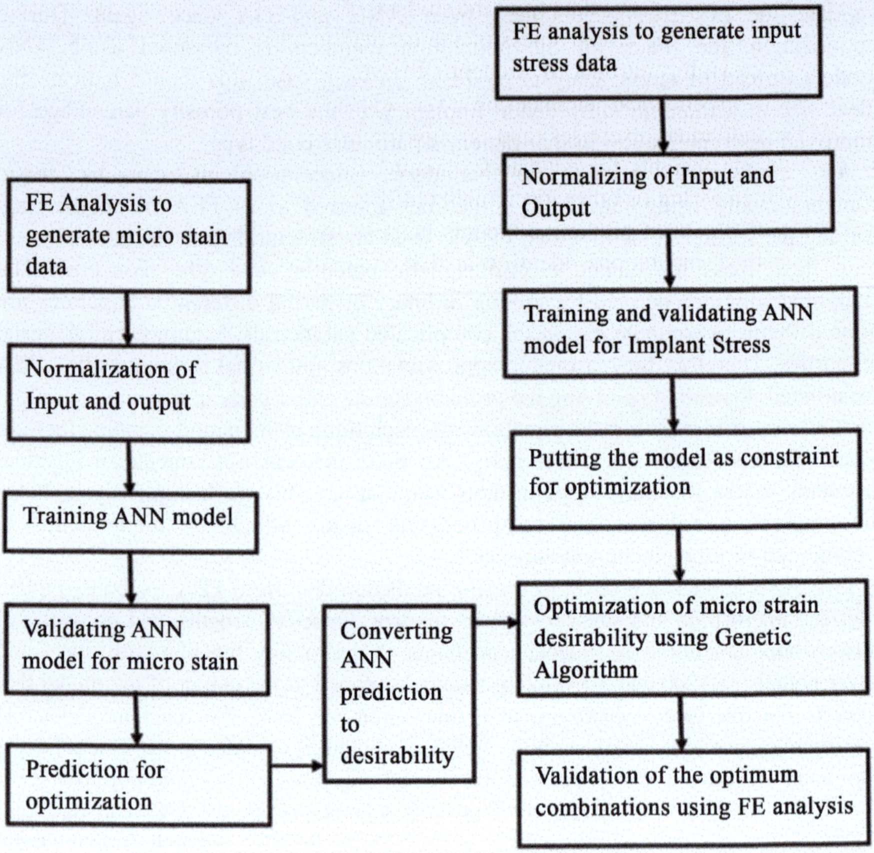


**Figure 12.19** The scheme of designing porous dental implant using finite element simulation, artificial neural network, and genetic algorithm in tandem.
Reprinted with permission from [46].

allocated. The literature contains very little information about the muscles used during mastication. Both of the mandible's condyle head zones are regarded as stationary or motionless in this investigation. The masseter muscles are analyzed at the appropriate anatomical zone and represented as a truss element. Membrane elements are modeled for the medial pterygoid and temporal muscles. These components contract to replicate muscular motions. After that, they are placed within the mandibular molar region, our area of interest, and the stress and strain that are visible there in the interface zone under loaded conditions are duly investigated. Subsequently, 180 unique 3D models of dental implants with different combinations of dimensions (e.g., dx1Lx2, d4L10, d5L9, and d6L12, where d is diameter, x1 is the diameter magnitude, L is length, and x2 is the length magnitude) and porosity are created (Fig. 12.21A and B).

In the molar region, each implant is placed in the exact spot where the natural molar tooth was once located. Following implant placement in the mandibular bone's molar position, the element and node file are imported into ANSYS Mechanical APDL and

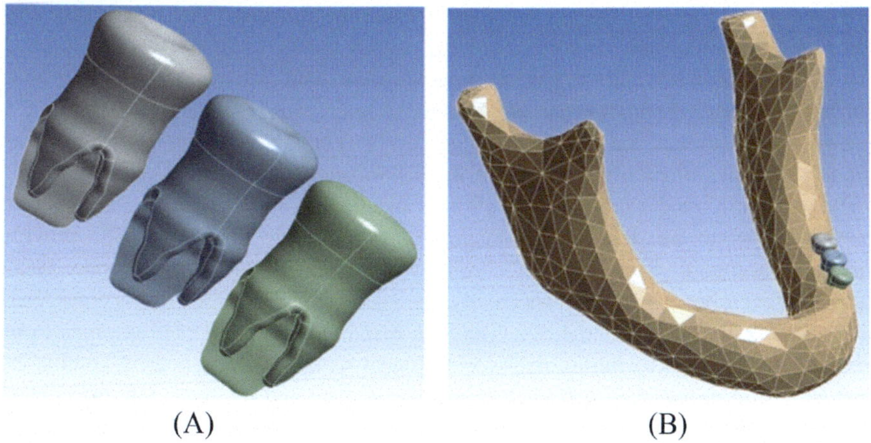


**Figure 12.20** Assembly of natural molar tooth (A) with 3D model of the mandible (B). Reprinted with permission from [46].

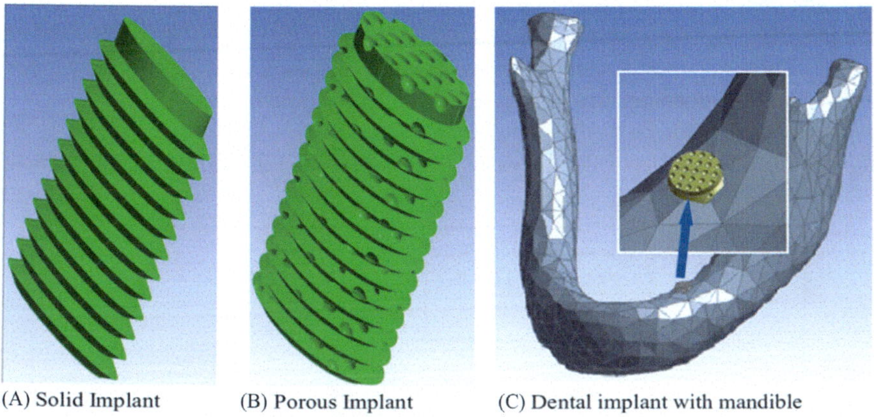


**Figure 12.21** 3D models used for the simulations using FEM (A) solid implant, (B) porous implant, and (C) dental implant with mandible.
Reprinted with permission from [46].

mesh with solid 187 elements in ANSYS workbench (Fig. 12.21C). The set of data about a natural molar tooth is compared with the reported interfacial stress and strain.

It is considered that the materials used in the analysis, for both the implant and the mandible, have linear elastic properties. Aspects such as bone resorption following tooth extraction are included while examining five different types of bone disorders. Eighty-nine (89) sets of CT scan data are collected and analyzed using MIMICS software in order to calculate Young's modulus, which is dependent on Hounsfield Units (HUs). A variance of approximately 22% in Young's modulus is observed on either side of the mean value, corresponding to typical bone density variations. An individual with an average bone density that is close to the mean is considered normal; instances, where the bone density is 10% or 20% greater than normal, are referred to as strong and very strong, respectively; instances where the bone density is 10% or 20% lower than normal are referred to as weak and very weak. Mandibles are said to have the following bone states: very strong, strong, normal, weak, and extremely weak. As each pixel in the CT scan image slice data has a known value for its Young's modulus (HU unit), the Young's modulus of each pixel point in the CT image data may be calculated.

The average Young's modulus for all the cancellous bone pixels in the very strong bone is found to be 4.369 GPa. Image processing tools, like MIMICS, provide immediate access to these data. Accordingly, for strong bone, normal bone, weak bone, and severely weak bone, respectively, the average Young's modulus is considered to be 3.745, 3.121, 2.497, and 1.872 GPa. The mandibular upper part is assumed to be fixed in all five cases to mimic real-world clinical scenarios. Moreover, a continuous bond is used to mimic the interface between the implant and the bone, and the contact element is employed in completely bonded circumstances. Without any relative motion at the interface, this suggests perfect osseointegration. Stated differently, all prosthesis material contacts exhibit a fixed and identical type of connection, indicating that the implant is firmly established in the bone. We observed the interface stress and strain on the dental implant with the appropriate limitations and an average biting force of 120 N. The interface stress and strain were also contrasted with the molar tooth's natural analysis. These parameters were taken into consideration for a total of 180 FE analyses. Here, ANN GA modeling was conducted using the analysis results.

As previously indicated, the microstrain output of the ANN model is converted into a unitless desirability value between 0 and 1, as shown in Fig. 12.22. The value is

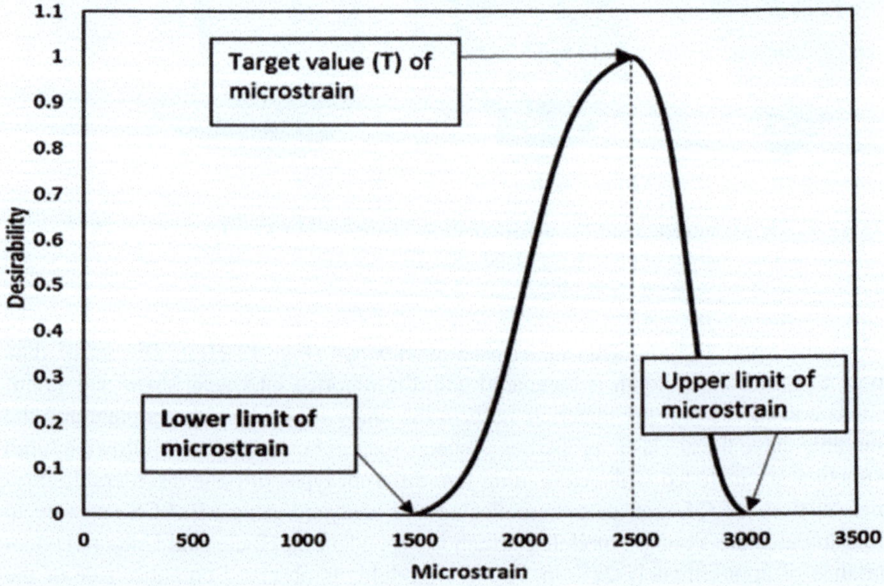


**Figure 12.22** Desirability function used for generating the desirability value of the microstrain at the bone-implant interface, as per the user defined desirability.
Reprinted with permission from [46].

0 for microstrain ≤1500 and ≥3000, and it is 1 for microstrain 2500. The objective function for the GA optimization is subsequently this ANN-desirability combined. For all the optimization tests presented in this work, crossover probability 0.95 and mutation probability 0.01 are utilized. Here, as previously stated, the goal of GA-based maximize is to identify the porosity and implant dimension combination that will provide the desired microstrain as near to 1. Fig. 12.23 displays the greatest desirability value attained through GA-based optimization under various bone circumstances. The plot shows that, for low bone quality, the desirability values are practically 1, up to a value of 2.75. This indicates that, under these circumstances, the microstrain approaches 2500, satisfying the constraint.

However, desirability ratings dramatically decline with increasing bone quality, that is, at 3. This means that even while the microstrain values that were obtained satisfied the restriction and fell within 1500 and 3000, they did not come close to the intended microstrain of 2500. With better bone quality, there is a significant decrease in microstrain at the implant-bone interface. The top fifteen ideal values for each category of bone quality, ranging from 2 to 4, are considered for further research. For the top 15 values of microstrain/desirability, Fig. 12.24 displays the variance in porosity and dimensions in various bone qualities. The 15 values' average, as well as their greatest and lowest values, are displayed in every instance.

The fluctuation of average porosity with bone quality in Fig. 12.24A illustrates that higher porosity is preferred with improved bone quality until it approaches a plateau at a bone quality of 2.75. Better bone quality results in narrower ranges, but worse bone quality results in significant variability in the solutions, suggesting that multiple porosity values could be used to get the high desired value microstrain. For different bone qualities, the average desired implant diameter variation is not that substantial; nevertheless, for lower bone quality, the ranges are once again large (Fig. 12.24B). As bone quality increases, the average value for the implant's length (Fig. 12.24C) often rises as well, plateauing at bone quality 3. The porosity scenario illustrated in Fig. 12.24A bears some resemblance to this pattern. The spectrum of options is

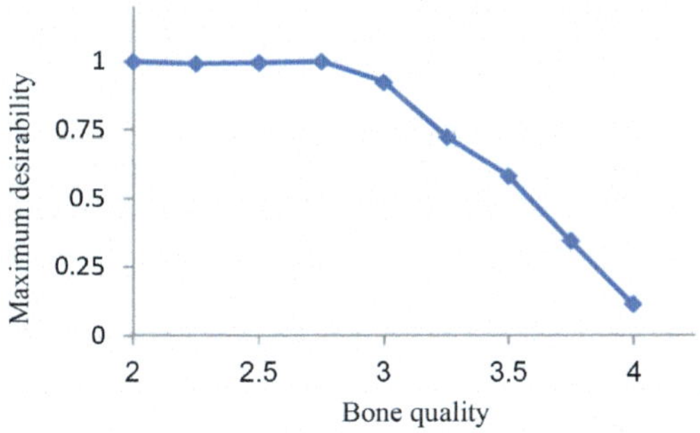


**Figure 12.23** The maximum desirability achieved using GA-based optimization using the ANN surrogate model at different bone conditions. *GA*, Genetic algorithms.
Reprinted with permission from [46].

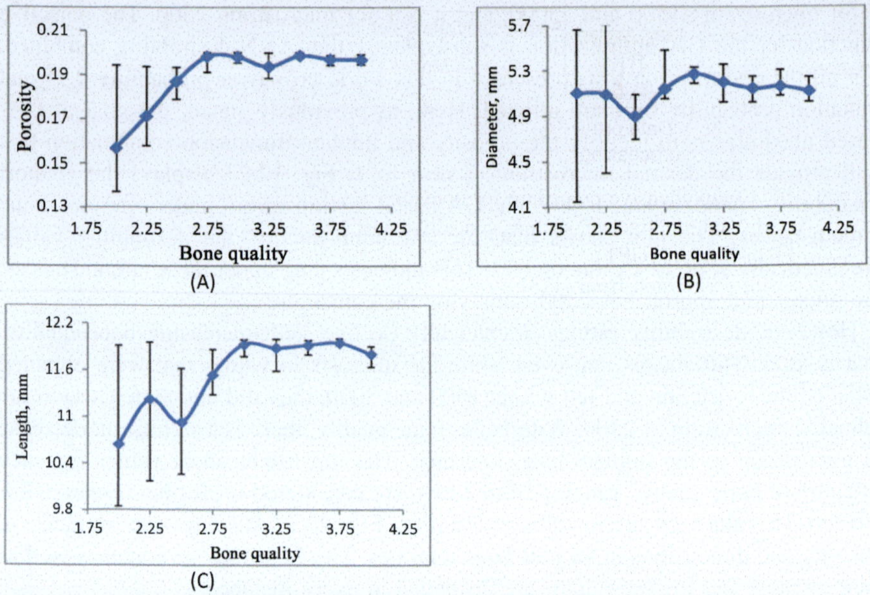


**Figure 12.24** The optimum values of the design variables (A) porosity, (B) diameter, and (C) length of the bone implant at different bone conditions, as found from the GA-based optimization of desirability of microstrain. GA, Genetic algorithms.
Reprinted with permission from [46].

likewise wide here for weaker bones. It appears that there are more design alternatives available for bones with lower porosity and size than for those with higher quality. When we contrast this result with that of Fig. 12.24, it becomes evident that microstrain may be obtained at lower bone quality levels, and that there are more ways to get that microstrain. Microstrain can be achieved very near to the desired value. However, the possibilities are limited and the microstrain values obtained are not close to the ideal value of 2500 in the case of superior bone quality.

So, it can be concluded that the dental implants can be designed using GA to produce the required implant stress and microstrain. An ANN-based surrogate model is found to be an effective way to translate the FEA results, and it can serve as the optimization process's objective function with less computing overhead. The hybridization of the ANN model with the intended function allows for the identification of the best solution within a reasonable range in the complex paradigm of dental implant design. It is noteworthy to observe that as bone quality improved, the ideal microstrain value gradually deviated from the desired value. An implant development guideline tailored to each patient is the result of the evolved optimal solutions. The range of the outcome is well within allowable bounds, according to the FEA-based validation of the best solutions.

## 12.5 Conclusions

According to a review of the published literature, even though many researchers have effectively used ANN, FL, and GA in a significant number of published works, the work's full potential has not yet been realized in the modeling and optimization of biomaterial properties. This is similar to other materials science and engineering domains. There has been a shift in materials scientists' preference for experimental work. Scientists are realizing more and more how cost- and time-effective it is to apply computational tools before tests. It is difficult to build a database that is appropriate for applying advanced ML techniques like ANNs because this is a relatively tiny field of study, necessitating complex experiments more frequently. In the realm of biomedical engineering, the volume requirement for novel materials is rather low when compared to other domains. Under current circumstances, the industry is not enough promoting the creation of newer and better materials. With increasing numbers of academics using CI techniques to find new materials, a better future becomes more possible. Regarding biomaterials, we will observe comparable trends in the coming days. Customized biomaterials are required because the properties of the materials used to create scaffolds and prostheses have to match exacting requirements for every particular application. Still, each individual has different requirements. When building material with a strict combination of qualities and a lower tolerance, there is greater relevance for applications of CI tools in this type of situation than materials used in other engineering applications. In these designs, constraints related to biocompatibility also need to be properly taken into account.

Polymer-based implants, or polymer composite implants, are being explored as potential replacements for metal or ceramic prostheses in many applications. Reductions in cost and density as well as increased biocompatibility are some of the expected advantages. It is difficult to achieve anisotropy in certain implants made of metals or ceramics. Nonetheless, the requirements can be satisfied by building continuous fiber-reinforced composites. Biomaterials built on an informatics basis can successfully meet all of these requirements with the appropriate use of CI approaches.

## Acknowledgment

To the best of the Editors' knowledge and authors' claims, no generative AI tools were used for substantive writing of chapters. Any AI-assisted language editing, if applied, was limited to grammar or style suggestions and did not alter the scientific content.

## References

[1] Olson GB. Designing a new material world. Science 2000;288(5468):993–8. https://doi.org/10.1126/science.288.5468.993.

[2] Pablo JJ, de, Jones B, Kovacs CL, Ozolins V, Ramirez AP. The Materials Genome Initiative, the interplay of experiment, theory and computation. Current Opinion in Solid

State and Materials Science 2014;18(2):99–117. https://doi.org/10.1016/j.cossms.2014.02.003.
[3] Homsy CA. Bio Compatibility in selection of materials for implantation. Journal of Biomedical Materials Research 1970;4(3):341–56.
[4] Sáenz A, Rivera E, Brostow W, Castaño VM. Ceramic biomaterials: an introductory overview. Journal of Materials Education 1999;21(5/6):267–76.
[5] Datta S, Chattopadhyay PP. Soft computing techniques in advancement of structural metals. International Materials Reviews 2013;58(8):475–504. https://doi.org/10.1179/1743280413Y.0000000021.
[6] de Pablo JJ, Jackson NE, Webb MA, Chen L-Q, Moore JE, Morgan D, et al. New frontiers for the materials genome initiative. npj Computational Materials 2019;5(1):41.
[7] Baudic G, Auger A, Ramiro V, Lochin E. Using emulation to validate applications on opportunistic networks. Advances in delay-tolerant networks (DTNs). Woodhead Publishing; 2021. p. 273–80.
[8] Papoulias SA, Grossmann IE. A structural optimization approach in process synthesis—I: utility systems. Computers & Chemical Engineering 1983;7(6):695–706.
[9] Zhang Q, Grossmann IE, Sundaramoorthy A, Pinto JM. Data- driven construction of Convex Region Surrogate models. Optimization and Engineering 2016;17:289–332.
[10] Akbari V, Tohid Nejad Ghaffar Borhani RA, Mohd Kamaruddin Abd Hamid AS, Mohamed AH. Evaluation of hydrodynamic behavior of the perforated gas distributor of industrial gas phase polymerization reactor using CFD-PBM coupled model. Computers & Chemical Engineering 2015;82:344–61.
[11] Keßler T, Christian K, Kevin MB, Nick M, Dennis M, Kai S, et al. Global optimization of distillation columns using explicit and implicit surrogate models. Chemical Engineering Science 2019;197:235–45.
[12] Mistry M, Letsios D, Krennrich G, Lee RM, Misener R. Mixed-integer convex nonlinear optimization with gradient-boosted trees embedded. INFORMS Journal on Computing 2021;33(3):1103–19.
[13] Grimstad B, Andersson H. ReLU networks as surrogate models in mixed-integer linear programs. Computers & Chemical Engineering 2019;131:106580.
[14] Schweidtmann AM, Mitsos A. Deterministic global optimization with artificial neural networks embedded. Journal of Optimization Theory and Applications 2019;180(3):925–48.
[15] Rao SS. Engineering optimization: theory and practice. John Wiley & Sons; 2019.
[16] Bhadeshia HKDH. Mathematical models in materials science. Materials Science and Technology 2008;24(2):128–36. https://doi.org/10.1179/174328407X213107.
[17] Olson GB. Computational design of hierarchically structured materials. Science 1997;277(5330):1237–42. https://doi.org/10.1126/science.277.5330.1237.
[18] Bozzolo G, Noebe RD, Abel PB, Vij DR. Applied computational materials modeling. Theory, simulation and experiment. NY: Springer New York; 2007.
[19] Raabe D. Computational materials science: the simulation of materials and microstructures and properties. Wiley-VCH; 1998.
[20] Yi Wang W, Li J, Liu W, Liu Z-K. Integrated computational materials engineering for advanced materials: A brief review. Computational Materials Science 2019;158:42–8. https://doi.org/10.1016/j.commatsci.2018.11.001.
[21] Doghri I, Lemoine G, Martiny P, Mathieu S, Wucher B, Adam L. Multiscaling-based integrated computational materials engineering: from academia to industry. International Journal for Multiscale Computational Engineering 2021;19(4):1–40. https://doi.org/10.1615/IntJMultCompEng.2021040073.

[22] Vinoth A, Datta S. Computational intelligence-based design of biomaterials. Computer Methods in Materials Science 2022;22(4):229–62.

[23] Kalidindi SR, De Graef M. Materials data science: current status and future outlook. Annual Review of Materials Research 2015;45:171–93. https://doi.org/10.1146/annurev-matsci-070214-020844.

[24] Mueller T, Kusne AG, Ramprasad R. Machine learning in materials science: recent progress and emerging applications. Reviews in Computational Chemistry 2016;29:186–273. https://doi.org/10.1002/9781119148739.

[25] Banerjee A, Bandyopadhyay T, Acharya P. Data analytics: hyped up aspirations or true potential? Vikalpa 2013;38:1–11.

[26] Datta S, Roy S, Davim JP. Optimization techniques: an overview, optimization in industry. Management and industrial engineering. Springer publications; 2019. p. 1–11.

[27] Deb K. Optimization for engineering design: algorithms and examples. Prentice Hall of India; 1995.

[28] Deb K. Multi-objective optimization using evolutionary algorithms. John Wiley & Sons; 2001.

[29] Booker L. Improving search in genetic algorithms. In: Davis In. L, editor. Genetic algorithms and simulated annealing. Morgan Kaufmann Publishers; 1987. p. 61–73.

[30] Deb K, Pratap A, Agarwal S, Meyarivan T. A fast and elitist multiobjective genetic algorithm: NSGA-II. IEEE Transactions on Evolutionary Computation 2002;6(2):182–96. https://doi.org/10.1109/4235.996017.

[31] Kurt HI, Oduncuoglu M. Application of a neural network model for prediction of wear properties of ultrahigh molecular weight polyethylene composites. International Journal of Polymer Science 2015;2015:1–11. https://doi.org/10.1155/2015/315710.

[32] Mukherjee M, Singh SB. Artificial neural network: some applications in physical metallurgy of steels. Materials and Manufacturing Processes 2009;24(2):198–208. https://doi.org/10.1080/10426910802612304.

[33] Anderson JA. An introduction to neural networks. A Bradford Book, MIT Press. 1995.

[34] Ganguly S, Patra A, Chattopadhyay PP, Datta S. New training strategies for neural networks with application to quaternary Al-Mg-Sc-Cr alloy design problems. Applied Soft Computing Journal 2016;46:260–6. https://doi.org/10.1016/j.asoc.2016.05.017.

[35] Mandal S, Sivaprasad PV, Venugopal S, Murthy KPN. Artificial neural network modeling to evaluate and predict the deformation behavior of stainless steel type AISI 304L during hot torsion. Applied Soft Computing 2009;9(1):237–44. https://doi.org/10.1016/j.asoc.2008.03.016.

[36] Arulraj V, Datta S, Davim JP. Natural computing-based designing of hybrid UHMWPE composites for orthopedic implants. Applied Sciences 2022;12:10408. https://doi.org/10.3390/app1220104.

[37] Prajapati DK, Tiwari M. Use of artificial neural network (ANN) to determining surface parameters, friction and wear during pin-on-disc tribotesting. Key Engineering Materials 2017;739:87–95. https://doi.org/10.4028/www.scientific.net/kem.739.87.

[38] Ding F, Chen T. Gradient based iterative algorithms for solving a class of matrix equations. IEEE Transactions on Automatic Control 2005;50(8):1216–21. https://doi.org/10.1109/TAC.2005.852558.

[39] Datta S, Banerjee MK. Mapping the input–output relationship in HSLA steels through expert neural network. Materials Science and Engineering: A 2006;420(1–2):254–64. https://doi.org/10.1016/j.msea.2006.01.037.

[40] Zadeh LA. Fuzzy sets. Information and Control 1965;8(3):338–53. https://doi.org/10.1016/S0019-9958(65)90241-X.

[41] Zadeh LA. Fuzzy logic. Computer 1988;21(4):83–93. https://doi.org/10.1109/2.53.
[42] Mamdani. Application of fuzzy logic to approximate reasoning using linguistic synthesis. IEEE Transactions on Computers, C 1977;26(12):1182–91. https://doi.org/10.1109/TC.1977.1674779.
[43] Sugeno M. Industrial applications of fuzzy control. Elsevier Science; 1985.
[44] Datta S, Mahfouf M, Zhang Q, Chattopadhyay PP, Sultana N. Imprecise knowledge based design and development of titanium alloys for prosthetic applications. Journal of the Mechanical Behavior of Biomedical Materials 2016;53:350–65. https://doi.org/10.1016/j.jmbbm.2015.08.039.
[45] Vinoth A, Dey S, Datta S. Designing UHMWPE hybrid composites using machine learning and metaheuristic algorithms. Composite Structures 2021;267:113898.
[46] Roy S, Dey S, Khutia N, Roy Chowdhury A, Datta S. Design of patient specific dental implant using FE analysis and computational intelligence techniques. Applied Soft Computing 2018;65:272–9.

# Biomaterials education through artificial intelligence-enabled product-based learning

13

*Ronald Marquez*[1,2], *Mariangeles Salas*[1], *Nelson Barrios*[1], *Laura Tolosa*[3], *Lokendra Pal*[1], *and Raine Viitala*[4]
[1]Department of Forest Biomaterials, North Carolina State University, Raleigh, NC, United States, [2]LEPAMAP-PRODIS Research group, University of Girona, C/Maria Aurèlia Capmany, Girona, Spain, [3]School of Chemical Engineering, University of Los Andes, Merida, Venezuela, [4]Department of Mechanical Engineering, School of Engineering, Aalto University, Aalto, Finland

## 13.1 Introduction

In 2019 global greenhouse gas (GHG) emissions reached 54 $GtCO_2$ equivalent annually, highlighting the significant environmental impact of human activities across various sectors [1]. Electricity, heat production, and transportation were responsible for 39% of these emissions, with industrial energy use contributing 21%, agriculture 24%, and other sectors making up the remaining 16% [2]. To address the challenge of global anthropogenic climate change, countries must transition to biomaterials to move away from linear economy and increase sustainability awareness while integrate their recycling systems into a more sustainable economic development model. One way to achieve this relies on the education of current and next generations to embrace the principles of the circular economy, which seeks to reduce waste and pollution while promoting economic development through the use of renewable resources [3]. The concept of the circular economy has received growing attention within academic and broader communities, recognized for its potential to significantly improve resource efficiency [4–6]. Its core objectives include fostering socio-economic development in harmony with ecological principles, redistributing resources to meet the needs of each economic agent, and breaking the link between resource consumption and quality of life improvements [7,8]. The circular economy encourages the design of products and systems for repair, reuse, recycle, or upcycle by promoting the sustainable use of resources [9,10]. In chemical engineering programs, there has been a shift toward utilizing renewable raw materials to foster sustainable and environmentally friendly resource use. As a response to this shift, the biorefinery concept has emerged, aiming to generate multiple products from renewable feedstocks and optimize biological resource use by transforming all input materials into valuable products [11].

The international community has begun to reassess the traditional "resources-products-waste" linear model, recognizing the circular economy as a systemic solution for enhancing resource efficiency [6,12]. Systematic innovation and adaptation are required across full

**Artificial Intelligence in Biomaterials Design and Development. DOI:** https://doi.org/10.1016/B978-0-323-95464-8.00018-9

supply chain from all stakeholders, including companies, policymakers, and educational institutions, to implement a circular economy framework [13,14]. Further, higher education institutions are crucial in implementing the United Nations' Sustainable Development Goals of the 2030 Agenda through basic and applied research, technological innovation, businesses, education, student training initiatives, and campus governance [15,16].

Biobased materials, offering advantages over fossil-based counterparts, are renewable and produce lower GHG emissions, often through carbon-neutral processes [17,18]. They also have the ability to sequester carbon during their lifecycle and stimulate economic growth in rural areas rich in renewable resources [19,20]. Consequently, biobased materials hold the potential to create new economic opportunities and stimulate economic growth in rural areas where renewable resources are abundant [21,22]. However, challenges to transitioning to a circular bioeconomy and the widespread use of biobased materials remain, including the need for infrastructure and technology, research and development investment, and new processes and technologies for large-scale production, while addressing sustainability and environmental impact concerns [23,24]. For instance, the production of certain biobased materials can negatively impact ecosystems or use land that could otherwise be used for food production [25,26]. In the following sections, we will explore the evolution of biorefineries, educational theories, and their connection to PBL strategies and artificial intelligence (AI). These elements are presented as tools to facilitate the transformation of traditional materials in Chemical Engineering courses into courses focused on biobased materials. To comprehend the shift toward incorporating biobased products within Materials in Chemical Engineering (ChE) courses, it is noteworthy that several leading universities globally have started to integrate circular bioeconomy principles into their curriculum at various levels (Table 13.1).

### 13.1.1 The evolution and significance of biorefineries within the chemical industry

The emergence of biorefineries is a response to the imperative for environmentally friendly industrial processes, aiming to harmonize economic growth with sustainable development [28,29]. These facilities process biomass to generate a diverse array of biobased products and energy, presenting a renewable alternative to traditional fossil fuel-dependent industries. Among these processes, the production of pulp, paper, and fibers from wood and agricultural residues can be mentioned [30,31], as well as the manufacturing of value-added biomaterials, which will be the focus of this chapter.

The concept of biorefineries has evolved from initial efforts to utilize biomass for energy and material production [32,33]. This notion received increased attention toward the end of the 20th century, driven by rising concerns over the depletion of fossil fuels and the impact of climate change. By the early 21st century, the scope of biorefineries had expanded beyond biofuel production to include the creation of value-added chemicals and materials, with the aim of achieving zero waste through circular economy principles [34]. The development of integrated biorefineries, capable of converting various feedstocks into a wide range of products, signifies a notable advancement in this domain [35–37]. Biorefineries hold the potential to contribute to economic development while mitigating environmental impacts. They

**Table 13.1** Examples of new educational programs focused on the circular bioeconomy in some of the top universities in the world [27].

| Country | University | School | Program | Contents | Web |
|---|---|---|---|---|---|
| *USA* | University of California Berkeley | School of Chemistry | Undergraduate school | Includes advanced concepts in bioprocessing, preparing students for careers in industries such as biopharmaceuticals, industrial biotechnology, and food technology | 1 |
| | MIT | School of Chemical Engineering | Graduate school | Research on converting carbon dioxide emissions into valuable chemicals or fuels | 2 |
| | California Institute of Technology | Resnick Sustainability Institute | Graduate school | Systems to create more affordable materials using sunlight in an experimental approach to create "solar fuels" | 3 |
| *Switzerland* | ETH Zurich | Department of Chemistry and Applied Biosciences | Graduate school | Control and recycling of plastic polymers | 4 |
| | ETH Zurich | Department of Mechanical and Process Engineering | Undergraduate school | Second-generation biofuels in hands-on classrooms | 5 |
| *Netherlands* | Eindhoven University of Technology | Department of Chemical Engineering and Chemistry | Graduate school | Biobased polymers. Conversion of $CO_2$ to useful chemical products | 6 |
| | Delft University of Technology | Online course | Biobased products | Covers topics such as biopolymers, bioenergy, bioflavors, and biosurfactants | 7 |
| *Australia* | Monash University | School of Chemistry | Graduate school | Development of muconic acids as starting materials for synthesizing value-added products | 8 |
| *Korea* | Korea Advanced Institute of Science & Technology | Department of chemical and biomolecular engineering | Graduate school | Manipulation of microbial metabolic pathways to produce sustainable and environmentally friendly chemicals | 9 |
| | Seoul National University | College of Chemical Engineering | Graduate school | Chemical convergence for energy and environment | 10 |
| *Japan* | University of Tokyo | Department of Biomaterials Chemistry | Research group | Biomaterials teaching through lectures in biochemistry, organic chemistry, and polymer science | 11 |
| *United Kingdom* | Imperial College London | Department of Chemistry | Research group | Developing and translating molecular tools and techniques for the application of green technologies | 12 |
| | University of Cambridge | EPSRC CDT | Research group | | 13 |

(*Continued*)

**Table 13.1** (Continued)

| Country | University | School | Program | Contents | Web |
|---|---|---|---|---|---|
| | | | | Hands-on teaching workshops that focus on learning how to quantify carbon emissions through carbon footprint tools in collaboration with companies | |
| *Singapore* | Nanyang Technological University | Center for Sustainable Materials | Research group | Uses biotechnology to produce biodegradable materials for efficient urban agriculture and environmental toxicology | 14 |
| *Chinese universities and European Institutions* | | MIX-UP project | Research group | Integrating biobased circular economy through teaching-experiment-based research | 15 |
| *Canada* | University of York | Graduate School | Research group | Utilization of unavoidable food waste in laboratory teaching and practice. Biobased Industry consortium fund to support the development of sustainable biobased solvents | 16 |

[1] https://chemistry.berkeley.edu/news/one-kind-course-aims-build-bioeconomy-workforce.
[2] https://news.mit.edu/2022/turning-carbon-dioxide-valuable-products-0907.
[3] https://eng.snu.ac.kr/node/9327.
[4] https://chab.ethz.ch/en/news-and-events/d-chab-news/2022/12/a-recipe-for-constructing-and-recycling-plastics.htm.
[5] https://ltr.ethz.ch/en/research/green_chemistry.html.
[6] https://research.tue.nl/en/organisations/technology-innovation-society.
[7] https://online-learning.tudelft.nl/courses/biobased-products-for-a-sustainable-bio-economy/.
[8] https://research.monash.edu/en/organisations/school-of-chemistry.
[9] https://personal.ntu.edu.sg/ali.miserez/.
[10] https://cbe.kaist.ac.kr/boards/view/news/672.
[11] http://www.fp.a.u-tokyo.ac.jp/cbm/detail.html.
[12] https://www.imperial.ac.uk/chemistry/research/research-themes/environmental-and-green-chemistry/.
[13] https://cdt.sensors.cam.ac.uk/news/new-sensors-cdt-workshop-looking-how-reduce-environmental-footprint-research.
[14] https://web.mse.ntu.edu.sg/susmat/#home-section.
[15] https://www.mix-up.eu/partner.
[16] https://www.york.ac.uk/chemistry/research/green/news/newsarchive/2017/atrioofgreensuccesses/.

facilitate enhanced energy security, reduced GHG emissions, and the promotion of rural development [38,39]. The production of biobased polymers, fibers, and composites from renewable sources further highlights the environmental and economic advantages of biorefineries, offering sustainable alternatives to materials derived from petrochemicals [40,41].

The influence of biorefineries on biomaterials science innovation, particularly in the context of pulp, paper, and fiber-based materials production, is significant. Since the early 20th century, fiber-based materials, such as pulp and paper, have evolved from simple machinery to complex energy-efficient operations, culminating in the modern biorefinery concept (Fig. 13.1). Advanced processing technologies have enabled the effective transformation of wood and agricultural residues into value-added materials, leading to innovations in packaging, paper, building materials, and textile industries [30,31,42,43]. The production of cellulose nanofibers and lignin-based products, such as films, nanoparticles, and 3D printing, among others, highlights the transformative potential of biorefineries in materials science [8,44,45], providing in some cases superior properties compared to synthetic materials in terms of strength, durability, reuse, recycling, and valorization [46–49].

As of 2024, the biorefinery sector has experienced considerable growth and diversification worldwide. The sector's market size was estimated at USD 150.4 billion in 2023 and is projected to expand to USD 268.3 billion by 2030, at a compound annual growth rate (CAGR) of 8.8% [50]. This expansion is driven by the adoption of advanced industrial biotechnology and thermochemical processing techniques, which are essential for converting biomass into various biofuels and biochemicals. The biorefinery industry growth is observed on a global scale, with significant contributions from the Americas, Asia-Pacific, and Europe (Table 13.2). Among the notable developments is the collaboration between Veolia and TotalEnergies on biomethane production [50].

The Americas are anticipated to dominate the market landscape, with significant investments and robust government support. Concurrently, the Asia-Pacific region, led by China and India, alongside Europe, with Germany, Sweden, and Finland leading, is making substantial contributions to the market's growth. This is partly due to the regions' commitment to environmental regulations and carbon emission reductions, which are amplifying investments in biorefinery technologies. Metsä Group, in collaboration with technology group ANDRITZ and Dow, is set to construct a demonstration plant for lignin bio-refining at its Äänekoski bioproduct mill, targeting a launch in late 2025 with a daily capacity of two tons [54].

Key players in this sector, including Renewable Energy Group Inc., Neste, Abengoa Bioenergy SA, ADM, POET Biorefining, USA Bioenergy, Valero Energy Corporation, and Honeywell International Inc., along with UPM, play critical roles in enhancing production capabilities and operational efficiencies of biorefineries. This aligns with global objectives for environmental preservation and carbon emission reduction [55].

### 13.1.2 Artificial intelligence and education

The educational landscape for biomaterials has undergone profound transformations, along with the evolution of materials science and the increasing focus on

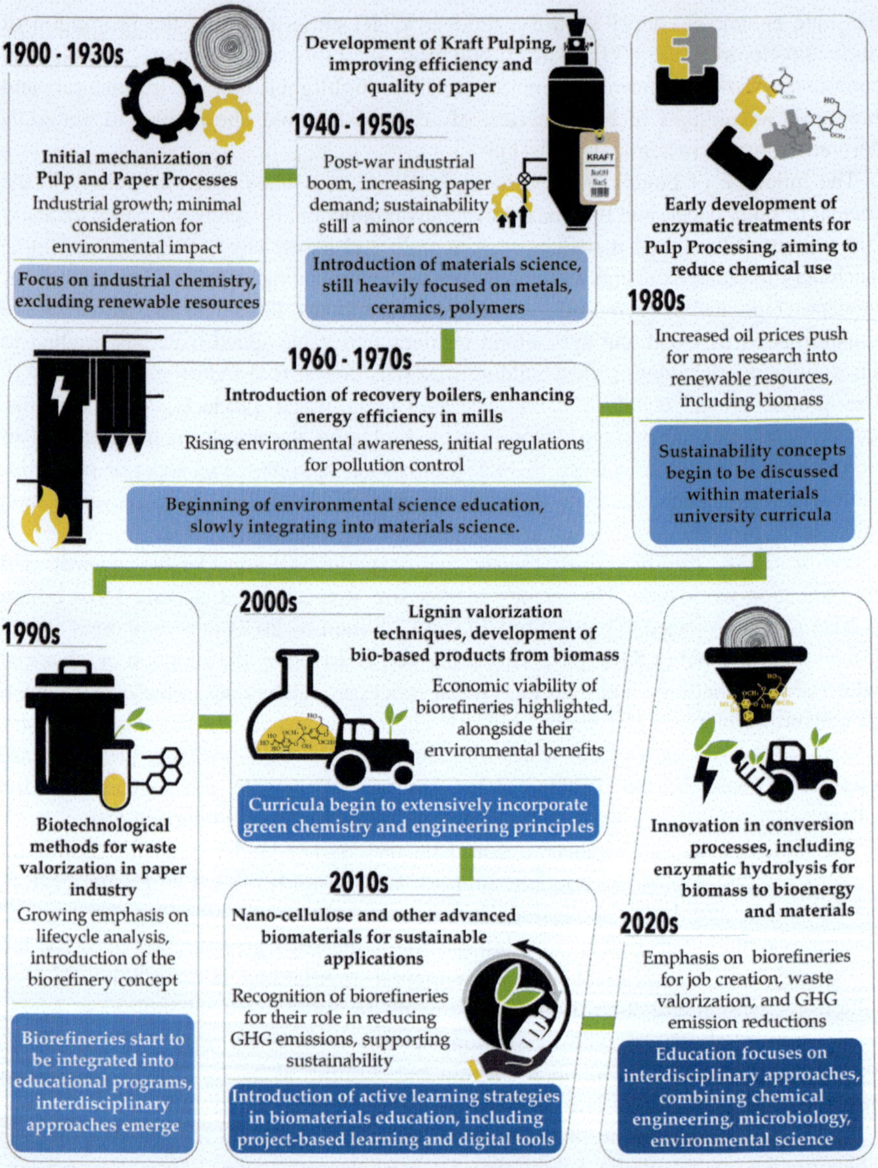


**Figure 13.1** Historical overview of biorefineries and fiber products from the pulp and paper industry.

sustainability. Historically, materials engineering education focused on traditional materials such as metals, ceramics, and polymers, with applications primarily within the medical and engineering fields. The curriculum was primarily structured around

**Table 13.2** Overview of recent biorefinery projects.

| Project location | Company/ consortium | Capacity and products | Investment and key dates | Additional information |
|---|---|---|---|---|
| Panama | SGP Bioenergy | 180,000 b/d; SAF, renewable diesel, etc. | Total: USD 7.7bn; Phase 1: USD 3.1bn; FID in Q4 2023, Phase 1 completion in Q1 2027 | Utilization of nonnarcotic industrial hemp oil and other fats; aims for zero-waste [51] |
| Malaysia | PETRONAS, Eni, Euglena | 12,500 b/d; SAF, HVO, bio-naphtha | Feasibility assessments ongoing, completion targeted by 2025 | Focused on nonfood chain raw materials; part of PETRONAS' biofuels space diversification [52] |
| Germany (Leuna) | UPM | 220,000 mt/year; wood-based biochemicals | Operational by end of 2023, ramp up in 2024 | Production of bio-monoethylene glycol, lignin-based renewable functional fillers, and other products from beechwood [53] |
| Austria (Schwechat) | OMV | 160,000 mt/year; SAF | SAF sales to increase to 700,000 mt/year by 2030 | Utilization of an innovative coprocessing method for converting liquid biomass into SAF [53] |

the properties, processing, and applications of these materials, with little emphasis on sustainability or renewable resources.

As the field of materials science expanded [34,56,57], so did the scope of education in biomaterials, incorporating broader principles of materials selection, design, and manufacturing [27,56,58]. This period witnessed the introduction of sustainability concepts into materials science curricula, emphasizing the development and use of renewable resources, life cycle analysis, smart manufacturing, and the principles of the circular economy [27,59]. The focus expanded to include biobased materials such as cellulose, lignin, and other biopolymers derived from biomass, aligning with the principles of green chemistry and sustainable engineering [12,60].

The concept of biorefineries introduced a new dimension to biomaterials education, necessitating a comprehensive understanding of the conversion of biomass into a wide array of materials and energy. Educational programs began to integrate courses on bioprocessing, bioenergy, and the valorization of waste streams, providing students with insights into the technological, economic, and environmental aspects of biorefineries. This interdisciplinary approach required the incorporation of principles from chemical engineering, material science and engineering, chemistry, biology, ecology, and environmental science into the biomaterials curriculum, which has evolved recently to the implementation of applied AI [27,34].

#### *13.1.2.1 Historical context of artificial intelligence related to education*

AI has become increasingly important in product research and development, capturing significant interest for its application in teaching chemical engineering, particularly concerning biobased and sustainable products [61]. This section offers an overview of AI's evolution, its current state, and capabilities, setting the stage for its role in educational frameworks.

AI, conceptualized as the simulation of human intelligence processes by machines, has its roots in the mid-20th century (Fig. 13.2) [62], starting with the first mathematical model for building a neural network by Warren McCulloch and Walter Pitts [63]. The foundational work of Alan Turing, which proposed the Turing Test as a criterion of intelligence, laid the foundational theories for AI [64]. The transformative phase of AI began in the 1980s when the interest in the connectionist or neural network approach resurges [65,66]. This model, inspired by the human brain's structure, uses vast networks of interconnected units to process data. The innovation of artificial neural networks marked this era, showcasing the ability to learn from and adapt to new data through backpropagation techniques [65,66].

The 1990s and 2000s witnessed significant progress in machine learning (ML) and natural language processing (NLP). This era saw the rise of ML algorithms trained on large datasets (big data), finding application in diverse fields such as image and speech recognition [65,67]. These developments have vast implications for education, from automating administrative tasks to enhancing student assessments. The advent of deep learning (DL) and neural networks in the 21st century generated a paradigm shift, enabling unprecedented capabilities in data analysis, pattern recognition, and

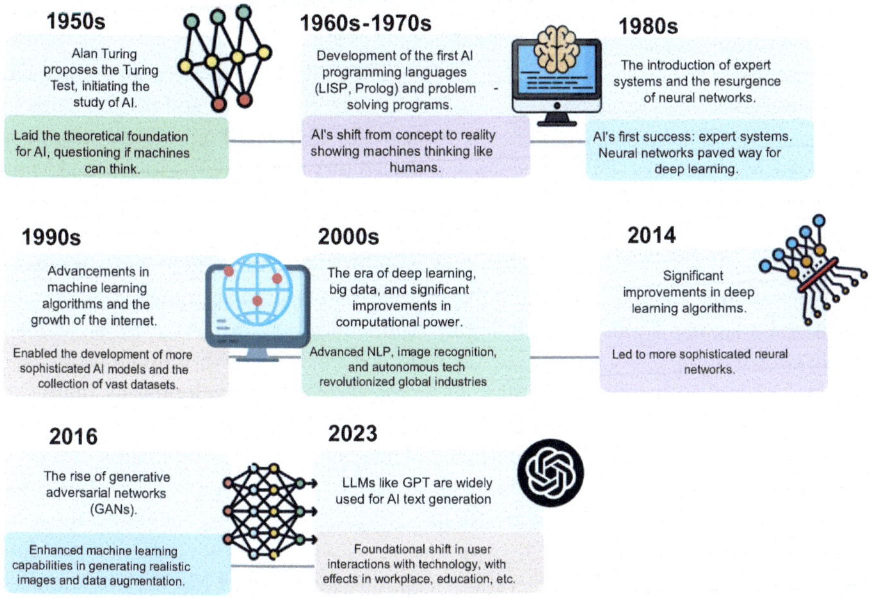


**Figure 13.2** Historical milestones in artificial intelligence and its impact on research and education.

autonomous decision-making [68,69]. Deep neural networks (DNNs), evolving from the foundational concepts of perceptrons and backpropagation, further pushed the boundaries of AI [68]. A notable advancement in this domain is generative adversarial networks (GANs) [70], which involve a competitive process between two networks. One network generates new data, while the other discerns generated data from real samples, enhancing the authenticity of AI-generated outputs.

In recent years, NLP technologies have advanced, enabling machines to comprehend and generate human-like text. The journey began before the 2010s, marked by Word2Vec [71], which was introduced by a team at Google in 2013 and was among the first technologies to use neural networks to understand word associations from large datasets. Shortly thereafter, the concept of sequence-to-sequence learning emerged, which was crucial for tasks like machine translation. In this approach, the model needs to understand an input sequence (a sentence in the source language) and produce an output sequence (the translated sentence in the target language).

The introduction of Transformers in 2017 was a key moment [72], leading to more efficient processing of language tasks. This had direct implications for educational tools, enabling faster and more accurate language translation services, summarization of academic papers, and the development of AI tutors that could understand and respond to student inquiries in natural language [73]. Following this advancement, the launch of generative pretrained transformers (GPT) models by OpenAI, particularly GPT-3.5 and its successor GPT-4, represents a leap forward in language processing. These models are trained on vast amounts of text, enabling them to perform complex tasks like language translation, answering queries, and creative writing with unprecedented proficiency [74].

Specifically, GPT is a type of Large Language Model (LLM) that uses a DL algorithm trained on a large amount of text data to learn patterns and relationships in language [74]. GPT models can generate human-like text based on a given prompt or context. LLMs, such as GPT-4, have been released by OpenAI [75]. Google and Meta have pursued their own directions in the development of LLMs and AI technologies. Google has introduced models like bidirectional encoder representations from transformers (BERT) [76] and text-to-text transfer transformer (T5) [77], focusing on understanding context and improving search results, among other applications. Google's Language Model for Dialogue Applications (LaMDA) [78] is another notable contribution, designed to generate more natural and conversational responses.

Meta AI has also been active in the AI research domain, developing its family of LLMs under projects such as Large Language Model by Meta AI (LLaMA) [79]. LLaMA is aimed at providing a more accessible and efficient foundation for NLP tasks, with an emphasis on enabling researchers and developers to push the boundaries of what is possible with AI in various applications, including those in educational and conversational AI. Incorporating advanced AI models, such as data analysis with Python, image generation technologies, and LLMs, holds immense potential for transforming educational settings. They can enhance students' interaction and visualization capabilities, significantly enriching the learning experience in PBL environments [27,75,80].

#### 13.1.2.2 Educational theories

The implementation of AI in the educational domain necessitates a reevaluation of pedagogical approaches and theoretical frameworks to optimize learning outcomes. AI not only enriches the learning experience on biomaterials but also aligns with contemporary educational theories that advocate for active and personalized learning environments. Constructivism indicates that learners construct their knowledge through experiences and interactions with their environment (Table 13.3).

AI-enhanced educational tools in biomaterials science facilitate such constructivist learning by offering simulated environments where learners can experiment, observe outcomes, and build understanding based on these experiences [81]. Connectivism extends this notion into the digital age, asserting that learning occurs across a network of connections facilitated by technology. AI serves as a bridge in connectivism settings, enabling learners to access, filter, and apply knowledge from diverse sources, thereby fostering a deeper understanding of complex concepts in biomaterials and biorefinery processes [82].

#### 13.1.2.3 Product-based learning pedagogical approaches

The development of teaching and learning theories has significantly evolved since the mid-twentieth century, with notable contributions from psychologists such as Jean Piaget, Ivan Pavlov, and John B. Watson. These pioneers laid the groundwork for various educational theories and models that still shape contemporary practices [88–90].

**Table 13.3** Educational theories and their implementation coupled with AI.

| Era | Theory | Application in AI-Assisted Learning | Impact | References |
|---|---|---|---|---|
| 1950s–1960s (Origins) | Constructivism | Early cognitive tools replicating problem-solving scenarios | Laid groundwork for experiential learning through simulation, promoting active engagement | [81] |
| 2000s (Digital Age) | Connectivism | Introduction of internet-based learning platforms | Marked a shift to learning through digital networks, enhancing access to and integration of knowledge | [82] |
| 2010s | Constructivism | Development of sophisticated simulations and virtual labs in biomaterials education | Allowed students to experiment and observe outcomes in a controlled, virtual environment | [83–85] |
| Late 2010s–Present | Connectivism | Use of AI to curate and filter relevant educational content from vast online resources | Facilitated personalized and contextual learning experiences, bridging knowledge gaps efficiently | [62,86] |
| 2020s | Both theories | Integration of AI in creating adaptive learning environments and collaborative platforms | Merged constructivist and connectivism principles, offering dynamic, interactive, and networked learning experiences | [87] |

The 1960s marked the emergence of instructional psychology as a separate field, influenced by the work of Robert Gagné, Leslie Briggs, and Jerome Bruner. This period introduced a comprehensive educational theory that aimed to integrate diverse teaching strategies with the complex nature of human learning. A key aspect of this approach was the view of learning as an active process, highlighting the vital role of student participation and interaction in the educational process [91,92]. Subsequent decades witnessed the introduction of additional theories and models, building upon and refining the earlier contributions. Notably, the development of group theory examined the impact of human interaction on creating meaningful learning experiences, emphasizing the significance of collaboration and social learning within the educational context [93,94].

Traditionally, materials engineering courses employed a transmission teaching model, characterized by a one-way flow of information from instructor to student, without the inclusion of practical, hands-on activities. However, recent trends have signaled a shift toward project and product-based learning (PBL), alongside other forms of experiential learning (Table 13.4) [99]. This transition reflects a growing consensus on the limitations of conventional classroom teaching methods in actively engaging students and equipping them with the requisite knowledge and skills for the dynamic demands of the modern workplace [100,101].

The integration of PBL and experiential learning methodologies within a biobased materials curriculum addresses these challenges by promoting critical thinking and problem-solving skills. Furthermore, it facilitates the development of essential competencies such as teamwork and effective communication, pivotal in driving research and product development toward a sustainable economy [99,102,103]. This approach aligns with the aspirations of newer generations inclined toward the adoption of renewable materials and resource conservation [17,18].

A notable implementation of a product-based educational model is the RAIS strategy, introduced at the Chemical Engineering School of Universidad de Los Andes [104]. RAIS fosters comprehensive knowledge management, transitioning from traditional teaching methods to a learning process characterized by the active information sourcing from digital and physical resources and the development of a product-oriented start-up-like classroom. The strategy encapsulates learning through construction and discovery, cooperative learning, project-based learning, and simulating an entrepreneurial environment within the classroom. RAIS aims to cultivate individuals with an entrepreneurial mindset and ethical consciousness, essential for thriving in interdisciplinary teams and contributing to collective creativity [99,105,106]. Such educational approaches are instrumental in preparing students for the demands and opportunities of the circular bioeconomy [58,107,108]. The integration of digital tools and resources has further enriched the educational experience, enabling access to a wider range of materials and facilitating collaboration across disciplines [27,109].

As the world's population is projected to reach at least 9 billion by 2050, industrial systems and economies must undergo a radical reevaluation to decouple economic development from the consumption of finite resources [9]. Education has the potential to effectively combine technology and social consciousness with the input of implicit and explicit knowledge and innovation [110]. Incorporating a circular bioeconomy framework into Chemical Engineering courses is a step toward meeting such a

**Table 13.4** Historical developments that have led to product-based learning application.

| Year | Methods | Description | Importance | References |
|---|---|---|---|---|
| Early 1900s | Introduction of project method | Initiated by John Dewey's educational reform, emphasizing learning through doing | Laid the foundational principles of PBL, promoting active engagement and practical knowledge acquisition | [95] |
| 1960s–1970s | Formalization of PBL in medical education | PBL becomes a core teaching method in medical schools, starting with McMaster University in Canada | Marked a significant shift in higher education toward problem-solving and critical thinking skills | [96] |
| 1980s–1990s | Expansion of PBL across disciplines | Adoption of PBL in engineering, business, and other fields | Demonstrated the versatility of PBL, enhancing interdisciplinary learning and collaboration | [97] |
| Early 2000s | Integration of digital tools in PBL | Introduction of computer-based simulations and virtual labs in PBL curricula | Facilitated a more interactive and immersive learning experience, utilizing technology for education | [98] |
| 2020s | AI-enhanced PBL in education | Incorporation of AI tools for personalized learning paths and simulation-based learning in PBL | Significantly enriched PBL with adaptive learning technologies, promoting individualized education | [27] |

challenge [111]. There is a limited number of reviews on the education of sustainable materials applications, with only a few researchers proposing a perspective on this issue, and most of them focusing on sustainability teaching [5,112]. Further research and analysis are required in this area to gain a more comprehensive understanding of the role of education in promoting a circular bioeconomy model.

### 13.1.3 Literature review

A literature review was performed, involving a comprehensive search in Dimensions and Scopus databases [113]. The search focused on the keywords "biobased" + "engineering" + "materials," resulting in 275 peer-reviewed journal articles from 2011 to 2023. The VoSviewer's text analytics software was used to obtain a visual mapping of bibliographic data, showing the major engineering innovation centers within the circular bioeconomy (Fig. 13.3). The analysis identified four primary research clusters, with the United States, China, Canada, and India leading. Notably, the collaboration between the European Union and China (red cluster) and between Canada and the "boreal alliance" countries (Finland and Sweden, blue cluster) highlights the international scope of these efforts. The geographical proximity between Canada and the United States accounts for the strong linkage depicted in the visual representation.

Table 13.5 lists the websites of top-tier undergraduate and graduate programs that focus on the circular bioeconomy, as identified through bibliographic analysis. These programs are aligned with the research clusters and countries highlighted in Fig. 13.3, underscoring the global academic commitment to integrating circular bioeconomy principles into engineering education.

### 13.1.4 Structure of the chapter

This chapter is organized into four main sections, focusing on the transition to biomaterials in materials science courses and the significant impact of AI in

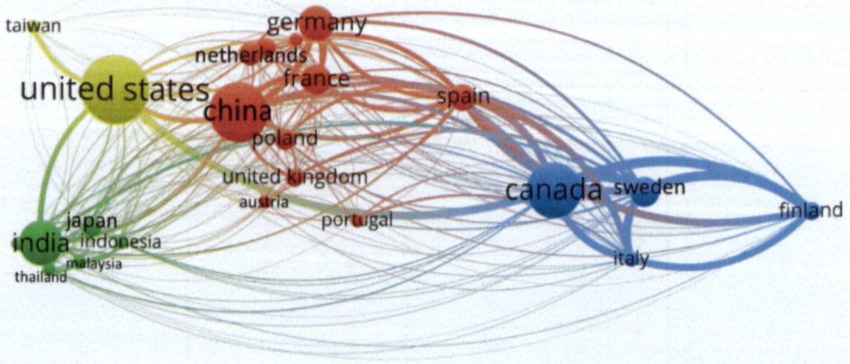


**Figure 13.3** Main countries in which the major engineering innovation centers within the circular bioeconomy have been established.

**Table 13.5** Examples of undergraduate and graduate programs which include circular bioeconomy principles, according to the analysis of bibliographical data.

| Country | University | Website |
|---|---|---|
| *United States* | University of South Florida | https://www.usf.edu/pcgs/research-and-initiatives/biofuels-and-bioproducts-development.aspx |
| | Iowa State University | https://www.biorenew.iastate.edu/ |
| *Canada* | North Carolina State University | https://cnr.ncsu.edu/fb/research/areas-of-research/biomaterials-research/ |
| | University of British Columbia | https://bpi.ubc.ca/ |
| | University of Guelph | https://www.bioproductscentre.com/ |
| *China* | South China University of Technology | http://www2.scut.edu.cn/sklppe/ |
| | Beijing University of Chemical Technology | https://www.buct.edu.cn/main.htm |
| *Sweden* | KTH Royal Institute of Technology | https://www.kth.se/ket/process-technology |
| | Chalmers University of Technology | https://www.chalmers.se/en/education/programmes/masters-info/Pages/Materials-Chemistry.aspx |
| *Germany* | RWTH Aachen University | https://www.cce.rwth-aachen.de/go/id/othcg/?lidx=1 |
| | Universität Greifswald | https://www.uni-greifswald.de/en/study/prior-to-studies/international-degree-courses/msc-bioeconomy/ |
| *India* | Visvesvaraya Technological University | http://www.vtu.ac.in/ |
| *Italy* | University of Perugia | http://biotecnologie.unipg.it/index.php/biotecnologie |
| *South Korea* | Advanced Institute of Science and Technology | http://efdl.kaist.ac.kr/research/res_04.php |
| *Finland* | Aalto University | https://www.aalto.fi/en/department-of-bioproducts-and-biosystems/bioproduct-chemistry |
| *Japan* | Hokkaido University | https://abse.bpe.agr.hokudai.ac.jp/en/ |
| *Austria* | Graz University of Technology | https://www.uni-graz.at/en/researching/organisation-plan/horizon-europe/ |

biomaterials education. Section 13.1 introduces biomaterials, the application of AI in education, and PBL strategies, including the literature review methodology. Section 13.2 examines the shift toward biomaterials, comparing the structure-properties-processing relationship in conventional materials with that of biomaterials, exploring the complexity of biomaterials' structure, and discussing the challenges in their processing. Section 13.3 presents an introduction to AI in engineering education. Section 13.4 addresses the integration of AI in biomaterials education, covering PBL approaches, AI's role in molecule discovery and structural analysis, and the application of GPT and LLMs, augmented reality (AR), and virtual reality (VR) in education. It also focuses on learning through AI-enhanced molecular simulations for developing advanced biomaterials and includes a case study on the processing of biomaterials in a fiber-based production facility. The chapter concludes with Section 13.5, which discusses the future directions of AI in enhancing biomaterials education, summarizing key findings and outlining potential implications.

## 13.2 Transition to biomaterials in materials science education

Traditionally, Chemical Engineering (ChE) education has emphasized the development, design, expansion, oversight, and regulation of industrial processes, with a significant focus on industries reliant on fossil fuels and the operations of oil refineries. This focus reflects a time when the chemical engineering profession was aligned with these sectors' needs. However, the landscape of the chemical industry has been evolving rapidly, requiring chemical engineers to broaden their skill sets and competencies to include aspects of product engineering. According to Prausnitz, the core of Chemical Engineering is defined by the activities of a chemical engineer, showcasing the profession's adaptability to the industry's evolving requirements [114]. Interestingly, a relatively small segment of Chemical Engineering graduates, roughly 20%, secure positions in the traditional chemical or oil refinery sectors [107,115]. The majority, especially those with advanced degrees, are currently employed in sectors that were either nonexistent or did not hire chemical engineers two decades ago [116].

Materials in Chemical Engineering courses, typically offered in the latter part of the curriculum, face several challenges, including providing insufficient training for students to develop the necessary skills and aptitudes for success in their professional careers [117]. This section explores the incorporation of fiber-based biomaterials, such as those used in pulp and paper, nanomaterials, and textiles, into the biobased materials education framework, underscoring the potential for producing sustainable and versatile materials. The proposed course program is designed to foster competencies in product and formulation engineering with an emphasis on new biomaterials. It encourages the development of multidisciplinary skills and a systemic approach to understanding phenomena and processes across different scales, from nano to macro [118–120]. The goal is for students to have the opportunity to develop a product for a specific application, by using the principles of circularity [22]. Fig. 13.4 outlines the four foundational axes of the course, which focus on education in circular bioeconomy and biomaterials, leveraging PBL strategies and AI models to achieve its objectives.

Incorporating lignocellulosic biopolymers into materials science education presents an avenue for exploring sustainable materials, contrasting with conventional material

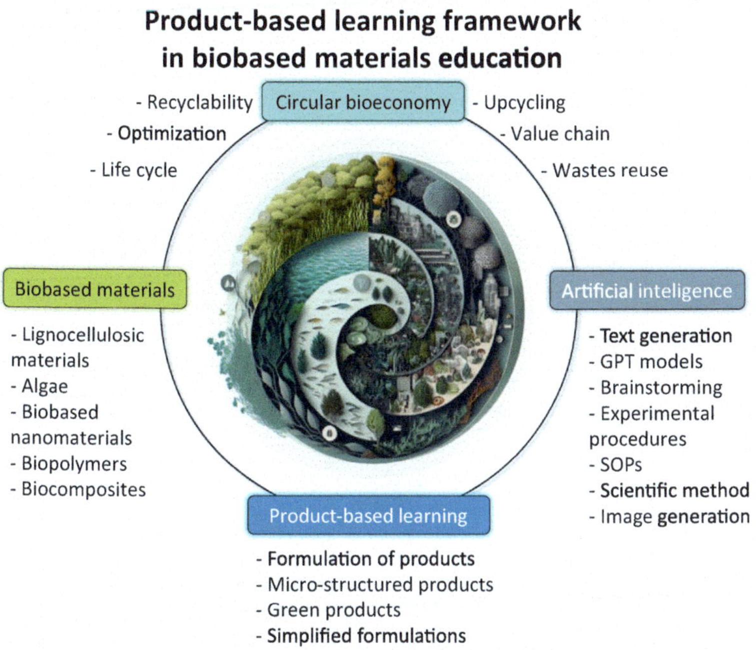


**Figure 13.4** The four axes essential for attaining the outlined objectives proposed in this chapter, which are centered around the education of circular bioeconomy and biomaterials. These axes integrate product-based learning and an artificial intelligence framework to provide a comprehensive approach to learning.
Reprinted with permission from [27].

counterparts derived from finite resources. Challenges in integrating these biomaterials into curricula include the need for an understanding of their unique structure-property relationships and overcoming preconceptions about the performance capabilities of biobased versus traditional materials. However, these challenges are outweighed by the advantages of exposing students to cutting-edge research areas, fostering innovation in sustainable material development, and cultivating a deeper understanding of materials environmental impacts [27].

### *13.2.1 Structure-properties-processing relationship in conventional materials versus biomaterials*

The structure-properties-processing relationship is a fundamental concept that explains how the molecular and macroscopic structure of these materials influences their physical and chemical properties, which in turn dictates the methods and conditions under which they can be processed. The relationship in conventional materials versus biomaterials is a complex and multidimensional area of study that spans various disciplines, including materials science, biology, and engineering

**Figure 13.5** Key properties, structure, and processing attributes that differentiate metallic, ceramic, polymeric materials, and biomaterials.

(Fig. 13.5). Conventional materials, such as metals, ceramics, and polymers, have been extensively studied for their mechanical, electrical, and thermal properties, which can be directly linked to their internal structure and the processing methods used to create them [121]. Biomaterials, on the other hand, include a broader range of materials designed for specific applications where their interaction with biological and chemical environments is critical [122].

Conventional materials have well-established process-structure-property relationships that allow for the tailoring of material properties through controlled processing techniques. For example, the mechanical properties of metals can be manipulated through processes such as alloying, heat treatment, and cold working, which alter the crystalline structure and defect distribution within the material [123].

On the other hand, the properties of ceramics are primarily determined by their ionic and covalent bonds, which make them hard, but brittle. Processing techniques like sintering affect the density and grain size, which in turn influences their mechanical properties [124]. Polymers exhibit a wide range of properties based on their molecular weight, crystallinity, and the types of monomer units. Processing methods such as extrusion and injection molding can change these factors, affecting the material's properties [125].

Biomaterials, such as cellulose, however, are characterized by their hierarchical structure from nano to macro scale (comprising crystalline and amorphous regions) directly impacting their mechanical strength, chemical reactivity, and thermal stability, thereby affecting their processability into various forms like fibers, films, or composites for applications in textiles, packaging, and bioplastics [126–129]. Similarly, the composition and structure of biomass (a mix of cellulose, hemicellulose, and lignin) determine its energy content, mechanical properties, and suitability for conversion processes like combustion, gasification, or bio-refining [130,131]. The choice of processing technique, whether mechanical, chemical, or biological, depends on the desired end-use properties of the biomaterial, highlighting the interdependence between structure, properties, and processing in designing and utilizing biomaterials effectively.

The link between structural properties and processing in conventional materials is well-established, with a direct correlation between processing conditions and the resulting material properties (Fig. 13.5). In contrast, the relationship for biomaterials derived from cellulose or biomass is more complex due to the variability in natural feedstocks and the multiscale organization of these materials. However, this complexity also offers a broader spectrum of tunable properties through processing, enabling the development of materials with tailored functionalities for specific applications [27,30].

A key difference lies in the goal of processing; whereas conventional materials often focus on achieving uniformity and specific mechanical properties, the processing of biomaterials emphasizes sustainability, recyclability, biodegradability, and functionality within biological systems. This shift necessitates innovative processing technologies that can maintain or enhance the desired properties of biomaterials without compromising their biocompatibility or environmental benefits [33,132]. The development of fully biodegradable polymer-cellulose composites for packaging, where cellulose acts as a reinforcement agent, exemplifies the successful application of understanding the relationship between structure, properties, and processing. Similarly, the use of biofabrication methods to create scaffolds for tissue engineering from cellulose demonstrates how processing can be tailored to produce structures with specific biological functionalities [133,134].

Understanding the intricate relationship between structural properties and processing is crucial for advancing material science, whether dealing with conventional materials or exploring the potential of biomaterials derived from cellulose or biomass. As the field progresses, the development of alternative processing techniques and the deeper understanding of material structures will continue to drive innovation, enabling the creation of materials that meet the evolving demands of technology, sustainability, and even areas such as health. The processing of metals, including methods such as forging, casting, and heat treatment, directly influences their crystalline structure [135,136]. These processes can alter the arrangement of atoms, affecting mechanical properties like strength, ductility, and hardness. For example, heat treatment can change the microstructure of steel, enhancing its toughness or wear resistance based on the cooling rate and subsequent tempering. The sintering process, pivotal for ceramics, affects their porosity and grain size, directly influencing mechanical strength and brittleness. Advanced ceramics processing techniques, like hot pressing, can produce materials with superior mechanical properties and thermal stability, suitable for applications in extreme environments. The properties of polymers are significantly influenced by their synthesis and processing conditions, which determine the polymer chain's length, branching, and cross-linking. Techniques such as injection molding and extrusion can induce orientation in polymer chains, affecting tensile strength, elasticity, and thermal behavior [125,135].

The transition to biomaterials, particularly those derived from cellulose or other biomass, introduces a set of complexities related to their natural origin and structural heterogeneity. Processing techniques for these materials, ranging from mechanical treatment to dissolve cellulose for regenerating fibers or chemical modification for enhancing compatibility with other materials, aim to exploit the inherent structural properties of biomass [10,137,138]. For instance, the controlled deconstruction of cellulose into nanocellulose through mechanical or enzymatic methods can produce materials with high strength and low weight, suitable for composite applications [30].

## 13.3 AI in biomaterials education

The incorporation of AI in educational settings is progressively transforming traditional teaching and learning [139]. The evolution of AI in education over the past two decades represents a profound transformation in how learning is delivered, experienced, and assessed (Fig. 13.6) [27,140].

### *13.3.1 Recent developments on AI applied to education in chemical engineering*

In Table 13.6 a summary of works on the implementation of AI in chemical engineering education is presented.

- **Mid-2000s:** Key technological innovations highlighted include virtual labs, remote labs, and hybrid delivery models, each playing a critical role in replicating and enhancing the laboratory learning experience outside the conventional classroom setting [143]. Virtual Labs utilize simulations and VR to allow students to conduct experiments in an entirely digital space, offering flexibility and safety without compromising on the learning outcomes [150]. Remote labs, on the other hand, provide a real-world experimentation experience by enabling students to control physical laboratory equipment from remote locations via the internet, integrating live video feeds for a comprehensive view of the experiments being conducted [150]. Hybrid labs merge the best of both virtual and remote laboratories, incorporating

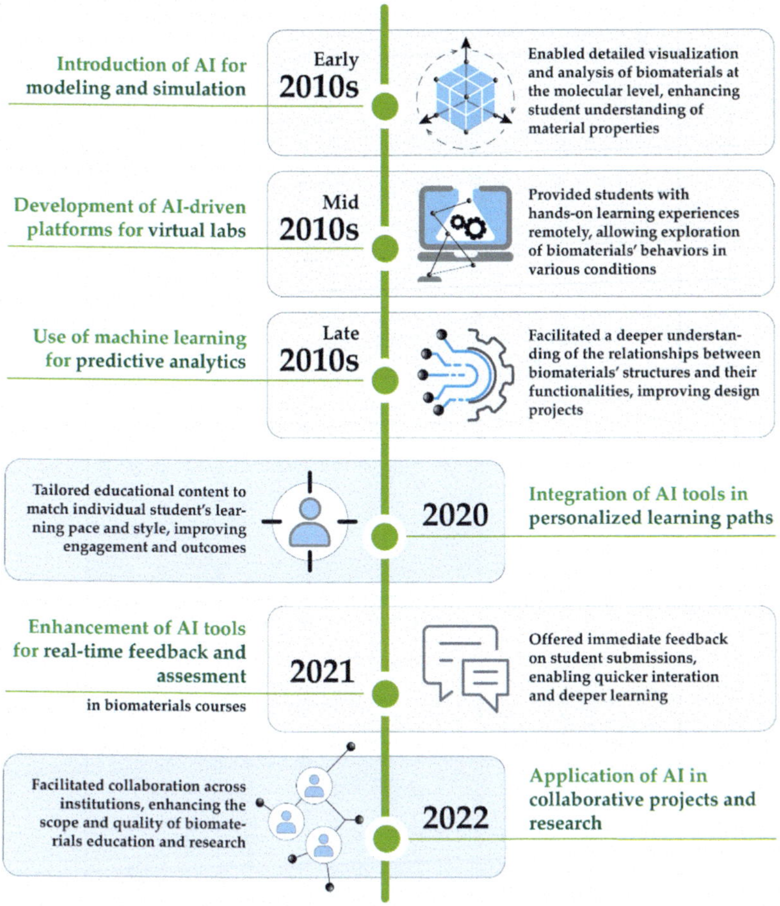


**Figure 13.6** Timeline of AI developments related to education in the last 20 years.

hands-on activities with digital simulations to offer a rich, multifaceted learning experience. This model particularly stands out for its adaptability, allowing for the preservation of essential hands-on skills while also embracing the technological advancements that facilitate remote learning. Emerging technologies such as the Internet of Things (IoT) and AR are identified as instrumental in enriching the laboratory experience further [151,152]. These technologies provide real-time data collection, immersive experiences, and enhanced interactivity, thereby augmenting both the effectiveness and engagement of laboratory sessions conducted in virtual or hybrid formats. Platforms such as learning management systems (LMS), online collaborative tools, and electronic lab notebooks support synchronous and asynchronous collaboration among students and faculty, fostering a community of learning despite physical separation. These technologies also enable effective assessment of student progress and competency in remote settings, ensuring that educational standards are maintained [150].

**Table 13.6** Perspective utilization of AI in chemical engineering education. The year of the innovation, the application of AI strategies, and their impact in materials engineering education are presented.

| Year | Innovation in PBL | AI application | Impact | References |
|---|---|---|---|---|
| Early 2000s | Introduction of digital modeling tools | Initial AI algorithms for predictive modeling in material science | Enabled the first steps toward simulating material properties and processing in educational settings | [141,142] |
| Mid-2000s | Development of virtual labs | Enhanced simulations for lab experiments, including biorefinery processes | Provided students with hands-on experience in a virtual environment, reducing resource constraints | [83,143] |
| Mid 2010s | Adoption of machine learning | Machine learning models to predict material behaviors under various conditions | Enhanced students' ability to predict and understand complex material interactions | [144] |
| 2019 | Introduction of AI-driven problem-solving platforms | Platforms utilizing AI to propose solutions to engineering challenges in biomaterials | Encouraged innovation and critical thinking by providing real-world problem-solving scenarios | [145] |
| 2021 | Expansion of AI in personalized learning | Personalized learning paths tailored by AI according to student performance and preferences | Improved student engagement and outcomes by adapting the learning experience to individual needs | [146,147] |
| 2023 | Utilization of generative AI for product development | Generative design algorithms to explore optimal biomaterial configurations | Fostered creativity and expanded the possibilities for product innovation in biomaterials education | [148,149] |

- **Mid-2010s:** The introduction of AI-driven analytics in 2016 for identifying learning gaps enabled educators to tailor teaching strategies to address specific student needs and improve outcomes [153]. Methodologies involving the development of specialized tools to facilitate real-time feedback and detailed tracking of students' engagement and understanding have been recently applied [154]. The research was conducted within a Chemical Engineering course at Texas A&M, comparing its impact against a control group through both qualitative and quantitative evaluations. A notable enhancement in learning outcomes was identified when compared to the control group. This suggests the potential of AI to positively influence student learning experiences. However, the study recognizes the substantial extra effort required to integrate these advanced tools into existing curricula, which could deter adoption by instructors [154].

In 2017, the expansion of VR and AR in education powered by AI, immersing students in interactive learning environments and enhancing engagement and understanding of complex subjects. The integration of VR technology was integrated into chemical and biochemical engineering education, highlighting its potential to bridge the gap between theoretical knowledge and real-world industrial experience. It emphasizes VR's capacity to offer immersive learning experiences that replicate the complexity of actual process plants, enabling students to visualize and interact with engineering concepts in a dynamic and engaging manner. Furthermore, the paper addresses the application of VR in the process industry for operator training, offering a realistic and safe environment to simulate various operational scenarios, including unexpected and hazardous situations that are difficult to replicate in traditional training settings [153].

- **Late 2010s:** Innovative AI courses have been designed for chemical engineering master's students, marking one of the first attempts of its kind in Europe [140]. The course is structured to offer both theoretical knowledge through frontal lectures and practical skills through hands-on exercises, focusing on modeling, optimization techniques via AI, and their applications in chemical engineering. The primary goal is to equip students with the ability to apply basic AI concepts in solving chemical engineering tasks. The curriculum was developed in response to the increasing relevance of AI and ML in process engineering and the chemical industry, addressing a significant gap in structured AI education within chemical engineering programs. The course content covers a broad spectrum of AI methodologies, including supervised learning, unsupervised learning, and reinforcement learning, with applications ranging from predictive modeling to process optimization and control. Feedback and performance data from the students who participated in the course were collected to assess the effectiveness of the curriculum. The results indicate that the course successfully introduced students to ML techniques and their potential applications in chemical engineering. The evaluation of student performances, based on individual exercises and group projects, alongside student feedback, offers valuable insights for educators planning to introduce similar AI courses in chemical engineering or other disciplines [140].

The development of predictive models in 2019 to improve student retention and success helped institutions identify at-risk students early, allowing for timely intervention and support [155]. This study investigates the effects of an online flipped classroom approach on student learning experiences and outcomes in process control and process design courses. Traditionally, these courses were taught in a flipped format to senior chemical engineering undergraduates, involving preclass online preparation, class meetings, and active tutorials. The sudden shift to completely online teaching due to COVID-19 lockdowns provided a unique opportunity to examine this educational model's efficacy in a remote learning environment. The study focused on two core courses offered to 54 chemical engineering undergraduates at the Technion, the Israel Institute of Technology, during the fall semester of 2020/2021. The transition to online teaching, necessitated by the pandemic, allowed for the collection of comprehensive data, including analytics from various online platforms and student surveys, offering insights into the teaching protocol's effectiveness and its impact on student engagement and learning outcomes. The findings from student surveys highlighted the significant value of active tutorials, with students reporting the highest confidence in their mastery following these sessions. Statistical analysis further confirmed that active student engagement positively correlated with final exam performance. Factors such as GPA, tutorial attendance, and lesson engagement emerged as critical determinants of exam scores. Notably, the shift to online teaching did not significantly affect learning outcomes compared to the face-to-face implementation of the flipped classroom, suggesting the online flipped approach's effectiveness in achieving similar educational results [155].

- **2020 to present:** In 2021, the implementation of AI in facilitating collaborative and interactive online learning environments replicates the dynamics of in-person classrooms in a virtual setting [156]. This research investigated the integration of digital tools within chemical engineering education, focusing on aligning these technologies with the core curriculum while addressing nontechnical barriers. The consensus among surveyed educators and industry experts highlights a preference for implementing accessible and user-friendly digital platforms, such as Excel and scripting languages, over more complex technologies like VR/AR. This preference is rooted in the importance of mathematical simplicity, ease of maintenance, and low initial investment costs as key factors influencing the adoption of digital tools in education. Interestingly, the survey indicates a growing interest in utilizing virtual laboratories/operator training simulators (OTS) and VR/AR technologies for specialized applications like process design and safety. These advanced tools provide immersive learning experiences that could significantly improve student comprehension of complex concepts. However, their adoption is constrained by concerns related to costs, maintenance, and the need for specialized expertise [156].

Since 2022, the integration of AI tutors and chatbots in educational platforms has provided students with on-demand assistance and feedback, enhancing learning efficiency [87]. This study showcases the integration of LLMs like ChatGPT into chemical engineering education, offering a novel approach to enhancing problem-solving and programming skills [27]. Utilizing LLMs for problem-solving has enabled chemical engineering students to improve their critical thinking abilities, gain a deeper understanding of core subjects, and prepare for Industry 4.0 with essential programming competencies. Feedback from students who participated in an

LLM-assisted experimental lecture indicates mixed perceptions, albeit recognizing its potential as an accessible tool for enhancing problem-solving efficiency. The research identifies common student misconceptions about LLMs in chemical engineering education and provides examples and strategies to aid their integration into the curriculum [157].

### 13.3.2 Additional types of AI-related techniques applied to an educational framework

Throughout the 20th century, unsupervised learning techniques have been instrumental in uncovering hidden patterns and structures within bioproduct datasets without the need for labeled data. In the educational context, unsupervised learning methods such as clustering and dimensionality reduction, enabled by tools like principal component analysis (PCA), allow students to explore the inherent variability and relationships among different bioproducts. For example, students can employ clustering algorithms to group similar bioproducts based on shared characteristics [158], thereby gaining a deeper understanding of their similarities and differences. Moreover, dimensionality reduction techniques PCA, which is a statistical technique that simplifies the complexity in high-dimensional data while retaining trends and patterns. In biomaterials science education, PCA can be utilized to analyze and interpret complex datasets, such as those arising from the characterization of biomaterials or the optimization of biorefinery processes. Similarly, clustering algorithms can identify patterns and groupings within data, such as categorizing biomaterials based on their properties or environmental impact. These methods provide students with hands-on experience in data analysis, fostering a deeper understanding of materials science principles [159].

However, supervised learning algorithms can be used by educators to provide students with hands-on experiences in predictive modeling, which is critical for the development of next-generation biomaterials. Linear regression, known for its straightforward interpretability, serves as an excellent starting point for students to grasp the basics of predictive modeling. Also, data preparation and organization techniques for AI/ML could be utilized. Through projects that require predicting biomaterial properties or optimizing processing parameters, students can apply linear regression to understand fundamental concepts before moving on to more complex algorithms. These algorithms can be applied to predict the properties of biomaterials based on their chemical composition and processing conditions or to forecast the outcomes of biorefinery processes [160].

Support vector machines (SVM) have shown exceptional promise in classifying materials based on their properties and predicting their performance in specific applications, as highlighted in the use of SVM for materials design [161]. This approach allows students to explore the relationship between materials' structural characteristics and their functional outcomes, an essential skill for PBL. By applying ML to model chemical reactivities, students can explore how changes in reactants or conditions influence the yield and efficiency of reactions [162], opening up new avenues for optimizing biomaterial production processes. This educational approach not only enhances students' analytical skills but also deepens their understanding of the material science principles underpinning the creation and application of advanced biomaterials, ultimately fostering innovation and advancement in the design of next-generation biomaterials.

Similarly, neural networks' ability to model complex, nonlinear relationships in large datasets enables students to tackle sophisticated design challenges in materials, from drug delivery systems to tissue engineering scaffolds. Incorporating semisupervised learning techniques for classifying materials synthesis procedures introduces students to the cutting edge of biomaterials research [163]. Students can learn to navigate and utilize large databases of synthesis procedures by engaging with algorithms capable of processing vast amounts of unlabeled data, an invaluable resource for product development.

Incorporating case studies and PBL that utilize AI algorithms offers students practical insights into real-world challenges in the field of biomaterials and biorefineries. For instance, analyzing case studies on the development of biobased polymers or the optimization of waste-to-energy processes provides a contextual understanding of how AI tools can drive innovation and sustainability in the industry. Such experiences prepare students for careers in biomaterials science, equipped with the knowledge and skills to apply AI in solving complex problems [164]. Recent empirical studies have shown the positive effects of AI on learning outcomes in STEM fields, including biomaterials science. For instance, research employing adaptive learning platforms powered by AI in materials science courses has shown significant improvements in student performance and retention of complex concepts. These platforms, which personalize learning content based on individual student's pace and understanding, facilitate a deeper comprehension of biomaterials' properties and applications [165].

## 13.4 Proposed educational approaches for AI-enabled product-based learning

In this section, six educational approaches will be presented as examples for AI-enabled PBL in biomaterials courses. The approaches include the application of GPT and LLMs coupled with PBL to develop methodological operating procedures to obtain products and molecules development. Additionally, this section discusses the integration of AI-enhanced intelligent fault diagnosis within fiber-based production facilities, as well as the incorporation of VR and AR to create immersive and interactive learning experiences within a biomaterials PBL-oriented classroom.

### *13.4.1 AI for molecules chemical structure discovery for specific applications*

DL and generative AI are significantly advancing molecule design, producing novel molecular structures with enhanced properties [166–168]. The application of ML and DL extends beyond mere molecular design to include the prediction and optimization of properties of polymers and biological molecules, among others. DL models can predict interactions within components, such as drugs and polymers, enhancing pharmaceutical formulations' stability, solubility, and bioavailability.

#### 13.4.1.1 Comprehensive AI-driven procedure for molecular design

A structured approach illustrated in Fig. 13.7 for deriving new molecule structures using generative AI includes:

1. **Advanced data collection and integration:** Gathering a broad spectrum of chemical and material datasets, including experimental results, literature findings, and proprietary databases. Integrating varied data types, such as quantum mechanical calculations and molecular dynamics (MD) simulations, first principle modelling, offers a holistic dataset for AI.
2. **Enhanced data preprocessing with AI:** Identifying data gaps, predicting missing properties, and generating synthetic data points to refine model training.
3. **Multiobjective optimization:** AI models could simultaneously optimize multiple objectives, such as the molecule technical performance and biodegradability, efficacy, and safety.
4. **Integrative model training with transfer learning:** Applying transfer learning and multitask learning to enhance the predictiveness of molecules by utilizing knowledge from related domains.
5. **Iterative design and synthesis loop:** AI not only helps to predict new molecular structures quickly but also suggests modifications to existing molecules for desired properties.
6. **Virtual screening and property prediction:** DL models virtually screen chemical spaces to identify promising candidates and predict critical properties.
7. **Experimental validation and feedback loop:** Conducting experimental testing on AI-predicted molecular structures to validate their properties, performance, and safety, refining AI predictions for future synthesis.

#### 13.4.1.2 Application of LLMs and GPT models in chemical synthesis

LLMs [169] and GPT models [167] are being explored as tools to optimize chemical synthesis and design new polymer molecules. Trained on diverse datasets from scientific publications, patents, and experimental records, LLMs can navigate and interpret extensive scientific literature and databases, aiding in the autonomous design, planning, and optimization of experiments [170–172]. This approach balances generative models' innovative output with the need for scientific accuracy and relevance, ensuring the generation of both novel and scientifically sound hypotheses

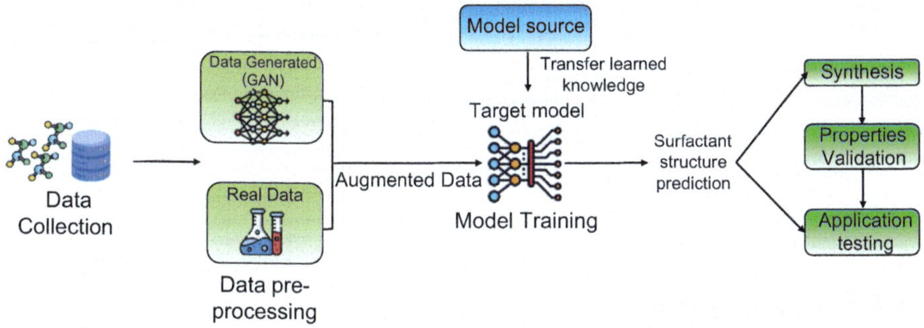


**Figure 13.7** Comprehensive procedure for obtaining a novel molecule structure using generative artificial intelligence, such as generative adversarial networks (GAN) or generative pretrained transformers (GPT).
Reprinted with permission from [173].

and experimental designs. Recently, DL models have been applied to the screening of millions of chemical compounds for potential antibiotic applications [168]. This AI-driven approach identified several compounds effective against drug-resistant pathogens, such as methicillin-resistant *Staphylococcus aureus* (MRSA) and vancomycin-resistant enterococci. Notably, the algorithm used in this study was designed for transparency, enabling researchers to understand its decision-making process and the biochemical basis for its predictions. This method could similarly be applied to the screening of (bio)surfactant molecules to identify those with optimized properties for specific applications, such as detergency or emulsification performance [168].

Generative AI, a subset of DL, is expanding the possibilities for molecular design, allowing for the generation of novel molecular structures with potentially enhanced properties. These models, capable of learning from extensive chemical compound datasets, are positioned to predict new surfactants meeting specific criteria, including biodegradability, low toxicity, and efficacy in targeted applications. The capacity to generate and screen thousands of potential surfactants in silico markedly reduces the time and cost associated with developing biobased surfactants. A comprehensive procedure for deriving new polymer molecule structures using generative AI involves several steps, from advanced data collection and integration to experimental validation and feedback. This procedure highlights the role of AI in simplifying data preprocessing, enabling a focus on higher-level thinking and the creative application of the information (Fig. 13.8) [167].

Generative AI also offers significant opportunities to enhance the production efficiency of biobased products and the design and operational efficiency of chemical processes. It assists in generating and refining process flowsheets, error correction, and hazard studies, leading to more effective data use, innovative problem-solving, and the creation of models that blend traditional knowledge with AI insights [174]. LLMs and GPT models have been proposed as tools to optimize chemical synthesis and design new polymer molecules. The body of knowledge created, particularly in the pharmaceutical field, suggests the application of DL and generative AI in other areas, such as the identification of molecules. LLMs, skilled in processing extensive scientific literature, can autonomously design, plan, and optimize experiments, significantly enhancing the efficiency of scientific research. However, balancing the innovative output of generative models with the stringent requirements for scientific accuracy and relevance poses a challenge, necessitating sophisticated model tuning [157]. Tables 13.7 and 13.8 present the learning outcomes of the strategy and the characteristics of the AI model, respectively.

### 13.4.2 Generative pretrained transformer and large language models in product-based learning education

GPT and LLMs like GPT-3.5 and GPT-4 have recently gained significant attention for their capabilities in text generation, presenting new opportunities and challenges in educational settings [175]. LLMs have been proposed recently as tools to be used

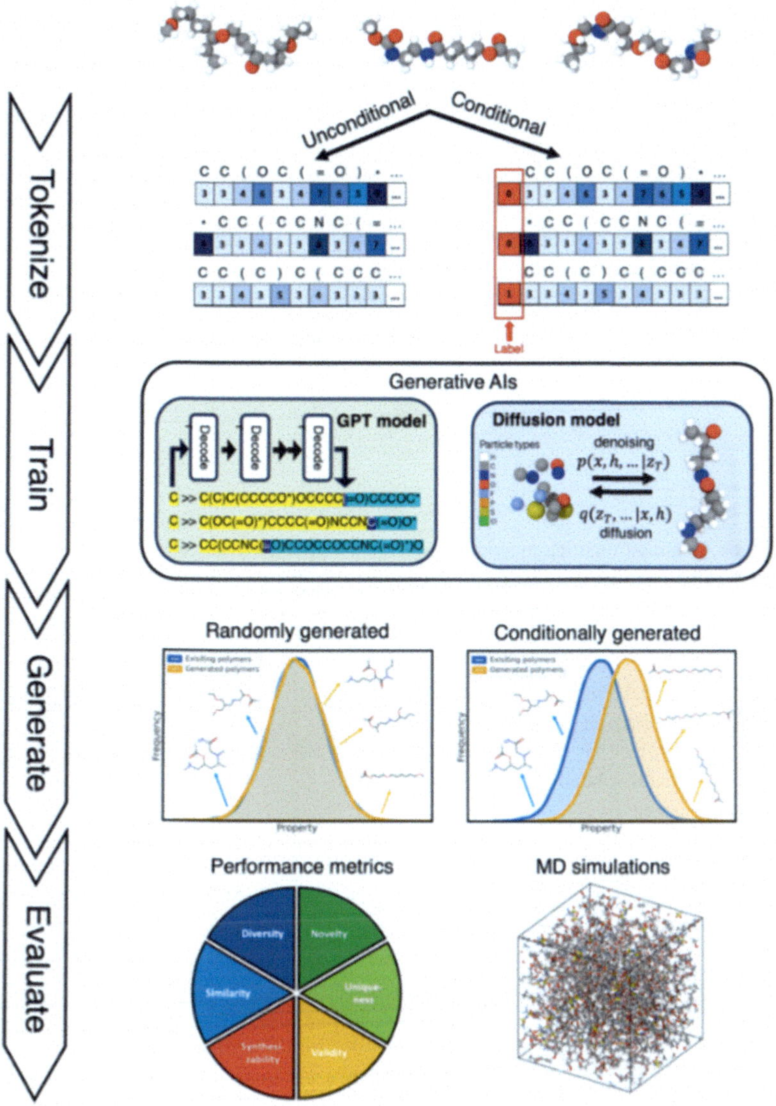


**Figure 13.8** Workflow for the use of GPT AI for new molecules discovery. The methodology begins with the high-throughput molecular dynamics (HTP-MD) dataset, wherein the SMILES codes representing the monomers of polymer electrolytes are tokenized. The generated polymer set is assessed using various metrics, and promising candidates exhibiting high conductivity from conditional generation are further validated through molecular dynamics simulations.
Reprinted with permission from [167].

**Table 13.7** Learning outcomes for AI in molecule design education.

| Outcome | After the course, the student | Evaluation method |
|---|---|---|
| 1. Molecular design | Understands the fundamental principles of molecular design | Lectures and virtual labs |
| 2. Data acquisition | Masters techniques of chemical data collection and integration | Practical sessions on data tools |
| 3. AI model deployment | Can implement and manage AI-based models for molecular prediction | Software proficiency tests |
| 4. Continuous improvement | Engages in iterative learning to refine molecular models with new data | Project-based assessment |

**Table 13.8** AI model characteristics for molecular structure discovery.

| Feature | Description | Relevance to education |
|---|---|---|
| Algorithm type | Utilizes generative pretrained transformers (GPT) and other LLMs | Introduce students to state-of-the-art generative models |
| Data processing | Handling and preprocessing of complex molecular datasets using advanced natural language processing (NLP) techniques | Teach data structuring and advanced NLP skills |
| Model training | Employs techniques such as few-shot learning and transfer learning | Illustrate the application of advanced training techniques in AI |
| Outcome analysis | Utilizes metrics like perplexity, accuracy, and generation quality | Quantify model performance and refine text-based generation techniques |

in ChE, enhancing their understanding of course content and relevant Industry 4.0 skills [157].

Examples of the use of text generation AI for the conception of ideas to develop products were proposed recently [27]. The Q&A session, performed with ChatGPT LLM AI, was proposed to identify suitable alternatives at various stages of the product development process in a Materials in Chemical Engineering course, including brainstorming, selection, and establishment of standard operating procedures (SOPs). Despite their potential, these technologies have sparked

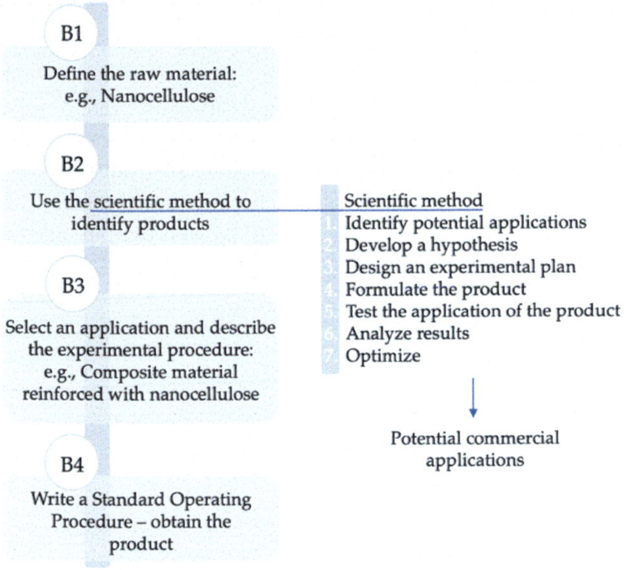


**Figure 13.9** Logical sequence of one interaction with the AI to develop a procedure to obtain nanocellulose products. Four stages are recommended, that is, B1. Define the raw material, B2. Use of the scientific method to identify products, B3. Select an application and product, B4. Write an SOP to produce the material.
Reprinted with permission from [27].

debates regarding their use in academic settings for writing of scientific literature, due to concerns regarding accuracy and originality [176–178]. Fig. 13.9 and 13.10 depict the logical sequence of an interaction with the GPT text generation AI to develop a procedure to obtain nanocellulose products [27].

### *13.4.2.1 Educational objectives and learning outcomes*

Students need to be introduced to the principles of prompt engineering, learning how to craft precise and effective prompts that guide ChatGPT to generate more targeted and relevant responses. Then, the critical analysis and revision stage involves students in the thorough examination of information and proposals generated by ChatGPT, identifying areas for enhancement or modifications, refining their queries based on initial outputs, and employing iterative prompting techniques to develop complex topics or to clarify ambiguities. This process refines critical thinking and analytical abilities, leading to the improvement of project proposals and designs through a process of iterative refinement. It enhances material comprehension and cultivates skills in evaluation and revision [27]. Afterwards students must apply the developed methodology to obtain the product within the framework of a PBL environment [27].

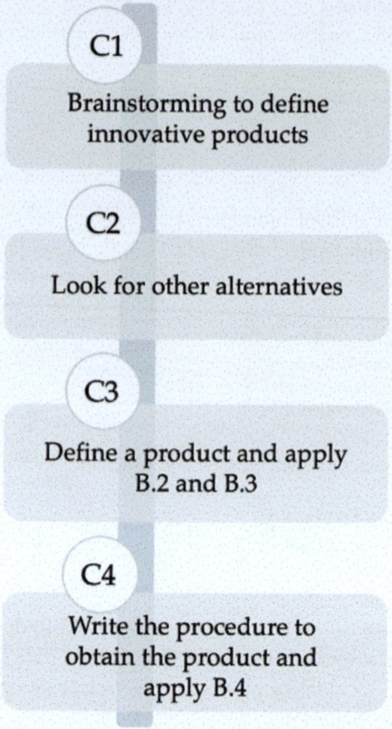


**Figure 13.10** Logical sequence to obtain alternatives through the interaction with the text generation AI.
Reprinted with permission from [27].

Tables 13.9 and 13.10 present the learning outcomes of the strategy and the characteristics of the AI model.

### 13.4.3 Learning through AI-enhanced molecular simulations to develop fourth-generation biomaterials

Computational simulations play a critical role across a vast spectrum of fields, including materials science, engineering, bioengineering, chemistry, and physics, enabling deep insights into the microscopic mechanisms behind a myriad of biological and material phenomena [179]. These phenomena range from ion transport across cell membranes and the flow of polymeric liquids to the stabilization of colloidal dispersions and the self-assembly of nanostructures. Among these, classical MD simulations stand out for their versatility in analyzing a wide array of material and chemical systems. MD simulations employ Newton's equations of motion to iteratively calculate the movement, velocity, and forces acting on particles over time [179]. However, the computational intensity of MD simulations, often scaling with the square of the particle count, requires significant

**Table 13.9** Learning outcomes for GPT and LLMs in chemical engineering education.

| Outcome | After the course, the student | Evaluation method |
|---|---|---|
| 1. Product conceptualization | Utilizes GPT and LLMs AI to generate new product ideas and enhance creativity | Group brainstorming sessions using AI tools |
| 2. Prompt engineering | Learns to utilize effectively AI prompts to obtain targeted outcomes | Practical exercises in prompt crafting in a product-based learning framework |
| 3. SOP development | Develops and refines standard operating procedures using AI-assisted text generation | Project documentation and SOP drafting |
| 4. Critical analysis | Engages in iterative refinement of AI-generated proposals to enhance product quality | Product development |

**Table 13.10** AI model characteristics for GPT and LLMs in chemical engineering education.

| Feature | Description | Relevance to education |
|---|---|---|
| Algorithm type | Utilizes generative pretrained transformers and other advanced LLMs | Introduce cutting-edge AI technologies |
| Data handling | Manages and processes vast amounts of textual data | Teach effective data management and utilization |
| Iterative learning | Supports dynamic learning and refinement based on user input | Emphasize the importance of feedback in AI interactions |
| Output analysis | Generates diverse outputs based on varied prompts and contexts | Illustrate the versatility of AI in generating creative and technical content |

computational resources. This challenge is typically overcome using high-performance computing (HPC) and parallel computing strategies like OpenMP and MPI, which significantly improve MD simulations' efficiency and feasibility.

Parallelized MD simulations unlock the potential to explore the dynamics of large particle systems under a diverse array of conditions [180]. These simulations not only pave the way for cutting-edge research but also serve as innovative pedagogical tools in computational science and engineering education. Despite the strategic selection of parallelization techniques tailored to the specific needs of a system's size and complexity, achieving precise outcomes from MD simulations can be time-intensive, ranging from mere minutes to several days, based on the intricacies of the system being modeled. This delay primarily stems from queue waiting times on computing clusters combined with the actual computational runtime. Consequently, the practical application of MD simulations in an academic context has predominantly been relegated to supplementary "outside-classroom" activities, such as homework assignments, where the extended duration of simulations is more manageable.

For MD simulations to be effectively integrated into classroom sessions, the supporting computational tools must be exceptionally responsive to address educational needs such as:

- Delivering simulation-based answers to student inquiries instantly.
- Streamlining the explanation of scientific principles through immediate access to precise simulation output trends.
- Conducting live, synchronous analysis of model system behavior alongside students.
- Creating an interactive learning space where students can conduct virtual experiments in class, allowing them to grasp concepts through direct observation of system responses under varied conditions.

Meeting these educational challenges can significantly enhance the teaching of computational science and engineering concepts in the classroom, thereby enriching student learning experiences.

The integration of ML techniques with HPC-driven simulations represents a cutting-edge approach to overcoming challenges encountered in teaching computational science and engineering courses, as recently investigated by Kadupitiya et al. [181]. Their study showcases the efficacy of employing ML surrogates, designed using artificial neural networks (ANN), to generate predictions that closely align with explicit simulations, but at significantly reduced time and computational expenses (Fig. 13.11). In this innovative methodology, an ML surrogate model is designed using data generated from completed runs of HPC-accelerated simulations, and then this model is deployed to approximate the complex relationships between the physical input parameters and the simulation output results. The ML surrogate bypasses the explicit computational evolution of the simulated model components, yielding accurate outputs within a fraction of the time and

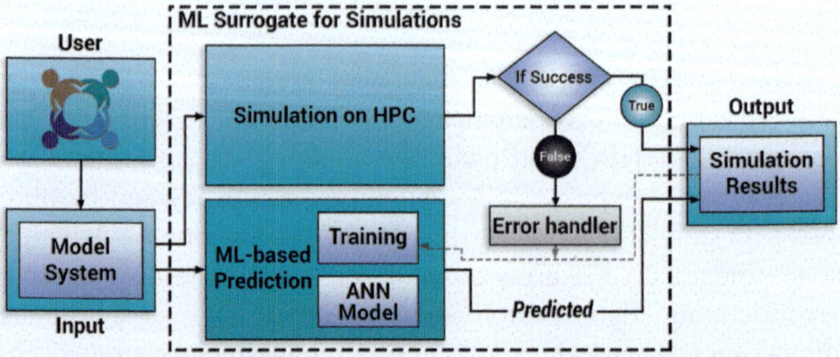


**Figure 13.11** Overview of the ML surrogate framework for simulation approach to generate rapid and accurate predictions of simulation outputs for classroom teaching.
Reprinted with permission from [182].

computational resources required by traditional methods. This approach underscores the effectiveness of employing ANN-based regression models, trained on data derived from completed runs of HPC-accelerated MD simulations, in emulating either partial or entire MD simulations.

Exposing this approach to a broader community of students, educators, and researchers requires hosting this application on a large online platform for educational materials. In that sense, the authors developed a web application hosted on nanoHUB, which hosts over 500 web applications for launching simulations and serves over 1 million users worldwide [183], featuring a user-friendly graphical user interface (GUI) that integrates both ML surrogate and MD simulation methodologies, as illustrated in Fig. 13.12 [182]. This ML-enhanced tool generates simulation outputs with remarkable accuracy, particularly in predicting density profiles, which closely align with results obtained through MD simulations. In

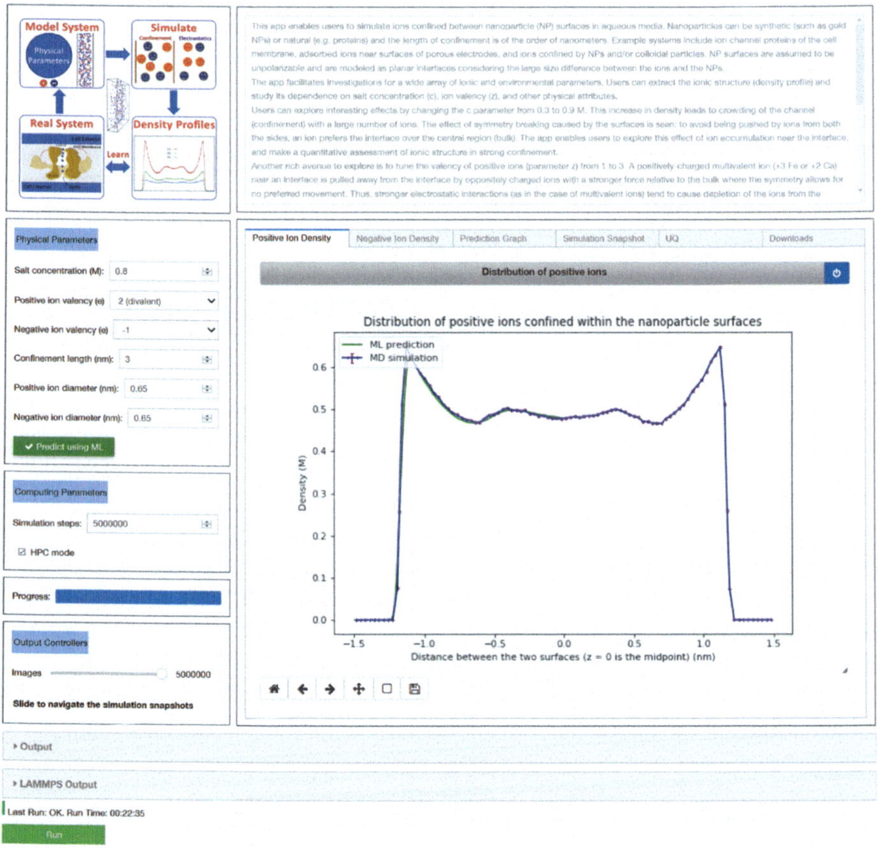


**Figure 13.12** Snapshot of the GUI of the ML-enhanced "Ions in nanoconfinement" nanoHUB tool. The GUI shows the density profile predicted by the ML surrogate (green line) and the result from completed runs of HPC-accelerated MD simulations (red markers). Reprinted with permission from [181].

addition to the high accuracy, ML inferences are made in a fraction of the time required by traditional MD simulations, approximately 0.2 seconds compared to an average of 36 minutes. This enhanced efficiency not only expedites the process but also enhances accessibility, rendering the tool invaluable for both in-classroom teaching and homework assignments. By leveraging this platform, students can immerse themselves in a wide array of chemical and physical phenomena, such as self-assembly, ionic behavior near interfaces, nanoscale material design, modeling, and simulation, and gain hands-on experience in biomaterials. The interactive GUI facilitates the examination of intricate relationships between specific parameters of biomaterials and their structural and dynamic behaviors, thereby fostering deeper comprehension and engagement in the subject matter.

Surveys and assessment studies indicate a notable enhancement in interactivity with simulation frameworks, marked by dynamic, real-time engagement and anytime access, thereby facilitating improved student comprehension of fundamental biomaterial concepts [184,185]. Additionally, survey feedback consistently highlights students' high satisfaction with simulation tools, rating them close to the highest level across user-friendliness, convenience, GUI layout, and consistency metrics [182]. Moreover, students attribute their increased conceptual and practical understanding of nanoscale simulations to several factors, including the user-friendly interface, ML-powered instantaneous predictions, and the availability of multidimensional input options. When comparing simulation-driven classroom teaching with traditional methods, students overwhelmingly express a preference for simulation-driven approaches in teaching computational science concepts. Furthermore, the survey responses underscore students' appreciation for the ability to manipulate various model parameters to probe system behavior. Additionally, they positively received output graphs as aids in their learning process.

The effectiveness of ML surrogates in generating accurate predictions of simulation outputs at a fraction of the time and computational cost of traditional methods presents a valuable avenue for students to study a wide array of chemical and physical phenomena, including self-assembly and nanoscale biomaterial design. With user-friendly GUIs of web applications on platforms like nanoHUB, students can engage directly with simulations, analyzing and adjusting model parameters in real time for deeper understanding. This integration of ML and simulation technologies promises to revolutionize classroom teaching, enhancing student learning experiences in computational science and biomaterials engineering.

Tables 13.11 and 13.12 present the learning outcomes of the strategy and the characteristics of the AI model.

### 13.4.4 AI-enhanced intelligent fault diagnosis for key bioproduct machinery

#### 13.4.4.1 Educational framework and objective

This section explores the strategic application of AI to develop an educational framework that equips students with the skills to deploy AI models for predictive

**Table 13.11** Learning outcomes for AI-enhanced molecular simulations in biomaterials education.

| Outcome | After the course, the student | Evaluation method |
|---|---|---|
| 1. Simulation proficiency | Understands and applies MD simulations to study biomaterials | Simulation labs and assignments |
| 2. Computation-al efficiency | Masters the use of high-performance computing (HPC) and parallel computing for simulations | Practical sessions on HPC usage |
| 3. ML integration | Can implement and interpret ML surrogate models for rapid simulations | Projects involving ML surrogates |
| 4. Real-time analysis | Engages in real-time analysis of simulations to understand dynamic behaviors | In-class interactive sessions |

**Table 13.12** AI model characteristics for enhancing molecular simulations with machine learning.

| Feature | Description | Relevance to education |
|---|---|---|
| Algorithm type | Utilizes machine learning surrogates such as ANN | Introduce advanced predictive modeling techniques |
| Data handling | Processes and integrates data simulation efficiently | Teach data management in a high-data environment |
| Model efficiency | Optimizes simulations to run with reduced computational resources | Emphasize efficient computing strategies |
| Output interpretation | Generates and interprets complex simulation outputs quickly | Illustrate real-time data analysis techniques |

maintenance in bioproduct smart manufacturing [186]. This approach allows students to be introduced to the utilization of condition monitoring to determine the longevity and efficiency of equipment with a test bench and AI model that is continuously updated with new data, leading to a constantly improving predictive model [187] (Fig. 13.13).

Students are first introduced to the fundamental operations and potential failure points of industry-specific machinery through hands-on laboratory experiments and simulations. In the case of bioproduct industries, typical

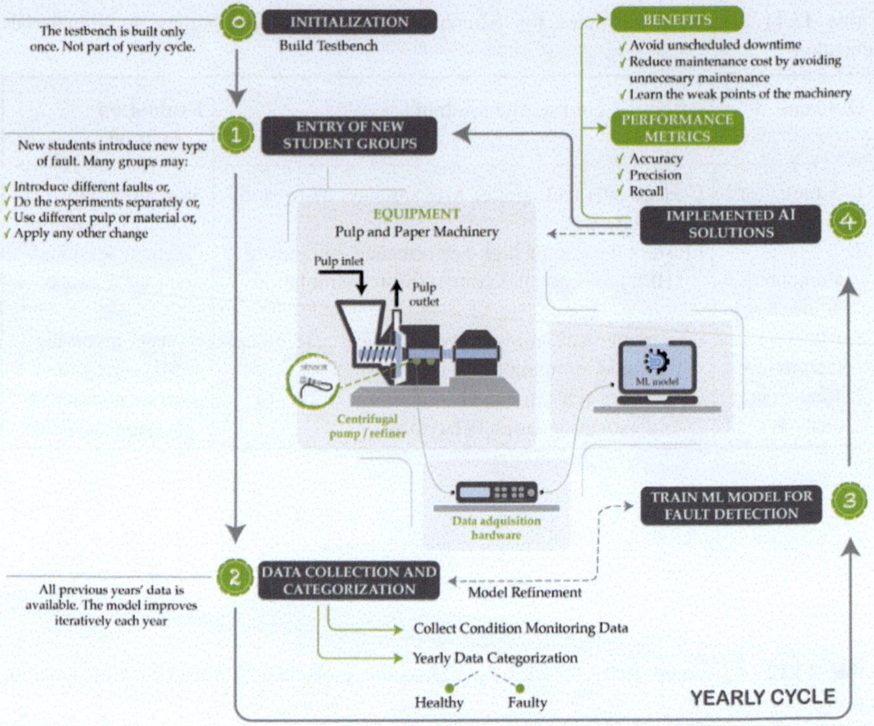


**Figure 13.13** Example of a bench-scale laboratory setting for the utilization of AI-enhanced intelligent fault diagnosis in a fiber-based production facility. (1) Testbench, (2) collection of data and characterization, (3) ML model training, and (4) implementation of AI solutions are presented.

examples could include bearings, seals, and impellers of centrifugal pumps and refiners. This part is critical in understanding the real-world implications of equipment malfunction and the importance of reliable machinery in the pulp and paper sector [188,189].

### *13.4.4.2 Data acquisition and handling*

A pivotal part of the coursework is to master data collection for condition monitoring, which includes understanding not only data handling but also the types of sensors available for this purpose and the practical considerations involved with their use [190]. Practical sessions on data handling impart the skill of managing the large time series datasets that are typical in AI applications. This forms the base for students to comprehend and engage with the world of predictive analytics. Students learn to implement AI-based diagnostic tools and are tested on their ability to manage this software. The goal is to integrate AI smoothly into the maintenance processes of the process industry, hence streamlining operations and maintenance tasks [191]. **The educational journey is characterized by continuous learning, where students**

**Table 13.13** Learning outcomes during the application of AI project and product-based learning strategies into pulp and paper machinery education.

| Outcome | After the course, the student | Evaluation method | Industry application |
|---|---|---|---|
| 1. Equipment mechanics | Understands fundamental operation principles and failure modes of some key pulp and paper machinery | Lab experiments and simulations | Enhance equipment reliability and reduce downtime |
| 2. Data acquisition | Masters techniques of data collection for condition monitoring | Practical sessions on data handling | Formulate the groundwork for predictive analytics |
| 3. AI model deployment | Can implement and manage AI-based diagnostic software | Software proficiency tests | Streamline maintenance processes through AI integration |
| 4. Continuous improvement | Can engage in iterative learning and model refinement with new data | Project-based assessment | Sustain a culture of perpetual advancement in operations |

**refine the AI model with new data every year**. Project-based assessments allow students to apply their learning in a real-world context, encouraging a mindset geared toward innovation and ongoing progress. The learning outcomes are presented in Table 13.13.

#### *13.4.4.3 AI model deployment and continuous improvement*

In Table 13.14 an example of the AI model characteristics is outlined. Initially trained on existing data to establish predictive accuracy, the model is then annually updated with new "healthy" and "faulty" data collected by students. This cyclical process mirrors the characteristics table of the AI model, deepening understanding of both the algorithmic foundations and data complexities. The resulting AI model not only serves an educational purpose but also provides data for academic research in condition monitoring and demonstrates the practical applicability of AI in industrial contexts.

### *13.4.5 VR in product-based learning education*

Through VR and AR, students can virtually interact with biomaterial structures at the molecular level or simulate biorefinery processes in a controlled, immersive

**Table 13.14** AI model characteristics during the application of AI project and product-based learning strategies into pulp and paper machinery education.

| **Feature** | **Description** | **Relevance to rducation** | **Impact on predictive maintenance** |
|---|---|---|---|
| Algorithm type | Supervised learning models such as SVM, random forest, CNN, and WDCNN | Introduce students to machine learning techniques | Accurate fault detection and classification |
| Data processing | Handling and preprocessing of large datasets | Teach data hygiene and preparation | Reliable input for model training |
| Model training | Iterative approach with cross-validation. Few-shot learning. | Illustrate the importance of model accuracy and generalization | Enhanced prediction of equipment failures |
| Outcome analysis | Performance metrics like accuracy, precision, and recall | Quantify learning outcomes and model efficacy | Informed decision-making in maintenance schedules |

environment. These interactive experiences, supported by AI, deepen learners' engagement and facilitate a more nuanced understanding of material science and engineering principles [192]. Simulation and digital twining of biorefinery operations is another area where AI algorithms can play a crucial role. Using a combination of ML models and process simulation software, students can explore the effects of various operational parameters on the efficiency and sustainability of biorefinery processes in VR settings [61].

VR has been proposed as a case study at Eindhoven University of Technology to be implemented into chemical engineering education. Initially, VR can be utilized for immersive learning experiences by integrating mathematical models with VR interfaces, leading to enhanced visualization of process plants and equipment and a better understanding of complex chemical processes. The pedagogical implementation stage foresees the adoption of VR to provide interactive learning experiences, allowing self-paced learning and a safe learning environment, though it may not suit all learners and could cause physical discomfort for some users [193].

VR has also been proposed to be utilized in operator training within chemical engineering.

In the Introduction to VR Environment phase, operators begin by acquainting themselves with VR controls, navigation, and the layout of virtual chemical plants.

This phase allows operators to become comfortable within the VR environment, effectively reducing initial disorientation. The primary advantage of this stage is the enhancement of spatial awareness and the mitigation of the learning curve associated with VR technology, though it may necessitate a period of adjustment for some operators, potentially delaying the onset of training [194]. During the Interactive Training Sessions phase, operators participate in hands-on training within the VR environment, where they practice operational procedures and respond to simulated emergencies. This engagement results in an improved understanding of operational procedures and emergency responses, alongside enhanced muscle memory for executing critical tasks. The ability to safely practice handling hazardous situations without real-world risks and the increase in engagement through interactive learning stand out as significant benefits. However, the development of high-quality VR content can be resource-intensive, and simulations might not capture the full complexity of real-life scenarios [194].

The continuous feedback and assessment phase is characterized by the provision of real-time feedback during VR training sessions, accompanied by assessments to gage operator performance and comprehension. This stage leads to the identification of improvement areas, ensuring operators reach a high level of proficiency prior to real-life application. The advantages include facilitating personalized learning and promoting rapid skill development, although it necessitates sophisticated VR software for meaningful feedback, which could be complex to develop [194]. Incorporation of game-based learning integration introduces game elements to increase motivation and engagement, applying learned skills in competitive or cooperative settings. This approach enhances operator motivation and engagement, leading to improved information retention and skill application in a gamified context. Making learning enjoyable and memorable, fostering competition and teamwork, presents a challenge in balancing educational content with game elements to maintain learning objectives without diminishing the fun aspect. Finally, the learning analytics implementation phase involves the collection and analysis of data regarding operators' performance and learning progress within the VR environment. This analysis offers insights into operators' strengths and weaknesses, facilitating targeted improvements in training programs. It supports data-driven decisions to augment training program effectiveness and personalized learning pathways. Nevertheless, the collection and interpretation of analytics demands advanced software tools and may introduce privacy concerns [194].

### 13.4.5.1 Educational objectives and learning outcomes

In Fig. 13.14, the use of virtual laboratories in chemical engineering education is presented. Each stage of the strategy, characteristics, outcomes, advantages, and limitations are explained in detail. One of the main takeaways of the application of these strategies is the increase of accessibility and inclusiveness in sites where laboratories are not available for diverse reasons [150,195]. The core content analysis of the example syllabus is presented in Table 13.15.

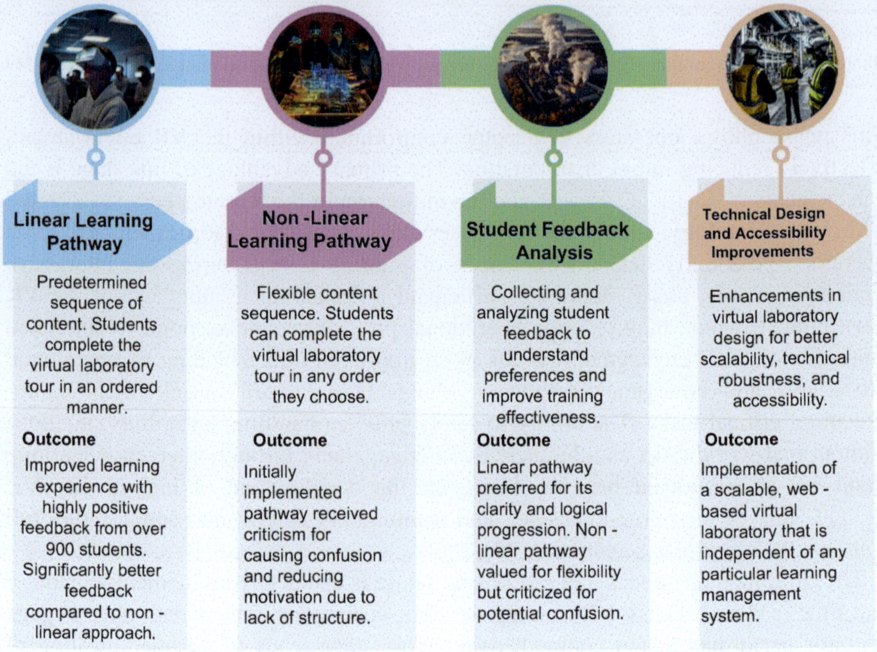


**Figure 13.14** Example of the application of virtual laboratories in chemical engineering education. Each stage's characteristics, outcomes, advantages, and limitations of the strategy application are shown.
Reprinted with permission from [150].

**Table 13.15** Core content analysis for virtual reality in product-based learning education.

| After the course, the student | Core content component | Description |
|---|---|---|
| Must know | Basics of VR | Students must grasp the fundamental technologies behind VR and their applications in chemical engineering. |
| | VR for process visualization | Understanding how VR can be used to visualize complex chemical processes and plant operations enhances theoretical knowledge and practical understanding. |
| Should know | Operational training via VR | Proficiency in using VR for operational training, including handling normal operations and emergency situations. |
| Could know | Game-based learning in VR | Familiarity with integrating game elements into VR training can make learning more engaging and effective, enhancing motivation and retention. |
| | Learning analytics in VR | Understanding how to collect and analyze data from VR training sessions to refine educational strategies and personalize learning. |

### 13.4.6 AR in product-based learning education

AR offers a transformative approach in chemical engineering education by providing enhanced visualizations of equipment and operational processes. It has been proposed recently to be implemented in laboratory settings. The strategy allows for attaining enhanced visualization of equipment and operations, enabling a better understanding of the stages of obtaining a product.

#### 13.4.6.1 Educational objectives and learning outcomes

In Fig. 13.15, the characteristics, outcomes, and advantages of each stage are shown. One of the main advantages is the online availability of these applications in smartphones, although the development of these types of apps is resource-intensive, with design complexities to simulate a high-quality environment [152,156]. In Table 13.16, the core content analysis on the application of AR in PBL education is presented.

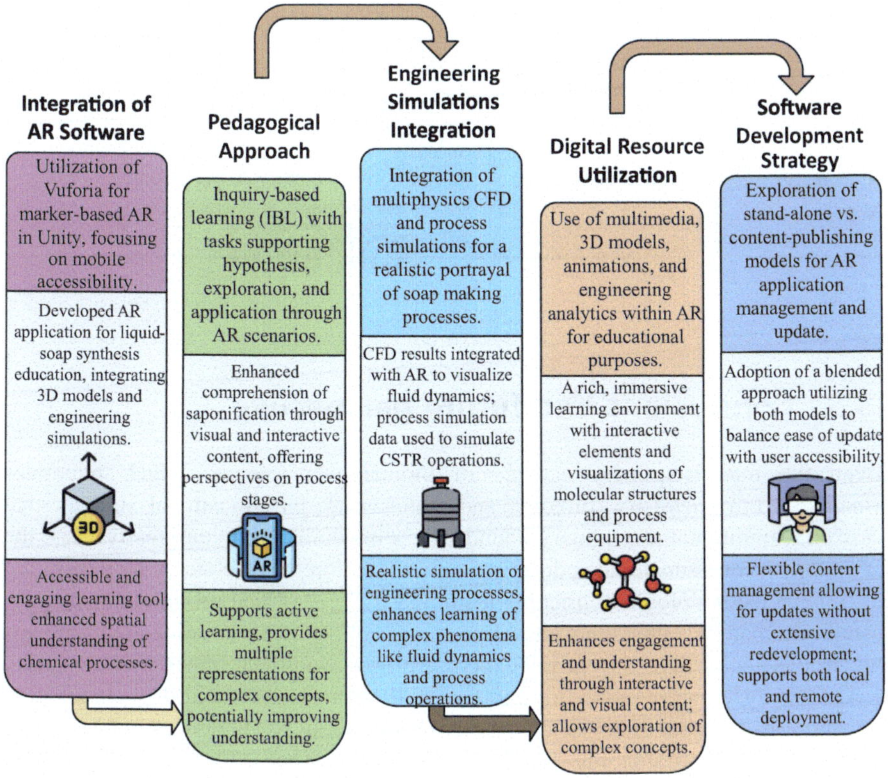


**Figure 13.15** Example of the application of augmented reality laboratories in chemical engineering education. Each stage's characteristics, outcomes, and advantages of the strategy application are shown.
Reprinted with permission from [196].

**Table 13.16** Core content analysis for augmented reality in product-based learning education.

| After the course, the student | Core content component | Description |
|---|---|---|
| Must know | Fundamentals of AR technology | Students must have a foundational understanding of AR technology and its applications in visualizing chemical engineering processes. |
| | Visualization of laboratory Procedures | Mastery of utilizing AR for visualizing complex laboratory procedures is essential to bridge the gap between theoretical knowledge and practical operations. |
| Should know | Operational process analysis | Proficiency in employing AR to analyze and understand operational processes within a simulated environment is crucial for fostering a deeper comprehension of chemical engineering principles. |
| | Interactive learning with AR | The ability to interact with virtual representations of laboratory settings and equipment is important for enhancing learning engagement and effectiveness. |
| Could know | Challenges in AR application design | Familiarity with the complexities involved in designing high-quality AR environments that accurately simulate real-world settings is advantageous. |

## 13.5 Conclusions and future perspective

Given the interdisciplinary essence of biomaterials science, which integrates principles from chemistry, biology, and engineering, an educational strategy that transcends traditional disciplinary boundaries is imperative. AI can greatly assist the forward path for biomaterials education within the biorefinery concept by generating educational methodologies, enriching learning experiences, and driving innovation in sustainable materials development. AI promotes collaborative learning environments and ensures access to resources and expertise from various disciplines. The capability of AI to analyze and integrate information from distinct fields will drive innovation and empower students to devise comprehensive solutions to challenges in biorefinery development and sustainability [197].

Developments in ML, NLP, and predictive analytics hold the promise of providing immersive learning experiences, which may include AR and VR simulations of biorefinery processes. These technologies allow students to gain a further understanding of complex biomaterial systems and their applications [198]. Anticipating the future of biomaterials education, there is an expected shift toward more personalized and adaptive learning strategies, with AI at the core of tailoring educational content to meet individual learner needs [199].

Assessment methods in the evolving educational landscape must also progress. Evaluations should prioritize critical thinking, the rationale behind decisions, and problem-solving strategies rather than mere memorization of facts. While oral evaluations pose scalability challenges, they are preferred for their effectiveness in measuring comprehension more accurately than written tests, which AI tools can easily generate [27]. LLMs' ability to integrate information from various sources into coherent, customized responses presents a significant improvement over traditional search techniques.

A critical component of AI-integrated education is teaching students how to formulate effective questions, a skill that is invaluable in both academic and professional contexts, where the right questions can lead to innovative solutions and insights. GPT-based AI models can enhance this skill by enabling interactive brainstorming sessions and providing rapid, relevant responses. Nonetheless, the integration of GPT AI in education presents challenges. Plagiarism detection is complicated with content that, while original, is generated by AI. Educators must therefore emphasize the creation of original work and the critical assessment of AI-generated content.

Concerns regarding the transparency and explainability of AI algorithms could impact the students' ability to critically evaluate the information provided by AI. Additionally, the potential for AI to perpetuate existing biases highlights the need for oversight and ethical usage of these technologies in educational settings. As AI technology continues to evolve, educators in chemical engineering and biomaterials must stay flexible, continuously updating teaching strategies to harness AI's potential while addressing its limitations and challenges.

Effective metrics to assess AI's impact on learning outcomes are essential to align its use with educational objectives, ensuring that AI serves as a valuable tool in the advancement of pedagogy [27]. Forging robust partnerships between academic institutions and industry is essential for the progression of biomaterials education and research. Joint projects and internships provide students with practical experience in applying AI to biomaterials development, bridging the gap between theoretical knowledge and practical application. Such collaborative efforts will also encourage the sharing of ideas and resources, stimulating innovation and the biorefinery concept in the biomaterials field [200].

## Acknowledgment

To the best of the Editors' knowledge and authors' claims, no generative AI tools were used for substantive writing of chapters. Any AI-assisted language editing, if applied, was limited to grammar or style suggestions and did not alter the scientific content.

## References


[1] Crippa M, Solazzo E, Guizzardi D, Monforti-Ferrario F, Tubiello FN, Leip A. Food systems are responsible for a third of global anthropogenic GHG emissions. Nat. Food 2021;2(3):198–209. https://doi.org/10.1038/s43016-021-00225-9.

[2] UN. GHG data from UNFCCC. Available from: https://unfccc.int/topics/mitigation/resources/registry-and-data/ghg-data-from-unfccc Accessed 2022 Sep 10.

[3] Li Y, Zambrano F, Wang Y, Marquez R. How China's foreign waste ban will reshape the U.S. Recycling supply chain: economic and environmental considerations towards a circular economy oriented paper recycling industry. BioResources 2022;17(2):3178–201. https://doi.org/10.15376/biores.17.2.3178-3201.

[4] Williams M, McDonough M, Edge S. Interdisciplinary circular economy design education through local and regional partnerships. Product Lifetimes and the Environment 2017:432–6.. https://doi.org/10.3233/978-1-61499-820-4-432. No. 2011.

[5] Romero-Luis J, Carbonell-Alcocer A, Gertrudix M, Gertrudis Casado M, del C. What is the maturity level of circular economy and bioenergy research addressed from education and communication? a systematic literature review and epistemological perspectives. Journal of Cleaner Production 2021;322:129007.

[6] Williams ID, Roberts KP, Shaw PJ, Cleasby B. Applying circular economy thinking to industry by integrating education and research activities. Detritus 2018;1(March):134–43. https://doi.org/10.26403/detritus/2018.11.

[7] Klarin T. The concept of sustainable development: from its beginning to the contemporary issues. Zagreb International Review of Economics and Business 2018;21(1):67–94. https://doi.org/10.2478/zireb-2018-0005.

[8] Kirchherr J, Reike D, Hekkert M. Conceptualizing the circular economy: an analysis of 114 definitions. Resources, Conservation and Recycling 2017;127:221–32. https://doi.org/10.1016/j.resconrec.2017.09.005.

[9] Harris S, Martin M, Diener D. Circularity for circularity's sake? scoping review of assessment methods for environmental performance in the circular economy. Sustainable Production and Consumption 2021;26:172–86.

[10] Vera R, Zambrano F, Suarez A, Pifano A, Marquez R, Farrell M, et al. Transforming textile wastes into biobased building blocks via enzymatic hydrolysis: a review of key challenges and opportunities. Clean Circular Bioeconomy 2022;3:100026. https://doi.org/10.1016/j.clcb.2022.100026.

[11] Ortiz M, Alvarado JG, Zambrano F, Marquez R. Surfactants produced from carbohydrate derivatives. A review of the biobased building blocks used in their synthesis. Journal of Surfactants and Detergents 2022;25:147–83. https://doi.org/10.1002/jsde.12581.

[12] Muranko Z, Andrews D, Chaer I, Newton EJ. Circular economy and behaviour change: using persuasive communication to encourage pro-circular behaviours towards the purchase of remanufactured refrigeration equipment. Journal of Cleaner Production 2019;222:499–510. https://doi.org/10.1016/j.jclepro.2019.02.219.

[13] Bertassini AC, Zanon LG, Azarias JG, Gerolamo MC, Ometto AR. Circular business ecosystem innovation: a guide for mapping stakeholders, capturing values, and finding new opportunities. Sustainable Production and Consumption 2021;27:436–48. https://doi.org/10.1016/j.spc.2020.12.004.

[14] Pieroni MPP, McAloone TC, Borgianni Y, Maccioni L, Pigosso DCA. An expert system for circular economy business modelling: advising manufacturing companies in

decoupling value creation from resource consumption. Sustainable Production and Consumption 2021;27:534–50.

[15] Paletta A, Bonoli A. Governing the university in the perspective of the United Nations 2030 agenda. International Journal of Sustainability in Higher Education 2019;20(3):500–14. https://doi.org/10.1108/IJSHE-02-2019-0083.

[16] Fernandez Rivas D, Boffito DC, Faria-Albanese J, Glassey J, Afraz N, Akse H, et al. Process intensification education contributes to sustainable development goals. Part 1. Education for Chemical Engineers 2020;32:1–14. https://doi.org/10.1016/j.ece.2020.04.003.

[17] Abad-Segura E, González-Zamar M-D. Sustainable economic development in higher education institutions: a global analysis within the SDGs framework. Journal of Cleaner Production 2021;294:126133. https://doi.org/10.1016/j.jclepro.2021.126133.

[18] Chen T-L, Kim H, Pan S-Y, Tseng P-C, Lin Y-P, Chiang P-C. Implementation of green chemistry principles in circular economy system towards sustainable development goals: challenges and perspectives. The Science of the Total Environment 2020;716:136998. https://doi.org/10.1016/j.scitotenv.2020.136998.

[19] Sun M, Wang Y, Shi L, Klemeš JJ. Uncovering energy use, carbon emissions and environmental burdens of pulp and paper industry: a systematic review and meta-analysis. Renewable and Sustainable Energy Reviews 2018;92:823–33. https://doi.org/10.1016/j.rser.2018.04.036.

[20] Remón J, Casales M, Gracia J, Callén MS, Pinilla JL, Suelves I. Sustainable production of liquid biofuels and value-added platform chemicals by hydrodeoxygenation of lignocellulosic bio-oil over a carbon–neutral Mo2C/CNF catalyst. Chemical Engineering Journal 2021;405(August 2020):126705. https://doi.org/10.1016/j.cej.2020.126705.

[21] Ubando AT, Felix CB, Chen W-H. Biorefineries in circular bioeconomy: a comprehensive review. Bioresource Technology 2020;299:122585. https://doi.org/10.1016/j.biortech.2019.122585.

[22] Tan ECD, Lamers P. Circular bioeconomy concepts—a perspective. Frontiers in Sustainability 2021;2(July):1–8. https://doi.org/10.3389/frsus.2021.701509.

[23] Vera R, Suarez A, Zambrano F, Marquez R, Bedard J, Vivas K, et al. Upcycling cotton textile waste into bio-based building blocks through an environmentally friendly and high-yield conversion process. Resources, Conservation and Recycling 2023;189:106715. https://doi.org/10.1016/j.resconrec.2022.106715353.

[24] Byrne EP. The evolving engineer; professional accreditation sustainability criteria and societal imperatives and norms. Education for Chemical Engineers 2023;43:23–30. https://doi.org/10.1016/j.ece.2023.01.004.

[25] Dudefoi W, Villares A, Peyron S, Moreau C, Ropers M-H, Gontard N, et al. Nanoscience and nanotechnologies for biobased mtcrials, packaging and food applications: new opportunities and concerns. Innovative Food Science and Emerging Technologies 2018;46:107–21. https://doi.org/10.1016/j.ifset.2017.09.007.

[26] Hairon Azhar NN, Ang DT, Abdullah R, Harikrishna JA, Cheng A. Bio-based materials riding the wave of sustainability: common misconceptions, opportunities, challenges and the way forward. Sustainability 2022;14:5032. https://doi.org/10.3390/su14095032.

[27] Marquez R, Barrios N, Vera RE, Mendez ME, Tolosa L, Zambrano F, et al. A perspective on the synergistic potential of artificial intelligence and product-based learning strategies in biobased materials education. Education for Chemical Engineers 2023;44:164–80. https://doi.org/10.1016/j.ece.2023.05.005.

[28] Bastidas-Oyanedel J-R, Schmidt JE. Biorefinery: integrated sustainable processes for biomass conversion to biomaterials, biofuels and fertilizers. New Jersey: Springer; 2019.

[29] Liu S, Abrahamson LP, Scott GM. Biorefinery: ensuring biomass as a sustainable renewable source of chemicals, materials, and energy. Biomass and Bioenergy 2012;39:1–4. https://doi.org/10.1016/j.biombioe.2010.12.042.
[30] Barrios N, Marquez R, McDonald JD, Hubbe MA, Venditti R, Lokendra P. Innovation in lignocellulosics dewatering and drying for energy sustainability and enhanced utilization of forestry, agriculture, and marine resources—a review. Advances in Colloid and Interface Science 2023;318:102936.
[31] Vera RE, Vivas KA, Urdaneta F, Franco J, Sun R, Forfora N, et al. Transforming non-wood feedstocks into dissolving pulp via organosolv pulping: an alternative strategy to boost the share of natural fibers in the textile industry. Journal of Cleaner Production 2023;429:139394. https://doi.org/10.1016/j.jclepro.2023.139394.
[32] Toor M, Kumar SS, Malyan SK, Bishnoi NR, Mathimani T, Rajendran K, et al. An overview on bioethanol production from lignocellulosic feedstocks. Chemosphere 2020;242:125080. https://doi.org/10.1016/j.chemosphere.2019.125080.
[33] Hassan SS, Williams GA, Jaiswal AK. Moving towards the second generation of lignocellulosic biorefineries in the EU: drivers, challenges, and opportunities. Renewable and Sustainable Energy Reviews 2019;101:590–9. https://doi.org/10.1016/j.rser.2018.11.041.
[34] Clark J, Deswarte F. The biorefinery concept. Introduction to chemicals from biomass. 2015. p. 1–29. https://doi.org/10.1002/9781118714478.ch1.
[35] He Q, Chen H. Increased efficiency of butanol production from spent sulfite liquor by removal of fermentation inhibitors. Journal of Cleaner Production 2020;263:121356. https://doi.org/10.1016/j.jclepro.2020.121356.
[36] Wang S, Mukhambet Y, Esakkimuthu S, Abomohra AE-F. Integrated microalgal biorefinery—routes, energy, economic and environmental perspectives. Journal of Cleaner Production 2022;348:131245. https://doi.org/10.1016/j.jclepro.2022.131245.
[37] Calvo-Flores FG, Martin-Martinez FJ. Biorefineries: achievements and challenges for a bio-based economy. Frontiers in Chemistry 2022;10:973417. https://www.frontiersin.org/articles/10.3389/fchem.2022.973417.
[38] Nanda S, Vo DVN, Sarangi PK. Biorefinery of alternative resources: targeting green fuels and platform chemicals. Singapore: Springer; 2020. https://doi.org/10.1007/978-981-15-1804-1.
[39] Saini R, Osorio-Gonzalez CS, Hegde K, Brar SK, Magdouli S, Vezina P, et al. Lignocellulosic biomass-based biorefinery: an insight into commercialization and economic standout. Current Sustainable Energy Reports 2020;7(4):122–36. https://doi.org/10.1007/s40518-020-00157-1.
[40] Ragauskas AJ, Williams CK, Davison BH, Britovsek G, Cairney J, Eckert CA, et al. The path forward for biofuels and biomaterials. Science (New York, N.Y.) 2006;311(5760):484–9.. https://doi.org/10.1126/science.1114736. *(80).*
[41] Davis R, Tao L, Tan ECD, Biddy MJ, Beckham GT, Scarlata C Process design and economics for the conversion of lignocellulosic biomass to hydrocarbons: dilute-acid and enzymatic deconstruction of biomass to sugars and biological conversion of sugars to hydrocarbons. National Renewable Energy Laboratory Technical Report NREL/TP-5100-60223. 2013;147.
[42] Tyagi P, Hubbe MA, Lucia L, Pal L. High performance nanocellulose-based composite coatings for oil and grease resistance. Cellulose 2018;25(6):3377–91. https://doi.org/10.1007/s10570-018-1810-7.
[43] Heinze T, Rojas OJ. Cellulose chemistry and properties: fibers, nanocelluloses and advanced materials. Advances in polymer science. Springer International Publishing; 2016.. https://doi.org/10.1007/978-3-319-26015-0. Vol. 271.

[44] Sandin G, Peters GM. Environmental impact of textile reuse and recycling—a review. Journal of Cleaner Production 2018;184:353–65. https://doi.org/10.1016/j.jclepro.2018.02.266.
[45] Otto S, Strenger M, Maier-Nöth A, Schmid M, Otto S, Strenger M, et al. Food packaging and sustainability—consumer perception vs. correlated scientific facts. Journal of Cleaner Production 2021;298:126733. https://doi.org/10.1016/j.jclepro.2021.126733.
[46] Hubbe MA, Alén R, Paleologou M, Kannangara M, Kihlman J. Lignin recovery from spent alkaline pulping liquors using acidification, membrane separation, and related processing steps: a review. BioResources 2019;14(1):2300–51. https://doi.org/10.15376/biores.14.1.Hubbe.
[47] Hubbe MA, Rojas OJ. Colloidal stability and aggregation of lignocellulosic materials in aqueous suspension: a review. BioResources 2008;3(4):1419–91.
[48] Tardy BL, Mattos BD, Otoni CG, Beaumont M, Majoinen J, Kämäräinen T, et al. Deconstruction and reassembly of renewable polymers and biocolloids into next generation structured materials. Chemical Reviews 2021;121(22):14088–188. https://doi.org/10.1021/acs.chemrev.0c01333.
[49] Li T, Chen C, Brozena AH, Zhu JY, Xu L, Driemeier C, et al. Developing fibrillated cellulose as a sustainable technological material. Nature 2021;590(7844):47–56. https://doi.org/10.1038/s41586-020-03167-7.
[50] PSM Market Research. Biorefinery market. Available from: https://www.psmarketresearch.com/market-analysis/biorefinery-market Accessed 2024 Mar 22.
[51] Argus Media. SGP plans 2024 FID for Panama biorefinery. Available from: https://www.argusmedia.com/en/news-and-insights/latest-market-news/2496 https://www.argusmedia.com/en/news-and-insights/latest-market-news/2496643-sgp-plans-2024-fid-for-panama-biorefinery Accessed 2023 Feb 22.
[52] Petronas. PETRONAS, Eni and Euglena to explore biorefinery opportunity in Malaysia. Available from: https://www.petronas.com/media/media-releases/petronas-eni-and-euglena-explore-biorefinery-opportunity-malaysia Accessed 2023 Feb 10.
[53] SPGlobal. Renewables projects in Europe. Available from: https://www.spglobal.com/commodityinsights/en/market-insights/latest-news/chemicals/072622-refinery-news-roundup-renewables-projects-in-europe Accessed 2023 Feb 10.
[54] Metsä Group. Metsä Group and ANDRITZ to construct a demo plant for developing new lignin products. Available from: https://www.metsagroup.com/news-and-publications/news/2024/metsa-group-and-andritz-to-construct-a-demo-plant-for-developing-new-lignin-products/ Accessed 2024 Mar 22.
[55] Brienzo M. Hemicellulose biorefinery: a sustainable solution for value addition to bio-based products and bioenergy. Singapore: Springer Nature; 2022.
[56] Ratner BD, Bryant SJ. Biomaterials: where we have been and where we are going. Annual Review of Biomedical Engineering 2004;6(1):41–75. https://doi.org/10.1146/annurev.bioeng.6.040803.140027.
[57] Anastas PT, Levy IJ. Green chemistry education changing the course of chemistry. American Chemical Society; 2009.
[58] Márquez R, Tolosa L, Gómez R, Izaguirre C, Rennola L, Bullón J, et al. Reproducción de Un Ambiente de Innovación En El Salón de Clase. Una Estrategia Para Promover La Creatividad En La Educación En Ingeniería Química. Educación Química 2016;27(4):249–56. https://doi.org/10.1016/j.eq.2016.07.001.
[59] Moraga G, Huysveld S, Mathieux F, Blengini GA, Alaerts L, Van Acker K, et al. Circular economy indicators: what do they measure? Resources, Conservation and Recycling 2019;146:452–61. https://doi.org/10.1016/j.resconrec.2019.03.045.

[60] Tolppanen S, Kang J, Riuttanen L. Changes in students' knowledge, values, worldview, and willingness to take mitigative climate action after attending a course on holistic climate change education. Journal of Cleaner Production 2022;373:133865. https://doi.org/10.1016/j.jclepro.2022.133865.

[61] Pistikopoulos EN, Barbosa-Povoa A, Lee JH, Misener R, Mitsos A, Reklaitis GV, et al. Process systems engineering—the generation next? Computers and Chemical Engineering 2021;147:107252. https://doi.org/10.1016/j.compchemeng.2021.107252.

[62] Chen L, Chen P, Lin Z. Artificial intelligence in education: a review. IEEE Access 2020;8:75264–78. https://doi.org/10.1109/ACCESS.2020.2988510.

[63] McCulloch WS, Pitts W. A logical calculus of the ideas immanent in nervous activity. The Bulletin of Mathematical Biophysics 1943;5(4):115–33. https://doi.org/10.1007/BF02478259.

[64] Turing AM. Computing machinery and intelligence. In: Epstein R, Roberts G, Beber G, editors. Parsing the turing test. Dordrecht: Springer Netherlands; 2009. p. 23–65. https://doi.org/10.1007/978-1-4020-6710-5_3.

[65] Qin SJ, Chiang LH. Advances and opportunities in machine learning for process data analytics. Comput. Chem. Eng. 2019;126:465–73. https://doi.org/10.1016/j.compchemeng.2019.04.003.

[66] Nabavi-Pelesaraei A, Bayat R, Hosseinzadeh-Bandbafha H, Afrasyabi H, Berrada A. Prognostication of energy use and environmental impacts for recycle system of municipal solid waste management. Journal of Cleaner Production 2017;154:602–13. https://doi.org/10.1016/j.jclepro.2017.04.033.

[67] Venkatasubramanian V. The promise of artificial intelligence in chemical engineering: is it here, finally? AIChE Journal: American Institute of Chemical Engineers 2019;65(2):466–78. https://doi.org/10.1002/aic.16489.

[68] LeCun Y, Bengio Y, Hinton G. Deep learning. Nature 2015;521(7553):436–44. https://doi.org/10.1038/nature14539.

[69] Nielsen MA. Neural networks and deep learning. San Francisco, CA, USA: Determination press; 2015. Vol. 25.

[70] Goodfellow I, Pouget-Abadie J, Mirza M, Xu B, Warde-Farley D, Ozair S, et al. Generative adversarial networks. Communications of the ACM 2020;63(11):139–44. https://doi.org/10.1145/3422622.

[71] Mikolov T, Chen K, Corrado G, Dean J. Efficient estimation of word representations in vector space. 1st International Conference on Learning Representations (ICLR) 2013 – Workshop Track Proceedings. 2013. p. 1–12.

[72] Vaswani A, Shazeer N, Parmar N, Uszkoreit J, Jones L, Gomez AN, et al. Attention is all you need. Advances in Neural Information Processing Systems 2017:30.

[73] Rasheed ASA, Masud MM, Abduljabbar M. A comparative study of transformer based pretrained AI models for content summarization. 2023 15th International Conference on Innovations in Information Technology (IIT). 2023. p. 79–84. https://doi.org/10.1109/IIT59782.2023.10366411.

[74] Floridi L, Chiriatti M. GPT-3: Its nature, scope, limits, and consequences. Minds and Machines 2020;30(4):681–94. https://doi.org/10.1007/s11023-020-09548-1.

[75] Heaven WD. GPT-4 is bigger and better than ChatGPT—but OpenAI won't say why. MIT Technology Review. Available from: https://www.technologyreview.com/2023/03/14/1069823/gpt-4-is-bigger-and-better-chatgpt-openai/ Accessed 2023 Mar 18.

[76] Devlin J, Chang MW, Lee K, Toutanova K. BERT: Pre-training of deep bidirectional transformers for language understanding. Proceedings of the 2019 Conference of the

North American Chapter of the Association for Computational Linguistics: Human Language Technologies. 2019; 1(Mlm):4171–4186.
[77] Raffel C, Shazeer N, Roberts A, Lee K, Narang S, Matena M, et al. Exploring the limits of transfer learning with a unified text-to-text transformer. Journal of Machine Learning Research: JMLR 2020;21:1–67.
[78] Thoppilan R, De Freitas D, Hall J, Shazeer N, Kulshreshtha A, Cheng H-T, et al. LaMDA: language models for dialog applications. 2022.
[79] Touvron H, Lavril T, Izacard G, Martinet, X, Lachaux M-A, Lacroix T, et al. LLaMA: Open and efficient foundation language models. 2023.
[80] Lund BD, Wang T, Mannuru NR, Nie B, Shimray S, Wang Z. ChatGPT and a new academic reality: artificial intelligence-written research papers and the ethics of the large language models in scholarly publishing. Journal of the Association for Information Science and Technology 2023;74(5):570–81. https://doi.org/10.1002/asi.24750.
[81] Piaget J. The construction of reality in the child. Routledge; 2013.
[82] Siemens G. Connectivism: a learning theory for the digital age 2004.
[83] Redel-Macías MD, Pinzi S, Martínez-Jiménez MP, Dorado G, Dorado MP. Virtual laboratory on biomass for energy generation. Journal of Cleaner Production 2016;112:3842–51. https://doi.org/10.1016/j.jclepro.2015.07.075.
[84] Dai X, Chen Y. Computational biomaterials: computational simulations for biomedicine. Advanced Materials 2023;35(7):2204798. https://doi.org/10.1002/adma.202204798.
[85] Redel-Macías MD, Pinzi S, Cubero-Atienza AJ, Dorado MP, Martínez-Jiménez MP. Biorefinery virtual lab-integrating E-learning techniques and theoretical learning. In: Herrero Á., Snášel V, Abraham A, Zelinka I, Baruque B, Quintián H, Calvo JL, Sedano J, Corchado E, editors. International Joint Conference CISIS'12-ICEUTE'12-SOCO'12 Special Sessions. Berlin, Heidelberg: Springer Berlin Heidelberg; 2013. p. 321–30.
[86] Blagoev I, Vassileva G, Monov V. From data to learning: the scientific approach to AI-enhanced online course design. 2023 International Conference on Big Data, Knowledge and Control Systems Engineering (BdKCSE). 2023. p. 1–5. https://doi.org/10.1109/BdKCSE59280.2023.10339693.
[87] Grubaugh S, Levitt G, Deever D. Harnessing AI to power constructivist learning: an evolution in educational methodologies. EIKI Journal of Effective Teaching Methods 2023;1(3):81–3. https://doi.org/10.59652/jetm.v1i3.43.
[88] Piaget J. Genetic epistemology. 1st ed New York, NY: Columbia University Press; 1970.
[89] Burman JT. The genetic epistemology of Jean Piaget. Oxford University Press; 2021. https://doi.org/10.1093/acrefore/9780190236557.013.521.
[90] Crawford C, Krebs D, Crawford C, Krebs D, editors. Foundations of evolutionary psychology. Psychology Press; 2008. https://doi.org/10.4324/9780203888155.
[91] Bruner JS. Toward a theory of instruction. Harvard University Press; 1966. Vol. 59.
[92] Gagne RM, Briggs LJ. Principles of instructional design. Oxford, England: Holt, Rinehart & Winston; 1974.
[93] Carretero M. Constructivismo y Educación. Tilde editora; 2021.
[94] Staver JR. Constructivism: sound theory for explicating the practice of science and science teaching. Journal of Research in Science Teaching 1998;35(5):501–20. https://doi.org/10.1002/(SICI)1098-2736(199805)35:5<501::AID-TEA3>3.0.CO;2-T.
[95] Dewey J. Democracy and Education. 1916. Vol 9.
[96] Barrows HS. A taxonomy of problem-based learning methods. Medical Education 1986;20(6):481–6. https://doi.org/10.1111/j.1365-2923.1986.tb01386.x.

[97] Chen J, Kolmos A, Du X. Forms of implementation and challenges of PBL in engineering education: a review of literature. European Journal of Engineering Education 2021;46(1):90–115. https://doi.org/10.1080/03043797.2020.1718615.
[98] Abdullah J, Mohd-Isa WN, Samsudin MA. Virtual reality to improve group work skill and self-directed learning in problem-based learning narratives. Virtual Real 2019;23(4):461–71. https://doi.org/10.1007/s10055-019-00381-1.
[99] Tolosa L, Marquez R, Rennola L, Sandia B, Bullon J. An overview of today's project-based learning and how it has been implemented in the chemical engineering school at Universidad de Los Andes. Educ. química 2018;29(4):36–48. https://doi.org/10.22201/fq.18708404e.2018.4.64701.
[100] Kiss AA, Webb C. The manchester perspective on using the design project to enhance the education of chemical engineering students. Journal of Chemical Technology and Biotechnology (Oxford, Oxfordshire: 1986) 2021;96(6):1453–64. https://doi.org/10.1002/jctb.6725.
[101] Salcedo Galán F, Buitrago Mora HM, Jiménez Heredia AT, Sierra Peñuela LL, González Barrios AF. Everyday chemical product design as platform for teaching transport phenomena. Education for Chemical Engineers 2018;25:9–15. https://doi.org/10.1016/j.ece.2018.09.001.
[102] Patete A, Marquez R. Computer animation education online: a tool to teach control systems engineering throughout the COVID-19 pandemic. Education Sciences 2022;12(4):253. https://doi.org/10.3390/educsci12040253.
[103] Ricaurte M, Viloria A. Project-based learning as a strategy for multi-level training applied to undergraduate engineering students. Education for Chemical Engineers 2020;33:102–11. https://doi.org/10.1016/j.ece.2020.09.001.
[104] Marquez R, Tolosa L, Gómez R, Izaguirre C, Rennola L, Bullón J, et al. Reproducing an innovation environment in the classroom. An strategy to promote creativity in chemical engineering education. Educación Química 2016;27(4):249–56. https://doi.org/10.1016/j.eq.2016.07.001.
[105] Sandia B, Gutiérrez D, Hernández D, Alvarado J, Parada J, Vergara M, et al. RAIS: Una Estrategia Para El Manejo Integral de Conocimiento. Experiencias En Ingeniería. Ciencia e Ingeniería 2011;32(1):115–22.
[106] Saldivia BES, Pinzone GDG, Monzón GAP. Enseñanza de La Ingeniería Reproduciendo El Ambiente industrial. Un Manejo Integral de Conocimientos. Educere 2011;15(51):379–88.
[107] Rugarcia A, Felder RM, Woods DR, Stice JE. The future of engineering education: part 1. A vision for a new century. Chemical Engineering Education 2000;34(1):16–25.
[108] Felder RM, Brent R. Random thoughts: learning by doing. Chemical Engineering Education 2003;37(4):282–3.
[109] Franco LFM, da Costa AC, de Almeida Neto AF, Moraes ÂM, Tambourgi EB, Miranda EA, et al. A competency-based chemical engineering curriculum at the university of campinas in Brazil. Education for Chemical Engineers 2023;44:21–34. https://doi.org/10.1016/j.ece.2023.04.001.
[110] Amirault RJ, Visser YL. The university in periods of technological change: a historically grounded perspective. Journal of Computer High Education 2009;21(1):62–79. https://doi.org/10.1007/s12528-009-9016-5.
[111] Burmeister M, Rauch F, Eilks I. Education for sustainable development (ESD) and chemistry education. Chemistry Education Research and Practice 2012;13(2):59–68. https://doi.org/10.1039/C1RP90060A.

[112] Gutierrez-Bucheli L, Kidman G, Reid A. Sustainability in engineering education: a review of learning outcomes. Journal of Cleaner Production 2022;330:129734. https://doi.org/10.1016/j.jclepro.2021.129734.
[113] Moher D, Liberati A, Tetzlaff J, Altman DG. Preferred reporting items for systematic reviews and meta-analyses: the PRISMA statement. Annals of Internal Medicine 2009;151(4):264–9. https://doi.org/10.7326/0003-4819-151-4-200908180-00135.
[114] Prausnitz JM. Chemical engineering and the postmodern world. Chemical Engineering Research and Design 2001;79(7):777–88. https://doi.org/10.1205/026387601753191957.
[115] Lenihan S, Foley R, Carey WA, Duffy NB. Developing engineering competencies in industry for chemical engineering undergraduates through the integration of professional work placement and engineering research project. Education for Chemical Engineers 2020;32:82–94. https://doi.org/10.1016/j.ece.2020.05.002.
[116] García-Serna J, Pérez-Barrigón L, Cocero MJ. New trends for design towards sustainability in chemical engineering: green engineering. Chemical Engineering Journal 2007;133(1):7–30. https://doi.org/10.1016/j.cej.2007.02.028.
[117] Bolton LW, Glassey J, Ventura-Medina E. Updating chemical engineering degree accreditation in changing times. Education for Chemical Engineers 2023;43:31–6. https://doi.org/10.1016/j.ece.2023.01.005.
[118] Costa R, Moggridge GD, Saraiva PM. Chemical product engineering: an emerging paradigm within chemical engineering. AIChE Journal. American Institute of Chemical Engineers 2006;52(6):1976–86. https://doi.org/10.1002/aic.10880.
[119] Kontogeorgis GM, Jhamb S, Liang X, Dam-Johansen K. Computer-aided design of formulated products. Current Opinion in Colloid and Interface Science 2022;57:101536. https://doi.org/10.1016/j.cocis.2021.101536.
[120] Rivera Gil JL, Serna J, Arrieta-Escobar JA, Narváez Rincón PC, Boly V, Falk V. Triggers for chemical product design: a systematic literature review. AIChE Journal 2022;68(4):e17563. https://doi.org/10.1002/aic.17563.
[121] Lemus-Ruiz J, Ceja-Cardenas L, Bedolla-Becerril E, H V. Production, characterization, and mechanical evaluation of dissimilar metal/ceramic joints. Nanocomposites with unique properties and applications in medicine and industry. InTech; 2011. https://doi.org/10.5772/21720.
[122] Silveira RL, Stoyanov SR, Kovalenko A, Skaf MS. Cellulose aggregation under hydrothermal pretreatment conditions. Biomacromolecules 2016;17(8):2582–90. https://doi.org/10.1021/acs.biomac.6b00603.
[123] Yang Q, Xia C, Deng Y, Li X, Wang H. Microstructure and mechanical properties of AlSi7Mg0.6 aluminum alloy fabricated by wire and arc additive manufacturing based on cold metal transfer (WAAM CMT). Materials 2019;12(16):2525. https://doi.org/10.3390/ma12162525.
[124] Barsoum MW. Fundamentals of ceramics. Boca Raton: CRC Press; 2002. https://doi.org/10.1887/0750309024.
[125] Montanari R, Varone A. Processing–structure–property relationships in metals. Metals 2019;9(8):907. https://doi.org/10.3390/met9080907.
[126] Yao J, Chen S, Chen Y, Wang B, Pei Q, Wang H. Macrofibers with high mechanical performance based on aligned bacterial cellulose nanofibers. ACS Applied Materials and Interfaces 2017;9(24):20330–9. https://doi.org/10.1021/acsami.6b14650.
[127] Mittal N, Ansari F, Gowda Krishne V, Brouzet C, Chen P, Larsson PT, et al. Multiscale control of nanocellulose assembly: transferring remarkable nanoscale fibril mechanics to

macroscale fibers. ACS Nano 2018;12(7):6378–88. https://doi.org/10.1021/acsnano.8b01084.
[128] Li T, Song J, Zhao X, Yang Z, Pastel G, Xu S, et al. Anisotropic, lightweight, strong, and super thermally insulating nanowood with naturally aligned nanocellulose. Science Advances 2018;4(3):eaas3724. https://doi.org/10.1126/sciadv.aar3724.
[129] Saba N, Safwan A, Sanyang ML, Mohammad F, Pervaiz M, Jawaid M, et al. Thermal and dynamic mechanical properties of cellulose nanofibers reinforced epoxy composites. International Journal of Biological Macromolecules 2017;102:822–8. https://doi.org/10.1016/j.ijbiomac.2017.04.074.
[130] Pasangulapati V, Ramachandriya KD, Kumar A, Wilkins MR, Jones CL, Huhnke RL. Effects of cellulose, hemicellulose and lignin on thermochemical conversion characteristics of the selected biomass. Bioresource Technology 2012;114:663–9. https://doi.org/10.1016/j.biortech.2012.03.036.
[131] Collard FX, Blin J. A review on pyrolysis of biomass constituents: mechanisms and composition of the products obtained from the conversion of cellulose, hemicelluloses and lignin. Renewable and Sustainable Energy Reviews 2014;2014:594–608. https://doi.org/10.1016/j.rser.2014.06.013.
[132] Chen C, Kuang Y, Zhu S, Burgert I, Keplinger T, Gong A, et al. Structure–property–function relationships of natural and engineered wood. Nature Reviews Materials 2020;5:642–66.. https://doi.org/10.1038/s41578-020-0195-z. Nature Research September 1.
[133] Hubbe MA, Ferrer A, Tyagi P, Yin Y, Salas C, Pal L, et al. Nanocellulose in thin films, coatings, and plies for packaging applications: a review. BioResources 2017;12(1):2143–233.
[134] Semple KE, Zhou C, Rojas OJ, Nkeuwa WN, Dai C. Moulded pulp fibers for disposable food packaging: a state-of-the-art review. Food Packaging and Shelf Life 2022;33:100908. https://doi.org/10.1016/j.fpsl.2022.100908.
[135] Mitchell BS. An introduction to materials engineering and science for chemical and materials engineers. John Wiley & Sons; 2004.
[136] Reshmy R, Paulose TAP, Philip E, Thomas D, Madhavan A, Sirohi R, et al. Updates on high value products from cellulosic biorefinery. Fuel 2022;308(March 2021):122056. https://doi.org/10.1016/j.fuel.2021.122056.
[137] Vera RE, Vivas KA, Urdaneta F, Franco J, Sun R, Forfora N, et al. Transforming non-wood feedstocks into dissolving pulp: an alternative strategy to mitigate the overuse of synthetic fibers in textile manufacturing. Journal of Cleaner Production 2023.
[138] Vera RE, Zambrano F, Marquez R, Vivas KA, Forfora N, Bedard J, et al. Environmentally friendly oxidation pretreatments to produce sugar-based building blocks from dyed textile wastes via enzymatic hydrolysis. Chemical Engineering Journal 2023;467:143321. https://doi.org/10.1016/j.cej.2023.143321.
[139] Griffiths M, Forcier LB. Intelligence unleashed 2016.
[140] Wu M, Di Caprio U, Vermeire F, Hellinckx P, Braeken L, Waldherr S, et al. An artificial intelligence course for chemical engineers. Education for Chemical Engineers 2023;45:141–50. https://doi.org/10.1016/j.ece.2023.09.004.
[141] Guo K, Yang Z, Yu C-H, Buehler MJ. Artificial intelligence and machine learning in design of mechanical materials. Materials Horizons 2021;8(4):1153–72. https://doi.org/10.1039/D0MH01451F.
[142] Huang JS, Liew JX, Ademiloye AS, Liew KM. Artificial intelligence in materials modeling and design. Archives of Computational Methods in Engineering 2021;28(5):3399–413. https://doi.org/10.1007/s11831-020-09506-1.

[143] Guzmán JL, Joseph B. Web-based virtual lab for learning design, operation, control, and optimization of an anaerobic digestion process. Journal of Science Education and Technology 2021;30(3):319–30. https://doi.org/10.1007/s10956-020-09860-6.
[144] Lavor V, de Come F, dos Santos MT, Vianna AS. Machine learning in chemical engineering: hands-on activities. Education for Chemical Engineers 2024;46:10–21. https://doi.org/10.1016/j.ece.2023.09.005.
[145] Coley CW, Thomas DA, Lummiss JAM, Jaworski JN, Breen CP, Schultz V, et al. A robotic platform for flow synthesis of organic compounds informed by AI planning. Science (New York, N.Y.) 2019;365(6453):eaax1566.. https://doi.org/10.1126/science.aax1566. (80).
[146] Tapalova O, Zhiyenbayeva N. Artificial intelligence in education: AIEd for personalised learning pathways. Electronic Journal of e-Learning 2022;20(5):639–53. https://doi.org/10.34190/ejel.20.5.2597.
[147] Maghsudi S, Lan A, Xu J, Schaar M, van der. Personalized education in the artificial intelligence era: What to expect next. IEEE Signal Processing Magazine 2021;38(3):37–50. https://doi.org/10.1109/MSP.2021.3055032.
[148] Bilgram V, Laarmann F. Accelerating innovation with generative AI: AI-augmented digital prototyping and innovation methods. IEEE Engineering Management Review 2023;51(2):18–25. https://doi.org/10.1109/EMR.2023.3272799.
[149] Bull C, Kharrufa A. Generative artificial intelligence assistants in software development education: a vision for integrating generative artificial intelligence into educational practice, not instinctively defending against it. IEEE Software 2024;41(2):52–9. https://doi.org/10.1109/MS.2023.3300574.
[150] Bhute VJ, Inguva P, Shah U, Brechtelsbauer C. Transforming traditional teaching laboratories for effective remote delivery—a review. Education for Chemical Engineers 2021;35:96–104. https://doi.org/10.1016/j.ece.2021.01.008.
[151] Oruganti RK, Biji AP, Lanuyanger T, Show PL, Sriariyanun M, Upadhyayula VKK, et al. Artificial intelligence and machine learning tools for high-performance microalgal wastewater treatment and algal biorefinery: a critical review. The Science of the Total Environment 2023;876:162797. https://doi.org/10.1016/J.SCITOTENV.2023.162797.
[152] Wang Y-H. Integrating games, e-books and AR techniques to support project-based science learning. Education and Technology Society 2020;23(3):53–67.
[153] Kumar VV, Carberry D, Beenfeldt C, Andersson MP, Mansouri SS, Gallucci F. Virtual reality in chemical and biochemical engineering education and training. Education for Chemical Engineers 2021;36:143–53. https://doi.org/10.1016/j.ece.2021.05.002.
[154] Kakosimos KE. Example of a micro-adaptive instruction methodology for the improvement of flipped-classrooms and adaptive-learning based on advanced blended-learning tools. Education for Chemical Engineers 2015;12:1–11. https://doi.org/10.1016/j.ece.2015.06.001.
[155] Lewin DR, Barzilai A. The flip side of teaching process design and process control to chemical engineering undergraduates—and completely online to boot. Education for Chemical Engineers 2022;39:44–57. https://doi.org/10.1016/j.ece.2022.02.003.
[156] Udugama IA, Atkins M, Bayer C, Carson J, Dikicioglu D, Gernaey KV, et al. Digital tools in chemical engineering education: the needs and the desires. Education for Chemical Engineers 2023;44:63–70. https://doi.org/10.1016/j.ece.2023.05.002.
[157] Tsai M-L, Ong CW, Chen C-L. Exploring the use of large language models (LLMs) in chemical engineering education: building core course problem models with Chat-GPT. Education for Chemical Engineers 2023;44:71–95. https://doi.org/10.1016/j.ece.2023.05.001.

[158] Stahl M, Mauser H, Tsui M, Taylor NR. A robust clustering method for chemical structures. Journal of Medicinal Chemistry 2005;48(13):4358–66. https://doi.org/10.1021/jm040213p.
[159] Jolliffe IT, Cadima J. Principal component analysis: a review and recent developments. Philosophical Transactions of the Royal Society A: Mathematical, Physical, and Engineering Sciences 2016;374:20150202.. https://doi.org/10.1098/rsta.2015.0202.20150202.
[160] Bishop CM, Nasrabadi NM. Pattern recognition and machine learning. Springer; 2006. Vol. 4.
[161] Lu W-C, Ji X-B, Li M-J, Liu L, Yue B-H, Zhang L-M. Using support vector machine for materials design. Advanced Manufacturing 2013;1(2):151–9. https://doi.org/10.1007/s40436-013-0025-2.
[162] Żurański AM, Martinez Alvarado JI, Shields BJ, Doyle AG. Predicting reaction yields via supervised learning. Accounts of Chemical Research 2021;54(8):1856–65. https://doi.org/10.1021/acs.accounts.0c00770.
[163] Vinoth A, Datta S. Computational intelligence based design of biomaterials. Computational Methods in Materials Science 2022;22(4):229–62. https://doi.org/10.7494/cmms.2022.4.0799.
[164] Huang M-H, Rust RT. Artificial intelligence in service. Journal of Service Research 2018;21(2):155–72. https://doi.org/10.1177/1094670517752459.
[165] Chou C-M, Shen T-CT-C, Shen T-CT-C, Shen C-H. Influencing factors on students' learning effectiveness of AI-based technology application: mediation variable of the human-computer interaction experience. Education and Information Technologies 2022;27(6):8723–50. https://doi.org/10.1007/s10639-021-10866-9.
[166] Cesaro A, Bagheri M, Torres M, Wan F, de la Fuente-Nunez C. Deep learning tools to accelerate antibiotic discovery. Expert Opinion on Drug Discovery 2023;18(11):1245–57. https://doi.org/10.1080/17460441.2023.2250721.
[167] Yang Z, Ye W, Lei X, Schweigert D, Kwon H-K, Khajeh A. De novo design of polymer electrolytes with high conductivity using GPT-based and diffusion-based generative models. arXiv 2023. arXiv2312.06470.
[168] Wong F, Zheng EJ, Valeri JA, Donghia NM, Anahtar MN, Omori S, et al. Discovery of a structural class of antibiotics with explainable deep learning. Nature 2024;626(7997):177–85. https://doi.org/10.1038/s41586-023-06887-8.
[169] Boiko DA, MacKnight R, Kline B, Gomes G. Autonomous chemical research with large language models. Nature 2023;624(7992):570–8. https://doi.org/10.1038/s41586-023-06792-0.
[170] Zheng Z, He Z, Khattab O, Rampal N, Zaharia MA, Borgs C, et al. Image and data mining in reticular chemistry powered by GPT-4V. Digital Discovery 2024;3(3):491–501. https://doi.org/10.1039/D3DD00239J.
[171] Zheng Z, Zhang O, Nguyen HL, Rampal N, Alawadhi AH, Rong Z, et al. ChatGPT research group for optimizing the crystallinity of MOFs and COFs. ACS Central Science 2023;9(11):2161–70. https://doi.org/10.1021/acscentsci.3c01087.
[172] Zheng Z, Alawadhi AH, Chheda S, Neumann SE, Rampal N, Liu S, et al. Shaping the water-harvesting behavior of metal–organic frameworks aided by fine-tuned GPT models. Journal of the American Chemical Society 2023;145(51):28284–95. https://doi.org/10.1021/jacs.3c12086.
[173] Marquez R, Ortiz MS, Barrios N, Vera RE, Patiño-Agudelo ÁJ, Vivas KA, et al. Surfactants produced from carbohydrate derivatives: Part 2. A review on the value chain, synthesis, and the potential role of artificial intelligence within the biorefinery concept. J Surfact Deterg. 2025;28:25–76. https://doi.org/10.1002/jsde.12766.

[174] Schweidtmann AM. Generative artificial intelligence in chemical engineering. Nature Chemical Engineering 2024;1(3):193. https://doi.org/10.1038/s44286-024-00041-5.
[175] Fryer LK, Nakao K, Thompson A. Chatbot learning partners: connecting learning experiences, interest and competence. Computers in Human Behavior 2019;93:279–89. https://doi.org/10.1016/j.chb.2018.12.023.
[176] Roose K. Don't ban ChatGPT in schools. Teach with it. The New York Times. Available from https://www.nytimes.com/2023/01/12/technology/chatgpt-schools-teachers.html Accessed 2023 Feb 02.
[177] Biswas S. ChatGPT and the future of medical writing. Radiology 2023;307:e223312. https://doi.org/10.1148/radiol.223312.
[178] Dowling M, Lucey B. ChatGPT for (finance) research: the bananarama conjecture. Finance Research Letters 2023;53:103662. https://doi.org/10.1016/j.frl.2023.103662.
[179] Frenkel D, Smit B. Understanding molecular simulation: from algorithms to applications. 3rd ed Academic Press; 2023. https://doi.org/10.1016/C2009-0-63921-0.
[180] Páll S, Zhmurov A, Bauer P, Abraham M, Lundborg M, Gray A, et al. Heterogeneous parallelization and acceleration of molecular dynamics simulations in GROMACS. The Journal of Chemical Physics 2020;153(13):134110. https://doi.org/10.1063/5.0018516.
[181] Kadupitiya JCS, Sun F, Fox G, Jadhao V. Machine learning surrogates for molecular dynamics simulations of soft materials. Journal of Computational Science 2020;42:101107. https://doi.org/10.1016/j.jocs.2020.101107.
[182] Jadhao V, Kadupitiya JCS. Integrating machine learning with HPC-driven simulations for enhanced student learning. 2020 IEEE/ACM Workshop on Education for High-Performance Computing (EduHPC). IEEE; 2020. https://doi.org/10.1109/EduHPC51895.2020.00009.
[183] Klimeck G, Mclennan M, Brophy SB, Adams GB, Lundstrom MS. NanoHUB.Org: advancing education and research in nanotechnology. Computing in Science and Engineering 2008;10(5):17–23. https://doi.org/10.1109/MCSE.2008.120.
[184] Brown CE, Alrmuny D, Williams MK, Whaley B, Hyslop RM. Visualizing molecular structures and shapes: a comparison of virtual reality, computer simulation, and traditional modeling. Chemistry Teacher International 2021;3(1):69–80. https://doi.org/10.1515/cti-2019-0009.
[185] Bennie SJ, Ranaghan KE, Deeks H, Goldsmith HE, O'Connor MB, Mulholland AJ, et al. Teaching enzyme catalysis using interactive molecular dynamics in virtual reality. Journal of Chemical Education 2019;96(11):2488–96. https://doi.org/10.1021/acs.jchemed.9b00181.
[186] Ahmad R, Kamaruddin S. An overview of time-based and condition-based maintenance in industrial application. Computers and Industrial Engineering 2012;63(1):135–49. https://doi.org/10.1016/j.cie.2012.02.002.
[187] Surucu O, Gadsden SA, Yawney J. Condition monitoring using machine learning: a review of theory, applications, and recent advances. Expert Systems and Applications 2023;221:119738. https://doi.org/10.1016/j.eswa.2023.119738.
[188] Koene I, Klar V, Viitala R. IoT connected device for vibration analysis and measurement. HardwareX 2020;7:e00109. https://doi.org/10.1016/j.ohx.2020.e00109.
[189] Turunen T, Miettinen J, Hämäläinen A, Karhinen A, Viitala R. Deep learning for centrifugal pump condition monitoring using data from variable frequency drive. In: Okada M, editor. Advances in mechanism and machine science. Cham: Springer Nature Switzerland; 2023. p. 905–14.
[190] Miettinen J, Haikonen S, Koene I, Keski-Rahkonen J, Viitala R. Comparing torsional and lateral vibration data for deep learning-based drive train gear diagnosis. Mechanical

Systems and Signal Processing 2023;203:110710. https://doi.org/10.1016/j.ymssp.2023.110710.

[191] Renforth L, Giussani R, Mendiola MT. A smart condition monitoring system for HV networks with artificial intelligence, augmented reality and virtual reality. In: 2018 IEEE Petroleum and Chemical Industry Technical Conference (PCIC); 2018; pp 325–332. https://doi.org/10.1109/PCIC31437.2018.9080444.

[192] Mikropoulos TA, Natsis A. Educational virtual environments: a ten-year review of empirical research (1999–2009). Computers in Education 2011;56(3):769–80. https://doi.org/10.1016/j.compedu.2010.10.020.

[193] Paszkiewicz A, Salach M, Dymora P, Bolanowski M, Budzik G, Kubiak P. Methodology of implementing virtual reality in education for industry 4.0. Sustainability 2021;13(9):5049. https://doi.org/10.3390/su13095049.

[194] Garcia Fracaro S, Chan P, Gallagher T, Tehreem Y, Toyoda R, Bernaerts K, et al. Towards design guidelines for virtual reality training for the chemical industry. Education for Chemical Engineers 2021;36:12–23. https://doi.org/10.1016/j.ece.2021.01.014.

[195] Girmay S, Yliniemi K, Nieminen M, Linnera J, Karttunen AJ. Enhancing 360° virtual laboratory safety training with linear learning pathway design: insights from student experiences. Education for Chemical Engineers 2024;47:12–21. https://doi.org/10.1016/j.ece.2024.02.002.

[196] Solmaz S, Dominguez Alfaro JL, Santos P, Van Puyvelde P, Van Gerven T. A practical development of engineering simulation-assisted educational AR environments. Education for Chemical Engineers 2021;35:81–93. https://doi.org/10.1016/j.ece.2021.01.007.

[197] Shneiderman B. Human-centered artificial intelligence: reliable, safe & trustworthy. International Journal of Human–Computer Interaction 2020;36(6):495–504. https://doi.org/10.1080/10447318.2020.1741118.

[198] Fabris CP, Rathner JA, Fong AY, Sevigny CP. Virtual reality in higher education. International Journal of Innovative Science and Mathematics Education 2019;27(8):69–80. https://doi.org/10.30722/ijisme.27.08.006.

[199] Kulik JA. Effects of using instructional technology in colleges and universities: what controlled evaluation studies say. Citeseer, 2003.

[200] Frey CB, Osborne MA. The future of employment: how susceptible are jobs to computerisation? Technological Forecasting and Social Change 2017;114:254–80. https://doi.org/10.1016/j.techfore.2016.08.019.

# Artificial intelligence in prosthodontic biomaterials

14

*Ahmad Al Jaghsi*[1,2,3]*, Dinesh Rokaya*[1,2]*, Pravin Kumar Shah*[4]*, Artak Heboyan*[5]*, Zohaib Khurshid*[6,7]*, Sara Zaky Mohammed*[8]*, and Viritpon Srimaneepong*[9]

[1]Clinical Sciences Department, College of Dentistry, Ajman University, Ajman, United Arab Emirates, [2]Center of Medical and Bio-Allied Health Sciences Research, Ajman University, Ajman, United Arab Emirates, [3]Department of Prosthodontics, Gerodontology, and Dental Materials, Greifswald University Medicine, Greifswald, Germany, [4]Boston University Henry M Goldman School of Dental Medicine, Boston, MA, United States, [5]Department of Prosthodontics, Faculty of Stomatology, Yerevan State Medical University after Mkhitar Heratsi, Yerevan, Armenia, [6]Department of Prosthodontics and Implantology, College of Dentistry, King Faisal University, Al-Hofuf, Saudi Arabia, [7]Center of Excellence for Regenerative Dentistry, Department of Anatomy, Faculty of Dentistry, Chulalongkorn University, Bangkok, Thailand, [8]Prosthodontics Department College of Dentistry, Ras Al Khaimah Medical and Health Science University, Ras Al Khaimah, United Arab Emirates, [9]Department of Prosthodontics, Faculty of Dentistry, Chulalongkorn University, Bangkok, Thailand

## 14.1 Introduction

Artificial intelligence (AI) is the ability of machines that exhibit a form of intelligence [1]. AI is described as “a branch of science and engineering concerned with the computational understanding of what is often referred to as intelligent behavior and the development of artifacts that display such behavior” [2]. AI utilizes machines to mimic intellectual human behavior and cognitive skills like problem-solving [1,3]. Key aspects of AI include machine learning (ML), neural networks (NNs), and deep learning (DL), as shown in Fig. 14.1 [1]. ML is part of AI, and it depends on algorithms that can predict outcomes from datasets. ML facilitates machines to learn from data, and they can resolve issues/problems without people’s involvement [1]. Similarly, NNs are a combination of algorithms that calculate signals through neurons that function like the human brain [1]. Finally, DL is a constituent of ML that operates the network with various computational layers in NNs to analyze the data, and DL constructs NNs to identify patterns to improve feature detection [1]. With the wide applications of materials ranging from information, transportation, construction, biomedicine, and biomaterials [4]. At present, AI has brought a new paradigm affecting various disciplines, including science and technology, touching our everyday life [4].

**Artificial Intelligence in Biomaterials Design and Development. DOI:** https://doi.org/10.1016/B978-0-323-95464-8.00016-5

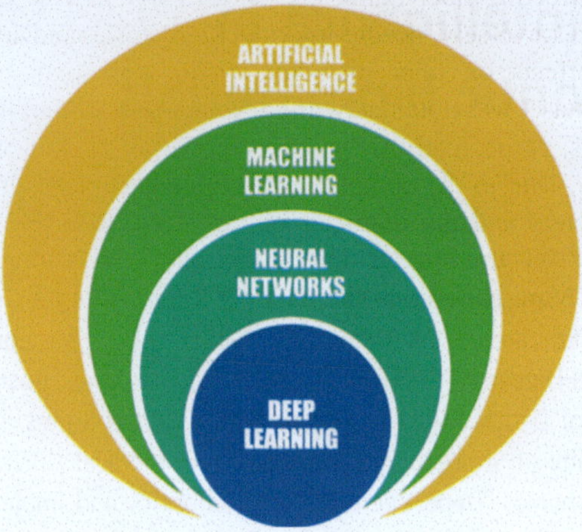


**Figure 14.1** Key aspects of AI.
Reprinted with permission from [1].

## 14.2 Artificial intelligence in medical sciences

AI has led to wide applications in the medical sciences and education [5,6]. Various applications of AI in medicine and dentistry are shown in Figs. 14.2 and 14.3 [4,7]. With the rising need for healthcare services, hospital needs are developing from traditional service-based to internet hospitals and smart hospitals (Fig. 14.2) [4]. AI can be implemented for the public health services in various ways. One good example is the digital health. Quick Response (QR) code, which uses a color coding system to detect COVID-19 cases and indicate the person's health status using mobile big data [8], has been adopted by various countries for the prevention and control of pandemic diseases (especially COVID-19) worldwide. AI in medical and dental imaging is one of the most developed areas for detection, classification, and splitting up tasks in computer vision [9]. AI computer algorithms have also been applied for computer-assisted diagnosis and treatment with computed tomography (CT) and electrocardiogram (ECG) repeatedly without fatigue [4,10]. The AI program anticipates the pathology or its prognosis by risk factor prioritization [7]. The first AI-based medical product permitted by the Food and Drug Administration (FDA) is IDx-DR, which uses an AI-based model from patient images to predict diabetic retinopathy [11]. Furthermore, the AI-based medical smartphone application SkinVision can precisely identify melanomas [12].

AI is extensively utilized in dentistry, where it serves a crucial function across various domains, including diagnosis and treatment planning, clinical care, laboratory processes, virtual assistant, treatment prognosis, educational training, administrative tasks, and research endeavors. In dentistry, AI is used in various specialties, that is, maxillofacial radiology, orthodontics, prosthodontics, dental implantology, etc. [9,10,13]. AI models

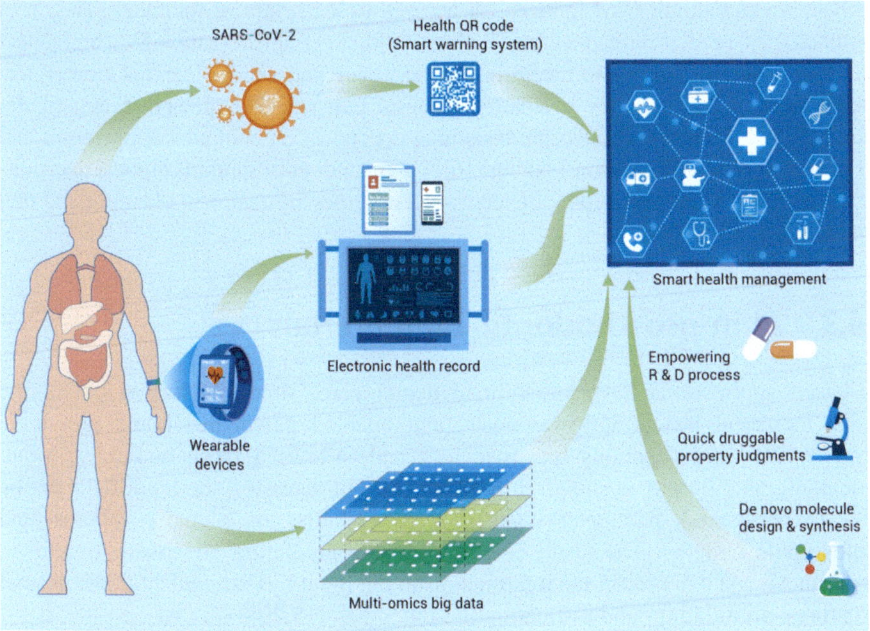


**Figure 14.2** Applications of AI in medicine.
Reprinted with permission from [4].

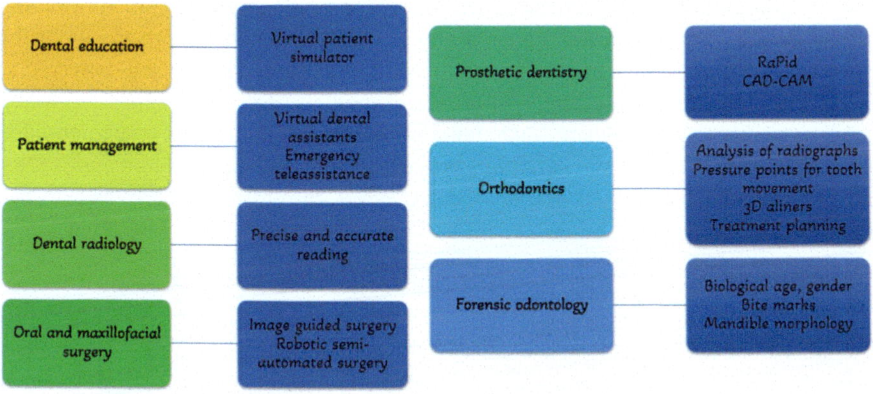


**Figure 14.3** Applications of AI in dentistry.
Reprinted with permission from [7].

can be used to diagnose dental caries, root fractures, maxillofacial cysts, salivary gland diseases, maxillary sinusitis, osteoporosis, cancerous lesions, lymph node metastasis, and alveolar bone loss [1,14]. In orthodontics, AI models can be used to detect the need for orthodontic treatments, predict orthodontic extractions, and perform cephalometric analysis. In endodontics, AI models can be used to locate apical foramen, assess root morphologies, predict retreatment predictions, predict periapical pathologies, and detect root fractures [14]. AI is also useful in biological age and gender identification [7,15]. Furthermore, AI is used for evaluating occlusal contacts and predicting mandibular morphology [1]. Hence, dentists are becoming dependent on computer applications and AI models for clinical decision-making [16,17]. This not only supports clinical decisions but also increases the precision, efficiency, and accuracy in treatment planning and oral rehabilitation [18].

## 14.3 AI in prosthodontic biomaterials

AI-based applications have streamlined dental care, simplified laborious routine tasks, increased health at lower costs, and enabled personalized and predictive dentistry [19]. AI functions like machines and follows a basic hierarchy: input, processing, and output as shown in Fig. 14.4 [7]. In dentistry, the input data can be data (experimental parameters and medical records) or pictures (photos and radiographic images). The result can be a disease prediction, diagnosis, treatment, or prognosis. AI can predict the treatment from the input by distinguishing the normal structures, stimulating, and evaluating the outcomes [18,20].

AI technology helps to examine a patient's oral structure and can customize the treatment based on the patient's condition [21]. AI is also able to recommend or suggest the most suitable biomaterials, designs, and technologies for prosthesis fabrication [22]. Such customized prostheses have the advantages of good fit, comfort, and function [23]. Furthermore, the incorporation of AI with 3D printing permits the fabrication of dental prostheses rapidly [22]. The zirconia prostheses can be produced in-office on the same day using a speed sintering technique and delivered to the patient, providing rapid and cost-effective solutions for their patients [24–27]. These use intraoral scanners and computer-aided design and computer-aided manufacturing (CAD/CAM) software programs for prostheses fabrication [26]. Furthermore, an application, RaPid, can be used in prosthodontics, and it has

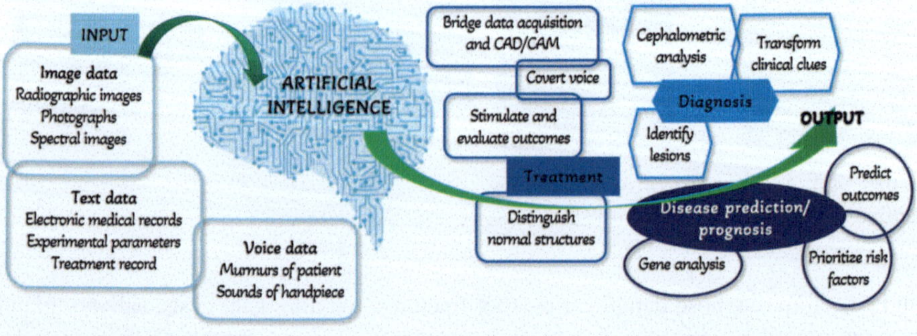


**Figure 14.4** Hierarchy of AI in medicine dentistry.
Reprinted with permission from [7].

combined various parameters such as ethnicity, anthropological calculations, face proportions, and patient preferences for optimal esthetics [7]. RaPid links knowledge-based systems, databases, and computer-aided manufacturing (CAM) by the unifying framework. With developments in NN, dental laboratories are applying AI to create advanced dental restorations with high standards of fit, function, and esthetics [7,28].

Over the past decades, a novel discipline within materials science has arisen, focusing on biomaterials. Biomaterials are substances, whether synthetic or natural in origin, that are utilized to enhance, treat, substitute, or regenerate tissues [29]. Currently, biomaterials have extensive applications in medicine and dentistry [30]. The trend is shifting from replacement toward regeneration (Fig. 14.5) [31].

Broadly, biomaterials can be classified as metals, polymers, ceramics (including carbon-based materials, ceramics, and glass), and composites [32,33]. The ceramic includes carbon-based materials, ceramics, and glasses. In the last half-decade, there has been an increasing interest in the field of biomaterials for application in dentistry, and numerous new biomaterials have been introduced for dental applications [34–36]. Various approaches in tissue engineering are shown in Fig. 14.6 [29].

### 14.3.1 AI in new materials design

With the wide applications of materials ranging from information, transportation, construction, and biomedicine [4], AI has been implemented in materials science. Recently, AI has made important improvements in rational design and speeded the

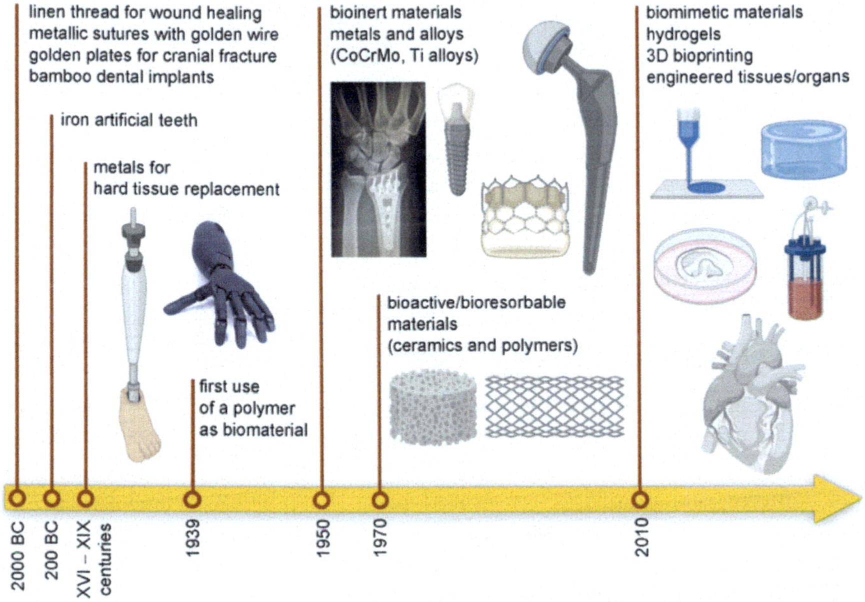


**Figure 14.5** The history and shift of biomaterials: from replacement to regeneration. Reprinted with permission from [31].

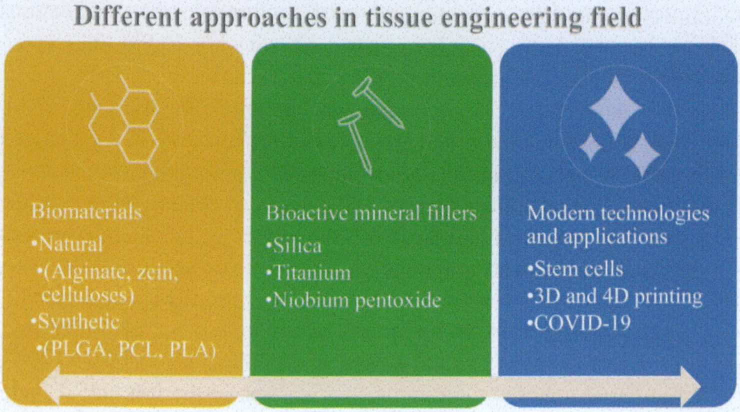


**Figure 14.6** Various approaches in tissue engineering.
Reprinted with permission from [29].

discovery of different biomaterials [4]. With the fast progress of data handling and algorithms, ML and DL are applied in the search for new biomaterials before actually producing them [37]. By incorporating various biomaterial data (such as the integral element, atomic weight and radius, lattice symmetry, magnetism, binding energy, polarization, electronegativity, band energy, and structural property), the machines are trained to think to improve the design of new materials and predict the properties cost-effectively (Fig. 14.7) [4]. Data-driven computing and algorithms can help simulation and ML in property prediction and material discovery.

AI tools can be adapted for experimental testing of materials and use computing, automation, and ML to calculate the material's properties, such as bulk, interface, and defects [38]. In the future, AI techniques can achieve the design of metals, superconductors, glasses, alloys, magnetocaloric materials, thermoelectric materials, polymeric materials, composite materials, 2D materials, and topological (electronic and phonon) materials [4]. A precise AI-based model needs to be made to forecast the formation energy of a compound to produce good predictive ability [39].

### 14.3.2 AI in fabrication of prostheses

AI with 3D printing techniques has been extremely valuable in transforming various data and images into the production of prostheses and devices [40]. Data collected from 3D instruments from various sources are computed using CAD models, designed from software, and prostheses are printed using 3D printing technology [41,42]. AI-supported 3D printing procedure supports the manufacture of different types of implants and prostheses [4,43]. The prostheses reproduce the normal anatomy precisely and can be customized to help improve the function and esthetics. AI can accelerate the fabrication process; hence, the reconstruction process is also quicker [44].

Apart from printing the maxillofacial anatomical structures, limbs (i.e., hands and legs) can also be printed [45,46]. The printed limbs can be supported with myoelectric

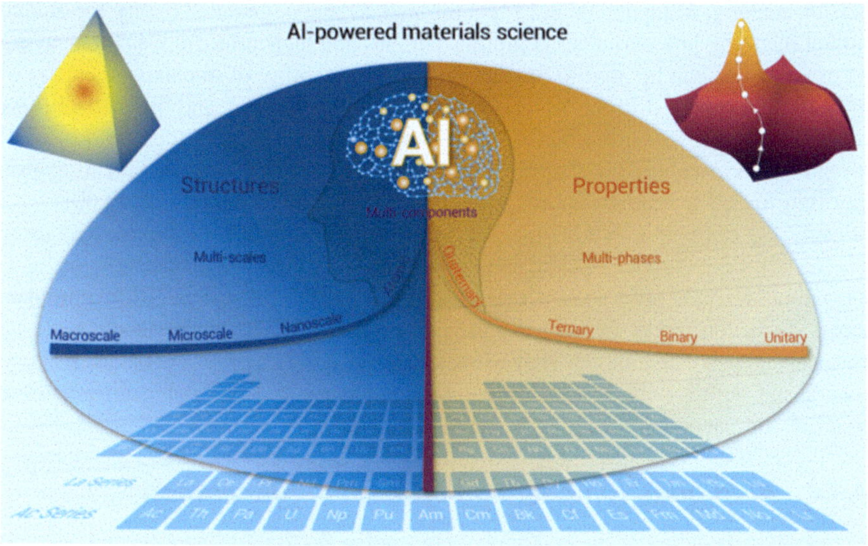


**Figure 14.7** AI-powered development in materials science.
Reprinted with permission from [4].

stimulation support [47,48]. Recent studies have also tried to print bionic ears in models simulating an artificial environment, but clinical trials are yet to come in the near future [49].

One advantage of AI is the prosthesis fabrication process in children. In children, the prosthesis needs to be changed frequently, which makes the process time-consuming and costly. However, with 3D printing technology using light printing materials, the time and cost can be reduced significantly, and the prostheses when needed [4]. 3D-printed prostheses in children have better functionality and movement [50].

### 14.3.3 AI in dental implant prosthodontics

AI has been used in dental implant prosthodontics. In implant dentistry, AI has helped in diagnostics, treatment planning, and patient outcomes [51]. In addition, AI can enhance the precision of treatment planning, enable differentiation of implant brands through ML, help in implant designs with finite element analysis, and predict the treatment outcome [51,52]. Furthermore, AI is a valuable tool for the detection of anatomical landmarks important for implant placement. AI helps in the detection of the mandibular canal using a deep convolutional neural network model [53–55]. This plays an important role in implant planning and helps to prevent pre- and post-operative neurovascular complications. Morgan et al. [56] used a convolutional neural network for the automatic segmentation of the maxillary sinus and it allowed for the precise reproduction of 3D models for the diagnosis and treatment planning.

For the prosthetically driven implant, a precise 3D placement of the dental implant is necessary [51]. AI helps in treatment planning in implantology by helping in decision-making. Mangano et al. [57] combined AI and augmented reality for guided implant planning in a partially edentulous patient, and their protocol was time-saving and efficient. AI can be used to predict the primary stability of implants (accuracy of 93.7%) based on the drilling protocols during implant surgery, and this is useful for young clinicians [58]. Furthermore, the AI can also help to identify the dental implant through the convolutional neural network of DL by forming an identification algorithm to detect spatial features such as shape, textures, and edges [59,60].

Finally, AI can help to predict the implant success and the risk of implant loss using NNs [61,62]. Dental implant failure shows the features of insufficient bone volume, bone loss, and unfavorable bone quality [63]. Zhang et al. [62] developed an effective implant success prediction model by studying the peri-implant alveolar bone pattern on dental periapical and panoramic films). They extracted features using a deep convolutional neural network and built a hybrid model to combine periapical and panoramic images. Both periapical and panoramic images showed that the prediction accuracy was 87%.

### 14.3.4 AI in bone remodeling and tissue regeneration

Regenerative medicine is an emerging field, and it focuses on auto-healing tissues. Bone regeneration is important in bone defect cases. Using 3D printing, native tissue mimics can be produced using biomaterials and living cells [64]. For tissue regeneration, various scaffolds are used that use biocompatible and biodegradable polymers as scaffolding biomaterials derived from natural (i.e., alginates, zein, and celluloses) or synthetic sources (i.e., polylactic acid, poly-lactic-co-glycolic acid, and polycaprolactone) [29,65,66]. Various approaches in the field of tissue engineering are shown in Fig. 14.8. Modern approaches, such as mesenchymal stem cells and 3D/4D printings, are applied in the tissue engineering field, as shown in Fig. 14.8 [29]. In many cases, conventional design and simulation methods cannot be used to design tissue engineering scaffolds due to the complexity of geometrical shapes, numerical mismatches, or manufacturing defects. Hence, AI and ML methods need to be used in such cases. They have proved to be transformative resources in tissue engineering

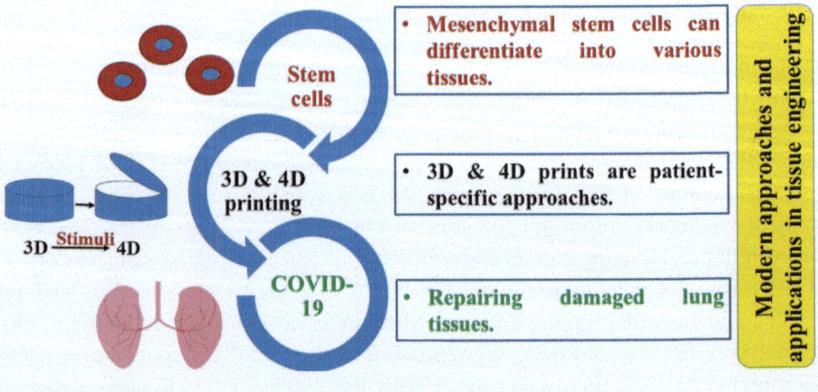


**Figure 14.8** Applications of tissue engineering.
Reprinted with permission from [29].

and regenerative medicine. In addition, 3D convolutional NN, trained using digital tomographies attained from the CAD models, is a powerful tool used in the prediction of the mechanical properties of designed scaffolds [67].

Similarly, AI with 3D printing has become a useful tool in bone regeneration which uses cells and biomaterial coalescence scaffold to re-establish the bony defects [4,68]. In addition, 3D printing can produce spongy scaffolds of the required shape and size by an incremental printing process [69,70]. The required CAD model (obtained from the CT or MRI) of scaffolds is prepared and printed using the printing technology with powder particles. The important considerations for producing a good scaffold are powder packing dentistry, flowability, layer thickness, and binder drop volume [4,71]. The features of the scaffolds are associated with pore size and pore volume, and the final properties of the scaffold depend on materials used to produce the scaffold [72–74]. Moreover, various features of the biomaterial are considered before printing, such as mechanical properties (strengths), chemical properties (connection between the cells), and biological properties (biocompatibility and cell growth) [75,76]. Recent advancements in the repair of bone defects include functioning scaffolds, cell planting, bone grafts, etc. [77–79]. The major advantages of 3D printing of bone tissue regeneration are its variety and ability to provide customized scaffolds [80]. Finally, AI with 3D printing technique is used in regenerative tissues that can be almost equally functional as natural tissues. The newer 3D bone platforms with interconnected 3D microvascular channels enhance bone tissue recovery with vascular progression [4,81,82].

## 14.4 Limitations and future perspectives

In dentistry, AI technologies can be used as an important tool for treatment planning, diagnosis, treatment result prediction, and patient-centered care. Although AI holds great promise, it also has several challenges and ethical considerations. AI in dentistry is rapidly exploring new uses of AI for electronic health records, image analysis, and prosthesis design [83]. Data safety, security, and privacy are critical aspects of integrating AI into healthcare [22,83]. Further long-term studies are needed before fully integrating AI into clinical practice.

Furthermore, important considerations are to instill knowledge of the basic knowledge and application of AI, examine current and potential ethical practices, and discuss its limitations [83,84]. Finally, although AI has wide applications in dentistry, dentistry performed by machines and without human interaction does not represent clinical care [7]. The human-to-human communication cannot be translated directly into computer language and coding [3].

## 14.5 Conclusion

The application of AI-based systems in dentistry and oral health keeps advancing. The incorporation of AI in prosthodontics using intraoral scanners and CAD/CAM software programs permits the rapid fabrication of the prosthesis and dental prostheses 3D printing in the office on the same day using a speed sintering technique and delivered to the patient, providing rapid and cost-effective solutions for their patients. In implant prosthodontics, AI has helped in diagnostics, treatment planning, and patient outcomes. In addition, AI can enhance the precision of treatment planning, enable differentiation of implant brands through ML, help in implant designs with finite element analysis, and predict the treatment outcome. AI combined with augmented reality is used for guided implant planning in a partially edentulous patient, and their protocol was time-saving and efficient. Similarly, prosthodontic biomaterials have a tangible influence to widen opportunities for clinicians as well as patients and can be used as an additional simple tool for assembling, handling, and establishing patient-related datasets to deliver individual, patient-centered, and personalized treatment. AI tools can be adapted for biomaterials testing of materials and use computing, automation, and ML to calculate the material's properties, such as bulk, interface, and defects. In the future, with the help of generative AI, dentists can prepare a patient-specific prosthesis for specific oral conditions. The application of AI-based technologies in prosthodontic biomaterials is desirable in various aspects from the clinicians' and patients' points of view.

## Acknowledgment

To the best of the Editors' knowledge and authors' claims, no generative AI tools were used for substantive writing of chapters. Any AI-assisted language editing, if applied, was limited to grammar or style suggestions and did not alter the scientific content.

## References

[1] Khanagar SB, Al-Ehaideb A, Maganur PC, Vishwanathaiah S, Patil S, Baeshen HA, et al. Developments, application, and performance of artificial intelligence in dentistry—a systematic review. Journal of Dental Sciences 2021;16(1):508–22.
[2] Shapiro SC. Encyclopedia of artificial intelligence. 2nd edn New Jersey, NY: Wiley; 1992.
[3] Shan T, Tay FR, Gu L. Application of artificial intelligence in dentistry. Journal of Dental Research 2021;100(3):232–44.
[4] Xu Y, Liu X, Cao X, Huang C, Liu E, Qian S, et al. Artificial intelligence: a powerful paradigm for scientific research. Innovation 2021;2(4):100179.
[5] Vodanović M, Subašić M, Milošević D, Savić Pavičin I. Artificial intelligence in medicine and dentistry. Acta Stomatologica Croatica 2023;57(1):70–84.
[6] Sarfaraz S, Khurshid Z, Zafar MS. Use of artificial intelligence in medical education: a strength or an infirmity. Journal of Taibah University Medical Sciences 2023;18(6):1553–4.
[7] Agrawal P, Nikhade P. Artificial intelligence in dentistry: past, present, and future. Cureus 2022;14(7):e27405.
[8] Huang Y, Wu Q, Wang P, Xu Y, Wang L, Zhao Y, et al. Measures undertaken in China to avoid COVID-19 infection: internet-based, cross-sectional survey study. Journal of Medical Internet Research 2020;22(5):e18718.
[9] Dashti M, Londono J, Ghasemi S, Tabatabaei S, Hashemi S, Baghaei K, et al. Evaluation of accuracy of deep learning and conventional neural network algorithms in detection of dental implant type using intraoral radiographic images: a systematic review and meta-analysis. The Journal of Prosthetic Dentistry 2024;133:137–46. In Press.

[10] Orhan K, Jagtap R. Introduction to artificial intelligence. In: Orhan K, Jagtap R, editors. Artificial intelligence in dentistry. Cham: Springer International Publishing; 2023. p. 1–7.
[11] Grzybowski A, Brona P. Analysis and comparison of two artificial intelligence diabetic retinopathy screening algorithms in a pilot study: IDx-DR and retinalyze. Journal of Clinical Medicine 2021;10(11):2352.
[12] Freeman K, Dinnes J, Chuchu N, Takwoingi Y, Bayliss SE, Matin RN, et al. Algorithm based smartphone apps to assess risk of skin cancer in adults: systematic review of diagnostic accuracy studies. BMJ (Clinical Research Ed) 2020;368:m127.
[13] Talesara V, Bennani V, Aarts J, Ratnayake J, Khurshid Z, Brunton P. Accuracy of digitally coded healing abutments: a systematic review. The Saudi Dental Journal 2023;35(8):891–903.
[14] Boreak N. Effectiveness of artificial intelligence applications designed for endodontic diagnosis, decision-making, and prediction of prognosis: a systematic review. The Journal of Contemporary Dental Practice 2020;21(8):926–34.
[15] Mohammad N, Ahmad R, Kurniawan A, Mohd Yusof MYP. Applications of contemporary artificial intelligence technology in forensic odontology as primary forensic identifier: a scoping review. Frontiers in Artificial Intelligence 2022;5:1049584.
[16] Schleyer TK, Thyvalikakath TP, Spallek H, Torres-Urquidy MH, Hernandez P, Yuhaniak J. Clinical computing in general dentistry. Journal of the American Medical Informatics Association 2006;13(3):344–52.
[17] Chae YM, Yoo KB, Kim ES, Chae H. The adoption of electronic medical records and decision support systems in Korea. Healthcare Informatics Research 2011;17(3):172–7.
[18] Khurshid Z. Digital dentistry: transformation of oral health and dental education with technology. European Journal of Dentistry 2023;17(4):943–4.
[19] Schwendicke F, Samek W, Krois J. Artificial intelligence in dentistry: chances and challenges. Journal of Dental Research 2020;99(7):769–74.
[20] Londono J, Ghasemi S, Hussain Shah A, Fahimipour A, Ghadimi N, Hashemi S, et al. Evaluation of deep learning and convolutional neural network algorithms accuracy for detecting and predicting anatomical landmarks on 2D lateral cephalometric images: a systematic review and meta-analysis. The Saudi Dental Journal 2023;35(5):487–97.
[21] Chadha U, Abrol A, Vora NP, Tiwari A, Shanker SK, Selvaraj SK. Performance evaluation of 3D printing technologies: a review, recent advances, current challenges, and future directions. Progress in Additive Manufacturing 2022;7(5):853–86.
[22] Heboyan A, Yazdanie N, Ahmed N. Glimpse into the future of prosthodontics: the synergy of artificial intelligence. World Journal of Clinical Cases 2023;11(33):7940–2.
[23] Alammar A, Kois JC, Revilla-León M, Att W. Additive manufacturing technologies: current status and future perspectives. Journal of Prosthodontics 2022;31(S1):4–12.
[24] Liu H, Inokoshi M, Xu K, Tonprasong W, Minakuchi S, Van Meerbeek B, et al. Does speed-sintering affect the optical and mechanical properties of yttria-stabilized zirconia? A systematic review and meta-analysis of in-vitro studies. The Japanese Dental Science Review 2023;59:312–28.
[25] Kongkiatkamon S, Peampring C. Comparison of regular and speed sintering on low-temperature degradation and fatigue resistance of translucent zirconia crowns for implants: an in vitro study. Journal of Functional Biomaterials 2022;13(4):281.
[26] Perlea P, Stefanescu C, Al-Aloul OA, Ionita C, Petre AE. Digital workflow for producing hybrid posts and cores. Healthcare (Basel, Switzerland) 2023;11(5):727.
[27] Saini RS, Alshadidi AAF, Gurumurthy V, Okshah A, Vaddamanu SK, Binduhayyim RIH, et al. Quantum mechanical analysis of yttrium-stabilized zirconia and alumina: implications for mechanical performance of esthetic crowns. European Journal of Medical Research 2024;29(1):254.

[28] Banerjee M. Artificial intelligence in dentistry: a ray of hope. CODS Journal of Dentistry 2021;13(2):58–60.

[29] Eldeeb AE, Salah S, Elkasabgy NA. Biomaterials for tissue engineering applications and current updates in the field: a comprehensive review. AAPS PharmSciTech 2022;23(7):267.

[30] Heboyan A, Bennardo F. New biomaterials for modern dentistry. BMC Oral Health 2023;23(1):817.

[31] Todros S, Todesco M, Bagno A. Biomaterials and their biomedical applications: from replacement to regeneration. Processes 2021;9(11):1949.

[32] Rokaya D. Advances in biomaterials for clinical applications. Journal of Chitwan Medical College 2022;11(4):1–3.

[33] Vaiani L, Boccaccio A, Uva AE, Palumbo G, Piccininni A, Guglielmi P, et al. Ceramic materials for biomedical applications: an overview on properties and fabrication processes. Journal of Functional Biomaterials 2023;14(3):146.

[34] Alqurashi H, Khurshid Z, Syed AUY, Rashid Habib S, Rokaya D, Zafar MS. Polyetherketoneketone (PEKK): an emerging biomaterial for oral implants and dental prostheses. Journal of Advanced Research 2021;28:87–95.

[35] Heboyan A, Zafar MS, Rokaya D, Khurshid Z. Insights and advancements in biomaterials for prosthodontics and implant dentistry. Molecules 2022;27(16):5116.

[36] Tuna EB, Oshida Y, Ozen B, Gjorgievska E, Tuzuner T. Biomaterials for dental applications. BioMed Research International 2017;2017:2520536.

[37] Mahmood A, Wang J-L. Machine learning for high performance organic solar cells: current scenario and future prospects. Energy and Environmental Science 2021;14(1):90–105.

[38] Correa-Baena J-P, Hippalgaonkar K, van Duren J, Jaffer S, Chandrasekhar VR, Stevanovic V, et al. Accelerating materials development via automation, machine learning, and high-performance computing. Joule 2018;2(8):1410–20.

[39] Liang Y, Chen M, Wang Y, Jia H, Lu T, Xie F, et al. A universal model for accurately predicting the formation energy of inorganic compounds. Science China Materials 2023;66(1):343–51.

[40] Qian C, Zheng B, Shen Y, Jing L, Li E, Shen L, et al. Deep-learning-enabled self-adaptive microwave cloak without human intervention. Nature Photonics 2020;14(6):383–90.

[41] Balestra D, Lowther M, Goracci C, Mandurino M, Cortili S, Paolone G, et al. 3D printed materials for permanent restorations in indirect restorative and prosthetic dentistry: a critical review of the literature. Materials 2024;17(6):1380.

[42] Amornvit P, Rokaya D, Sanohkan S. Comparison of accuracy of current ten intraoral scanners. BioMed Research International 2021;2021:2673040.

[43] Dimitrova M, Vlahova A, Kalachev Y, Zlatev S, Kazakova R, Capodiferro S. Recent advances in 3D printing of polymers for application in prosthodontics. Polymers (Basel) 2023;15(23):4525.

[44] Cortes C, Vapnik V. Support-vector networks. Machine Learning 1995;20(3):273–97.

[45] Ten Kate J, Smit G, Breedveld P. 3D-printed upper limb prostheses: a review. Disability and Rehabilitation. Assistive Technology 2017;12(3):300–14.

[46] Vujaklija I, Farina D. 3D printed upper limb prosthetics. Expert Review of Medical Devices 2018;15(7):505–12.

[47] Rimaneepong V, Heboyan A, Syed AUY, Trinh HA, Amornvit P, Rokaya D. Recent advances in myoelectric control for finger prostheses for multiple finger loss. Applied Sciences 2021;11(10):4464.

[48] Kumar DK, Jelfs B, Sui X, Arjunan SP. Prosthetic hand control: a multidisciplinary review to identify strengths, shortcomings, and the future. Biomedical Signal Processing and Control 2019;53:101588.

[49] McCulloch WS, Pitts W. A logical calculus of the ideas immanent in nervous activity. The Bulletin of Mathematical Biophysics 1943;5(4):115–33.
[50] Freund Y, Schapire RE. Experiments with a new boosting algorithm. Machine learning: proceedings of the thirteenth international conference. 1996. p. 148–56.
[51] Altalhi AM, Alharbi FS, Alhodaithy MA, Almarshedy BS, Al-Saaib MY, Al Jfshar RM, et al. Al-Harbi NH: the impact of artificial intelligence on dental implantology: a narrative review. Cureus 2023;15(10):e47941.
[52] Amornvit P, Rokaya D, Keawcharoen K, Thongpulsawasdi N. Stress distribution in implant retained finger prosthesis: a finite element study. Journal of Clinical and Diagnostic Research: JCDR 2013;7(12):2851–4.
[53] Kwak GH, Kwak EJ, Song JM, Park HR, Jung YH, Cho BH, et al. Automatic mandibular canal detection using a deep convolutional neural network. Scientific Reports 2020;10(1):5711.
[54] Jindanil T, Marinho-Vieira LE, de-Azevedo-Vaz SL, Jacobs R. A unique artificial intelligence-based tool for automated CBCT segmentation of mandibular incisive canal. Dento Maxillo Facial Radiology 2023;52(8):20230321.
[55] Lahoud P, Diels S, Niclaes L, Van Aelst S, Willems H, Van Gerven A, et al. Development and validation of a novel artificial intelligence driven tool for accurate mandibular canal segmentation on CBCT. Journal of Dentistry 2022;116:103891.
[56] Morgan N, Van Gerven A, Smolders A, de Faria Vasconcelos K, Willems H, Jacobs R. Convolutional neural network for automatic maxillary sinus segmentation on cone-beam computed tomographic images. Scientific Reports 2022;12(1):7523.
[57] Mangano FG, Admakin O, Lerner H, Mangano C. Artificial intelligence and augmented reality for guided implant surgery planning: a proof of concept. Journal of Dentistry 2023;133:104485.
[58] Sakai T, Li H, Shimada T, Kita S, Iida M, Lee C, et al. Development of artificial intelligence model for supporting implant drilling protocol decision making. Journal of Prosthodontic Research 2023;67(3):360–5.
[59] da Mata Santos RP, Vieira Oliveira Prado HE, Soares Aranha Neto I, Alves de Oliveira GA, Vespasiano Silva AI, Zenóbio EG, et al. Automated identification of dental implants using artificial intelligence. The International Journal of Oral and Maxillofacial Implants 2021;36(5):918–23.
[60] Revilla-León M, Gómez-Polo M, Vyas S, Barmak BA, Galluci GO, Att W, et al. Artificial intelligence applications in implant dentistry: a systematic review. The Journal of Prosthetic Dentistry 2023;129(2):293–300.
[61] Huang N, Liu P, Yan Y, Xu L, Huang Y, Fu G, et al. Predicting the risk of dental implant loss using deep learning. Journal of Clinical Periodontology 2022;49(9):872–83.
[62] Zhang C, Fan L, Zhang S, Zhao J, Gu Y. Deep learning based dental implant failure prediction from periapical and panoramic films. Quantitative Imaging in Medicine and Surgery 2023;13(2):935–45.
[63] Rokaya D, Srimaneepong V, Wisitrasameewon W, Humagain M, Thunyakitpisal P. Peri-implantitis update: risk indicators, diagnosis, and treatment. European Journal of Dentistry 2020;14(4):672–82.
[64] Saini G, Segaran N, Mayer JL, Saini A, Albadawi H, Oklu R. Applications of 3D bioprinting in tissue engineering and regenerative medicine. Journal of Clinical Medicine 2021;10(21):4966.
[65] Khayatan D, Bagherzadeh Oskouei A, Alam M, Mohammadikhah M, Badkoobeh A, Golkar M, et al. Cross talk between cells and the current bioceramics in bone regeneration: a comprehensive review. Cell Transplantation 2024;33. 09636897241236030.

[66] Rokaya D, Srimaneepong V, Sapkota J, Qin J, Siraleartmukul K, Siriwongrungson V. Polymeric materials and films in dentistry: an overview. Journal of Advanced Research 2018;14:25–34.
[67] Bermejillo Barrera MD, Franco-Martínez F, Díaz Lantada A. Artificial intelligence aided design of tissue engineering scaffolds employing virtual tomography and 3D convolutional neural networks. Materials 2021;14(18):5278.
[68] Rokaya D, Kongkiatkamon S, Heboyan A, Dam VV, Amornvit P, Khurshid Z, et al. 3D-printed biomaterials in biomedical application. In: Jana S, Jana S, editors. Functional biomaterials: drug delivery and biomedical applications. Singapore: Springer Singapore; 2022. p. 319–39.
[69] Zhang Q, Zhou J, Zhi P, Liu L, Liu C, Fang A, et al. 3D printing method for bone tissue engineering scaffold. Medicine in Novel Technology and Devices 2023;17:100205.
[70] Do AV, Khorsand B, Geary SM, Salem AK. 3D printing of scaffolds for tissue regeneration applications. Advanced Healthcare Materials 2015;4(12):1742–62.
[71] Lee SS, Du X, Kim I, Ferguson SJ. Scaffolds for bone-tissue engineering. Matter 2022;5(9):2722–59.
[72] Suamte L, Tirkey A, Barman J, Jayasekhar Babu P. Various manufacturing methods and ideal properties of scaffolds for tissue engineering applications. Smart Materials in Manufacturing 2023;1:100011.
[73] Velasco MA, Narváez-Tovar CA, Garzón-Alvarado DA. Design, materials, and mechanobiology of biodegradable scaffolds for bone tissue engineering. BioMed Research International 2015;2015:729076.
[74] Loh QL, Choong C. Three-dimensional scaffolds for tissue engineering applications: role of porosity and pore size. Tissue engineering. Part B, Reviews 2013;19(6):485–502.
[75] Huzum B, Puha B, Necoara RM, Gheorghevici S, Puha G, Filip A, et al. Biocompatibility assessment of biomaterials used in orthopedic devices: an overview (Review). Experimental and Therapeutic Medicine 2021;22(5):1315.
[76] Mitragotri S, Lahann J. Physical approaches to biomaterial design. Nature Materials 2009;8(1):15–23.
[77] Amini AR, Laurencin CT, Nukavarapu SP. Bone tissue engineering: recent advances and challenges. Critical Reviews in Biomedical Engineering 2012;40(5):363–408.
[78] Xue N, Ding X, Huang R, Jiang R, Huang H, Pan X, et al. Bone tissue engineering in the treatment of bone defects. Pharmaceuticals 2022;15(7):879.
[79] Wei H, Cui J, Lin K, Xie J, Wang X. Recent advances in smart stimuli-responsive biomaterials for bone therapeutics and regeneration. Bone Research 2022;10(1):17.
[80] Cybenko G. Approximation by superpositions of a sigmoidal function. Mathematics of Control, Signals, and Systems 1989;2(4):303–14.
[81] Nguyen LH, Annabi N, Nikkhah M, Bae H, Binan L, Park S, et al. Vascularized bone tissue engineering: approaches for potential improvement. Tissue engineering. Part B, Reviews 2012;18(5):363–82.
[82] Barabaschi GD, Manoharan V, Li Q, Bertassoni LE. Engineering pre-vascularized scaffolds for bone regeneration. Advances in Experimental Medicine and Biology 2015;881:79–94.
[83] Kim CS, Samaniego CS, Sousa Melo SL, Brachvogel WA, Baskaran K, Rulli D. Artificial intelligence (AI) in dental curricula: ethics and responsible integration. Journal of Dental Education 2023;87(11):1570–3.
[84] Orhan K, Gülbeş MM, Jadhav A, Jagtap R. Medico-legal problems of artificial intelligence. In: Orhan K, Jagtap R, editors. Artificial intelligence in dentistry. Cham: Springer International Publishing; 2023. p. 259–82.

# Artificial intelligence applications in electrospinning of biocompatible polymers

15

*Mojtaba Nasirinezhad, Sara Etminanrezaeieh, and Saba Abbasi Sedaghat*
Chemical Engineering Group, Faculty of Chemical Engineering and Advanced Materials, Urmia University of Technology, Urmia, Iran

## 15.1 Introduction

Different types of micron-sized protein fibers produced by spiders and silkworms inspired humans to use and produce fibers. Fibers are a fundamental part of human life, and the use of fibers has been observed before civilization. Fiber production by humans dates back to 5000 years ago. Rayon was the first semisynthetic man-made fiber that is extracted from cellulose fibers of cotton and wood. In 1938 the DuPont Company commercialized nylon as the first synthetic fiber, which was widely accepted by the public. From that date on, other types of synthetic fibers, such as polyester, were introduced to the society [1].

To make fibers from synthetic polymer sources, the polymer chains must have sufficient mobility for processing, and after the formation of the fibers, the mobility is given to them by solidification to take the final shape of the fibers. Based on this, various methods were developed to make fibers from wet, dry, molten, and gel states. In all these methods, first, a jet of polymer is made under a force field (external shearing force or mechanical drawing) when passing through spinnerets until the initial shape is created; then, fibers are formed by solidification. In all these methods, the fibers' diameter ranges are typically between 10 and 100 microns, which cannot be achieved with thinner fibers by increasing the intensity of the field [2,3].

The concept of electrospinning process goes back to the work done in 1600 by William Gilbert. He observed the formation of a cone-shaped (known as Taylor cone) water drop by using an electric field. This observation later led to the creation of the electrospraying machine, which was first used with water molecules. In 1887 Charles V. Boys reported that viscoelastic liquids could be drawn into fibers using an electric force. In electrospinning, the same concepts as the electrospraying method are used, but the difference is in the viscosity and viscoelastic properties of the liquid that comes out in the form of a jet under a high-voltage electric field. In electrospinning, the process is continuous, but in electrospraying, the process is discrete, and the liquid breaks into droplets and makes particles instead of fibers [1].

Electrospinning was first reported in 1934 and has received a significant revival of interest in recent years due to its potential to produce ultrafine fibers with diameters in the nanometer to submicrometer range (thinner than 500 nm). Electrospun fibers are excellent candidates for tissue engineering scaffolds and wound dressings due to their

**Artificial Intelligence in Biomaterials Design and Development. DOI:** https://doi.org/10.1016/B978-0-323-95464-8.00013-X

high specific surface area and porous structure [4–7]. In recent years, we have seen amazing advances in combining artificial intelligence (AI) with materials science. This has led to new and innovative developments in various industries. Artificial Neural Networks (ANN), or in other words, neural networks, are modern computing systems and methods for machine learning (ML), displaying knowledge and data, and finally applying the obtained data to predict the output responses from complex systems. The main idea of such networks is largely inspired by the way the biological nervous system works to process data and information in order to learn and create knowledge. Among these exciting applications, AI has been integrated into a process called electrospinning, particularly to create specific materials in medicine, drug delivery, and tissue engineering. Electrospinning with AI is a significant advance because it allows us to make very precise biomaterials that are functional and cost-effective. Instead of using traditional trial-and-error methods, AI helps us take a systematic and data-driven approach. AI algorithms help us control critical factors in real time and predict how materials will look and behave. This use of AI with electrospinning opens up new opportunities to create highly precise nanofibers (NFs) from biodegradable materials in nature. Electrospinning is a well-known method of making fibers and is used in the medical field to create materials that are well adapted to the body. Biopolymers obtained from natural sources are of special importance due to their compatibility with the environment. However, working with electrospun biopolymers can be challenging because there are many factors to control. This chapter explores how AI can help in this process. AI is a branch of computer science that makes machines learn, adapt, and make decisions based on data. When we add AI to the electrospinning of biopolymers, we can change the way we make materials for medicine and tissue engineering [8,9].

AI makes the process more accurate and efficient, which is very important. This chapter looks deeply at this fascinating topic, discussing the latest research, noteworthy findings, how AI can be used in practical ways, and real-life examples. It is intended to be a guide for researchers, engineers, and scientists who are interested in using AI to create better and more functional NFs with biopolymers. By combining AI, biopolymers, and electrospinning, we hope to create materials that will improve medicine, tissue engineering, and other industries. This chapter aims to be a valuable resource for those who want to explore the possibilities of these technologies and push the boundaries of what is possible with biopolymers. The review and analysis of various materials used in numerous articles related to the electrospinning process show that materials, including polymers, nanoparticles (NPs), and hybrid compounds, have wide applications in various fields.

## 15.2 Electrospinning

Electrospinning is a complex and advanced technique in materials and polymer science, which is specifically used to produce very thin NFs from polymer solutions. This process, by creating a strong electric field between a needle filled with polymer solution and a metal collecting part, transforms the dispersed liquid polymer into NFs so that by increasing the voltage to a critical level, the polymer droplet formed at the tip of the needle as a Taylor cone, which, after being stretched in an electric field and removing the solvent, it turns into a very fine and thin nanofiber. Fig. 15.1 represents a simple schematic of electrospinning process. NFs produced through electrospinning have unique physical and chemical properties due to their special structure. In addition, these NFs have a high surface-to-volume ratio, high porosity, and favorable mechanical strength, which make them suitable for various applications such as tissue engineering, drug delivery, membranes, food packaging, and making various composites. This process is important from the point of view of the ability to precisely control the characteristics of the manufactured NFs, including diameter, type of polymer, surface structure, and arrangement. These capabilities allow researchers and engineers to create new materials with better performance and properties and to be used in various industries [10–13]. Adding AI to the electrospinning process is very smart and has opened new horizons in the optimization and development of this technology. Using ML and AI algorithms, process parameters can be automatically optimized and used to produce NFs with custom-designed properties. AI is able to do this by analyzing countless data obtained from various experiments and simulations to discover and investigate complex patterns that may remain hidden from human sight. This optimization of the electrospinning process with the integration of AI not only increases the quality and stability of NFs but can also significantly reduce production time and costs and, in addition, produce new, more advanced, and more efficient NFs [14].

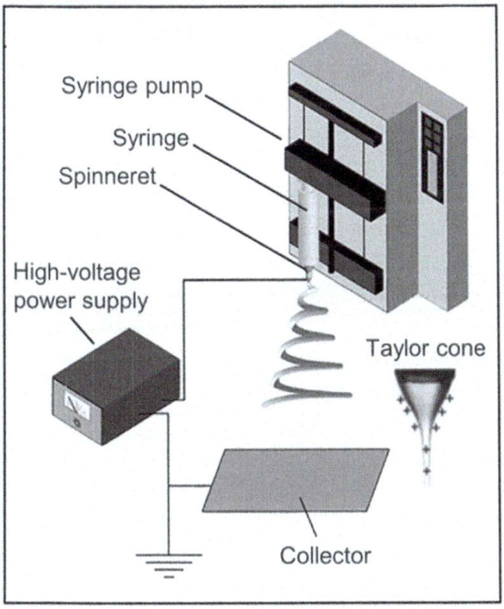


**Figure 15.1** Schematic representation of the electrospinning process.
Reprinted with permission from [15].

### 15.2.1 Effects of parameters on electrospinning

The electrospinning process is a process in which the production of fibers with a nanosize diameter is expected. Despite the simplicity of the mechanism, this process has certain process complications. Various parameters are effective in this process. With proper control of these parameters, smooth and bead-free NFs can be achieved. Usually, these parameters are classified into three categories: environmental, process, and material parameters. Temperature and relative humidity are considered as environmental parameters. The relative humidity of the environment can be effective in the morphology and diameter of the fibers. As the humidity increases, the diameter of the fibers will decrease. Pilepenko et al. reported the reduction of fiber diameter from 667 to 161 nm with increasing humidity from 4% to 60% [16]. Temperature in the electrospinning process has two opposite effects. As the temperature increases, the evaporation rate increases, and, on the other hand, the viscosity of the solution will decrease. In general, the performance of these two phenomena together leads to a reduction in the diameter of the fiber [17].

Process parameters include applied voltage, flow rate, distance between the collector and nozzle, and nozzle diameter. The voltage at which the spherical droplet of polymer becomes a Taylor cone is called the critical voltage. Digital images in Fig. 15.2 show these steps by increasing the voltage in polyvinylpyrrolidone droplet. At this voltage, ultrathin fibers are formed in the collector. This voltage has a different value from one polymer to another. By increasing in the applied voltage, the amount of repulsion in the Taylor cone increases, which will lead to a change in the diameter and morphology (bead formation) of the fibers. Also, the increase in jet velocity can also be due to the increase in voltage above the critical voltage value [17]. In various articles, the increase or decrease of fiber diameter with increasing voltage has been reported [18,19]. The morphology of NFs can be changed by altering the flow rate of polymer solution. At the critical flow rate, uniform bead-free NFs are formed, which is different from polymer to polymer system [17]. Increasing the flow rate can lead to the formation of beaded fibers [20]. By increasing the flow rate, the evaporation of the solvent also decreases, which will lead to the formation of unspun fibers [21]. An increase in fiber diameter distribution has also been observed at high flow rates [22]. Therefore, it is recommended to set the flow rate at the minimum value. The distance of the nozzle from the collector and its diameter can play a key role in the morphology of electrospun NFs because of effects on the evaporation rate, deposition time, and whipping or instability interval. Therefore, there is a critical distance for each system in which smooth and bead-free fibers are formed [17]. However, there are several reports that the distance did not play a role in the diameter of the fibers [23].

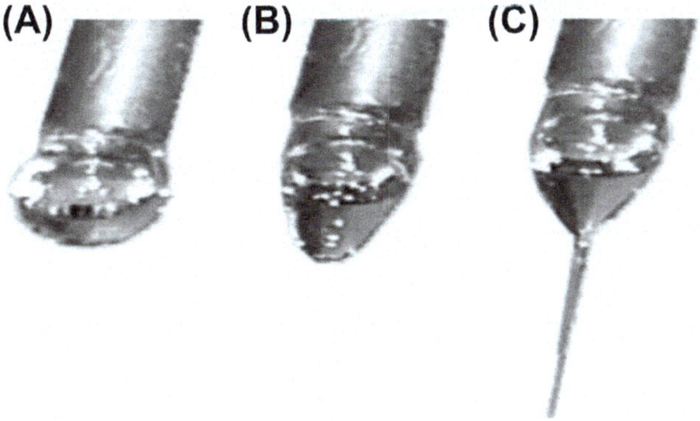


**Figure 15.2** Digital images of deformation a polyvinylpyrrolidone by increasing electrical field. Reprinted with permission from [24].

Material parameters are viscosity, electrical conductivity, concentration, and molecular weight of polymer and the selected solvent. The electrospinning process is based on the unidirectional stretching of the charged jet. The stretching of the charged jet of polymer solution is affected by the concentration of the solution. Increasing the concentration of the polymer solution will increase the entanglement of the chains, which, in addition to increasing the viscosity of the solution, will overcome the surface tension, which will produce smooth and bead-free fibers [17]. On the other hand, at low concentrations of the solution, the entangled chains cannot overcome the electric field and surface tension, and as a result, they break into fragments, which will cause beads in the fibers [17,25]. Increasing the concentration of the solution to more than the critical value will inhibit the solution flow in the nozzle, resulting in beaded fibers. Koski et al. showed that in the electrospinning of polyvinyl alcohol NFs, the molecular weight of polymer, in addition to the concentration, could be effective in the cross-sectional shape of the fibers. As the concentration increases, the cross-section of the fibers will change from circular to flat. The lower the molecular weight of the polymer, the sooner this change will occur at higher concentrations [26]. As the viscosity changes, the fiber morphology changes from interconnected round droplets to elongated droplets and then to smooth fibers [22]. The electrical conductivity of the solution not only causes the Taylor cone to form but also determines the diameter of the fibers. In solutions with low electrical conductivity, fibers will not form due to the lack of Taylor cone formation. By increasing the electrical conductivity of the solution, it not only increases the electric charge on the surface of the droplet but also causes a reduction in the diameter of the fibers [27]. On the other hand, by increasing the electrical conductivity again beyond the critical value, the Taylor cone will not form. Therefore, the electrical conductivity of the polymer solution should be controlled by adding salts [17]. In the solvent selection, two things should be taken into consideration: firstly, the polymer should be completely dissolved in it, and secondly, the solvent should have a moderate boiling point. The choice of solvent should be made in such a way that it is not so volatile that it evaporates at the tip of the nozzle before the start of the process and hinders the flow of the solution. On the other hand, it should not have a high boiling point that prevents the drying of the fibers during the flight from the tip of the nozzle to collector [28].

### 15.2.2 Different nanofiber morphologies in electrospinning

The electrospinning process is a simple process that can achieve fibers with different morphologies by changing the methods and tools. Fig. 15.3 shows the types of morphologies of manufactured NFs.

Based on this, different types of NFs are classified as follows:

- Normal electrospun fiber
- Spring/helical electrospun fiber
- Porous electrospun fiber
- Core-shell electrospun fiber
- Hollow electrospun fiber
- Janus electrospun fiber
- Triaxial electrospun fiber

Fig. 15.4 depicts typical morphologies of electrospun fibers.

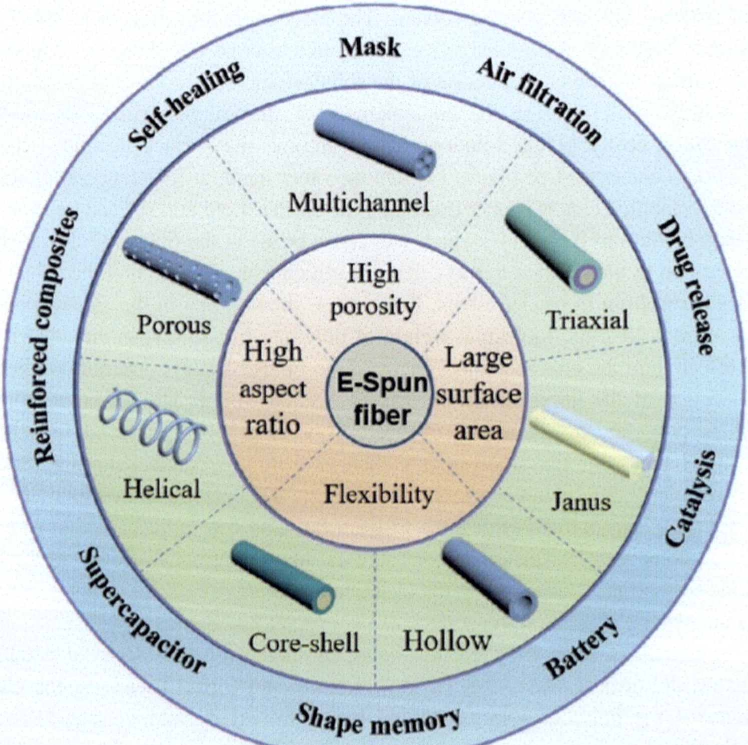


**Figure 15.3** The characteristics, structures, and applications of electrospun fiber with different structural design.
Reprinted with permission from [29].

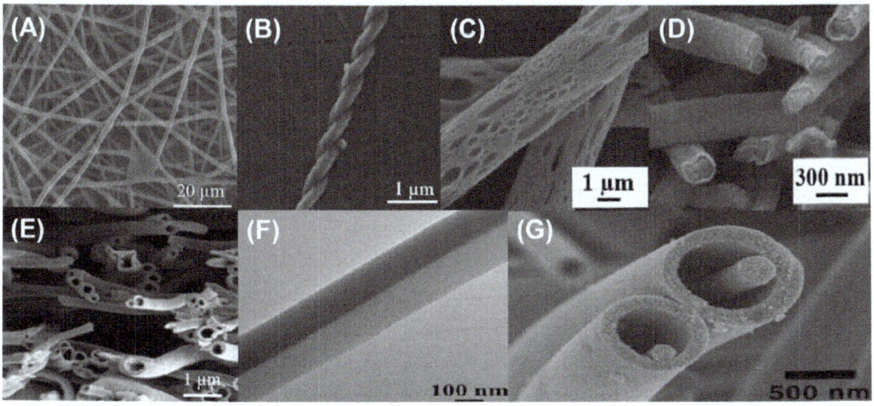


**Figure 15.4** Different morphologies of electrospun fibers. (A) Normal, (B) spiral, (C) porous, (D) core-shell, (E) hollow, (F) Janus, (G) triaxial.
Reprinted with permission from [29].

## 15.2.3 Various electrospinning set-ups

From the point of view of the industry, the production of high-volume fibers is very important, and therefore, the production process must be able to produce a sufficient amount of fibers compared to other traditional methods, such as dry spinning. Despite the existence of various patents in electrospinning machine set-up design since 1900, in the last decade, the academia has entered into the design of various set-ups. Fig. 15.5 depicts various set-ups of electrospinning [30].

All set-ups are designed with the aim of more production, better control in fiber alignment, simplicity, and more area for fiber production. However, some cases, such as the interference of jets, the limited length of the fibers, the slowness of the process, the concentration of the deposition of fibers in some areas, and the lack of production of thicker layers, can also be considered among the disadvantages of the above methods [30].

## 15.2.4 Materials of electrospun fibers

The most common materials for making electrospun fibers include organic polymers in solution or molten state. The condition for the successful use of organic polymers is the presence of a sufficiently high molecular weight and a suitable solvent for their dissolution. In the case of polymers that do not have the ability to dissolve under normal conditions (such as polypropylene), the melt electrospinning method is used. In this case, the melt must have sufficient electrical conductivity and viscosity that is suitable for electrospinning. The glass transition temperature and the polymer degradation temperature should also be considered [1].

Small molecules can also be electrospun directly if they have proper and sufficient entanglement. In these materials, there should be suitable intramolecular interactions for self-assembly to keep the molecules together in the charged jet, so that continuous

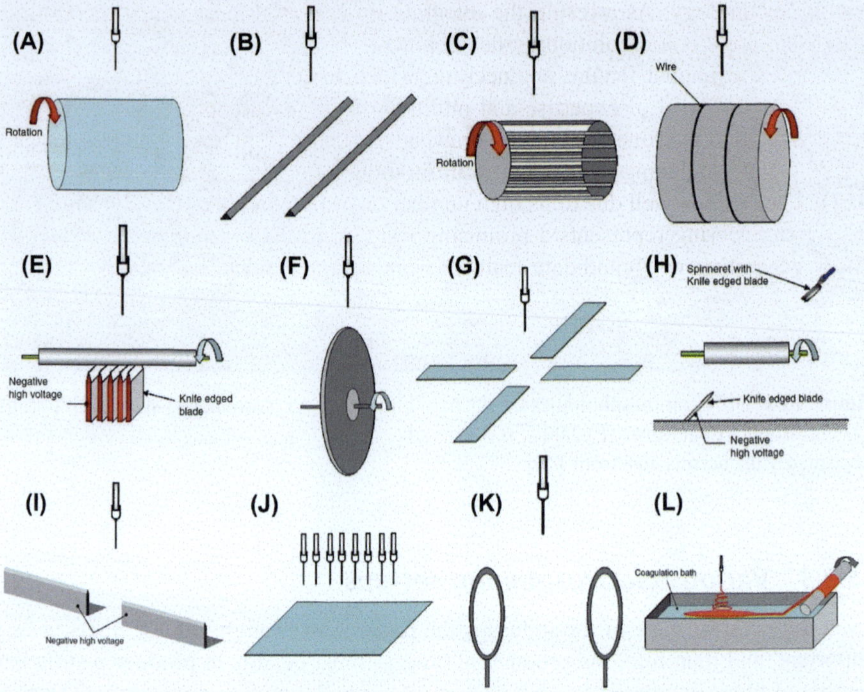


**Figure 15.5** Schematics of various electrospinning set-ups. (A) Rotating drum, (B) parallel electrodes, (C) rotating wire drum collector, (D) drum collector with wire wound on it, (E) rotating drum collector with knife-edge electrodes below, (F) disk collector, (G) array of counter electrodes, (H) controlling electrospinning jet using knife-edge electrodes, (I) blades placed in line, (J) multiple spinnerets, (K) ring collector placed in parallel, (L) yarn collection using water bath.
Reprinted with permission from [30].

fibers can be prepared. For example, we can mention the solution of cyclodextrin derivatives in dimethylacetamide solvent at a concentration of 120%, which has good solution viscosity and viscoelastic behavior due to the presence of many hydrogen bonds [31].

With the introduction of sol-gel chemistry, these materials have the ability to produce electrospun composite fibers. Colloids, as a biphasic material with sufficient entanglements to keep the charged gel in a continuous form, can also be used for electrospinning. For example, a silica sol, which is made from tetraethylorthosilicate, distilled water, ethanol, and hydrochloric acid, aged at 80°C for 30 minutes, is used to make fibers with a diameter of 0.4–1 micron [32].

In composite materials, two sol-gel states or nanomaterials inside the polymer matrix are used to make NFs. In the sol-gel state, the reactions of hydrolysis, condensation, and gelation of the precursor initiate in the jet in contact with the surrounding air. So, a network of continuous inorganic phase is formed inside the polymer matrix, which makes organic-inorganic composite fibers. For example, titanium tetraisopropoxide, as a precursor of $TiO_2$, was added to the polyvinylpyrrolidone (PVP) solution in ethanol, and PVP/$TiO_2$ composite fibers were made during electrospinning [33]. As mentioned, composite fibers with added nanomaterials, such as gold nanorods, gold and silver nanowires, carbon nanotubes, and other nanomaterials inside the polymer solution, are also prepared. The formulation in these cases, which depends on the type, size, and concentration of the nanomaterial, will determine the morphology of the electrospun fibers [34].

## 15.3 Artificial intelligence and machine learning

### 15.3.1 Collection and preparation of data

ML is a subset of AI where models act as dynamic engines that orchestrate and execute a set of tasks. While data plays the role of fuel that drives these models, any given ML model has an operational performance that is based on the existence of a sufficient amount of data, which makes it a prerequisite for optimal system performance. Emphasizing that the importance of data goes beyond sheer quantity, the quality of data is equally important to the effective implementation of an ML model. For this reason, significant amounts of data are critical to the ML result. It is very important that both the quantity and the reliability of the available data are properly recognized, and this directly affects the final results of the ML models. Significantly, the quantitative and qualitative training datasets used in the learning process affect the accuracy of a prediction model [35,36]. So, to ensure optimal results, a holistic approach to generating training datasets is essential. Often, the preparation of educational data includes three main methods. The first approach includes data extraction from published literature. It can be said that the data obtained in this way, in addition to serving as a valuable resource in that it provides insights into practical applications, is also relevant. The second method involves the use of experiments or high-throughput calculations to collect data. Subsequently, the third method involves collecting data from open databases accessible on various repository websites [37,38]. In these databases, datasets from experimental tests and computational simulations, including failed data, are integrated as theoretical and experimental research is continuously progressing. It should be noted that the basic principle underlying these repositories is data sharing, according to which access to essential information is simplified.

After proper and accurate data collection, data preprocessing is performed, which includes tasks such as formatting and cleaning. Unprocessed datasets of collected data pose a challenge for analysis, often rendering them unusable due to noise, inconsistency, and missing values. Maintaining a quality standard is essential to portray a suitable dataset for use. Data cleaning is used as an operation that is applied to the existing dataset and its purpose is to reach the peak of refinement and correction of anomalies. This process of data collection includes reconciliation of inconsistencies, elimination of errors, and standardization of data in a unified and uniform format. By using formatting, the quality of the data will be improved, and the data will have a framework. Data cleaning is done by filling in missing data values and inconsistencies, identifying outliers in the dataset, noise correction, and systematic noise reduction. Various common techniques, including clustering, regression, and binning, are used to smooth the noise [39]. In the ML engineering process, the stage of integrated data preparation is of particular importance. Subsequently, for the selected algorithm used, the process of converting the raw data into specific features is given as input, which is an essential step in achieving accurate results. This effective step not only helps to understand more about the model but also increases the accuracy of learning [40,41].

In building ML models, rational feature selection is a critical determining factor. In addition, different conditioning factors may influence each acquisition pattern, and if not, all of these factors are important for the features. To maintain the uniformity of all extracted values, some features are removed during the cleaning step, and data quality is guaranteed. For example, when evaluating the prediction of lithium-ion conductivity, it may be influenced by multiple internal and external factors. However, of the four factors, only a subset is directly related to decision characteristics, such as experimental temperature, ion diffusion, medium volume, and transition temperature. For this reason, it is essential that an appropriate feature selection method be adopted in the process of identifying the subset of features considered for integration in the final evaluation. Keep in mind that the process of rationally selecting these features can often be both resource-intensive and challenging. In past studies, the feature selection task has been done traditionally and manually, which had limitations, such as preventing the ability to identify the expected features. So, in recent times, automatic feature engineering has been developed and has been increasingly considered. This new technique involves creating potential features automatically by analyzing the data and then selecting the most optimal and relevant ones to train the model, eliminating the challenges of the manual method [41–43].

### *15.3.2 Machine learning models selection*

A suitable ML algorithm is used after collecting and modifying a sufficient dataset to build an ML model. Basically, the ML model building acts as a process black box and communicates between the input data and the output data through the interaction of special nonlinear or linear functions. ML provides a mechanism to use samples of the objective function and to discover the coefficients, thereby allowing the determined mapping function to approximate the objective function. Also, the purpose of the ML model is to determine the correlation between the input characteristics and the predicted outputs in the collected data sample. The knowledge obtained through the use of ML not only is useful for further applications, especially for the prediction of target properties but is also readily available [44,45]. This part of the book evaluates the different ML models available. Fig. 15.6 shows the structure of different ML models [46]. Considering that it is related to the selection of a suitable ML algorithm, prediction accuracy also emphasizes its key role in the dominant ML workflow. Usually, ML algorithms are built using specialized libraries such as sci-kit-learn, Keras, PyTorch, TensorFlow, or mlpack, each of which is proficient in different

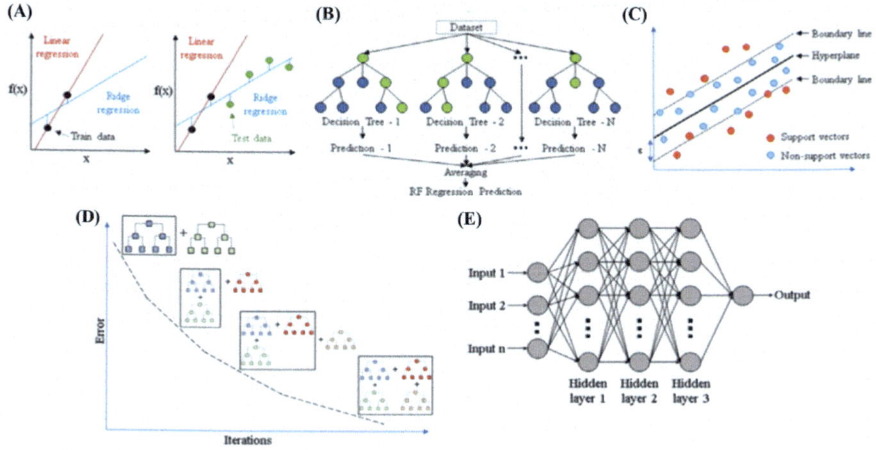


**Figure 15.6** Different ML models' structures: (A) Kernel ridge regression, (B) Random forest regression, (C) Support vector regression, (D) Gradient boosting regression, and (E) Artificial neural networks.
Reprinted with permission from [46].

programming languages, including Python, C++, and R. The following section describes the most common ML algorithms. A brief explanation is given for the use case. The techniques play an important role in modifying the support vector regression (SVR) model by applying penalties to the mentioned Slack variables and thereby reducing the impact of each of them on the performance of the model. The main goal of this process is to enhance the margin, and optimization is equal to minimizing a designed function of uniformly decreasing weights [47–49].

### 15.3.2.1 *Linear/multiple regression*

Regression is an excellent and common technique in ML for prediction. The linear regression (LR) model represents the linear relationship between a dependent variable and one or more independent variables. This technical model presents a linear relationship between variables, which is usually shown as a straight line in the picture. According to the LR model, it tries to fit a straight line to the given dataset. However, it is often questioned due to structural limitations of reliability and accuracy of regression. In LR analysis, it is called simple in scenarios where a single variable is considered, but when we deal with more than one variable, the approach of the method becomes multiple linear regression. As a valuable tool, MLR works by considering various parameters to predict the outcome of a dependent variable. An equation of the results and information obtained from the prediction model is obtained through MLR. It is important to mention that MLR has certain limitations; among these limitations, it is unable to ensure accuracy in achieving desired results [50,51].

### 15.3.2.2 Support vector regression

SVR vector regression support is part of support vector machine (SVM) category. The ability to discover complex patterns in datasets is the core function of SVR. This is done by using a superplane that effectively contains the maximum allowed number of data points and also maintains a known tolerance margin. Some data points in the dataset managed by SVR fall beyond the defined tolerance margin, which are called loose variables. Using these variables, the amount of divergence of specific observations from the complete hyperplane is shown. To increase the accuracy of the SVR model, several optimization techniques are used. These optimization techniques play an important role in modifying the SVR model and thus reduce their impact on the performance of the model. Enhancing the margin is the main goal of this optimization process, which is equal to minimizing a designed function of weights that are uniformly decreasing [48,52,53].

### 15.3.2.3 Kernel ridge regression

Kernel ridge regression (KRR) is inspired by SVR as an advanced iteration of SVR. It is alternatively called Least Squares Support Vector Regression (LSSVR) and represents a nonparametric approach that obtains the target directly based on the input. KRR is adept at handling nonlinearity in data using regularization techniques, quite unlike traditional regression methods. The metaparameters are the parameters that refer to the parameters governing the learning process, and the size of the training data plays an important role in identifying the effectiveness of the KRR learning model. The advanced management of trade-off bias comes from the significant advantages of the KRR model, which causes a slight bias in it and enables a significant reduction in variance. It ensures the optimal performance and generalizability of the model in different datasets, which results from its fine balance. The strength of this model lies in its ability to provide more accurate predictions for long-term unseen test data, which reduces the complexity of the problem and helps to overfit the model, while the KRR model may not perfectly match the training data [54–56].

### 15.3.2.4 Random forest regression

In the ensemble learning approach using multiple decision trees (DTs) for meaningful generation, random forest regression (RFR) is used as a technique rather than the final output being dependent on a single DT. In the RF ML model, the DT is trained on a randomly selected subsample of the dataset. Then, through the process of averaging the outputs produced by DTs, the final prediction is obtained. This technique protects against overfitting, a problem often encountered when using DT, so it can be used when its accuracy is compromised in predicting the results of new input data. Although these models exhibit low training error rates, it is not uncommon for the testing error to be significantly larger. One of the effective solutions to this challenge is the use of RFR, which, with its exceptional speed and ability handles, high-dimensional datasets as well as larger input datasets when evaluating with alternative approaches [57,58].

### 15.3.2.5 Gradient boosting regression

This regression is an ensemble learning technique that combines and uses weak learners to form a strong learner collectively. This algorithm gradually integrates weak learners into the group, with each subsequent learner focusing on correcting their previous errors. The group training process is facilitated through a gradient descent algorithm, and most poor learners are usually DT. Compared to other ML algorithms, such as DT, RF, and SVR, gradient boosting regression (GBR) typically has higher accuracy, attributed to the algorithm's capacity to absorb insights from the errors of previous poor learners, and subsequently increase its prediction accuracy over time. It improves. XGBoost, AdaBoost, LightGBM, and CatBoost. XGBoost is a popular GB algorithm. GB regression performs a DT using a strategy of calculating the difference between the base learner result and the actual generated value with the aim of reducing the variance between the model output and the observed value. XGBoost is highly adaptable and has the ability to customize loss functions to meet specific needs. Among its many features, XGBoost has attracted a lot of attention, especially for its exceptional performance [59–61].

### 15.3.2.6 Artificial neural networks

The models used in ML are called ANNs if they are inspired by the biological structure and function of neural networks. Depicted in Fig. 15.7, these models are strategically organized to process the input data and produce the corresponding output, as they are composed of layers of interconnected nodes. The order of input data in the forward direction in the field of ANNs is called a feedforward neural network. In a feedforward neural network, the output of each node is subjected to multiplication factors before entering the input layer, where it is subjected to a nonlinear activation function. Connections within ANNs play a central role, as these connections define edges, and their weights are actively adjusted during the learning process. In the structure of an ANN, each connection that is created between two nodes represents a certain weight value that shows the strength of the signal passing through that connection and effectively corresponds to the call of ANNs [62,63]. Various transformations are performed on the inputs as they pass through the different layers of the network. ANNs consist of three main components in their structure: input layer, hidden layer (middle), and output layer. The input layer plays the role of the input point for the input parameters and transfers them in both stages of model training and testing. The hidden layer plays a role as a central component in the overall architecture of ANNs and plays a key role in facilitating data connections and interactions between the input and output layers, and is also placed between the input and output layers of the hidden layers. Each hidden layer in the structure of an ANN includes a set of neurons that contribute to the complexity and adaptability of the network by facilitating them. Finally, the output layer is given the responsibility of producing the result or final result of the project [64,65].

ANNs are trained on samples with known inputs and outputs, along with probabilistic weighted connections embedded in the network's data structure, using evaluation. The process of training ANNs relies on measuring the difference between the processed

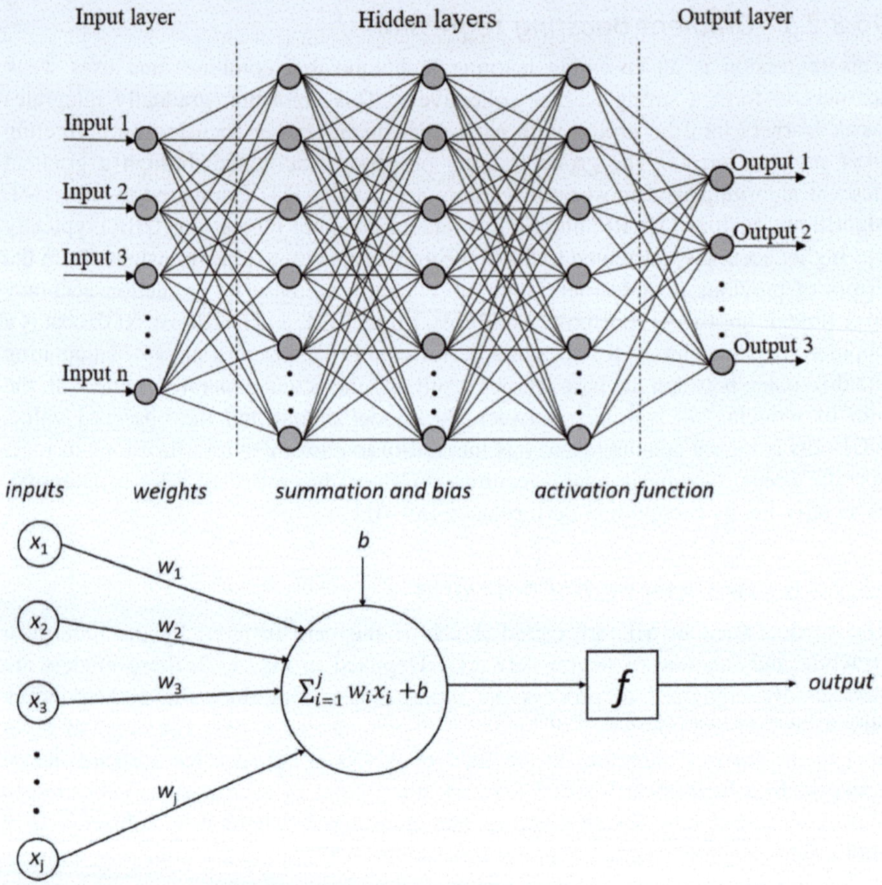


**Figure 15.7** Artificial neural network: (Up) scheme of a three-layer network; and (Down) operation of a single neuron.
Reprinted with permission from [62].

output and the expected target output, which is usually referred to as the error. This error value is considered as an important criterion to guide the adjustment of weighted communication of ANNs. The ANN makes these adjustments with a learning rule, along with the error value. In networks, the iterative adjustment of network weights is a complex task when providing training data to the network. Minimizing the difference between the current output generated by the network and the predetermined target output is the main objective of this network weight adjustment. This training process is iterative in nature, and repeated changes in the network parameters are necessary until the results are completely identical to the desired results [66].

An important step in modeling neural networks is to identify the number of hidden layers and neurons in the network structure. This decision-making process is of great importance because the capacity of the model to handle nonlinear and complex problems is effectively impaired when the number of hidden layers is insufficient. Increasing the number of hidden layers and neurons in the neural network can do the opposite and increase the training time. This increase in structural complexity in the model may lead to poor performance by learning irrelevant network behaviors instead of capturing accurate relationships between parameters. ANNs are widely used in planning scenarios, including the evaluation and determination of the probability of events. Primarily, ANNs are driven by providing experimental data and are used with learning and mapping. These networks can be used to address various problems with a focus on predictive tasks, especially in the domain of complex systems that either challenge modeling or pose significant modeling challenges [67–69]. It should be noted that this model is not without flaws; even if the ANNs ML model is considered as a powerful tool to address complex challenges in engineering and science. Among the unwanted disadvantages of this network, we can mention the convergence, lengthening the time required for training, and multiplying multiple parameters.

#### 15.3.2.7 Response surface method

The response surface method (RSM) was developed by Box and colleagues in the 1950s. This term is used from the graphical perspective created after fitting the mathematical model, and it was widely used in the chemometrics literature. The RSM model includes a group of mathematical and statistical techniques that are based on fitting empirical models with experimental data obtained in relation to experimental design. To achieve this goal, linear or quadratic polynomial functions are used to describe the studied system and thus to explore (modeling and shifting) the experimental conditions until their optimization. The steps of applying RSM as an optimization technique are, firstly, the selection of independent variables that have major effects on the system through screening studies and determining the limits of the experimental area, according to the purpose of the study and the researcher's experience. Second, the selection of the experimental plan and conducting the experiments according to the selected experimental matrix. The third step is mathematical and statistical processing of experimental data obtained through fitting a polynomial function. Assessing the fit of the model is the fourth step. The fifth step is to examine the necessity and possibility of making a shift in the direction of the optimal region, and finally, the last step is to obtain the optimal values for each studied variable [70–72].

### 15.3.3 Evaluation of machine learning model

A model fitted with data is expected to perform admirably not only on familiar datasets but also on new and unseen data. The abstract errors of the models are measured through calculation-based tests in the normal evaluation paradigm and play a key role in determining the optimal model results. Among the various ML models, the diverse features and wide applications collectively contribute to their merit as powerful predictive tools. To achieve its main goal, each ML model in this field adheres to a distinct framework that is designed. Identifying weak points in previous models continuously and improving their learning acts as an acceleration, and new and more efficient models are invented day by day [73]. Evaluating the performance and accuracy of ML model predictions is done by evaluating an algorithm, an important aspect that involves testing it to gauge its performance. Where experimental data are systematically compared with their predicted counterparts is where the expansion of model prediction accuracy assessment is observed. Coefficient of determination ($R^2$), root mean square error (RMSE), mean percentage error (MPE), mean absolute error (MAE), mean absolute percentage error (MAPE), mean square error (MSE), and RMSE of ML models are evaluated by performance criteria. These metrics provide valuable information about the model's skill in revising mean values, its resilience in the face of outliers, and the degree of inherent uncertainty in its predictions, among other relevant details, and serve as statistical indicators and insights. They provide comprehensive information on various aspects of model performance. Below are detailed mathematical equations that define each of these performance measures [47,74].

$$R^2 = 1 - \frac{\sum_{i=1}^{n} (y_i - f(x_i))^2}{\sum_{i=1}^{n} (y_i - \bar{y})^2} \tag{15.1}$$

$$MAE = \frac{1}{n} \sum_{i=1}^{n} |y_i - f(x_i)| \tag{15.2}$$

$$MAPE = 100 \times \frac{1}{n} \sum_{i=1}^{n} \left| \frac{y_i - f(x_i)}{y_i} \right| \tag{15.3}$$

$$MSE = \frac{1}{n} \sum_{i=1}^{n} (y_i - f(x_i))^2 \tag{15.4}$$

$$RMSE = \sqrt{\frac{1}{n} \sum_{i=1}^{n} (y_i - f(x_i))^2} \tag{15.5}$$

$$MPE = \frac{1}{n} \sum_{i=1}^{n} \frac{y_i - f(x_i)}{y_i} \tag{15.6}$$

As a pivot measure, the $R^2$ value from 0 to 1 serves to assess the accuracy of the model, with a value of 1 indicating the most accurate and 0 indicating no correlation. In fact, $R^2$ shows the degree of accuracy in the predictions made by the model. It is necessary to note that it indicates the inefficiency of a model when the value of $R^2$ is 0 and indicates the inability to predict labels with satisfactory accuracy. If the value of $R^2$ is 1, it indicates that the predictive capacity is strong; this means the superiority of the model in producing very accurate results. $R^2$ distinguishes itself in these performance measures as a dimensionless quantity, while sharing the same dimensions as the output values examined by MAE. It evaluates the absolute difference between the predicted and actual values with MAE, adopts a linear approach in penalizing the errors, and thus treats those deviations [75,76]. Although MAE can be converted to a percentage-based metric known as MAPE, which standardizes the error of each measurement against the corresponding true value, MSE takes a quadratic approach to penalizing errors. In that case, errors are penalized in proportion to the square of their magnitude. Importantly, due to the quadratic nature of the MSE penalty function, outliers have a significant impact on MSE compared to MAE. A challenge associated with MSE is observed in reporting its errors, which are expressed in terms of the squared units predicted by the model [77]. RMSE has a square root transformation to ensure consistency with the units considered. From a statistical point of view, to show sensitivity to deviations of significant magnitude, RMSE works as a characteristic indicator of large errors, even in a single prediction. In contrast, MAE provides an overall deviation and shows no sensitivity to the effect of isolated large errors [78].

### 15.3.4 Advantages of using machine learning for electrospun nanofibers

In the fabrication of NFs, the integration of ML with electrospinning has several advantages. One of the most important advantages that has been addressed is the optimization of the process parameters involved in the electrospinning process. The integration of these two items not only optimizes the quality and consistency of the produced NFs but also significantly reduces manufacturing costs. Traditional methods used for optimization rely on determining the best settings for process parameters through extensive trial-and-error experiments. These methods are performed by repeatedly adjusting the parameters and conducting several tests until reaching the optimal conditions, which is very inefficient, long, and expensive. Not surprisingly, the trial-and-error process is costly due to the high cost of materials used for each experiment and the labor-intensive nature of conducting and analyzing these experiments. However, ML algorithms have a more advanced and efficient approach by analyzing past and published data from various experiments. One of the important advantages of algorithms is processing and evaluating large amounts of data to identify patterns and relationships between different process parameters, nanofiber properties, and influencing factors for a wide range of applications [42,79]. ML significantly reduces the use of expensive materials, and it minimizes process waste by identifying the optimal combination of process parameters using historical and published data from previous experiments. This advanced predictive capability leads to process optimization, increased production, and savings by reducing material consumption, producing more stable materials, and minimizing experimental waste [80].

One of the important and significant advantages of integrating ML with the electrospinning process is its accuracy. ML models can be trained on large datasets, enabling them to achieve high accuracy in predicting process results and electrospinning parameters. This leads to improved control over the targeted properties of electrospun NFs. The ability to accurately predict and control fiber diameter is critical, as it directly affects critical properties such as specific surface area, mechanical strength, and electronic conductivity. For example, precise control of mechanical strength is critical for tissue engineering applications, while electronic conductivity and specific surface area are critical for use in sensors. In other cases, in energy storage devices, a high level of precision is ensured so that the fabricated electrospun NFs meet the necessary standard requirements for each relevant application consistently [81,82]. It cannot be overstated that the innovative potential of ML in this field not only increases the accuracy and reliability of the electrospinning process but also opens new avenues for research and development. ML provides a deeper insight into the electrospinning process by discovering hidden patterns and relationships in complex and high-number datasets, leads to the discovery of new parameter combinations and manufacturing techniques, and can have better control over the properties of NFs. It was unattainable in traditional methods. ML algorithms identify the design of experiments with the most accurate and relevant data needed to optimize process parameters. Significantly, this approach reduces the number of tests required and speeds up the overall development process. The resulting integration designs experiments that systematically vary several process parameters simultaneously, enabling them to effectively identify their combined effects on fiber diameter and alignment. In addition, the use of ML can improve the microstructure of electrospun NFs. It defines the microstructure of fibers on a microscopic scale by including complex structural details and is important for determining the overall performance of NFs in various applications. Among the important aspects of microstructure, we can mention surface roughness, porosity, fiber diameter, and alignment. Therefore, ML significantly increases the accuracy and control in the process of making electrospun fibers, and as a result, electrospun NFs will have stable and exceptional microstructural qualities [83–85].

## 15.4 Approaches of machine learning in electrospinning

The integration of AI has played a significant role in the selection of materials and the use of biocompatible polymers in electrospinning. AI offers unprecedented precision and efficiency, enabling researchers to tailor materials for specific applications with a level of exclusivity previously unattainable. For example, the central role of AI algorithms focuses on the selection of biological materials that are compatible with the human body, the required thermal properties, or even the combination of several materials to increase efficiency. These materials include polycaprolactone, gelatin, and polyvinyl alcohol with cellulose in acetic acid buffer, which leads the choice of each study in another direction. This means that the choice of material should be intelligent and consider all aspects [47,86,87]. New opportunities have been opened with the concept of ML for refining and optimizing electrospinning processes. While the basic principles of electrospinning remain unchanged, ML represents successful tools for further control of nanofiber properties and process parameters involved in electrospinning. In the past few years, various ML models have been widely used in materials science to predict the diameter, mechanical properties, biological properties, and other measurables in electrospun NFs. Aiming to increase various vital properties of fibers, including mechanical flexibility, surface area, permeability, wettability, and porosity, researchers have made many efforts to modify fiber diameter and other predictable aspects of NFs for various applications, all of which are essential for their performance [88–90].

### 15.4.1 Prediction of nanofiber diameter

ML models and empirical equations have been widely used to predict the diameter of electrospun NFs and save resources, costs, and time. ANNs play an important role in developing new procedures, increasing efficiency, and changing organizational strategies and approaches in the production of NFs. As mentioned earlier, ANNs use a nonlinear mapping structure inspired by the human neural network and are particularly useful for modeling methods where data is large and multiple input processing parameters affect the expected response. Optimizing the desired response by accurately predicting the effects of different input variables is the main goal of using ANNs in this field. This capability demonstrates the suitability of ANNs for electrospinning applications, where the number of parameters to be considered is large and several parameters must be tuned to achieve optimal nanofiber properties. The diameter of the fibers is controlled by the flow of the polymer solution and the applied voltage. To define these stability domains, a combination of analytical expressions is used depending on the location along the jet travel. In the vicinity of the nozzle, an expression is used that links the diameter of the fiber with the kinematic viscosity of the polymer solution, nozzle-collector distance, solution density, liquid flow, electric current and electrostatic field intensity. At larger distances from the nozzle, the fiber diameter can be expressed as a function of solution density, liquid flow, applied electrostatic field intensity, and distance from the nozzle. Close to the collector, the diameter of the fiber can be expressed according to the surface tension of the polymer solution, dielectric permittivity, liquid flow and electric current intensity. Under certain constraints, the superposition of graphs obtained from these mathematical expressions is used to determine the stability range of fiber diameter, where the diameter can be controlled by two process parameters, that is, applied voltage and polymer solution flow [91–93].

Faridi Majidi and colleagues. Among many studies, ANN was used as an ML model in their research, and the primary factors influencing the fiber diameter of electrospun nylon-6, 6 NFs have been evaluated. They used ANN as ML model in their research. This study combined four key process parameters such as polymer concentration, needle-to-collector distance, solution feed rate, and applied voltage, as input process parameters, with the resulting fiber diameter as output. The ML model generated in this study facilitated an in-depth exploration of the complex interactions between input variables and their effect on fiber diameter. The findings of this evaluation showed that solution feed rate and polymer concentration appear as important factors affecting fiber diameter, which show inverse and direct relationships, respectively. Conversely, needle-to-collector distance and applied voltage have slight but direct effects on fiber diameter. Using the ANN model, an optimal prediction model dataset was obtained with $R^2$ values of 0.92 and 0.91 for the training and testing datasets, respectively. $R^2$ metric serves as an indicator of ML model prediction accuracy. Due to the complex and highly complex relationships between the process parameters and the diameter of the electrospun NFs, these $R^2$ values indicate the successful training of the model, thus indicating its efficiency in capturing the underlying patterns in the data [94].

In order to increase control over the diameter of the fibers, in the study of Cramariuc et al., a method was proposed to determine the stability areas of the process, in which the diameter of the electrospun fibers can be predetermined and also controlled by the flow of the polymer solution and the applied voltage. To define these stability areas, a combination of analytical expressions depending on the location along the travel jet was used. In the vicinity of the nozzle, an expression was used that links the diameter of the fiber with the kinematic viscosity of the polymer solution, nozzle-collector distance, solution density, liquid flow, electric current, and electrostatic field intensity. At larger distances from the nozzle, the fiber diameter can be expressed as a function of solution density, liquid flow, applied electrostatic field intensity, and distance from the nozzle. Close to the collector, the diameter of the fiber can be expressed according to the surface tension of the polymer solution, dielectric permittivity, liquid flow, and electric current intensity. Under certain constraints, the superposition of graphs obtained from these mathematical expressions is used to determine the stability range of fiber diameter, where the diameter can be controlled by two process parameters, that is, applied voltage and polymer solution flow [93].

In Naghibzadeh et al.'s study, ANNs have been used, as can be seen in Fig. 15.8 to predict the diameter of electrospun gelatin NFs. By using the available knowledge and data, a data structure can be designed that acts like a brain neuron. So, by creating a network of interconnected artificial neurons, a training algorithm for the network is created, and this algorithm is applied to the network in the form of Hayden Lear. Apply and teach. The results showed that the ANN method, with high accuracy and low error, predicted the diameter of NFs in different electrospinning conditions with three hidden layers [13].

Another study introduces the use of the Simplified Encoding Molecular Input Line Input System (SMILES) method for material representation, along with ML algorithms, to model the relationships between material properties, electrospinning

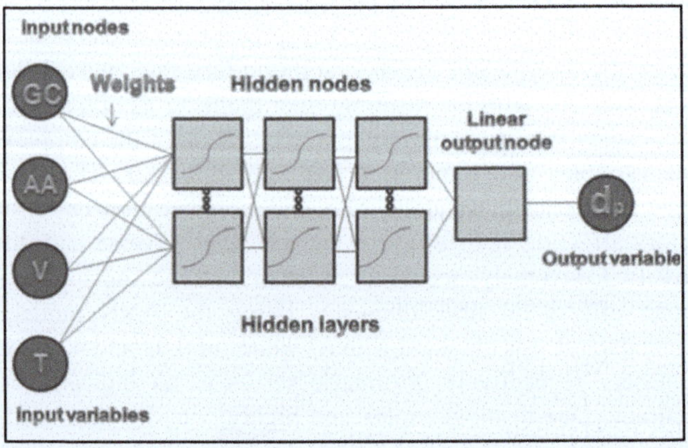


**Figure 15.8** The designed artificial neural network model using prediction of nanofibers diameter.
Reprinted with permission from [13].

parameters, and physical properties of scaffolds. The diameter of the fibers and the conductivity of the scaffolds have been predicted for the first time using this approach. In the classification task, the vote classifier predicted fiber diameter with a balanced accuracy score of 0.9478. In the regression work, a neural network regression was built to learn the relationships between parameters and predict the diameter of fibers with $R^2 = 0.723$. In the case of fiber conductivity, regression and classifier models were used for prediction, but performance fluctuated due to insufficient information in published data and collected datasets. Finally, the accuracy of the model prediction was confirmed by experimental electrospinning of a biocompatible polymer (i.e., polyvinyl alcohol and polyvinyl alcohol/polypyrrole). Field emission scanning electron microscope (FE-SEM) images were used to measure fiber diameter. The results confirmed the effectiveness of the proposed model in the study of predicting the diameter of polymer NFs and reducing the parameter space before the scoping exercises [95]. In another study, O.S. Yördem et al. investigated the effects of material and process parameters on the diameter of electrospun polyacrylonitrile fibers experimentally. RSM was used to design the experiments in the settings of solution concentration, voltage, and collector distance. Also, the importance of each parameter on the resulting fiber diameter was evaluated. Investigations were carried out in bivariate process domains of several collector spacings as applied voltage and solution concentration varied at constant polymer molecular weight. Average diameter and coefficient of variation were modeled by polynomial response surfaces as a function of solution concentration and voltage at each collector distance. The effect of the applied voltage on the micron-scale fiber diameter was almost negligible when the solution concentration and the collector distance were high. However, all three factors were statistically significant in the production of nanoscale fibers. The response surface predictions showed parametric interactions for the resulting fiber diameter and showed that there was a negative correlation between the mean diameter and the coefficient of variation for the fiber diameter. A subdomain of the parameter space consisting of solution concentration, applied voltage, and collector spacing was proposed for potential nanoscale fiber production [96]. Moreover, Ko et al. understood that Poly (ε-caprolactone) (PCL) 14k, 45k, and 70k Mw have different crystallization temperatures and thus slightly different properties that affect fiber diameter. To observe these behaviors, the fiber was produced at each stage of 10°C for each molecular weight, and its diameter was measured. In addition, the fiber was fabricated on a cooled ground plane to observe the change in fiber diameter compared to a conventional ground plane. In the case of molecular Mw 14k PCL, the diameter increased with increasing temperature. For Mw 45k PCL, the fiber diameter decreased with increasing temperature. From Mw 70k PCL, the fiber diameter also decreased with increasing temperature. When the experiment was performed on the cold collection plate, the data did not change significantly from the previous experiments [97].

The model of ANNs by Khatti et al. aims to predict the diameter of PCL fiber obtained by the electrospinning technique [98]. This study focused on evaluating key process parameters such as polymer concentration, applied voltage, and needle-to-collector distance. The table was designed and trained using the back-propagation

**Table 15.1** The performance measures of trial-error and artificial neural network (ANN) [100].

| Performance measures | Training | Test | All data |
|---|---|---|---|
| Trial-error-$R^2$ | 0.5667 | 0.5551 | 0.564 |
| ANN-$R^2$ | 0.9679 | 0.9452 | 0.9594 |

algorithm, the ANN model through a set of input-output patterns to effectively record the complex relationships within the data. The R correlation coefficient values for these sets were 0.987, 0.989, and 0.998, respectively, which showed a perfect fit between the predicted and observed values. It is evident that the MSE of the network undergoes a decreasing trend, indicating that the network nest is effectively learning and improving over time. The ANN model shows a significant performance with $R^2$ value of 0.97 and RMSE of 3.81, which shows its efficiency in accurately predicting PCL diameter. In addition, this model has an MAE of 14.58, which further shows its predictive ability. A critical evaluation measure that quantifies the difference between model or statistical estimator predictions and actual values is RMSE, and it always appears as a comparison parameter in most studies [99].

As it is known, in the electrospinning process, the diameter of the produced NFs plays an important role in their final properties. In this study, ANN and multiple regression (MLR) models were used to predict the diameter of PCL and gelatin NFs. The results of Table 15.1 showed that the ANN model with high accuracy ($R^2$=0.959) performs better compared to the MLR model ($R^2$=0.564). The analysis of the available information has shown that the weight ratio of polymers, the distance between the needle and the collector, the injection rate, and the applied voltage are the most important to the least important parameters affecting the diameter of NFs, respectively. The use of the ANN model to predict the diameter of NFs can be used as a decision support system in the production process of NFs, which reduces time and costs, and increases the accuracy of data analysis. Also, the use of the aforementioned forecasting models, such as ANN, has improved the accuracy of predicting the diameter of NFs and optimizing the production process. These advanced models consider several variables and a high number of data simultaneously, allowing the creation of biopolymers with very specific properties. By adjusting polymer chain length, functional group composition, or cross-linking density, AI can help develop materials that are biodegradable, responsive to environmental stimuli, or have unique mechanical properties tailored to the intended application [100].

Polycaprolactone/chitosan NFs were made with different weight ratios, and another studied sample was in the fiber diameter analysis, which was performed by Andrade del Olmo et al. and showed significant antibacterial performance that is suitable for wound healing applications [101]. Salehi et al. used the ANN model to optimize the properties of electrospun polyacrylonitrile/poly (vinylidene fluoride) (PAN/PVdF) NFs from the ANN model. This ANN model was used to predict the fiber diameter and its standard deviation in electrospun NFs. First, the electrospinning technique was used to produce PAN/PVdF NFs, which made it possible to establish a quantitative relationship between specific process parameters, such as applied voltage, solution concentration, and PVdF concentration, and the diameter of the resulting fibers. The fiber diameter of the produced NFs was changed from 116 to 379 nm. The observations show that the fiber diameter decreases with higher PVdF concentration and increases with higher solution concentration. Interestingly, the applied voltage appeared to have little effect on the fiber diameter. The most optimal structure of the ANN model consists of two hidden layers, each of which contains five neurons in a 3–5-5-3 structure [102].

Tissue engineering, which is another field that has received increasing attention, is important because the extracellular matrix (ECM) has a nanoscale structure. The use of nanomaterials in tissue engineering allows the production of tissue scaffolds that are more similar to the ECM form. Therefore, the success rate of tissue engineering will increase because it provides a more favorable environment for cell growth. In another study conducted by Sara et al., an ANN model based on multilayer perceptron (MLP) is presented to predict the average fiber diameter (AFD) of electrospun gelatin/bioactive glass (Gt/BG) scaffold. The experimental results previously published in the literature, which include a solution parameter (BG content) as well as two process parameters (tip-to-collector distance and solution flow rate) related to the production of electrospun Gt/BG NFs, were compared with the results of this paper. According to this study, the average values of the error percentage between the average diameter of the predicted and experimental fibers have been obtained as 3.27%. The results obtained from the proposed model were also confirmed by comparison with AFD expression results reported elsewhere. It was shown that the AFD of Gt/BG electrospinning can be predicted by the model presented here without the need for complex knowledge or complex mathematical and physical background [103,104].

For a better understanding, a table of research is given below (Table 15.2); the aim of these articles was to optimize and predict the diameter of polymers. In this table, the algorithm used, the polymer used, the evaluated parameter, the efficiency of the model, and finally its application are listed.

### 15.4.2 Prediction of properties of nanofiber

One of the most interesting aspects of AI and AI methods in polymer selection is its ability to adjust different properties of materials to meet specific needs. AI-based optimization techniques can adjust the molecular structure of biopolymers to achieve desired properties, including high mechanical strength, biodegradability, and biocompatibility. Generative algorithms, for example, adversarial networks (GANs) and variational autoencoders (VAEs), can design new biopolymer structures by generating hypothetical materials and iteratively improving them based on desired criteria. It is evident that Yao et al.'s study focuses on predicting and producing the diameter of NFs from synthetic and natural polymers. This article especially deals with PCL and gelatin (Gt) polymers and how to improve the properties of these polymers through their combination. The combination of these two polymers has been done

**Table 15.2** A detailed review of using machine learning (ML) models for predicting the fiber diameter of electrospun nanofibers.

| ML model | Polymer | Evaluated parameter | ML model performance | Application | References |
|---|---|---|---|---|---|
| XGBoost model using kNN data | Poly (lactic-co-glycolic acid) (PLGA) | Diameter/particle size | $R^2$= 0.91 | Drug delivery or tissue engineering | [105] |
| Artificial neural network (ANN) | Chitosan/polyethylene oxide (PEO) blend | Diameter | MSE = 0.0707 and $R^2$ = 0.9630 | For desired shapes and sizes | [106] |
| Response surface method (RSM) and ANN | Polycaprolactone-Gelatin (PCL-GT) blend | Diameter | $R^2$>0.92, and MAPE<0.057 | Tissue engineering and industrial fields | [107] |
| Decision tree (DT), extra trees regression (ETR), kernel ridge regression (KRR), random forest (RF), support vector regression (SVR), and XGBoost (XGB) | Various polymers (unspecified) | Diameter | RF $R^2$ = 0.9468 and ETR $R^2$ = 0.9421 | Using a web server (ENDP) for user collaboration and input | [108] |
| RSM and ANN | Polymethyl methacrylate (PMMA) | Diameter | ANN outperformed RSM in terms of accuracy and prediction | Mechanical, electrical, and optical Applications | [109] |
| Group method of data handling (GMDH) and ANN | Silk fibroin | Average diameter | GMDH = 3.56%, ANN = 2.28% | Wound dressings | [110] |
| ANN | Polyethylene oxide (PEO) | Mean diameter | High predictive accuracy with $R^2$ between predicted and actual values (exact value not specified) | For controlled fabrication | [111] |

| | | | | | |
|---|---|---|---|---|---|
| RSM | Chitosan-collagen composite | Diameter | $R^2 \geq 0.9666$ | Wound healing and tissue engineering applications | [112] |
| ANN and convolutional neural network (CNN) | Poly (vinyl alcohol) (PVA) | Production of aligned nanofibers (binary classification), orientation, angle, and diameter of nanofibers (regression models) | ANN for binary classification: accuracy = 0.94 (training set), accuracy = 0.90, F1-score=0.87 (validation set) | For biomedical and electronic devices | [113] |
| Adaptive neuro-fuzzy inference system (ANFIS) | Polyethersulfone (PES) | Diameter | $R^2 > 0.94$ and RMSE<0.064 | Various applications | [114] |
| RSM based on Box–Behnken design (BBD) | Gelatin/chitosan/PVA | Mean diameter | High accuracy with good accordance between experimental results and BBD predictions | Wound healing applications | [115] |
| ANN | Polyethylene | Diameter | The ANN model achieved an average error of 2.29% between predicted and actual nanofiber diameters. | Various applications | [116] |
| ANN | Poly (glycerol sebacate) (PGS), poly (glycerol sebacate-co-caprolactone) (P[GScoCL]), Gelatin, Peptide | Diameter | The model effectively predicted and optimized electrospinning parameters. | Biomedical scaffolds | [117] |
| ANN | Polycaprolactone | Diameter | $R^2 = 0.97$, RMSE = 3.81 and MAE = 14.58% | Tissue engineering | [98] |

*(Continued)*

**Table 15.2** (Continued)

| ML model | Polymer | Evaluated parameter | ML model performance | Application | References |
|---|---|---|---|---|---|
| ANN | Polyacrylonitrile | Diameter | $R^2$ = 0.99 and MAE = 1.6% | Biomedical applications | [118] |
| ANN | Ferrofluid/polyvinyl alcohol | Diameter | $R^2$ = 0.79 (training), $R^2$ = 0.94 (testing) and MSE = 0.000085 | Biomedical applications | [119] |
| ANN | Chitosan/polyethylene oxide | Diameter | $R^2$ = 0.963 and MSE = 0.0707 | Biomedical applications | [106] |
| ANN | Polyethylene oxide | Diameter | $R^2$ = 0.9992 | Biomedical application | [120] |
| ANN | Polyacrylonitrile/poly (vinylidene fluoride) | Diameter | $R^2$ = 0.99 (training), $R^2$ = 0.99 (testing) and $R^2$ = 0.99 (validation) | Electrolyte in lithium batteries | [102] |
| ANN | Polycaprolactone | Diameter | $R^2$ = 0.97 (training) and $R^2$ = 0.98 (testing) | Tissue engineering | [121] |
| ANN | Polyamide-6 | Diameter | $R^2$ = 1.00, MSE=0.00 (training), $R^2$ = 0.9946 and MSE = 0.0021 (testing) | Air filtration | [122] |
| ANN | Polyurethane | Diameter | $R^2$ = 0.990 | Wound dressing | [123] |
| ANN | Polyacrylonitrile | Diameter | $R^2$ = 1.00 (training), $R^2$ = 0.908 (validation), and $R^2$ = 0.979 (comprehensive) | Biomedical applications | [124] |
| ANN | Polyacrylonitrile | Diameter | $R^2$ = 0.9936 (training), $R^2$ = 0.9944 (testing), and $R^2$ = 0.9936 (comprehensive) | Energy conversion and storage | [125] |

| | | | | | |
|---|---|---|---|---|---|
| Least squares support vector regression (LSSVR), LW-KPLSR, and FL | Polyvinyl alcohol/acetic acid/chitosan | Diameter | LSSVR $R^2$ = 0.5945, MAE = 20.3188 nm, RSME = 25.5405 nm (training), $R^2$ = 0.7354, MAE = 18.6228 nm, RMSE = 22.757 nm (testing) LW-KPLSR $R^2$ = 0.8534, MAE = 12.8781 nm, RSME = 16.6615 nm (training), $R^2$ = 0.7509, MAE = 21.0767 nm, RMSE = 23.2845 nm (testing) FL $R^2$ = 0.9199, MAE = 12.9889 nm, RSME = 16.1874 nm (training), $R^2$ = –0.8718, MAE = 42.2333 nm, RMSE = 50.5757 nm (testing) | Drug delivery | [86] |

(*Continued*)

**Table 15.2** (Continued)

| ML model | Polymer | Evaluated parameter | ML model performance | Application | References |
|---|---|---|---|---|---|
| LSSVR, LW-KPLSR, and FL | Chitosan/silver nanoparticles colloid and polyethylene oxide | Diameter | LSSVR $R^2$ = 0.999, MAE = 4.7538 nm, RSME = 5.2597 nm (training), $R^2$ = 0.6616, MAE = 51.3537 nm, RMSE = 79.5503 nm (testing) LW-KPLSR $R^2$ = 0.9989, MAE = 3.1167 nm, RSME = 5.6667 nm (training), $R^2$ = 0.8115, MAE = 33.6509 nm, RMSE = 42.5396 nm (testing) FL $R^2$ = 0.8877, MAE = 51.3636 nm, RSME = 64.9678 nm (training), $R^2$ = 0.6224, MAE = 64.6667 nm, RMSE = 72.1757 nm (testing) | Drug delivery | [126] |
| ANN | Polymethyl methacrylate | Diameter | $R^2$ = 0.98588, MAE = 1.26% (training), MAE = 5.76% (testing) | Biomedical applications | [127] |

| | | | | | |
|---|---|---|---|---|---|
| ANN | Poly(Ɛ-caprolactone) (PCL), Poly (lactic acid) (PLA), and *Nigella sativa* (NS) extract | Diameter | The ANN model demonstrated an average goodness value of 1.992, outperforming the Response Surface Methodology (RSM) model, which had a value of 1.823 | Wound treatment | [128] |
| ANN | Polyvinyl alcohol/ chitosan | Diameter | $R^2$ = 0.93866 and MSE = 0.09008 | Biomedical applications | [129] |

using the electrospinning method under specific conditions. PCL and gelatin polymers have been combined to create a new material with improved properties. The combination of these polymers has led to the improvement of physical and mechanical properties due to their different and complementary properties. PCL is a synthetic polymer with biocompatible, semicrystalline, and hydrophilic properties, and gelatin is a natural polymer with high biocompatibility, biodegradability, and low-cost properties [130]. The combination of these two polymers has led to improved mechanical and chemical properties as well as better biocompatibility (resulted from Fig. 15.9) [130]. The combination of PCL and gelatin has created a new composite material with improved physical and mechanical properties.

In Islam et al. study, Poly (vinyl alcohol) (PVA)/alginate (Alg) NFs were prepared using electrospinning method in aqueous solutions with PVA (10% by weight)/Alg

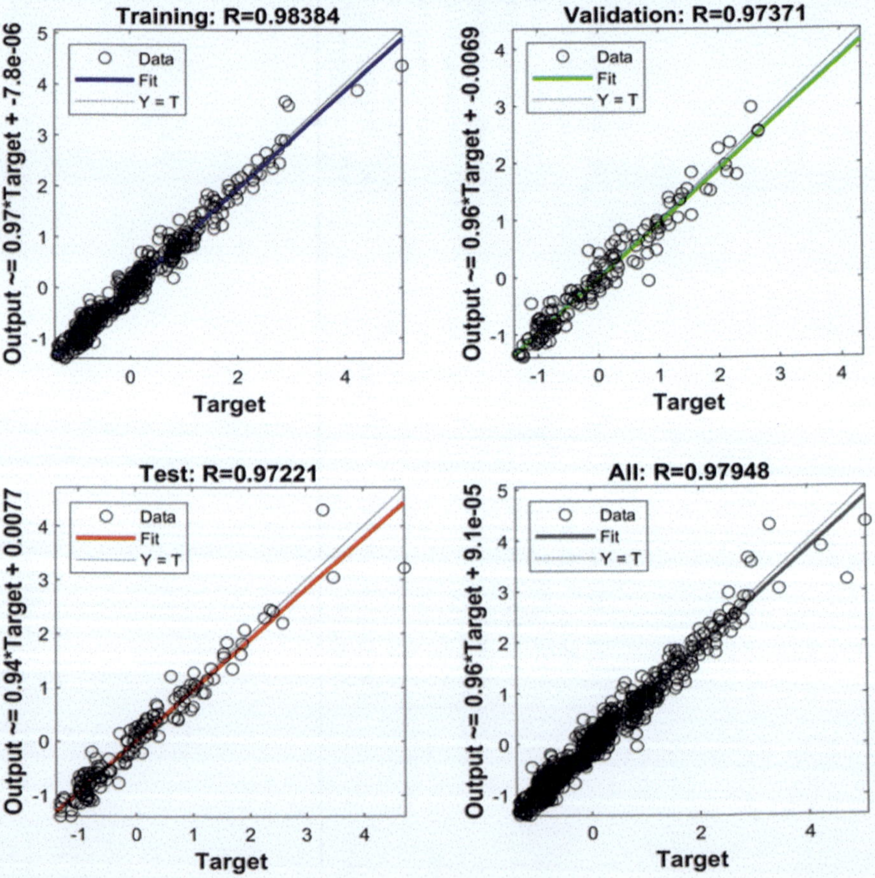


**Figure 15.9** Scatter plots of output versus target predict the diameter of PCL/Gt nanofibers values by artificial neural network (ANN).
Reprinted with permission from [130].

(2% by weight) mixed system in different volume ratios. Due to its biocompatibility and nontoxicity, PVA can be used in many fields. Alginate is an interesting natural biopolymer due to its many advantages and good biological properties. Using XRD, FTIR, and DSC data, it was shown that there are good interactions between PVA and Alg, probably due to hydrogen bonds. This study showed that with a higher percentage of Alg in PVA/Alg composite NFs, a superior degradation onset temperature and higher thermal stability can be achieved above 350°C. In addition, the composite NFs show improved mechanical properties compared to pure electrospun PVA with the addition of Alg [131]. Reddy et al. consumed electrospun polycaprolactone (PCL) scaffolds widely in tissue engineering applications due to their superior biomechanical properties and compatibility with the cellular matrix. The properties of PCL scaffolds depend on electrospinning parameters. The relationships between electrospinning process parameters and scaffold properties are complex and nonlinear. In this study, we used an ANN technique to estimate the tensile strength and suture retention of PCL scaffolds as a function of electrospinning parameters (polymer concentration, solution feed rate, applied voltage, and nozzle-to-collector distance). An independent ANN software was developed, and the predicted properties were in good agreement with the experimental data. Excellent learning accuracy was observed for training and testing datasets in this model. ANN model calculated the minimum tensile strength of NFs and suture retention as 0.70 MPa and 4.20 N/mm. The results can be obtained with 10% polymer concentration, feed rate of 2.0 ml/h, high voltage of 20 kV and nozzle to collector distance of 140 mm. Reddy's model has been an efficient technique to optimize the process parameters for the biomechanical properties of the desired scaffold. It was difficult to predict the biomechanical properties of electrospun NFs due to their complex interactions between different parameters. This problem was solved by imaginary electrospinning to quantitatively estimate the effect of electrospinning parameters on the properties. It was a new and simple technique to identify the importance of input parameters on the properties of nanofibrous scaffolds. Accurate predictions showed that this model can adequately estimate the relationships between electrospinning parameters and properties of PCL scaffolds [132].

In another study by Chen et al., ANN was used to predict the tensile moduli of carbon nanofibers (CNF)/epoxy composites. Tensile properties of CNF/epoxy composites made by different dispersion techniques were evaluated by tensile tests. Tensile properties were found to be significantly affected by CNF fraction, sonication time, and mechanical stirring time. According to the test results, ANN was trained and used to predict the tensile moduli of CNF/epoxy composites. The combination of ultrasonication and mechanical stirring improved the dispersion of CNF in epoxy resin and resulted in a significant increase in tensile modulus. We can see that the MSE reaches the target after 16 calculation cycles. Three groups of test samples were used to verify the trained network; the test results are listed in Table 15.3. It shows that the error of tensile moduli between ANN and experimental results does not exceed 5.0%. Therefore, the use of ANN to predict the results is more favorable and reduces the time and cost of testing. The predicted values were compared with the experimental data, and it was concluded that the postdiffusion ANN model can be a promising tool for predicting the properties of composites [133].

**Table 15.3** Experiment data and predicted outputs from the artificial neural network (ANN) network [133].

| CNF fraction | Ultrasonication time (h) | Mechanical stirring time (h) | Tensile moduli (GPa) | | |
|---|---|---|---|---|---|
| | | | Experiment | ANN | error |
| 1.0 | 3 | 1 | 4 | 3.8 | 5.0% |
| 2.0 | 2 | 3 | 3.8 | 3.9 | 2.6% |
| 2.5 | 4 | 1 | 4.4 | 4.5 | 2.3% |

The ability of AI to tune biopolymer properties has practical implications for biomedical applications. In tissue engineering, AI-optimized biopolymers can be spun into scaffolds that mimic the ECM and induce cell adhesion, proliferation, and differentiation. These scaffolds can be customized to support the growth of specific cell types, such as osteoblasts for bone regeneration or chondrocytes for cartilage repair, or in tissue engineering. AI-enhanced biopolymers can be engineered in drug delivery to form NFs with calculated drug release profiles. By manipulating polymer composition and fiber structure, AI can help design drug delivery systems that release therapeutic agents at controlled rates, reduce side effects, and increase treatment efficacy, while speeding up data analysis and polymer materials increase. Specifically, Khedri et al. used electrospun NFs loaded with curcumin and optimized parameters that affect the physicochemical properties of these NFs with the help of AI. Curcumin, as a natural substance with antioxidant, antiinflammatory, and antitumor properties, is widely used in drug delivery systems and tissue engineering, and improves drug delivery systems. However, due to problems such as low solubility and poor stability, the need for new formulation and improvement of existing preparation techniques is felt to increase its efficiency and effectiveness. In this study, electrospun NFs have been investigated as an efficient method for loading curcumin and improving its mentioned properties. Using ML methods, the production of NFs loaded with curcumin was optimized. Through library research, the required data was collected, and the effective parameters were divided into two categories: machine-related parameters and material-related parameters. According to the results, polymers with high density have a lower release rate of curcumin, while the encapsulation efficiency (EE) of curcumin increases with the increase of polymer density. As a result, the smallest diameter, the highest EE, and the highest percentage of drug release are obtained in a molecular weight between 100 and 150 kDa and a curcumin concentration of 10%–15% by weight with a polymer density in the range of 1.2 up to 1.5 g/ml. According to Fig. 15.10, parameters related to materials include concentration, viscosity, electrical conductivity, and type of solvent, while machine conditions include voltage, flow rate, and needle-to-collector distance. Furthermore, the final characteristics of the electrospinning process can be summarized in AFD, drug release percentage (DR%), and EE [79].

Moreover, AI can help select biopolymers that have a favorable interaction with target tissues, improve the biological properties of the polymer, and improve targeting

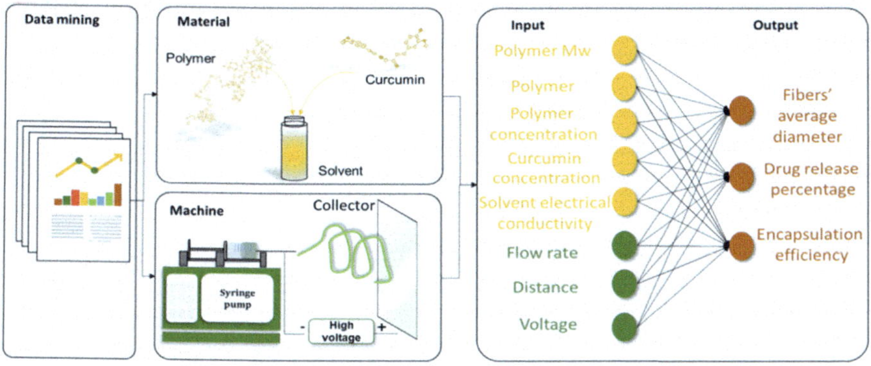


**Figure 15.10** Schematic of the workflow in the study to determine the effective parameters in the preparation of nanofibers regarding inputs and outputs in the machine learning system. Reprinted with permission from [79].

accuracy. Furthermore, the role of AI extends to personalized medicine, where patient-specific data can inform the selection and customization of biopolymers. By integrating genomic, proteomic, and clinical data, AI algorithms can predict how patients will respond to different biopolymer materials, enabling the design of personalized biomedical devices and treatments. In short, the use of AI can help to improve the production processes and optimize the properties of drugs at the nanoscale. Using advanced algorithms and optimization techniques, researchers can design biopolymers with unprecedented precision, paving the way for new biomedical applications. Advances in AI and materials science are accelerating the development of next-generation biomaterials, improving patient outcomes, and pushing the boundaries of medical technology. Customized samples can be obtained by adapting the morphology and architecture of NFs for specific applications, including using different parameters such as electrospinning voltage, solution viscosity, and polymer concentration. Recent advances in 3D modeling and computer-aided design (CAD) have enabled researchers to predict and visualize the structure of nanofiber mats prior to fabrication and optimize their properties for various applications. In recent studies, researchers have combined polyvinyl alcohol NFs with different amounts of silver NPs by adjusting electrospinning parameters such as voltage, distance between nozzle and collector, polymer solution concentration, and solution flow rate, and this work has increased the antibacterial properties of these fibers and, to an extent, has improved significantly. The diameter of the bacterial growth inhibition zone in the samples containing silver NPs was about two times higher than the samples without silver NPs. Agar Diffusion Test has been used to measure the antibacterial properties of these NFs. This method includes nanofiber samples on the surface of agar containing desired bacteria (such as *Escherichia coli* and *Staphylococcus aureus*) and is used to measure the areas of inhibition of bacterial growth around the samples [109]. Comparative studies between RSM and ANN methods to find the effects of electrospinning parameters on the

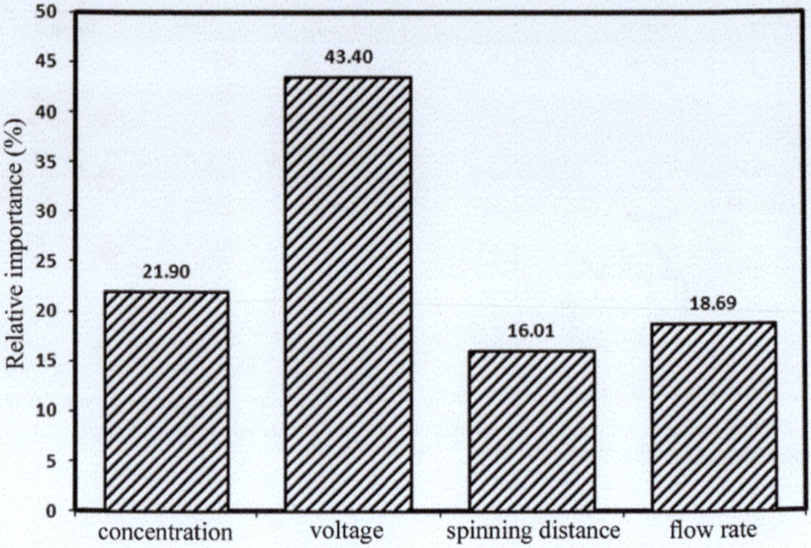


**Figure 15.11** Relative importance of the input variables on the value of the nanofiber mat porosity.
Reprinted with permission from [134].

porosity of nanofiber mats were conducted by Hadavi Moghadam et al. Solution concentration (weight), applied voltage (kV), rotation distance (cm), and volumetric flow rate (ml/h) were the four important electrospinning parameters studied in this scientific research. It was confirmed that applied voltage and solution concentration are two key parameters that affect the porosity of NFs (Fig. 15.11). The two approaches were compared for modeling and optimization capabilities with RSM modeling capability showing superiority over ANN with relatively lower error values. The average relative error for RSM and ANN models was 1.97% and 2.62%, and the RMSE was 1.50 and 1.95, respectively. Comparison of predicted porosity using RSM and ANN models showed that the former had higher modeling performance than the latter. Its high prediction accuracy and the ability to calculate the combined effects of electrospinning factors on the porosity of nanofiber mats have been the superiority of the RSM-based approach. Increasing the concentration of the solution led to a decrease in the porosity of the NFs, while increasing the applied voltage increased the porosity of the NFs [134].

It is clear that NFs have great potential in the field of drug delivery and provide a versatile platform for the controlled release of therapeutic agents. By incorporating drugs into the polymer matrix during the electrospinning process, researchers can create biocompatible and renewable drug delivery systems that provide sustained and controlled release profiles. This section evaluates design considerations for the development of nanofiber-based drug delivery systems, including the type of biopolymers, drug loading techniques, and drug release kinetics. For example, in a

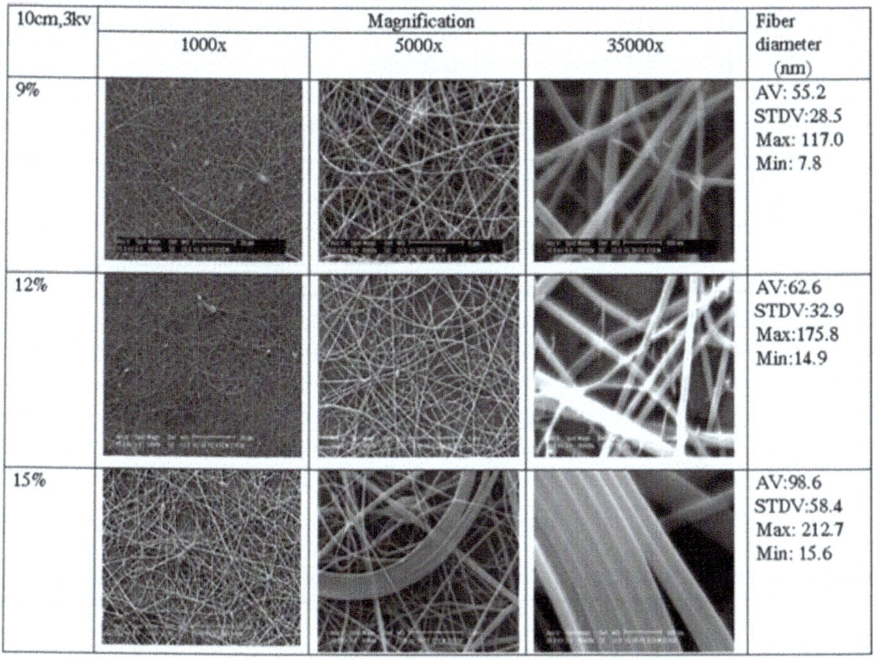


**Figure 15.12** Electrospun silkworm silk fibers captured in field emission scanning electron microscope micrographs with the matching processing parameters of 3 kV/cm electric field, 10 cm spinning distance, and 9%, 12%, and 15% concentrations, respectively.
Reprinted with permission from [135].

drug delivery study, silk fibroin, a type of biopolymer, was used. Silk fibroin, obtained from regenerated Bombyx mori silk, is chosen as an excellent material for drug delivery applications due to its high biocompatibility and biodegradability properties. This material is dissolved in formic acid, and then it is converted into NFs with a diameter of less than 100 nm to perform the electrospinning process. The micrograph of electrospun NFs in different concentrations is shown in Fig. 15.12. These polymer NFs have suitable mechanical and structural properties for the controlled release of drugs. Case studies in this field provide successful applications in the treatment of various medical conditions. It also shows the transformative effect of nanofiber science in improving disease outcomes, especially in targeted treatment with minimal side effects. In most of these studies, AI is used to optimize the electrospinning process and analyze the data. Using ML algorithms, various parameters, such as electric field, silk fibroin concentration, and rotation distance, were optimized to produce NFs with the desired diameter and suitable structure for drug delivery. In addition, these algorithms can automatically identify the relationships between input and output parameters, which are very complex, and naturally improve the process of nanofiber production [135,136].

## 15.5 Challenges and limitations in electrospinning mixed with artificial intelligence

The integration of AI in the electrospinning of biopolymers provides significant advances in the field of nanofiber electrospinning, but it is not without limitations and challenges. AI requires high-quality, accurate, and correct data to provide accurate analysis. If the data is incomplete, inaccurate, or out of order, the results of the data processing may be incorrect or misleading. Protection of patient data and proprietary research information in the field of medical applications and biopolymers is of particular importance. In the European Union and the United States, respectively, there are strict regulations, such as the General Data Protection Regulation (GDPR) and the Health Insurance Portability and Accountability Act (HIPAA), that govern and protect data. This problem can lead to the production of the wrong NFs. The need for frequent updates of algorithms is another challenge in this field that requires frequent adjustments. Privacy and data security problems may arise in the widespread use of AI in the electrospinning process. The use of AI in the electrospinning process requires technical expertise, deep knowledge, and computational challenges that must be overcome. Companies may face a shortage of skilled professionals in this field. It is critical to address these societal challenges by providing adequate support and training for workers to transition into new roles. In addition, developing and maintaining strong AI systems is costly for companies, and companies must make significant human and technical investments in this field, such as computers with high graphics and specialized hardware, like graphics processing units (GPUs) or more equipped infrastructure, such as processing units. Addressing these and other possible barriers is very important for the ethical and sustainable development of AI-based technologies in the field of electrospinning [98,102,123,137]. Table 15.4 is another listed information from the research, whose aim was to optimize and predict other characteristics and required properties of polymers. In this table, the algorithm used, the polymer used, the evaluated parameter, the efficiency of the model, and finally its application are mentioned.

## 15.6 Prospective of future

Collecting accurate and comprehensive data on process parameters related to electrospinning, fiber diameter, and other properties plays an important role. It is important to note that existing datasets on electrospinning process parameters, fiber diameter, and fiber properties remain relatively small-scale, often lacking standardization in characterization methods, and are not accessible to the general public. The introduction of noise into the dataset and the optimal results can be from variations in data collection processes, equipment, and measurement techniques. For this reason, the expansion of ML models to predict the target fiber diameter of electrospun NFs requires a change in the data processing approach. The potential to expand the horizons of ML can be achieved by a continued and determined effort toward the deliberate collection of data by academic journals or increased data sharing by

**Table 15.4** A review of using machine learning (ML) models for predicting the properties of electrospun nanofibers.

| model | Polymer | Evaluated parameter | ML model performance | Application | References |
|---|---|---|---|---|---|
| Artificial neural network (ANN) | Polyvinylpyrrolidone (PVP) and alginate | Diameter/particle size | The ANN accurately predicted increases in porosity and elastic modulus with higher $TiO_2$ weight percentages | Dental and bone regeneration applications. | [138] |
| Deep neural network (DNN) | Polyvinyl alcohol (PVA) and gelatin | Compressive stress-strain responses of porous hydrogels | The DNN effectively predicted and captured the compressive stress-strain responses of the hydrogels based on the concentrations of the constituent materials and the duration of mechanical tests. | Biomedical applications | [139] |
| ANN | Hyaluronic acid (HA) | Elastic modulus, compressive strength, impact resistance | New combinations of HA and facades properties successfully predicted | Enhanced durability of building facades with HA nanofiber coatings | [140] |
| ANN | Chitosan (Cs) with royal Gel (RG) | Mechanical properties (elastic modulus, tensile modulus, porosity) | Improved elastic modulus (from 32 to 62 MPa), tensile modulus (from 1.4 to 3.9 MPa), and porosity (from 76% to 85%) with 5 wt.% RG | Wound dressing application | [141] |

*(Continued)*

**Table 15.4** (Continued)

| model | Polymer | Evaluated parameter | ML model performance | Application | References |
|---|---|---|---|---|---|
| XGBoost, gradient boosting, extra trees classifier, random forest classifier, lightGBM, fully connected neural network | Various biomaterials (natural and synthesized) | Cell response, printability, scaffold quality | Superior performance in classification tasks, achieving higher accuracy and F1 scores | Tissue engineering | [142] |
| RSM and ANN | Composites, blends, and polymer membranes | Optimization of material characteristics | RSM is shown to be relevant in determining the effect of variables on single/multiple responses compared with ANN for effectiveness. | Polymerization and manufacturing | [143] |
| ANN | Chitosan (Cs) particulates encapsulating insulin | Particle stability, insulin release profile | Optimized parameters to prevent burst release in acidic medium (pH=1.20) and provided sustained release in PBS medium (pH=7.40) | Drug delivery | [144] |

researchers. This proactive approach to data access bypasses the need to resort to ethically uncertain and unethical methods, such as web scraping to extract data. Standardization related to the description, analysis, and presentation of process parameters related to electrospinning provides the potential to facilitate the community of larger datasets. Such standardized approaches simplify data collection efforts and increase the accessibility of accumulating comprehensive datasets. It is important to recognize that the features, especially the parameters inherent to the electrospinning process, are chosen correctly because they play a fundamental role in determining the accuracy and efficiency of ML models. According to the studies conducted, electrospinning of biopolymers based on AI will continue to evolve, especially in the medical industry and environmental issues, including food packaging; there are several promising ideas that will be expanded. These scientific paths not only transform the boundaries of current knowledge but also strengthen interdisciplinary collaborations. For example, in a study, electrospinning technology has drawn increasing attention to various aspects of biotechnology. The fabrication of electrospun NFs containing antibacterial agents for antimicrobial applications has increased significantly in recent years. In Liu et al.'s review, different electrospun NFs with antimicrobial properties were introduced and investigated, which is promising in the area of NFs used in the field of medicine and can be used in various cases. The focus in this study is on the developments and applications of antimicrobial electrospun NFs with various antimicrobial agents, including metal NPs, antibiotics, quaternary ammonium compounds, triclosan, plant extracts, carbon nanomaterials, and antimicrobial biopolymers that have antimicrobial properties. The results showed that electrospun NFs containing antimicrobials have enhanced antimicrobial performance with various biomedical applications compared to traditional antimicrobial materials used [145]. The future of biopolymer electrospinning based on AI is bright and full of prospects. Predictable areas for the development of biopolymers obtained by the electrospinning method derived from AI in the future include the development of advanced AI algorithms to increase the capabilities of electrospinning systems and increase the efficiency of production biopolymers. The discovery and development of novel biopolymers with unique properties by AI to produce new biopolymer materials will be another vision of the future and lead to innovative applications in fields such as medicine, food packaging, environmental improvement, and production. The material will be sustainable and beyond. Even this field can be expanded and integrated with other fields; for example, biopolymers produced by the electrospinning method and integration of AI can be used in 3D printing technology. As a result, the integration of AI with biopolymer electrospinning technology is a revolutionary development.

At present, manual feature engineering, which includes feature filtering, usually depends on the level of expertise and intuition of the researcher. It should be noted that this method is prone to potential drawbacks, such as ignoring important features and potentially inducing overfitting, resulting in the model's ability to generalize the data not being seen well due to its high number or complexity. Conversely, automated feature engineering represents a promising solution to these problems. By independently generating new candidate features from data and selecting the most relevant ones for model training, automated feature engineering has the potential to efficiently and acceptably address the current challenges associated with manual feature engineering. Despite significant progress, there are several limitations in using ML to predict the target fiber diameter of electrospun NFs. Considering these limitations, the following suggestions can be made as effective avenues for future research efforts.

- ML models have the potential to be used more widely in various fields beyond their current scope. While the conducted research has mainly focused on the development of ML models to predict the fiber diameter of electrospun NFs, many other topics need further exploration and investigation. Among them are the development of mathematical and physical models, the analysis of degradation mechanisms, the diagnosis of failures, and the clarification of the relationships between the properties of materials at the micro- or nanoscale and the performance at the macro-scale, which require more studies that are comprehensive. Further research in these directions can bring valuable insights and advances in various fields beyond nanofiber prediction. Many challenges in fields such as mathematical modeling, experimental analysis, and numerical simulation often cause significant obstacles in traditional approaches.
- There is an opportunity to further refine and improve ML models to meet the specific needs of predicting the target fiber diameter of electrospun NFs, including increasing their ability to maintain high levels of accuracy and efficiency in learning and training, especially when dealing with datasets. In addition, exploring the combination of various ML algorithms for data preprocessing can be useful and valuable. Such approaches can help improve the accuracy of ML models and optimize decision-making processes in this field.

## 15.7 Conclusion

This chapter of the book is proof that AI with the biopolymer electrospinning process creates a synergistic effect that adjusts parameters in real time for optimal conditions, improving overall efficiency, optimizing energy consumption, and recyclability of biopolymers and materials development, monitoring, and regulation, and promotes environmental friendliness. Electrospinning is a new and very efficient method for producing polymer NFs in various fields; integration with polymer algorithms has made the work of scientists and engineers easier by collecting and analyzing many data. Important parameters, such as diameter, mechanical, and thermal properties, are expected. This chapter of the book is a collection and comparison of past studies that emphasize how to use AI to predict electrospinning using prior knowledge about the polymer and solvent. Discovering new materials, processing large amounts of data and learning from it, and optimizing existing materials with rapid ML enable this in a wide range of industries where high-performance materials are in demand. It is widely used in medicine, drug delivery, food, environment, biological materials, and other cases. This has profound implications for industries from healthcare to the environmental sciences, where the demand for high-performance, sustainable materials is growing by the day.

## Acknowledgment

To the best of the Editors' knowledge and authors' claims, no generative AI tools were used for substantive writing of chapters. Any AI-assisted language editing, if applied, was limited to grammar or style suggestions and did not alter the scientific content.


## References


[1] Xue J, et al. Electrospinning and electrospun nanofibers: methods, materials, and applications. Chemical Reviews 2019;119(8):5298–415. Available from https://doi.org/10.1021/acs.chemrev.8b00593.

[2] Gupta V, Kothari V. Manufactured fibre technology. Springer Science & Business Media; 2012.

[3] Luo C, et al. Electrospinning versus fibre production methods: from specifics to technological convergence. Chemical Society Reviews 2012;41(13):4708–35. Available from https://doi.org/10.1039/C2CS35083A.

[4] Villarreal-Gómez LJ, et al. Electrospinning as a powerful technique for biomedical applications: a critically selected survey. Journal of Biomaterials Science, Polymer Edition 2016;27(2):157–76. Available from https://doi.org/10.1080/09205063.2015.1116885.

[5] Karatepe UY, Ozdemir T. Improving mechanical and antibacterial properties of PMMA via polyblend electrospinning with silk fibroin and polyethyleneimine towards dental applications. Bioactive Materials 2020;5(3):510–5. Available from https://doi.org/10.1016/j.bioactmat.2020.04.005.

[6] Hoque ME, et al. Electrospun matrices from natural polymers for skin regeneration. Nanostructured polymer composites for biomedical applications. Elsevier; 2019. p. 87–104. Available from https://doi.org/10.1016/B978-0-12-816771-7.00005-3.

[7] Santschi M, et al. Decellularized matrix as a building block in bioprinting and electrospinning. Current Opinion in Biomedical Engineering 2019;10:116–22. Available from https://doi.org/10.1016/j.cobme.2019.05.003.

[8] SalehHudin HS, et al. Multiple-jet electrospinning methods for nanofiber processing: a review. Materials and Manufacturing Processes 2018;33(5):479–98. Available from https://doi.org/10.1080/10426914.2017.1388523.

[9] Arumugam M, et al. Electrospinning cellulose acetate/silk fibroin/Au-Ag hybrid composite nanofiber for enhanced biocidal activity against MCF-7 breast cancer cell. Materials Science and Engineering: C 2021;123:112019. Available from https://doi.org/10.1016/j.msec.2021.112019.

[10] Gu J, et al. Dielectric thermally conductive boron nitride/polyimide composites with outstanding thermal stabilities via in-situ polymerization-electrospinning-hot press method. Composites Part A: Applied Science and Manufacturing 2017;94:209–16. Available from https://doi.org/10.1016/j.compositesa.2016.12.014.

[11] Su S, et al. Coaxial and emulsion electrospinning of extracted hyaluronic acid and keratin based nanofibers for wound healing applications. European Polymer Journal 2021;142:110158. Available from https://doi.org/10.1016/j.eurpolymj.2020.110158.

[12] Ma L, et al. Electrospinning of polycaprolacton/chitosan core-shell nanofibers by a stable emulsion system. Colloids and Surfaces A: Physicochemical and Engineering Aspects 2019;583:123956. Available from https://doi.org/10.1016/j.colsurfa.2019.123956.

[13] Naghibzadeh M, Adabi M. Evaluation of effective electrospinning parameters controlling gelatin nanofibers diameter via modelling artificial neural networks. Fibers and Polymers 2014;15:767–77. Available from https://doi.org/10.1007/s12221-014-0767-x.
[14] Brooks H, Tucker N. Electrospinning predictions using artificial neural networks. Polymer 2015;58:22–9. Available from https://doi.org/10.1016/j.polymer.2014.12.046.
[15] Wang Y, Yokota T, Someya T. Electrospun nanofiber-based soft electronics. NPG Asia Materials 2021;13(1):22. Available from https://doi.org/10.1038/s41427-020-00267-8.
[16] Pelipenko J, et al. The impact of relative humidity during electrospinning on the morphology and mechanical properties of nanofibers. International Journal of Pharmaceutics 2013;456(1):125–34. Available from https://doi.org/10.1016/j.ijpharm.2013.07.078.
[17] Baumgarten PK. Electrostatic spinning of acrylic microfibers. Journal of Colloid and Interface Science 1971;36(1):71–9. Available from https://doi.org/10.1016/0021-9797(71)90241-4.
[18] Sill TJ, Von Recum HA. Electrospinning: applications in drug delivery and tissue engineering. Biomaterials 2008;29(13):1989–2006. Available from https://doi.org/10.1016/j.biomaterials.2008.01.011.
[19] Megelski S, et al. Micro-and nanostructured surface morphology on electrospun polymer fibers. Macromolecules 2002;35(22):8456–66. Available from https://doi.org/10.1021/ma020444a.
[20] Zhenyu L, Wang C. Effects of working parameters on electrospinning. One-dimensional nanostructures. Springer; 2013. Available from https://doi.org/10.1007/978-3-642-36427-3_2.
[21] Zargham S, et al. The effect of flow rate on morphology and deposition area of electrospun nylon 6 nanofiber. Journal of Engineered Fibers and Fabrics 2012;7(4):42–9. Available from https://doi.org/10.1177/155892501200700414.
[22] Zhang C, et al. Study on morphology of electrospun poly (vinyl alcohol) mats. European Polymer Journal 2005;41(3):423–32. Available from https://doi.org/10.1016/j.eurpolymj.2004.10.027.
[23] Laudenslager MJ, Sigmund WM. Electrospinning. Encyclopedia of nanotechnology. 2012. p. 769–75.
[24] Haider A, Haider S, Kang I-K. A comprehensive review summarizing the effect of electrospinning parameters and potential applications of nanofibers in biomedical and biotechnology. Arabian Journal of Chemistry 2018;11(8):1165–88. Available from https://doi.org/10.1016/j.arabjc.2015.11.015.
[25] Pillay V, et al. A review of the effect of processing variables on the fabrication of electrospun nanofibers for drug delivery applications. Journal of Nanomaterials 2013;2013(1):789289. Available from https://doi.org/10.1155/2013/789289.
[26] Koski A, Yim K, Shivkumar S. Effect of molecular weight on fibrous PVA produced by electrospinning. Materials Letters 2004;58(3-4):493–7. Available from https://doi.org/10.1016/S0167-577X(03)00532-9.
[27] Sun B, et al. Advances in three-dimensional nanofibrous macrostructures via electrospinning. Progress in Polymer Science 2014;39(5):862–90. Available from https://doi.org/10.1016/j.progpolymsci.2013.06.002.
[28] Lannutti J, et al. Electrospinning for tissue engineering scaffolds. Materials Science and Engineering: C 2007;27(3):504–9. Available from https://doi.org/10.1016/j.msec.2006.05.019.
[29] Yang X, et al. Structural design toward functional materials by electrospinning: a review. e-Polymers 2020;20(1):682–712. Available from https://doi.org/10.1515/epoly-2020-0068.

[30] Teo WE, Ramakrishna S. A review on electrospinning design and nanofibre assemblies. Nanotechnology 2006;17(14):R89. Available from https://doi.org/10.1088/0957-4484/17/14/R01.
[31] Celebioglu A, Uyar T. Electrospinning of nanofibers from non-polymeric systems: polymer-free nanofibers from cyclodextrin derivatives. Nanoscale 2012;4(2):621–31. Available from https://doi.org/10.1039/C1NR11364J.
[32] Geltmeyer J, et al. The influence of tetraethoxysilane sol preparation on the electrospinning of silica nanofibers. Journal of Sol-Gel Science and Technology 2016;77:453–62. Available from https://doi.org/10.1007/s10971-015-3875-1.
[33] Li D, Xia Y. Fabrication of titania nanofibers by electrospinning. Nano Letters 2003;3(4):555–60. Available from https://doi.org/10.1021/nl034039o.
[34] Zhang C-L, Yu S-H. Nanoparticles meet electrospinning: recent advances and future prospects. Chemical Society Reviews 2014;43(13):4423–48. Available from https://doi.org/10.1039/C3CS60426H.
[35] Moses B, Gavish L, Vorwerck M. Data quality fundamentals. O'Reilly Media, Inc; 2022.
[36] O'Donnell F. A survey of data quality requirements that matter in ML development pipelines. Journal of Data and Information Quality 2023;15(2):11. Available from https://doi.org/10.1145/3592616.
[37] Kairuz T, Crump K, Brien AO. Tools for data collection and analysis. Pharmaceutical Journal 2007;278:371–2.
[38] Taherdoost H. Data collection methods and tools for research; a step-by-step guide to choose data collection technique for academic and business research projects. International Journal of Academic Research in Management (IJARM) 2021;10(1):10–38.
[39] Uddin MF, et al. Proposing enhanced feature engineering and a selection model for machine learning processes. Applied Sciences 2018;8(4):646. Available from https://doi.org/10.3390/app8040646.
[40] Krenn M, et al. On scientific understanding with artificial intelligence. Nature Reviews Physics 2022;4(12):761–9. Available from https://doi.org/10.1038/s42254-022-00518-3.
[41] Holmes J, Sacchi L, Bellazzi R. Artificial intelligence in medicine. Annals of the Royal College of Surgeons of England 2004;86:334–8. Available from https://doi.org/10.1007/978-3-319-19551-3.
[42] Xu Y, et al. Artificial intelligence: a powerful paradigm for scientific research. The Innovation 2021;2(4):100179.
[43] Sak J, Suchodolska M. Artificial intelligence in nutrients science research: a review. Nutrients 2021;13(2):322. Available from https://doi.org/10.3390/nu13020322.
[44] Choudhary K, et al. Recent advances and applications of deep learning methods in materials science. npj Computational Materials 2022;8(1):59. Available from https://doi.org/10.1038/s41524-022-00734-6.
[45] Schmidt J, et al. Recent advances and applications of machine learning in solid-state materials science. npj Computational Materials 2019;5(1):83. Available from https://doi.org/10.1038/s41524-019-0221-0.
[46] Dai H, et al. Structural reliability assessment by local approximation of limit state functions using adaptive Markov chain simulation and support vector regression. Computer-Aided Civil and Infrastructure Engineering 2012;27(9):676–86. Available from https://doi.org/10.1111/j.1467-8667.2012.00767.x.
[47] Singh SK, Rai N, Subramanian A. Machine learning-informed predictive design and analysis of electrohydrodynamic printing systems. Advanced Engineering Materials 2023;25(19):2300740. Available from https://doi.org/10.1002/adem.202300740.

[48] Hurtado JE. Filtered importance sampling with support vector margin: a powerful method for structural reliability analysis. Structural Safety 2007;29(1):2–15. Available from https://doi.org/10.1016/j.strusafe.2005.12.002.

[49] Subeshan B, Atayo A, Asmatulu E. Machine learning applications for electrospun nanofibers: a review. Journal of Materials Science 2024;59:14095–140. Available from https://doi.org/10.1007/s10853-024-09994-7.

[50] Wang J, et al. Efficient structural reliability analysis based on adaptive Bayesian support vector regression. Computer Methods in Applied Mechanics and Engineering 2021;387:114172. Available from https://doi.org/10.1016/j.cma.2021.114172.

[51] Ma X, et al. A comprehensive review of the development of land use regression approaches for modeling spatiotemporal variations of ambient air pollution: a perspective from 2011 to 2023. Environment International 2024;183:108430. Available from https://doi.org/10.1016/j.envint.2024.108430.

[52] Hoek G, et al. A review of land-use regression models to assess spatial variation of outdoor air pollution. Atmospheric Environment 2008;42(33):7561–78. Available from https://doi.org/10.1016/j.atmosenv.2008.05.057.

[53] Poguluri SK, Bae YH. Enhancing wave energy conversion efficiency through supervised regression machine learning models. Journal of Marine Science and Engineering 2024;12(1):153. Available from https://doi.org/10.3390/jmse12010153.

[54] Abdulla H, et al. Truncated Newton kernel ridge regression for prediction of porosity in additive manufactured SS316L. Applied Sciences 2022;12(9):4252. Available from https://doi.org/10.3390/app12094252.

[55] Maalouf M, Homouz D. Kernel ridge regression using truncated newton method. Knowledge-Based Systems 2014;71:339–44. Available from https://doi.org/10.1016/j.knosys.2014.08.012.

[56] Maalouf M, et al. Accurate prediction of gas compressibility factor using kernel ridge regression. Fourth International Conference on Advances in Computational Tools for Engineering Applications (ACTEA). IEEE; 2019. Available from https://doi.org/10.1109/ACTEA.2019.8851106.

[57] Kirasich K, Smith T, Sadler B. Random forest vs logistic regression: binary classification for heterogeneous datasets. SMU Data Science Review 2018;1(3):9.

[58] Muchlinski D, et al. Comparing random forest with logistic regression for predicting class-imbalanced civil war onset data. Political Analysis 2016;24(1):87–103. Available from https://doi.org/10.1017/pan.2018.40.

[59] González S, et al. A practical tutorial on bagging and boosting based ensembles for machine learning: algorithms, software tools, performance study, practical perspectives and opportunities. Information Fusion 2020;64:205–37. Available from https://doi.org/10.1016/j.inffus.2020.07.007.

[60] Chen S, et al. Enhancing rutting depth prediction in asphalt pavements: a synergistic approach of extreme gradient boosting and snake optimization. Construction and Building Materials 2024;421:135726. Available from https://doi.org/10.1016/j.conbuildmat.2024.135726.

[61] Sutton CD. Classification and regression trees, bagging, and boosting. Handbook of Statistics 2005;24:303–29. Available from https://doi.org/10.1016/S0169-7161(04)24011-1.

[62] Jadidi M, et al. An artificial neural network for the low-cost prediction of soot emissions. Energies 2020;13(18):4787. Available from https://doi.org/10.3390/en13184787.

[63] Xia J, et al. Using feed-forward perceptron artificial neural network (ANN) model to determine the rolling force, power and slip of the tandem cold rolling. ISA Transactions 2023;132:353–63. Available from https://doi.org/10.1016/j.isatra.2022.06.009.

[64] Dongare A, Kharde R, Kachare AD. Introduction to artificial neural network. International Journal of Engineering and Innovative Technology (IJEIT) 2012;2(1):189–94.
[65] Anderson D, McNeill G. *Artificial neural networks technology*. Technical Report 258. Kaman Sciences Corporation.1992. p.1–83.
[66] Ahmad A, Cotsovos DM, Lagaros ND. Framework for the development of artificial neural networks for predicting the load carrying capacity of RC members. SN Applied Sciences 2020;2:1–21. Available from https://doi.org/10.1007/s42452-020-2353-8.
[67] Haritha K, et al. A novel neural network model with distributed evolutionary approach for big data classification. Scientific Reports 2023;13(1):11052. Available from https://doi.org/10.1038/s41598-023-37540-z.
[68] Csáji BC. Approximation with artificial neural networks. [Master's thesis]. Budapest: Faculty of Sciences, Etvs Lornd University; 2001.
[69] Goel A, Goel AK, Kumar A. The role of artificial neural network and machine learning in utilizing spatial information. Spatial Information Research 2023;31(3):275–85. Available from https://doi.org/10.1007/s41324-022-00494-x.
[70] Bezerra MA, et al. Response surface methodology (RSM) as a tool for optimization in analytical chemistry. Talanta 2008;76(5):965–77. Available from https://doi.org/10.1016/j.talanta.2008.05.019.
[71] Lenth RV. Response-surface methods in R, using rsm. Journal of Statistical Software 2009;32(7):1–17. Available from https://doi.org/10.18637/jss.v032.i07.
[72] Mohamad Said KA, Amin MAM. Overview on the response surface methodology (RSM) in extraction processes. Journal of Applied Science and Process Engineering 2015;2(1):8–17. Available from https://doi.org/10.33736/jaspe.161.2015.
[73] Hu Y, et al. A five-year milestone: reflections on advances and limitations in GeoAI research. Annals of GIS 2024;30(1):1–14. Available from https://doi.org/10.1080/19475683.2024.2309866.
[74] Johnson NS, et al. Invited review: machine learning for materials developments in metals additive manufacturing. Additive Manufacturing 2020;36:101641. Available from https://doi.org/10.1016/j.addma.2020.101641.
[75] Hoxha J, et al. Prediction of transportation energy demand in Türkiye using stacking ensemble models: methodology and comparative analysis. Applied Energy 2023;350:121765. Available from https://doi.org/10.1016/j.apenergy.2023.121765.
[76] Hoc HT, et al. Comparing stacking ensemble and deep learning for software project effort estimation. IEEE Access 2023;11:60590–604. Available from https://doi.org/10.1109/ACCESS.2023.3286372.
[77] Robeson SM, Willmott CJ. Decomposition of the mean absolute error (MAE) into systematic and unsystematic components. PLoS One 2023;18(2):e0279774. Available from https://doi.org/10.1371/journal.pone.0279774.
[78] Willmott CJ. Some comments on the evaluation of model performance. Bulletin of the American Meteorological Society 1982;63(11):1309–13. Available from https://doi.org/10.1175/1520-0477(1982)063%3C1309:SCOTEO%3E2.0.CO;2.
[79] Khedri M, et al. Artificial intelligence deep exploration of influential parameters on physicochemical properties of curcumin-loaded electrospun nanofibers. Advanced NanoBiomed Research 2022;2(6):2100143. Available from https://doi.org/10.1002/anbr.202100143.
[80] Huang T, et al. Application and development of electrospun nanofiber scaffolds for bone tissue engineering. ACS Biomaterials Science and Engineering 2024;10(7):4114–44. Available from https://doi.org/10.1021/acsbiomaterials.4c00028.

[81] Bhattarai RS, et al. Biomedical applications of electrospun nanofibers: drug and nanoparticle delivery. Pharmaceutics 2019;11(1):5. Available from https://doi.org/10.3390/pharmaceutics11010005.
[82] Vimal Samsingh R, Sam Raj RB, Akash S. Python inspired AI modelling of process parameters of electro spinning system. Materials Today: Proceedings 2022;62:1197–204. Available from https://doi.org/10.1016/j.matpr.2022.04.384.
[83] Abdolrasol MG, et al. Artificial neural networks based optimization techniques: a review. Electronics 2021;10(21):2689. Available from https://doi.org/10.3390/electronics10212689.
[84] Javaid M, et al. Significance of machine learning in healthcare: features, pillars and applications. International Journal of Intelligent Networks 2022;3:58–73. Available from https://doi.org/10.1016/j.ijin.2022.05.002.
[85] Basheer IA, Hajmeer M. Artificial neural networks: fundamentals, computing, design, and application. Journal of Microbiological Methods 2000;43(1):3–31. Available from https://doi.org/10.1016/S0167-7012(00)00201-3.
[86] Pervez MN, et al. Electrospun nanofiber membrane diameter prediction using a combined response surface methodology and machine learning approach. Scientific Reports 2023;13(1):9679. Available from https://doi.org/10.1038/s41598-023-36431-7.
[87] Toscano JDet al. A machine learning approach to model the electrospinning process of biocompatible materials. ASME 2020 15th International Manufacturing Science and Engineering Conference. 2020. Available from https://doi.org/10.1115/MSEC2020-8362.
[88] Wu Z, et al. Investigation of a novel poly (lactic acid) porous material toughened by thermoplastic polyurethane. Journal of Materials Science 2022;57(9):5456–66. Available from https://doi.org/10.1007/s10853-022-06951-0.
[89] Jiang Y, et al. Preparation of hierarchical porous polyacrylonitrile-based fiber sponges and electrochemical performance study. Journal of Materials Science 2023;58(45):17326–39. Available from https://doi.org/10.1007/s10853-023-09124-9.
[90] Zhang C, et al. Surface porous carbon nanofibers based on coaxial electrospinning with improved mechanical strength and cycle stability for freestanding anode in Li-ion batteries. Journal of Materials Science 2021;56(36):19996–20007. Available from https://doi.org/10.1007/s10853-021-06532-7.
[91] Ziabari M, Mottaghitalab V, Haghi AK. A new approach for optimization of electrospun nanofiber formation process. Korean Journal of Chemical Engineering 2010;27(1):340–54. Available from https://doi.org/10.1007/s11814-009-0309-1.
[92] Ziabari M, et al. Measuring electrospun nanofibre diameter: a novel approach. Chinese Physics Letters 2008;25(8):3071. Available from https://doi.org/10.1088/0256-307X/25/8/090.
[93] Cramariuc B, et al. Fiber diameter in electrospinning process. Journal of Electrostatics 2013;71(3):189–98. Available from https://doi.org/10.1016/j.elstat.2012.12.018.
[94] Faridi-Majidi R, et al. Use of artificial neural networks to determine parameters controlling the nanofibers diameter in electrospinning of nylon-6,6. Journal of Applied Polymer Science 2012;124(2):1589–97. Available from https://doi.org/10.1002/app.35170.
[95] Golbabaei MH, et al. Machine learning-guided morphological property prediction of 2D electrospun scaffolds: the effect of polymer chemical composition and processing parameters. RSC Advances 2024;14(22):15178–99. Available from https://doi.org/10.1039/D4RA01257G.
[96] Yördem OS, Papila M, Menceloğlu YZ. Effects of electrospinning parameters on polyacrylonitrile nanofiber diameter: an investigation by response surface methodology. Materials and Design 2008;29(1):34–44. Available from https://doi.org/10.1016/j.matdes.2006.12.013.

[97] Ko J, et al. Effects of molecular weight and temperature on fiber diameter of poly (ε-caprolactone) melt electrospun fiber. Journal of the Korean Society of Manufacturing Technology Engineers 2015;24(2):160–5. Available from https://doi.org/10.7735/ksmte.2015.24.2.160.
[98] Khatti T, Naderi-Manesh H, Kalantar SM. Application of ANN and RSM techniques for modeling electrospinning process of polycaprolactone. Neural Computing and Applications 2019;31:239–48. Available from https://doi.org/10.1007/s00521-017-2996-6.
[99] Yan G, et al. A comparative study of machine learning models for respiration rate prediction in dairy cows: exploring algorithms, feature engineering, and model interpretation. Biosystems Engineering 2024;239:207–30. Available from https://doi.org/10.1016/j.biosystemseng.2024.01.010.
[100] Vatankhah E, et al. Artificial neural network for modeling the elastic modulus of electrospun polycaprolactone/gelatin scaffolds. Acta Biomaterialia 2014;10(2):709–21. Available from https://doi.org/10.1016/j.actbio.2013.09.015.
[101] Andrade del Olmo J, et al. Alternating current electrospinning of polycaprolactone/chitosan nanofibers for wound healing applications. Polymers 2024;16(10):1333. Available from https://doi.org/10.3390/polym16101333.
[102] Salehi M, et al. Intelligently optimized electrospun polyacrylonitrile/poly (vinylidene fluoride) nanofiber: using artificial neural networks. eXPRESS Polymer Letters 2020;14(11):1003–17. Available from https://doi.org/10.3144/expresspolymlett.2020.82.
[103] Yilmaz C, Ustun D, Akdagli A. Usage of artificial neural network for estimating of the electrospun nanofiber diameter. International Artificial Intelligence and Data Processing Symposium (IDAP). IEEE; 2017. Available from https://doi.org/10.1109/IDAP.2017.8090329.
[104] Pezeshki-Modaress M, Zandi M, Mirzadeh H. Fabrication of gelatin/chitosan nanofibrous scaffold: process optimization and empirical modeling. Polymer International 2015;64(4):571–80. Available from https://doi.org/10.1002/pi.4843.
[105] Wang F, et al. Machine learning predicts electrospray particle size. Materials and Design 2022;219:110735. Available from https://doi.org/10.1016/j.matdes.2022.110735.
[106] Ketabchi N, et al. Preparation and optimization of chitosan/polyethylene oxide nanofiber diameter using artificial neural networks. Neural Computing and Applications 2017;28:3131–43. Available from https://doi.org/10.1007/s00521-016-2212-0.
[107] Khatti T, Naderi-Manesh H, Kalantar SM. Prediction of diameter in blended nanofibers of polycaprolactone-gelatin using ANN and RSM. Fibers and Polymers 2017;18:2368–78. Available from https://doi.org/10.1007/s12221-017-7631-8.
[108] Sukpancharoen S, et al. Data-driven prediction of electrospun nanofiber diameter using machine learning: a comprehensive study and web-based tool development. Results in Engineering 2024;24:102826. Available from https://doi.org/10.1016/j.rineng.2024.102826.
[109] Khanlou HM, et al. Prediction and optimization of electrospinning parameters for polymethyl methacrylate nanofiber fabrication using response surface methodology and artificial neural networks. Neural Computing and Applications 2014;25:767–77. Available from https://doi.org/10.1007/s00521-014-1554-8.
[110] Chomachayi MD, Solouk A, Mirzadeh H. Electrospun silk-based nanofibrous scaffolds: fiber diameter and oxygen transfer. Progress in Biomaterials 2016;5(1):71–80. Available from https://doi.org/10.1007/s40204-016-0046-6.
[111] Mirzaei E, et al. Artificial neural networks modeling of electrospinning of polyethylene oxide from aqueous acid acetic solution. Journal of Applied Polymer Science 2012;125(3):1910–21. Available from https://doi.org/10.1002/app.36319.

[112] Amiri N, et al. Modeling and process optimization of electrospinning of chitosan-collagen nanofiber by response surface methodology. Materials Research Express 2018;5(4):045404. Available from https://doi.org/10.1088/2053-1591/aaba1d.
[113] López-Flores FJ, et al. Data-driven machine learning approach for modeling the production and predicting the characteristics of aligned electrospun nanofibers. Industrial and Engineering Chemistry Research 2024;63(22):9904–13. Available from https://doi.org/10.1021/acs.iecr.4c00075.
[114] Mohamadi M, Aliasghary M. Fabrication, integrated modeling, and quantitative estimation of fiber diameter in electrospun polyethersulfone as a function of material and process parameters. Journal of Polymer Research 2023;30(7):273. Available from https://doi.org/10.1007/s10965-023-03645-2.
[115] Hadipour-Goudarzi E, Hemmatinejad N, Shokrgozar MA. Fabrication and DOE optimization of electrospun chitosan/gelatin/PVA nanofibers for skin tissue engineering. Macromolecular Materials and Engineering 2023;308(5):2200562. Available from https://doi.org/10.1002/mame.202200562.
[116] Solis-Rios D, et al. A neural network approach to reducing the costs of parameter-setting in the production of polyethylene oxide nanofibers. Micromachines 2023;14(7):1410. Available from https://doi.org/10.3390/mi14071410.
[117] Moghadamifar S, Bahrami SH, Goodarzi V. Optimization and investigation of physical, chemical, and biological properties of nanofibers produced from (poly glycerol Sebacate-co-caprolactone)/gelatin/peptide and scaffold's cellular behavior. The Journal of the Textile Institute 2024:1–15. Available from https://doi.org/10.1080/00405000.2024.2364310.
[118] Nasouri K, et al. Modeling and optimization of electrospun PAN nanofiber diameter using response surface methodology and artificial neural networks. Journal of Applied Polymer Science 2012;126(1):127–35. Available from https://doi.org/10.1002/app.36726.
[119] Maurya AK, et al. Modeling the relationship between electrospinning process parameters and ferrofluid/polyvinyl alcohol magnetic nanofiber diameter by artificial neural networks. Journal of Electrostatics 2020;104:103425. Available from https://doi.org/10.1016/j.elstat.2020.103425.
[120] Sarkar K, et al. A neural network model for the numerical prediction of the diameter of electro-spun polyethylene oxide nanofibers. Journal of Materials Processing Technology 2009;209(7):3156–65. Available from https://doi.org/10.1016/j.jmatprotec.2008.07.032.
[121] Lakshmi Narayana P, et al. Correlating the 3D melt electrospun polycaprolactone fiber diameter and process parameters using neural networks. Journal of Applied Polymer Science 2021;138(37):50956. Available from https://doi.org/10.1002/app.50956.
[122] Sohrabi M, et al. Exercising hybrid model to design an optimized electrospun polyamide-6 nanofibrous mat for air filtration applications. The Journal of the Textile Institute 2023;114(11):1667–81. Available from https://doi.org/10.1080/00405000.2022.2145440.
[123] Rabbi A, et al. RSM and ANN approaches for modeling and optimizing of electrospun polyurethane nanofibers morphology. Fibers and Polymers 2012;13:1007–14. Available from https://doi.org/10.1007/s12221-012-1007-x.
[124] Ma M, et al. Analysis and prediction of electrospun nanofiber diameter based on artificial neural network. Polymers 2023;15(13):2813. Available from https://doi.org/10.3390/polym15132813.
[125] Samadian H, Zakariaee SS, Faridi-Majidi R. Evaluation of effective needleless electrospinning parameters controlling polyacrylonitrile nanofibers diameter via modeling artificial neural networks. The Journal of the Textile Institute 2019;110(4):477–86. Available from https://doi.org/10.1080/00405000.2018.1532781.

[126] Thirugnanasambandham K, Sivakumar V. Preparation of chitosan based nanofibers: optimization and modeling. International Journal of Chemical Reactor Engineering 2016;14(1):283–8. Available from https://doi.org/10.1515/ijcre-2015-0029.
[127] Sadan MK, et al. Quantitative estimation of poly(methyl methacrylate) nano-fiber membrane diameter by artificial neural networks. European Polymer Journal 2016;74:91–100. Available from https://doi.org/10.1016/j.eurpolymj.2015.11.014.
[128] Sharifi M, et al. Modeling and optimization of poly(lactic acid)/poly(Ɛ-caprolactone)/*Nigella sativa* extract nanofibers production for skin wounds healing by artificial neural network and response surface methodology models. International Journal of Biological Macromolecules 2023;253:127227. Available from https://doi.org/10.1016/j.ijbiomac.2023.127227.
[129] Karimi MA, et al. Using an artificial neural network for the evaluation of the parameters controlling PVA/chitosan electrospun nanofibers diameter. e-Polymers 2015;15(2):127–38. Available from https://doi.org/10.1515/epoly-2014-0198.
[130] Yao R, et al. Electrospun PCL/gelatin composite fibrous scaffolds: mechanical properties and cellular responses. Journal of Biomaterials science, Polymer Edition 2016;27(9):824–38. Available from https://doi.org/10.1080/09205063.2016.1160560.
[131] Islam MS, Karim MR. Fabrication and characterization of poly (vinyl alcohol)/alginate blend nanofibers by electrospinning method. Colloids and Surfaces A: Physicochemical and Engineering Aspects 2010;366(1-3):135–40. Available from https://doi.org/10.1016/j.colsurfa.2010.05.038.
[132] Reddy B, et al. Modeling tensile strength and suture retention of polycaprolactone electrospun nanofibrous scaffolds by artificial neural networks. Materials Today Communications 2021;26:102115. Available from https://doi.org/10.1016/j.mtcomm.2021.102115.
[133] Chen XK. Prediction of tensile properties of CNF/epoxy composites using artificial neural network. Advanced Materials Research 2014;898:111–4. Available from https://doi.org/10.4028/www.scientific.net/AMR.898.111.
[134] Moghadam BH, et al. Computational-based approach for predicting porosity of electrospun nanofiber mats using response surface methodology and artificial neural network methods. Journal of Macromolecular Science, Part B 2015;54(11):1404–25. Available from https://doi.org/10.1080/00222348.2015.1090654.
[135] Ayutsede J, et al. Regeneration of Bombyx mori silk by electrospinning. Part 3: characterization of electrospun nonwoven mat. Polymer 2005;46(5):1625–34. Available from https://doi.org/10.1016/j.polymer.2004.11.029.
[136] Elakkiya T, et al. Curcumin loaded electrospun Bombyx mori silk nanofibers for drug delivery. Polymer International 2014;63(1):100–5. Available from https://doi.org/10.1002/pi.4499.
[137] Ong HT, Dilley RJ. Novel non-angiogenic role for mesenchymal stem cell-derived vascular endothelial growth factor on keratinocytes during wound healing. Cytokine and Growth Factor Reviews 2018;44:69–79. Available from https://doi.org/10.1016/j.cytogfr.2018.11.002.
[138] Jiang L, et al. Fabrication of porous polymeric-based scaffold for dental tissue repair in fracture healing: RVE simulation and ANN optimization. Materials Science and Engineering: B 2023;297:116770. Available from https://doi.org/10.1016/j.mseb.2023.116770.
[139] Khalvandi A, et al. Data-driven supervised machine learning to predict the compressive response of porous PVA/Gelatin hydrogels and in-vitro assessments: employing design of experiments. International Journal of Biological Macromolecules 2023;253:126906. Available from https://doi.org/10.1016/j.ijbiomac.2023.126906.

[140] Lei L, Song S, Wang Y. Enhancing structural surface durability in building facades with hyaluronic acid nanofiber coatings. Iranian Journal of Chemistry and Chemical Engineering 2024;43:2203–19. Available from https://doi.org/10.30492/ijcce.2024.2016810.6337.

[141] Liang H, et al. Effect of royal gel addition to chitosan matrix for wound dress applications: fabrication, characterization and artificial neural network analysis. Environmental Technology and Innovation 2023;30:103077. Available from https://doi.org/10.1016/j.eti.2023.103077.

[142] Rafieyan S, Ansari E, Vasheghani-Farahani E. A practical machine learning approach for predicting the quality of 3D (bio)printed scaffolds. Biofabrication 2024;16(4):045014. Available from https://doi.org/10.1088/1758-5090/ad6374.

[143] Boublia A, et al. State-of-the-art review on recent advances in polymer engineering: modeling and optimization through response surface methodology approach. Polymer Bulletin 2023;80(6):5999–6031. Available from https://doi.org/10.1007/s00289-022-04398-6.

[144] Safdar R, Thanabalan M. Preparation of chitosan-tripolyphosphate formulated insulin microparticles, their characterization, ANN prediction, and release kinetics. Journal of Pharmaceutical Innovation 2023;18(3):1047–64. Available from https://doi.org/10.1007/s12247-023-09707-8.

[145] Liu M, et al. A review: electrospun nanofiber materials for lithium-sulfur batteries. Advanced Functional Materials 2019;29(49):1905467. Available from https://doi.org/10.1002/adfm.201905467.

# Index

*Note*: Page numbers followed by "*f*" and "*t*" refer to figures and tables, respectively.

C

**N**

## Q

# THE GOSPEL WAY OF LIFE



*by*

Sr. Rosena Marie

A BOOK FOR YOUNG PEOPLE

*Edited by*

JAYNE DILLON

FAITH PUBLISHING COMPANY

*Published by*

FAITH PUBLISHING COMPANY

P.O. BOX 237

Milford, Ohio 45150

Printed in the U.S.A.

Published by Faith Publishing Company
P.O. Box 237
Milford, OH 45150

For additional copies of this book, bookstores and book distributors should contact Faith Publishing Company.

Individuals may order from:
The Riehle Foundation
P.O. Box 7
Milford, OH 45150

Library of Congress No.: 94-061405

ISBN No.: 1-880033-17-8



Cover photo by: Joe Mixan. Taken in Medjugorje. For additional Medjugorje photographs call 402-731-4398.

# *Table of Contents*

## Part IV: The Divine Healing of Sin



## Part V: Re-Making Our Lives



## Part VI: The Gospel Way of Life

## *Preface*

In the doubt and confusion of our times, the faith of the average believer runs the risk of being severely shattered. This is especially true of young people, who seem to be losing that fundamental sense of security which the Faith is supposed to provide. A growing sense of uncertainty is beginning to be felt by those experiencing continuous upheaval, as the most fundamental doctrines of the Faith are being daily called into question. Many young people no longer seem to know what they must believe, or what is changeable or unchanging in the Church's practice or worship.

The danger of this growing sense of uncertainty is the fact that without a clear concept of the Faith and its fundamental doctrines, uninformed youth may quickly drift into skepticism or complete atheism. This book has been written to strengthen their wavering faith.

It is intended to be a book of basic instruction in the fundamental principles of Christian morality, the A-B-C's of the Ten Commandments, which Jesus made an integral part of His New Law. It discusses those basic moral values which can never change, regardless of the shifting emphasis on various points of doctrine in any given age, and shows that it is not the shirking of responsibility or the gratification of personal whims that provide true happiness, but rather a faithful and reasonable obedience to the Divine Law. This law was first engraved on human hearts by God Himself, and afterwards given to Moses on Mt. Sinai. Jesus reinforced the

validity of the law, by making it an integral part of His own New Law, when He said: *"I came not to destroy the Law but to bring it to perfection"* (*Matthew* 5:17).

The wisdom contained in the Ten Commandments is often overlooked by those who are impressed by more sophisticated sources of moral teaching. Yet when we think about it, all moral teaching ultimately comes from the basic source of the natural law, which is essentially contained in the Ten Commandments. To prove this point, we can reflect on Jesus' reply to the rich young man when asked what should be done to possess eternal life. Jesus simply replied, *"If you will enter into life, keep the Commandments"* (*Matthew* 19:17). He also said, *"If you continue in My word you shall know the Truth, and the Truth will make you free"* (*John* 8:31-32).

This book is designed specifically to answer the questions of young people today regarding the basic principles of Christian morality. It endeavors to show that the happiness which our hearts crave, is to be found in God alone. He draws us to Himself, by the fascination of His grace, to find in the depths of His own Divine Mystery the truth that can make us free.

The Commandments are a listing of that truth which governs moral life. If we follow their counsel, we will have found the pearl of great price which Jesus spoke of in the Gospel, that changeless moral truth which shapes our lives and can lead to that fullness of life for which we long.

This work is in complete agreement with Church teachings and can be of interest to any adult reader, though it is intended primarily for young people. If it helps to strengthen the faith of even a few of its readers, it will have fulfilled the purpose for which it was written.

# PART I

## The Question of Sin: Its Nature, Origin and Healing as Explained by the Church

*"Other foundation no man can lay,*
*but that which is laid:*
*which is Christ Jesus"*
(*1 Cor.* 3:11).

## *Chapter 1*

# The Mystery of the Wheat and the Weeds: A Consideration of the Problem of Sin

Today's society is preoccupied, as it has been in every previous age, with the mystery of evil in the world. It is a reflection within our moral lives of the mystery of light and darkness throughout the material universe. Jesus referred to this in the Parable of the Wheat and the Weeds, and the Church formally speaks of it as the mystery of sin.

In considering the problem of sin, society is divided into two opposing camps, namely those who deny and those who believe in the reality of sin. The disbelief often comes from denial of the existence of God, Who is the source of all good. Without this understanding, the basis of all moral law is swept away. Without moral guidelines, chaos follows.

The philosophy which denies the reality of sin could be summed up in the phrase "God is dead." According to this opinion there is no God and no afterlife. There is no absolute norm of conduct, no good or evil in principle, since there is no absolute authority to provide such a norm. There is no ultimate reward for good or punishment for evil since there is no Supreme Being to decree either one. Good and evil depend on circumstances.

Moral behaviors which come from this philosophy include the Epicurean ideal: "Let us eat and drink for tomorrow we die." This philosophy, however, makes us no better than animals, content to find happiness in physical gratification alone, and depriving us of the possibility of true self-fulfillment. Most tragic of all, it destroys the very happiness which we so desperately seek, and produces only bitter disillusionment and remorse.

Then we have the philosophy of "the end justifies the means," which says, in effect, that individuals may do as they please in order to get what they want. This can make us tyrants, without thought for the rights or needs of others, and would sanction lawlessness, vice, and every kind of evil under the cover of achieving a desired goal. These philosophies may be convenient for a time, but sooner or later, those who live by them will experience the tragedy of moral death.

Those, on the other hand, who admit to the reality of sin have a better grasp of reality, for whether we accept or reject it, sin is a fact. We may call it by another name, but it is sin just the same. Our very nature reveals the reality of sin, for we perceive a moral imbalance in our otherwise excellent natures, a sort of chronic moral illness. We have in ourselves at the same time, a love of good and a tendency towards evil. We are attracted by the beauty of virtue, and realize that we are made better by accepting its challenge, yet at the same time we are conscious of a moral imbalance which makes evil attractive, and often leads us to do things which are unworthy of our dignity as human beings. We are aware of this, yet frequently feel powerless to resist it, even when we know that it brings both moral and physical suffering. There have been many theories over the years regarding this behavior. Which is the right one? Where must we look to find the true explanation to this puzzling problem?

There is only one source which can supply a valid answer, and that source is the formal teaching of the Church which has been established by Christ, the guardian and interpreter of God's Revelation to man. This Divine Revelation is the

testimony which God gave to us for all times, concerning His own nature and His divine purpose in creation, particularly in regard to mankind itself.

The author of Hebrews summed up the history of Divine Revelation when he said: *"In times past, God spoke in partial and various ways to our ancestors through the prophets; in these last days, He spoke to us through a Son"* (*Hebrews* 1:1-2). With the coming of Christ, mankind received the most perfect knowledge of God and His purpose in creation, that it is possible to have in this life.

From this trustworthy source, in virtue of the command received from Christ, to teach all people (*Cf. Matthew* 28:19-20; *John* 20:21), the Church gives the history of our destiny, as received from God through Divine Revelation. When the Church speaks, it is the voice of truth we hear. The Church does not give its own private opinion in these matters, but rather truths received from God. When the Church speaks in this way it can truly say what Jesus said, *"My doctrine is not mine, but His that sent Me"* (*John* 7:16). In the exercise of its formal teaching office the Church is, as St. Paul observed, *"the pillar and foundation of truth"* (*1 Timothy* 3:15).

Let's consider what the Church has to say about the moral disorder within each of us, how it was caused, and how it can be most effectively treated.

# *Chapter 2*

# The Question of Sin

The Church explains the nature of sin as being like a wound dealt by mankind to its own nature, which wounded the integrity of humanity. The effects of this action are still felt today. In the beginning God created human beings with perfect integrity and gave them a number of gifts to prepare them for the destiny which God had willed for them. This destiny was the gift of eternal life in the face-to-face vision of God's glory in Heaven, in the enjoyment of His divine company and friendship. This blessed vision of God is called the Beatific Vision.

The gifts which God gave to human beings to prepare them for this destiny were of three kinds; natural, preternatural and supernatural. A natural gift is an endowment that goes with nature, as for example, the gift of sight; a preternatural gift is an expansion of a natural gift, such as, immortal life for the body; a supernatural gift is something beyond human nature. Sanctifying grace and the gift of the Beatific Vision are supernatural gifts.[1]

In the natural order God gave Adam physical integrity, which meant freedom from illness or suffering. The crowning gift of this physical integrity was the preternatural gift of immortality, that is, exemption from death, which is the

natural end of life in the universe. Humans were destined to live forever without ever having to die. Commenting upon this gift of immortality St. Augustine said, "God made man in such a way that as long as he did not sin he would remain immortal, so that he himself might be his own decider as to whether he should have life or death."[2]

In addition to these physical gifts, God bestowed on Adam the gift of a sharp intellect with vast and profound powers of comprehension. This was necessary to him as the first teacher of mankind. Another gift was to have natural law planted deep within his soul to perfect his intellect and will.[3] The natural law was like a compass designed to point him toward God. It enabled him to acknowledge a Supreme Being, to distinguish good from evil, to do good and avoid evil, and to honor benefactors. It is this law which causes us to yearn for God in our hearts and which constantly urges us to seek, love, and possess the Divine Being in whose likeness we are made.

The natural law is so deeply embedded in our nature that no sophistication of culture or system of education can ever erase it. It is found in every race and civilization throughout history and it explains why great natural virtue can often be found in the lives of those who do not admit the existence of God. It also explains why those who have led a life of sin will often, in their last moments, turn to God in sincere repentance. This final conversion is the soul's last supreme attempt to make an ultimate choice for the infinite good which it was created to possess. The natural law could best be explained perhaps as the mysterious attraction by which God, the Divine Magnetic Star, eternally draws us to Himself.

As the greatest of all gifts, God gave mankind, at creation, the gift of sanctifying grace.[4] This gift, because of its transcendent nature, is difficult to explain. It is the supernatural life-force of the soul, as the soul itself is the natural life-force of the body. The Church defines sanctifying grace as the communicated presence of God in the depths of a soul; a most mysterious, yet nonetheless very real presence. This presence permeates the soul as light through a prism, so that each

person becomes a living temple of God.[5]

This presence of God living within the soul, by its very nature, raises us to a supernatural plane. That is, it enables humans to live and operate on a plane which is above our nature as rational creatures. It entitles us to move in a spiritual realm which, according to our nature, we could never hope to enter. Jesus referred to this indwelling presence of God in the soul of mankind when He said: *"Whoever loves me will keep my word, and my Father will love him, and we will come to him and make our dwelling with him"* (*John* 14:23).

The first effect of sanctifying grace in the soul is that it gives us an active likeness to God. We have a two-fold likeness to God, first a natural likeness, in the possession of a rational nature (intellect and free will), secondly a supernatural likeness in the possession of sanctifying grace.[6] This gift of sanctifying grace elevates us to the dignity of adopted children of God and by this very fact we gain the right to inherit eternal life in the kingdom of Heaven, to enjoy the face-to-face vision of God's glory. For this reason sanctifying grace is often referred to as mankind's divine birthright.[7]

The effect of sanctifying grace upon the soul might be compared to the effect of fire upon iron, or light passing through a prism, or the change which took place in the body of Jesus at the Transfiguration. It fills the soul with beauty and plants within it the seeds of virtue. In the possession of grace we are made worthy to become the friend of God, worthy of His love and esteem.

Although mankind was given these wonderful gifts, we were not immediately granted the gift of seeing our Creator face-to-face. Adam was given a specially gifted mind, but he did not fully see or understand God because this ability is a supernatural gift, and even in the garden of Eden, mankind only possessed natural or preternatural gifts. This face-to-face vision of God was designed to be His final gift to mankind. The blessed in Heaven have been granted this gift, called Beatitude, of truly understanding God as He is.[8]

In our original state of integrity, humans were physically, morally and intellectually perfect. Human nature was like a

finely tuned instrument without the slightest imperfection to mar its integrity, but the preservation of this integrity rested with Adam himself,[9] for God would not force His gifts unwillingly upon His creature. Out of respect for mankind's rational nature God allowed His creation to make a free choice of accepting or rejecting Him as the Supreme Good, Friend and Benefactor. Sacred scripture says that God placed our first parents on trial to allow them to make such a free choice: this trial is represented in Scripture as a divine order not to eat the fruit of the Tree of Knowledge-of-Good-and-Evil. In essence, this forbids mankind to sin, since the knowledge of good and evil in its fullest sense understands all aspects of the whole moral law.[10] This decree also obliged Adam and Eve to respect God through friendship and holiness, and to acknowledge His sovereign dominion. Since the humans possessed free will their destiny was within their own power: they could obey the divine precept or reject it. As it happened the humans disobeyed it, having been tempted by the serpent who suggested doing evil under the guise of good.

Interpreting the scriptural account of the Fall, the Church says that the serpent signified the Devil, the leader of the fallen angels who is called elsewhere in scripture, Lucifer and Satan (*Apocalypse* 12). He was envious of mankind, seeing them appointed to that destiny which he himself had forfeited by his rebellion against God. It was of the Devil that Jesus said: *"He was a murderer from the beginning and he stood not in the truth because the truth is not in him. When he speaks a lie he speaks of his own for he is a liar and the father thereof"* (*John* 8:44).

Satan's plan caused our first parents to question God's motive for prohibiting them from eating the fruit of this tree. *"You certainly will not die!"* he said to them, *"No. God knows well that the moment you eat of it your eyes will be opened and you will be like gods who know what is good and what is bad"* (*Genesis* 3:4-5). This lie, presented under the disguise of good, was acceptable to them. It was the spark that ignited their ambition to be like God, the same ambition

which first led the tempter himself to rebel against God. It seemed a greater good to be equal to God, rather than to remain a mere creature.

Of their own free choice they disobeyed God's command because of ambition and this ill-advised decision was the first sin. It is called by the Church, original sin from the word origin which means source or beginning. In essence it was a sin of pride and disobedience, as St. Paul said: *"By the disobedience of one man, many were made sinners"* (*Romans* 5:19).

Describing the first sin, it is said: *"The woman saw that the tree was good for food, pleasing to the eyes, and desirable for gaining wisdom. So she took some of its fruit and ate it; and she also gave some to her husband, who was with her, and he ate it. Then the eyes of both were opened..."* (*Genesis* 3:6-7). Once they gave in to the deceitful suggestion of the tempter, they found only disillusionment and death. This is the psychology of all sin.

Temptation to do evil, whether it comes from our own fallen nature or from the suggestion of the Devil, always presents itself under the disguise of good. Like the forbidden fruit, it appears *"good for food, pleasing to the eyes, and desirable for gaining wisdom"* (*Genesis* 3:6). But when we give in, our eyes are opened and we find only the bitterness of death, that is, we experience the remorse of sin.

The essential nature of sin, both the original sin and all subsequent sin, was explained by the Second Vatican Council when it said: "Although he was made by God in a state of holiness, from the very dawn of history man abused his liberty, at the urging of personified Evil. Man set himself against God and sought to find fulfillment apart from God. Although he knew God he did not glorify him as God but his senseless mind was darkened and he served the creature rather than the Creator" (*Cf. Romans* 1:21-25).

As God had warned (*Genesis* 2:17), the Divine judgment quickly followed mankind's sin. Because the humans refused to subject their intellects and wills to God, the divinely bestowed hierarchy of gifts were destroyed and so Adam, Eve, and in them, the whole human race, fell from grace.

# *Chapter 3*

# The Punishment of Sin

The injury to human nature which resulted from the Fall occurred essentially in the supernatural order, but it had repercussions for the entire nature.[1] We might say that human nature was covered by the dark shadow of sin as a sunlit landscape is covered by dark storm clouds. Although mankind suffered because of the Fall, our first parents were as much human beings after sinning as they were before.

The most important and most immediate loss was the destruction of supernatural life within the soul, the loss of sanctifying grace.[2] This meant that the communicated presence of God, which was the supernatural principle of life in the soul was withdrawn and by that very fact mankind broke friendship with God.[3] Because of this withdrawal all preternatural gifts vanished and the harmony of human nature was disrupted. On every level of human nature the effects of sin were felt.[4]

Thus, on the bodily level, human beings lost the perfection of their physical nature and became subject to suffering and death. On the intellectual level, human understanding was darkened and the will rendered weak.[5] From then on it required mental labor to acquire knowledge which could have been easily understood before the Fall. In moral nature they experienced a strong inclination to evil. As a result of these

many defects, mankind quickly discovered that even though by nature they were prepared to be "lords of the universe," they were now no longer even masters of themselves. They were like a bird with a broken wing that by its nature wants to fly upward but by its infirmity is constantly drawn downward.

Drawn toward God, the Supreme Good, by the very nature of our being, people now also experienced an attraction toward sin. We are now constantly being torn in two directions, toward God and toward sin, as St. Paul expressed it: *"For I do not do the good I want, but I do the evil I do not want. Now if [I] do what I do not want, it is no longer I who do it, but sin that dwells in me. So, then, I discover the principle that when I want to do right, evil is at hand. For I take delight in the law of God, my inner self, but I see in my members another principle at war with the law of my mind, taking me captive to the law of sin that dwells in my members. Miserable one that I am! Who will deliver me from this mortal body?"* (*Romans* 7:19-24).

These effects of sin were destined to be transmitted to the entire human race since Adam was the father of all mankind, as St. Paul also said: *"By one man sin entered the world and by sin, death, and so death passed upon all men, in whom all have sinned"* (*Romans* 5:12). Indeed, the effects of this moral imbalance would be felt in every aspect of human history throughout time.

On a spiritual plane, in the loss of sanctifying grace, mankind was deprived of the divine birthright which entitled them to inherit eternal life in the glory of the Beatific Vision. This life of blessedness implies much more than simply beholding the glory of God from without. It implies, rather, the total immersion of one's being in the infinite ocean of God's mystery so that in contemplating the mystery of God's Being and Life, our intellect reaches the fullness of its capacity for knowing and our will reaches the fullness of its capacity for loving, yet without exhausting the infinite ocean of mystery which it explores. And since only the infinite and incompre-

hensible ocean of God's Being and Nature can satisfy humans as rational creatures, we can reach the total fulfillment of our being only in the enjoyment of the Beatific Vision, for in possessing God we will have come into the possession of the Infinite Good for whom we were made. The magnitude of this loss of the gift of sanctifying grace, therefore, was beyond understanding, for we could never hope to recover our privileges by any effort of our own.

With the loss of sanctifying grace, we also lost the gift of immortality. This gift was like a precious fruit which we held in our hands but had not yet tasted, for it was to follow the completion of earthly life, when, without having to experience death, we would begin to enjoy eternal life. But before we had the opportunity to experience this gift, we fell from grace and were deprived of it.

The gift of immortality was symbolized by the "Tree of Life" in Eden. *"The moment you eat from it you are surely doomed to die"* (*Genesis* 2:17).[6] The withdrawal of the gift of immortality was signified by the Divine judgment upon Adam: *"See! The man has become like one of us, knowing what is good and what is bad! Therefore, he must not be allowed to put out his hand to take fruit from the tree of life also, and thus eat of it and live forever"* (*Genesis* 3:22). The scriptural account of the Fall concludes with a description of the expulsion of our first parents from Eden. It says: *"The Lord God therefore banished him from the garden of Eden, to till the ground from which he had been taken. When He expelled the man, He settled him east of the garden of Eden; and He stationed the cherubim and the fiery revolving sword, to guard the way to the Tree of Life"* (*Genesis* 3:23-24).

## *Chapter 4*

# God's Promise of a Redeemer

Without our original inheritance, mankind stood in an impoverished state before God after the fall from grace. In this fallen state, God could have abandoned us and condemned us to live forever in the alienation and misery which we had brought upon ourselves. But instead, God willed to redeem us from the consequences of sin because of His faithful love. As St. Paul says, *"His gifts are without repentance"* (*Romans* 11:29). So, even as God pronounced a sentence of just punishment upon mankind, and the serpent who had deceived us, He promised us a Saviour, one through whom we would be reconciled to God and recover our lost inheritance.

This formal "Promise of Salvation" was contained in the sentence of Divine judgment upon the serpent: *"I will put enmities between you and the woman and your offspring and her offspring: He shall crush your head and you shall lie in wait for his heel"* (*Genesis* 3:15). Interpreting this passage, the Church says that the "woman" referred to prophetically signified Mary, mother of the promised Redeemer. Through her Son, the Saviour, the serpent's head would be crushed and mankind would be redeemed.

In promising a Saviour to mankind, God did not reveal the Messiah's identity or the manner in which redemption would

be accomplished. He merely signified that the Saviour would be a member of the human race, a true Son of Man, and that there would always be enmity between Him and Satan and their respective followers. It was only when He came that we discovered that He was the well-beloved and only begotten Son of the Eternal Father, who was born of the Virgin Mary, so that in His human nature He might redeem mankind by His death on the Cross.

The Church says that this original "Promise of Salvation" was fulfilled in Christ. It was the first gospel or "good news" given to fallen mankind. In this connection it is interesting to note that at His birth the angel said to the shepherds: *"Behold, I bring you good tidings of great joy which shall be to all the people. For this day is born to you a Saviour who is Christ the Lord, in the city of David"* (*Luke* 2:10-11). St. John best expressed the mystery of Christ's coming by saying: *"The Word was made flesh and dwelt among us and we saw His glory, the glory that was His as the only-begotten of the Father, full of grace and truth"* (*John* 1:14).

Before Jesus' birth the angel explained to St. Joseph the reason for Christ's coming: *"He shall save His people from their sins"* (*Matthew* 1:21). Christ's mission was to restore to mankind their original destiny and to reopen the gates of Heaven which had been closed to mankind since the Fall. Jesus Himself revealed this to Nicodemus at the beginning of His public life, when He said: *"No one has gone up to heaven except the one who has come down from heaven, the Son of Man. And just as Moses lifted up the serpent in the desert, so must the Son of Man be lifted up, so that everyone who believes in Him may have eternal life. For God so loved the world that He gave His only Son, so that everyone who believes in Him might not perish but might have eternal life. For God did not send His Son into the world to condemn the world, but that the world might be saved through Him"* (*John* 3:13-17). His salvation was to be for all people throughout time. As all people shared in Adam's gift, so, likewise, all were to partake in the grace of redemption.

It was part of Jesus' mission of redemption to provide a way of life which would enable us to serve God, live in His friendship and love, and lead us by a sure course to eternal life. This way was also intended to give us, even during our earthly lives, the fullness of life we longed for. *"I have come that they may have life and may have it more abundantly,"* He said (*John* 10:10). For His way, faithfully followed, would help us reach the complete self-fulfillment which God intended for us in the natural order.

This way of life is what the Church calls the "New Law" and is found throughout the gospels, particularly in the Sermon On the Mount. It is essentially the Mosaic Law brought to perfection by Christ as He Himself said: *"I came not to destroy the Law but to bring it to perfection"* (*Matthew* 5:17). The Ten Commandments, therefore, are an integral part of the New Law of Christ, and like the Mosaic Law, the New Law was summed up by Jesus in the two Great Commandments: *"You shall love the Lord, your God, with all your heart, with all your soul, and with all your mind. This is the greatest and the first commandment. The second is like it: You shall love your neighbor as yourself. The whole law and the prophets depend on these two commandments"* (*Matthew* 22:37-40).

On the night before His death, at the Last Supper, He summed up the New Law for His apostles when He said: *'A new commandment I give you: that you love one another as I have loved you. By this shall all men know that you are my disciples, if you have love one for another"* (*John* 13:34-35).

The previous chapters provided a brief look at the Church's teaching on the origin of sin and its healing as prescribed by God. It is worthwhile to look more deeply into the teaching of Christ as explained by the Church, in order to find that fullness of life and healing which Jesus alone can give.

# PART II

## On the Love and Service of God

*"You shall love the Lord your God*
*with your whole heart and with your whole soul,*
*and with your whole mind.*
*This is the greatest and the First Commandment"*
(*Matthew* 22:37-38).

## *Chapter 5*

# Christ the Light of the World

The mission of Christ as Savior and Teacher of mankind could best be summed up in His own words to the Apostle John, *"Behold, I make all things new"* (*Revelations* 21:5). As Savior, He was to remove the curse of the Fall, restore all that we had lost by sin, and to give us a new law by which to live, that we might have "the fullness of life," even during this earthly pilgrimage. His coming changed human history, for He brought to mankind the light of Truth from the Source of Truth Itself, as St. John said: *"He was the true light which enlightens every man that comes into this world"* (*John* 1:9).

When Jesus came, He laid His credentials before the world, stating clearly who He was, and why He had come. He had much to say about His mission as Savior and Teacher of men, which will help us to better understand the true nature and depth of His Gospel message.

Concerning the most important aspect of His mission, that of Savior, He said: *"I came from God and am here; I did not come on my own, but He sent me* (*John* 8:42). *For God so loved the world that He gave His only Son, so that everyone who believes in Him might not perish but might have eternal life. For God did not send His Son into the world to condemn the world, but that the world might be saved through Him* (*John* 3:16-17). *And just as Moses lifted up the*

*serpent in the desert, so must the Son of Man be lifted up, so that everyone who believes in Him may have eternal life''* (*John* 3:14-15).

*''I am the Good Shepherd. The Good Shepherd gives His life for His sheep. This is why the Father loves me, because I lay down my life in order to take it up again. No one takes it from me, but I lay it down on my own. I have power to lay it down and power to take it up again. This command I have received from my Father* (*John* 10:11, 17-18). *I do just as the Father has commanded me''* (*John* 14:31).

Jesus had been foretold by Moses and the prophets as the teacher of mankind. Before his death, Moses had spoken to the children of Israel of their obligation to listen to Christ's teaching. Moses said: *''A prophet like me will the Lord, your God raise up from among your own kinsmen; to him you shall listen. . .And the Lord said to me, '. . .[I] will put My words into his mouth; he shall tell them all that I command him. If any man will not listen to My words which he speaks in My name, I Myself will make him answer for it' ''* (*Deuteronomy* 18:15, 17-19). Joel, also, had foretold Christ's mission as teacher when he said, *''And do you, O children of Zion, exult and rejoice in the Lord, your God! He has given you the teacher of justice''* (*Joel* 2:23).

Christ identified Himself as this teacher sent by God. He said: *''For this I was born and for this I came into the world, to testify to the truth. Everyone who belongs to the truth listens to my voice* (*John* 18:37). *I am the way, and the truth, and the life* (*John* 14:16). *I am the light of the world. Whoever follows me will not walk in darkness, but will have the light of life* (*John* 8:12). *My teaching is not my own but is from the one who sent me* (*John* 7:16). *I came so that they might have life and have it more abundantly''* (*John* 10:10).

Having revealed the nature of His Redemptive mission, Jesus warned of the serious obligation of every individual to receive Him; no one could remain neutral in regard to Him. He said: *''Whoever is not with me is against me, and whoever does not gather with me scatters''* (*Matthew* 12:30). He spoke to both friends and enemies of the importance of this personal

decision in His regard, and of the reward or punishment which it would bring. He said to His enemies who challenged or denied His claims:

*"You search the scriptures, because you think you have eternal life through them; even they testify on my behalf. But you do not want to come to me to have life. I do not accept human praise; moreover, I know that you do not have the love of God in you. I came in the name of my Father, but you do not accept me; yet if another comes in his own name, you will accept him. How can you believe, when you accept praise from one another and do not seek the praise that comes from the only God? Do not think that I will accuse you before the Father: the one who will accuse you is Moses, in whom you have placed your hope. For if you had believed Moses, you would have believed me, because he wrote about me. But if you do not believe his writings, how will you believe my words?"* (*John* 5:39-47).

Having presented His credentials, He set forth the basic principles of His gospel of salvation against the various false philosophies of the world. This gospel way of life is specifically designed by God to bring to mankind that fullness of life which we so greatly desire. The principles of His way are to be found throughout the Gospels, particularly in the Sermon on the Mount (*Matthew* 5-7; *Luke* 6). Here is a brief cross section of its most important aspects.

*"No one can serve two masters. He will either hate one and love the other, or be devoted to one and despise the other. You cannot serve God and mammon [wealth]* (*Matthew* 6:24). *Not everyone who says to me, 'Lord, Lord,' will enter the kingdom of heaven, but only the one who does the will of my Father in heaven"* (*Matthew* 7:21).

*"Enter through the narrow gate; for the gate is wide and the road broad that leads to destruction, and those who enter through it are many. How narrow the gate and constricted the road that leads to life. And those who find it are few* (*Matthew* 7:13-14). *Whoever wishes to come after me must deny himself, take up his cross, and follow me. For whoever wishes to save his life will lose it, but whoever loses his life*

*for my sake will find it. What profit would there be for one to gain the whole world and forfeit his life? Or what can one give in exchange for his life?''* (*Matthew* 16:24-26).

*''I am the resurrection and the life; whoever believes in me, even if he dies, will live, and everyone who lives and believes in me will never die''* (*John* 11:25-26).

Then, having set forth the basic principles of His gospel, He goes on to speak of the reward. *''If you remain in my word, you will truly be my disciples, and you will know the truth, and the truth will set you free* (*John* 8:31-32). *I solemnly assure you: if any man keep My word, he will never see death''* (*John* 8:51).

The Second Vatican Council had much to say about this freedom promised by Christ. It said for example: "To be free means achieving the fruits of truth, acting in truth. To be free also means knowing how to give in, to submit oneself to truth, and not to submit truth to oneself, to one's own designs, to one's own interests, to one's own circumstances. To be free according to the program of Christ and His kingdom, does not mean pleasure, but toil, the toil of freedom. At the cost of this toil man does not 'scatter' but together with Christ 'stores up.' At the cost of this toil, man also acquires in himself that unity which is characteristic of the Kingdom of God.[1] This is the true fulfillment, 'the fullness of life' " (*Cf. John* 10:10).

The rewards which would follow the faithful observance of His gospel way of life were to be received in eternity. Jesus spoke of these rewards in very clear and absolute terms. In the parables and elsewhere in the Gospels, He showed that eternal life was a homecoming to everlasting happiness with God, a reward for fidelity during periods of earthly trial. We could sum up this aspect of His teaching with these observations made to His disciples at the Last Supper. He said:

*''I came from the Father and have come into the world. Now I am leaving the world and going back to the Father* (*John* 16:28). *In my Father's house there are many mansions, if not I would have told you, because I go to prepare a place for you. And if I go and prepare a place for you, I will come*

*again and take you to myself, so that where I am, you also may be''* (*John* 14:2-3). What joys await us in the Father's house! St. Paul was granted a vision which led him to say: *''Eye has not seen, nor ear heard: neither has it entered into the heart of Man, what things God has prepared for those that love Him''* (*1 Corinthians* 2:29).

His final word of assurance to His disciples was that He could give all that He promised in reward: *''I am Alpha and Omega, the First and the Last, the Beginning and the End''* (*Revelations* 22:13).

We look at the gospel of Christ in contrast to the philosophies of the world, and see how vastly they differ. What earthly philosophy can compare with His teaching? What earthly philosopher could dare to make the claims that He made, demand the allegiance that He asked, or promise the rewards that He promised? Yet He alone could say in perfect truth: *''I am the Truth''* (*John* 14:6). We compare His gospel with the philosophies of men and see their true value. One promises life, but in reality gives death; the other, the gospel of Christ, counsels death to self, that we may find true life; and somehow, when we ponder them both, the gospel rings true. It instructs us to cultivate a habit of balanced and prudent resistance rather than self-indulgence.

Jesus knew, however, that the demands of His gospel teaching might prove difficult to human nature in its fallen state. So He gave His disciples a new law which would be a sure guide for their way, and enable them to discern the true from the false, the right from the wrong. We will consider this new law in the following chapters.

## *Chapter 6*

# A Consideration of Sin

The Church defines sin as any willful thought, word or deed contrary to the Law of God.[1] We know whether or not an act is sinful by finding out whether it violates any of God's Commandments. Some sins are easily recognizable, others have to be learned from the Church.

When considering sin, questions might naturally arise concerning the use of our free will. Since God has given us this gift, why can't we use it freely, to do either right or wrong as we please? The answer is simply that the gift of free will does not mean that we may do as we please; although, in a sense, it gives us the power or capability to do as we please. In considering the matter of free will, we must be careful to remember that although we have the power to do evil, we do not have the "right" to do evil.[3] To claim such a right would be the abuse of free will.[4] To claim that we may do as we please, is equivalent to removing God's authority over us.

We may not do as we please because human reason, our own good, and the good of others forbid it. Were we to transgress the Law of God at will, we would bring suffering and confusion into our own lives and the lives of others. We do not possess all the rights; others have rights also, and these hold us responsible for our actions. Both conscience and the

Law of God tell us that we may not do as we please, and when we act contrary to these two authoritative councilors, we are guilty of sin.[5]

The Church says that we commit sin in four different ways; namely, by thought, word, deed and omission.[6]

1). By thought—by thinking about or desiring what is evil.
2). By word—by using improper or evil speech, such as cursing or lying.
3). By deed—any sinful action which transgresses the Law of God, such as stealing, murder, etc.
4). By omission—by neglecting to do our duty.

We can also cause someone else to sin in various ways. These will be discussed in the chapter dealing with the Fifth Commandment, but I will mention them here also for convenience sake. They are: by counsel, by command, by consent, by provocation, by praise, by concealment, by being partner to another's sin, by silence, by defending the evil done.[7]

All sin is divided into two basic categories, namely, Mortal sin and Venial sin.[8]

Mortal sin is defined as a serious offense against God's Law.[9] The word "mortal" means "death-bringing." It is called mortal sin because it brings death to the soul by depriving it of the supernatural life of sanctifying grace. If unrepented, it brings everlasting death and damnation to the soul.[10] Everlasting death means exclusion from Heaven; damnation means condemnation to Hell.[11]

Three things are necessary for a sin to be mortal sin.[12] The matter must be serious, you must have full knowledge at the time of committing the sin that it was a mortal sin, and it must be done deliberately, with full consent of the will. This means that you are willing to desire, think about, or do what you know to be seriously sinful.[13] If any one of these three conditions is missing, the sin is not mortal. For example, if the matter was not serious, the sin is not mortal. Or if you were to commit a sinful action but did not know it was sinful, you would not be guilty of mortal sin. If you were to commit a sinful action, having no chance of freedom to consent or

to refuse consent, for example, the victim of violent assault, you would not be guilty of sin.[14] The most serious mortal sins are sins against the Holy Spirit. These are the following: despair and presumption, opposition to the truth, obstinacy in sin, envy of another's spiritual good, final impenitence.[15]

"Despair" is a loss of hope in God's mercy.[16] To refuse to trust in God's mercy is like denying the truth of His word. It is like refusing to believe that He is infinitely good, kind, and compassionate, or that He is able by His infinite power to forgive any offense of sin. We know from scripture that God in His infinite goodness will never refuse to pardon any sin no matter how enormous, if one is truly sorry. The parables of the Lost Sheep and of the Prodigal Son clearly reveal this truth, while the story of Mary Magdalen or the Good Thief on the Cross prove it in actual fact. These living parables teach us that no one is ever condemned to Hell except of his own free choice; hence, to doubt the goodness and mercy of God is a most grevious sin. Cain and Judas are examples of despair.

"Presumption" is foolishly expecting Salvation, without properly using the means necessary to obtain it.[17] Presumption means to take a thing for granted. If, for example, you were to believe that God would not allow you to be lost, or that you were free to continue to live a life of sin because God would undoubtedly give you time to repent at the end, you would be guilty of presumption. It would also be presumption to think that your faith or virtue was so strong, that you could expose yourself to occasions of sin without danger, for Scripture says: *"He who loves the danger shall perish therein."*

Other serious sins which are usually referred to are: willful murder, sodomy, oppression of the poor, the widow and the orphan, and defrauding a laborer of his wages.[18]

When mortal sin is committed over a long period of time, so as to become a habit, it is called a vice.

Venial sin, on the other hand, is defined as a light offense against the Law of God. It is an offense committed without sufficient reflection or full consent of the will.[19] Venial means

pardonable. Venial sins lessen our friendship with God, but do not deprive us of God's friendship. Multiple venial sins do not add up to a mortal sin, nor do they take away sanctifying grace from the soul. But venial sin is not something to be treated lightly, for its danger lies in the fact that it makes our love for God grow lukewarm, thus opening the door to greater temptations which may ultimately lead to mortal sin.

In fact, a sin which ordinarily would be venial, might become mortal if it is committed in defiance of God or religion, or if it is followed by serious consequences.[20] Comparing mortal and venial sin, we could say that mortal sin is the death of the soul, while venial sin continuously and carelessly committed without any sense of repentance, is like a sickness which could ultimately lead to death.

## *Chapter 7*

# What Causes Sin?

Sin is always caused by giving in to temptation. Temptations are evil thoughts or inspirations, and they can come from any of these sources—the world, the flesh, or the Devil. Temptations in themselves are not sinful; in fact God allows everyone to be tempted, but never beyond one's strength. Handling temptation well can be very beneficial to our souls, to our whole personalities, and may even become a source of great merit. It can make us conscious of our own weaknesses and of the need for dependence on God's grace. Temptations teach us to be constantly vigilant and active in repelling their first assaults. They also make us more compassionate and understanding of the faults of others. It is only when we knowingly and willingly yield to temptation that it becomes a sin.

Let's look at the basic sources of temptation. First there is the world, which from the very dawn of history has been a source of temptation to mankind. By "the world" the Church usually means the desire for wealth, and a fascination with success, fame, and power. These things are alluring, but they can never satisfy our deepest yearnings.

The second source of temptation is "the flesh," by which the Church means the evil inclinations of our fallen nature. These are our passions, when they urge us to evil.[1]

At the risk of over simplification, we could define the passions as powers of reaction to external stimuli, which are inherent to our natures and assist us in our quest for happiness. They regulate our activities in our pursuit of good, enabling us basically to choose good and avoid evil. There are eleven passions, or emotions, and they are divided into two basic categories, the first having six passions, the second group, five.[2] Those in the first category are called "Concupiscible" or ordinary passions, from the Latin verb "concupiscere," which means to desire. They are concerned with our pursuit of good and avoidance of evil, in a simple sense.

The five passions in the second category are called "Irascible passions," from the Latin word "ira," meaning anger. These are also concerned with the pursuit of good, but a good which is difficult to attain, or with the shunning of evil which is difficult to avoid. They are emergency passions, called into service when we must take action to achieve a difficult good or avoid a difficult evil.[3]

Coming back now to the first group, the consupiscible or ordinary passions: love, desire, joy, hatred, aversion, and sorrow. The first three have to do with simple good, the last three with simple evil.

We could define "love" as an inclination to a good, whether present or absent. "Desire" is an inclination to an absent good. "Joy" is contentment in the possession of a good.

"Hatred" is repulsion for an evil, whether present or absent. "Aversion" is retreat from a present evil. "Sorrow" is restless possession of an unavoidable evil.

The second group, the irascible or emergency passions, are: hope, despair, courage, fear, and anger. The first three are concerned with a difficult good, the last two are concerned with a difficult evil.

We could define "hope" as a confident impulse for overcoming obstacles. "Despair" is surrender before insurmountable obstacles. "Courage" is daring in the face of evil.

"Fear" is receding in the face of evil. "Anger" is battling with present evil.[4]

Without passions we would not be human; with them, when they are exercised reasonably, human life and good are both increased and perfected. Unfortunately, we do not always control or use our passions in the right way. When we allow them to urge us to do evil instead of good, we are guilty of sin.

The many sins we are capable of committing can be classified under seven major headings which are called the "Seven Capital" sins, or the "Seven Deadly" sins. They are called "Capital" from the Latin word "caput" which means "head," because they are the cause or source of many other sins. In fact, all other sins could be listed as subheadings of these seven major categories. These capital sins are really seven evil inclinations of the heart,[5] resulting from mankind's fallen nature. They are an exaggeration of something good and useful, but are harmless as long as they are kept under control. They are named as follows: pride, covetousness, lust (impurity), anger, gluttony, envy, and sloth.[6]

"Pride" is a sinful exaggeration of self respect. It is the cause of presumption, ambition, vainglory, boasting, insolence, ostentation, hypocrisy, etc. It is a false idea of one's own goodness or excellence.

"Covetousness" is a sinful exaggeration of providing for the future, and is seen in the desire to gain and hoard up wealth simply for its own sake. Covetousness causes hardness of heart, injustice, faithlessness, fraud, and deceit.

"Lust" is the sinful exaggeration of pure love between a man and a woman. It is the cause of all sins against purity and innocence.

"Anger" is the sinful exaggeration of justice to oneself or others. It causes quarrels, strife, insult, injustice, abuse and violence.

"Gluttony" is the sinful exaggeration of the appetite for food; eating or drinking too much, simply for pleasure. It is the cause of intemperance.

"Envy" is the sinful exaggeration of self-love. It is sadness, bitterness or displeasure at the good fortune or success of another, at the advantages which others possess, and of which

oneself is deprived. Envy causes hatred, detraction, calumny, rash judgment, suspicion, and injustice.

"Sloth" is the sinful exaggeration of necessary rest for body or soul. Sloth is the cause of idleness, laziness, dislike for work, neglect of duty, etc. It opens the heart to temptation.

It is easy to see that we are constantly experiencing in many ways the tragic effects of original sin in our whole natures. These effects require constant vigilance and strenuous effort to resist their persistent demands, so that we may preserve the integrity of our natures.

We come now to the third and last source of temptation, namely, the Devil. The Devil may tempt us directly or indirectly, through the world or through our own fallen natures. We cannot minimize the power or presence of the Devil in the world. Jesus continually spoke of him as a very real being, a fallen angel, jealous of mankind's life and happiness, both here and in eternity. Many times during His public life Jesus had to free people who were possessed by the Devil. The two most notable examples are the man possessed by the legion of devils, and Mary Magdalen. St. Peter warned the Faithful that *"the Devil goes about like a roaring lion, seeking whom he may devour,"* and he cautioned them to resist Satan (*Cf. 1 Peter* 5:8-9). St. Paul also reminded the Church that our wrestling is not against flesh and blood, but against the fallen angels, of whom the Devil is the leader (*Cf. Ephesians* 6:12).

Regarding Satan's method of tempting us, we could say that the story of Eden is repeated in every human life, for he strives by every means in his power to draw the individual soul, and indeed the whole human race, away from God, as in the case of our first parents. Sometimes he tries to tempt the individual soul openly, so that it is easy to recognize his temptations. In this role the Church refers to him as the "Noonday Devil" (*Cf. Psalms* 91:6), but at other times, as St. Paul observes, he can transform himself into an angel of light, to tempt us to evil under the disguise of good (*Cf. Corinthians* 11:14). It is here that we have to be vigilant in order to recognize his presence and avoid his snares.

The Devil can harass a person from without; this is called obsession. He can assume control over a person's body; this is called possession.[7] But the Church teaches that the Devil can never possess the soul of an individual, nor deprive us of our liberty or free will, though he may interfere with the person's control over his body.[8] Jesus has given the Church the power to expel the Devil from a person's body, and she uses this power when she performs exorcisms (*Cf. Matthew* 10:1). The Church teaches that we have nothing to fear from the Devil as long as we remain in the friendship of God, for the Devil is powerless against God, and flees in terror at His name. To call upon God for help, to invoke the holy Name of Jesus, to make the Sign of the Cross, or sprinkle Holy Water, any of these holy practices will overcome the Devil completely. Like the world, or our own fallen nature, the Devil can tempt, but never compel us to sin.

In regard to actually committing sin, it is comforting to know that most people sin through weakness, ignorance, or lack of proper instruction rather than through malice.

Since sin is such an important matter in the life of any individual, capable of destroying even our natural happiness and integrity, it is good to reflect on the counsel which the Church gives us about the best means of avoiding it. In order to avoid sin effectively, we must seek to control our emotions by the practice of constant vigilance and self control. We must learn to judge what is right and then live by it. This forms a good character. We must keep ourselves constantly occupied, and avoid every occasion of sin. This brings us to a consideration of the occasions of sin.

The Church defines an occasion of sin as any person, place, or thing that would lead us to commit sin. Experience, or the natural evilness of a thing, usually cause us to recognize what is an occasion of sin to us personally. It is good to remember that what constitutes an occasion of sin to one person may be perfectly harmless for another, but some occasions are dangerous for all. The most common occasions of sin are: bad companions, bad books, curiosity, idleness, and the neglect of prayer.[9] The Church distinguishes two types

of occasions of sin— "immediate" and "remote."

An immediate occasion of sin is anything which we know by experience almost always leads us to commit sin. A remote occasion of sin is that which we know by experience has sometimes, though not often, led us to commit sin.

An occasion of sin may be "necessary" or "unnecessary."[10] It is necessary when we cannot avoid it without very great loss, such as the loss of our lawful means of living. An occasion of sin is unnecessary when we could avoid it without any great loss. We are bound, under pain of mortal sin, to avoid all unnecessary immediate occasions of mortal sin. If an immediate occasion of mortal sin is necessary, we must try with the help of God's grace to change it into a remote occasion. To do this, we must go to Confession and Holy Communion regularly, pray earnestly for strength to keep from sin, ask the advice of our confessor, and use our common sense to preserve ourselves from sin. If, for example, we are tempted to steal at our work place, we should try never to be there alone, since that would lessen the temptation. If we find, however, that we still continue to fall frequently into mortal sin, we must avoid the occasion at all costs.[11]

The last and **most important** means of avoiding temptation is to pray constantly and to receive the sacraments of Penance and Holy Communion frequently. In regard to temptation, the importance of the sixth petition of the "Our Father" cannot be overestimated: *"Lead us not into temptation,"* for if those who rush headlong into physical and moral danger had the wisdom to pray that petition sincerely, many lives would be saved daily and hourly from ruin. When we try to keep our lives free from sin, then happiness begins to enter, and with it the beginning of that fullness of life for which we constantly yearn. For when sin has been cast out, God enters in to take possession of the heart that is rightfully His. In fact it should be the desire and prayer of every individual.

## *Chapter 8*

# A Consideration of the First Commandment

*"To be near God is my good"* (*Psalms* 73:28).

The Church teaches that human beings were created to know, love and serve God here on earth, and afterwards to be happy with Him forever in Heaven. Because of this we are obliged, by the very reason for our existence, to worship God. But how exactly do we worship God? The Church says that we worship God by faith, hope, and charity, by prayer and sacrifice.[1]

To have a clearer idea of what the worship of God entails, we must reflect on the first three Commandments, because these regulate all that pertains to our direct service of God. They set forth in detail what the first Commandment prescribes in general.

The first Great Commandment says: *"You shall love the Lord your God with all your heart and with all your soul, and with all your strength and with all your mind"* (*Luke* 10:27). This love of God put into practice, is true worship.

The first three Commandments of the *Decalogue* [Ten Commandments] describe our duties of personal worship to God, and by implication show us what they prohibit. The First Commandment says: *"I am the Lord your God: you*

*shall not have strange gods before Me."* This Commandment lays the foundation of all our worship, for it commands us to acknowledge and honor God above all things.

The Second Commandment says: *"You shall not take the name of the Lord your God in vain."* The Third says: *"Remember that you keep holy the Sabbath Day."* Let us now consider how we worship God by faith, hope, and charity, by prayer and sacrifice.

What is faith? "Faith" is a divine virtue by which we firmly believe all the truths that God has revealed.[2] "Hope" is a divine virtue by which we firmly trust that God will give us eternal life, and the means to obtain it.[3] "Charity" is a divine virtue by which we love God above all things for His own sake, and our neighbor as ourselves for the love of God.[4] Charity is sometimes called "love." These three virtues are called the "Theological" virtues, because they have God as their object. They are supernaturally infused virtues given as a free gift to us by God, implanted in our souls, at Baptism. They cannot be acquired by our own efforts, but can be strengthened and made perfect by repeating certain acts.

Faith is the foundation of all the virtues.[5] We could compare it to the eye of the soul which discovers God, and having learned what kind of being He is, accepts on His word alone, all the truths He has revealed, because He is truth itself Who can neither deceive nor be deceived.

Hope comes from faith.[6] By hope we reach out to God Whom we have discovered by faith. We trust in His goodness, that He will give us eternal life and the means to obtain it.

Charity comes of faith and hope.[7] All other virtues come from charity, (love of God).[8]

Faith and hope will end with this life, for in Heaven, faith will be changed into sight, and hope will be changed into possession, but charity will last forever. Charity, therefore, is the most excellent of all the virtues (*Cf. 1 Corinthians* 13:8-13). By charity the soul embraces God.

Faith, hope, and charity are the three most fundamental ways by which we can adore or worship God. The Church advises us to make frequent acts of faith, hope, and charity,

to foster the love of God in the soul. These are interior acts of adoration, such as prayer.

The two other basic ways by which we can worship God, namely, prayer and sacrifice will be covered in subsequent chapters.

Now that we know what the First Commandment requires of us, let's see how it can be broken.

The Church says that the First Commandment may be broken by giving to a creature the honor due to God alone; by false worship, or by acting as if a creature has characteristics which belong to God alone.[9] The first reference is to idolatry, which is comparatively rare today, and which would pertain to pagan areas which have not yet heard the word of God. There is one form of idolatry, however, which is becoming common today even in Christian countries, namely devil-worship. This is a terrible and dangerous offense, and shows that the First Commandment is as relevant today as in the days of Moses.

By false worship we mean heresy. The Church defines a heretic as someone who willfully changes the teaching of the Church,[10] or who does not accept or believe all the doctrines of the Catholic faith as officially taught by the Church. Christ founded the Church to guard the true meaning of His teachings and to make those teachings known throughout the world. He also sent the Holy Spirit to guide the Church in its teaching mission. Because of God's loving protection of His Church, we are confident that the Church teaches only God's truth. Anything which is opposed to the Church's teaching is potential heresy and should not be believed in light of the First Commandment.

The third way in which the First Commandment may be broken is by attributing God's power to other people or things. This refers to the practice of superstition, a problem which has troubled the Church throughout history. People have always been intrigued by the world beyond, and in an endeavor to penetrate the spirit world, they have resorted to various unlawful, though futile, means in order to communicate with spirits or with the souls of the dead, or to learn

the secrets of the future, either in regard to themselves or others. All such activity is strictly forbidden by the First Commandment, because it attributes to mere creatures knowledge and abilities which belong to God alone. God can know the future with perfect clarity, since He is the "Author of Time" and can see past, present, and future as an ever present "now."

People who break the First Commandment in this manner are: those who believe in charms and spells; those who believe in dreams; those who believe in mediums, spiritists, or fortune-tellers; all those who themselves practice these arts.[11]

Now let's clarify what these various titles mean. What are spells, for example? "Spells" are words that are supposed to have a magical, preternatural power.[12] "Charms" are objects that are believed to have the same powers.[13] "Spiritists" are those who try to communicate with spirits: "mediums" try to act as the mouthpiece of spirits. "Fortunetellers" pretend to learn the future from dreams, palms of hands, the stars, etc.

The practice of these occult arts not only breaks the First Commandment, but even endangers the very sanity of those who become involved in them. For these two reasons the Church vigorously condemns all such practices and counsels the Faithful carefully to avoid them.

In addition to the above mentioned ways in which the First Commandment may be violated, there are the sins against faith, hope, and charity which offend against it, because all such sins deny God the honor that is His due.[14]

There are many ways in which a person may sin against faith, namely; by not trying to know what God has taught, by refusing to believe all that God has taught, and by neglecting to profess belief in what God has taught.

One fails to try to know what God has taught by neglecting to learn Christian doctrine. It is a sin to be indifferent to faith, or to endanger one's faith. This can be done by reading books against faith or morals, by associating with bad

company, sometimes by mixed marriages, or by joining anti-Christian societies.

Those who refuse to believe all that God has taught, are: heretics—those who willfully change or who do not accept all the teachings of the Church, schismatics—those who refuse to submit to Church authority, infidels—those who reject Christianity, agnostics—those who doubt the existence of God, rationalists—those who make human reason their God.[15]

The Church teaches that a person who neglects to profess belief in God cannot expect to be saved.[16] Jesus said: *''Whoever denies me before others, I will deny before my heavenly Father''* (*Matthew* 10:33). We are obligated to profess our faith openly as often as God's honor, the spiritual welfare of our neighbor, or our own spiritual welfare requires it. For Jesus also says: *''Everyone who acknowledges me before others I will acknowledge before my heavenly Father''* (*Matthew* 10:32).

Regarding the virtue of hope, the Church teaches that sins against hope are despair and presumption. As we discussed in chapter 6, despair is a loss of hope in God's mercy.[17] Cain and Judas are usually cited as examples of despair because they did not look for God's forgiveness. Peter also denied Jesus, but he sought and accepted Jesus' forgiveness and mercy. We should never doubt or mistrust the goodness of God.

Presumption is the opposite of despair. As was mentioned earlier, presumption is to take salvation for granted, as for example, when a person thinks that God will not allow him to be lost, or that He will at least give time for repentance before death, without regard of how this person lives. It is also presumption to think anyone is strong enough in faith that they can expose themselves to the occasions of sin without any danger.

In regard to charity, or the love of God, one sins against it by every sin, but particularly by mortal sin.[18]

Before concluding our reflections on what is commanded or forbidden by the First Commandment, we must consider

two other matters which are often misunderstood; these are the veneration of the saints, and the use of sacramentals. The Church not only permits but even encourages both of these practices as being good.

Honoring the saints is not forbidden but rather encouraged by the First Commandment, because in honoring them we honor God Who gave them their holiness. They were the special friends of God, and for this reason the Church encourages us to ask the help of their intercession. We do not adore the Saints, for adoration belongs to God alone; we merely honor them.

We give Mary, the Mother of Jesus, special honor, because God Himself honored her in a special manner, and because when dying on the Cross He made her the mother of all mankind.

We believe that the saints can help us by their intercession, because we are all members of the One Church—we, of the Church on earth, they of the Church in Heaven. God reveals our prayers,[19] and listens to their intercession on our behalf. We know this, because of Jesus' words in the Parable of the Lost Sheep: *"I tell you. . .there will be more joy in Heaven over one sinner who repents than over ninety-nine righteous people who have no need of repentance"* (*Luke* 15:7).

This communion which exists between the members of the Church in Heaven, earth, and Purgatory, is called "the Communion of Saints." It is established and made possible through Christ, who is the Head of the Church (*Cf. Collosians* 1:18). For, as St. Paul observed: *"we being many, are one body in Christ"* (*Cf. 1 Corinthians* 10:17: *Ephesians* 4:25). Since this mutual assistance is possible only through Christ, the invocation of the saints in no way denies the fact that Jesus is the one mediator between God and mankind.[20]

It is good to mention, however, that although the Church encourages the faithful to pray to the saints, it strictly forbids anyone to offer Mass to any saint, even to the Blessed Virgin Mary. The Liturgy of the Eucharist is offered to God alone. It may be offered to God in honor of a saint, that is to thank God for the grace and glory He bestowed on that privileged soul, but it is always offered directly to God.

Besides petitioning the saints to ask their intercession on our behalf, the Church also allows and promotes the honor paid to the relics of the saints. "Relics" are the bodies of the saints, or objects directly connected with them, such as their clothing, books, or other articles which they used. Relics also include objects directly connected with Jesus, for example, the Holy Shroud of Turin. The First Commandment in no way forbids this honor, for it helps us to call to mind the virtues and merits of the saints, of Mary the Mother of Jesus, and of Jesus Himself. In honoring the relics of the saints, however, it is good to remember that we ask the help and intercession of the saint who is in Heaven, not of his or her relics.[21]

The Church also states that pictures, statues, and images of Jesus, of Mary, His Mother, and of the saints, be treated with reverence and respect, because they are memorials of those they represent. The same instinct which prompts us to raise memorial statues to great heroes of history in the public squares of cities, or to display photographs of family and friends in a prominent place in the home, underlies the honor and reverence paid by the Church to the relics of the saints, or memorials of them, whether they be pictures or statues. Relics venerated in public must be approved by the proper Church authority, and no superstitious use may be made of them.[22]

It is not right to pray to a crucifix, or to images or relics of the saints, for they have neither life, nor sense, nor power to hear or help us.[23] We may pray in front of these images to help our devotion, or strengthen our faith and trust in God, by remembering the merits of Jesus or of the saints, and thereby being encouraged to imitate their virtues.[24]

Now let's consider the Church's use of sacramentals. Sacramentals are objects or actions which the Church uses to obtain favors, especially spiritual favors.[25] In this way they are similar to Sacraments. Perhaps we could define a sacramental more clearly by saying that a sacramental is anything set apart or blessed by the Church, to inspire good thoughts, to increase devotion, and through these movements

of the heart, to remit venial sin.[26] Sacramentals are worlds removed from charms or spells because it is the blessing of the Church that makes them effective. In fact the Church says that in order to be effective, they must be used with reverence and piety, and with sorrow for sin; not superstitiously believing that they can help us, apart from the Church's blessing or our own piety.[27]

Jesus gave the Apostles power to cast out devils and to heal illnesses (*Matthew* 10:1); the Church exercises this power in the sacramentals.[28] The Church blesses persons or things; in order to dedicate them to the service of God, to protect or bring benefit to the individual, or to drive out the Devil by exorcism.[29] Sacramentals are of no benefit to those who persist in sin, just as the Ark of the Covenant was of no help to the Israelites in their fight against the Philistines (*1 Samuel* 4).

Sacramentals differ from sacraments in significant ways. The sacraments were instituted by Christ but sacramentals were instituted by the Church. If no obstacles are put in their way, sacraments give grace. Sacramentals, on the other hand, inspire us to holiness in our hearts which leads us to obtain grace, but sacramentals do not give graces of themselves.[30]

There are a wide variety of sacramentals recognized by the Church. Specific prayers, such as, the "Our Father," the words of Scripture, the prayers at Mass, and the "Liturgy of the Hours," which many religious groups pray, are used to inspire individuals to holiness. Other sacramentals include blessings given by priests or bishops on objects or people. Blessed candles, medals, crucifixes, ashes, palms, and holy water have been traditionally placed in Christian homes and work places as reminders of the faith.[31]

The Church uses the Sign of the Cross as its primary sacramental. The Sign of the Cross is made by putting the right hand to the forehead, then to the heart, then to the left and right shoulders while saying: "In the name of the Father, and of the Son, and of the Holy Spirit. Amen." Making the Sign of the Cross shows that we are Christians and professes our faith in God. It expresses the main mysteries of our faith;

the mystery of the Blessed Trinity—Father, Son, and Holy Spirit, and the mystery of the Incarnation—where the Son of God became man, died on the cross, and rose again for our salvation.

The image of a cross has been a significant sacramental since the time of Christ's crucifixion. A crucifix differs from a simple cross because it has a figure of Christ attached to it. The initials "I.N.R.I." inscribed on every crucifix mean "Jesus of Nazareth, King of the Jews." Pilate ordered this inscription be placed on Christ's cross on Calvary. It is a good practice to place a cross or crucifix in your home, office, or school as a reminder of what Christ has done for us all.

Another important sacramental which is used in church and in homes or offices is holy water. It is natural water mixed with salt and blessed by a priest. A solemn prayer is used for the blessing to beg God's gifts for those who use it, and to ask His protection from the powers of darkness.[37] It has great power over evil spirits and should be used often, particularly when experiencing trials, or around the dying.

The Church also encourages individuals in the sacramental wearing of scapulars.[39] Scapulars are usually two pieces of cloth, joined by strings, and worn around the neck. They represent the "habit," a type of uniform, of different religious orders and provide an exterior symbol of an interior prayer and commitment to God. Individuals who commit to wearing the scapular usually become enrolled in the scapular by means of special prayers and blessings administered by a priest or member of a particular religious order. Once they are enrolled, individuals share in the prayers and good works of the members of the order and also gain special privileges and indulgences.

The Brown Scapular of Our Lady of Mount Carmel is the most commonly used scapular. It was given by the Blessed Mother to St. Simon Stock and is connected with the Carmelite Order. On July 16, 1251, Mary promised St. Simon Stock that, *"Whosoever dies clothed in this scapular shall not suffer eternal fire."* This promise has been handed down

throughout history and even now people remain devoted to wearing the scapular according to the Blessed Mother's wishes.

The Green Scapular was given by Our Lady to Sr. Justine Bisqueyburu on September 8, 1840, with a promise that it would contribute to the conversion of many souls, especially those without faith, and they would have a happy death. Scapulars are a tangible sign of a prayerful devotion to God's love and protection. Wearing or carrying a scapular reminds us to trust in God's mercy.

Sacramentals are also used during church services, such as the blessed palm carried on Palm Sunday or holy oils used during the administration of the sacraments. These oils are made of pure olive oil, except for the oil of "chrism," which has balm mixed with it. The holy oils are blessed by the bishop on Holy Thursday.[33] There are three separate oils. The Oil of Chrism is used at Baptism and Confirmation, and at the consecration of a bishop; also at the consecration of altar stones and sacred vessels.[34] The Oil of Catechumens is used in Baptism.[35] The Oil of the Sick is used in the Anointing of the Sick.[36]

This information gives us a general idea of how we as members of the Church can express our faith in God through liturgical life and sacramental practices. There are many ways available for Christians to actively give honor to God and thus live up to the directive of the First Commandment.

## *Chapter 9*

# A Consideration of the 2nd and 3rd Commandments

*"In Holiness and Justice before Him"* (*Luke* 1:75).

The Second and Third Commandments regulate our direct personal service of God through our words and actions. The Second Commandment says: *"You shall not take the name of the Lord your God in vain."*[1]

To take God's name in vain, means to use it carelessly or lightly, without due reverence. We are commanded by the Second Commandment, to speak of God, of the saints, and of all holy things with reverence; and to keep our lawful oaths and vows. The very first petition of the "Our Father" is: "Hallowed by Thy name." *"Do not be deceived"* St. Paul said in his epistle to the Galatians, *"God is not mocked"* (*Galatians* 6:7). The punishment of King Belshazzar (*Daniel* 5), or of the sons of Eli (*1 Samuel* 4), are graphic examples of the swift judgment of God upon those who refuse to treat Him with proper reverence. The expulsion of the money changers from the Temple (*John* 2), is a similar example in the New Testament.

The Second Commandment also forbids all false, rash, or unnecessary oaths, as well as cursing, blaspheming, or profane words.[2]

An oath is the calling on God to witness that what we say is true. The taking of an oath is called swearing; the taking of a false oath is called perjury. An oath is an act of faith in the omnipotence, justice, and holiness of God. To take an oath on the Bible, is the same as calling upon God directly. The words "So help me, God," mean that you renounce God's help, and therefore your salvation, if your oath is not true.[3]

It is sometimes lawful and necessary to take an oath, for example, when ordered to do so by a lawful authority, or when the honor of God, our own, or our neighbor's good require it. For an oath to be lawful, it is necessary that what one swears be true, and that there be sufficient cause for taking an oath. An oath is the strongest proof one can give of the truth of what one affirms or denies, or of the sincerity of one's promise.

An unjust oath is one that causes offense to God, or injury to one's neighbor. An unnecessary oath is an oath taken without sufficient reason.

We are commanded by the Second Commandment to keep our lawful oaths and vows. It is forbidden to take an unjust or unnecessary oath, and if this has been done, we must not keep it.

A vow is a deliberate promise made to God, to do something that is pleasing to Him.[4] Sinful or trivial things are not subject matter for vows, because they do not honor God.[5] Private vows are entirely personal, that is, they do not involve the Church or her authority. They should be made, however, on the advice of one's confessor. Public vows are made on the authority of the Church. They are usually made by members of religious orders or institutes, or during a sacrament, such as Marriage.

A vow differs from a good intention or resolution, in that it is a definite promise to be kept under pain of sin.[6] By a vow one gives God a right to the things promised. It is a sin not to fulfill a vow; the sin may be mortal or venial, according to the nature of the vow, and the intention one had in making it.

To curse, which is also forbidden by the Second Commandment, is to ask God to inflict harm on oneself or others. To blaspheme, means to scorn or ridicule God, or sacred things. To use profane words means to use irreverent or unholy language when speaking of God or of sacred things. This would include the taking of rash or unlawful oaths. The most common example of profane language is the taking of the name of God in vain. It can become a bad habit if repeatedly done through impatience or as a joke. Profanity is usually a venial sin of irreverence to God. It differs from coarse or vulgar language or from slang, which is an uncultured use of speech.

The Third Commandment regulates our formal worship of God on the Sabbath Day, both on a personal and social level. It says: *Remember that you keep holy the Sabbath Day.*[7]

In the Old Testament, the Sabbath Day was Saturday, the last day of the week. In the New Testament, the Sabbath Day of the Christian Church is Sunday, the first day of the week; it is commonly called "The Lord's Day." The change from Saturday to Sunday was made by the Apostles,[8] through the authority which they received from Christ to govern the Church. This change was made because Jesus rose from the dead on the first day of the week—Sunday.[9] His Resurrection is the foundation and central point of the Christian Faith. He also sent the Holy Spirit to the Apostles on Sunday, the first Christian Pentecost, which is regarded as the birthday of the Church.[10]

Since the Third Commandment is general, the Church, by virtue of her governing authority, determines how Christians are to keep Sunday holy. Thus the Church requires each individual member to attend Mass (the Liturgy of the Eucharist) on Sundays and on Holy Days of Obligation, unless prevented by a legitimate reason.[11] Due to changes in modern lifestyles, the obligation to attend Mass on Sunday may be fulfilled by attending Mass on Saturday evening.

The Church says that anyone who neglects to attend Mass on a Sunday or a Holy Day of Obligation, without sufficient reason, is guilty of serious sin.[12] Anyone who prevents some-

one in their care from attending Mass on such days is also guilty of serious sin.[13]

Holy Days of Obligation are days set aside by the Church to call to mind the great mysteries of our religion, and the virtues and gifts of the saints.[14] Many of the Holy Days of Obligation which were originally celebrated on week days are now celebrated on Sundays, to relieve the burden of obligation from those who, because of work or business, find it difficult to attend Mass during the week. Holy Days of Obligation vary from country to country. Some are celebrated by the universal Church, others by certain nations or regions. Check with your pastor or diocesan office to find out which days are celebrated in your diocese.

The following are the Holy Days which are celebrated by the universal Church. The Church teaches that Holy Days are to be kept in the same way as the Sabbath.[15] Some of these feast days are celebrated on Sundays and therefore are not listed as Holy Days of obligation.

Christmas Day—December 25th, celebrates the birth of Christ.

New Year's Day—January 1, is a day set aside to honor Mary which is called, the Solemnity of Mary.

The Annunciation—March 25th, is a remembrance of Jesus' conception.

Easter Sunday—This is celebrated on the first Sunday after the first full moon after the Spring equinox. It recalls Jesus' triumphant resurrection from the dead.

The Ascension—Forty days after Easter, is the day Jesus ascended into Heaven.

Pentecost Sunday—Fifty days after Easter, is a celebration of the day Christ sent His Holy Spirit to the Apostles. This signifies the Church's birthday.

Feast of the Blessed Trinity—The Sunday after Pentecost.

Corpus Christi—Celebrated the Sunday after Trinity Sunday, focuses on the gift of the Holy Eucharist.

The Assumption of Mary—August 15th, remembers the day Mary was assumed into Heaven.

All Saint's Day—November 1st, is a celebration in remembrance of all saints.

The Immaculate Conception—December 8th, recalls the day Mary was conceived without original sin.

The Church instructs us that these days are kept holy by: attending Mass, prayer, reading Scripture, benediction of the Blessed Sacrament, spiritual reading, and other good works. Sunday and other "days of rest" are gifts from God whereby we maintain our human dignity and keep from becoming working machines or slaves to labor. Sundays should call to mind that we are children or God and lords over His kingdom. The Lord Himself rested on the seventh day of creation as an example for His children to follow. Many modern stress related diseases could be avoided by respecting the Third Commandment. Those who violate the Sabbath not only sin against God by refusing to give Him honor, but they also foolishly work against their own dignity.[16]

Other devotions to God are encouraged, but the Mass, also called the Liturgy of the Eucharist, is mandatory for Roman Catholics. The Liturgy of the Eucharist is the holiest of all prayers and infinite in value. It is the renewal of the sacrifice on Calvary, without the shedding of blood.[17] It is the Church's ultimate act of worship, since it offers to the Father, His only begotten Son. This is done according to Jesus' request at the Last Supper and so everything involved with this sacrifice signifies majesty and dignity.

The bread and wine used during the Mass at consecration must be prepared according to Church law; the bread must be made of wheat flour, leavened or unleavened, brown or white; the wine must be pure grape wine.[18]

The sacred vessels must also fulfill the Church's requirements. The most important sacred vessels are: the paten, which holds the Sacred Host; the chalice, which contains the Precious Blood of Our Lord after the Consecration; and the ciborium, which holds the consecrated Hosts to be given to the Faithful in Holy Communion.

The priest's vestments indicate the dignity and exclusive nature of the priesthood, and the awe inspiring magnificence of the Eucharistic Sacrifice.[19] They, also, must fulfill all the liturgical laws of the Church. The most important of the

vestments are: the alb, which is a plain white tunic; the stole, a band or sash worn around the neck as an official emblem of the priestly office; and the chasuble, an outer vestment of specific cut and design, which varies in color according to the liturgical season, or the particular feast being celebrated on a given day.

The traditional colors of the priest's vestments in the Roman Catholic Church are: white for purity, red for love, green for hope, purple for penance, and black for mourning.[20]

White vestments are worn on feasts of Our Lord, Our Lady, and some saints. Red are worn on feasts of the Holy Spirit, Pentecost for example, and on feasts of the martyrs. Violet—purple, are worn during the seasons of Advent and Lent. Black vestments used to be worn on Good Friday, and at the Mass of the Dead. Since the Second Vatican Council, however, violet may be worn on Good Friday and white at Masses for the Dead, since the Church wishes to place greater emphasis on the mystery of mankind's future resurrection. Green vestments are worn on Sundays after the Epiphany and after Pentecost, or on week days when no special feast day occurs.[21]

The Eucharistic Sacrifice should be offered on an altar if at all possible; if it is not possible, an altar stone should be used. An altar stone is consecrated by a bishop, and contains relics of the saints and martyrs.[22] The altar upon which the Holy Sacrifice is offered, should be covered with clean linen cloths, and should have a crucifix, at least two lighted candles, a stand or a pillow for the Mass Book or Missal, and the Missal itself.

The Holy Sacrifice is offered according to a prescribed formula or rule, called a rite.[23] The Latin Rite is that of the Roman Catholic Church. Other rites include, the Greek, Syrian, Armenian, and Ukrainian Rites.[24] In the Latin Rite, prior to the Second Vatican Council, the Latin language was always used, but since the revision of the Liturgy, following the Council, the vernacular, that is, the language spoken by the people in each region is now used. In certain instances the Latin language is still permitted, though even then, the

Eucharistic Sacrifice must be offered according to the New Revised Latin Rite.[25]

The two basic divisions of the Eucharistic Sacrifice, according to the New Revised Rite, are: the Liturgy of the Word, and the Liturgy of the Eucharist. The Liturgy of the Word includes: all the introductory prayers, Scripture readings both from the Old and New Testaments, responsorial Psalms, the reading of the Gospel, and the homily or sermon, usually upon the Gospel theme.[26]

Next comes the Liturgy of the Eucharist, which includes the offertory, the Consecration, and the Communion service. The Consecration is the most important part of the Mass. The parts of the Mass which immediately precede and follow it, from the Preface to the "Our Father," form the "Canon" of the Mass.[27] Previously there was only one canon, but now, there is a choice of four different canons. The Eucharistic Sacrifice concludes with the rite of dismissal of the congregation.

In order to make the Mass the inspirational experience that it is intended to be, we should be respectful and devout when participating.[28] This includes being attentive during the recitation of the prayers, the singing of the hymns, and the common responses. It also includes arriving on time and staying until the Mass is concluded. We should remember that we are actually visited by Christ's real presence in the Eucharist. This makes the Mass more special than a visit with even our closest friend. Our participation, or lack of participation, influences the experience we have, as well as the experiences of those in our community.

The Church offers the Holy Sacrifice to adore God, to thank Him for His blessings, in reparation for sin, and to ask for all our needs.[29] These are the same reasons Jesus offered Himself on Calvary. Since the Mass is of infinite value it may be offered for any number of intentions, both personal and communal. It is a good practice, therefore, to join our personal intentions to the intentions of the Church. All who participate in the Mass receive infinite graces.[30]

All of those facts show us how important it is to keep the

first three Commandments, for they regulate the entire prayer-life of the Church and each of its individual members. Prayer guides our lives toward God, the Source and End of our beings. This in turn helps us realize the goal of true happiness, for everything falls into true perspective, and life becomes truly meaningful, when God is its center. When anchored in God, the heart finds rest, for the peace and security which logically flow from this establishment in God, can never be destroyed by the uncertainties of life. Neither the failure of friends, nor the pain of adversity can overwhelm the soul, for it realizes that when every earthly support is taken away, there still remain the Everlasting Arms,[31] to comfort and uphold it.

# PART III

## On the Love and Service of Self and Neighbor

*"You shall love your neighbor as yourself"*
(*Matthew* 22:39).

## *Chapter 10*

# Reflections on the Fourth Commandment

*"Honor your Father and your Mother, that you may have a long life in the land which the Lord, your God, is giving you."*

Now we come to the second basic division of the Decalogue, namely, that which deals with our love and service of self and neighbor. This section includes the Fourth through the Tenth Commandments. The first of these is the Fourth Commandment: *"Honor your father and your mother, that you may have a long life in the land which the Lord, your God, is giving you.*[1]*"* This divine teaching given by God, from Whom all parenthood in Heaven and on earth comes, establishes forever the excellence and dignity of parenthood against the worldly philosophies that would try to degrade it. It is noteworthy that God commands us to honor our father and mother, even in preference to the phrase to "love," though undoubtedly in this context honor includes love. However, honor gets first preference here, because of the serious obligation which binds every individual person to respect those who, in the natural order, have given him the gift of life.

To honor means to acknowledge and publicly proclaim the excellence of another, and who more than one's parents is

worthy of such respect? For parenthood has an intrinsic excellence in itself; it is a reflection of the Divine Fatherhood of God and of human participation in His creative power.

Parents assist God by building up the Church through the foundation and preservation of a home. In a real sense, the home is the rock foundation on which the Church rests. The service they give, in the establishment of a home and the raising of children, can never be supplied by another in exactly the same way. They are the first apostles the child will encounter in life. Parents set little feet on the path of virtue, and turn young hearts to God.

In building up the secular state, they play an equally important role, for where there is good family life, there is also a strong and prosperous nation. Conversely, where there is an absence of good family life, there is inevitable moral decline, and social disintegration which can lead to a nation's ruin.

Implicit in the Fourth Commandment is the responsibility of parents towards their children. It is the duty of parents to feed, clothe, and educate their children, to the best of their abilities, to protect them against physical and moral danger, and to direct and counsel them by word and example. In the spiritual or moral sphere they are obligated to instruct them, or to have them instructed, in the Catholic Faith, to advise and counsel them regarding the dangers to Faith and morals which they will encounter in life, and to encourage them in the practice of Christian virtue.

The children, for their part, are bound to love, honor, and obey their parents; this is dictated by the natural law itself. Parents have a unique claim to the love and respect of their children, because they represent the authority of God to the child, mirror His supreme parenthood, and reflect His providence over His creation, in providing for their material needs.

Children show love for their parents by showing esteem for them, and by taking care of them in sickness or old age, according to the parents' need and their own ability to help. They honor parents by showing them respect, by avoiding snobbishness, or anything in their attitude or demeanor that

might hurt a parent's feelings. Children obey their parents by doing their parents' will in lawful things. A child would not be obliged, however, but rather forbidden, to obey a parent, or anyone else, if the request were sinful, that is, if it were contrary to the law of God.

Now let's look at what the Fourth Commandment forbids. The Fourth Commandment forbids all disobedience, contempt, or stubbornness towards parents or lawful superiors, that is, towards all those who exercise lawful authority over them. This includes both religious and civil authority. People with such authority would be, for example: bishops, pastors, priests, teachers, government officials, police officers, employers, guardians, or grandparents. In regard to religious authority, Jesus said: *"He who hears you, hears me,"* and in regard to civil authority, He said: *"Give to Caesar the things that are Caesar's"* (*Matthew* 22:21).

Here we come to the question of the short-comings of parents, or of serious parental neglect. Do these things justify contempt or dishonor on the part of the children? We must answer "no." Even serious matters do not in any way lessen the obligation of children to respect their parents,[2] for no fault, however terrible, can ever outweigh the wonderful gift they have made to their children in giving them the gift of natural life. This is the supreme gift in a natural sense, and without it no other gift would be possible, even that of eternal life.

We know that there can be serious neglect of duty on the part of parents. We can only imagine the number of people throughout history, who have suffered as a result of parental neglect? Equally tragic is the fact that many lives have been embittered or warped irreparably, by harsh, unjust, or tyrannical conduct on the part of parents. Yet, despite all this, God spoke without qualification: *"Honor your father and your mother."* We must remember that all misconduct on the part of parents is a deviation from the law of nature. For God has placed in the hearts of parents, a deep natural love for their children, which urges them to be concerned for their children's well being.

Parental neglect can come from a lack of maturity on the part of the parents, who are not sufficiently developed either on emotional or psychological levels to care for a child. They do not always understand the responsibilities of their role. Another factor in abuse is the fact that some otherwise capable parents are addicted to substances that keep them from adequately performing their duties as parents. Such problems can easily cause resentment on the part of the child. It is important for children in such situations to receive help if necessary so that they can turn any bitterness toward their parents into compassion.

The Lord gave us the commandments to live by because, as our Creator, He knows human nature better than we do. He knows that we were created for love and not hatred. Since the family unit was designed to teach us about His love for us, any unresolved pain in the family keeps us from truly understanding His divine love for us, His children.

When God sent His Son into the world, He sent Jesus into a family. As a human child, Jesus honored and respected His parents. As the Son of God, it could easily be said that Jesus possessed an understanding in excess of his earthly parents. But He never treated them as inferiors. This is seen in the episode when Jesus was twelve years old and His parents mistakenly left Him behind in the temple. After three days of frantic searching they found Him teaching in the temple. *"When His parents saw Him, they were astonished, and His mother said to Him, 'Son, why have you done this to us? Your father and I have been looking for You with great anxiety.' And He said to them, 'Why were you looking for me? Did you not know that I must be in my Father's house?' But they did not understand what He said to them. He went down with them and came to Nazareth, and was obedient to them . . . And Jesus advanced* [in] *wisdom and age and favor before God and man"* (*Luke* 2:48-52).

In this example Jesus follows the Fourth Commandment by being obedient to Joseph and Mary. This commandment is the only commandment which also guarantees immediate rewards for following it. In this case, Jesus grows in wisdom.

The commandment grants *"a long life in the land which the Lord, your God, is giving you."* To the Jewish people this promise meant great blessings from the Lord. Fidelity to the Fourth Commandment is a hallmark of a good home life because good parents are loved and cherished by God, and good children are the joys of their lives.

# *Chapter 11*

# Reflections on the Fifth and Eighth Commandments

*"You Shall Love Your Neighbor As Yourself"*
(*Matthew* 19:19).

When the rich young man asked Jesus what he should do to possess eternal life, Jesus simply replied: *"If you wish to enter into life, keep the Commandments."* The young man said to Him: *"Which ones?"* Jesus replied: *"You shall not kill; you shall not commit adultery; you shall not steal; you shall not bear false witness; honor your father and your mother; and you shall love your neighbor as yourself"* (*Matthew* 19:16-19). He also said this in the "Sermon on the Mount," at the beginning of His public life when He said: *"Do to others whatever you would have them do to you"* (*Matthew* 7:12; *Luke* 6:31).

St. Paul, in his letter to the Romans, thought it necessary to remind the early Christians of this when he said: *"Pay to all their dues, taxes to whom taxes are due, toll to whom toll is due, honor to whom honor is due. Owe nothing to anyone, except to love one another; for the one who loves another has fulfilled the law"* (*Romans* 13:7-8).

The Fifth Commandment is concerned with the physical well-being and protection of our own and our neighbors'

lives. It says: ''*You shall not kill.*''[1] This Commandment establishes the right and duty to protect our own body and soul, as well as those of others, from harm. Our body and soul belong to God by right of creation and redemption and we must give an account to Him of our use or abuse of them. All forms of cruelty, whether mental or physical, offend against this commandment[2]; it includes even cruelty to animals.[3]

We are commanded by the Fifth Commandment to live in peace and harmony with our neighbors, to respect their rights, to seek their spiritual and temporal welfare, and to take proper care of our own lives. This means that God expects us to take care of our physical health. We must, for example, receive sufficient rest and food, eat in moderation, be physically active, exercise to stay healthy, and use legal remedies to restore us to health when we are ill.

It also requires that we protect our lives against physical dangers, including dangerous occupations, entertainment and sports, the use of drugs, and the excessive use of alcohol. Anything, in effect, which would prove harmful or fatal to physical life at any stage from fertilization until natural death, comes under the Fifth Commandment. Every individual has the right and duty to protect themselves. Self-preservation is the strongest instinct of all living things. This self-protection allows even the taking of life if necessary.[4]

Looking now at the reverse side of the coin, so to speak, we find that the Fifth Commandment includes all quarreling, fighting, anger, hatred, revenge, willful murder, abortion, euthanasia, and the giving of bad example. All these evils are closely connected, and one can follow upon another. Quarreling and fighting usually lead to anger, and if allowed to go uncontrolled, can lead to hatred, revenge, and even murder.

Anger may sometimes be justified, but it takes prudence and discretion to know when it is lawful. Usually the day-to-day trivialities which provoke us to anger, are not sufficient to justify a loss of temper. Yielding to anger frequently may lead to serious consequences both for oneself and others.

Hatred is an even greater evil than anger. The church defines anger as a strong but passing feeling of displeasure against those whom we believe to have done us wrong,[5] but hatred is a settled dislike of others, with the desire of injuring them.[6] Uncontrolled anger can easily become hatred, and therein lies its greatest danger.

Every additional outburst of anger will make it increasingly difficult to control one's temper if provoked, because the habit of anger will have become stronger and more habitual. On the other hand, a sincere and determined effort to remain calm and self-controlled when provoked will help to build up a strong and noble character. To control one's temper and keep from answering sharply in difficult circumstances is not a sign of weakness, but of great moral strength, and in the end this will contribute greatly to both mental and physical health.

Now we'll consider the sin of willful murder which is often the tragic outcome of uncontrolled anger or hatred. The Church formally teaches that it is a serious sin to commit willful murder, that is to take one's own life or the life of another. There are only three instances in which it is lawful to take human life: in a just war, in the execution of a criminal, and in self defense. When it is a question of self-defense, however, one must not kill if it is possible to defend oneself by disabling or inflicting a lesser injury on one's assailant.[7] This principle of self-defense applies also to State law.[8]

In regard to the control of anger or hatred, it is good to follow the advice St. John Bosco gave the first members of his religious family while on his deathbed:

"Love your enemies, and do good to those who hate you. It will be a beautiful day for you, when you will succeed in overcoming an enemy by kindness, or in making a friend of him. May the sun never set on your anger, and may you never recall forgiven offenses to mind, or remember injuries, or recall to mind the forgotten wrong. Let us always say with all our hearts: 'Forgive us our trespasses, as we forgive those who trespass against us.' Let us really and definitively forget all that may have been of insult to us, and let us love every-

body with a brotherly love."[9] If this golden rule were faithfully practiced, many broken lives and broken hearts might be spared the need of healing.

How about the question of bad example, a sin which is also forbidden by the Fifth Commandment? Bad example is often called "scandal," which means "a stumbling block," because it causes our neighbor to stumble and fall on the way to eternal life. To give scandal means to lead others into sin, which is the death of the soul, and is forbidden by the Fifth Commandment.

There are three kinds of scandal: direct, indirect, and pharisaical scandal.[10]

Direct scandal is to do or say anything with the intention of causing others to sin. This kind of scandal is malicious, and must be avoided at all costs. To realize its evil, we should remember the dreadful words of condemnation spoken by Jesus against those who are guilty of it: *"He that shall scandalize one of these little ones that believe in Me, it were better for him that a millstone should be hanged about his neck, and that he should be drowned in the depths of the sea"* (*Matthew* 18:6).

Indirect scandal means to do what is wrong, or to do something that appears to be wrong, with no intention in either case of causing others to sin, but knowing, nonetheless, that our action is likely to do so.[11] An example of this would be making a harsh criticism of someone. Your criticism may be the truth, but saying it in certain circumstances may lead others into malicious gossip. We are obligated to remove the danger of scandal from our actions by explaining them if there is room for misinterpretation. If this cannot be done the action should be entirely avoided. In the example of harsh criticism, the comment should not be made in front of people who might use your comments as ammunition against the person being discussed. If a situation cannot be avoided, however, you would be justified in performing the action.

Pharisaical scandal is scandal which occurs when innocent actions are turned into occasions of sin by the person who observes them. This often happens because of jealousy or bad

feelings.[12] It is named after the Pharisees who took offense or scandal at the words and actions of Jesus. In pharisaical scandal the fault lies with the person who takes offense and not with the person whose actions are under scrutiny.

There are nine ways in which we act scandalously, that is, in which we might cause others to stumble or sin[13]: by counsel, command, consent, provocation, praise, concealment, silence, being partner to another's sin, and by defending sinful actions. An example of scandalous counsel is advising someone to read a dirty book. A scandalous command would be ordering someone to sin, such as ordering a person to steal. When a parent knowingly allows their child to associate with drug dealing friends, this is an example of scandalous consent. An example of provocation is irritating someone just to make them angry. Telling a person that they are brave or clever for doing something wrong is an example of scandalous praise. Not telling the proper authorities about something, such as child abuse, because you want to protect an individual or the community is an example of scandalous concealment. Failure to correct or instruct a child when they lie would be scandalous silence. Engaging in adultery would mean being partner to another's sin, and siding with someone justly convicted of a crime is an example of defending a sinful action.

Obviously, the Fifth Commandment is very comprehensive in scope. When we consider the Eighth Commandment, which is closely allied with it, we find that the concern for the physical well-being of ourselves and of our neighbor which the Fifth Commandment prescribes, finds its complement in the care and honor of one's good name, which is prescribed by the Eighth.

The Eighth Commandment says: *"You shall not bear false witness against your neighbor."*[14] This tells us to speak the truth in all things, and to be careful of the honor and reputation of our neighbor.[15]

A good reputation is a precious possession, and no one has a right to deprive another of this honor. Everyone has a right to be thought well of, unless he has been proven guilty

of a crime.[16] We protect our own good name because it is the testimony of a life of integrity. Without such a testimony, we would be deprived of the respect and good wishes of the community. The Eighth Commandment, therefore, forbids all false testimony, rash judgments, lies, backbiting, calumny, detraction, and anything in fact that would injure a neighbor's reputation. Let's examine these titles in greater detail.

First, there is false testimony; this means to swear falsely in a court of justice. It is always a grevious sin. Rash judgment means forming a bad opinion of others without sufficient reason. A lie means to say anything contrary to what we think is true. It is the intent to deceive that constitutes a lie, not the actual statement itself.[17] For example, if a person makes a false statement, but thinks it is true, he is not guilty of a lie, since he thinks he is telling the truth, and has no intention of deceiving. On the contrary, if a person intends to deceive, and makes a statement which is actually true, without his being aware of it, he is nevertheless guilty of lying.

There are four categories of lies.[18] *Jocose* lies are told for humor or in fun. The category commonly referred to as "little white lies" are *officious* lies, those lies told to excuse oneself or others, to escape some evil or to acquire some good. *Malicious* lies are told specifically to injure someone else and *sacrilegious* lies are told in the Sacrament of Confession or as an oath. A lie told in Confession would only be sacrilegious if it involves the confession of a mortal sin.[19]

*Backbiting* means to speak evil of others in their absence. *Calumnly* or *slander* means to tell lies about one's neighbor with the intent of injuring their character. Anyone who has been guilty of this sin, must try to repair the injury done to the neighbor, as far as possible, otherwise the sin will not be forgiven. In this instance it is just as important to make restitution of the character or good name of the person injured, as it would be to make restitution of stolen goods. Since it is difficult, however, to make such restitution, one should be all the more careful not to harm a neighbor's character either by word or action.

*Detraction* means to make known the hidden sins of another. We cannot make known the hidden sins of others to any or everyone. If you have knowledge of another's sins, or are aware that they are gravely tempted, or in serious moral danger, you would be wise to make these matters known to someone who would be in a position to help them; otherwise, silence is strictly required. If a person has committed a sin of detraction, they are obligated to make restitution as much as is possible, by trying to restore the good opinion which others had of the injured party.

To keep the Eighth Commandment faithfully, it is necessary to keep a strict guard over one's tongue, especially in regard to anything that touches the good name of a neighbor; and to cultivate a habit of speaking the truth at all times and under all circumstances, even in little things. The peace which will follow from this self imposed discipline will be its greatest reward.

# *Chapter 12*

# Reflections on the Seventh and Tenth Commandments

*"As you would have others do to you."*

We come now to consider a very important aspect of our neighbors' well-being, namely the care of their property and possessions, and this is the subject matter of the Seventh and Tenth Commandments. The Seventh Commandment says: *You shall not steal.*[1] The Tenth Commandment says: *You shall not covet your neighbor's goods.*[2] What the Seventh Commandment forbids in action, the Tenth Commandment forbids in thought. Both are concerned with protecting a person's lawful possessions.

We are commanded by the Seventh Commandment to give all people what belongs to them, and to respect their property.[3] This commandment touches, therefore, on the whole question of private property, and the acquisition of wealth. What does the Church say about these matters?

To begin with, the Church teaches that the natural law prompts an individual to provide for himself and his dependents, to save, and to acquire possessions. This instinct to provide for personal and family needs, against future shortages, is found even in the animal kingdom, where, for

example, the squirrel stores nuts for winter food. This noble instinct was placed in our hearts by God Himself; without it no progress or civilization would be possible.

It is good to remember that Jesus never condemned wealth in itself, since the instinct to provide for future need prompts us to set aside surplus wealth. What He condemned was an unreasonable attachment to wealth, and an excessive preoccupation with material things. He showed in His parables, that it is the abuse of wealth, like that of any other good, that becomes an evil. When, for example, a person becomes so attached to materials that he unscrupulously violates the rights of others in gaining or preserving wealth, he becomes the slave of that which he was intended to govern.

Because of the dangerous temptations that accompany the acquisition of wealth in any form, the Church lays down strict principles regarding both its acquisition and preservation. The Church insists that the rights and needs of others must always be respected, and timely assistance given to those who cannot provide for themselves. She also teaches that in the acquisition, preservation, and distribution of wealth, all are equal, being by their very nature brothers and sisters under God.

Therefore, the wealth of any nation should belong in part to all the citizens and not be the privileged possession of a chosen few. The right to acquire personal property, and to benefit by the advantages of social and educational advancement, should also be the privilege of all, without exception.

Unfortunately, in ages past, this basic right was often ignored, but today the Church and the civil governments alike, in almost every nation, are coming to realize more clearly that equality and social justice under God are the surest guarantee of a prosperous and happy nation.[4] In light of this growing realization, both are striving to correct past wrongs by taking effective steps to ensure the application of social justice.

In view of our natural right to gain and possess personal property, the Seventh Commandment forbids all unjust taking or keeping of what belongs to another.[5] This would include

*theft,* secretly taking another's property; *robbery,* taking with open violence; *fraud,* cheating in the buying or selling of items, or pretending an inferior product is actually of superior quality. Also included would be neglecting to do the work for which you are paid, unjust lawsuits, willfully destroying another's property, and charging too high an interest for borrowed money, with is called *usury.*[6] Keeping what belongs to another includes such things as charging unjust prices, not paying a wage to employees, not paying one's debts, refusing to give back what was unjustly taken, not returning what was left in your care, not taking the proper steps to find the owner of found merchandise, buying or receiving stolen goods, and squandering wealth.[7]

Merchandise which has been received in an unlawful way may not be kept but must be returned to the owner or the owner's heirs. If the item in question cannot be returned, then the equal value of the missing merchandise should be given to the rightful owner. If the owner or the owner's heirs cannot be located, then restitution can be given to charity. However, this cannot be considered restitution if no attempt is made to first locate the injured individual or his family.[8] If someone has damaged another's property, they are obligated to repair the damage.[9]

If a sin of injustice is mortal, it would be a mortal sin not to make restitution.[10] If this sin is confessed in Confession, absolution will take away the sin, but not the need to make restitution.[11]

While the Seventh Commandment is concerned with respect for another's possessions, the Tenth Commandment forbids us even to covet our neighbor's possessions. It says: *"You shall not covet your neighbor's goods."*

The Tenth Commandment tells us to be content with what we have, and to rejoice in our neighbor's well being. It forbids all "desire" to take or keep unlawfully what belongs to another. Indirectly, therefore, it touches upon the question of poverty, whether individual or corporate poverty, and upon the question of personal industry and the use of talents.

To begin with, the Tenth Commandment calls us to rejoice

in our neighbor's well-being. Unfortunately, due to mankind's fallen nature, it is often easier to be compassionate to our neighbor in misfortune, than to rejoice in their success. When we stop to analyze it, however, what often makes it psychologically difficult to rejoice at another's success is the subconscious fear that, somehow, this achievement has detracted from our own. What makes us, for example, covet the possessions of another, except the fact that we do not possess these things ourselves? Yet, our personal lack does not of itself justify depriving our neighbor of what is rightfully theirs. This brings us to a consideration of the whole question of poverty.

In itself, poverty is not a good. When it becomes destitution it is a positive evil, unworthy of human dignity.[12] It is a serious obligation, therefore, on the part of the Church, the State, as well as on the part of every individual, to strive to eradicate this evil from society, so that no one will have any need to covet the possessions of another. Yet, even when we have tried our best, we know that the problem of poverty will still remain, for Jesus said: *"The poor you have always with you"* (*John* 12:8). This comes naturally due to the dynamics of human society. There are always the sick, the elderly and the orphaned to provide for, as well as others who through misfortune or circumstances beyond their control are prevented from earning an honest livelihood, even though they would sincerely like to do so. Toward all these classes of society, both the Church and State should exercise a sharp vigilance, to ensure that their needs are being met, since circumstances prevent them from providing adequately for themselves.[13]

When dealing with the question of poverty, however, it is good to remember that even though it is an evil in itself, it possesses one essential element of good, for it is a natural challenge to mankind to acquire by his own talent and industry the necessities of life which he lacks. Every nation on earth can list among its most honored heroes individuals who were born in poverty, but who overcame the deprivations of life. Therefore, the Tenth Commandment indirectly points to

one very efficient remedy for material poverty, namely, the cultivation and diligent use of one's talents by personal industry.

In regard to the matter of personal industry, Jesus clearly showed in the Parable of the Talents (*Matthew* 25:14-30), and other parables, that God will require of each individual soul a strict account of the use or misuse he has made of his personal talents. For, besides helping a person to acquire sufficient material items, the diligent use of an individual's talents will also help him to achieve self-fulfillment, to realize his highest ambitions, and to discover his true dignity as a child of God.

When an industrious person has acquired sufficient material things due to personal hard work, he will feel less inclined to envy the prosperity of a neighbor, or to take another's possessions unlawfully. Pride in personal achievements will lead a person to be content with what he has, and to rejoice in the good fortune of others. In doing this a person becomes spiritually rich, having come into the possession of that peace which is the inheritance of those only who are truly free. Jesus referred to these people in the Sermon on the Mount, when He said: *"Blessed are the poor in spirit, for theirs is the Kingdom of Heaven"* (*Matthew* 5:3).

# *Chapter 13*

# Reflections on the Sixth and Ninth Commandments

## Moral Integrity Of Life

In previous chapters we have seen that the Fifth and Eighth Commandments are concerned with the physical and mental health of ourselves and others, while the Seventh and Tenth are concerned with our material well being in regard to property and possessions. The Sixth and Ninth Commandments deal with moral integrity, that is purity of heart and pure lives.

These commandments regulate the use of the gifts given to mankind by God whereby we join Him in the act of creation. These instincts are of great importance because they were given to ensure the preservation and perpetuation of the human race. They were designed by God to be governed by their own specific laws, and when utilized within these boundries they achieve the noble end for which they were intended. Used independently of these laws, however, they can cause moral devastation on the life and soul of the individual or society at large.

As we have seen before, one commandment forbids in action what the other forbids in thought. In this case the Sixth Commandment, *"You shall not commit adultery,"*[1] forbids

the action and the Ninth, *"You shall not covet your neighbor's wife,"*[2] forbids unclean thoughts.

Both protect purity of mind and body. The obligation to remain pure comes from the fact that we are made in the image and likeness of God. Having created us for His own glory, God requires that we should live in a way which is worthy of our dignity as His children. St. Paul reminded the early Christians of this fact in his letters to the churches: *"Do you know that you are the temple of God, and that the Spirit of God dwells in you? If anyone destroys God's temple, God will destroy that person; for the temple of God, which you are, is holy* (*1 Corinthians* 3:16-17). *For you have been purchased at a price. Therefore glorify God in your body* (*1 Corinthians* 6:20). *What profit did you get then from the things of which you are now ashamed? For the end of those things is death. But now that you have been freed from sin and have becomes slaves of God, the benefit that you have leads to sanctification, and its end is eternal life. For the wages of sin is death, but the gift of God is eternal life in Christ Jesus Our Lord"* (*Romans* 6:21-23)..

Deep in the nature of every individual God has engraved a natural love of integrity or moral wholeness. This is true even of those who, through human frailty, fail to achieve the ideals of a morally good life. Many who have fallen morally, and continue in an immoral lifestyle, do so initially because of lack of proper instruction in the Faith, a lack of home training, bad environment, or the bad example and counsel of others. Even in the most depraved life, however, deep beneath the surface, there is hidden an essential recognition of the value, nobility, and beauty of the virtue of purity. Even the most disgusting invididual would not want to be called by a subhuman or insulting term.

There are many interesting things about the virtue of purity which, in a sense, set it apart from all the other virtues. There are many, for example, who think it is difficult to practice or preserve, yet those who have abandoned it are often regarded as social outcasts. Purity has a beauty and a charm distinctly its own. Other virtues often have to be discovered;

patience, honesty, or kindness, for example. But purity is self-revealing; it cannot hide itself even if it would.

If purity of heart and life are so desirable, we might wonder why the majority of people today seem to throw it aside as nothing, something outmoded or something of which we might be ashamed. We can trace the reasons for this mistaken outlook to various causes.

First, there is the attractiveness of the good things of life which are not evil in themselves. Among these good things are the foundation and preservation of a family and home, which involves the lawful use of the physical powers designed by God to achieve this end. Often, however, these procreative powers are used unlawfully and for their own sake, independent of their role as intended by God. Since humans have a natural desire for happiness, people reach out to whatever appears to offer what they seek. This is especially true in moral matters, where we are led on by attractive appearances. It can be easy to cast aside all moral restraint and plunge headlong into sin in a mistaken pursuit of happiness, only to learn when it is too late that a lack of control in the reckless pursuit of pleasure has brought only bitterness and moral death. It is the story of Eden repeated all over again; we are reminded of St. Paul's rebuke to the Romans: *"What profit did you get then from the things of which you are now ashamed? For the end of those things is death."* (*Romans* 6:21).

There is also the modern philosophy of life which says that without complete freedom to act in moral matters, we can never reach full maturity. This philosophy rejects as absurd or even morally injurious, any attempt at restraint or obedience to the restrictions of law in matters of morality. It sees these things as destructive to the natural development of the personality. It maintains that any such moral restraint inhibits the individual, shatters his emotional system, and leaves him unfulfilled. Therefore, restraint in any form is to be avoided as an evil and abolished as something outmoded, for the good of the individual and of society.

It does not take much observation or reflection to see what a mistake this philosophy is, for the results are abundantly

evident in the tragedies of our society today. If lack of moral restraint leads to maturity, then where is the maturity to which it leads? We cannot find it. Most of our society is made up of those who having reached adult life cannot or will not assume the responsibility of family or parenthood. The high divorce rate, with its consequent result of broken lives and broken homes, is proof of this. If lack of moral restraint brings happiness, then where is the happiness that it brings?

Against this false philosophy, which in reality is nothing more than the advocate of license and debauchery, there stands the voice of God, as shown through divine revelation, particularly as found in the Gospels.

Jesus' teachings on self-control could be summed up in the following Gospel passages: "*Whoever wishes to come after me must deny himself, take up his cross, and follow me. For whoever wishes to save his life will lose it, but whoever loses his life for my sake will find it. What profit would there be for one to gain the whole world and forfeit his life? Or what can one give in exchange for his life?* (*Matthew* 16:24-26). *Enter through the narrow gate; for the gate is wide and the road broad that leads to destruction, and those who enter through it are many. How narrow the gate and constricted the road that leads to life. And those who find it are few* (*Matthew* 7:13-14). *Do not give what is holy to dogs, or throw your pearls before swine, lest they trample them underfoot, and turn and tear you to pieces* (*Matthew* 7:6). *The lamp of the body is the eye. If your eye is sound, your whole body will be filled with light; but if your eye is bad, your whole body will be in darkness. And if the light in you is darkness, how great will the darkness be* (*Matthew* 6:22-23). *Blessed are the clean of heart, for they will see God* (*Matthew* 5:8). *So be perfect, just as your heavenly Father is perfect* (*Matthew* 5:48)."

These Christian teachings are often obscured by the "values clarification" philosophy which encourages people to take action according to whatever feels good at any particular moment. The "narrow way" Jesus spoke of is self control

and obedience to the laws of nature. The "broad way" is the permissiveness of modern philosophies. Because of misinformation, many young people today are led into immoral lifestyles that do not bring true happiness. A pattern of selfishness and irresponsibility is formed that does not tolerate the sacrifices necessary for family or community life. Human beings were designed by God to live together: *"The Lord God said: 'It is not good for the man to be alone. I will make a suitable partner for him"* (*Genesis* 2:18). The commandments and teachings of Christ provide guidelines so that we can live together in the best way possible according to human nature.

The Church teaches that each person is a gift of inestimable value and dignity. All of an individual's mental and physical abilities are holy since they were created by God to glorify Himself. We were each created to honor God from the first moment of our lives to our last. It is our duty to preserve the sacredness and dignity of our lives, no matter what path of life we take. Since we belong to God, we will be asked to explain how we used the gift of life He gave us. This is referred to in the Parable of the Talents (*Matthew* 25).

In order to protect the gift of a pure life, we need the assistance of God's grace. Temptations against purity are persistant because Satan hates mankind and wants to rip away all the dignity that God has given us. Each individual must work diligently to avoid temptations and seek God's grace in every situation. Due to our fallen nature, we are easily led away from God's protection; by following the Sixth and Ninth Commandments we are supplied with specific guidelines which keep us close to God.

These commandments regulate our moral conduct both in regard to ourselves and our neighbors. In the matter of moral integrity we have a responsibility toward others. In this area we can say that God has appointed us "our brother's keeper." Every individual has a right to personal integrity. This is the most personal of an individual's possessions. No one, therefore, has the right to deprive another of this integrity by any means whatsoever.

Both the Sixth and the Ninth Commandments require that we be pure in thought, word, and action; modest in speech, conduct, and attire. They forbid any dishonor to oneself or others by an impure action. They also forbid, whether in thought or action, all unchaste freedom with another's wife or husband, not only for the sake of preserving personal integrity of life, but also to protect the integrity of family life, which is next to individual human life in importance.

When it is a question of purity, the Church teaches that most deliberate sins against the virtue of purity are mortal sins.[3] Here, however, as in the case of all the other Commandments, we have to distinguish between "temptation" and "willful consent." Temptation is any evil thought or desire which might come to mind. It is not sinful in itself, in fact, it may be a source of merit if we resist it. It is only when we deliberately consent to temptation and take sinful delight in it, that it becomes a mortal sin. If we neglect temptation, or are slow in resisting it, or if we give partial consent before actually rejecting it, it is a venial sin.[4]

To combat temptations the Church recommends the following practices: to avoid carefully all occasions of sin; to practice self denial; to be moderate in eating and drinking; to practice the virtue of modesty; to keep guard over the imagination; to pray constantly—this would include the frequent reception of the Sacraments of Confession and Holy Communion; and the cultivation of a love and reverence for Mary, the Virgin-Mother of Jesus; to practice living always in the presence of God.

# PART IV

## The Divine Healing of Sin

*"Those who are well do not need a physician, but the sick do"*

(*Matthew* 9:12).

# *Chapter 14*

# A Consideration of Guilt and Punishment

*"The wages of sin is death, but the gift of God is eternal life in Christ Jesus our Lord"* (*Romans* 6:23).

To be convinced of the reality of sin, we need only look at the tragic face of human society to see the pain and misery which inevitably follows in the wake of sin. The impoverishment and loneliness of sin is engraved on the faces of young and old, rich and poor, learned and unlearned. But even in the darkness, goodness silently grows in the midst of evil. The mystery of this spectacle provokes the thoughtful observer to reflection.

Why is it, for instance, that some individuals seem destined to live their entire lives untouched by sin, while others seem never to have encountered virtue along their life's path? Saints and scholars throughout history have pondered this baffling riddle, without finding a satisfactory answer. For in truth, there is no human solution to the mystery; it is the secret of God's eternal counsel. From the teaching of Jesus, in the Parable of the Wheat and the Weeds, we know that this basic pattern of human society will always remain the same (*Matthew* 13:24-30).

When it comes to the question of sin, no one can presume to say, like the Pharisee in the Gospel: *"Oh God, I thank you that I am not like the rest of humanity"* (*Luke* 18:11). In truth we are all sinners. St. John observed that: *"If we say, 'we are without sin,' we deceive ourselves, and the truth is not in us"* (*1 John* 1:8). As human beings we share a common fallen nature, and if we have been kept from excessive sin it is not because of our personal abilities, but a pure gift of God's mercy. Those who have been preserved from sin are just as capable of falling as those who have already sinned. St. Paul warned us to be humble: *"Do not become haughty, but stand in awe"* (*Romans* 11:20). He told the Corinthians: *"Whoever thinks he is standing secure should take care not to fall"* (*Corinthians* 10:12).

Why God preserves one person from sin and allows another to fall into sin is not ours to know. Certainly, God can always keep a soul from falling into sin, but He will never force a person to accept the grace He offers. Perhaps God lets us fall so that we can learn to trust in His strength and not our own. We do not know why things happen the way they do in God's plan, but we must always trust that the Lord brings good out of evil whenever we sincerely ask Him to do so. God knows the needs of each soul as no one else can and deals with each according to its need; in love and wisdom He draws each soul in the way that will most surely lead to Himself. So it remains a profound mystery why God leads some by the way of grace or innocence, and others by the way of repentance, to ultimate salvation.

When we do sin we are brought to repentance in two ways: through a sense of guilt and through appropriate punishment.[1] What is guilt? Essentially, it is a sense of having done wrong, and it develops from the innate love of good which is permanently engraved in human nature by the natural law. Since we are made in the image and likeness of God, we can never feel at home with evil. Though all the philosophies of this world might reassure us that we have done no wrong when we sinned, this natural goodness of our own nature would react to condemn us. This is the essence of guilt. But let

us say a word here about the natural law, since it has to do with the question of guilt.

What is the *natural law?* Quite simply, we could say that it is human reason, which acts like a judge for our actions telling us whether they are good or bad, right or wrong, indicating what should be done and what should be avoided.[2] When reason acts as judge of our actions in this manner, it is called the voice of *conscience.*[3] If it approves our actions as good, it is called the "Testimony of Conscience"; if it disapproves them as evil, it is called "Remorse of Conscience."[4] This latter is a sense of guilt.

From this we can realize that the whole question of sin is the story of Eden repeated in every human life. Eve looked at the forbidden Tree, and saw that its fruit was *"good to eat, and fair to the eyes, and delightful to behold"* (*Genesis* 3:6). So she ate the fruit, hoping to find pleasure; instead she found the bitterness of death. St. Paul expressed the tragedy of that first disillusionment, and of all that have followed since, when he said: *"The wages of sin is death"* (*Romans* 6:23). That is the story of all sin. It appears to be desirable, but once committed, it brings only misery and regret.

So it happens that when we do evil, our consciences rebuke us. This reprimand is a sharp wound of nature, intended however, not to kill but to heal, to preserve our moral integrity, not to destroy it. No one can escape from this disapproving voice of conscience, since we cannot escape from ourselves. This sense of guilt is found only in humans; it is absent from the animal kingdom, and it is perhaps the most acute and inescapable type of punishment to come from sin. However, it is not the only type of punishment brought on by sin, for the Church teaches that all sin brings punishment which may be either temporal or eternal, depending upon the nature of the offense.[5]

Temporal punishment lasts only for a while—it will end either in this life or in Purgatory.[6] Eternal punishment lasts forever in Hell—it is reserved for those who die in the state of unrepented mortal sin.[7] But punishment must be suffered

for all sin, even after the sin has been forgiven. We see examples of this in Scripture itself; Adam, Moses, Aaron and David were forgiven their sins, but punished nevertheless.[8]

When a person becomes aware of a sense of guilt, he immediately seeks a remedy to relieve his inner misery; unfortunately he often seeks a wrong or inadequate one. He may, for example, turn to purely natural means to relieve this mental anguish, such as the remedies offered by natural science. This has a certain value since the mind, like the body, may at times need treatment by a competent physician. But if a person relies solely on natural remedies for the healing of his soul, he will ultimately be disappointed because no natural treatment can provide the relief needed.

When dealing with moral or spiritual ills, all natural remedies prove inadequate beyond a certain point. The soul of every individual is a closed kingdom, into which no other human can enter, unless freely invited by the individual himself. A physician or professional counsellor can only comfort or advise, according to the amount of knowledge they have of the patient's illness or moral need. This knowledge depends on the patient's willingness to reveal the true state of his soul, and even then there are depths to the human soul which no natural science can reach. No matter how perfect or comprehensive the treatment of moral ills by medical science can prove to be, no human remedy can remove the guilt of our sin.

In a desperate attempt to find relief from moral misery, people sometimes seek escape into the world of fantasy by means of drugs or alcohol, or they try to quiet the voice of conscience in an endless round of pleasure. Thus people spend lifetimes of trying to ignore or suppress an oppressive sense of guilt. The danger of this is self evident; the guilt smoulders like a volcano which can errupt at any moment to destroy all mental balance. In fact, when a person realizes the inadequacy of these dangerous remedies he often turns to suicide, seeking to end the misery in what he believes to be the oblivion of death.

This is especially tragic because God has given us a remedy for all our anguish. This wonderful medicine of the soul, which the Church calls The Sacrament of Reconciliation or Penance, will be the subject of our next chapter.

*Chapter 15*

# The Sacrament of Reconciliation: The Healing Balm of Sin

Having created human hearts, God alone knows their hidden depths. He alone can know the intensity of a heart's anguish and its basic need for healing when someone has sinned. Knowing this, He has supplied an authentic remedy which can give the healing and true peace for which a sinner longs. This remedy is the Sacrament of Reconciliation, formerly called the Sacrament of Penance, or more commonly the Sacrament of Confession.

It was of this Sacrament that the prophet Zachariah spoke, when he said: *"In that day* (the time of Christ), *there shall be a fountain open to the house of David* (the Church), *for the washing of the sinner."* (*Zacharias* 13:1). It is in this Sacrament, likewise, that the word of God spoken through the prophet Isaiah is most wonderfully fulfilled: *"If your sins be as scarlet, they shall be made as white as snow."* (*Isaiah* 1:18). The Sacrament of Reconciliation requires not that we run from God and hide our guilt as Cain did, but rather, that, like the Prodigal Son, we return to Him and acknowledge our sins with sorrow. This is sufficient to merit the Divine forgiveness and the complete removal of the guilt of our sins.

The Church defines the Sacrament of Reconciliation as a sacrament in which the sins committed after Baptism are forgiven.[1] There are four parts to this sacrament, namely *contrition* or sorrow for sin; *confession* of sins; *satisfaction,* or atonement for sin; and *absolution* from sin.[2] Let's look at each of these four elements.

The Church defines *contrition* as a hatred for sin and a true grief of soul for having offended God, with a firm purpose to sin no more.[3] Contrition is the most important part of the Sacrament of Reconciliation because without sorrow God will never forgive sin.[4] True contrition includes not only sorrow for the past, but a firm resolution not to sin again. There are two kinds of contrition—perfect and imperfect. *Perfect Contrition* is sorrow for sin arising purely from the love of God.[5] *Imperfect Contrition* is sorrow for sin arising from any less perfect supernatural motive, such as the fear of God's punishment, or the hope of reward.[6] We see from this, that perfect and imperfect contrition are different in their motives, and so will be different in their effects.[7] The motive for perfect contrition is Love: we think only of God, so it is, therefore, unselfish. The various motives for imperfect contrition are gratitude to God, hope of eternal reward, or fear of God's punishment; it is, therefore, partly a self-centered sorrow.[8]

Perfect contrition will take away all sin, even without Confession, if it is not possible to go to confession, but nevertheless one is bound to tell all one's mortal sins in the next confession.[9] Imperfect contrition will take away sin only with the Sacrament of Reconciliation.[10]

Contrition, whether perfect or imperfect, should be sincere and from the heart; it should come from a supernatural motive, not from any natural consideration, such as loss of health or reputation. Such natural sorrow would not help to obtain forgiveness of sin.[11] We should be sorry for all of our mortal sins, and regard sin as the greatest of all misfortunes. True sorrow for sin should be accompanied by a sincere purpose of amendment, which should lead us to take practical steps with the help of God's grace to avoid all mortal sin, and every occasion of sin.

Confession is the second part of the Sacrament of Reconciliation. The Church defines *confession* as the telling of one's sins to a duly authorized priest for the purpose of obtaining forgiveness.[12] A priest is authorized if he has the permission from the Bishop.[13]

The Church formally teaches that the Sacrament of Reconciliation was instituted by Our Lord Himself (*Cf. Matthew* 16:18-19; *John* 20:21-23). It was Jesus who made this sacrament an obligation for all.[14] The Church believes that the power to forgive or refuse forgiveness of sin would be useless, if we could appeal directly to God for the forgiveness of sin without the Sacrament of Reconciliation.[15] Regarding the actual confession of sins, so much must be said that it seems best to deal with this personal aspect of the sacrament in a separate chapter.

After hearing the confession of sins, the priest imposes a penance, so that the penitent may atone for his sins. This part of the sacrament is called *satisfaction*. We may wonder why is atonement necessary at all? In the chapter on Guilt and Punishment, we mentioned that the Church teaches that every sin brings its own bitter reward, namely guilt and punishment. The punishment which grave sin merits is called eternal punishment; it means being condemned to Hell for eternity if the person dies in unrepented mortal sin. Lesser offenses merit temporal punishment which must be suffered either in this life or in the next in Purgatory. The obvious question is: is there any way in which this punishment could be forgiven or cancelled so that a person would not have to suffer for his sins? The answer is "Yes."

The Sacrament of Reconciliation takes away eternal punishment due to sin when it takes away the guilt of sin, otherwise it would be impossible to be justified or reinstated as children of God.[16] But it does not always take away the temporal punishment which God requires as atonement for sin.[17] He requires this temporal punishment not because He is harsh or merciless, but rather because He is kind. This punishment is God's way of teaching us the great evil of sin, not only as an offense against His Divine Majesty, but also as a great

injury to ourselves, and thereby preventing us from falling into sin again.

However, the Church says that there are various ways in which we may pay our debt of atonement to God and be free from the obligation of enduring temporal punishment due to our sins.[18] There are so many different ways in fact, that we will address them in a separate chapter dealing with atonement for sin. Suffice it to say here, that the penance given by the priest in the Sacrament of Reconciliation is one of the easiest and yet most important ways of making satisfaction for our sins. It is an important and integral part of the sacrament, and it is wrong to willfully omit it.[19] It usually consists of some prayers to be said or some good work to be done. It is good to remember, however, that once the priest has pronounced the words of absolution, our sins are forgiven, even before we have performed the penance.[20] If we neglect to perform our penance, our confession still remains good, but we must confess our willfull neglect in our next confession.

Having imposed a penance, the priest then gives absolution by the power which he has received from the Church. This power comes directly from Christ, who instituted the Sacrament of Reconciliation on the evening of His Resurrection. The Church believes and teaches that Jesus instituted this most valuable Sacrament, when He came to His Apostles in the Upper Room and said to them: *"As the Father has sent Me, so I send you."* and *"when He had said this, He breathed on them and said to them, Receive the Holy Spirit Whose sins you forgive are forgiven them, and those sins you shall retain are retained"* (*John* 20:21-23). With the granting of absolution, the Sacrament of Reconciliation is complete.

We know, therefore, that Jesus instituted the Sacrament of Reconciliation, but it is the Church who regulates how often individuals are to confess their sins. The Church teaches that each individual member of the Church should confess his or her sins at least once a year.[21] This means that they are bound under pain of mortal sin to go to Confession at least once a year to fulfill the will of Christ.[22] That, however, is only the minimum; for those who desire to lead a good Christian

life, weekly Confession, or at least monthly Confession is very beneficial and to be highly commended.

Children should go to Confession as soon as they reach the age of reason, which is generally supposed to be about the age of seven years,[23] for then they are capable of committing sin.

Now that we have investigated the basic doctrinal aspects of the Sacrament of Reconciliation; in the following chapters we can consider the more personal aspects of Confession, to discover how marvelously effective is this divine remedy designed by God Himself to be the true healing balm of sin.

## *Chapter 16*

# Preparing For Confession

In any consideration of the Sacrament of Reconciliation or Confession, the first question we must consider is whether the confession of sins is really necessary or beneficial. Because of all we hear today, we might be inclined to think that it is not; yet the Church with the wisdom of the ages, and guided by the grace of the Holy Spirit, declares unconditionally that it is valuable for both young and old alike. Sin is the root cause of an individual's estrangement from God, and it leaves the soul in need of healing. Since each individual shares in the fallen nature of Adam, each enters the world with the guilt of Original Sin upon his soul. It is not a question of entering the world in innocence and later making the acquaintance of sin; rather, it is the other way around. We enter the world tainted by sin; then by Baptism the guilt of Original Sin is removed, but the weakness of sin, that is, of our fallen nature, remains with us. This means that we are all liable to sin, no matter what age we are.

Confession is very necessary, therefore, for any individual, but especially for young people who experience many influences working to draw them away from virtue. A good home environment, adequate religious instruction or good moral training can prove important factors in combating these influences. But they cannot guarantee immunity from sin,

since the inclination to evil is rooted in fallen nature itself. Besides, if a child or young person has no moral protection, they are all the more liable to failure. It is a mistake to think that they can take care of themselves entirely. They can instinctively discern between good and evil, in a broad sense, but they lack the wisdom which comes from experience to make the finer distinctions between right and wrong. Since they have limited life experiences, they have no authentic sense of direction, and depend on others to lead the way. If they lack proper guidance, they may easily take the wrong road. If they are led to evil they will probably do evil, but if they are led to good they will probably do good.

In today's society, many young people sin through ignorance or due to lack of proper instruction. Surrounded by influences which are designed to undermine virtue, they become confused and find it difficult to distinguish between what is false and what is true, with the result that they give away the precious gift of virtue before they are old enough to realize its incredible value, and at an early age find their lives a moral ruin. This is a tragedy, yet the picture is not one of total darkness. Part of the beauty of childhood lies in the fact that it is pliable and easy to bend. Once a child or young person discovers their mistake, they can more easily adjust and reform their lives. Their sense of remorse may be more intense than that of an adult, and this in turn makes them all the more eager to accept the challenge of virtue and remold a misguided youth into a life of virtue.

Adult confession is no less important. Sooner or later the burdened conscience comes to realize that no professional treatment or counseling, however efficient or praiseworthy, can ever give the healing or sense of security for which it longs. The soul seeks restored peace through the healing of Confession.

Now we come to the question of how to go to confession. To receive the Sacrament of Reconciliation worthily we must do these five important things: make a careful examination of conscience, confess one's sins to a priest, make a sincere act of contrition (sorrow for sin), make a firm resolution not

to sin again, accept the penance which the priest imposes; and ask for absolution. We shall consider each of these headings in greater detail, beginning in this chapter with the examination of conscience.

What is an examination of conscience? This is a sincere effort to call to mind all of the sins we have committed since our last confession. Before we begin we should pray for the grace to know our sins and be sorry for them. Next we should think about God's Commandments, the teachings of the Church, the seven Capital Sins, and the duties of our state in life. As we consider each of these areas we should look at the ways in which we have failed to live up to the kind of life they describe. It is good to remember that we sin against God by every sin we commit.[1] We sin against our own dignity by failing to take proper care of our soul or body,[2] and by failing to control our passions.[3] We sin against the love of neighbor by fault finding, unkindness, rudeness and being hard-hearted. Refusal to forgive and neglecting to help the needy also fall into this category.[4]

Since all sins against the Ten Commandments are sins against love of God, self, or others,[5] here are some examples of sins that fall under each of the commandments. They may be helpful in the examination of conscience.

Sins against the First Commandment include: atheism; a lack of faith in God; a lack of hope; putting other things, such as money, ahead of God in importance; not receiving the sacraments; being superstitious; using charms, crystals, spells, or practicing idolatry; believing fortune-tellers, dreams or horoscopes; having confidence in our own abilities over the abilities of God; ridiculing religious practices or beliefs; committing sacrilege by giving someone else the honor God deserves; practicing simony, which is the buying or selling of spiritual things; and not trusting in God's mercy.

Things considered sins against the Second Commandment include: using the Lord's name with disrespect; blasphemy, to ridicule God or abuse holy things; false oaths, perjury or taking unnecessary oaths; to curse; or to break a vow. The

Third Commandment involves: failure to attend Mass on Sundays or Holy Days without a valid reason; being late or disrespectful in Mass; not allowing proper time to rest or give God reverence; engaging in unnecessary work on Sundays or Holy Days; or forcing someone else to work on these special days.

In regard to the Fourth Commandment, it is sinful for children: to show disrespect, disobedience or anger toward parents; to be ungrateful; to refuse to help the family as needed; to do things secretly that they know the parents would forbid; and to refuse to care for elderly parents or family members in need, if they are able to provide for them. For parents, it is sinful under this commandment: to neglect to provide proper food, clothing and necessities for children; to be over indulgent toward the children; to be abusively strict with the children; to neglect religious training or other education; to set a bad example; to knowingly allow mental, physical, moral or emotional harm to come to a child; or to abort a child. This commandment also regulates general family matters, such as, the way spouses should treat each other. Spouses should not: be thoughtless or inconsiderate toward each other, they should not be unfaithful to each other; deceive each other; be abusive, violent, or domineering toward each other; or neglect to support each other or the home.

To sin against the Fifth Commandment includes: murder; abortion; euthanasia; suicide or assisting in a suicide; injuring or endangering your own life or that of others; anger, hate, and envy; degrading human life; or prompting others to sin through scandal. The Sixth and Ninth Commandments collectively consider sinful: a lack of chastity according to one's state in life; masturbation; fornication; pornography; homosexual practices; divorce; adultery; polygamy; living together out of marriage; dressing or behaving immodestly; willingly reading about, watching or talking about immodest things; contraception; direct sterilization; or working against the sanctity of human life and marriage.

Finally, we sin against the Seventh and Tenth Command-

ments when we: steal; rob; cheat; defraud others; enslave others; squander our resources; refuse to give alms; refuse to pay our debts; pay unjust wages or demand unjust prices; accept payment for wasted time or poor work; or cause another to lose work. We sin against the Eighth Commandment: by lying; by being a hypocrite; through rash judgment; revealing the hidden faults of others, which is detraction; by making unfavorable and false comments about someone to ruin their reputation, which is calumny; to pry into someone's secrets; to gossip; or to eavesdrop.

It is also helpful when making an examination of conscience to consider the seven Capital Sins. These sins are: *pride,* which displays inflated feelings of self worth; *avarice,* also called "covetousness," it is an exaggerated desire for material things; *envy,* resentment because of another's possessions or abilities; *wrath,* uncontrolled or unjustified anger; *lust,* uncontrolled passions; *gluttony,* excessive eating or drinking; *sloth,* laziness or neglect of natural talents and abilities.

Another guideline for reflection includes the sins against the Holy Spirit: presumption of God's mercy; despair of His grace; speaking against known Christian truths, and so injuring the Faith; envy of another's spiritual good; and final impenitence.

By considering all of these items we can discover the areas in which we need prayer to eliminate sinful behaviors. We should take time in our examination of conscience to remember sins we have committed since our last Confession. If a person does not understand why a certain behavior offends God, or does not feel regret for their actions, it is a good practice to pray for the grace to be truly penitent. We should make a sincere act of contrition and receive the Sacrament of Confession. This sacrament gives us the graces needed to combat our sinful natures.

*Chapter 17*

# The Confession of Sins

In regard to the confession of sins, it is noteworthy that neither God nor the Church who interprets the Gospel, requires public confession of sins. In fact, the Church safeguards the privacy of the individual's conscience in every possible way, and forbids any superior in authority, in the religious life for instance, to require an exposure of conscience from a person.

The absolute silence, which the Church requires from the priest in regard to all sins confessed, gives the penitent a sense of complete security. A person can speak in Confession about matters of conscience which they would never mention to their dearest earthly friend. This absolute secrecy is called by the Church the *seal of confession*. This guarantee of secrecy is necessary; every individual has a basic need to unburden himself in this searching and personal manner. God created the human heart in such a way that it cannot bear an excess of joy or pain alone: it must share with others, or else it breaks beneath the burden of pent-up feelings. Confession gives us the opportunity we need to share our anxiety or internal distress with someone who has been empowered by God to really help, by forgiving the guilt of sin.

Although assured of security in the confession of our sins, for some the idea of making one's sins known to another,

be he priest or layman, is extremely embarrassing, and a great price to pay for peace of heart. There is an inevitable sense of embarrassment which accompanies the confession of our sins. It would be strange if this were not so, but to think it is too great a price to pay for peace of heart is a mistake, for anything that is truly valuable costs dearly.

We should not be discouraged or embarrassed in telling our sins as they really are, for the priest has been trained to cope with every problem that can trouble the human mind. If we have difficulty explaining ourselves, we should make this known to the priest who will be only too glad to help us. We should confess our sins truthfully, accusing no one but ourselves. It is good to remember, that we go to confession to confess our sins, not our virtues, for in doing the latter, we would simply be like the Pharisee in the Gospel who went into the Temple not to praise God but himself; he acquitted himself very well, but he gained neither mercy not forgiveness.

We do not accomplish anything by masking our true selves in Confession. We neither deceive nor impress the priest by a recital of our virtues. It is encouraging to know, however, that while absolute truthfulness and sincerity are required on the part of the penitent, the Church treats him with the greatest dignity and respect. The priest asks no questions, except those which are necessary to make the confession clearer, or to enable him to know what counsel to give the penitent.

It is evident from this, that it would be a terrible mistake to conceal or minimize a mortal sin in Confession, but in so doing, we would not only make a sacriligous confession, but likewise deprive ourselves of the peace and consolation that the sacrament is designed to give.

Now we come to the actual confession of sins. What exactly are we bound to confess? We are bound to confess all our mortal sins, if we have committed any. If we have no mortal sins to confess, we must confess and be sorry for at least one venial sin, in order to receive Absolution.[1] Except in the

case just cited, we are not bound to confess venial sins in Confession, because they do not destroy sanctifying grace in the soul, and they can be forgiven through good works and prayer.[2] When it is a question of mortal sin, however, we must confess all our mortal sins of thought, word, deed, and omission, and any circumstance that would change the nature of the sin; together with the number of times each sin was committed.[3]

We must tell our sins honestly and exactly, neither exaggerating nor excusing them, with a sense of our own unworthiness, and sincere sorrow for having offended God. If we cannot remember the exact number of our sins, we should tell the number as nearly as possible, or how long we have been in the habit of committing the sin in question. If through no fault of our own we forget a mortal sin, our confession is good, and the sin is forgiven; but we must confess it in Confession if it again comes to mind.

The Church says that it is a terrible offense to willfully conceal a mortal sin in Confession, because by doing so we tell a lie to the Holy Spirit, and make our confession worthless. If we have concealed a mortal sin in Confession, however, we must not only confess it when we approach the Sacrament of Reconciliation again, but we must also confess all the mortal sins we have committed since our last good (worthy) confession.

We have finally come to the actual confession itself, so let us consider the practical details of Confession here, that is, what we do when we go to Confession.

Immediately before entering the confessional, it is good practice to say the *Confiteor,* that is, a general confession of sins made to God, and to the whole court of Heaven, both angels and saints. It begins with the words: *I confess to Almighty God*... and will be given in a later chapter.

In regard to the procedure which is usually followed when we enter the confessional, it will be necessary to give the two different methods now in use since Vatican Council II, namely the older or pre-vatican II method, and the new post-conciliar method. Let us begin with the older form, for both

are equally valid even today.

Upon entering the confessional, it is customary to kneel, make the Sign of the Cross and say: "Bless me, Father, for I have sinned." You may add: "I confess to Almighty God, and to you Father, that I have sinned."

Next say: "It is a week, a month, or whatever length of time it has been, since my last confession." "I said my penance and went to Holy Communion," if you did so. If Absolution was refused in one's last confession, this must be made known.

Then you proceed to tell your sins, carefully, distinctly, and truthfully.

After having confessed your sins, you conclude by saying: "I am sorry for these and for all the sins of my past life, especially (here you may mention one or more sins of your past life for which you are particularly sorry)." Then you say: "I ask pardon of God, and absolution of you, Father."

Having finished the confession of your sins, you should listen to the advice which the priest gives you, and to the penance he imposes, then you say your act of contrition, after which he gives you absolution. We have already mentioned, that the penance which the priest gives in Confession is a very important part of the Sacrament, and should not be omitted. It is given to enable us to satisfy or atone to God for the temporal punishment due to our sins.[4]

If the priest mentions any special time in which to perform our penance we should be careful to carry this out. If he does not mention any special time, we can say it at any time, but it is best to say it before leaving the Church. It should be said carefully and devoutly, but we should not keep repeating it, for fear that it was not properly said. It is the first time that counts for the sacramental penance. The saying of our act of contrition before the priest is also very important, because it is by this that he knows we are sorry for our sins, and therefore worthy of absolution.

After having listened to our act of contrition, the priest pronounces the words of absolution. The word "absolution" means to forgive or pardon, and comes from the words

spoken by the priest— "I absolve you. . ." Absolution is not a mere declaration that our sins are forgiven, but an actual forgiving of our sins.[5] We have already said that only God can forgive sins, but He has granted this power to the Church, to be exercised in His name, and she in turn has invested the priest with this power.[6]

One would have to reflect for a long time, to understand what the forgiveness of sins really means. It means that the guilt of sin is actually removed from the soul of the penitent, in the same way that a person might have a burden removed from their shoulder, or wash away a dark ink stain from a snow white table cloth. The burden or the stain of guilt is no longer there. The Scriptures explain this cleansing of guilt as the *"washing of one's robes white, in the Blood of the Lamb"* (*Revelations* 7:14).

In the absolution given by the priest in Confession, *"the power of the keys"* (*Cf. Matthew* 16:18-19), is most marvelously felt, and this is what constitutes the great difference between the Sacrament of Reconciliation, and any mere natural remedy for alleviating moral misery. For this wonderful Sacrament heals the wounds of sin and guilt, and brings deep and abiding peace to the burdened soul. Here, God receives His prodigal child back into His friendship, gives him innocence once again and presents him with the kiss of divine forgiveness.

The true and abiding peace which a good Confession brings is a superabundant compensation for any difficulty a person may experience in revealing one's sins in Confession. For this Sacrament can rekindle the most degraded existence into a new and beautiful life. Many of the greatest saints of the Church were once great sinners who were transformed by the grace of God through the Sacrament of Confession.

With absolution by the priest, the Sacrament of Reconciliation is complete.

This formula or ceremonial for private Sacramental Confession is still the standard for the reception of the Sacrament. In response to changes in society, the Church at Vatican II instituted an alternative ceremony for Confession. In this case

the Sacrament of Penance is framed in a communal celebration where people prepare for the Sacrament as a group. A liturgy of the word is conducted with readings and a homily. The examination of conscience and request for forgiveness are done simultaneously by the group, but confession of sins and absolution are conducted individually. After this, an *Our Father* and act of thanksgiving are prayed by the community.

It should be noted that the Church specifically requests the use of personal, individual Confessions. The communal celebration of Reconciliation is reserved for those occasions where the number of penitents and lack of priests make individual confessions impractical.

The essential elements of the Sacrament of Reconciliation always remain the same.

Those who are not personally attracted to a communal celebration of the Sacrament, are always free to go to Confession privately at another time. Whichever method is employed, the effects are always the same. With the absolution of the priest, God receives His wayward child back again into the embrace of His divine love, and thus the soul finds peace.

# *Chapter 18*

# Atonement for Sin

We have mentioned that every sin incurs punishment, which may be eternal or temporal, according to the nature of the offense. The Sacrament of Reconciliation always removes the eternal punishment due to sin, but it does not always remove the temporal punishment, which must be endured either in this life or in Purgatory, unless we can find another way to pay out debt. The Church offers this through a variety of means. First among those means is the penance which the priest gives us in the Sacrament of Reconciliation, and of which we have already spoken.[1] Then there is prayer, the humble petition of a contrite heart asking a complete pardon for sin. An example of this is Jesus pardoning the Good Thief who prayed on the Cross. In addition to these, there is fasting, almsgiving and indulgences.[2] Sacred Scripture draws our attention to these excellent means of making atonement for sin when it says: *"Prayer and fasting are good, but better than either is almsgiving accompanied by righteousness. A little with righteousness is better than abundance with wickedness. It is better to give alms than to store up gold; for almsgiving saves one from death and expiates every sin"* (*Tobias* 12:8-9).

The Church requires that we fast and abstain on the days prescribed. The motive for fasting and abstinence is to curb

our desires and atone for our sins.[3] From apostolic times the practice of fasting has held an important place in the life of the Church. It usually included abstinence from meat. In recent times, however, especially since the Second Vatican Council, the laws of fasting and abstinence have been lessened due to changing lifestyles. Radical changes in the lives of the people of all nations, greatly alter their physical, psychological and emotional needs, and make them less capable of enduring the rigors of the traditional form of fasting.

Presently, the Church requires that members fast, which means eating less than you usually eat, and abstain, which means to avoid certain food, particularly meat in this situation. This is called for on only two days of the year: Ash Wednesday, the first day of Lent; and Good Friday, the day of Our Lord's crucifixion. The fasting rule applies to all Catholics ages 21 to 59 who are in good health. The law of abstaining from meat applies to any Catholic ages 14 to 59. It is generally held that Catholics abstain from meat on each Friday during the Lenten season.

The Church does not require strict fasting in the manner it had for previous generations. But fasting and abstinence are still encouraged for personal devotion. The Church especially recommends practices of self-denial during the season of Lent, a time of prayer, good works, and private devotions.[4]

In the category of praiseworthy good deeds and almsgiving (the gift of time) the Church includes the spiritual works of mercy and the corporal works of mercy. The spiritual works of mercy include: to admonish the sinner; to instruct the ignorant; to counsel the doubtful; to comfort the sorrowful; to bear wrongs patiently; to forgive injuries; to pray for the living and the dead.[5] The corporal works of mercy include: to feed the hungry; to give drink to the thirsty; to clothe the naked; to ransom the captive; to shelter the homeless; to visit the sick; to bury the dead.[6]

There is also value in patiently suffering the difficulties of life. This includes suffering all natural and spiritual afflictions, poverty, illness, and misfortune. It is accepting any difficulty permitted by God to refine the soul and cleanse it from sin.

Lastly there is the question of indulgences, a doctrine of the Catholic Faith which has been misunderstood, due in part to abuses which had arisen in regard to the gaining of indulgences, and partly to ignorance of what an indulgence really means. To remove all misunderstanding it might be good to begin by stating what an indulgence is not, rather than what it is. An indulgence is not a pardon for sins already committed, nor a license to commit future sin, for mortal sin must be forgiven, and a person must be in the state of grace, before he can even hope to gain an indulgence.[7]

The Church defines an indulgence as the remission, in whole or in part, of the temporal punishment due to sin.[8] Indulgences are concerned only with the "temporal" punishment due to sin, for the Sacrament of Reconciliation always takes away the "eternal" punishment due to sin; in some cases where Confession is not possible, an act of perfect contrition will take eternal punishment away. This is true, for example, of those outside the Catholic Faith, who do not have the benefit of the Sacrament of Reconciliation.

The word *indulgence* means a releasing of the temporal punishment due to sin.[9] It is not a right, but a favor or an act of mercy which the Church grants to the Faithful in virtue of the power which she has received from Christ.[10] The Church received this power when Jesus said to His Apostles: *"Whatever you loose on earth shall be loosed in heaven"* (*Matthew* 16:19). With these words, spoken specifically to Peter, but intended also for the Twelve, He gave the Apostles power to loose, that is, to release individuals from the guilt of sin and the punishment due to sin. The Church exercises this power when she grants an indulgence.[11] Those who are unwilling to acknowledge the power of the Church to grant indulgences, might be helped by reflecting on its greater power to forgive sin and the resulting eternal punishment.

There are two kinds of indulgences, namely, plenary and partial. A plendary indulgence is the full remission of temporal punishment due to sin.[12] The word *plenary* means full or complete. To gain a plenary indulgence a person must be free from mortal sin, and fulfill all the conditions prescribed

by the Church for its reception.

The conditions for gaining a plenary indulgence usually are: confession, the reciting of the prayers prescribed, or the performance of the good works prescribed, if any.[13] Those who go to confession twice a month fulfill the conditions of Confession for all indulgences, except jubilee indulgences, or those granted as jubilee indulgences.[14] For the gaining of a jubilee indulgence, confession within eight days before or after the indulgence day is usually required.[15]

A partial indulgence is the remission in part of the temporal punishment due to sin. To gain a partial indulgence, a person must be free from mortal sin, and fulfill the conditions prescribed for gaining the indulgence, namely, the prayers and good works.[16]

The prayers prescribed for either a plenary or partial indulgence are usually for the intentions of Our Holy Father the Pope. These intentions are: for the exaltation of the Church, for the propagation of the Faith, for the destruction of heresy, for the conversion of sinners, for peace and concord among Christian nations. Usually, six "Our Fathers" and six "Hail Marys" are said for these intentions.[17]

In granting an indulgence, the Church does not attempt to cancel the temporal punishment due to sin, but rather applies to the soul of the individual the merits of Jesus and of the saints.[18]

The satisfaction or atonement offered by Jesus to the Father was infinite in value, and, therefore, infinitely more than sufficient to satisfy for all sin. Then there was Mary, His Virgin-Mother, who was sinless, and yet was the Queen of Martyrs. Many of the saints and martyrs also suffered more than was necessary to atone for their own sins. All of these superabundant merits are gathered together by the Church to form a spiritual treasury or what we might call her bank of merit,[19] from which she draws when she grants indulgences.

How did the Church begin this practice of granting indulgences? It is important to mention here that the Church did not "invent" indulgences, rather they grew and developed naturally with the unfolding of Church destiny. We can trace

their origin to the very early days of Church history, which we shall briefly outline here.

In early times, when a Bishop visited a Church and saw people doing canonical (public) penances for serious sins, he would occasionally release them from part of their penance if appropriate.[20] This was a "partial indulgence."

Likewise, martyrs who were going to suffer death, were allowed to send to the Bishop the names of penitents whom they wished to have released from canonical penance.[21] This is the authority which the Church exercises, though in a different manner, when granting indulgences.

The prayer which the Church offers continually for the Faithful, whether it be collective or individual, formal or informal, public or private, ascends before the throne of God like incense, and brings down the blessings of Divine mercy and forgiveness. This is always God's response to a sincere plea for complete forgiveness and an earnest effort to make adequate atonement for sin. This mystery of the Church's prayer of intercession and of the Divine response was shown to St. John in the revelations of Patmos which he described as follows: "*. . .and another angel came and stood before the altar, having a golden censer; and there was given to him much incense, that he should offer of the prayers of all the saints, upon the golden altar which is before the throne of God. And the smoke of the incense of prayers of the saints ascended up before God from the hand of the angel. And the angel took the censer and filled it with fire of the altar, and cast it on the earth* (*Revelations* 8:3-5).

We can see that God in His wisdom and goodness has placed the elements for the healing of sin, side by side with the very punishment which He has decreed as the effect of sin. It remains only for the individual soul to reach out and take advantage of these spiritual riches.

# PART V

## Re-Making Our Lives

*"Go, now and sin no more"*
(*John* 8:11).

## *Chapter 19*

# Beginning Again

When the penitent steps out of the confessional, joyful in the knowledge that his sins have been forgiven, his thoughts turn naturally to the future. What must be done to rebuild a shattered life? Certainly this person can never return to former behavior if he wishes to preserve this new-found peace, for true conversion of heart is shown in a sincere amendment of life. His first concern, therefore, is to part company with sin, as Jesus told the sinful woman when her accusers slipped away: *"Go now and sin no more"* (*John* 8:11).

St. Paul explained Jesus' meaning in greater detail in a letter to the Colossians, in which he said: *"I say this so that no one may deceive you by specious arguments. For even if I am absent in the flesh, yet I am with you in spirit, rejoicing as I observe your good order and the firmness of your faith in Christ. So, as you received Christ Jesus the Lord, walk in Him, rooted in Him and built upon Him and established in the faith as you were taught, abounding in thanksgiving. See to it that no one captivate you with an empty, seductive philosophy according to human tradition, according to the elemental powers of the world and not according to Christ"* (*Colossians* 2:4-9).

*"If then you were raised with Christ, seek what is above,*

*where Christ is seated at the right hand of God. Think of what is above, not of what is on earth. For you have died, and your life is hidden with Christ in God. When Christ shall appear, who is your life, then you too will appear with Him in glory.*

*"Put to death, then, the parts of you that are earthly: immorality, impurity, passion, evil desire, and the greed that is idolatry. Because of these the wrath of God is coming* [upon the disobedient]. *By these you too once conducted yourselves, when you lived in that way. But now you must put them all away: anger, fury, malice, slander, and obscene language out of your mouths. Stop lying to one another, since you have taken off the old self with its practices and have put on the new self, which is being renewed, for knowledge, in the image of its creator. Here there is not Greek and Jew, circumcision and uncircumcision, barbarian, Scythian, slave, free; but Christ is all and in all.*

*"Put on then, as God's chosen ones, holy and beloved, heartfelt compassion, kindness, humility, gentleness, and patience, bearing with one another and forgiving one another, if one has a grievance against another; as the Lord has forgiven you, so must you also do. And over all these put on love, that is, the bond of perfection. And let the peace of Christ control your hearts, the peace into which you were also called in one body. And be thankful. Let the word of Christ dwell in you richly, as in all wisdom you teach and admonish one another, singing psalms, hymns, and spiritual songs with gratitude in your hearts to God. And whatever you do, in word or in deed, do everything in the name of the Lord Jesus, giving thanks to God the Father through Him"* (*Colossians* 3:1-17).

This as we see is a very comprehensive program of amendment, covering the entire Decalogue. It involves the resolute walking away from sin and a turning to God. Once that first resolution to reject sin has been made, the next step naturally follows, namely the clasping of God's hand in prayer, and setting out on the path of virtue which will lead us in the end to a truly holy life.

In order to effectively turn away from sin, we must resolve to avoid occasions of sin. Among these temptations the Church lists: bad companions, bad books, curiosity, idleness, and the neglect of prayer.[1]

In regard to the choice of companions, great prudence is necessary because our friends can quickly lead us to good or to evil, depending on the kind of companions they are. In choosing friends we should remove false ideas about what true friendship means. Jesus Himself said that we should be wise as serpents but simple as doves (*Matthew* 10:16). We are often attracted by the simplicity of the dove, forgetting that the wisdom of the serpent is also necessary to guard virtue. This is especially true in the choice of our companions.

It is essential to our own spiritual and material well-being, to choose friends who live good moral lives. There are certain definite signs by which true friendship can be recognized. A friendship that is genuine will always include respect. If this respect is not present, then there is something very wrong with that friendship; in fact it is no friendship at all but disguised malice. Once we are sure of this, the only way to handle such an evil is a complete severing of the friendship. We should not be deceived into thinking that such a decision offends against the love of neighbor; nothing could be farther from the truth. Such false reasoning, or delay in acting promptly, may end in spiritual or moral ruin for ourselves.

If we doubt this, we should remember that Jesus warned about the danger of bad companions. He said: *''Do not fear those who kill the body, and are not able to kill the soul; rather fear the one who can destroy both soul and body in Hell. Yes, I say to you: fear him''* (*Matthew* 10:28; *Luke* 12:5).

*''If your right eye causes you to sin, tear it out and throw it away. It is better for you to lose one of your members than to have your whole body thrown into Hell''* (*Matthew* 5:29). His words should not be taken literally. Instead, we should take this as an example of how important it is to sever any

friendship, no matter how close we are, if this friendship proves to be an occasion of sin. Friends have a mutual obligation to show respect and reverence for each other. They are gifts from God and should help bring us to Heaven and not take us in another direction. If we reject a bad friendship out of loyalty to God, He will send us positive companions.

Everyone has experienced an occasion where they have been part of a group that was not a positive influence. Everything from gossip to illicit behavior is harder to resist when under peer pressure. But the Lord provides us with an instinctive knowledge of right and wrong, an ability to recognize dangerous situations. This instinct is similar to an animal's ability to sense danger. It operates separately from any reasoning process and is often more effective since reason can be deceived by false information and misguided thinking. If a person is in a group and senses danger, it would be wise to leave the situation. If this is not possible, we should keep a clear mind, a resolute will, and should refuse to be coerced into doing anything against our will. Since God can bring good from all situations, it is possible that the strength the Lord gives us in such situations may protect our companions' virtue as well as our own.

Like all gifts from the Lord, we are free to reject this sense of danger. But if we are wise we will cultivate these instincts by safeguarding the gift of purity. The virtue of modesty is the natural guardian of purity; this virtue is an innate protector of all things regarding the body.[2] A person remains modest by refusing to dress, act, or even speak in a manner that might lead themselves or someone else to sinful thoughts or actions. Refusing to become a source of temptation shows respect for everyone's dignity and protects the gift of purity.

Human experience has proven time and again that tragic consequences can come from association with bad companions. We have only to think of St. Augustine's cry of deep remorse for his wasted years to be convinced of this: "too late have I known Thee, too late have I loved Thee, oh Beauty ever ancient and ever new!" He is only one of a countless multitude who have had a like experience.

Another, who lived a little nearer to our own times, though who perhaps is less well known than Augustine, is St. Peter Canisius, S.J. (1521-1597), who was canonized in 1925. Born of devout Catholic parents, Peter knew the security of a wealthy middle-class home, yet, as an old man looking back at years of a marvelous life in the service of the Church, he confessed to the moral carelessness of his childhood and early youth. He told of these squandered years, sincerely blaming himself, yet also clearly acknowledging that neglect of vigilance on the part of his otherwise dutiful parents, was in no small part responsible for his lack of cooperation with grace.

His bitter words of remorse could have been written by many young people of today. These words are a warning and a deep consolation because Peter perceived the error of his ways while still young and immediately resolved to make amends for the mistakes of his youth by a life of true Christian virtue. Through faithfulness to grace, he became not only a great defender of the Faith and light of the Church, but a great saint as well.

Peter's example of walking away from the path of moral danger may be an incentive for many modern young people to do the same. Here is the main part of his confession. He said:

> "What shall I say about these first years of my wretched, senseless boyhood which I spent foolishly and without purpose, more asleep than awake? In truth, many were the things, shameful for a Christian child, which in those days I thought, planned, and performed. Very often I deserved not only reproof but severe chastisement. Boyhood has its own graces, modesty, candor and innocence, but they were not mine to boast of; and it has also its special faults, with which oh Lord, I even then began to stain my nuptial robe, which Thou gavest me.
>
> "Woe is me, how many profitless hours, days, nights, weeks, months and years I have squandered!

> How empty, indigent and stupid I have been, living without Thy fear or Thy love, as though I knew Thee not at all, the Giver, the Guide, and the Preserver of my being. . .I grew [angry] with the counsels of wisdom, and gave my temper rein. I loved to annoy, and was full of envy and pride. There was spite in my heart too, and as far as I could at that tender age I carried out schemes of revenge. How often did I not then despise and offend my parents, my nurses, my playmates, and any who dared admonish me! Only tardily and reluctantly would I do what was required of me, led away as I was by vanity, and I know not what foolish whims.
>
> "But now I implore Thy grace, Lord Jesus, who when Thou wert a boy didst grow more than all other boys in wisdom and grace before God and men, a Child conceived and born and brought up without shadow of sin, in whom all other children are blessed. O Lord, who art glad when children come to Thee with their sins, remember not the transgressions of my youth and ignorance. Let Thy mercies speedily prevent me, wretched, miserable, ignorant, frail, empty, stupid man that I have ever been. . . What else can I offer Thee for those first slippery years with their countless falls, but that by which Thou art gladly appeased, the sacrifice of a contrite and humble heart?"

Continuing his account, he related how on one occasion while praying before the Blessed Sacrament, by an intuition of grace, he suddenly understood the lying vanities of the world and the grave perils which surround us on every side, and he resolved to live a more virtuous life in the future. As a matter of fact, he did so for a long time, but gradually began to slip back into his careless ways as the memory of that former grace began to fade from his mind. In his confession, he told the story of his relapse as follows.

"Alas, if only my heart and all the ways of my young life had stood fast in that boyhood simplicity! But with increasing years my wickedness grew. A greater inclination to sin possessed me, and corruption of various kinds infected my heart. I used to sin, and it was accounted no sin but sometimes a thing to be proud of, that wrecking my youthful innocence I became more and more arrogant, thinking myself a knowing fellow, and despising others in comparison. It used to be my desire to express my opinion on the weightiest matters, and I would hold forth as the saying is, like a blind man discoursing on colors. Nor would I give in easily if at any time advised or admonished, so swollen had I become, and so much did impudence, self-love, folly and obstinacy possess my soul. And what am I to say about my contentiousness, my fits of anger, my jealousies and secret hatreds? According to Thy mercy and not according to my perversity, remember Thou me, for Thy goodness' sake, oh Lord.

"When the time came for me to leave home for school, the change only made my disease worse, for there I fell in with companions who taught me the license of sin both by word and example. . .I do not accuse them oh Lord, in order to excuse or cover my own iniquity. They sinned, and I was party to their sins. They merited chastisement and so did I. It shames me now to confess what I was not then ashamed to do. I beg for mercy because I fear Thy judgment, knowing that the greater the sin, the greater the penalty, and that lesser sins too, will have their appointed retribution.

"Now, therefore, while there is yet time to be merciful, let Thy power conquer our weakness, Thy wisdom our ignorance, Thy goodness our iniquity, so that to none of us may be imputed the evil done secretly or openly against Thy law by me, on account of those comrades, or by them on account

of me. Help us oh God our Savior, and for the glory of Thy name oh Lord deliver us, and forgive us our sins...

"Open oh Lord, the eyes of blind and foolish parents and masters, that they may no longer lead blind and foolish children to perdition. Make them see the danger to themselves and to their charges, that lies in their most criminal carelessness. Cause them to realize how prone youth naturally is to rush headlong into all manner of evil, and how as a rule, it can hardly be turned to virtuous courses without strenuous effort. Let them reflect that the flower of virginity is the loveliest and most commendable of boyhood's graces, but that it is also the most fragile and perishable of flowers. Once it falls, it falls forever, and the earliest regret is too late, because it is irrecoverable.

"Oh, if only young people knew the good things they possess in their purity, with what care and diligence would they not hedge around and guard their golden treasure, what fierce battles would they not fight to defend it and what cautious watch would they not keep on their domestic foe, the flesh, to suppress its rebellions. Never would they permit modesty to suffer damage, or holy chastity to be violated by their own or another's action. Rather like alert and well armed soldiers, they would at once take the field against the enemy, burning with holy indignation, the moment he appeared with his allurements.

"As for me, though I cannot glory, I yet declare the grace Thou hast conferred on me in saving my body from fornication...For this I thank Thee the Author of all good, with my whole heart..."[3]

This admirable confession should be sufficient to convince even the most liberal of the danger of association with bad companions, and a compelling warning to avoid them.

## *Chapter 20*

# Further Reflections on Avoiding the Occasions of Sin

*"I said, I Will Watch My Ways"* (*Psalms* 39:2).

The Church places the reading of improper literature and all associated materials on the list of occasions of sin. This would include pornographic books, magazines or videos and books promoting ungodly philosophies. A person cannot be too careful about the things they read, because nothing can pollute the mind more quickly than immoral reading or viewing. Our mind, with its powers for comprehension, is what makes us like God. It was designed to glorify God, so any input that degrades our dignity as children of God or blasphemes against Our Lord Himself, deprives the mind of its natural function.

Reading is an important source of knowledge, and whether good or bad, once acquired, knowledge cannot be lost. We cannot get rid of harmful information, even if this is what we want. Our brains are so complex that even if we cannot immediately call a situation to mind, the information is still filed away waiting for the correct stimuli to trigger its memory. Information that is distressing or disturbing can surface when we least expect it and cause unfortunate consequences. This is why it is so important to guard our innocence and

keep a vigilant watch over everything that enters our minds. There is a multitude of enlightening, positive, and entertaining books, magazines, and videos to choose from, so there is no need to investigate degrading material.

It is curiosity which most often leads people to immoral materials and it is curiosity that is next on the list of occasions of sin. Curiosity is a subtle enemy which disguises itself as something necessary for enlightenment. It is good, however, to remember St. Paul's words: *"Everything is lawful for me, but not everything is beneficial"* (*Corinthians* 16:12).

Although knowledge is essential to survival in society, it is important to discern what is necessary and what is merely self-indulgent. The unrestrained indulgence of curiosity can be a foolish and dangerous waste of time if it leads to investigating immoral matters. But curiosity which is balanced with a wise pursuit of information for a moral good is worthwhile. Many great inventions have come about due to curiosity, but many lives were morally ruined due to a lack of control; as the saying goes, "curiosity killed the cat."

Fourth on the list of dangerous occasions, is idleness, a dangerous enemy of virtue, since it opens the door to many temptations. Our nature is constituted so that we cannot remain idle for long without tending towards good or evil, and unfortunately, when not sufficiently occupied, evil can often prove more attractive. An effective way to guard against idleness is to develop a habit of being regularly occupied with either work, study, or healthful recreation. Besides protecting virtue, this is also an effective means of developing talents, while at the same time safeguarding physical and mental health.

To avoid the dangers that might arise from idleness, we should keep a constant guard over our senses and imagination. Actions dangerous to chastity always involve the senses, since this is how all knowledge enters the mind. Sight and touch are particularly important. Failure to guard our eyes from anything that might arouse temptation can quickly lead to serious sin. Vigilance over our speech is also important. Suggestive or immoral conversation can greatly dim the

beauty of purity. We should not only refrain from unbecoming speech, but should likewise refuse to listen to such conversations on the part of others. Control of the sense of touch also requires great vigilance. In all our actions, whether alone or with others, we should be reserved, modest, reverent, and careful.

In order to keep control of our senses, it is also necessary to keep control over our imagination. Because of its nature and function, the imagination may prove difficult to control, especially at first. If the mind dwells on sinful things, it may help to cultivate the habit of interrupting sinful thoughts with thoughts of natural beauty, such as, sunsets, mountain ranges and other gifts from God. But even more effective would be training an imagination to abandon sinful thoughts and concentrate on the beautiful face of Jesus. In His presence, love of purity will naturally grow, while impurity in any form will lose its attraction and reveal itself as evil. This pattern will also strengthen our prayer life. **Prayer is the most effective defense against temptation;** neglect of prayer is one of the main causes of a sinful life.

As in the case of all virtues, the response to the Divine invitation to be pure of heart, will differ in the degree of its intensity according to each individual soul. We will recall the Parable of the Sower (*Matthew* 13), in which Jesus described the varying response to grace on the part of individual souls. Even when the seed fell on "good ground" there were different degrees in the yield of fruit, thirty, sixty or a hundred fold (*Matthew* 13:23).

For some, the response to the Divine invitation to observe purity of life, may consist in a sincere effort to avoid serious sin, for others it may consist in a life of average virtue, with a sincere respect for purity of heart, but in those who give a complete response to the call of Divine grace, the beauty of purity will radiate and add beauty to the Church. Wherever purity is found, it exudes an aura of holiness which cannot fail to win the admiration and respect of all who experience it.

It is purity of heart and life which wins enduring respect and affection because virtue is the loveliest adornment of any personality. The reward of purity was revealed by Jesus Himself in the Sermon on the Mount, where He said: *''Blessed are the clean of heart, for they shall see God''* (*Matthew* 5:8).

# *Chapter 21*

# Clasping God's Hand: Reflections on Prayer

When after years of restless wandering and searching, St. Augustine at last found God, he cried out in lament for his wasted life. In finding God he had found all, and his heart became anchored in the Lord's goodness and love.

This hunger for God was not, however, peculiar to St. Augustine alone; it is common to all mankind for it reveals the mysterious action of God, eternally drawing our hearts to Himself. The following passage, taken from the Liturgy of the Hours, eloquently describes this universal longing to encouter the Supreme Being, in whose likeness we are made. It says:

> "Insignificant man, escape from your everyday business for a short while, hide for a moment from your restless thoughts, break off from your cares and troubles, and be less concerned with your tasks and labors. Make a little time for God, and rest awhile in Him. Enter into your mind's inner chamber, shut out everything but God, and whatever helps you to seek Him. Speak now to God, and say with your whole heart: 'I seek Your face, Your face oh Lord, I desire.'

"Lord my God, teach my heart where and how to seek You, where and how to find You. Lord if You are not here, where shall I look for You in Your absence? Yet, if You are everywhere, why do I not see You when You are present? But surely You dwell in light inaccessible. And where is light inaccessible? How shall I approach light inaccessible? Or who will lead me and bring me into it that I may see You there? And then, by what signs and under what forms shall I seek You? I have never seen You, Lord my God: I do not know Your face.

"Lord, most High, what shall this exile do, so far from You? What shall Your servant do, tormented by love of You, and cast so far from Your face? He yearns to see You, and Your face is too far from him. He desires to approach You, and Your dwelling is unapproachable. He longs to find You, and does not know Your dwelling place. He strives to look for You, and does not know Your face.

"Lord, You are my God and You are my Lord, and I have never seen You. You have made me and remade me, and You have given me all good things I possess, and still I do not know You. I was made in order to see You, and I have not yet done that for which I was made.

"Lord, how long will it be? How long oh Lord will You forget us? How long will you turn Your face away from us? When will You look upon us and hear us? When will You enlighten our eyes, and show us Your face? When will You give Yourself back to us? Look upon us Lord, hear us and enlighten us, show us Your very self. Restore Yourself to us, that it may go well with us, whose life is so evil without You. Take pity on our efforts and our striving towards You, for we have no strength apart from You.

"Teach me to seek You, and when I seek You, show Yourself to me, for I cannot seek You unless

> You teach me, nor can I find You unless You show Yourself to me. Let me seek You in desiring You, and desire You in seeking You, find You in loving You, and love You in finding You.'"[1]

It is only by prayer that we can enter into personal contact with God. The Church defines prayer as the lifting up of the heart and mind to God, to adore Him, to thank Him for His benefits, to ask forgiveness for our sins, and to ask for every need of soul and body.[2] Personal prayer to God is an absolute requisite for every individual, and will admit no substitute, for no work, however praiseworthy, can ever take the place of this personal meeting with God. Being Lord of all, He has no need of our works, rather what He seeks is our love. It is only by personal prayer that we get to know God intimately as our Father, Friend and Benefactor, from Whom we receive every good that we possess.

**Prayer is necessary to salvation,** and without it, as a component of faith, no one can be saved.[3] Without prayer one's love for God would grow quickly cold, and virtue would lose its attraction. This in turn would lead to a life of indifference or possibly even of sin. Without this personal contact with God, we would no longer be vigilant, and would consequently be totally unaware of the dangers that surround us, and threaten to destroy virtue. Thus, we would become an easy prey to temptation and gradually drift away from God. In losing God, we would have lost everything, both virtue and happiness.

Since prayer is so important, it is very necessary to know when we should pray. Turning to the Commandments, we find that the First and Third Commandments regulate our duties in regard to prayer. By the First Commandment we are commanded to worship God; by the Third Commandment we are commanded to keep holy the Sabbath Day—Sunday—that it may be given especially to His divine service and adoration. Here we come to the question of religion.

Religion is the love and obedience which we give to God. Worship is religion put into practice; it is the submission,

love and respect which we offer to God. Adoration is the love of God put into practice. Good works also honor God, but not as directly as adoration.

Jesus said that we ought to pray always; this means that we should pray regularly and that we should cultivate a habit of prayer. We should pray more at certain set times, namely on Sundays and Holy Days of Obligation, every morning and every night, and in all dangers, temptations, and afflictions. It is also praiseworthy to pray before and after meals, as St. Paul counselled when he said: *"Whether you eat or drink, or whatever you do, do everything for the glory of God"* (*1 Corinthians* 10:31).

An important prayer that can be said daily upon awakening, is the Morning Offering, by which we offer ourselves and our whole day to God, so that our day may be sanctified, and all we do may be a prayer.

Next comes the question of where we should pray. Since prayer is lifting up the heart to God, it cannot be restricted to any set place or time, yet to ensure the continuous practice of formal prayer, both for the individual and for the community, the Church says that the best place for formal prayer, whether liturgical or communal, is the house of God.[4] It was God Himself Who ordained that He should be worshiped solemnly in His own Temple, the description of which He gave to Moses. The Church has followed that divine ordinance in appointing the house of God as the formal place of prayer.

Now we should consider how to prepare ourselves for prayer in order to approach God. Jesus had much to say on this matter, for it was on this point that He changed mankind's whole attitude towards God. According to His teaching, prayer was to be the loving conversation of a child with God, his much loved Father. Still, we can never treat God as an equal. Everything in our attitude should reflect the dignity, reverence, and modesty which is His due. Posture is especially important; kneeling, standing, or folding one's hands in prayer, honor God and help an individual's devotion.

Our prayer should be simple, without bragging or doing

anything calculated to bring attention to ourselves. In the Sermon on the Mount Jesus said: *"When you pray, do not be like the hypocrites, who love to stand and pray in the synagogues and on street corners so that others may see them. Amen, I say to you, they have received their reward. But when you pray, go to your inner room, close the door, and pray to your Father in secret. And your Father who sees you will repay you. In praying do not babble like the pagans, who think that they will be heard because of their many words. Do not be like them. Your Father knows what you need before you ask Him. This is how you are to pray:*

*Our Father in Heaven, hallowed be your name, your kingdom come, your will be done, on earth as in Heaven. Give us today our daily bread; and forgive us our debts, as we forgive our debtors; and do not subject us to the final test, but deliver us from the evil one"* (*Matthew* 6:5-13).

Simplicity and reverence were the keynotes of Jesus' teaching on prayer. There was to be nothing strained or unnatural about our communication with the Father. It is noteworthy that He who is Lord and Creator of the human heart and Who knows its hidden depths, never recommended any difficult or complex preparation for prayer. We look in vain for any involved formulas of preparation for prayer in His teaching. The man-made systems of prayer prescribe, for example, trying to make one's mind a complete blank; God never intended the mind to be in such a state. He created it to be filled with thought and imagery, so that everything in creation might reveal some aspect of His divine perfections to us. If therefore, Jesus never advised such extravagant methods of preparation for prayer, it seems wholly unnecessary, and indeed a waste of time, to seek out such methods, which have been devised by fallible and mortal men.

Distractions during prayer should be avoided as much as possible, though some will usually be there. It shows a lack of reverence to God. Summing up her teaching on prayer, the Church says that we should pray with attention and devotion, with fervor and perseverance, with a sincere desire to obtain what we ask of God, with a sense of our own helpless-

ness and dependence on Him, and with complete trust in His goodness.

Jesus stressed the great need of perseverance in prayer during the Sermon on the Mount, in which He said: *"Ask and it shall be given you, seek and you shall find, knock and it shall be opened to you"* (*Matthew* 7:7). Again He emphasized this teaching in the Parable of the Widow, who by her perseverance compelled the unjust judge to listen to her in the end, and to judge her case favorably, which at first he refused to do (*Luke* 18:1-8). The story of the woman of Canaan is also a graphic example of the wonderful effects of perseverance in prayer (*Matthew* 15). Though seemingly rejected by Jesus, Who in reality was only testing her faith, she persevered in her request, until Jesus Himself marveled at her faith and granted all she asked.

Faith is an essential element of prayer; Jesus explicitly said that the prayer of the faithful can move mountains (*Matthew* 17:19). No prayer is ever made in vain, though sometimes God may delay in answering it, because the person may not be worthy, or the request may really be harmful to one's true good. Nevertheless our prayer is always heard, either by the granting of the favor we have asked, or something more beneficial instead.

The Church says that we should not hesitate to ask for many things in prayer: for all our spiritual and temporal needs, for parents, relatives, friends and superiors, for benefactors, for the sick and for the dead. We should pray also for the holiness of the Church, for the intentions of the Pope, and for all who neglect to pray for themselves.

Let's consider prayer in itself. Prayer is divided into two basic categories, namely mental and vocal prayer. Mental prayer is that which is said in the silence of the heart; vocal prayer is that which is expressed audibly in words. All vocal prayer, however, must have a basic element of mental prayer, otherwise it would be a useless utterance.

There are many forms of vocal prayer, for instance the psalms, hymns, and Scripture readings of the Liturgy. Mental prayer, on the other hand, instead of a variety of forms has

a variety of degrees. We could think of these various degrees as a ladder of seven steps, leading the soul upward towards ultimate union with God, or as St. Teresa of Avila explained it, they are like seven mansions of the interior castle of the soul.

The most basic form of mental prayer is meditation. This consists of reflection on some truth of the Faith, some passage of the Scriptures, especially the Gospels, or some mystery of the Life of Jesus. This meditation is usually made in order to discover how the subject of our meditation might affect us personally, or what lesson it might teach us. This in turn should lead us to make good resolutions to grow in virtue.

The highest type of prayer is contemplation, but this form of prayer is more the result of God's immediate action upon the soul, than the efforts of the individual. We can prepare or open ourselves for this Divine action, but we can never merit it as a just reward for personal effort; it is a pure gift of God. Since contemplation involves the direct action of God upon the soul, it is difficult to explain. The most we can do is to make comparisons, but these, of their very nature, fall short of reality. At the risk of over simplification we could perhaps explain contemplation as differing from meditation, in the following way.

In meditation, the individual works diligently to achieve a desired goal, namely, a greater knowledge of God as revealed in His works. The labor involved in this type of prayer, largely our work and in a certain sense, the result of our labor, is equal to our efforts. It is something like the efforts of a person who tries to study the heavens with unaided vision. A person can learn a great deal from simple observation but there is also a great deal which can never be discovered in that way. Meditation is something like that.

With contemplation it is different; here God takes the initiative, and does the work Himself. We could explain His divine action in this way. Suppose the person who had studied the heavens with unaided vision suddenly found himself a guest in an observatory, examining the universe through a powerful telescope. Think what a difference it would make. There is

no comparison between the vast range of vision that would be opened up to him by means of the telescope, and the restricted view which he previously enjoyed. In a similar manner, under the influence of the Divine action, the soul finds new and undreamt of horizons, and perceives the works of God in an entirely new light. By contemplation the soul becomes united with God in a most marvelous manner, in the most perfect way possible in this life.

The object of all prayer is not only to give God the homage and adoration which is His due, but also to establish between God and mankind, a relationship of friendship that will reach its completion in Heaven. With this relationship of love firmly established, our hearts are set towards God, its true goal, and thus oriented towards Him. We set the course of our lives towards the goal of true happiness.

# *Chapter 22*

# Reflections on the Basic Christian Virtues

*"Be You Therefore Perfect"* (*Matthew* 5:48).

Once having parted company with sin, and having, through grace, clasped God's hand in prayer, the soul which had been a wilderness begins to blossom in spiritual beauty. This beauty reveals itself in a desire to avoid sin, in the practice of mental and vocal prayer and in the practice of the basic virtues of the Christian life. In fact, we can say that the practice of virtue is a basic necessity for anyone who aspires to lead a good Christian life. In this chapter we shall consider briefly some of the most fundamental virtues which are the basic foundation of a holy life. It might be helpful to consider the virtues which are opposed to the seven capital sins, since that would ensure a fairly comprehensive survey.

Beginning now with pride, we must first define it, in order to discover what virtues will help to heal it. The Church defines pride as a sinful exaggeration of self-respect.[1] It makes one presumptuous, ambitious, vain, boastful, insolent, ostentatious and hypocritical.[2] It is an interesting fact that no one feels drawn to a proud person. Pride repels rather than attracts, and it should find no place in the life of one who is striving for holiness.

The virtue which tempers pride is *humility,* an often misunderstood virtue, since many erroneously think that it requires denial that we possess any good, are capable of any achievement, or are worthy of any respect. This is a completely false and dangerous concept, for the virtue of humility is concerned with truth, and a sense of proportion. It consists in having a true knowledge of ourselves, neither exaggerating nor depreciating ourselves, but rather recognizing that all we have or are, is a gift of God. Humility requires that we recognize the good we possess, whether it be in the way of virtue, talent, or material possessions, acknowledging that we owe these gifts to God, the Giver of all good. Humility requires also, that we recognize that others are similarly blessed, and perhaps more so than we, though in a different manner. This clear perception of truth prevents us from becoming boastful or arrogant. It makes us rather unassuming in manner, and kind and courteous towards others, with a sincere sympathy for those who may be less fortunate than ourselves.

A commonly held misconception in regard to humility is that it destroys self-esteem, which is a good and beneficial instinct placed in our hearts by God Himself. Nothing could be farther from the truth, because humility, far from destroying self-esteem, regulates and guards it. Everyone should have a true knowledge and appreciation of their own intrinsic dignity and worth as a human person, and this dignity deserves to be recognized and respected by others. The awareness of this basic excellence in no way detracts from humility, rather it constitutes the very essence of self-respect which is a God given instinct in mankind. It is this consciousness of personal worth as an inalienable right to respect, that needs to be regulated and controlled, if one is to avoid the vice of pride. For if an individual becomes too demanding of his right to respect and esteem, he may take undue offense at the least transgression against his dignity on the part of others, or become arrogant and intolerant in his preoccupation with the idea of his own importance. Here is where humility acts as a guide.

On the one hand, humility keeps us from being proud,

haughty, boastful, arrogant or conceited; on the other hand it restrains us from self-depreciation, self-defamation, or lack of self respect in any form. The sense of balance and proportion which it fosters in the soul makes us realize what we are in the sight of God, and that is what really counts. When we come to think of it, it is not really necessary to advertise our virtue or lack of it to those with whom we live. If virtue is present, it is usually self-evident and needs no publicity. If it is absent, that, too, is painfully evident.

True humility produces many positive effects both in our souls and in our exterior actions. In our souls it causes: a reverent fear of God; acceptance of God's will; obedience to our superiors for the love of God, whether these superiors be parents, teachers, religious superiors, civil or ecclesiastical authorities; overlooking slights from our companions; willingness to lend a helping hand with the humbler kinds of work when this is necessary; a sincere conviction of our own unworthiness in the sight of God.[3]

To sum up, we could say that a humble person is one to whom we would like to talk when we are troubled or sorrowful. Such a person is noble-minded without pretense. Jesus is the perfect example of a humble person. Who was more humble than Jesus, yet who was more majestic than He? And it was He who said to us: *"Learn of Me, because I am meek and humble of heart"* (*Matthew* 11:29).

The second capital sin is covetousness, a sinful exaggeration of providing for the future.[4] It causes hardness of heart, injustice, faithlessness, fraud, and deceit. The virtue which overcomes covetousness is *generosity* in giving.[5]

While covetousness is sinful, the virtues which counterbalance it do not exclude the right and duty of a person to provide prudently and adequately for his own present and future needs. Jesus proclaimed and upheld this right throughout the Gospel, especially in the Parable of the Talents (*Matthew* 25). The virtues which overcome covetousness, however, prevent people from becoming slaves of wealth, and makes them conscious of their obligations of justice and charity to others. It enables them to be honest in their business

dealings, and faithful in the payment of debts.

The third capital sin is that of lust, the sinful exaggeration and abuse of true love.[6] It is the cause of all sins against purity and innocence.[7] The virtues which are opposed to lust are *chastity* and *purity* in their many forms, as well as self denial of which we shall speak in a separate chapter.

The fourth capital sin is anger, which is a sinful exaggeration of justice to ourselves or others.[8] It causes quarrels, strife, insult, injustice, and violence.[9] The virtue which overcomes anger is *meekness,* that is, slowness to take offense, and readiness to forgive.[10] Other virtues which help to overcome the sin of anger are: carefulness of speech, prudent silence and patience under provocation, carefulness not to harbor a grudge or to seek revenge, to bear no hatred or ill-will towards those who have wronged us, and to pray for our enemies.

The fifth capital sin is gluttony, a sinful exaggeration of the desire for food and drink.[11] This vice causes intemperance in eating and drinking. The virtue which overcomes gluttony is *temperance* or moderation. We should not confuse moderation in eating and drinking with fasting. There is nothing wrong with eating and drinking in themselves, because food and drink were ordained by God as the natural elements by which the life and vitality of all living things should be sustained. They should therefore be received with gratitude as the gifts of a provident Creator, because to enjoy good food can be a means of praising the goodness and bounty of God, as St. Paul advises us when he said: *"Whether you eat or drink, or whatever else you do, do all for the glory of God"* (*1 Corinthians* 10:31).

It is moderation in food that is required of us, not severe and perpetual abstinence. For the average person, such abstinence could have a very harmful effect. The very idea of perpetually denying any gratification of taste in food or drink, could easily fill a person with dismay, and lead him to abandon all effort at moderation, or even drive him to excess. Moderation in the use of food can, on the other hand, prove beneficial to both soul and body.

The sixth capital sin is envy or jealousy, which is a sinful exaggeration of the love of oneself.[12] Envy causes sadness over the good things that others possess and which we ourselves lack. This sin causes hatred, calumny, detraction, rash judgment, suspicion, and injustice. The virtue which heals envy is *charity* or love of neighbor.[13]

This very human and all too common failing reveals an inferiority complex in those who are its unhappy victims. We should, therefore, feel the most sincere sympathy for such persons, realizing that their mental anguish must be very great. Yet, if only they were aware of it, the remedy for this torment is close at hand, for all they have to do is to turn their eyes upon their own blessings, which may be far greater than those they envy in others. There is a marvelous equity in the distribution of God's gifts, so that when we look beneath the surface everything balances evenly in the end. Those who seem less richly endowed in one area are most marvelously blessed in another, and it is this variety that makes the beautiful harmony and balance of nature, and of human society. Besides, the world is large enough to hold this vast complexity of talent, allowing each individual sufficient room to exercise his divinely bestowed gifts without harm to any one else.

The seventh and last capital sin is sloth, which is a sinful exaggeration of necessary rest for soul and body. It causes laziness, dislike for work, neglect of duty, and it leaves the way open to temptation. The virtue which counterbalances sloth is *diligence.* Diligence is a great preservative of both mental and physical health, for it closes the door to temptation and promotes success in every personal undertaking; if not material success, it at least provides the deep satisfaction of having made an honest effort to do well in the performance of the work undertaken.

From these brief considerations we can see that the practice of these basic virtues will quickly set the soul, who has turned away from sin, on the path of Christian perfection.

# *Chapter 23*

## Reflections on Self Denial

*"If Anyone Will Come After Me"* (*Matthew* 16:24).

After prayer, self denial is perhaps our greatest defense against sin. Like humility, this excellent virtue has been much misunderstood, for many think that self denial restricts one's freedom and prevents a person from achieving self-fulfillment. Actually the reverse is true, for self denial is the guardian of true freedom. If we observe closely, we will discover that anyone who consistently gives in to himself, becomes the slave of his own whims. We can also see that where there is lack of self denial there is also a lack of consideration for the rights of others, with a constant manifestation of selfishness, rudeness, irresponsibility, and a host of other failings against justice and charity.

Self denial always involves self control, for it entails a constant and systematic resistance to evil in any form, in order to preserve virtue, and to prove one's love for God. This principle of self control by means of resistance is often seen in nature. We know, for instance, that the sun tries to draw the planets toward itself by attraction. The planets resist this attraction by a counter-attraction of their own. It is this law of counter-attraction which maintains them in perfect position relative to the sun. This law is operative not only throughout

the Solar System, but throughout the entire universe to preserve the balance and harmony of the whole cosmos. It is a graphic image of what self denial effects in the moral order.

Unfortunately, however, there are many who fail to practice self denial, because they do not understand its true nature. They falsely believe that it consists of extreme practices which are beyond their physical or moral strength. In the face of such an obstacle they abandon all attempt at self denial of any kind, and content themselves with a life of mediocrity, or even of sin. This is unfortunate because self denial does not consist of extreme strictness, but in a systematic and constant curbing of one's natural impulses at all times, by a gentle restraint. It is noteworthy that Jesus never counselled extremes, but simple self-control. *"If anyone will come after Me," He said, "let him deny himself, take up his cross and follow Me; for he that shall save his life shall lose it, and he that shall lose his life for My sake shall find it"* (*Matthew* 16:24-25).

The most beneficial form of self denial is the keeping of the Commandments. It is a penance which does not grow easier through the years and which, for the most part, passes unnoticed. This is its greatest advantage, perhaps, because it is a natural safeguard against pride.

Another excellent form of self denial is to patiently bear life's disappointments. This can prove beneficial in helping forward the work of personal sanctification, for the endurance of mental anguish, physical illness, material deprivation or adverse circumstances of any kind, when accepted for the love of God, can serve to beautify and enoble our nature, rather than warp or embitter it.

The consistent denial of self gratification in little things, gradually builds up our moral strength and molds our character into a beautiful and pleasing personality. It helps us to be strong without being rigid, gentle without being weak, and kind without being sentimental. It helps us to be cultured in speech and manner, noble and upright in character. It enables us to bend before the storms of life rather than be broken by them, to stand firm against the onslaughts of temptation,

and continue on our way resolute and strong, when the tempest has past. In a word, we learn by experience from the faithful practice of self denial in little things, that it is self restraint and not self indulgence that leads to true freedom, and the effects of a consistent self denial will become evident in a pure and virtuous life. Thus we see the practical proof of the age-old proverb that virtue is its own reward.

# *Chapter 24*

# The Renewal of Our Christian Life

*"Come Away And Rest Awhile"* (*Mark* 6:31).

When considering the question of holiness of life, we must admit that since we possess a fallen nature, it is difficult to walk the path of perfection for a long time without experiencing some slackening of fervor, and this constitutes a danger, or at least a source of discouragement for us. Despite our best intentions, the cares of the world, or our fascination with earthly glory, tend to distract us from the pursuit of perfection. Realizing this danger, the Church provides many ways to keep the devotion of the faithful active and zealous. She recommends, for example: the frequent reception of the Sacraments of Confession and Holy Communion; regular attendance at Mass, daily if possible; frequent attendance at Church devotions; the reading of good books which are designed to promote the spiritual life; the prayerful reading of the Scriptures; sanctifying each day by cultivating the habit of living in the presence of God.

We will speak of these praiseworthy practices later. Here we will consider a very important means provided by the Church as an excellent way of fostering a devout life, namely, the periodic making of a retreat.

Let's begin by explaining what a retreat is. A retreat is a brief time set apart from the ordinary routine of daily life,

to reflect on the eternal truths which give meaning to life and which are the source of authentic happiness. It is a time to reflect upon God, our personal relationship with Him and the eternal destiny to which He has called us.

A person who makes a retreat is like a pilgrim who sits down by the roadside to rest before continuing on his journey. Sitting alone, he looks back at where he has been in order to evaluate his present position. He also considers the need to make further plans to enable him to reach his journey's end in safety. On a spiritual level this is what we do during a retreat. We look back over the past to see what mistakes we have made, then we use the present opportunity to set right whatever needs to be changed. In the light of past experience, we make wise plans for the future.

A retreat is not an obligation, but rather a devotion highly recommended by the Church to all the Faithful, whether adults, young people, or children, for it provides a period of silence in which the individual can be alone with God. Such a time is necessary for everyone, no matter of what type of character or temperament they may be, for we know that though humans by nature are social beings, we also experience within ourselves a need for privacy at certain times. We delight in friendship and a social life, yet nevertheless, if we get caught up in an endless round of external activity we grow weary of it, and long for the relaxation of silence. We are made that way, for while we love joy and laughter, we also feel the need for deep and serious reflection.

To be convinced of this we need only to reflect on our own experiences. Sometimes we grow tired of everyone and everything, restless for something we cannot seem to name. While this weariness can sometimes be traced to physical causes, it may also be due to spiritual need. In reality it may be God Who is knocking at the door of our hearts, reminding us that we were made for Him alone and that He alone can satisfy us.

A retreat is a very important spiritual exercise, for it enables us to draw closer to God, and gives us the opportunity to make a searching examination of conscience, to discover how we may have failed to live up to the ideals of a good

Christian life. It also is an excellent opportunity to make a fresh start if we find that we have fallen behind.

If, after a sincere examination of conscience, we find that we have tried to lead a truly virtuous life, we should be grateful to God, realizing that it was His grace alone that enabled us to continue in this way. If, on the other hand, we discover that we have grown lazy, that we have, for example, become neglectful of prayer, or have begun to take chances with virtue, even to the point of having offended God in grave matters, or we discover that our love for God has begun to grow cold, then the time has come to make a fresh beginning. The discovery of such a slackening of virtue should not be a cause for discouragement, but rather a matter of thanksgiving, since the admission of our failures is the first step on our return journey to God.

Admission of our mistakes should lead naturally to a sincere effort toward change. The most effective way to set matters right is to make a good confession. This should be done immediately; do not put it off until tomorrow for tomorrow may be too late. Then, having settled our accounts with God by means of a sincere confession, we should renew our purpose of amendment and begin again. Resolutions such as the following might be particularly helpful at this time.

Never be ashamed to profess our belief in God and to give Him the first place in our lives.

Never to be ashamed to profess our wholehearted belief in the Divinity and in the Humanity of Christ.

To accept unconditionally the complete Gospel of Jesus, as taught and interpreted by the teaching Magisterium of the Church—not just those parts of the Gospel which may prove convenient or personally attractive.

To be faithful to our duties to God, as expressed by the Church, for example, to attend Mass regularly, to receive the Sacraments of Confession and Holy Communion frequently, and to be faithful to prayer.

To make a sincere and persistent effort to avoid the dangerous occasions of sin, and to live a life of moral integrity.

To faithfully carry out our duties to our parents and to our

neighbor, and to make an earnest effort to make our life successful both on a natural and supernatural plane.

By means of resolutions such as these, taken seriously and thoughtfully, we shall regain true peace of heart, and relieve ourselves of the burden of guilt and misery which no human remedy can ever fully alleviate. At the same time, we will have begun to reshape our lives into something beautiful and good. Once we take steps toward a new way of life, we should never look back, but rather trust in the goodness and mercy of God to help us persevere in the way of virtue. Undoubtedly, we will experience some moments of discouragement, as well as the temptations which normally assault any beginner, but God's helping grace will always be at hand to assist us.

In view of these facts it might be good to reflect briefly on some of the more common temptations which might trouble the beginner setting forth on the way toward perfection, and to study the remedies which the Church offers to combat them.

To begin with, we may feel strongly inclined to make up for past sins by excessive corporal penance which is really beyond our strength. This is a big mistake, for when we attempt penance that is utterly beyond us, we may abandon all penance, and even return to a life of indifference. If we force ourselves to continue in the practice of severe physical penance, despite what is understood through common sense, we may seriously injure our physical health and make ourselves incapable of helping ourselves or others in any way.

It is good to remember that rarely is anyone called by God to a life of extreme penance, but when He does, He gives this individual grace which fits this person's needs. For most people, however, the simple penance of keeping the Commandments is the safest of all. It is good to also remember that the penance given in Confession, as atonement for sin, is all that is required by the Church, and that sincere repentance of heart is a safer way to holiness than any corporal penance done for its own sake. In fact, such repentance can prove more powerful an incentive to the love and service of

God, than any form of external penance. This is not to devalue corporal penance in itself, for it too, when practiced with moderation and fidelity, can prove to be a powerful aid to holiness. But for a beginner, corporal penance should not be undertaken without the advice and guidance of a prudent spiritual director or confessor.

Another temptation that might trouble the beginner is the question of God's love. Does He love someone less because of past unfaithfulness to grace, than He would have loved that person if he had never sinned? On this point the Church assures us that God can love anyone, be he saint or sinner. We can see this from the parables, especially those of the Laborers in the Vineyard (*Matthew* 20), or the Prodigal Son (*Luke* 15).

In the former, God gave the same payment to the laborer who had worked only one hour, as to those who had worked all day. It is evident that the servant who had worked only one hour had not earned the same amount as the others, but because the Lord of the Vineyard was good, He gave as a free gift to that servant what He gave as a just wage to the others. If we think of that gift as "love," we have solved our problem. God can give an equal or even greater amount of love to a sinner than to someone who has never sinned, and this because He is God. *"Am I not free to do as I wish?"* (*Matthew* 20:15).

We can see from this that God's love for every soul is personal and unique. The love He gives differs from one individual to another. God's love is for each soul individually. He is our dearest and truest friend, the happiness of our life and our eternal blessing.

# PART VI

## The Gospel Way Of Life

*"I have come so that they might have life, and may have it more abundantly"*
(*John* 10:10).

# *Chapter 25*

# Vocation in Life

Once having experienced the happiness of a life of virtue, a person naturally begins to wonder how to serve God in a permanent manner throughout their entire life, and this touches upon the question of a vocation. What is a vocation? It is the mysterious call of God to the individual soul, to serve Him in a particular way or state of life. We could express it in another way by saying that it is the mysterious action of Divine Grace attracting the individual soul to God in a specific way.

The various ways in which God exercises this attraction upon the human heart are as numerous as the types of people He created. Every soul is unique, and therefore, must come to God by its own unique path. One thing is certain, however, there is an element of mystery in every vocation, regardless of the state to which the individual is called. For a vocation implies two things, namely, the mysterious action of God's grace on the one hand, and the free response of the individual soul on the other. But overall, a vocation is far more the work of God than the work of humans. Jesus clearly showed this when He said to His Apostles at the Last Supper: *"You have not chosen Me, but I have chosen you, and have appointed you, that you should go and bring forth fruit and your fruit should remain"* (*John* 15:16).

A vocation in life always implies stability or permanence, and the many diverse vocations are brought into a basic unity by the Church, in the various "states of life" which she formally recognizes. When considering the concept of a vocation, we can think of the Church as the Vineyard of God (*Matthew* 20), in which every soul is appointed by Him to its own specific task. There is work for everyone to do, and each work has its own specific value, beauty, and dignity. No one is ever compelled by God or by the Church to embrace any specific vocation, rather each is free to make their own personal choice.

A natural attraction to a particular role, together with an aptitude for the specific obligations of that position, constitutes a vocation. Why a person feels drawn to one vocation rather than another is truly a mystery, ultimately unexplainable on a natural basis. In reality this attraction is the mysterious call of God, drawing the individual soul to Himself in the way He wills. The Church says that each individual is best for the life to which he feels called by God.

There are two basic states of life, virginity for the sake of the kingdom of Heaven, and marriage. Both of these roles are holy, since God designed them, and each has a specific function in the mystery of the Church. They are meant to reinforce each other and give glory to God according to His plan for mankind. Our relationship with Jesus Christ is the primary relationship of our lives.

Let's begin with a consideration of the basic state of virginity, which is also a virtue. True virginity involves the preservation of perfect moral integrity both of soul and body. We could express it in another way by saying that a true virgin is one who has never committed a serious sin against chastity. True virginity, therefore, is a rare and precious gift of God. It is like the pearl of great price of which Jesus spoke in the Gospel. A man, having found this gem hid it, and because of the joy it brought him, went and sold all that he had to buy this treasure (*Matthew* 13:45-46).

The rare and unique nature of virginity can be inferred from St. John's vision on Patmos where he saw on the one

hand, a multitude whom no one could count, standing before the throne of God, clothed with white robes and with palm branches in their hands. These, he was told, were the multitude of the Redeemed who had washed their robes and made them white in the Blood of the Lamb (*Revelations* 7:9-14): and on the other hand was a choir of virgins, only 144,000 who followed the Lamb where He went, singing a hymn which none but they could sing (*Revelations* 14:1-5). This symbolic vision describes the rare and precious nature of true virginity.

For the Church says that: "There has always been an affinity between angels and virginity. To live in the body while transcending the body, is not an earthly life but a heavenly one. And it is a greater thing to acquire angelic glory than merely to have it. To be an angel indicates happiness, but to be a virgin indicates virtue. For virginity acquires by its power, what the angel possesses by nature. Both angel and virgin then, fulfill a function that is not human but divine."[2] We could say that virginity, whether considered as a virtue or a state of life, mirrors the holiness of God.

Explaining the excellence of virginity the Church says that in the virginal state one belongs exclusively to God, and is occupied in serving Him directly, while in the married state one must, of necessity, serve Him indirectly by the foundation and preservation of a home. Thus St. Paul observed that: *"I should like you to be free from anxieties. An unmarried man is anxious about the things of the Lord, how he may please the Lord. But a married man is anxious about the things of the world, how he may please his wife, and he is divided. An unmarried woman or a virgin is anxious about the things of the Lord, so that she may be holy in both body and spirit. A married woman, on the other hand, is anxious about the things of the world, how she may please her husband"* (*1 Corinthians* 7:32-34).

Jesus Himself set the supreme seal of excellence on the value of virginity,[3] when He said: *"In the Resurrection, they shall neither marry nor be married, but shall be as the angels*

*of God in heaven''* (*Matthew* 22:30).

In proclaiming the value of virginity the Church cites many striking examples of God's encouragement for this beautiful virtue. In the Mystery of the Incarnation, the Eternal Father willed that His beloved Son should become human by being born of a virgin, without detriment to her virginity. The Church believes and teaches that Mary's divine motherhood, in no way removed but rather consecrated her virginity. She always remained a virgin.[4]

St. John the Baptist was also a striking example of virgin holiness, being sanctified before his birth, at the moment of his first meeting with Jesus.

It is Jesus Himself, however, the giver of all purity and holiness Who is the most glorious example of virginity. In this respect it is significant that at the beginning of His public life He allowed the devil to tempt Him to pride, ambition, and even idolatry, but not to impurity. Also, He permitted the Scribes and Pharisees to accuse Him of lawbreaking, sedition, blasphemy and sacrilege, but never of impurity.[6] *''Can any of you charge me with sin?''* He challenged them (*John* 8:46), and no one was able to answer Him.

Virginal integrity becomes all the more precious by the fact that once lost, it can never be recovered in the physical order. It is like a priceless gem which once destroyed can never be duplicated. Yet, God does not request that all should live in the state of perpetual virginity as a way of life. Jesus clearly indicated that it is a gift of God, when He said to His Apostles: *"Not all can accept this word, but only those to whom it is granted''* (*Matthew* 19:11). He recommended it, however, to those who perceive and value its merit and feel called by grace to adopt it as a way of life. (*Cf. Matthew* 19:12).

Following His teaching, the Church has always held the role and virtue of virginity in the highest esteem,[7] and in imitation of Jesus. Countless souls throughout the ages have consecrated their virginity to God. The Church is careful to note, however, that it is virginity chosen for the love of God that makes it precious in the eyes of God.[8] Those, therefore, who

freely choose to consecrate their virginity to God by vow, whether in the religious life or the secular life, do something praiseworthy and noble, which the Church endorses and blesses, for she says that virginity is the highest degree of chastity.[9] Thus St. Augustine says: "What we praise in virgins, is not the mere fact of their being virgins, but their consecration to God."[10]

The Church is careful to note that virginity is preferred to marriage only when the motive for such a voluntary choice or dedication is love of the things of God.[11] In regard to this matter, the Council of Gangres decreed that "if anyone preserves continence or virginity, not because of the beauty or sanctity of this virtue, but because he avoids marriage as something execrable, let him be anathema (accursed ) (*Canticles* 9).[12]

The Church regards celibacy with the same respect it gives consecrated virginity. Celibacy is choosing to remain unmarried, regardless of prior lifestyle, and remaining completely chaste.[13] Consecrated chastity, whether in religious life or in secular life, is placed in the same category as consecrated virginity if it is done for love of God.[14]

While physical virginity as a way of life is not required of anyone by God, chastity is required of all. Chastity is being pure in thoughts and actions and abstaining from unlawful sexual conduct. This beautiful virtue is different for each person depending on their state of life.[15] The nature and degree of chastity required of a person who has made religious vows, for example, will differ from that of an unmarried secular person, or married people.[16] All, however, are required to live chaste and pure lives. Although many people choose to live lives of consecrated chastity in the world, most who wish to consecrate their lives to God by a vow of chastity enter religious life.

What exactly do we mean by the religious life? We could define it as a state of life freely chosen by those who desire and feel called by God to strive for a higher state of perfection than that required of the ordinary Christian.[17] Every member of the Church has the duty to strive for Christian perfection,

as Jesus clearly indicated in the Sermon on the Mount when He said: *"Be you therefore perfect, as also your Heavenly Father is perfect"* (*Matthew* 5:48). The basic elements of this perfection are the love of God and neighbor, and the avoidance of over attachment to worldly things. This involves the keeping of the Commandments and the conscientious fulfillment of the duties of one's state in life.[18]

Anyone wishing to strive for a higher state of perfection over and above what is signified by these requirements, is recommended, though not commanded, to follow the "Christian Counsels."[19] Foremost among these are the "Evangelical Counsels" of Poverty, Chastity, and Obedience.[20] These three virtues are called this because they are recommended by Jesus in the Gospels.[21] The invitation to follow Him is clear, for example, in His words to the rich young man: *"If you will be perfect, go sell what you have and give to the poor, and you shall have treasure in heaven; and come follow me"* (*Matthew* 19:21).

The incentive to consecrate one's life to God through the vow of Obedience, is found in the obedience of Jesus Himself. The Gospel says that: *"He went down with them and came to Nazareth and was obedient to them"* (*Luke* 2:51). Jesus constantly spoke of His obedience to His Father in all things, as for example, when He said: *"I do always the things that please Him"* (*John* 8:29).

In pondering the mystery of this obedience, St. Paul said: *"Have among yourselves the same attitude that is also yours in Jesus Christ, Who though He was in the form of God, did not regard equality with God something to be grasped. Rather, He emptied Himself, taking the form of a slave, coming in human likeness; and found human in appearance, He humbled Himself, becoming obedient to death, even death on a cross. Because of this, God greatly exalted Him and bestowed on Him the name that is above every name, that at the name of Jesus every knee should bend, of those in heaven and on earth and under the earth, and every tongue confess that Jesus Christ is Lord, to the glory of God the Father"* (*Philippians* 2:5-11).

Having its root and origin in the Gospels and other books of the New Testament, and having been counselled by Jesus Himself, the religious life is proven to be a valid and authentic way of life, greatly to be desired and beneficial not only to those who choose it, but to the whole Church and to secular society as well. The Counsel of Evangelical Poverty, when understood and faithfully observed, gives a sense of freedom to the heart, which is not possible to the same degree in secular life, for it frees the mind from perpetual preoccupation with material concerns, particularly the amassing and preservation of wealth.

The vow of Virginity or Chastity likewise frees the soul, and aids rather than prevents true self-fulfillment. For it enables the individual to love and serve all impartially, without being personally obliged to anyone.

The vow of Obedience as understood by the Church is designed to make the individual not weak and worthless, but strong. To understand this, we can consider secular life, where every member of society has to be obedient to the civil authority for the good of the nation. Without such obedience, the whole social fabric would crumble, and the whole social order would disintegrate in violence and anarchy.

True obedience makes the individual, whether in religious life or secular society, strong and dependable. On the battlefield, who is the dependable soldier, the one who scoffs at authority and shirks his duty, or the one who faithfully obeys the commands of higher authority? It is the same in the spiritual order. The vow of religious Obedience makes an individual strong, reliable, and prudent, and in the end makes him holy, like Jesus Himself.

The religious life, by which those who feel called by God freely choose to live a life of consecrated virginity or celibacy, in the service of God and neighbor, has continued in the Church since the days of the Apostles. Those who enter religious life usually take the three vows of Poverty, Chastity, and Obedience, but the manner of observance, and the degree in which they are practiced, differs from one religious institute to another, depending upon the goals or works of the order.[22]

We could sum up by saying that the religious life is the salt which preserves the life of the Church. It is essentially adaptable to every age and culture, and will be found in the Church in one form or another until the end of time. In every age there are people who are called by God to go aside from the normal way of life, to follow a more perfect path. It is God Who attracts the soul to the religious life, as He attracts every individual to its own proper vocation, and this attraction is what the Church calls a religious vocation.

# *Chapter 26*

# The Married State

The second basic state of life, marriage, is the call of many. It is the consecration of the natural vocation of parenthood, which was designed by God and is necessary for all created life. Since God established parenthood, it is sacred and holy, being a reflection of God's own Fatherhood, from which as St. Paul observes *"all paternity in heaven and on earth is named"* (*Ephesians* 3:15). Jesus raised marriage to the dignity of a sacrament in order to Divinely approve of this essential state of life, and to show its intrinsic goodness and excellence. This sacramental character and grace, sanctifies human life at its very source.

The Church defines the Sacrament of Matrimony as a sacrament which unites a Christian man and woman in lawful marriage.[1] It is thus a contract between a man and woman to live in life-long partnership with each other, and a sacrament to bestow God's grace on this human contract.[2]

The laws by which the Church governs the married state, in accordance with Christ's teachings, are not intended as restrictions to human freedom, but rather as safeguards to human dignity. They are designed to protect the honor of each person involved in the marriage contract, namely, the honor of each parent and of each child. Like every member of the Church, those who enter the married state are required to

live pure and chaste lives.

Following the teachings of Christ, the Church teaches that marriage is a consecration of the lives of one man and one woman before God. Marriage is indissoluble, the contract binds both parties until death. For serious reasons the Church will sometimes grant a separation, that is, it can sometimes permit husband and wife to live apart, but neither is free to marry another while the other partner is still living. After the death of husband or wife they are free to marry.

An annulment is something entirely different. It is a formal declaration by the Church that a marriage is null and void, that is, invalid. In other words, it is an official declaration that there was no real marriage there from the beginning, in spite of outward appearances.[3]

The marriage contract lasts only until death; at death every soul will enter eternal life as the exclusive possession of God, regardless of the state they had chosen in life. With all human ties severed and all obligations dissolved, the elect in Heaven will be bound to one another only by the bonds of charity, that is, by their common love of God, and their love of one another in God.

The Church says that the love between husband and wife in the Sacrament of Matrimony is a symbol of the love between God and the individual soul, or between God and the Church. Jesus gave Divine approval to the married state by being Himself present with His mother and the Apostles at the wedding feast of Cana (*John* 2). He worked the first great miracle of His public life at the wedding, by changing water into wine in order that the joy of the festivities might not be spoiled by a shortage of wine. The primary work of those who enter marriage is the foundation and preservation of a home. The care, protection and upbringing of children which is a vital part of this parental vocation, mirrors the Fatherhood of God. Parents share in God's creative power in the manner and amount willed by Him, and reflect His providence over creation, in the raising and training of their children. The excellence and value of virtuous married life cannot be over emphasized, for as we have already said, parents give wonderful service to

God and to human society in the establishment and preservation of a good home life. This is the foundation upon which both the Church and the State rest.

We now come to the question of the choice of a state in life, a matter which sooner or later confronts every responsible individual. Because the two basic roles of virginity and marriage have to do with the sources of human life, God has given every person the potential to choose either one. He is just to all, no one is ever compelled by Divine Law to embrace either; in the choice of a state of life, the individual must decide for himself. And so, for each person, the time comes when childhood fades away, and the young person looks at life with the eyes of an adult. This time of transition can present difficulties of its own. For instance, the awareness that one is about to leave behind the security and irresponsibility of childhood, and to step into adult life, may cause a sense of anxiety or uncertainty in regard to the best choice of vocation.

When deciding which is our personal choice of a state in life, we should first pray earnestly for guidance to make the right decision. Since we have only one life to live, we should make every effort to make it a happy and successful one both on a natural and supernatural plane.

In deciding on a vocation, our choice should be free and self-determined, since we are free and intelligent agents. Besides, if God Himself respects the free will of the individual, no human being should be allowed to coerce or unduly influence us in deciding such an important matter. A parent, friend, or spiritual director can counsel or encourage us regarding a vocation, but the final decision must always be our own.

It would be unfair to favor one type of vocation to the exclusion of another. Unfortunately, this can happen in the society of today. To ensure, therefore, that the counsel given to the one seeking advice is adequate, just, and beneficial, the dignity, excellence and desirability of every vocation should be thoughtfully discussed, leaving to the individual concerned, the ultimate personal choice.

While no state is completely exempt from suffering, the contentment that springs from the knowledge that we have made a correct choice, and are in the vocation in which we truly belong, will make the burdens of life much easier to bear. In choosing a state of life, therefore, we should always do so with regard to those eternal values which shape our destiny, and make for our true and lasting happiness both on earth and in eternity.

# *Chapter 27*

# The Blossoming Wilderness

## Reflections on the Living of a Christian Life

*"The land that was desolate and impassable shall be glad: and the wilderness shall rejoice and shall flourish like the lily"* (*Isaias* 35:1). Isaiah said this to describe the change the Messiah would make in Israel by the grace of His presence. It can be applied to any individual soul who has turned from sin and resolved to follow Jesus. True holiness in life is the gift which comes from faithfulness to the teachings of Christ, as interpreted by the Church. It was to that holiness of life that Jesus Himself referred when He said: *"You are the light of the world. A city set on a mountain cannot be hidden. Nor do they light a lamp and then put it under a bushel basket; it is set on a lamp stand, where it gives light to all in the house. Just so, your light must shine before others, that they may see your good deeds and glorify your heavenly Father"* (*Matthew* 5:14-16).

It was to this holiness that St. Paul called the early Christians when he wrote: *"So be imitators of God, as beloved children, and live in love, as Christ loved us and handed Himself over for us as a sacrificial offering to God for a fragrant aroma. Immorality or any impurity or greed must not even be mentioned among you, as is fitting among holy ones,*

*no obscenity or silly or suggestive talk, which is out of place, but instead, thanksgiving. Be sure of this, that no immoral or impure or greedy person, that is, an idolater, has any inheritance in the kingdom of Christ and of God. Let no one deceive you with empty arguments, for because of these things the wrath of God is coming upon the disobedient. So do not be associated with them. For you were once in darkness, but now you are light of the Lord. Live as children of light, for light produces every kind of goodness and righteousness and truth. Try to learn what is pleasing to the Lord''* (*Ephesians* 5:1-9).

*''Do not be yoked with those who are different, with unbelievers. For what partnership do righteousness and lawlessness have? Or what fellowship does light have with darkness? What accord does Christ have with Beliar? Or what has a believer with an unbeliever? What agreement has the temple of God with idols? For we are the temple of the living God; as God said: 'I will live with them and among them, and I will be their God and they shall be my people. Therefore, come forth from them and be separate,' says the Lord, 'and touch nothing unclean; then I will receive you and I will be a Father to you, and you shall be sons and daughters to me, says the Lord Almighty' ''* (*2 Corinthians* 6:14-18).

*''Rejoice in the Lord always. I shall say it again: rejoice! Your kindness shall be known to all. The Lord is near. Have no anxiety at all, but in everything, by prayer and petition, with thanksgiving, make your requests known to God. Then the peace of God that surpasses all understanding will guard your hearts and minds in Christ Jesus. Finally, brothers, whatever is true, whatever is honorable, whatever is just, whatever is pure, whatever is lovely, whatever is gracious, if there is any excellence and if there is anything worthy of praise, think about these things. Keep on doing what you have learned and received and heard and seen in me. Then the God of peace will be with you. My God will fully supply whatever you need, in accord with His glorious riches in Christ Jesus''* (*Philippians* 4:4-9, 19).

Holiness reveals itself in every aspect of the daily life of a true follower of Jesus, in the day's plans, and even in the atmosphere of the home. A good Christian life is oriented towards God.

Observing such a life, we can see that the faithful Christian always gives God first place in his life, being faithful to prayer, and in the completion of religious duties; attendance at Mass on Sundays, and frequently receiving the Sacraments of Confession and Holy Communion.

In obligations to self and neighbor this Christian is no less diligent, seeing these as indirect service to God. This person also exercises self respect, which is the basic right and duty of every individual. This reveals itself in moral integrity, in the careful preservation of his own good name, in reasonable care for his physical health, and in the avoidance of anything that might endanger his life whether work or recreational activity. Self respect also reveals itself in the dignity and modesty of a person's attire, behavior, and in the cultivation of talents as a means of providing for personal needs.

Towards his neighbor the Christian shows the concern required by the Divine Precept: "You shall love your neighbor as yourself." First among his obligations to neighbor are his duties of respect and affection towards his own parents, regardless of their personal failures or shortcomings, and a sincere effort to provide for their needs in illness or old age.

Toward others, the Christian shows concern and charity, which are the spirit of the Gospel teaching. This sincerity is shown in the truthfulness and honesty of all social and business dealings with a neighbor and in the avoidance of quarreling, anger, hatred, revenge, or anything which might injure the physical or moral well-being of the neighbor, whether friend or enemy. It leads a person to be wise in his speech, especially in regard to the character of another, so that he may never defame or injure another's good name. This guarded speech leads to a conscientious practice of truthfulness even in little things, and a detestation of lying in any form.

Concern for the well-being of a neighbor shows itself in

a practical manner by fidelity and honesty in work, by the payment of just wages to those one has employed, and by sincere happiness at a neighbor's success.

Most importantly, love of neighbor reveals itself in a conscientious desire to avoid anything that would injure or destroy the moral integrity of those with whom a Christian associates, or who in any way might come within the influence of his life or work. The prayer of St. Ignatius becomes the permanent concern of the Christian's life: "May no one be less good for having come under my influence, no one less pure, less true, for having been a fellow traveler on the journey towards eternal life."

Christian perfection reveals itself not only in the personal conduct of the good Catholic, but even in the atmosphere of his home. There everything gives silent witness to this love for God, and to the enduring values of the Gospel. It has rightfully been said that the home is a mirror in miniature of the Church, but this is true only if the presence of God can be seen there in the spirit of the household. No matter what evidence of refinement and culture may be in a home, if the spiritual dimension of God's presence is absent, it leaves a strange sense of emptiness in the visitor.

Yet wealth, good taste, and refinement in the material objects of a home are both acceptable and desirable for they were intended by God to play an important role in the social life of His people. The elegance and atmosphere of dignity and culture which fine furnishings create, help to glorify God since they charm and elevate the mind. But if they do not convey the sense of God's presence, they are at most lifeless and dead.

In order to create a positive atmosphere, the Church encourages its members to use Christian symbols and sacramentals within the home, that they may be a constant reminder of God's grace and immediate presence. The proper use of Christian art, such as pictures or statues, can greatly contribute to creating an atmosphere of peace and holiness in the home, since they constantly bring to mind scenes of the Mystery of Salvation. The Crucifix, as the most sacred

symbol of salvation should have an honored place in every household, while the use of holy water, sprinkled throughout the home, brings the blessing and protection of God against the snares of the devil. The use of flowers or lights placed before a statue of Jesus, Mary, or the saints, to recall their memory or honor their virtues, and thus glorify God for the works He completed through them, is also an age-old custom in Catholic countries.

Sacred music is also an excellent way to keep in touch with the life of the Church and live in the presence of God.

Here are some suggested elements of an ideal schedule for a good Christian. It is good to begin the day thinking of God. This means praying a short prayer such as, 'My God I love Thee above all things,' or by simply kissing the Crucifix. After preparing to begin the day, some commonly said prayers are: the Morning Offering; acts of Faith, Hope, and Charity; the Our Father; the Hail Mary; the Apostles' Creed; the Confiteor; the prayer to the Angel Guardian; the Act of Contrition and a general confession of sins. These can be found in most prayer books, but we will also list them in the back of this book.

Daily Mass is another important practice. If you are unable to go every day, a few extra times a week, or whenever possible, will provide extra graces for the week. Receiving Jesus' Eucharistic presence on a regular basis encourages the practice of living in God throughout the day. We should speak to Him often in the silence of our hearts and do everything for His glory. The habit of saying short prayers of praise or love of God is an excellent way to become aware of Our Lord's continued presence in our lives. An example of this brief type of prayer would be, 'Most Sacred Heart of Jesus, I trust in Thee.'

Other practices recommended by the Church include reading of the Gospels or the Sacred Scriptures either alone or with others. Mental prayer, or a short meditation on some event in the life of Christ can also be beneficial. Praying the Rosary, that age-old prayer of the Faithful, can also be very

effective, for the Rosary is in reality a brief but comprehensive reflection on the mystery of salvation.

The activities of the day should close with night prayers before sleeping. These can be the same as those said in the morning, and are usually said kneeling, though any respectful posture may be assumed. Thus sitting or even saying one's prayers in bed may sometimes be necessary.

With the day thus sanctified by prayer and the remembrance of the presence of God, the individual soul can begin to find true self-fulfillment, and that fullness of life for which everyone naturally longs, because his life will be directed towards God.

## *Chapter 28*

# A Last Word: Let Science Speak

There are many, however, who to use the expression of Jesus *"do not receive this word"* (*Cf. Matthew* 19:11). They refuse to admit the existence of God, and they look upon His testimony as merely a myth devised to fulfill the needs and desires of primitive peoples, unworthy of acceptance by the educated, especially by the intellectual elite of this sophisticated era.

Such an outlook often shows a lack of sufficient knowledge of the historical background of the Deposit of Divine Revelation, particularly of that portion of it which is contained in the Sacred Scriptures. It is not an uninvestigated myth, handed down by uncritical minds from generation to generation, but rather as we have said, a great reservoir of authentic knowledge of God and His works, given to us by God Himself throughout history, carefully preserved by the Patriarchs as moral tradition, and from the days of Moses onward in the writings of the Sacred Scriptures, then finally perfected by the Revelation of Christ, and given by Him to the leaders of the Church.

Far from being an uninvestigated source, this Deposit of Divine Revelation has been tried in the fire of fierce intellectual controversy, from which it has triumphantly emerged unscathed.

From the beginning, the Church received this information as the word of God, on faith alone, relying not on the testimony of human science or scholarship, but on the truth of God's infallible word. All Christians did this until the end of the fifteenth century; then with the beginning of the Renaissance Period, that is from about 1500 A.D. onwards, a wave of atheistic disbelief began to sweep over the intellectual élite of Europe, and the whole question of the Sacred Scriptures was brought under attack. The atheistic thinkers rejected the Bible as unworthy of acceptance either from a historical or an intellectual point of view. They denied the Mosaic authorship of the first Five Books—the *Pentateuch,* as well as the authenticity of various other books of the Bible. They likewise denied the Divine inspiration and inerrancy of the Sacred Scriptures.[1]

Toward the end of the last century the situation became so serious that the Church was compelled to take an official stand in the defense of the Faith. Leo XIII, who was then the Supreme Pontiff, took up the challenge of the skeptics, for he realized that since Divine Revelation was the word of God it had nothing to fear from intellectual investigation. He first studied the nature and extent of the attack and then rose in defense. He first issued an encyclical entitled *''Providentissimus Deus''* in November 1893, in which he set forth and defended the Church's doctrine on the truth of the inspired Scriptures. Then he laid down certain principles for the guidance of Catholic scholars, insisting on a close adherence to the Catholic tradition of interpretation. At the same time, he advocated the use of all modern helps and methods in the pursuit of higher biblical studies. This great document may be regarded as the Magna Charta of present day biblical studies.

Ever since that time Catholic scholars in various academic fields have labored in the cause of the Sacred Scriptures. Their investigations have been made on a strictly professional basis, according to the most scientific methods of modern research, and have been all embracing in their nature and scope. The secular sciences such as literature, history,

astronomy, archeology, etc. have been employed to aid in this great enterprise which has now continued for almost a century.

The aim of this vast program of research has been to establish the reliability of the Sacred Scriptures on a natural level for those who do not accept the testimony of Faith, and on a natural level to be able to give to the unbelieving *"a reason for the hope that is in us"* (*Cf. 1 Peter* 3:15).

The result of this formal investigation has been rewarding, for as Pope Pius XII observed, confidence in the historical value and in the authority of the Bible which in certain cases was undermined by the ferocity of the atheistic attacks, is today completely restored among Catholics.[2] In fact, it has shown that the Scriptures are composed of the various elements of human history, in which from the very beginning, everything was being ordered by God towards a determined goal. That goal was the mystery of Christ, the Son of God and Savior of Mankind (*Cf. Romans* 10:4).

The Deposit of Divine Revelation is now seen to be the answer given by God to the deeply perplexing questions which have confronted mankind since the very dawn of human history; He used the doubt and disbelief of men to reveal the truth of His testimony. We might sum up the outcome of this great intellectual attack upon the Scriptures in the words of Jesus Himself. *"...the rain fell and the floods came, and the winds blew, and they beat upon that house (the Church), and it fell not, because it was founded on a rock"* (*Matthew* 7:25). The rock was God, the Eternal Truth.

Yet, despite this impressive evidence there are some who are still not convinced. Among the arguments which they give to support their skepticism, is the familiar one which asserts that people of this modern age are not the same as people of former ages. This is the age of nuclear science and space navigation, so we must let science speak, for modern people cannot be expected to receive the Church's explanation of those basic and perplexing problems of life, such as sin, suffering and death, as the people of former ages did.

This is perhaps a hasty conclusion, for sharp intellectual

inquiry is not the exclusive possession of the space age. To say that only this present age is intellectually alert is to ignore the testimony of universal history.

To begin with, both science and scholarship today are beginning to realize that people of the most remote ages of antiquity were similar to people of today.[3] From the very beginning mankind translated the concepts of the mind into the external realities of language, music, painting, sculpture, etc.,[4] fashioned tools and made noteworthy carvings in bone and ivory. All of these artifacts show that humans thought and acted very much like his far distant descendants of today.

Although people lived in caves, these caves were homes and not dens. Humans adorned the walls of their caves with beautiful drawings and frescoes. Their activity did not remain static, as that of the animals, rather it progressed from the fundamentals to the perfected.

There is also the marvelous similarity discernible in the moral life of mankind in every age. The basic needs and desires of all people are essentially the same. Every person thirsts for happiness, that sense of fulfillment and well-being which we could best express as *"the fullness of life"* (*Cf. John* 10:10). Humans want to love and to be loved, to be accepted by others, and treated with dignity and respect. Without such love and acceptance, life would not be worth living.

As we scan the ages, therefore, we can plainly see from history that since the very dawn of time, mankind has pondered, questioned, investigated, reasoned, and concluded as he does today. The fact that science has today achieved such a sophisticated level of discovery, in no way dwarfs the intellectual genius of yesterday. Rather we could more truly say that this age of nuclear science and space technology is just the apex of human achievement, the crowning point of a pyramid of knowledge which has been slowly building up throughout the ages, each age contributing its own share of critical investigation and discovery.

If this is true on a material level, it is also true in the spiritual. The scientific discoveries of today in no way dwarf

or minimize the vitality and value of the eternal truths contained in the Deposit of Divine Revelation.

To worship science with an unquestioning and unqualified submission is to mistake its true nature and function. For what is science? It is nothing more than the discovery of laws which have been present in the Universe since the very origin of Creation. These laws have been operative from the beginning, but have escaped the notice of mankind. Today people have discovered them, but they have not invented them; they are the work of the Creator. It is the function of science to study these laws and to employ them in the service of mankind: it is the function of Divine Revelation to reveal the Author of these laws and His purpose in establishing them, for they are like arrows pointing back to Him Who is their Creator. For those, therefore, who are inclined to regard science as the only reliable basis of faith or knowledge, it might be interesting to hear the conclusions to which science itself led two masterminds of this sophisticated age.

Sir Isaac Newton, for example, literally affirmed that "an intelligent being. . .governs all things, not as the soul of the world, but as the Lord of the universe, and because of His rule He is called 'The Lord God,' 'Pantocrator.' "[5]

Einstein maintained that "science without religion is lame, and religion without science is blind." He also said: "I want to know how God created the world. I am not interested in such and such a phenomenon nor in the spectrum of a chemical element. I want to know God's thought, the rest is a detail."[6]

If Einstein had only realized it, however, the Church has the answer he so sincerely sought, in the Deposit of Divine Revelation, particularly in the Revelation of Christ.

Jesus not only instructed us in the Divine purpose of all God's works, but also revealed the manner of life which would enable us to achieve that "fullness of life" for which we long. Many atheists and agnostics, having sought the answer to life's perplexing problems from the false philosophies of the world, were led to admit that the Church alone has a rational and satisfying answer, for she is the voice

of Truth, or more accurately still, the voice of God, the Eternal Truth. Since she speaks to us with the voice and authority of Christ, and since it is His doctrine that she teaches, let us always contemplate Jesus, the Teacher, Lawgiver and Savior, Whom the Father sent into the world to lead mankind back to Him.

# Common Prayers of the Church

### *Our Father*

Our Father, Who art in heaven, hallowed be Thy name; Thy Kingdom come; Thy will be done, on earth, as it is in heaven. Give us this day our daily bread; and forgive us our trespasses, as we forgive those who trespass against us; and lead us not into temptation, but deliver us from evil. Amen.

### *Hail Mary*

Hail Mary, full of grace; the Lord is with thee; blessed art thou among women, and blessed is the fruit of thy womb, Jesus. Holy Mary, Mother of God, pray for us sinners, now and at the hour of our death. Amen.

### *Glory be to the Father*

Glory be to the Father, and to the Son, and to the Holy Spirit. As it was in the beginning, is now, and ever shall be, world without end. Amen.

### *The Apostle's Creed*

I believe in God, the Father Almighty, Creator of heaven and earth; and in Jesus Christ, His only Son, our Lord; Who

was conceived by the Holy Spirit, born of the Virgin Mary, suffered under Pontius Pilate, was crucified, died and was buried. He descended to the dead, the third day He rose again. He ascended into heaven, sits at the right hand of God, the Father Almighty; from thence He shall come to judge the living and the dead. I believe in the Holy Spirit, the holy Catholic Church, the communion of Saints, the forgiveness of sins, the resurrection of the body, and life everlasting. Amen.

## SPIRITUAL COMMUNION

*By a rescript of November 24, 1922 the Sacred Congregation of Indulgences approved the following formula for a spiritual communion:*

O Jesus I turn toward the holy tabernacle where You live hidden for love of me. I love you, O my God, I cannot receive you in Holy Communion. Come nevertheless and visit me with Your grace. Come spiritually into my heart. Purify it. Sanctify it. Render it like unto Your own. Amen.

Lord, I am not worthy that thou shouldst enter under my roof, but only say the word and my soul shall be healed.

## GUARDIAN ANGEL PRAYER

Angel of God, my guardian angel dear, to whom God's love commits me here; ever this day be at my side, to light and guard, to rule and guide. Amen.

## ACT OF CONTRITION

O my God, I am heartily sorry for having offended You. I detest all my sins because I dread the loss of heaven and the pains of hell.

But most of all because they offend You, my God, Who are all good and deserving of all my love.

I firmly resolve, with the help of Your grace to sin no more and to avoid the near occasions of sin. Amen.

## AN ACT OF FAITH

O my God, I firmly believe that You are one God in three Divine Persons, Father, Son, and Holy Spirit; I believe that your Divine Son became man and died for our sins, and that He will come to judge the living and the dead. I believe these and all the truths which the Holy Catholic Church teaches, because You revealed them, who can neither deceive nor be deceived. *(Partial indulgence)*

## AN ACT OF HOPE

O my God, relying on Your infinite goodness and promises, I hope to obtain pardon of my sins, the help of Your grace, and life everlasting, through the merits of Jesus Christ, my Lord and Redeemer. *(Partial indulgence)*

## AN ACT OF LOVE

O my God, I love You above all things, with my whole heart and soul, because You are all-good and worthy of all love. I love my neighbor as myself for the love of You. I forgive all who have injured me, and I ask pardon of all whom I have injured. *(Partial indulgence)*

Lord Jesus Christ, Son of the Living God,
Have mercy on me, a sinner.

### *Confiteor*

I confess to almighty God, and to you, my brothers and sisters, that I have sinned through my own fault in my thoughts and in my words, in what I have done, and in what I have failed to do; and I ask blessed Mary, ever virgin, all the angels and saints, and you, my brothers and sisters, to pray for me to the Lord our God.

# *Footnotes*

# PART I

## 2: The Question of Sin

1. Cf. St. Thomas Aquinas O.P.: *Summa Theologica,* volume I: literally translated by the Fathers of the English Dominican Province: New York: Boston: Cincinnati: Chicago: San Francisco: Benziger Bros. Inc. 1947), p. 461, Q 91, Art. 1 ff. for a detailed treatment of this subject matter.
2. Cf. Pierre Conway O.P. *Theology For The Layman,* no. 22, "When Man Was Right" (July 1946), p.8. Theology For The Layman is a series of 47 pamphlets on the Summa Theologica, published by the Dominican Fathers of St. Joseph's Province, U.S.A. (1942-54).
3. Cf. Edward P. Farrell O.P.: *Theology For The Layman,* no. 41, "An Obliging Teacher" (1952), p. 30; John Fearon O.P. op. cit. no. 42, "The Path Of Reason" (May 1952), p. 18 ff.
4. Cf. *Summa Theologica I,* p. 482, Q 95, Art. 1 ff.; Matthew Hyland O.P.: *Theology For The Layman,* no. 21, "Adam The Magnificent" (1946), p. 26 ff.
5. Cf. *Summa Theologica I,* p. 482, Q 95, Art. 1 ff; William Hill O.P. *Theology For The Layman,* no. 46, "In The Foothills Of Glory" (1954), p. 7 ff.
6. Cf. Orchard, Dom Bernard et al.: *Catholic Commentary On Holy Scripture:* (Toronto: New York: Edinburgh: Camden, N.J.: Thomas Nelson & Sons, 1953 ed.), p. 185
7. Cf. Hill, op. cit. p. 8 ff.
8. Op. cit. p. 10; Cf. Hyland, op. cit. p. 21
9. Cf. Hyland, op. cit. p. 27
10. Cf. *New Revised Catholic Commentary On Holy Scripture* (1969 ed.), p. 178

### 3: The Punishment of Sin

1. Cf. Hyland, op. cit. p. 27
2. Loc. cit.
3. Loc. cit.
4. Loc. cit.
5. Loc. cit.
6. Cf. *Catholic Commentary On Holy Scripture,* (1953 ed), p. 184; Cf. Pierre Conway, op. cit. p. 7 ff.

## PART II

### 5: Christ the Light of the World

1. Cf. John Paul II: *L'Osservatore Romano:* English ed.: "The Resurrection Confirmed The Truth Of Christ's Words"; (Vatican City: Italy, April 21, 1981), p. 4

### 6: A Consideration of Sin

1. For further reading on the subject matter of this chapter cf. *Summa Theologica I,* p. 897, Q 71, art. 1 ff.; Cf. Deck, Rev. E.M.: *Baltimore Catechism II:* (Buffalo, N.Y.: Rauch & Stoeckl Inc. 1933), p. 31
2. Op. cit. p. 29
3. Loc. cit.
4. Loc. cit.
5. Cf. op. cit. p. 30
6. Cf. *Catechism Notes:* (Dublin: The Anthonian Press, 1959), p. 21
7. Op. cit. p. 33; Deck, op. cit. p. 32
8. Cf. Deck, op. cit. p. 32; *Catechism Notes,* p. 21
9. Deck, op. cit. p. 33
10. Ibid.
11. Loc. cit.
12. Op. cit. p. 33; *Catechism Notes,* p. 21
13. Ibid.
14. Deck, op. cit. p. 31
15. Op. cit. pp. 33-34
16. Op. cit. p. 137
17. Ibid.
18. Op. cit. p. 34
19. Loc. cit.
20. Op. cit. p. 33

### 7: What Causes Sin?

1. For further reading on the subject matter of this chapter cf. *Summa Theological I,* p. 919 ff.; Deck, op. cit. p. 32

2. Cf. Francis L. B. Cunningham O.P. et al: *The Christian Life:* (Dubuque, Iowa: The Priory Press, 1959), p. 78 ff. for the passions; Deck, op. cit. p. 32
3. Cf. *The Christian Life,* p. 78 ff.
4. Op. cit. p. 85
5. Deck, op. cit. p. 34
6. Ibid.
7. Op. cit. p. 25
8. Loc. cit.
9. *Catechism Notes,* p. 67
10. Ibid.
11. Op. cit. p. 68
12. Ibid.
13. Ibid.
14. This hymn was published in the ''Hymn'' magazine, July 1976

## 8: A Consideration of the First Commandment

1. Deck, op. cit. 134; For further reading on the subject matter of this chapter cf. *Summa Theologica I,* p. 1039, Q 100, Art. 4 ff.
2. Deck, op. cit. p. 54
3. Loc. cit.
4. Loc. cit.
5. *Catechism Notes,* p. 117
6. Loc. cit.
7. Loc. cit.
8. Loc. cit.
9. Deck op. cit. p. 135
10. Op. cit. p. 136
11. Op. cit. p. 135
12. Ibid.
13. Ibid.
14. Loc. cit.
15. Op. cit. p. 136
16. Op. cit. p. 136 ff.
17. Op. cit. p. 137
18. Loc. cit.
19. Op. cit. p. 139
20. Op. cit. p. 140
21. Ibid.
22. Loc. cit.; Abbott, Walter M. S.J. et al.: *Documents Of Vatican II:* (New York: Guild Press: American Press: Association Press, 1966), p. 170
23. Deck, op. cit. p. 141
24. Loc. cit.
25. *Catechism Notes,* p. 111

26. Deck, op. cit. p. 123
27. *Catechism Notes,* p. 112
28. Deck, op. cit. p. 123
29. Loc. cit.
30. Op. cit. p. 122
31. *Catechism Notes,* p. 111 ff.
32. Deck, op. cit. p. 123
33. *Catechism Notes,* p. 112
34. Loc. cit.
35. Loc. cit.
36. Loc. cit.
37. Op. cit. p. 112 ff.; Deck op. cit. p. 125
38. *Catechism Notes,* p. 113
39. Ibid.

## 9: A Consideration of the 2nd and 3rd Commandments

1. For further reading on the subject matter of this chapter cf. *Summa Theologica I,* p. 1040, Q 100, Art. 4 ff.; Deck, op. cit. 141
2. Op. cit. p. 143
3. Op. cit. p. 142
4. Ibid.
5. Ibid.
6. Op. cit. p. 143
7. Ibid.
8. Op. cit. p. 144
9. Ibid.
10. Op. cit. p. 144, 57
11. Op. cit. p. 153
12. Loc. cit.
13. Loc. cit.
14. Op. cit. p. 154
15. Ibid.
16. Op. cit. p. 143
17. Cf. op. cit. p. 98 ff.
18. *Catechism Notes,* p. 51
19. Cf. *Documents Of Vatican II,* p. 174 ff
20. Deck, op. cit. p. 108 ff.
21. Loc. cit.
22. Op. cit. p. 108; *Catechism Notes,* p. 114
23. Deck, op. cit. p. 109
24. Loc. cit.
25. Cf. *Documents Of Vatican II,* p. 150 ff.
26. Cf. *Documents Of Vatican II,* p. 146 ff.
27. Deck, op. cit. p. 108; *Catechism Notes,* p. 57
28. Ibid.

29. Op. cit. p. 107
30. Op. cit. p. 109
31. Cf. Deut. 33: 27

# PART III

## 10: Reflections on the Fourth Commandment

1. Deck, op. cit. p. 145
2. Op. cit. p. 146

## 11: Reflections on the Fifth and Eighth Commandments

1. For further reading on the subject matter of this chapter cf. *Summa Theologica I,* Q 100, Art. 5 ff.; Deck op. cit. p. 147
2. Loc. cit.
3. Loc. cit.
4. Ibid.
5. Cf. *Catechism Notes,* p. 32
6. Ibid.
7. Op. cit. p. 32
8. Deck, op. cit. p. 147
9. Lemoyne, J. B. S.C.: *A Character Sketch Of The Venerable Don Bosco:* (New Rochelle, New York: Salesian Press, 1927), p. 32
10. *Catechism Notes,* p. 32
11. Op. cit. p. 33
12. Loc. cit.
13. Loc. cit.
14. Deck. op. cit. p. 150
15. Loc. cit.
16. Ibid.
17. Cf. *Catechism Notes,* p. 35
18. Loc. cit.
19. Loc. cit.

## 12: Reflections on the Seventh and Tenth Commandments

1. For further reading on the subject matter of this chapter cf. *Summa Theologica I,* p. 1049, Q 100, Art. 11 ff.; Deck, op. cit. p. 1049, Q 100, Art. 11 ff.
2. Op. cit. p. 151
3. Op. cit. p. 149
4. Cf. *Documents Of Vatican II,* p. 183 ff. 584, 634
5. Deck, op. cit. p. 149
6. Op. cit. p. 149; *Catechism Notes,* p. 34
7. *Catechism Notes* p. 34
8. Deck, op. cit. p. 150

9. Cf. *Catechism Notes,* p. 35
10. Loc. cit.
11. Deck, op. cit. p. 150
12. Cf. *Documents Of Vatican II,* p. 303, 202 ff.
13. Op. cit. p. 229

## 13: Reflections on the Sixth and Ninth Commandments

1. For further reading on the subject matter of this chapter cf. *Summa Theologica I,* p. 1049, Q 100, Art. 11 ff.; Deck op. cit. p. 148
2. Deck, op. cit. p. 151
3. Op. cit. p. 148
4. Ibid.

# PART IV

## 14: A Consideration of Guilt and Punishment

1. For further reading on the related subject matter of this chapter cf. *Summa Theologica I,* p. 662, Q 18, ff.; *Catechism Notes,* p. 22 p. 966, Q 85 ff.
2. Deck, op. cit. p. 30; Farrell, op. cit. supra, ''An Obliging Teacher'' p. 18 ff.
3. Deck, op. cit. p. 30
4. Loc. cit.
5. *Catechism Notes,* p. 22
6. Loc. cit.
7. Loc. cit.
8. Deck, op. cit. p. 92

## 15: The Sacrament of Reconciliation

1. For further reading on the subject matter of this and the following three chapters cf. *Summa Theologica II,* p. 2529, Q 84, Art. 1 ff.; Deck, op. cit. p. 84
2. Cf. *Catechism Notes,* p. 65 ff.
3. Deck. op. cit. p. 87
4. Cf. *Catechism Notes,* p. 65
5. Op. cit. p. 66
6. Loc. cit.
7. Loc. cit.
8. Loc. cit.
9. Ibid.
10. Ibid.
11. Deck, op. cit. p. 87
12. Op. cit. p. 90
13. Op. cit. p. 85, 90

14. Op. cit. p. 90
15. Loc. cit.
16. Deck, op. cit. p. 92
17. Op. cit. p. 92, 95
18. Cf. op. cit. p. 93
19. Deck, op. cit. p. 92
20. Cf. *Catechism Notes,* p, 69
21. Deck, op. cit. p. 153, 157
22. Op. cit. p. 157
23. Op. cit. p. 158

## 16: Preparing for Confession

1. Deck, op. cit. p. 181
2. Ibid.
3. Loc. cit.
4. Loc. cit.
5. Loc. cit.
6. Loc. cit.

## 17: The Confession of Sins

1. Cf. *Catechism Notes,* p. 69
2. Deck, op. cit. p.90
3. Deck, op. cit. p. 91; *Catechism Notes,* p. 68
4. Deck, op. cit. p. 92
5. Op. cit. p. 84
6. Op. cit. p. 85

## 18: Atonement for Sin

1. Deck, op. cit. p. 92
2. Op. cit. p. 93
3. Op. cit. p. 157
4. Ibid.
5. Op. cit. p. 93
6. Loc. cit.
7. Op. cit. p. 95
8. Ibid.
9. *Catechism Notes,* p. 70
10. Op. cit. p. 71
11. Deck, op. cit. p. 96
12. Ibid.
13. Op. cit. p. 97; *Catechism Notes,* p. 71
14. Deck, op. cit. p. 157; *Catechism Notes,* p. 71 ff.
15. Deck, op. cit. p. 157 ff.

16. Op. cit. p. 96 ff.
17. Op. cit. p. 97
18. Op. cit. p. 96
19. *Catechism Notes,* p. 71
20. Ibid.
21. Loc. cit.

# PART V

## 19: Beginning Again

1. *Catechism Notes,* p. 67
2. Deck, op. cit. p. 148
3. Rev. J. Broderick S.J.: *St. Peter Canisius S.J.:* (Baltimore, Maryland, The Carroll Press, 1950), p. 6 ff.

## 21: Clasping God's Hand

1. *Liturgy Of The Hours I:* (New York: Catholic Book Publishing Co. 1963), p. 184
2. Deck, op. cit. p. 125
3. Op. cit. p. 126
4. Ibid.

## 22: Reflections on the Basic Christian Virtues

1. Deck, op. cit. p. 34
2. Loc. cit.
3. Cf. Msgr. Charles H. Doyle: Pride, *The Thief Of The Holocaust:* (Milwaukee: Bruce Publishing Co. 1959), p. 68
4. Deck, op. cit. p. 34
5. Loc. cit.
6. Op. cit. p. 35
7. Loc. cit.
8. Ibid.
9. Ibid.
10. Ibid. *Catechism Notes,* p. 120
11. Deck, op. cit. p. 35
12. Ibid.
13. Ibid.

# PART VI

## 25: Vocation in Life

1. For further reading on the subject matter of this chapter cf. *Summa Theologica II,* p. 1802, Q 151 ff.; *Documents Of Vatican II,* p. 447; Doyle, op. cit. p. 34

2. *Breviary Of The Order Of Preachers I:* English ed.: (Dublin: St. Savior's, 1967), p. 188 ff.
3. Doyle, op. cit. p. 36
4. Op. cit. p. 35
5. Op. cit. p. 36
6. Op. cit. p. 35
7. Op. cit. p. 32 ff.; *Documents Of Vatican II,* 75 ff., 466 ff.
8. Doyle, op. cit. p. 34 ff.
9. Op. cit. p. 36
10. Op. cit. p. 34
11. Op. cit. p. 35
12. Ibid.
13. Op. cit. p. 34
14. Ibid.
15. Op. cit. p. 32
16. Loc. cit.
17. *Documents Of Vatican II,* p. 466 ff., 74 ff.; Deck, op. cit. p. 55
18. Deck, op. cit. p. 55
19. Ibid.
20. Loc. cit.
21. Loc. cit.
22. *Documents Of Vatican II,* p. 468 ff.

## 26: The Married State

1. For further reading on the subject matter of this chapter cf. *Summa Theologica II,* p. 1808, Q 152, Art. 4 ff.; Deck, op. cit. p. 117
2. Loc. cit.
3. Deck, op. cit. p. 118
4. Author uncertain, probably Rev. Thomas a Kempis Reilly, O.P. (1879-1957).

## 28: A Last Word: Let Science Speak

1. For the main outline of the controversy on the Scriptures, especially during the last century cf. *Catholic Commentary On Holy Scripture* (1953 ed.), p. 61 ff.
2. Cf. op. cit. p. 109
3. Cf. Odell, M. E.: *Preparing The Way:* (This is vol I of The New Library Of Catholic Knowledge): (New York: Hawthorn Books Inc. 1963), p. 13
4. Ibid.
5. Cf. Pope John Paul II: *L'Osservatore Romano,* (English ed.): (Vatican City, Italy, April 21, 1981), p. 4
6. Ibid.
7. Stoddard, John L.: *Rebuilding A Lost Faith:* (New York: P. J. Kennedy & Sons, 1922), p. 183

# *Bibliography*


Abbott, Walter M. S.J. et al.: *Documents Of Vatican II:* New York: Guild Press: America Press: Association Press, 1966

Bible, *Douay Version:* New York: The Douay Bible House, 1944

*Breviary Of The Order Of Preachers I,* (English ed.): Dublin: St. Savior's, 1967

Broderick, Rev. J. S.J.: *St. Peter Canisius S.J.:* Baltimore, MD.: The Carroll Press, 1950

*Catechism Notes:* Dublin: The Anthonian Press, 1959

Cunningham, Rev. Francis L. B. O.P. et al.: *The Christian Life:* Dubuque, Iowa: The Priory Press, 1959

Deck, Rev. E. M.: *Baltimore Catechism III:* Buffalo, NY: Rauch & Stoeckl Printing Co. Inc. 1933

Doyle, Msgr. Charles Hugo: *Pride, The Thief Of The Holocaust:* Milwaukee: The Bruce Publishing Co. 1959

Farrell, Rev. Walter M. O.P. et al. *Theology For The Layman,* a series of 47 pamphlets published by the Dominican Fathers of St. Joseph's Province U.S.A. (1942-54), on the Summa Theologica of St. Thomas Aquinas. Only a few pamphlets have been used as reference: 21, 22, 41, 42, 46.

Fuller, Rev. Reginald C. et al.: *A New Catholic Commentary On Holy Scripture:* London, Melbourne, Johannesburg, Ontario, Camden, NJ.: Nelson, Thomas & Sons, 1969.

Le Moyne, J. B. S.C.: *A Character Sketch Of The Venerable Don Bosco:* New Rochelle, NY: Salesian Press, 1927

*Liturgy Of The Hours I* (ICEL text): New York: Catholic Book Publishing Co., 1976

*L'Osservatore Romano* (English ed.): Vatican City, Italy, April 21, 1981

Odell, M. E.: *Preparing The Way:* (This is vol. 1 of The New Library Of Catholic Knowledge): New York: Hawthorn Books Inc. 1963

Orchard, Dom Bernard et al.: *Catholic Commentary On Holy Scripture:* Toronto, New York, Edinburgh, Camden NJ: Nelson, Thomas & Sons, 1953

Stoddard, John L.: *Rebuilding A Lost Faith:* New York: Kennedy, J. P. & Sons, 1922

# THE RIEHLE FOUNDATION...

The Riehle Foundation is a non-profit, tax-exempt, charitable organization that exists to produce and/or distribute Catholic material to anyone, anywhere.

The Foundation is dedicated to the Mother of God and her role in the salvation of mankind. We believe that this role has not diminished in our time, but, on the contrary has become all the more apparent in this the era of Mary as recognized by Pope John Paul II, whom we strongly support.

During the past four years the foundation has distributed books, films, rosaries, bibles, etc. to individuals, parishes, and organizations all over the world. Additionally, the foundation sends materials to missions and parishes in a dozen foreign countries.

Donations forwarded to The Riehle Foundation for the materials distributed provide our sole support. We appreciate your assistance, and request your prayers.

IN THE SERVICE OF JESUS AND MARY
All for the honor and glory of God!

**The Riehle Foundation**
**P.O. Box 7**
**Milford, OH 45150**

# *The Gospel Way of Life*

## A Book for Young People

*by* **Sr. Rosena Marie**

What makes a sin mortal? What is venial sin? How do you make an examination of conscience? What is entailed in the Ten Commandments?

Chances are that if you were raised before the 1960s in the Roman Catholic Church you can probably answer these questions. But they remain a mystery to most young people.

Many of today's young adults were raised during a time of great changes in the Catholic Church. As the Church sought to implement Vatican II, schools often failed to teach some of the fundamentals of Catholicism which are still pillars of the Faith.

Sr. Rosena Marie has provided a comprehensive study of such topics as original sin, the Ten Commandments, virtues and vices, and the choice of vocations. She clarifies misconceptions regarding the Church's consistent view of sin by using frequent Scriptural references, and the teachings of historical Church leaders.

This book is an excellent companion to the new *Catechism of the Catholic Church* and is a guide for anyone seeking the truth of the Catholic Faith.

Faith Publishing Company

ISBN: 1-880033-17-8

$6.00

Printed and bound by CPI Group (UK) Ltd, Croydon, CR0 4YY

28/08/2026

02205841-0005